The Structure of Scientific Theories

UNIVERSITY OF ILLINOIS PRESS
Urbana Chicago London

The Structure of Scientific Theories

Second Edition

Edited with a Critical Introduction and an Afterword by

FREDERICK SUPPE

To
MAX HAROLD FISCH
on his retirement

Manufactured in the United States of America
Second Edition

Second printing, 1979

LIBRARY OF CONGRESS CATALOGING IN PUBLICATION DATA

Main entry under title:

The Structure of scientific theories.

Bibliography: p.
Includes indexes.
1. Science—Philosophy—Congresses. I. Suppe, Frederick.
Q174.S87 1977 501 77-4411
ISBN 0-252-00655-0
ISBN 0-252-00634-8 pbk.

Preface to the Second Edition

Response to the first edition has been very satisfying; sales have been brisk and critical reviews have been most kind. Even more gratifying to me personally is the fact that both the Press and I have been inundated with requests (sometimes bordering on demands) that my long editorial introduction be made available in an inexpensive form suitable for use as a text in philosophy of science courses. Meeting this request posed certain problems, not the least of which is that my introduction had become somewhat dated as a result of rather dramatic developments in philosophy of science since the 1969 symposium. Accordingly, in bringing out a paperback edition we decided to update it by adding a substantial Afterword which details how the post-positivistic confusion and disarray within philosophy of science at the time of the symposium (displayed graphically in the symposium portion of this volume) is becoming resolved and has led to the more coherent state of the field today. The Afterword also expands the scope of the volume (hence its usefulness as a textbook) by including discussions of developments on issues such as explanation and induction which received only slight attention in the introduction. In addition to the Afterword errata have been corrected and changes have been made at a few places in my editorial introduction. The Bibliography which Rew A. Godow, Jr., compiled for the first edition has been revised and expanded substantially. Hopefully these changes and the addition of the Afterword will provide a more comprehensive and up-to-date account of where philosophy of science is today and how it got there, thus increasing the usefulness of the volume.

In an effort to make the paperback cost sufficiently low to permit use of the volume in the classroom, in producing the second edition we have attempted to minimize the resetting of type. Hence we opted for an Afterword rather than an extensive revision and expansion of my editorial introduction; and a separate supplementary index has been provided for the Afterword. In preparing the second edition I owe special debts to Edward C. Mascotti; Gertrude C. Suppe; my colleagues Lindley Darden,

Michael Gardner, and especially Dudley Shapere; and my former secretary, Margaret-Mary Ryan. Again it has been a pleasure to work with the University of Illinois Press and have Ms. Bruce McDaniel as my copy-editor. Financial support for doing the revision was provided by a grant from the University of Maryland General Research Board, and some of the research reported was supported by NSF grant GS-39677.

FREDERICK SUPPE
Washington, D.C.
February, 1977

Preface

This volume is an outgrowth of a symposium on the structure of scientific theories held in Urbana, March 26 to 29, 1969. The call for the symposium was as follows:

> Traditionally philosophers of science have construed scientific theories as axiomatic calculi in which theoretical terms and statements are given a partial observational interpretation by means of correspondence rules. Recently the adequacy of this analysis has been challenged by a number of philosophers, historians of science, and scientists. A number of alternative analyses of the structure of theories have been proposed and discussed. The purpose of this symposium is to bring together a number of the main proponents and critics of the traditional analysis, proponents of some of the more important alternative analyses, historians of science, and scientists to explore the question "What is the structure of a scientific theory?"

The views held by the various participants in the symposium are fairly representative of the current spectrum of philosophical thinking about the nature of scientific theories, and so the symposium proceedings offer a revealing picture of what philosophers currently think about the nature of theories and their roles in the scientific enterprise. A revised and edited version of the symposium proceedings constitutes the bulk of this volume. Each author has had the opportunity to revise both his papeı and his remarks during the discussions; editorial interpolations (always clearly indicated) have been inserted to resolve any incompatibilities resulting from such revisions. For various reasons three of the participants were unable to prepare revised manuscripts for publication; in two of these cases I have supplied whatever material was necessary to preserve the continuity of the proceedings (clearly indicating where this was done), and in the third case a replacement paper has been included. In a few cases it seemed desirable to alter the order of the discussions or pare the discussions, and I have done so without giving any indications when it has been done. As such the proceedings published here do not purport to be a historically accurate account of what transpired at the symposium, though it does claim to be an accurate representation of the views held by the symposiasts. As an aid to the reader I have freely added footnotes to the discussions; some of these are citations of works obliquely referred to in the discussions, and others are substantive footnotes giving details of scientific experiments or theories referred to where the average reader might not be familiar with them. In addition to the proceedings the volume contains a lengthy critical introduction by the editor, a retrospective postscript on the symposium by Stephen Toulmin (who originally was scheduled to attend but could not), and a comprehensive bibliography of the philosophical literature concerning the structure of theories. This bibliography contains virtually all sources cited in the volume as well as other related writings on the subject.

One thing that was particularly revealing about the symposium was the extent of interest by nonphilosophers in what philosophers have to say about the structure of scientific theories. The Departments of Chemistry, History, Physics, and Psychology at Illinois provided generous financial support for the symposium, and sessions of the symposium drew audiences as large as 1,200 persons. But interest in what the philosopher of science has to say is not sufficient to understand what he says. During the symposium a number of nonphilosophers said to me, "I can see that what's going on is relevant to my work as a scientist and should be of use to me, but I don't have sufficient philosophical background to follow it in detail or see exactly how it affects my work; as such I don't get the answers I need." To serve the interests of such interested nonphilosophers it was decided to include a lengthy introduction which would provide the philosophical background needed both to understand in detail what transpires in the symposium and also for further excursions into the philosophical literature on theories. This introduction presents a critical survey of the main philosophical literature of this century relating to the structure of theories. Although it has been written for the purpose of introducing the nonphilosopher-of-science to the main philosophical literature on theories, to the best of my knowledge it is as comprehensive a critical survey of the philosophical literature on theories as has been published; as such it could be used as a textbook in a philosophy of science course. Hopefully the philosopher of science also will find things of interest in it. In short, the conception of the book is that the combination of the editor's introduction and the proceedings of the symposium will provide a comprehensive account of past and present philosophical thinking about the nature of scientific theories.

Since a number of works are cited by several contributors to the volume, it was decided to include a comprehensive bibliography on the structure of theories rather than repeat bibliographic information. All citations in material prepared by the editor refer to that bibliography, as do citations in a majority of the papers in the symposium proceedings. These citations consist of the author's last name followed by a date in brackets. Thus "Hempel [1970]" refers to the work by Carl Hempel published in 1970 listed in the bibliography at the end of the volume. When the bibliography contains more than one work for a given year by an author, lower case letters have been added to the ends of dates to distinguish the works. Several contributors preferred to follow some other format for citation and they were allowed to do so; in such cases virtually all the works cited in their contributions have been included in the bibliography at the end of the volume.

My debts in organizing the symposium and preparing this volume for publication are many. The symposium was financed through the support of the George A. Miller Committee and the Departments of Chemistry, History, Philosophy, Physics, and Psychology at the University of Illinois, Urbana. In organizing the symposium, I was aided by Professor Alan H. Donagan, who served as co-chairman of the organizing committee, and Professors B. J. Diggs, David Pines, Robert C. Stalnaker, and Frederick L. Will, who were members of that committee. Jack Lynes was my extremely able administrative assistant, and without his help the symposium would not have run smoothly, if at all. Professors Wilbur Applebaum (History, Illinois), Roger C. Buck (History and Philosophy of Science, Indiana), Don E. Dulany (Psychology, Illinois), Max H. Fisch (Philosophy, Illinois), Leonard K. Nash (Chemistry, Harvard), Raymond P. Stearns (History, Illinois), and Frederick L. Will (Philosophy, Illinois) graciously undertook the sometimes difficult, and invariably unrewarded, task of moderating sessions. Professor Max Fisch, to whom this volume is dedicated, is responsible for the idea of organizing the symposium. In preparing the volume for publication, I have relied on a bevy of secretaries, of whom Marjorie Beasley, Maria Bonial, Sheila Clair, Alice Dennis, and Diane Hiither deserve special mention. Rew A. Godow and Richard Wright were able research assistants; Mr. Godow aided in editing the proceedings and prepared the bibliography; Mr. Wright proofread manuscripts and helped see the volume through press. Professor Max Fisch has read and commented on a portion of the introduction, and Professor Thomas Nickles has read the entire draft of the introduction and provided copious comments. None of these persons is responsible for any errors which remain. To the participants in the symposium I am grateful for their cooperation in revising their manuscripts, and in several instances for their patience in waiting for others to complete their revisions. I am particularly grateful to the staff of the University of Illinois Press for the care they have bestowed on the manuscript: Frank Williams, Assistant Director, and Richard Wentworth, Associate Director, have proved willing and invaluable sources of help and advice; and my copy editor, Ms. Bruce A. McDaniel, has showered the manuscript with even more devotion than I have been able to muster. My most immediate personal debt is to Edward C. Mascotti. I also wish to thank Professor David Turner. A number of the contributions to this volume have been written under the support of the National Science Foundation, which is gratefully acknowledged. Financial support for preparation of the volume was provided by two grants from the University of Illinois Research Board and a Faculty Summer Research Fellowship.

FREDERICK SUPPE
Urbana, Illinois
April, 1973

Contents

The Search for Philosophic Understanding of Scientific Theories

FREDERICK SUPPE

Proceedings of the Symposium

SESSION I

SESSION II

SESSION III

Afterword — 1977

FREDERICK SUPPE

THE SEARCH FOR PHILOSOPHIC UNDERSTANDING OF SCIENTIFIC THEORIES

Frederick Suppe

Introduction

If any problem in the philosophy of science justifiably can be claimed the most central or important, it is that of the nature and structure of scientific theories, including the diverse roles theories play in the scientific enterprise. For theories are the vehicle of scientific knowledge, and one way or another become involved in most aspects of the scientific enterprise. It is only a slight exaggeration to claim that a philosophy of science is little more than an analysis of theories and their roles in the scientific enterprise. A philosophy of science's analysis of the nature of theories, including their roles in the growth of scientific knowledge, thus is its keystone; and should that analysis prove inadequate, that inadequacy is likely to extend to its account of the remaining aspects of the scientific enterprise and the knowledge it provides. At the very least, it calls for a reassessment of its entire account of scientific knowledge.

The centrality of the nature of theories to an understanding of the scientific enterprise is attested to by the recent histories of both science and the philosophy of science. The last century has provided science with some of its most spectacular, controversial, and revolutionary theoretical episodes in all branches of science — physical, biological, and social. Traditionally the philosophy of science has been concerned to either vindicate, evaluate, make sense of, or improve the practice of the then contemporaneous science; thus it is no surprise that recent philosophy of science has undergone intellectual revolutions nearly as spectacular as the theoretical science it has studied, evaluated, and commented on.

In consideration of, and in response to, recent developments in physics, in the 1920s it became commonplace for philosophers of science to construe scientific theories as axiomatic calculi which are given a partial observational interpretation by means of correspondence rules. This analysis, commonly referred to as *The Received View on Theories*,[1] has been widely assumed by philosophers of science in dealing with other

[1] The name 'the Received View' was first introduced in Putnam [1962]. Citations in this Introduction are in accordance with the system described in the Preface.

problems in the philosophy of science. It is little exaggeration to say that virtually every significant result obtained in philosophy of science between the 1920s and 1950 either employed or tacitly assumed the Received View. In the 1950s, however, this analysis began to be the subject of critical attacks challenging its very conception of theories and scientific knowledge.[2] These attacks, which continued well into the 1960s, were of two sorts: First, there were attacks on specific features of the Received View (for example, the notion of partial interpretation and the observational-theoretical distinction) designed to show they were defective beyond repair.[3] Second, there were alternative philosophies of science advanced by Hanson, Kuhn, Feyerabend, and others which rejected the Received View out of hand, and proceeded to argue for some other conception of theories and scientific knowledge.[4] These two lines of attack were so successful that by the late 1960s a general concensus had been reached among philosophers of science that the Received View was inadequate as an analysis of scientific theories; derivatively, the analyses of other aspects of the scientific enterprise (for example, explanation) erected upon the Received View became suspect and today virtually have succumbed to skeptical criticism.[5]

Although these various proposed alternative philosophies proved successful in undercutting the Received View, they too were subject to significant critical attack,[6] and by the late 1960s were coming into increased disrepute. The result was that the Received View had been dethroned, but none of the proferred alternatives had gained widespread acceptance among philosophers of science. Philosophy of science thus fell into a state of acute intellectual disarray.

At this point the 1969 Illinois Symposium on the Structure of Scientific Theories (whose proceedings constitute the central portion of this volume) was convened to bring together leading figures in philosophy of science, and allied disciplines, to sort out prevailing chaos and to search for new, productive intellectual directions to follow. Those proceedings graphically portray not only the chaos of the field then, but also the informed efforts of its leaders to sort things out in a productive manner.

[2] The Received View had, of course, been the subject of various criticisms designed to force changes in its details (see Sec. II below), but these did not call into question the basic conception of the Received View. The challenge of its basic conception conveniently can be construed as beginning with Toulmin [1953].

[3] See, for example, the attacks in Achinstein [1963], [1965], and Putnam [1962].

[4] See, for example, Hanson [1958a], Kuhn [1962], and Toulmin [1953].

[5] Consider, for example, the recent controversy over Hempel's covering-law model analysis of scientific explanation which tacitly is based on the Received View. This and other analyses based on the Received View will be considered in the Afterword.

[6] See, for example, Achinstein [1968], Ch. 6; Scheffler [1967]; and Shapere [1964] and [1966].

Since that pivotal conference the field has begun to make sense of both science and its recent past, and a new intellectual movement is emerging that rapidly is providing an improved philosophic understanding of scientific theories and the scientific enterprises they occur in; the seeds of these more recent developments are found in the proceedings of the 1969 Illinois symposium. Focusing on that conference at a "crisis state" of the field, the present volume attempts to provide a clear understanding of recent developments in philosophy of science — its current state and how it came to it. The volume parcels the story into three parts — the first, my critical introduction, traces the main developments in philosophy of science concerning theories and theorizing prior to the symposium, telling in critical detail how these developments emerged, developed, and led to the crisis in philosophy of science addressed by the 1969 Illinois symposium. The second part, the symposium proceedings, details how leading figures in the field attempted to grapple with, and make sense of, the chaos wrought by the rejection of the recently dominant intellectual view of science, the Received View. And the third part, my Afterword written for the second edition, details how the profession worked itself out of the crisis evidenced in the symposium proceedings, and found a new direction — to such an extent that a new movement in the field can be discerned as rapidly coalescing.

In my main contributions to the telling of this story — this introduction and the Afterword — I trace and critically assess the main episodes and developments in this story, attempting to make recent developments in philosophy of science, including the symposium, accessible to the seriously interested scientist or student first encountering the philosophy of science; at the same time, the philosopher of science hopefully will find new insights and perspectives which are of interest and value.

I. Historical Background to the Received View

Although the Received View continued to enjoy wide acceptance after logical positivism had been rejected, it is the product of logical positivism and cannot be understood if divorced from the tenets of that movement.[7] Merely knowing the tenets of logical positivism is not sufficient for understanding the Received View and its rationale; it is necessary also to understand the problems and influences which prompted the positivists to adopt the philosophical position they did and which prompted them to make the Received View so central to their epistemology. Logical positivism was influenced by a number of developments in nineteenth and early twentieth century science and philosophy, and was a response to problems raised by these developments; it cannot be understood in isolation from these developments.

It is often said that positivism emerged as a response to the metaphysical excesses of Hegel and his neo-Hegelian successors (for example, MacTaggart, Bradley and others) who sought to explain reality in terms of abstract metaphysical entities (for example, Entelechy and the Absolute) which did not admit of empirical specification.[8] While it certainly was an important goal (pursued with messianic fervor) of logical positivism to eliminate such metaphysical entities from philosophy and science, it seems to me that its role in the inception of the

[7] That the Received View survived so long after logical positivism had been rejected initially seems rather surprising. The explanation of this lies, I think, in the fact that positivism unreasonably had tried to force all empirical knowledge into the scientific mold, and many who rejected positivism as a general epistemology did so on the ground that not all empirical knowledge was like scientific knowledge; thus, in rejecting logical positivism as a general epistemology, they were willing to concede that positivism was adequate as an analysis of scientific knowledge (see Wheelwright [1954] for an example of this attitude). Logical positivism thus became philosophy of science, and continued to survive as a philosophy dealing with a restricted range of empirical knowledge—scientific knowledge.

[8] Compare, for example, Passmore [1957], Ch. 16, for an historical treatment which gives this impression.

movement tends to be exaggerated,[9] and that giving it too central an importance tends to obscure the true origins of the positivistic doctrines. Logical positivism is the philosophy which emerged from the Vienna Circle and Reichenbach's Berlin School, whose memberships consisted almost exclusively of scientists, mathematicians, and scientists turned philosophers; while the rejection of traditional metaphysics was common among them, they showed more important common bonds—namely, they were concerned with foundational issues in science of a philosophical nature raised by recent scientific developments, and also shared some general agreement how these problems were to be dealt with. Therein lies the genesis of logical positivism.

Logical positivism is a Germanic movement, and to understand its genesis certain features of the German scientific establishment in the nineteenth and early twentieth century must be considered.[10] In the German university departments were organized around a single professor (occasionally two) who had virtually dictatorial control over the affairs of the departments, including the hiring of teaching and research faculty. Typically the professor hired faculty whose scientific interests and empirical philosophy reflected his own, and so faculties of departments reflected the scientific interests and approaches of their professors. An analogous situation obtained in the various research institutes such as the Kaiser Wilhelm Institutes. Thus the German scientific establishment tended to break into various schools surrounding a few main figures holding professorships or directorships of institutes; and the members of these schools tended to share the scientific interests and approaches of the professor or director. In a given field there often were substantial and basic differences in the positions of the different schools. In physics after 1870 the differences in schools were not confined just to scientific issues, but also included philosophical and political orientation; which school one belonged to determined which philosophy of science one embraced.

In the period between 1850 and 1880 German science was dominated

[9] That its role has been exaggerated is not surprising, for it does tend to dominate the early manifestos issued by the positivists (for example, Hahn, *et al.* [1929], Carnap [1932]) and occupies a central place in Ayer's [1946] popularization of the movement, through which logical positivism is best known. Carnap [1963b] indicates, however, that while the members of the Vienna Circle rejected traditional metaphysics, they wasted little time in polemics against it, concentrating more on ways of avoiding its introduction in dealing with other, more central problems (p. 21).

[10] My understanding of the German scientific establishment in this period has been enhanced by the work of a student of mine, Dr. David Preston. The account which follows is heavily indebted to his doctoral dissertation, Preston [1971]; see esp., Chs. III and VII.

by *mechanistic materialism* which was a blend of Comptean positivism, materialism, and mechanism.[11] The position is aptly characterized by its chief spokesman, Ludwig Büchner, who writes, "Science . . . gradually establishes the fact that macrocosmic and microcosmic existence obeys, in its origin, life, and decay, mechanical laws inherent in things themselves, discarding every kind of super-naturalism and idealism in the exploration of natural events. There is no force without matter; no matter without force." [12] Thus, according to mechanistic materialism science can present a picture of the world firmly based on empirical inquiry, rather than upon philosophical speculation. In this picture matter is primary, and there is no doubt that a real, objective world exists independent of individual perceivers; science is the discovery of the mechanisms in this objective world whereby animate and inanimate matter behaves and realizes itself. The product of science will be mechanistic laws governing life and the world—that is, mechanistic laws governing matter in motion. The scientific method yields immediate and objective knowledge of these laws, and is capable of doing so by empirical investigation without any recourse to philosophical speculation. Thus there is no place for a priori elements in natural science or in empirical knowledge. Observation of the world is immediate in the sense that no a priori or conceptual mediation is involved in obtaining observational knowledge; observation in accordance with the procedures of natural science is sufficient to yield knowledge of the world's mechanistic nature.

By the 1870s mechanistic materialism began to be challenged—largely as a result of developments in physiology and psychology which cast doubt on its doctrines of the external world and the ability of scientific theory to adequately describe that world. For example, the work of Helmholtz on the physiology of the senses (Helmholtz [1863] and [1927]) indicated that an adequate philosophy must make provision for the activity of the thinking subject in the growth of scientific knowledge—something mechanistic materialism did not do. The mediation of the senses in the apprehension of the world was seen as incompatible with mechanistic materialism's doctrine that science provided immediate knowledge of the external world.

In the German scientific community mechanistic materialism gradually gave way to a neo-Kantian philosophy of science developed initially

[11] Although this was the dominant philosophy held by scientists in this period, it was in opposition to the "official" philosophy of the German state and the state universities, which was a watered-down version of Hegelianism; see Passmore [1957], p. 33.

[12] Büchner [1855]; quoted in Passmore [1957], p. 34.

by Helmholtz and (more importantly) Hermann Cohen and his Marburg School, and revised later by Ernst Cassirer.[13] Cohen combined an interest in Kant with an interest in mathematics and logic to form a neo-Kantian epistemology of the natural sciences. Science is concerned to discover the general forms or structures of sensations; the knowledge science yields of the "external world" is seen as webs of logical relations which are not given, but rather exemplified (*ausgegeben*), in sensory experience. That is to say, sensations have forms or structures which are revealed when one digs down through the superficialities of the given sensations; these forms are structures of phenomena, not structures of the thing-in-itself. These structures have a Platonic sort of absoluteness, being a sort of ideal world structure which exemplifies itself in structured phenomena. The job of science is to discover the structure of this ideal world, the structure of phenomena. Scientific laws will describe this structure. Accordingly, scientific knowledge is absolute, not relativistic. By 1900, this sort of neo-Kantianism had become the dominant philosophy of the German scientific community; it was the essence of German scientific common sense—a common sense that virtually precluded acceptance of both relativity theory and quantum theory.[14]

Neo-Kantianism was not the only philosophy of science adopted in reaction against mechanistic materialism; another school, which had a significant but less widespread influence on German science, stemmed from Ernst Mach; its influence was limited primarily to a few schools (especially Göttingen, Berlin, and the Kaiser Wilhelm Institutes). Ernst Mach initially held a neo-Kantian position wherein every scientific theory contains an a priori element of a purely formal character as far as its fundamental principles are concerned.[15] Later he came to reject this, maintaining that one must reject any a priori elements in the constitution of our knowledge of things: science is no more than a conceptual reflection upon facts whose elements are contents of consciousness given to us by sensation. Mach's neo-Kantianism thus gave way to a neo-positivism wherein there is no place for a priori elements in science. In particular there was no place for a doctrine of absolute

[13] See Helmholtz [1921]; H. Cohen [1871], [1902–12]; Cassirer [1910].

[14] The vast majority of the German scientific community remained hostile to both theories until the Nazi period, largely due to its neo-Kantian position and antisemitic bias directed to the new theories which were the epitome of "Jewish science"; see Preston [1971], Ch. VII. Although neo-Kantianism of the Marburg variety continued to dominate German science well into the 1930s, it did not exert that much influence among philosophers, being supplanted by non-Platonic and more conventional or pragmatic positions such as those of Friedrich Lange [1866] and Hans Vaihinger [1911].

[15] This position is maintained in Mach [1868].

space and time.[16] Scientific statements must be empirically verifiable, which is to say that all empirical statements occurring in a scientific theory must be capable of being reduced to statements about sensations. In Mach [1886] he tries, rather unsuccessfully, to develop this approach into an analysis which construes the principles of science as nothing but abbreviated descriptions of sensations. His lack of success in carrying out this program stems partially from the fact that abbreviated descriptions of sensations cannot account for the fact that scientific principles contain mathematical relationships not reducible to sensations alone. Later modifications or developments of his basic approach by Clifford [1885], Pearson [1892], and Hertz [1894] gradually loosened things to allow the inclusion of an a priori element in science, but construing it as being a conceptual element without factual content. A similar position was developed by Poincaré [1902].

By the turn of the century, the three main philosophic positions held in the German scientific community were mechanistic materialism, neo-Kantianism, and Machian neo-positivism, with neo-Kantianism being the most commonly held. Which philosophy one held depended largely on the scientific school one belonged to. At the same time, however, theoretical physics was coming into its own, and the physical sciences were developing much more theoretical and mathematical branches. In 1905 Einstein published his special theory of relativity, and shortly thereafter the old quantum theory was well on its way in development. Relativity theory and quantum theory were thought to be incompatible with all three of these philosophies of science, and acceptance of them seemed to require abandonment of these philosophical positions. In Germany the neo-Kantian and mechanistic materialistic schools of physics typically opposed the replacement of classical physics by relativity and quantum theory—largely on neo-Kantian or mechanistic materialistic grounds.[17] Primary German support for the new physics came from those schools which were sympathetic to Machian positivism;[18] but embracement of the new physics did require abandonment of a strict adherence to Mach's positivism.

With the gradual acceptance of the new physics, a philosophical crisis emerged: the new physics was incompatible with the prevailing notions of scientific common sense—the philosophies of science previously held. What then was the nature of the scientific enterprise?

[16] This denial of Mach's strongly influenced Einstein—see Einstein and Infeld [1947].

[17] Included in the schools taking this position were those at Heidelberg, Würzburg, Jena, and Munich.

[18] Göttingen and Berlin were the primary schools in this camp.

What new philosophy of science was to be adopted? Several directions were followed in attempting to end the crisis. One approach was to produce a modified neo-Kantianism which could accommodate the new physics; the most important attempt along these lines was that of Ernst Cassirer [1910]. The other, and ultimately philosophically more influential, approach was to embrace a weakened version of Mach's neo-positivism.

The latter approach was tried by groups of interested philosophers and scientists in Berlin under the influence of Hans Reichenbach (his Berlin School) and in Vienna under the influence of Moritz Schlick (the Vienna Circle). Both groups agreed that Mach was correct in insisting on verifiability as a criterion of meaningfulness for theoretical concepts, but concluded he was mistaken in not allowing a place for mathematics. Poincaré's observation that scientific laws often are nothing more than conventions about facts of science (for example, the law of conservation of energy was for Poincaré nothing other than an agreement or convention how science would talk about phenomena)[19] provided the means for introducing mathematics: following Mach, the subject matter of scientific theories is phenomenal regularities; but theories characterize these regularities in terms of *theoretical terms.* Following Poincaré, these theoretical terms are nothing other than mere conventions used to refer to phenomena, in the sense that any assertion made using them could be made in phenomenal language as well. That is, theoretical terms are to be *explicitly defined* in terms of phenomena (or phenomenal language), and are nothing other than abbreviations for such phenomenal descriptions. The definitions of theoretical terms were to be such that theoretical terms could be mathematical. For example, the theoretical term 'mass' might be defined as being a numerical quantity obtained by performing such and such a measurement on certain kinds of phenomena.[20] Since the laws of a theory are formulated using the theoretical terms, this enables one to express the laws mathematically. But since statements using theoretical terms can be eliminated in favor of equivalent statements in phenomenal language, these mathematical laws are nothing other than conventions for expressing certain relations holding between phenomena.

This is almost, but not quite, the Received View on theories. Mathematicians formed a large portion of the Vienna Circle membership;

[19] Poincaré [1902]; much the same position had been advanced earlier by Hertz [1894a], but received much less notice.

[20] Thus operational definitions are a species of explicit definition; see Sec. II–A below.

and most of these mathematicians, as well as some of the philosophers in the group, were quite taken by recent developments in mathematics by Frege, Cantor, and Russell[21] culminating in Whitehead and Russell's *Principia Mathematica* (Whitehead and Russell [1910–13]). *Principia Mathematica* was a coherent development of mathematical logic which also axiomatized much of mathematics in terms of that logic; it thus made a convincing case that all of mathematics can be done in terms of logic, and that logic provides the essence of mathematics. That this is so suggested to the members of the Vienna Circle that the mathematical statements of scientific laws and also the definitions of theoretical terms could be given in terms of mathematical logic, and they proceeded to modify their synthesis of Mach's and Poincaré's positions accordingly. The result was *the original version of the Received View*: A scientific theory is to be axiomatized in mathematical logic (first-order predicate calculus with equality). The terms of the logical axiomatization are to be divided into three sorts: (1) logical and mathematical terms; (2) theoretical terms; and (3) observation terms which are given a phenomenal or observational interpretation. The axioms of the theory are formulations of scientific laws, and specify relationships holding between the theoretical terms. Theoretical terms are merely abbreviations for phenomenal descriptions (that is, descriptions which involve only observational terms). Thus the axiomatizations must include various explicit definitions for the theoretical terms of the form:

$$Tx \equiv Ox$$

where 'T' is a theoretical term and 'O' is an observation term.[22] Such explicit definitions are called *correspondence rules* since they coordinate theoretical terms with corresponding combinations of observation terms. The observation terms are taken as referring to specified phenomena or phenomenal properties,[23] and the only interpretation given to the theoretical terms is their explicit definition provided by the correspondence rules. The earliest published version of the Received View seems to be that of Carnap [1923].

The Received View occupies a central place in logical positivism,

[21] See Frege [1879], [1884], and [1893–1903]; Cantor [1932]; Russell [1903].

[22] '$\equiv$' is to be read "if and only if"; other symbolic logic notation used in this essay will include '$\supset$' ("if . . ., then . . ."), '$\sim$' ("not"), '$\vee$' ("or"), '$\cdot$' ("and"), '(x)' ("for every x"), '$=$' ("equals" or "is identical to"), and '$(\exists x)$' ("there is an x such that").

[23] Initially this was so; later phenomenal characterizations were replaced by characterizations in physicalistic language (see below); I am using "phenomenal" here loosely to encompass phenomenal and physicalistic language characterizations.

the philosophy developed by the Vienna Circle, and many of positivism's other doctrines were consequences of the Received View. To mention just a few: the members of the Vienna Circle, through their partial acceptance of Mach, were opposed to the introduction of metaphysical entities in science and philosophy. For science the Received View provided a means of avoiding the introduction of such metaphysical entities. Since metaphysical entities are not phenomenal or observational entities, the terms used to describe them cannot be observation terms, and so must be theoretical terms. But, theoretical terms are allowed only if they can be provided with correspondence rules which give them an explicit phenomenal definition, and so the objectionable metaphysical entities cannot be introduced into scientific theories. On the other hand, legitimate theoretical terms such as 'mass,' 'force,' and so on, can be introduced because they do admit of explicit phenomenal or observational definition; this solves the troublesome *problem of theoretical entities* without allowing the admission of metaphysical entities. If the Received View could eliminate the introduction of objectionable entities in scientific theories, why could it not be extended to philosophy and all discourse? Seeing no reason why it should not be, and being influenced by Wittgenstein's [1922] doctrines of a logically perfect language, the Received View was broadened into a general doctrine of *cognitive significance*:[24] the only meaningful discourse was that done either in terms of phenomenal language or using terms which were abbreviations for (that is, could be rephrased equivalently as) expressions in phenomenal language; any assertions failing to meet these conditions were metaphysical nonsense. This doctrine was summarized in the slogan, "The meaning of a term is its method of verification," since theoretical terms were defined in terms of the phenomenal conditions by means of which assertions employing them could be verified. The doctrine was known as *the verification theory of meaning*.[25] It was held that ordinary language was not used in accordance with the verification theory, hence that much of what was said lacked cognitive significance and covertly was about metaphysical entities (an idea due to Wittgenstein [1922]). As a means of avoiding such errors through use of ordinary language, much ingenuity was exercised trying to develop a "logically

[24] Judging from Carnap's [1963b] comments (p. 25), it was here that Wittgenstein was most influential; he also exerted an influence in the use of mathematical logic in the Received View as a result of his doctrine that logical truths are devoid of factual or empirical content.

[25] Actually, some earlier versions of the verifiability criterion were attempted; these will not be considered here, since they were not directly incorporated into the Received View.

perfect" language which automatically would make such errors impossible and guarantee the cognitive significance of whatever was said using it.[26]

All cognitively significant discourse about the world must be empirically verifiable. Under the original version of the Received View, all assertions of a scientific theory are reducible to assertions about phenomena in the observation language. In the extension of the Received View to language in general, all factual assertions are reducible to assertions in *protocol language* about phenomenal experience. Thus the problem of verification of assertions is reduced to the question how observation language and protocol language assertions are to be verified. Two cases need to be distinguished: the verification of particular assertions about experience and the verification of generalizations about experience.[27] By means of characterizing the latter, logical positivists attempted to develop an inductive logic.[28] For particular assertions, two different theses were advanced initially. Some members of the Vienna Circle favored a phenomenalistic approach. Under this proposal, the observation or protocol language would be a sense datum language which would provide a phenomenalistic characterization of experience. There then would be no problem verifying observation or protocol language assertions since, by standard sense-data doctrines, the phenomenal descriptions of sense data are incorrigibly known to be true in virtue of one's sensory experience.[29] The other proposal was that the observation or protocol language would be a *physicalistic language* or a thing-language where one speaks of material things and ascribes observable properties to them. Since the properties ascribed to things are observable properties, physicalistic language thus is intersubjective, and there is no problem in determining the truth of assertions in physicalistic language—one merely observes and sees whether the thing has the claimed property; if it does, the assertion is verified; if not, it is falsified. Ultimately

[26] See Carnap [1932], where he distinguishes the *material* and the *formal* mode of speech. Physical language there is introduced as a universal language in the formal mode in which anything cognitively significant can be said of the world. See also Carnap [1932a].

[27] It should be noted that for early positivism theoretical generalizations are just abbreviations for generalizations in the observation language.

[28] The most noteworthy attempts were Carnap [1950] and [1952], and Reichenbach [1938]; it should be noted that these attempts were rather late in the development of logical positivism. In the early stages not too much consideration was given to problems involved in the verification of generalizations.

[29] Carnap [1928] employs this approach; for a critical discussion of sense data theories and the alleged incorrigibility enjoyed by knowledge of sense data, see Suppe [1973b].

physicalism won out, and the observation terms in the Received View were interpreted as referring to material things and observable properties. The verification of physicalistic assertions was taken as nonproblematic. So interpreted, the Received View embodies physicalism as a doctrine of perceptual knowledge.

Gradually the positivistic doctrine that language consists of observation sentences whose only nonlogical terms are observation terms and assertions using theoretical terms explicitly defined in terms of them began to take on an historical dimension among positivists, being construed as an analysis of the process whereby humans acquire language: one initially acquires an observation vocabulary learned by ostensive definition; later nonobservation vocabulary is introduced by definition. At times the Received View is construed analogously as characterizing the way science develops: initially science consists of empirical generalizations formulated using observation terms. Later, as the science advances, theoretical terms are introduced by definition and theoretical laws or generalizations are formulated in terms of theoretical terms. Thus science proceeds "upward" from particular facts to theoretical generalizations about phenomena, this upward process proceeding in an essentially Baconian fashion.[30]

While the above by no means constitutes a comprehensive treatment of the origin of logical positivism or its doctrines, it does suffice to indicate the various philosophical, scientific, and mathematical developments which were synthesized together as the Received View on theories, and to indicate the various philosophical doctrines embedded into that analysis.[31] In the next section we will see that a number of modifications were made in the Received View as defects in the analysis were discovered; we also will see that these changes did not seriously affect a number of the basic positivistic doctrines, and hence that the Received View continues to be essentially positivistic throughout its philosophical life.

[30] That is, it is the inductive method of doing science advocated by Bacon [1620], Bk. I. Carnap [1939], p. 65, indicates that this upward procedure "corresponds to the way in which we really obtain knowledge about physical states by our observations"; on p. 69 he indicates this corresponds to the historical procedure science has followed.

[31] For more comprehensive discussions of the development of logical positivism, see Ayer [1959], pp. 3–28; Carnap [1963b]; Feigl [1956]; Jørgensen [1953]; Passmore [1957], Ch. XVI; and Kraft [1953]. A recent assessment of logical positivism is to be found in Achinstein and Barker [1969]. Ayer [1959] contains translations of a number of the more important papers written by logical positivists.

II. Development of the Received View

We have seen the main features of the Received View as initially presented by the Vienna Circle. In essence that initial version of the Received View construed scientific theories as axiomatic theories formulated in a mathematical logic L meeting the following conditions:

(i) The theory is formulated in a first-order mathematical logic with equality, L.

(ii) The nonlogical terms or constants of L are divided into three disjoint classes called *vocabularies*:

  (a) The *logical vocabulary* consisting of logical constants (including mathematical terms).

  (b) The *observation vocabulary*, V_O, containing observation terms.

  (c) The *theoretical vocabulary*, V_T, containing theoretical terms.

(iii) The terms in V_O are interpreted as referring to directly observable physical objects or directly observable attributes of physical objects.[32]

(iv) There is a set of theoretical postulates T whose only nonlogical terms are from V_T.

(v) The terms in V_T are given an *explicit definition* in terms of V_O by *correspondence rules* C—that is, for every term 'F' in V_T, there must be given a definition for it of the following form:

$$(x)(Fx \equiv Ox),$$

[32] Initially clause (iii) would not have been put this way; indeed it probably would have been omitted. When the Received View first was formulated, logicians had no clear idea of the semantic-syntax distinction, and did not clearly see the need for giving an explicit semantic interpretation to terms in a logical system; for example, in Whitehead and Russell [1910–13] and Carnap [1934] the necessity for a semantic interpretation is not seen. It is only with Gödel [1931] and [1934], and Tarski [1936], that the syntax-semantic distinction is clearly seen. Clause (iii) is a statement of the substance of the basic observational-theoretical term distinction as it should have been stated in accordance with the syntax-semantic distinction.

where '*Ox*' is an expression of *L* containing symbols only from V_O and possibly the logical vocabulary.

It is a corollary to this characterization that all theoretical terms are cognitively significant in the sense that they each satisfy the verification criterion of meaningfulness. The set of axioms *T* is the set of theoretical laws for the theory, and the set *C* of correspondence rules stipulate the allowable applications of the theory to phenomena; the theory is identified with the conjunction *TC* of *T* and *C*.

As the Vienna Circle investigated further the nature of scientific knowledge, the Received View underwent considerable modification and evolution; changes were made in clauses (i) to (iii) and (v) of the initial version of the Received View. These modifications will be traced in the next several subsections.

A. Correspondence Rules and Cognitive Significance

Correspondence rules[33] serve three functions in the Received View: first, they define theoretical terms; second, they guarantee the cognitive significance of theoretical terms; third, they specify the admissible experimental procedures for applying a theory to phenomena. Thus if a correspondence rule defines 'mass' (a theoretical term) as the result of performing measurements *M* on an object under circumstances *S* (where *M* and *S* are specified using observation terms), this specifies an empirical procedure for determining mass, defines 'mass' in terms of that procedure, and does so in a way to guarantee the cognitive significance of the term 'mass.' These three functions of correspondence rules are intimately related in virtue of being tied to the form (for example, an explicit definition) of the correspondence rules. If it is shown that the admissible forms for correspondence rules cannot accommodate legitimate experimental methods, new forms will have to be allowed; since correspondence rules define theoretical terms, new kinds or forms of definition must be countenanced as a result; and since theoretical terms are cognitively significant if defined by admissible correspondence rules, the criterion of cognitive significance also will be changed as a result of introducing new forms for correspondence rules. The most significant modifications made in the Received View concerned the admissible forms for correspondence rules,

33 Correspondence rules also are referred to variously as coordinating definitions, dictionaries, interpretative systems, operational definitions, epistemic correlations, and rules of interpretation.

and thus involved changes in the criterion of cognitive significance and the canons of experimental methodology.

Initially correspondence rules had to have the form of explicit definitions which provide necessary and sufficient observational conditions for the applicability of theoretical terms; theoretical terms were cognitively significant if and only if they were explicitly defined in terms of the observation vocabulary (all terms in the observation vocabulary being cognitively significant), and sentences were cognitively significant if and only if all their nonlogical terms were cognitively significant.[34] Carnap [1936–37][35] pointed out that dispositional terms do not admit of explicit definitions in terms of observational terms, but clearly are cognitively significant. If one were to try to explicitly define the dispositional term 'fragile' in terms of observables, one would have to stipulate something like:

> An object x is fragile if and only if it satisfies the following condition: for any time t, if x is sharply struck at t, then x will break at t.

Since clause (i) of the Received View requires that the theory and correspondence rules be axiomatized in a first-order predicate calculus with equality, this definition must be rendered as follows:

$$Fx \equiv (t)\ (Sxt \supset Bxt)$$

where 'F' is the theoretical term "fragile," 'S' is the observation term "is struck at time," and 'B' is the observation term "breaks at time." But this does not define the dispositional property *fragile*; for '$(t)(Sxt \supset Bxt)$' will be true of any object which is never struck.[36] And so by the definition any object which is never struck will have the property F. But since some of these objects are not fragile, F is not the property *fragile*. Thus explicit definition will not work for dispositional theoretical terms.

A special case version of the requirement that correspondence rules be explicitly defined is that they be *operationally defined.* This version was popularized by the physicist, P. W. Bridgman, and was widely

[34] Actually, logical positivism attempted some earlier criteria of cognitive significance—the criteria of complete verifiability and of complete falsifiability; as these do not directly influence the correspondence rules, they will be omitted from consideration here. See Hempel [1965b] for detailed discussion of these criteria. My discussion of cognitive significance relies heavily on Hempel's very excellent article. For a later, more comprehensive, treatment of the issues, see Scheffler [1963], Pt. II.

[35] Sec. 7.

[36] A sentence of form $(\varphi \supset \psi)$ is false if and only if φ is true and ψ is false; otherwise it is true; thus the assertion depends upon features of '$\supset$' in symbolic logic.

adopted in the social and biological sciences; it enjoys an undeserved degree of allegiance among scientists today.[37] According to Bridgman, "The concept of length is therefore fixed when the operations by which length is measured are fixed: that is, the concept of length involves as much as and nothing more than the set of operations by which length is determined. In general, we mean by any concept nothing more than a set of operations; *the concept is synonymous with the corresponding set of operations.*"[38] Thus the requirement of operational definition for correspondence rules is nothing other than a special version of the requirement that correspondence rules be explicitly defined. Moreover, operational definitions clearly are dispositional, being in terms of what *would* be the result of performing the operations in question (cf. Hempel [1954]). As such, the requirement of operational definition encounters the same problems defining dispositional properties (or concepts) as does the requirement of explicit definition. But it encounters additional difficulties as well. Often there is more than one experimental procedure used to determine, for example, an object's mass. Since concepts or properties are identified with unique combinations of operations, each different experimental procedure defines a distinct concept, and so there are as many distinct concepts of *mass* as there are procedures for determining it. In actual scientific practice, however, these different procedures are taken as measuring the same thing, *mass*; thus operational definition is unsatisfactory as an analysis of the meaning (hence the cognitive significance) of theoretical terms. To this objection, Bridgman replies that science is just confused, that they really are different concepts and science typically equivocates them illegitimately.[39] However, even if science is confused, it remains the case that science views the different concepts of, for example, *mass* defined by different operations as being equivalent, and uses them interchangeably; moreover it could not go about its business if it did not allow such interchange. Thus, if Bridgman's position is to be maintained and physical theory is not to be dismissed as metaphysical nonsense, some proviso must be made for the interchange of the

[37] It seems to be characteristic, but unfortunate, of science to continue holding philosophical positions long after they are discredited. Thus, for example, Skinner's radical behaviorism, which insists on operational definition, came into prominence and dominated behavioral psychology well after most philosophers had abandoned the doctrine of operational or explicit definitions; taxonomists today strongly insist on operational definitions for taxa; see Suppe [1973c] for discussion of this case.

[38] Bridgman [1927], p. 5; italics Bridgman's.

[39] *Ibid.*, pp. 6, 23–24. Bridgman paradoxically finds the proliferation of concepts one of the virtues of his analysis.

different concepts of, for example, *mass*; the only ways this could be accomplished would be to introduce some sort of super theoretical term or concept 'mass' which integrates the various operationally defined concepts of *mass* or else to introduce various laws stipulating their equivalence. The former procedure is unsatisfactory for two reasons; the reason for its introduction precludes its being operationally defined, and so the super-concept will fail to be cognitively significant, and thus will be illegitimate; second, if the super-concept were operationally definable, then there would be no need for all the other different operationally defined concepts of, for example, *mass*. Thus the second proposal must be followed. These laws presumably will take the form that if a given body is measured using operational procedures O_1 and O_2, for $mass_1$ and $mass_2$, the numerical results will be indistinguishable within measurement error.[40] This, unfortunately, will not work in all cases since the different operational procedures for determining *mass* do not apply to the same objects; and for cases where the operational procedures for a concept are not applicable to exactly the same objects, there seems no way of interpreting such laws so as to make them empirically verifiable, and hence cognitively significant. There seems, then, no satisfactory way of integrating the various operationally defined concepts for *mass*; and so operational definition is unsatisfactory as a criterion of cognitive significance, as is the requirement that correspondence rules be operational definitions.[41] Even if these problems could be circumvented, there still would be the problem that every time a new procedure was developed for measuring a given theoretical property, the definitions of theoretical terms would have to be changed or else additional laws identifying the operationally defined concepts, for example, of *mass* would be required; this seems unreasonable: the concepts are the same, we've just learned new ways of experimentally working with them.[42]

Our consideration of correspondence rules as explicit or operational definitions shows two sorts of defects are encountered: (1) dispositional theoretical terms are not explicitly definable if the theory is to be axiomatized in first-order predicate calculus with equality; (2) alternative experimental procedures for measuring the same theoretical property make it unreasonable to identify the theoretical property with

[40] Bridgman [1927] suggests this criterion on p. 23.

[41] For a classic discussion of operationalism's defects, see Hempel [1952] and [1954]. For criticisms of Hempel's discussion, and a different perspective on why operationalism is unworkable, see Suppe [1973e].

[42] Essentially this problem continues to plague the Received View in all its versions, for the theory is identified with *TC* and so any change in correspondence rules (that is, any new experimental procedure) is a change in theory.

any one experimental procedure or even any specified set of alternative procedures. The first defect can be circumvented in two different ways: Either the requirements for definitional forms of correspondence rules can be relaxed so that dispositions need not be explicitly defined (that is, change clause (v) above); or else, allow the theory to be axiomatized in a modal logic capable of expressing subjunctive conditionals. Although the second alternative is reasonable, at the time no adequate modal logic with subjunctive conditionals existed, and so this approach was not attempted.[43] Rather, the first approach was followed. To remedy the second defect, it is necessary that no particular experimental procedure or particular observational condition be made a necessary condition for the applicability of a theoretical term; at most correspondence rules need only supply sufficient observational conditions for the applicability of theoretical terms.

Carnap [1936–37] incorporated these approaches to avoiding the defects resulting from the construal of correspondence rules as explicit definitions into the requirement that correspondence rules be *reduction sentences* which "partially define" theoretical terms. A *bilateral reduction sentence* for 'Q_3' is a universal sentence of the form:

$$Q_1 \supset (Q_2 \equiv Q_3),$$

provided that '$(x) \sim Q_1x$' is not valid. Correspondence rules must be bilateral reduction sentences[44] such that 'Q_3' is a term in V_T, and 'Q_1' and 'Q_2' are terms in V_O or logical combinations of such terms.[45] Thus, for example, the dispositional property *fragile* would be defined by the following reduction sentence:

$$(x)(t)[Sxt \supset (Bxt \equiv Fx)],$$

where 'S', 'B', and 'F' are as above. Unlike the explicit definition case, if a is a nonfragile object which is never sharply struck, it is not implied that 'Fa' is true; but '$Sat \supset (Bat \equiv Fa)$' will be true. Thus the defect of explicit definition is avoided. The reason it is avoided is that a re-

[43] Later, however, it was attempted; these attempts will be considered briefly in Sec. II–C.

[44] This is, strictly speaking, incorrect since Carnap also allows other forms of reduction sentences to be correspondence rules; for simplicity these other forms will not be considered here; see Carnap [1936–37], Sec. 5, for discussion of them. Explicit definitions are equivalent to a form of bilateral reduction sentence, and so continue to be admissible correspondence rules.

[45] Carnap [1936–37] allows that 'Q_1' and 'Q_2' also may be theoretical terms which have been previously introduced in what he calls a reduction chain; this in fact does not add to the number of theoretical terms which can be introduced, and so the complication will be ignored here—but see the next note.

duction sentence does not completely define what it is for something to be fragile; rather it merely stipulates a test condition which is applicable only under certain circumstances (here when an object is sharply struck).

Going over to reduction sentences as the form for correspondence rules may appear to be nothing more than a technical logical trick used to get around the limitations of material implication ('⊃'), and get something of the effect of subjunctive conditionals without having to develop a modal logic of subjunctive conditionals. This certainly is part of what was involved, but the changes were far more significant. First, by allowing correspondence rules to be reduction sentences, it no longer can be required that correspondence rules completely define the meaning of theoretical terms; rather, correspondence rules only *partially* define them since more than one reduction sentence (correspondence rule) is possible for the same theoretical term. To continue our *fragile* example: fragile objects break if twisted sharply (T) or if subjected to certain high frequency sounds (P). Thus in addition to the above reduction sentence, we could introduce the following reduction sentences as correspondence rules:

$$(x)(t)[Txt \supset (Bxt \equiv Fx)]$$

$$(x)(t)[Pxt \supset (Bxt \equiv Fx)].$$

Each of these reduction sentences specifies a test condition, the passing of which is sufficient for being fragile; but it is not necessary that an object actually pass any of these test conditions to be fragile; all that is required is that it *would* if the test actually *were* carried out. A finite collection of reduction sentences for a theoretical term F collectively constitutes an explicit definition if and only if the disjunction of the various test conditions (for example, those corresponding to 'T', 'S', 'P' above) either is logically valid or else is a logical consequence of the theory the reduction sentences occur in. As a finite collection of reduction sentences rarely if ever meets this requirement, collections of reduction sentences generally do not completely or explicitly define theoretical terms; rather they only provide *partial definitions* for theoretical terms: Each reduction sentence is a partial definition of its constituent theoretical term (unless the reduction sentence is equivalent to an explicit definition). Correspondence rules thus only provide partial definitions of theoretical terms.

Since allowing reduction sentences to be correspondence rules eliminates both defects of the explicit definition requirement, by 1936 clause (v) of the Received View had been replaced by:

(v′) The terms in V_T each are given a partial interpretation in terms of V_O by reduction sentences.

Adopting (v′), of course, required a change in the criterion of cognitive significance. The criterion now became: Every term with empirical significance must be capable of introduction, on the basis of observation terms, through chains of true reduction sentences.[46] These reduction sentences were claimed to be analytic sentences. Just as (v) had been viewed as characterizing the historical processes whereby language was acquired and science developed (see Sec. I), with this change in the Received View (v′) also was interpreted as characterizing those historical processes.

Although the change from (v) to (v′) eliminated the defects of explicit definition, the latter has its own defects. For not all theoretical terms in science are introduced by reduction sentences; indeed, such terms as the ψ function in quantum mechanics do not even seem amenable to definition by reduction sentences. More generally, metrical theoretical concepts such as 'mass', 'mass point', 'rigid body', 'force', 'absolute temperature', 'pressure', 'volume', 'Carnot process', 'electron', 'proton', etc., are never introduced by introductive chains of reduction sentences. Rather, as Hempel [1952] observes (p. 32),

> Terms of this kind are not introduced by definition or reduction chains based on observables; in fact they are not introduced by any piecemeal process of assigning meaning to them individually. Rather, the constructs used in a theory are introduced jointly, as it were, by setting up a theoretical system formulated in terms of them and by giving this system an experimential interpretation, which in turn confers empirical meaning on the theoretical constructs.

And the claim here is not merely that science *does not* introduce these terms by reduction sentences, but that it *cannot* for such metrical concepts. For,

> suitable reduction sentences for the phrase 'length $(u, v) = r$' would have to specify for every theoretically permissible value of r, a necessary and a sufficient condition, couched in terms of observables, for an interval (u, v) having a length of exactly r cm. But it is not even possible to formulate all the requisite sufficient conditions; for this would

[46] A chain of reduction sentences is a sequence of reduction sentences such that every nonlogical term in a given reduction sentence either is in V_O or else occurs in a previous reduction sentence in the sequence. See Carnap [1936–37], Sec. 6. It can be shown that any reduction sentence introduced through a chain of reduction sentences is equivalent to a reduction sentence involving only one theoretical term—the one being partially defined; thus allowing chains of reduction sentences does not add to the class of theoretical terms which may be introduced.

> mean the establishment, for every possible value of *r*, of a purely observational criterion whose satisfaction by a given interval (u, v) would entail that the interval was exactly *r* cm. long. That a complete set of such criteria cannot exist . . . is obvious [since the total number of defining expressions that can be formed from the finite vocabulary available is denumerably infinite, whereas the class of all theoretically permissible *r*-values has the power of the continuum].[47]

On the basis of such arguments it was concluded that it is unreasonable to require that theoretical terms be defined individually by introductive chains of reduction sentences and also unreasonable to require that being so introducible should be the criterion for cognitive significance.[48]

[47] Hempel [1952], p. 32.

[48] The arguments were taken as conclusive, but it does not seem to me that they are. Specifically Hempel's argument just quoted fails to make its case. In the passage just quoted, Hempel's argument turns crucially on the claim that under (v′) reduction sentences would have to specify necessary and sufficient conditions, couched in terms of observables, for every theoretically permissible value of *r*. Note that there is an obscurity in the claim: is 'length $(u, v) = r$' a sentence in L_T, a formula (sentence form) with free variables in L_T, or is it a relational theoretical term? If it is a sentence, then Hempel's claim amounts to a requirement that the reduction sentences for the theory be such that each sentence in L_T involving theoretical terms has a unique observational consequence. But this claim does not follow from (v′). All that (v′) requires is that each theoretical term be specified in terms of observational consequences which will occur in at least one circumstance or test situation. If this condition is met by each theoretical term, in L_T, then according to Carnap's reduction sentence proposal, any L_T sentence involving the theoretical terms will be cognitively significant. And it is consistent with this that there be L_T sentences which have no testable consequences. For example, suppose that we have the L_T sentence '$(x)(T_1x \supset T_2x)$', where 'T_1' and 'T_2' have been introduced only by the following two reduction sentences

$$S_1x \supset (O_1x \equiv T_1x)$$
$$S_2x \supset (O_2x \equiv T_2x),$$

where it is physically impossible for x to be both S_1 and S_2 at the same time. Then '$(x)(T_1x \supset T_2x)$' will be cognitively significant but will have no testable or observable consequences. On this reading of 'length $(u, v) = r$,' Hempel's claim thus would be false. If 'length $(u, v) = r$' is a formula with free variables, then Hempel's claim amounts to a requirement that the reduction sentences be such that every instance of it (where 'u', 'v', and 'r' are replaced by constants designating real numbers) has a unique observable consequence; again, the same objections as above are forthcoming. [Note that there is a certain artificiality about these two cases since they presuppose that there are separate constants designating each real number—which is impossible since L is a first-order predicate calculus.] Finally, suppose 'length $(u, v) = r$' is a relational theoretical term. In this case 'length $(u, v) = r$' is a misleading way of writing it; for it is nothing other than a three-place predicate, and 'u', 'v', and 'r' strictly speaking are not a part of the term. (As written it is an atomic formula—which suggests the first two readings we have considered.) It would be more accurate to write it 'length (—, – – –) = . . .'. Condition (v′) only requires for the introduction of this term that there be a reduction sentence which enables one to observationally determine the applicability of the term in at least one situation. Suppose now that I describe a measuring situation S where measurements are accurate to three decimal places

Again (v) was weakened still further so as to allow correspondence rules which were not reduction sentences, (v′) being replaced by:

(v″) The correspondence rules C constitute an *interpretative system* satisfying the following conditions:

(a) The set C of rules must be finite.
(b) The set of rules C must be logically compatible with the theoretical postulates (axioms) of the theory.
(c) C contains no nonlogical terms not belonging to either V_O or V_T.
(d) Each rule in C must contain at least one V_O term and at least one V_T term essentially or nonvacuously—that is, is not equivalent to a rule which does not contain at least one V_O term or else does not contain at least one V_T term.
(e) The rules in C must be such that TC is cognitively significant.[49]

Underlying (v″) is the idea that the theory as a unit has various observable consequences which makes it testable; but these consequences are not definitional of any particular theoretical terms, being rather the empirical manifestations of theoretical entities interacting in the ways specified by the laws or axioms of the theory. The correspondence rules may be construed as the sum total of admissible experimental procedures for applying the theory to observable phenomena. They do not provide complete definitions of theoretical terms;

---

and where the measurements are read out on a numerical counter which truncates all digits beyond the third decimal place; let r' be the value obtained from the counter. Let 'O_1' be an observation-language predicate describing the situation and the output of the counter, and let 'O_2' be an observation-language description of the paper-and-pencil process of subtracting one number r from another r' and finding that $| r-r' | \leq .0001$. Then form the reduction sentence

$$S(u, v) \supset (O_1(u, v)r' \cdot O_2 rr' \equiv \text{length}\ (u, v) = r),$$

where '(u, v)' is used to designate the interval being measured. This qualifies as a legitimate reduction sentence and also enables 'length (—, – – –) = . . .' to be real-valued. Thus condition (v′) is satisfied, and so any sentence or formula of L_T involving 'length (—, – – –) = . . .' will be cognitively significant under (v′). Thus Hempel is incorrect in his crucial claim—not only in this case, but no matter how 'length $(u, v) = r$' is construed. Indeed, the ability to make that claim is exactly what is given up in going from (v) to (v′); it is the price of allowing partial interpretation. And without assuming that claim, his case cannot be made. I conclude therefore that his arguments fail to make his case. I do think Hempel's observations in the quotation immediately preceding the argument just criticized are sound, however.

[49] For a discussion of interpretative systems, see Carnap [1963c], [1956]; Hempel [1963], [1958], [1965b]. The doctrine was anticipated in Schlick [1918]; see Feigl [1956] for other anticipations.

rather, together with the theoretical postulates *T*, they provide the theoretical terms with a partial observational interpretation. It is obvious that adopting (v″) requires abandonment of the earlier doctrines about language acquisition and theory development, though it does allow retention of the claim that the observation language is the source of empirical significance.

The greatest difficulty with (v″) is specifying condition (e). Under (v″) it is the theory as a whole (that is, the conjunction of the theoretical postulates *T* and correspondence rules *C*) which must be cognitively significant. A number of attempts were made to specify what this consists in. It was suggested that the theoretical system (*TC*) is cognitively significant if and only if it is partially interpreted to at least such an extent that none of its primitive sentences is isolated, where an isolated primitive sentence *S* is a sentence in *TC* such that the omission of *S* from *TC* does not affect the class of observation sentences deducible from *TC*. This proposal has been shown defective in that it allows the possibility of there being two logically equivalent formulations of a theoretical system such that one may qualify as cognitively significant whereas the other will contain an isolated sentence among its primitives, and thus will fail to be cognitively significant.[50] To avoid this defect, the criterion was revised, namely: A theoretical system *TC* is cognitively significant if and only if it is partially interpreted by correspondence rules *C* to such an extent that in no system equivalent to it is any primitive sentence isolated. It can be shown, however, that this criterion in effect requires that cognitively significant theories not contain postulates employing V_T terms. Since science is not this Machian, the criterion fails.[51] Other attempts to find a satisfactory criterion of cognitive significance for clause (e) of (v″) have been made, but none of these has proved satisfactory. As a result, most adherents to the Received View abandoned the search for cognitive significance and have deleted (e) from (v″). In doing so they have tended to abandon the analytic-synthetic distinction and no longer maintain that the correspondence rules *C* are analytic truths (see Sec. IV-B-1 for related discussion).[52] Thus, in the final version of

[50] Suppose *TC* contains sentences *S′*, *S″*, . . ., where only *S′* is isolated. Let *T′C* be just like *TC* except that *S′* and *S″* are replaced by the single sentence (*S′·S″*). *T′C* will fail to have any isolated primitive sentences. See Hempel [1965b], pp. 115–116.

[51] See Hempel [1965b], p. 116.

[52] The one exception was Carnap, who continued to look for criteria of cognitive significance; see Carnap [1956], Secs. VI to VIII; [1963c], pp. 960–961, 963–966; [1966], Chs. 27, 28. As will be seen in Sec. IV–B–1, he did give up the claim that the correspondence rules are analytic truths.

the Received View, (v) is replaced by (v″) with (e) deleted. Correspondence rules thus specify the admissible experimental procedures for applying the theory to observational phenomena; at the same time they, in conjunction with the theoretical postulates, partially interpret the terms in V_T by specifying their observational content. No other observational interpretation is given to the terms of V_T other than that supplied by *TC*.

B. Interpretation of Theories: The Status of Theoretical Terms

The successive weakenings in the requirements on correspondence rules culminates in the following picture of scientific theories. A scientific theory *TC* is an axiomatized system where *T* are the theoretical postulates or basic laws of the theory formulated in L_T, and *C* are correspondence rules specifying the admissible applications of *T* to observable phenomena. The inclusion of *C* in the theory enables *T* to be used to make predictions about what will be observed subsequently. For example, suppose *TC* is a version of classical mechanics. To apply *TC* to predict the subsequent behavior of a ball released on an inclined plane, we would first have to determine certain features of the experimental situation such as the mass of the body, the angle of inclination of the plane, and the relative location of the ball when released. These various features can be determined by performing various observable operations such as noticing what number on a balance the pointer coincides with when the ball is being weighed. These various observable operations can be specified in terms of V_O, and then incorporated into correspondence rules which correlate these observable operations with various theoretical terms from V_T; thus we obtain correspondence rules such as the following:

> If object *x* is placed on a balance and the pointer of the balance coincides with numeral *y*, then the mass of *x* is the number designated by numeral *y*.

Given that we have performed this operation and found that the pointer indicated '32' on a gram scale when the ball was weighed, we know by the correspondence rule that the mass of the ball is 32 grams. More generally, what we are doing here is the following: (1) various operations or experimental procedures are carried out which may be described by the true V_O sentences $O_1, \ldots, O_n$. (2) Using correspondence rules $C_1, \ldots, C_m$ in *C*, $O_1, \ldots, O_n$ are correlated with various assertations $T_1, \ldots, T_k$ in L_T—for example, 'The mass of the object is 32 gm.'. (3) The set of theoretical assertions $T_1, \ldots, T_k$ constitutes a theoretical characterization of the inclined plane experiment in its initial configuration at the instant the ball is released. Using the theoretical laws, T, together with $T_1, \ldots,$ T_k various predictions can be made about the configuration of the inclined plane at subsequent times—for example, we could deduce T' as a logical consequence of T and $T_1, \ldots, T_k$, where T' says that the velocity of the object will be 16 cm./sec. 3 seconds after release. Having obtained T' we can use rules in C to "translate" T' into a V_O statement O' about the distance the ball has traveled after 3 seconds; for example, O' might say, 'when the hand of the stopwatch clicked at release reaches 3, the ball will be at a point which coincides with such and such mark on a yardstick lain on the path of the ball with its tip coinciding with the point where the ball was released.' The theory TC thus is able to make predictions about observable phenomena; both T and C are essentially involved in such predictions. Since most adherents to the Received View also subscribe to the covering-law model of explanation wherein prediction and explanation are formally the same, the only difference being that prediction is before the fact and explanation is after the fact,[53] TC also is capable of providing scientific explanations in essentially the same manner.[54]

One function, then, of theories TC is to make predictions of, and provide explanations for, observable phenomena expressible in V_O statements. So regarded, TC serves to establish various lawlike regularities between observable phenomena; it does so by enabling the deduction of a number of V_O statements of the form:

$$O_1 \cdot O_2 \cdot \ldots \cdot O_n \supset O',$$

where $O_1, \ldots, O_n, O'$ belong to V_O.[55] These conditional observation

[53] See Hempel and Oppenheim [1948] for discussion of this doctrine; the identification of prediction and explanation recently has come under considerable attack, and Hempel [1965a] surveys and addresses itself to these attacks. In this article Hempel retreats somewhat from the identification of prediction and explanation, and he now leaves open the question whether every prediction potentially is an explanation; he still maintains the converse however. The article includes an extensive bibliography on the problem of explanation.

[54] The above account of the use of TC in prediction and explanation is overly simple, and will not work for cases where the laws in T are essentially statistical—for example, in quantum theory or statistical mechanics. The modifications required to accommodate such cases need not be considered here. The discussion in Secs. 3.2, 3.3 of Hempel [1965a] can be considered as one approach to making the modifications.

[55] That this is so easily can be seen. By the above discussion, O' is a valid consequence of $O_1, \ldots, O_n \cdot TC$; hence by the deduction theorem for first-order predicate calculus, '$O_1 \cdot O_2 \cdot \ldots \cdot O_n \supset O'$' is a valid consequence of TC.

statements are statements about the regularities which hold between observable phenomena, and they constitute *TC*'s predictions about the regularities in observable phenomena which may be experienced. Let T_O be the class of all observation statements (statements whose only nonlogical terms are from V_O) which are valid consequences of *TC*. Then T_O consists of all observable consequences of *TC*—that is, all of the predictions the theory *TC* can make about observable phenomena. If *TC* is empirically true, it is necessary that all the observation statements in T_O be true of the world.

Is the truth of all the statements in T_O a sufficient condition for *TC* being empirically true? Whether it is depends on the empirical status accorded to *T*, and hence to the terms in V_T. Two different statuses are possible for the terms in V_T. First, one may allow that the theoretical terms refer to real but nonobservable physical entities or their attributes; for example, 'electron jump' as a term in V_T refers to a behavioral characteristic of a nonobservable object, an electron, which really exists. This is the *realist interpretation* of theories, and under it, the statements in T_O being true is a necessary but not a sufficient condition for *TC* being empirically true: in addition the laws *T* of the theory must be empirically true generalizations about the behavior of the nonobservable entities referred to by the V_T terms. *C* then will include empirically true or false statements how these theoretical entities manifest themselves in observable ways.[56] Since it is possible that all the statements in T_O may be true but *T* or *C* will be false, the statements in T_O being empirically true is not a sufficient condition for *TC* being empirically true. Second, one can deny that the terms in V_T refer to any nonobservable entities which really exist; if this denial is made, then sentences involving V_T terms will not be true or false, and so *TC* is not empirically true or false. Rather, *TC* is nothing more than a set of rules for making observable predictions; that is, it is simply a set of rules for specifying T_O. In this case the issue is not whether *TC* is true, but rather whether it is *adequate* in the sense that T_O contains all and only those V_O statements which are empirically true. This second view is called the *instrumentalist interpretation* of theories. On the instrumentalist interpretation, to say that *TC* is empirically true

[56] More precisely, *C* in conjunction with *T* provides a partial specification of the meanings of V_T terms and also makes factual assertions about the observable manifestations of the referents of the V_T terms. According to the doctrine that the Received View incorporates the analytic-synthetic distinction (see Sec. IV–B–1 below), every sentence of *L* either specifies meanings, hence is analytic and not factually true or false, or makes factual assertions, hence is factually true or false. Thus part of the content of *C* is empirically true or false, and part of it consists of analytic meaning contents.

is just a loose and elliptical way of saying TC is adequate in this sense. The Received View can be maintained both with a realist interpretation and with an instrumentalist interpretation.

Maintaining an instrumentalist interpretation of the Received View[57] poses a problem, however: Why are theoretical terms necessary? Even if they cannot be explicitly defined, they are not necessary in the sense that all they do is enable one to define the class T_O. But, then, why can one not just specify T_O directly, without recourse to V_T terms, without recourse to TC? Many adherents to the Received View have thought this possible, arguing that if the terms and general principles of a scientific theory serve their purpose by establishing definite connections between observable phenomena, then they can be dispensed with; for any definite connections established by TC could be established or specified by a law which does not employ any statements from V_T (for example, the class T_O of observation statements establishes exactly the same connections). Taking this position leaves one with a question, namely, why does science continue to use TC formulations—why does it continue to employ V_T terms in its theories when it does not need them? Hempel observed that this question could be posed as a dilemma, which he calls the *theoretician's dilemma*: "If the terms and principles of a theory serve their purpose, they are unnecessary, as just pointed out; and if they do not serve their purpose they are surely unnecessary. But given any theory, its terms and principles either serve their purpose or they do not. Hence the terms and principles of any theory are unnecessary." [58] Thus, the instrumentalist interpretation apparently leads to the theoretician's dilemma, and there seems no need for V_T; hence there is no need for the mechanism of the Received View.

The theoretician's dilemma also arises if one maintains that initial version of the Received View wherein only explicitly definable theoretical terms are allowed and theoretical assertions are construed as abbreviated descriptions of phenomena. This version can be construed as providing a realistic interpretation to TC wherein theories are confined to the observational or phenomenal level.[59] On this version

[57] Persons who have done so include Ramsey [1931], pp. 194–255, and Schlick [1938], pp. 67–68. Toulmin's [1953] alternative to the Received View also maintains an instrumentalism, as does Ryle [1949]. The Copenhagen interpretation of quantum theory also can be construed as an instrumentalist account; see Hooker [1972a].

[58] Hempel [1958], Sec. 5. The discussion which follows of this dilemma borrows heavily from Hempel's article; however, some of the points are not made in Hempel's paper, and my development of the problem is somewhat different.

[59] Note that it is also possible to construe the explicit definition version of the Received View instrumentally. If one allows the theoretical terms to be mathemat-

theoretical terms in principle are dispensable, and so by the above considerations are unnecessary. It may seem that the dilemma can be disposed of for this case on the grounds that the problems considered in the last section require the rejection of the explicit definition thesis. But to dismiss the theoretician's dilemma in this case on such grounds would be illegitimate. For scrutiny of Section II-A will indicate that the reasons for loosening the restrictions on correspondence rules, the reasons for allowing them to be only partial definitions of the terms in V_T, were that the theoretical terms actually used in science did not all admit of explicit definition or even of definition by reduction sentences. All this establishes is that *if V_T terms have a place in theories,* they do not all admit of explicit definition. Thus the considerations of the last section leave the theoretician's dilemma unchallenged.

Is the theoretician's dilemma a genuine dilemma? Is it true that the V_T terms and principles of theories are unnecessary? If not, then one of the horns of the dilemma must be false. The nature of the dilemma is such that only the first horn could be false; so if the dilemma is to be attacked, the attack will have to center on the claim that "If the terms and principles of a theory serve their purpose, they are unnecessary." The basis for this claim is the observation that on the instrumentalist interpretation or the explicit definition version, all *TC* does is define T_O.[60] This, by itself, does not establish the first horn of the dilemma. For if T_O cannot be defined except by recourse to *TC*, it does not follow that the terms and principles of *TC* are unnecessary. That

---

ical and *T* to include mathematical apparatus it is not clear that one can maintain that theoretical assertions are merely abbreviated descriptions of phenomena. (Recall here from Sec. I that one of the changes introduced by the positivists in Mach's view, which did hold that they were merely abbreviated descriptions of phenomena, was to allow mathematical conventions in *T* which could not be reduced to the phenomenal level.) In this case an explicity defined theoretical term, whose conditions of applicability are equivalent to those for a specified observable condition, may not mean the same thing as the observation terms; when this is coupled with a refusal to allow an independent semantic interpretation of theoretical terms, one obtains an instrumentalism wherein theoretical terms have no referents even though explicitly defined in terms of the observation language. Thus, by the previous argument for instrumentalist interpretations, the theoretician's dilemma obtains; when coupled with the discussion which follows, we obtain the result that the theoretician's dilemma results from any version of the explicit definability thesis. More or less contemporary formulations of explicit definition versions of the Received View are found in Bergmann [1957], MacCorquodale and Meehl [1948], and Skinner [1953]; it is not entirely clear whether these versions are to be taken instrumentally or realistically.

[60] On a realistic interpretation (except when explicit definitions are required) *TC* clearly does more: it describes various nonobservable entities and their systematic interactions.

is, the first horn is true only if T_O could be defined without recourse to anything like *TC*, if it could be defined using just V_O terms and logic. The considerations raised thus far do not show that this is possible.

How might one demonstrate that T_O can be defined without recourse to anything like *TC*? One suggestion is that a result in logic, Craig's Theorem, demonstrates this possibility. Put overly simply, Craig's Theorem says that if the nonlogical vocabulary of a logical system *S* is bifurcated into two classes, *A* and *B*, and if T' is the class of theorems of *S* such that the only nonlogical terms occurring in them are from *A*, then there exists a logical system S' whose only nonlogical terms are from *A* such that the theorems of S' are exactly the sentences in T'.[61] If we let *A* be V_O, *B* be V_T, T' be T_O, and *S* be *TC*, then Craig's Theorem says that there does exist a theory S' whose nonlogical symbols are just those of V_O and whose theorems are just the sentences in T_O. This does establish that there exists a theory which can be axiomatized independently of *TC* which has T_O as its theorems. However, the S' established by the proof of Craig's Theorem will not be finitely axiomatizable. S' will have an infinite number of axioms, and these axioms cannot even be specified by a finite number of axiom schemata.[62] Indeed, every sentence in T_O will be an axiom of S' or else will be logically equivalent to an axiom of S'. That is, the axioms of S' will be a set of sentences equivalent to the sentences in T_O, and so the only nonaxiom theorems will be sentences equivalent to axioms. In effect, then, S' is little more than a listing of the sentences in T_O, a listing which can never be written down completely. Thus, S' can be completely specified only by showing how to construct S' from TC (that is, by giving an instance of the proof of Craig's Theorem), so Craig's Theorem fails to show that *TC* can be dispensed with in practical applications.[63]

Another approach to establishing the first horn of the theoretician's dilemma is to employ the Ramsey sentence. Ramsey [1931] (pp. 212–236) observed that by using a higher-order logic[64] V_T terms could be

[61] See Craig [1956] for a more detailed heuristic treatment of Craig's Theorem; the full proof of the theorem is in Craig [1953]; for a more comprehensive treatment of Craig's Theorem and Lyndon's generalizations of it, see Robinson [1963], Ch. 4.

[62] It can be shown that if a theory in first-order predicate calculus is axiomatizable by a finite number of axiom schemata, then there exists an equivalent system which uses a finite number of axioms, but has additional inference rules.

[63] See Maxwell [1962], pp. 17–18, for substantially the same point.

[64] First-order logic allows quantification only over individual variables; higher-order logics allow quantification over predicates and relational variables as well; see Church [1956], Ch. 5, for details.

eliminated in a theory *TC* where *TC* has a finite number of axioms. The procedure is as follows: Let $\alpha_1, \ldots, \alpha_n$ be all the different theoretical terms which occur in the axioms $\psi_1, \ldots, \psi_m$ of *TC*. Then *TC* may be construed as a logical system with one proper axiom:

$$\psi_1 \cdot \ldots \cdot \psi_m.$$

Let $\psi_1', \ldots, \psi_m'$ be formulas just like $\psi_1, \ldots, \psi_m$ except that every occurrence of a V_T term α_i $(1 \leq i \leq n)$ has been replaced by the predicate variable β_i (where $\beta_1, \ldots, \beta_n$ all are different). Then form the *Ramsey-sentence for TC*,

$$(\exists \beta_1) \ldots . (\exists \beta_n) (\psi_1' \cdot \ldots \cdot \psi_m'),$$

and let TC^R be the theory which is obtained from *TC* by replacing

$$\psi_1 \cdot \ldots \cdot \psi_m$$

by the Ramsey sentence for *TC*. All of the theorems of T_O will be theorems of *TC* and of TC^R, but unlike *TC*, there will be no theorems in TC^R which contain terms from V_T—the reason being that the V_T terms in *TC* have been replaced by existentially quantified predicate variables. That is, whereas '$\psi_1 \cdot \ldots \cdot \psi_m$' uses V_T terms to assert that, for example, electrons have such and such observable properties or manifestations, the Ramsey sentence merely asserts that there exist entities which have such and such observable properties or manifestations. Thus, TC^R avoids the use of theoretical terms only by refusing to mention them; it just refers to theoretical entities without explicitly mentioning them. As Hempel [1958] summarizes it, the Ramsey-sentence for *TC* "still asserts the existence of certain entities of the kind postulated by *TC*, without guaranteeing any more than does *TC* that those entities are observables, or at least fully characterizable in terms of observables. Hence, Ramsey-sentences provide no satisfactory way of avoiding theoretical concepts." [65] Moreover, it is clear that TC^R can be formulated only relative to *TC*, and so the use of Ramsey sentences fails to show that science can dispense with theoretical terms or principles.[66]

None of the techniques attempted have succeeded in showing that theoretical terms and principles are dispensable with in the sense that

[65] Page 81; notational changes have been made in the quotation to make it compatible with the notation I am using here. It should be noted that Ramsey's approach almost succeeds in construing theories realistically; it only fails to do so because there are no V_T terms. As such it is rather paradoxical that Ramsey thought of theories as being instrumentalistic (see, for example, Ramsey [1931], pp. 1944ff. and 237–255).

[66] See also Carnap [1966], Ch. 26, for related discussion of Ramsey sentences and theorizing.

one could formulate a theory S' with theorems T_O without prior knowledge of TC. But even if some other technique were found which could do this, it would not itself be sufficient to establish the first horn of the theoretician's dilemma. To be useful a scientific theory must provide an economical statement of the regularities which hold between observable phenomena, in the sense that it has a high degree of systematic economy and its formulation is heuristically fertile in suggesting experiments and indicating possible extensions.[67] Thus, to establish the first horn of the theoretician's dilemma, it is necessary to show that T_O can be formulated or characterized without recourse to theoretical terms or principles in such a way as to yield a high degree of systematic economy and heuristic fertility; those who argue that theoretical principles and laws are not necessary have failed to show that T_O can be so formulated; thus they have not made their case. Moreover, the whole history of science indicates that the means whereby a high degree of systematic economy and heuristic fertility is obtained is through the use of theoretical principles involving nonobservational concepts. Thus it seems that the first horn of the theoretician's dilemma is false, and a case cannot be made for it. The theoretician's dilemma is a pseudo-dilemma.

Commitment to an instrumentalist interpretation thus does not call for the eliminability of theoretical terms. In fact, Hempel's dissolution of the theoretician's dilemma shows that theoretical terms generally are necessary under the instrumentalist interpretation of theories; and one of the attractions of an instrumentalism is that one is allowed to introduce whatever theoretical terms one needs to obtain a fruitful theory which permits the economical prediction of observable phenomena without having to be concerned with the question whether they designate anything real.[68] Nonetheless, to allow theoretical terms while holding an instrumentalism leaves one in the uncomfortable position of holding that theoretical terms are necessary, but they do not mean anything or refer to anything. Rather than maintain such a position, most people who accept the legitimacy of theoretical terms in scientific theorizing also commit themselves to the position that they have real referents in the world. To use Quine's dictum, "to be is to be the value of a bound variable," [69] and so to countenance theoretical terms is to commit oneself to the existence of theoretical (that is, non-

[67] See Hempel [1958], Sec. 10, for development and defense of these claims.

[68] This, of course, is not the only motivation for adopting an instrumentalism. In Sec. V–B–1–a we will consider some theoretical arguments advanced by Toulmin [1953] in support of the contention that all laws and theories must be construed instrumentally. Ryle [1949] also argues for the same contention.

[69] Quine [1953], pp. 12–14.

observable) entities. Thus, most adherents to the Received View who countenance theoretical terms eschew instrumentalism and commit themselves to a realist interpretation of theories.

Whereas the instrumentalist's problem with theoretical entities and terms was how to dispense with them, the realist's problems are how to account for those entities and the meanings of the theoretical terms which designate them. On the Received View the correspondence rules provide the solution to these problems: theoretical entities may be countenanced whenever they are referred to by theoretical terms which have been introduced by correspondence rules; and such introduction of theoretical terms provides them with empirical meaning. More specifically, the correspondence rules C together with the theoretical postulates T for a theory TC provide a partial interpretation of the terms in V_T, and thus only provide a partial specification of their meaning. Moreover, "all the interpretation (in the strict sense of this term, i.e., observational interpretation), that can be given for [the terms in V_T] . . . is given in the C rules." [70] In particular, it is forbidden to give the terms of V_T an independent observational semantic interpretation.[71] This, however, raises a new problem about the meaning of theoretical terms: Where does the rest of the meaning of V_T terms come from if TC only partially specifies it, and no independent observational semantic interpretation may be given?

The answer lies in the fact that the meaning of the theoretical terms is not wholly observational; thus TC could not specify the full meaning of theoretical terms. To fully specify the meaning of V_T terms, recourse must be made to a richer metalanguage.[72] Thus, if the theoretical term t in V_T is interpreted as meaning *electron,* then a full specification of t's meaning would be a full specification of the meaning of 'electron'; but only part of the meaning of 'electron' concerns the observational manifestations of electrons; indeed, only part of its meaning is empirical. In addition 'electron' has various other associations, and so on, of a nonempirical sort which contribute to its meaning. Thus, when a scientist employs the theoretical term 'electron' in a theory TC, he is asserting that something exists which has the observable manifestations specified by TC; but he is not committed to these observable manifestations exhausting the meaning of the term 'electron'; all he is

[70] Carnap [1956], p. 45.

[71] Note that clauses (i) to (v) of the initial version of the Received View make no provision for such an independent interpretation.

[72] Hempel [1963], p. 695; Carnap [1939], p. 62; see also what Hempel says on p. 260 below. A metalanguage is a language used to talk about another language (called the object language) and to specify the syntax and semantic interpretations of sentences in the object language.

committed to is the claim that it captures at least part of the empirical meaning of the term.[73] That is, the correspondence rules C together with theoretical principles T provide only a partial interpretation of the terms in V_T by specifying properties of the theoretical entities which manifest themselves observationally. But this is only a partial interpretation since the observational properties of theoretical entities do not exhaust the meaning of the theoretical terms designating them; they need not even exhaust the empirical meanings of the terms. Full specification of the meanings of theoretical terms requires recourse to a richer metalanguage.

C. Logic of the Conditional

Under the realistic interpretation, the Received View asserts that a scientific theory is a deductively connected bundle of laws which are applicable to observable phenomena in ways specified by the correspondence rules. Clause (i) of the initial version of the Received View requires that these laws be axiomatized in a first-order logic with equality; since such logics are extensional,[74] scientific laws are extensional. The difficulties of defining dispositionals in the indicative mood, the fact that scientific laws resemble dispositions, and difficulties encountered in attempts to characterize scientific laws extensionally,[75] called into question the Received View's commitment to laws being extensional (clause (i) above). Clearly, some modification of (i) seemed necessary.

That scientific laws have a subjunctive character is obvious since they describe not only what *has* happened or what *will* happen, but also describe what *would* happen under various circumstances. As

[73] Hempel [1958], p. 70; it will capture all of the empirical meaning of the term only if no more correspondence rules are possible and all theories which employ the term are reducible to TC. The nonempirical portion of its meaning still will be unspecified; using techniques developed in Suppe [1973a] it is possible to show that the empirical content is extensional whereas the nonempirical part is intensional. The issue raised here will be discussed further in Sec. IV–C below; a much more thorough and detailed discussion is to be found in Suppe [1971].

[74] To say that a logic is extensional is to say that the principle of substitution *salva veritate* holds for the logic: whenever S' is a sentence just like S except that a subsentence A in S has been replaced by a sentence B in S' then S and S' will have the same truth-value if A and B do. Intuitively, an extensional logic is one whose expressive powers are confined to the indicative mood.

[75] See, for example, Chisholm [1946] and Goodman [1947].

such, laws employ the so-called *counterfactual conditional.*[76] The counterfactual conditional is not the material conditional, '$\supset$', of mathematical logic. For '$(P \supset Q)$' will be true whenever 'P' is false regardless whether 'Q' is true or false. Thus if the counterfactual conditional in

If this fragile glass were dropped it would break,

were the material conditional, then it will be true of any fragile glass which is not dropped; but

If this fragile glass were dropped it would not break,

also would be true of any such glass. But the latter is false and the former true of undropped fragile glass, and so the counterfactual conditional here cannot be the material conditional.[77]

This does not show, however, that the counterfactual conditional cannot be defined in terms of the material conditional and the other apparatus of first-order logic; that is, it does not show that the counterfactual conditional is not extensional. Dispositional properties are specifiable by counterfactual conditionals; for example, the property *fragile* can be specified by the counterfactual

If this were dropped it would break.

The facts that dispositionals can be specified by reduction sentences (see II, A above) and reduction sentences employ only the extensional apparatus of first-order logic suggest that the counterfactual conditional can be specified extensionally in terms of the material conditional. Reduction sentences fail to be a specification of the counterfactual conditional, however, as Chisholm has shown:[78] For a reduction sentence

$$Q_1 \supset (Q_2 \supset Q_3)$$[79]

for the dispositional term 'Q_3' only specifies a sufficient condition for being Q_3, and in the absence of those sufficient conditions being met (namely Q_1 and Q_2), it does not specify what it is to be Q_3. Although a number of different reduction sentences may be given for Q_3, there

[76] Counterfactual conditionals are not always contrary-to-fact; they may be any subjunctive conditional. It is standard, however, to refer to both sorts as counterfactual conditionals, and so I will use this somewhat misleading locution. Counterfactual conditionals often are referred to simply as counterfactuals.

[77] See Chisholm [1946], Sec. II, for substantially the same point.

[78] *Ibid.*

[79] This is not a bilateral reduction sentence, but is an allowable form; see Carnap [1936–37].

always will be conditions in which a thing has the disposition Q_3 but none of the sufficient conditions are realized—namely those circumstances where the disposition fails to manifest itself. Thus there will be a "region of indeterminateness" where it is not specified what it is to be Q_3. As the reduction sentences define the meaning of 'Q_3', we will have to say that 'Q_3' is meaningless in this "region of indeterminateness"; for example, when an object is not being dissolved, the dispositional predicate 'is soluble' will be meaningless.[80] But, this is, of course, absurd. We know perfectly well what 'is soluble' means under such circumstances—namely that if certain conditions *were* met, the substance *would* dissolve. Accordingly, reduction sentences do not provide a means for extensionally specifying the counterfactual conditional. Reduction sentences do, however, capture some of the force of the counterfactual. This fact, when coupled with the observation that reduction sentences implicitly involve causal modalities,[81] suggests that the counterfactual conditional is a causal relationship, and hence is the relationship characteristic of causal scientific laws.

Goodman [1947] explored the idea that the nature of counterfactual conditionals could be specified in terms of scientific laws. He begins by observing that the truth of a counterfactual conditional requires that a certain connection obtain between the antecedent and the consequent of the conditional, but that the consequent rarely if ever follows from the antecedent by logic alone. For example, when we say,

(*) If that match had been scratched, it would have lighted,

we are asserting that conditions are such that 'that match lights' can be inferred from 'that match is scratched', where the relevant conditions include the match being well made, dry enough, and oxygen being present. Thus the consequent follows from the conjunction of the

[80] One might object to this step of Chisholm's argument as follows: It thus follows that the reduction sentence account leaves 'Q_3' meaningless for the "region of indeterminateness" only if one assumes that reduction sentences provide full or explicit definitions—which, of course, they do not. Since reduction sentences only partially define the terms they are used to introduce, the most one can claim for the "region of indeterminateness" is that the meaning of 'Q_3' is not specified; this does not mean that 'Q_3' is meaningless. This objection seems to be substantial, but can be gotten around. Chisholm's conclusion is forthcoming if the remainder of the argument is replaced by the following: It is characteristic of the counterfactual conditional that its truth does not depend upon whether the conditions in the "if clause" are actually met; even when these conditions are not realized (for example, in this "region of indeterminateness") it is possible in principle to determine the truth of the conditional. However, reduction sentences do not enable one to determine the truth of the conditional in this "region of indeterminateness," and so reduction sentences cannot be used to specify the counterfactual conditional.

[81] Hempel [1963], p. 690–691.

antecedent and statements of these relevant conditions; but even here it does not follow by logic alone—for 'that match lights' is not a logical consequence of

> that match is scratched and is dry enough; enough oxygen is present, etc.

Rather, it follows only in virtue of a natural law holding between these conditions being met and matches lighting.[82]

Since the truth of the counterfactual depends upon the generally unstated relevant conditions elliptically present in the antecedent, Goodman first attempts to specify the truth conditions for counterfactuals by imposing restrictions on the conjunction of the relevant conditions with the antecedent. The attempt here is to provide an extensional account of counterfactuals, the general form of the account being that a counterfactual conditional is an elliptical statement of a conditional of the form '$A \cdot S \supset C$' (where 'A' is the antecedent of the counterfactual conditional, 'S' is a statement of the relevant conditions, and 'C' is the consequent), where '$A \cdot S$' meet the following conditions. . . . Through a number of ingenious arguments, Goodman concludes that these conditions must include 'A' being cotenable with 'S' as well as certain further requirements—where 'A' is *cotenable* with 'S' if it is not the case that 'S' would not be true if 'A' were. But then he observes,

> In order to determine whether or not a given S is cotenable with A, we have to determine whether or not the counterfactual "If A were true then S would not be true" is itself true. But this means determining whether or not there is a suitable S_1, cotenable with A, that leads to $\sim S$ and so on. Thus we find ourselves involved in an infinite regressus or a circle; for cotenability is defined in terms of counterfactuals, yet the meaning of counterfactuals is defined in terms of cotenability. In other words to establish any counterfactual, it seems that we first have to determine the truth of another. If so, we can never explain a counterfactual except in terms of others, so that the problem of counterfactuals must remain unsolved.[83]

Accordingly, if counterfactual conditionals are to be specified, it will have to be in terms of the natural laws which sanction the inference from '$A \cdot S$' to 'C'.

Goodman then turned to the problem of specifying the general form of natural or scientific laws in hopes that this would provide a solution to the problem of counterfactual conditionals. On such a solution, the

[82] Goodman [1947], p. 116.
[83] *Ibid.*, p. 121.

counterfactual (*) would be true if and only if there is a true natural law such as

> Every match that is scratched, well made, dry enough, in enough oxygen, etc., lights.

However, not every generalization of this sort supports or sanctions a counterfactual conditional—for example,

> Everything in my pocket on V-E day was silver.

does not sanction the counterfactual

> If *P* had been in my pocket on V-E day, *P* would have been silver.[84]

The reason for this, Goodman asserts, is that the coin generalization is not a causal law; thus, if we are to characterize counterfactuals in terms of laws, we will have to distinguish lawlike empirical generalizations. One mark of difference is that lawlike generalizations can be used to make predictions whereas accidental ones cannot, and Goodman attempts to determine what conditions an empirical generalization must meet to gain predictability; he concludes that lawlike generalizations must be capable of inductive confirmation, where the confirmation depends upon the determination of no particular instance of the generalization. Thus such generalizations as

> Everything that is in my pocket or is a dime is silver.

do not qualify as lawlike generalizations. However, the statement of this criterion is inadequate since we do not yet know which empirical generalizations are capable of inductive confirmation in a way that does not depend on the determination of any particular instance of the generalization. Thus, Goodman concludes, we are in the following situation: Any attempt to specify counterfactuals must involve either the notion of cotenability or of lawlike generalizations. But the former cannot be specified without getting into an infinite regress or circularity; and the latter requires developments in confirmation theory which have not yet been obtained.

A large but inconclusive body of literature followed in response to Chisholm's [1946] and Goodman's [1947] articles.[85] The responses largely were attempts either to show that Goodman's problem of cotenability could be circumvented or that Chisholm's arguments that

84 *Ibid.*, pp. 122–123.

85 The literature is too excessive to mention here; a comprehensive bibliography is to be found in Meehl [1970], n. 11, pp. 385–387.

an extensional account of the counterfactual conditional could not be given failed to make their cases; at the same time various inconclusive attempts were made to solve the problems in confirmation theory which, according to Goodman, are the key to the problem of counterfactuals.[86] However, none of these attempts exerted any significant influence on the Received View's formulation, and so do not require any further treatment here—however interesting and significant they are in their own right.

Goodman's and Chisholm's works did prompt another sort of response, however, which did influence and result in alteration of the Received View. Some philosophers interpreted Goodman's and Chisholm's papers as having the following moral: The notions of scientific law and the counterfactual conditional are fundamentally nonextensional, and can be specified only using nonextensional logics; moreover, these notions are fundamentally causal, and so laws and counterfactuals will have to be developed using a logic of the causal modalities. This possibility had been noted by Carnap in his early work on defining dispositions (see II-A above), but had not been attempted then since little was known about modal logic[87] and reduction sentences seemed capable of dealing with his immediate problems concerning the definition of dispositional terms. But the later failure of reduction sentences, combined with the moral drawn from Goodman's and Chisholm's articles and more comprehensive developments in modal logic by Ruth Barcan Marcus and others (for example, J. C. C. McKinsey),[88] prompted a number of attempts to develop causal logics which could characterize counterfactual conditionals and natural laws.[89] Basically, these attempts consisted in augmenting first- and second-order logics with causal operators having a modal force, and attempting to model the causal implicative features which are characteristic of dispositions and scientific laws. By far the most important attempts were those made by Arthur Burks and Hans Reichenbach.[90] These attempts were not wholly successful, however, since the

[86] A comprehensive review of these is to be found in Scheffler [1963], Pt. III.

[87] Lewis and Langford [1932] was representative of what was then known.

[88] See Barcan [1946a], [1946b], and [1947].

[89] Carnap [1947] devoted considerable attention to modal logic, but apparently did not do his work in response to Chisholm's and Goodman's articles; Carnap's work was prompted more from problems concerning semantics and meaning. He does not devote much attention to the causal modalities or natural laws, although he was concerned with the applicability of his work to problems of dispositionals.

[90] See Burks [1951], [1955]; Reichenbach [1947], [1954]; see also von Wright [1951], and Sellars [1958].

various systems of causal implication were subject to various paradoxes.[91] More recently, using semantic techniques for interpreting modal logics developed by Saul Kripke, attempts have been made to characterize conditionals and laws in terms of possible states of affairs.[92] While not wholly successful, these developments have been sufficiently impressive to convince many philosophers of science that an adequate treatment of scientific theories must construe laws non-extensionally as involving causal modalities. Accordingly, in 1956, Carnap altered clause (i) of the initial version of the Received View, replacing it by

(i′) The theory is formulated in a first-order mathematical logic with identity, L, possibly augmented by modal operators.[93]

I want to digress from tracing the development of the Received View for a moment to make a few critical and speculative comments on the replacement of (i) by (i′) in the Received View; for the *motivation* behind the change seems to me to be fundamentally misguided. Insofar as the problem of counterfactual conditionals has been concerned with scientific theorizing, it has concerned the nature of the counterfactual in theoretical laws (the T of a theory TC). However, if one looks at a theory under the Received View, one finds that the theoretical laws T typically are formulated as mathematical equations such as '$F = ma$' or the Schrödinger wave equation. Quâ mathematical relationships, such laws clearly are extensional and do not involve anything remotely like a counterfactual conditional. Thus if such mathematically formulated laws involve counterfactual conditionals, this counterfactual nature must be a result of the physical or empirical interpretation given to the mathematical relationships in them. Differently put, the mathematically formulated laws by themselves are not counterfactual, but they can be given an empirical interpretation such that they relate counterfactually to the world. Since the correspondence rules C are what relates the theoretical laws T to the world on the Received View, these observations suggest that the C are counterfactual but the T are not; if so, then of course TC is counterfactual.

[91] See Sellars [1958] and Burks [1973], Ch. 5, for discussions of these. More recent developments forthcoming in Burks [1973] apparently have succeeded in avoiding these paradoxes and defects.

[92] See Stalnaker [1968]; Kripke's results are succinctly summarized in Lyndon [1966]. Stalnaker's idea of using possible states of affairs is not new, it being implicit in the earlier developments by Carnap, Burks, and others; Stalnaker's treatment of it is new, however.

[93] Carnap [1956], p. 42.

This suggestion is supported by a consideration of actual theories in physics. Consider, for example, classical particle mechanics. When divorced from the correspondence rules, the laws of the theory can be construed as describing an idealized world populated by isolated systems of extensionless point masses in a vacuum where the only properties relevant to the behavior of these point masses are their positions and momenta. This idealized world contains every such system which is consistent with the laws of the theory. So interpreted every statement the theory can make will be a description of an actual state of affairs in the idealized world. As such, none of the laws stand in a counterfactual relationship to *this* world.[94] This indicates that the laws by themselves do not essentially require counterfactual conditionals in their statements. This idealized world cannot be the real world for two reasons: First, the real world does not contain isolated systems of extensionless point masses in a vacuum; second, not every causally possible system or phenomenon is actually realized in the real world, whereas this isolated world contains all possible systems consistent with the laws in *T*. Nonetheless, *T* is applied counterfactually to the world in two ways. First, the idealized systems described by *T* can be employed as idealized replicas of actual phenomena occurring in the world. Using various experimental procedures and introducing some degree of experimental control, data about an actual phenomenon are gathered; then using various correction procedures one shapes the data until it is in a form representative of what the phenomenon *would have been had it been* an isolated system of extensionless point masses in a vacuum. But this data then describes the actual behavior of one of the systems in the idealized world described by *T*, and so that idealized system now serves as an idealized replica of the phenomenon observed in the real world. Furthermore, it does so by standing in a counterfactual relationship to the actual phenomenon—where that counterfactual relationship is determined by the experimental procedures used to connect the phenomenon with the idealized system. But on the Received View the correspondence rules describe the ways in which the laws *T* are to be applied to the world,

[94] It might be objected here that the Received View makes no provision for such a direct interpretation of *T*. In Section IV–C below we will see that such direct interpretations must be allowed if a coherent account is to be given of the notion of partial interpretation. See also Hempel's assertion, in Session I's discussion below, to the effect that such direct interpretations were allowed. In terms of the more detailed account given of partial interpretation in Suppe [1971], it follows from the accounts of partial interpretation and empirical truth given there that such an interpretation implicitly is given under the Received View.

and so this experimental procedure must be described by one of the sentences in *C*; this sentence will say that if such and such experimental procedures are performed with such and such results, then one obtains the following data—where these data describe one of the idealized systems. Thus the correspondence rule describes what the phenomenon would have been had it been one of the idealized systems, and so is fundamentally counterfactual. Since the correspondence rules *C* are counterfactual, so is *TC*—even though *T* itself is not. There is a second way the theory can be applied counterfactually to phenomena. Suppose one wishes to apply the theory to a phenomenon which does not actually occur but could have—for example, suppose a cannon ball is flying and hits nobody, but one wonders with what force it would have hit a man had he been in its path. In this case, one hypothetically characterizes the phenomenon; the correspondence rules are not involved in this step. Then one applies the theory to this postulated phenomenon in the way just indicated. In this case the application of the theory would be doubly counterfactual—the phenomenon did not occur, and even if it had it would have related counterfactually to the laws of the theory. These observations strongly support the suggestion that the correspondence rules are counterfactual in a theory whereas the laws are not, and thus that the source of the counterfactual nature of theories is the correspondence rules.[95]

It is important to be clear about what is and is not being suggested here. It is not being suggested that *TC* (the physically interpreted theory) does not require counterfactual conditionals for its formulation; it is granted that *TC* does involve counterfactual conditionals. The question is whether the counterfactuals are required to formulate *T* or *C* or both, and the suggestion here is that only *C* requires counterfactuals for its formulation. This becomes a criticism of the replacement of (i) by (i′) only to the extent that the change was made *because* it was thought that counterfactual conditionals were required to formulate *T*; indeed, if my suggestions are sound, it follows that the replacement of (i) by (i′) is required—the only difference being that they are needed to formulate *C* and not *T*. To put the suggestion

[95] In Section IV–E below we will consider objections to the Received View's account of correspondence rules which argue that some correspondence rules specify causal relationships; that they do lends further support to the suggestion that correspondence rules are counterfactual. Although the observations just given have been made in the context of the Received View, they do not depend essentially on that account of theories. For a defense of the perspective presented here which is not tied to the Received View, see Suppe [1972b], [1973d], and [1973e]; the perspective presented here figures centrally in the analysis of theories discussed in Sec. V–C.

epigrammatically, laws are not counterfactual, although their particular applications may be.[96]

This suggestion, if correct, leads to the further suggestion that the key to understanding the counterfactual conditional, insofar as it functions in scientific theorizing (but not necessarily in general), lies in the experimental procedures used to apply the formalism of the theory (the principles T) to the phenomena within the theory's scope. If this suggestion is viable, it promises two advantages over the procedures outlined above for attempting to deal with the counterfactual —namely, that on the one hand this may enable one to determine the counterfactual nature of scientific theories without solving the general problem of counterfactuals and, on the other hand, the understanding of counterfactuals in theoretical contexts may provide some illumination which will help solve the more general problem of counterfactuals. Since none of the approaches discussed above enjoy widespread acceptance as solutions to either the problem of counterfactuals or the problem of scientific laws,[97] this alternative proposal warrants further consideration.

D. Observational-Theoretical Distinction

Clause (iii) of the initial version of the Received View stipulates that the terms in the observation vocabulary V_O are interpreted as referring to directly observable physical objects or directly observable attributes of physical objects; except for (iv), this clause underwent the least modification of any of the five clauses. In section I it was indicated that there was some early disagreement among members of the Vienna Circle whether V_O terms should be given a phenomenalistic sense-data interpretation (as was done in Carnap [1928]) or a physicalistic interpretation, that the two proposals came to be viewed as equivalent in the sense of being just alternative ways of talking about the same

[96] Note that it is conceivable that there might be the theories wherein the idealized systems described by T actually occur in the world; in this case one would not need recourse to counterfactual conditionals in formulating C. Counterfactual conditionals still would be needed to apply the theory to phenomena which might have occurred but did not, but such counterfactual conditionals would not occur in the correspondence rules.

[97] That this is so is evidenced by the fact that much of the problem involved in assessing Hempel's covering-law models of explanation centers on the question what it is to be a scientific law (either deductive or inductive-statistical); see Hempel [1965a]; the developments introduced in Suppe [1973d] are of direct relevance to the proposal just introduced.

thing,[98] and that the Vienna Circle opted for physicalistic language very early. This choice is reflected in (iii). After the decision to employ physicalistic language was made, remarkably little attention was devoted to further development or specification of the notion of being directly observable.

In Carnap [1936-37], the notion of what it is to be directly observable was given as full a specification as it ever got. There Carnap wrote,

> A predicate 'P' of a language L is called [directly] *observable* for an organism (e.g., a person) N, if, for suitable arguments, e.g., 'b', N is able under suitable circumstances to come to a decision with the help of a few observations about a full sentence, say 'P(b)', i.e. to a confirmation of either 'P(b)' or '∼P(b)' of such a high degree that he will either accept or reject 'P(b)'.
> This explanation is necessarily vague. There is no sharp line between observable and non-observable predicates because a person will be more or less able to decide a sentence quickly, i.e. he will be inclined after a certain period to accept the sentence. For the sake of simplicity we will here draw a sharp distinction between observable and non-observable predicates. By thus drawing an arbitrary line between observable and non-observable predicates in a field of continuous degrees of observability we partly determine in advance the possible answers to questions such as whether or not a certain predicate is observable by a given person. . . .
> According to the explanation given, for example, the predicate 'red' is observable for a person N possessing a normal colour sense. For . . . say a spot [*c*] on the table before N, N is able under suitable circumstances —namely, if there is sufficient light at *c*—to come to a decision about the full sentence "the spot *c* is red" after few observations—namely by looking at the table. On the other hand, the predicate 'red' is not observable by a colour-blind person. And the predicate 'an electric field of such and such an amount' is not observable to anybody, because, although we know how to test a full sentence of this predicate, we cannot do it directly, i.e. by a few observations; we have to apply certain instruments and hence to make a great many preliminary observations in order to find out whether the things before us are instruments of the kind required.[99]

In later writings, advocates of the Received View typically took the notion of being directly observable as nonproblematic and generally understood, giving little in the way of characterization of the distinction other than examples. For example, Carnap [1956] merely writes "The terms of V_O are predicates designating observable properties of events or things (for example, 'blue', 'hot', 'large', and so on) or

[98] See Carnap [1963b], pp. 50–51.

[99] Sec. 8 (pp. 63–64 in the Feigl and Brodbeck [1953] reprinting).

observable relations between them (for example, 'x is warmer than y,' 'x is contiguous to y.', and so on)."[100]

At one point, however, Carnap did address himself to the criticism that his observational distinction did not correspond to that actually employed in science. He replies,

> Philosophers and scientists have quite different ways of using the terms "observable" and "non-observable." To a philosopher, "observable" has a very narrow meaning. It applies to such properties as "blue", "hard", "hot". These are properties directly perceived by the senses. To the physicist, the work has a much broader meaning. It includes any quantitative magnitude that can be measured in a relatively simple, direct way. A philosopher would not consider a temperature of, perhaps, 80 degrees centigrade, or a weight of 93 1/2 pounds, an observable because there is no direct sensory perception of such magnitudes. To a physicist, both are observables because they can be measured in an extremely simple way. The object to be weighed is placed on a balance scale. . . . Magnitudes that can be established by relatively simple procedures—length with a ruler, time with a clock, or frequency of light waves with a spectrometer—are called observables [by the physicist]. The philosopher might object that the intensity of an electric current is not really observed. Only a pointer position was observed. . . . Certainly the current's intensity was not observed. It was *inferred* from what was observed! . . . There is no question here of who is using the term "observable" in a right or proper way. There is a continuum which starts with direct sensory observations and proceeds to enormously complex, indirect methods of observation. Obviously no sharp line can be drawn across this continuum; it is a matter of degree. . . . In general the physicist speaks of observables in a very wide sense compared with the narrow sense of the philosopher, but, in both cases, the line separating observable from non-observable is highly arbitrary. It is well to keep this in mind whenever these terms are encountered in a book by a philosopher or scientist. Individual authors will draw the line where it is most convenient, depending on their points of view, and there is no reason why they should not have this privilege.[101]

This clarifying passage together with the long passage previously quoted constitute the fullest development of the observational-theoretical distinction given by adherents to the Received View. It is clear from these passages that while the distinction was clarified somewhat no significant changes were made in (iii) in the course of developing the Received View.

Carnap's presentation of the observational-theoretical distinction masks a number of characteristics built into it, features which need

[100] P. 41.
[101] Carnap [1966], pp. 225–226.

to be clearly displayed if we are to be able to assess the critical attacks the distinction later was subjected to (see Sec. IV–B–2 below). Carnap's observational-theoretical distinction is actually a double dichotomy. First, there is a distinction between those objects or entities, their properties, and the relationships they enter into which are amenable to direct observation (that is, can be directly perceived by the senses augmented at most by very simple instruments) and those which are not. This is a bifurcation of the world's constituents and their attributes on the basis of normal human sensory abilities. Second, there is a division of the nonlogical (that is, empirical) vocabulary of a theory into observation terms and nonobservational (or theoretical) terms. This division says that certain empirical words in a scientific language (for example, the language of physics) are to be put into V_O and the rest will be put in V_T. However, clause (iii) imposes the further requirement that this division into V_O and V_T must be such that the terms in V_O are all and only those words in the scientific language whose meanings are such that they refer to or designate directly observable entities or things, or their attributes. Accordingly, clause (iii) implicitly asserts the existence of two dichotomies—one of objects and their attributes, the other of terms in scientific languages —which, given the meanings of the terms, are coextensive. Whether such dichotomies can be drawn for any existing scientific language is, of course, an empirical claim for which adherents to the Received View have supplied no evidence or support. The degree of arbitrariness Carnap claims in drawing the distinction is limited by the requirement that the two dichotomies will be coextensive in this manner.[102]

Clause (iii) implicitly involves a claim about perceptual knowledge as well. Suppose that the coextensive dual dichotomies can be drawn. Then, according to the Received View, the assertions which can be made using terms from V_O as their only nonlogical terms will be intersubjectively nonproblematic with regard to truth: any two observers who possess the words from V_O used in the assertions, regardless of their scientific or theoretical background, will be able to agree upon the truth of such V_O assertions. Differently put, such assertions are scientifically and theoretically neutral, and nonproblematic with respect to truth.[103]

These two doctrines implicit in (iii)—that the coextensive dual

[102] For more detailed discussion of this interpretation of the observational-theoretical distinction, and for supporting further evidence that this is implicit in (iii), see Suppe [1972b].

[103] That this is so follows from the physicalist doctrine discussed in Sec. I above.

dichotomies can be drawn and that V_O assertions will be nonproblematic with respect to truth—are two of the features of the Received View subjected to most severe criticism by opponents to the Received View (see Sections IV–B and V–B–1 below).

One other development relating to (iii) deserves mention in passing. Since assertions having V_O terms as their only nonlogical terms are supposed to be capable of confirmation by a very few observations (see the first quotation above), some restrictions must be imposed upon the logical form and complexity of these assertions. In Carnap [1956], sublanguages are distinguished for the languages L used to axiomatize scientific theories (cf. clause (i)). One of these, the *observation language* L_O, has V_O terms as its only nonlogical terms, and has a restricted logical apparatus and syntax intended to guarantee that L_O assertions can be confirmed by a very few observations. These restrictions are designed to get around the fact that the use of modal operators, unrestricted use of quantifiers, and so on, with V_O terms will allow V_O assertions which are not directly confirmable or verifiable.[104] These requirements include the explicit definability of non-V_O terms introduced into L_O, nominalism, finitism, constructivism, and extensionality, and in effect constitute a requirement that L_O sentences be cognitively significant under the verification criterion of meaningfulness ("A sentence is empirically significant if and only if it is not analytic and is capable, at least in principle, of complete verification by observational evidence"); thus L_O is required to meet the verifiability requirement of cognitive significance even though the changes in (v) no longer require that the scientific language L be cognitively significant in this way. Since L_O has much more restricted syntax and logical power than L, Carnap also introduces a *logically extended observation language*, L_O', which is just like L_O except that it possesses the full logical apparatus of L, and its sentences thus do not satisfy the verification criterion of cognitive significance. The details of Carnap's characterizations of L_O and L_O', will be indicated in the next section; the rationale behind their specifics will not be considered since they do not figure essentially in subsequent discussion, criticism, and evaluation of the Received View.[105] Carnap also includes a *theoretical language*, L_T, which has V_T terms as its only nonlogical terms and posseses the full logical apparatus of L.

[104] For a discussion of these problems, see Hempel's [1965b] discussions of the failure of the verifiability criterion of cognitive significance.

[105] See Carnap [1956], Secs. II and IX, for their detailed formulation and justification.

E. Final Version of the Received View

In tracing the development of the Received View I have concentrated primarily on the developments and changes made by Carnap and Hempel. While these two together were the main authors of the Received View in its final and most sophisticated form, they were not the only proponents of the Received View. Other versions were developed by a number of other philosophers including Bergmann [1957], pp. 31–32; Duhem [1954], p. 19; Braithwaite [1953], Ch. II; Reichenbach [1962], Ch. 8; Campbell [1920], Ch. 6; Ramsey [1931], pp. 212–236; Margenau [1950]; Northrop [1947], Ch. 8; Nagel [1961], pp. 90ff.; and Kaplan [1964], pp. 298–299, to name some of the more prominent versions. These various versions of the Received View can be considered as being variations on stages in the development of the Received View sketched above; as their distinctive features do not make them any less vulnerable to the criticisms made against the Carnap-Hempel version, their details do not require separate consideration here.[106]

When the modifications in (i) to (v) discussed above are incorporated into a coherent account, we obtain *the final version of the Received View* which construes scientific theories as having a canonical formulation satisfying the following conditions:

(1) There is a first-order language L (possibly augmented by modal operators) in terms of which the theory is formulated, and a logical calculus K defined in terms of L.

(2) The nonlogical or descriptive primitive constants (that is, the "terms") of L are bifurcated into two disjoint classes:
V_O which contains just the observation terms;
V_T which contains the nonobservation or theoretical terms.
V_O must contain at least one individual constant.

(3) The language L is divided into the following sublanguages, and the calculus K is divided into the following subcalculi:

(a) The *observation language*, L_O, is a sublanguage of L which contains no quantifiers or modalities, and contains the terms of V_O but none from V_T. The associated calculus K_O is the restriction of K to L_O and must be such that any non-V_O terms (that is, nonprimitive terms) in L_O are explicitly defined in K_O; furthermore, K_O must admit of at least one finite model.

[106] The only exceptions will be those of Nagel and Campbell who are considered in Sec. IV–B below.

(b) The *logically extended observation language, L_O'*, contains no V_T terms and may be regarded as being formed from L_O by adding the quantifiers, modalities, and so on, of L. Its associated calculus K_O' is the restriction of K to L_O'.

(c) The *theoretical language*, L_T, is that sublanguage of L which does not contain V_O terms; its associated calculus, K_T, is the restriction of K to L_T.

These sublanguages together do not exhaust L, for L also contains *mixed sentences*—that is, those in which at least one V_T and one V_O term occur. In addition it is assumed that each of the sublanguages above has its own stock of predicate and/or functional variables, and that L_O and L_O' have the same stock which is distinct from that of L_T.

(4) L_O and its associated calculi are given a *semantic interpretation* which meets the following conditions:

(a) The domain of interpretation consists of concrete observable events, things, or things-moments; the relations and properties of the interpretation must be directly observable.

(b) Every value of any variable in L_O must be designated by an expression in L_O.

It follows that any such interpretation of L_O and K_O, when augmented by appropriate additional rules of truth, will become an interpretation of L_O' and K_O'. We may construe interpretations of L_O and K_O as being *partial semantic interpretations of* L and K, and we require that L and K be given no observational semantic interpretation other than that provided by such partial semantic interpretations.

(5) A *partial interpretation* of the theoretical terms and of the sentences of L containing them is provided by the following two kinds of postulates: the *theoretical postulates* T (that is, the axioms of the theory) in which only terms of V_T occur, and the *correspondence rules* or postulates C which are mixed sentences. The correspondence rules C must satisfy the following conditions:

(a) The set of rules C must be finite.

(b) The set of rules C must be logically compatible with T.

(c) C contains no extralogical term that does not belong to V_O or V_T.

(d) Each rule in C must contain at least one V_O term and at least one V_T term essentially or nonvacuously.

Let T be the conjunction of the theoretical postulates and C be the conjunction of the correspondence rules. Then the scientific theory based on L, T, and C consists of the conjunction of T and C and is designated by 'TC'.[107] As this is the most sophisticated and satisfactory version of the Received View developed, it will be assumed in our subsequent discussion.

Before concluding our discussion of the development of the Received View, it should be observed how much the final version differs from the initial version of the Received View. Initially the Received View was an account of theories which attached little importance to the theoretical apparatus, TC, its function being little more than a means for introducing mathematics into science. In its final version, theories are construed realistically as describing systems of nonobservables which relate in incompletely specifiable ways to their observable manifestations; as such the theoretical apparatus is central to its analysis, and the emphasis is on how the theoretical apparatus connects with phenomena.

It also needs to be emphasized that other versions of the Received View continued to be held after Carnap and Hempel developed the final version. Thus, for example, versions of the Received View were advanced contemporaneously with the final version, wherein there was a total prohibition on providing V_T with a semantic interpretation, rather than Hempel's and Carnap's weaker prohibition on supplying it with an *observational* semantic interpretation. In calling Carnap's and Hempel's version the final version, and limiting my critical assessment below to the final version, I am making a value judgment as to the relative merits of the various later versions of the Received View. And my assessment here is that what I call the final version is

[107] No single comprehensive account of Carnap's and Hempel's most recent formulation has been published. This formulation of the Received View is extracted from Carnap [1956], [1959], [1963c], pp. 859–1013, [1966]; and Hempel [1958], [1963]. My formulation of conditions in clauses (2) to (4) is more explicit in certain respects than either of these authors explicitly require but are necessary if the restrictions on the sublanguages L_O and L_O' imposed on pp. 41–42 of Carnap [1956] are to be met. To meet these restrictions, different additional conditions could have been imposed, but I have selected the ones given here because they are the most conservative. The detailed arguments in support of these additional requirements will be omitted as the particular choice of these restrictions in no way affects subsequent discussion. Carnap and Hempel disagree as to the requirements to be imposed on the rules of correspondence. Hempel would replace clause (d) by "C contains every element V_O and V_T essentially—i.e., C is not logically equivalent to some set of sentences in which at least one term of V_O or V_T does not occur at all" (Hempel [1963], p. 692), and so is more restrictive than Carnap's version. Carnap also would require that the theory be cognitively significant, whereas Hempel doubts that a satisfactory criterion of cognitive significance can be given.

the most sophisticated and least vulnerable version of the Received View: it is the version for which the strongest case can be made. Thus, for example, it will be seen in IV–C and IV–D below that the final version escapes certain criticisms which are telling for other versions.

F. Development of Science on the Received View: Theory Reduction

I want to close this section by giving brief consideration to a doctrine which strictly speaking is not a part of the Received View, but is closely allied with it; this is the positivistic treatment of *theory reduction.* According to most proponents of the Received View, theories are subjected to empirical test and if a theory passes a sufficient variety of such tests it enjoys a high degree of confirmation. However, the history of science is full of theories which once were highly confirmed, but later were supplemented by new theories. According to the Received View, this phenomenon can be understood when it is seen that scientific progress occurs in three ways. First, although a theory was widely accepted as highly confirmed, subsequent developments (for example, technological advances which drastically improve the accuracy of observation and measurement) displayed places where the theory was predictively inadequate, and so the degree of confirmation was eroded. Although historically inaccurate, the Copernican Revolution sometimes is advanced as an example of this.[108] Second, while the theory continues to enjoy confirmation for systems in its original scope, it is seen how to expand the theory to encompass a larger scope of systems or phenomena. An often-cited example of this is the extension of classical particle mechanics to rigid body mechanics. Third, various disparate theories, each enjoying high degrees of confirmation, are included in, or *reduced to,* some more inclusive theory.

In the main, positivists maintain the thesis that, except in the initial consideration of new theories, scientific progress comes largely via the latter two kinds of development. The rationale behind this thesis seems to be the following: When a theory is initially advanced and tested for its adequacy, predictive failures will result in its rejection or disconfirmation; but if the theory successfully passes a sufficient variety of experiments for its initial scope, the theory comes to enjoy a high degree of confirmation for that scope. Once it enjoys a high

[108] That it is historically inaccurate can be easily seen by looking at the negligible role of experimental discovery (Galileo not withstanding) in the Copernican Revolution; for an authoritative account of the evidence, see Kuhn [1957].

degree of confirmation it is highly unlikely that the theory ever can be disconfirmed. For if a theory is to be disconfirmed it will have to fail in its predictions, and this is unlikely for any of the sorts of phenomena in its initial scope since the theory *is* highly confirmed for that scope; rather, subsequent disconfirmations would have to come as a result of predictive failures for new sorts of phenomena different from what have been tested previously. However, the fact that such phenomena are different means that new techniques of instrumentation, and so on, will be required to perform the tests, and these must be introduced into *TC* as additional correspondence rules. But to do so is to replace *TC* by a closely related new theory *TC′* which is tested; and any disconfirmation that occurs will be of *TC′*, not *TC*. Thus, once it enjoys a high degree of confirmation, a theory *TC* is unlikely to be disconfirmed; rather, any disconfirmation will be of extensions of *TC* to scopes wider than that of *TC*. Once a theory is accepted, then, scientific progress concerning it is of the second sort, consisting of attempts to expand *TC* to a wider scope—that is, in the production of *TC′*, *TC″*, and so on. Each of these expanded versions of *TC* is a new theory which must undergo empirical tests before it is accepted, but once it passes its tests and enjoys a high degree of confirmation, it too is relatively isolated from disconfirmation. This expansion of the scope of a theory is a form of *theory reduction*. Nagel characterizes such reduction, thusly, "the laws of the *secondary science* [*TC*] employ no descriptive terms that are not used with approximately the same meanings in the *primary science* [*TC′*]. Reductions of this type can be regarded as establishing deductive relations between two sets of statements that employ a homogeneous vocabulary." [109] Essentially the same form of reduction is involved if *TC* is expanded to a wider scope by augmenting the theoretical principles *T* by additional ones which use the same theoretical terms as *TC*, thus obtaining *T′C* or *T′C′* (depending whether new correspondence rules are involved as well). Thus the development and expansion of a theory is via this first form of theory reduction, and consists in the replacement of *TC* by closely related, more comprehensive theories.

Scientific progress sometimes involves a second form of theory reduction which occurs in science when a theory *TC* is absorbed into a more inclusive or comprehensive theory—for example, the reduction of thermodynamics to statistical mechanics or the reduction of Kepler's laws to Newton's dynamics. "The phenomenon of a relatively autonomous theory being absorbed by, or reduced to, some more inclusive

[109] Nagel [1961], p. 339; emphasis added.

theory is an undeniable and recurrent feature of the history of modern science."[110] Unlike the first sort of reduction considered above, "in reductions of this type the secondary science [that is, the theory being reduced to another] employs in its formulations of laws and theories a number of distinctive descriptive predicates that are not included in the basic theoretical terms or in the associated rules of correspondence of the primary science [that is, the theory the secondary one is being reduced to]."[111] That the terms V_T of the secondary theory are not all contained in the theoretical vocabulary of the primary theory is what makes this form of reduction problematic. For this form of reduction to occur, the following conditions must be met: (a) the theoretical terms for both theories must have "meanings unambiguously fixed by codified rules of usage or by established procedures appropriate to each discipline";[112] (b) for each theoretical term *a* of the secondary theory not in the vocabulary of the primary theory, assumptions must be introduced which postulate relations between whatever is signified by *a* and traits represented by theoretical terms in the primary theory's vocabulary; (c) with the help of these additional assumptions, all of the laws of the secondary theory must be logically derivable from the theoretical premises and their associated correspondence rules in the primary theory; (d) these additional assumptions used must have adequate evidential support.[113] When the conditions are met all of the laws and observable consequences of the secondary theory can be deduced from the primary theory, and so the secondary theory has been reduced to, or incorporated into, the primary theory. As such the reduction is "the explanation of a theory or a set of experimental laws established in one area of inquiry, by a theory usually though not invariably formulated in some other domain."[114] For example, Kepler's planetary laws are claimed to have been reduced to, and explained by, Newton's laws of motion in this way.

The thesis of reduction thus results in the following picture of scientific progress or development: science establishes theories which, if highly confirmed, are accepted and continue to be accepted relatively free from the danger of subsequent disconfirmation. The development of science consists in the extension of such theories to wider scopes

[110] *Ibid.*, p. 337.
[111] *Ibid.*, p. 342.
[112] *Ibid.*, p. 345.
[113] *Ibid.*, pp. 353–354, 358. Nagel's analysis is based in part on Kemeny and Oppenheim's [1956] classic treatment of the subject, though he does introduce significant improvements over their analysis.
[114] Nagel [1961], p. 338.

(the first form of theory reduction), the development of new highly confirmed theories for related domains, and the incorporation of confirmed theories into more comprehensive theories (the second form of theory reduction). Science thus is a cumulative enterprise, extending and augmenting old successes with new successes; old theories are not rejected or abandoned once they have been accepted; they are just superceded by more comprehensive theories to which they are reduced.

This view of scientific development, which I call the *thesis of development by reduction*, and the Received View clearly go hand in hand. As indicated above, it is crucial to the thesis of development by reduction that highly confirmed theories are relatively immune from subsequent disconfirmation, and this follows in virtue of requiring that the correspondence rules be individuating components of theories. In addition, the thesis of development by reduction requires that reduction does not affect the meanings of theoretical terms (see requirement (a) above). The thesis of development by reduction thus presupposes the Received View. More important, we will see in Section V–B–1 that rejection of the thesis of development by reduction does tend to cast serious doubts on the tenability of the Received View. Indeed, rejection of the thesis of development by reduction is at the heart of Feyerabend's, Hanson's, Kuhn's, and Bohm's rejections of the Received View.

III. Status of the Received View

What is being claimed when proponents of the Received View assert that scientific theories have canonical formulations meeting conditions (1) to (5) above? Many proponents of the Received View write as if they were giving a descriptive account how theories actually are formulated.[115] But even a cursory look at the formulations of scientific theories actually employed in science makes it clear that such theories are not formulated axiomatically in accordance with the Received View. Indeed, they are rarely formulated axiomatically at all outside of foundational studies in certain branches of physical science and in certain mathematical branches of social science; and there the axiomatizations usually are not in accordance with the Received View's requirements. Even less frequently does one find explicit and comprehensive formulations of correspondence rules—the only place where one finds them being those branches of science such as radical behaviorism in psychology that deliberately have tried to model their theorizing on Bridgman's operationalist version of the Received View. Clearly, then, the Received View could not have been advanced as an accurate descriptive account of typical scientific theories as actually formulated in science.

What, then, is the status of the Received View analysis? I take it as being reasonably clear from Carnap's and Hempel's writings that they intend their analysis to provide an *explication* of the concept of a scientific theory. Since our task here is to critically evaluate the challenges made against the adequacy of the Received View analysis, it will help if we first become clear about the nature of explication. Carnap gives us his clearest statement of what he means by an explication in Carnap [1950]—be it an explication of scientific theories, confirmation, probability, or whatever.

> The task of *explication* consists in transforming a given more or less inexact concept into an exact one, or rather, in replacing the first by the

[115] For example, Nagel's [1961] introduction to his version of the Received View (p. 90) conveys this impression, though I doubt Nagel intended to.

> second. We call the given concept (or the term used for it) the *explicandum,* and the exact concept proposed to take the place of the first (or the term proposed for it) the *explicatum.* . . . The explicatum must be given by explicit rules for its use, for example, by a definition which incorporates it into a well-constructed system of scientific either logico-mathematical or empirical concepts.[116]

He then raises the question of what requirements an adequate explicatum must meet, and tells us that an adequate explicatum must be (1) similar to the explicandum; (2) the rules of its use must be given in an exact form; (3) it must be fruitful, which is to say useful for the formulation of many universal statements; and (4) it must be as simple as the first three requirements permit.[117]

All of this is rather vague as to the desired relationship in which the explicatum should stand to the explicandum; fortunately, however, Carnap also tells us that his notion of explication includes C. H. Langford's notion of an analysis as a special case,[118] and so it will be helpful in understanding the notion of an explication if we look at Langford's notion of analysis. Langford [1942] defines the *analysandum* to be that which is to be analyzed and the *analysans* as that which does the analyzing. "The *analysis* then states an appropriate relation of equivalence between the analysandum and the analysans" (Langford [1942], p. 323). Langford's question is what equivalence relation must hold between the analysandum and the analysans in order that the latter should correctly analyze the former. The obvious suggestion is that the equivalence should be one of meaning or content, but this leads immediately to the *paradox of analysis*: If the verbal expression representing the analysandum has the same meaning as the verbal expression representing the analysans, the analysis then states a bare identity and is trivial; but if the two verbal expressions do not have the same meaning, the analysis is incorrect.[119] Langford's problem is to present an analysis of the concept of an analysis which avoids this paradox. For our purposes it will not be necessary to give detailed consideration to his discussion;[120] rather it will suffice to state his conclusion which can be put

116 Carnap [1950], p. 3.

117 *Ibid.*, pp. 5–7.

118 *Ibid.*, p. 3; see Langford [1942] for details of this analysis of analyses.

119 *Ibid.*, p. 323.

120 Most of the difficulties in his discussion center round the fact that his discussion prior to p. 335 is confined to analyses of concepts, and *not* the verbal expressions which one uses to express these concepts, and the fact that his account is in terms of "having the same truth conditions," "having the same meanings," "having the same denotation," and so on. While these notions are reasonably well defined with respect to verbal expressions, it is not at all clear that they make any sense when applied to concepts or ideas, and if so what their sense is. Accordingly

as follows: The analysandum and the analysans expressions will have the same denotation or extension, but they will have different intentions or senses. Moreover, the analysans must be such that it is better and more precisely understood than the analysandum.[121]

Having looked at Langford's notion of an analysis, let us return to Carnap who tells us that explication often is analysis, but not always—the difference being that the explicatum "often deviates from the explicandum but still takes its place in some way." [122] These deviations are prompted by the fact that where an explication is really needed, the explicandum is so vague that we never can determine whether the explicandum and explicatum do have the same denotation, and so we cannot always require that they have the same denotation in an adequate explication. And wherever we cannot, an explication will not be an analysis.[123] This, however, does not make it clear in what ways the explicandum and the explicatum may differ, and Carnap has little more to say on the matter. However, Chomsky [1957] presents an adequacy criterion which stipulates how the explicatum and the explicandum may differ, and his criterion seems to be in accord with Carnap's position. Chomsky says that in an adequate explication we determine the clear-cut instances and the clear-cut noninstances of the explicandum, and we demand that the explicatum denote all the clear-cut instances, and none of the clear-cut noninstances. For the vague cases where it is not clear whether they should be counted as an instance of the explicandum or not we do not concern ourselves with the problem, but rather let the explicatum decide for us whether to count them as instances.[124] That is, we restrict the requirement that the explicandum and the explicatum statements have the same denotation to just the clear-cut instances and noninstances of the explicandum.

All of this suggests that Carnap probably would accept the following

---

it is somewhat difficult to make his discussion coherent. The problem is compounded further by the fact that at the bottom of p. 335, he suddenly shifts his attention to verbal expressions, considering what he calls "logical analysis," and although he seems to think there is an intimate connection between that discussion and his preceding discussion of the analysis of concepts, it is not at all clear what this connection is. If we construe concepts as properties, relations, and functions—as Carnap [1950] does on p. 8—then it is possible to give a coherent reconstruction of Langford's discussion in terms of intensional and extensional specification of concepts in a manner which seems to be faithful to Langford's intentions. My statement of Langford's conclusion reflects such a reconstruction, but a detailed consideration of these issues here would take us too far afield.

121 This, I take it, is the import of his discussion on the bottom of p. 337, where he maintains that the analysans must be "less idiomatic" than the analysandum.

122 Carnap [1950], p. 3.

123 *Ibid.*, pp. 4–5.

124 Chomsky [1957], pp. 13–14.

characterization of an explication. An adequate explication consists of an explicandum statement together with an explicatum statement, and satisfies the following requirements: (1) Restricted to clear-cut instances and noninstances of the explicandum concept, the explicandum and explicatum statements must have the same denotation (or extension). (2) The explicandum and explicatum statements must have different senses, with that of the latter being more precise and better understood than that of the former. (3) the explicatum must be fruitful relative to the purposes of the explication in that it leads to interesting and useful consequences and results. (4) The explicatum must be as simple as is consistent with requirements (1) to (4).[125] Furthermore we note that explications are not true or false, but rather are accepted or rejected as being more or less adequate. Even if an explication satisfies adequacy conditions (1) to (4) it will be rejected as inadequate if there exists an alternative explication which is more adequate.

The realization that the Received View is intended to be an explication of the concept of a scientific theory together with our discussion of the concept of an explication gives us a better idea of what is being claimed of the Received View analysis, and hence how to assess its adequacy. In particular we now are in a position to understand the relation claimed to hold between actual scientific theories and the Received View's characterization. The Received View begins by specifying a canonical formulation for theories in terms of an axiomatic calculus and rules of correspondence. This canonical formulation is claimed to stand in the following relation to any scientific theory: Any given scientific theory could be reformulated in this canonical manner, and such a canonical formulation would capture and preserve the conceptual and structural content of the theory in such a manner as to reveal most clearly and illuminatingly the conceptual or structural nature of that theory.

In light of these considerations we see that the following paths are open in attempting to show the inadequacy of the Received View. (a) It can be demonstrated that there are clear-cut examples of scientific theories which do not admit of the required canonical formulation, or else show that certain clear-cut examples of nonscientific theories fit their analysis; in this manner it is shown that requirement (1) for explications is violated. (b) It can be shown that various of the concepts or distinctions employed in the explicatum are excessively vague or else are unintelligible; if so, then adequacy requirement (2) is violated.

[125] For further discussion of Carnap's notion of explication, see Goodman [1951], Ch. 1, and Hanna's [1968] illuminating discussion.

(c) It can be shown that the analysis misconstrues or obscures a number of characteristic conceptual features of scientific theories, and thus that requirement (3) is not satisfactorily met. (d) It can be shown that the analysis is incompatible with accepted analyses of other related concepts, and thus does not satisfactorily meet requirement (3). (e) It can be shown that the analysis introduces unwarranted complications, thereby violating requirement (4). Finally, (f) one can show the analysis inadequate by presenting an alternative analysis which avoids the inadequacies of the analysis in question and at the same time is more illuminating about the explicandum.

In the next sections we will consider the attacks which have been made on the Received View; these attacks attempt to show it inadequate in ways (a) to (e). The discussion of various proposed alternatives to the Received View in Section V can be construed partially as attempts to show the Received View inadequate in way (f).

IV. Criticism of the Received View

In the course of its development, a number of criticisms were raised against various features of the Received View; these largely were criticisms raised by its proponents with an eye toward refining and improving the analysis. These were considered in Section III. In this section I want to turn to a variety of criticisms raised with the intent of showing that the Received View is fundamentally untenable and must be abandoned in favor of some alternative analysis. These criticisms, together with the alternative analyses of theories to be considered in Section V, ultimately were successful in bringing about the general rejection of the Received View.

A. How Adequate Is the Received View as a General Analysis of Scientific Theories?

The Received View was advanced by its proponents as an adequate explication of all scientific theories—the claim being that if a theory does not admit of a canonical reformulation meeting the conditions of the final version of the Received View, it is not a genuine scientific theory.[126] Rather surprisingly, the various criticisms made of the Received View have left this claim essentially unchallenged.[127] Before considering the more detailed criticisms made of the Received View, I want to consider whether the Received View has any plausibility as a

126 A very explicit version of the claim for the initial version of the Received View is found in Carnap [1932], Secs. 5, 7; in the addenda to the English translation in Alston and Nakhnikian [1963], Carnap reaffirms this claim in its essential form.

127 The closest things to a challenge seem to be Achinstein's [1968] arguments intended to show that scientific theories exhibit so much diversity that there are no deep and general properties common to all theories (pp. 121–129), Rapoport's [1958] taxonomy of theories which indicates that only certain theories are amenable to the Received View's treatment, and Kaplan's [1964] claim (pp. 298–299) that the Received View applies only to one kind of theory. Achinstein's and Rapoport's claims are considered in Sec. V–A below.

general analysis of theories.[128] My approach is to raise the question whether every clear-cut example of a scientific theory can be reformulated axiomatically in the canonical manner required by the Received View. Any attempt to answer this question faces considerable difficulty. For to answer it one needs to have agreement on what qualifies as a clear-cut example of a scientific theory, and no such agreement exists today among philosophers of science. Some would maintain that theories in physics are scientific but those in sociology are not, while others would maintain that all these are as well as Freudian psychology.[129] The problem is complicated further by the fact that various decisions as to what counts as a scientific theory often are motivated in large part by which analysis of theories one accepts—thus running a danger of circularity in any attempt to assess the adequacy of the analysis. In order to avoid getting sidetracked into the seemingly hopeless task of delimiting the class of theories which are to be accepted as being clearly scientific, and hence which must admit of the canonical reformulation prescribed by the Received View, I shall take the following approach. I shall begin by asking the general question whether all those entities which typically are referred to as scientific theories can be reformulated axiomatically; and I will invoke a variety of such theories in support of the contention that they cannot. Although there will be readers who will want to reject some of these theories as not properly qualifying as scientific, few readers will wish to reject all of them as being unscientific. Thus without attempting to delimit the class of theories which properly qualify as being scientific, I will establish that not all scientific theories admit of the canonical axiomatic formulation required by the Received View. Then I shall argue that some theories do admit of the required canonical formulation, thereby establishing that the Received View is plausible for some but not all scientific theories.

To demonstrate that not all theories commonly referred to as scientific admit of the canonical reformulation required by the Received View, it will suffice to show that some of these theories cannot be axiomatized fruitfully. The question here is not whether all theories can be axiomatized—for it is the case that any theory, scientific or otherwise, can be "axiomatized" in a trivial fashion by the mere listing of symbolizations of all known results—but rather whether they all can be axiomatized fruitfully.

[128] The discussion which follows is an altered version of pp. 38–45 of Suppe [1967].

[129] For a consideration of the issues and difficulties involved, see Gallie [1957] and Harrah's [1959] reply.

I begin by considering what is characteristic of a fruitful axiomatization on the Received View. It is characteristic of scientific theories that they systematize a body of empirical knowledge by means of a system of interrelated concepts. For the purposes of explicating the structure of scientific theories, the Received View clearly intends that to be fruitful an axiomatization of a theory must reflect this systematic character of the theory by having the following features: Of the various concepts occurring in the pre-axiomatic version of the theory, a small number of these concepts are selected as basic; axioms are introduced which specify the most fundamental relations holding between these basic concepts; and definitions are given specifying the remaining concepts of the theory in terms of these basic ones. The relations specified by the axioms and definitions do not explicitly state the entire content of the theory, but if the axiomatization is fruitful and adequate, it will be possible to deduce the remaining content of the theory from the axioms and definitions by a process of logical manipulation. That is, a fruitful axiomatization will reduce the content of the theory to a compact axiomatic basis in such a way as to display the systematic interconnections between the various concepts in the pre-axiomatic version of the theory.[130]

For such fruitful axiomatization to be possible, rather extensive knowledge of the interconnections between the component concepts of the pre-axiomatic theory must be on hand. The axiomatic method in effect is a method for introducing order into an already well-developed body of knowledge; in particular, fruitful axiomatization of a theory is possible only if the theory to be axiomatized embodies a well-developed body of knowledge for which the systematic interconnections of its concepts are understood to a high degree. Without these conditions being met, any attempt at axiomatization will be premature and fruitless.[131]

It is manifest that the systematic interconnections among the concepts occurring in any of the following theories at present are insufficiently well known or understood to admit of fruitful axiomatization: Hebb's theory of the central nervous system, Darwin's theory of evolution, Hoyle's theory on the origin of the universe, Pike's tagmemic the-

[130] Carnap [1963b], p. 58, critically relates an attempt by Neurath to axiomatize Freudian psychology by presenting a sentence-by-sentence symbolization of Freud's writings. Part of Carnap's criticism of this attempt is that it is fruitless in the sense just specified.

[131] For a similar discussion of fruitful *vs.* premature axiomatization, see Copi [1958], pp. 115–116; in his discussion he cites several examples of premature and fruitless attempts to axiomatize portions of linguistics and psychology.

ory of language structure, Freud's psychology, Heyerdahl's theory about the origin of human life on Easter Island, or the theory that all Indo-European languages have a common ancestor language, proto-Indo-European.[132] Furthermore, it is manifest that most theories in cultural anthropology; most sociological theories about the family; theories about the origin of the American Indian; most theories in paleontology; theories of phylogenetic descent; most theories in histology, cellular and microbiology, and comparative anatomy; natural history theories about the decline of the dinosaur and other prehistoric animals; and theories about the higher processes in psychology, all are such at present that any attempts at axiomatization would be premature and fruitless since they are insufficiently developed to permit their reduction to a highly systematic basis in the manner described above which is required for fruitful axiomatization.[133] We conclude, then, that a large number of the theories usually referred to as scientific do not admit of the canonical axiomatic reformulation required by the Received View for the simple reason that they presently admit of no fruitful axiomatization.

Some theories do admit of fruitful axiomatization, however. The most successful examples of fruitful axiomatization come from physics, and include the axiomatizations of such theories as classical particle

132 The reader doubting that axiomatization of these theories at present would be premature and fruitless is invited to consult the relevant literature. For Hebb's theory, see Hebb [1949]; for Hoyle's theory, see Hoyle [1961]; and for a bibliography of Pike's work, see Pike [1966]. Darwinian evolutionary theory can be found in any good text on genetics and natural selection. For Easter Island, see Heyerdahl [1950]; for Freud, see Freud [1961]; and for discussion of proto-Indo-European, see Gleason [1961], Ch. 28.

133 Another way of putting the point is that all these theories are such that given their current development they are relatively vague and schematic; and any attempt at axiomatization at present will unwarrantedly transcend the data and knowledge upon which they are based—the situation being somewhat analogous to computing a calculation to seven decimal places when the data is accurate to only two places. Or, to put the point differently: given the state of development of the theories cited, if an axiomatization were advanced having the required systematic properties, it would deviate from the informal theory so much that it could not plausibly be construed as being a *re*formulation of that theory. Rather, it would be a different theory which displayed a certain similarity to the original informal theory. And being so precise, it would be significantly less well supported by the known facts than the vaguer informal theory. It does not follow, however, that attempts at axiomatization of the informal theory necessarily will be without value, for the attempt at axiomatization may provide hypotheses the testing of which might lead to further articulation of the theory. But this is not the sort of fruitfulness required for the purposes of the Received View. Another view of the issue is suggested by Rudner [1966], pp. 47–53, where he argues for the necessity of partial formalizations of theories in much of social science.

and rigid body mechanics, relativistic mechanics, and so on by McKinsey, Suppes, and others.[134] These axiomatizations do not have the form that the Received View requires, but it seems clear that they could be modified so as to meet the requirements imposed by the Received View—provided, of course, that these requirements are coherent ones.

Subject to the assumption that the various requirements imposed on axiomatizations by the Received View are coherent ones, we thus conclude that some, but not all, of the theories commonly referred to as scientific theories do admit of the canonical axiomatic formulation required by the Received View analysis. There is no reason to doubt a priori that the more mathematical scientific theories can be given canonical axiomatic formulations of the sort required by the Received View. We conclude, then, that the Received View is an initially plausible analysis for a number of scientific theories, including the class of exact scientific theories. Since certain of our examples above of theories for which axiomatization would be premature and fruitless will qualify as scientific under any reasonable account of which so-called scientific theories really are scientific, we also conclude that the Received View is not plausible as an analysis of the structure of *all* scientific theories. Our subsequent critical and analytic discussion thus can be construed as raising the question whether the Received View is adequate even for those scientific theories which do admit of fruitful axiomatization.[135]

B. Observational-Theoretical Distinction

Some of the strongest and most influential attacks on the Received View have been aimed at its reliance on the observational-theoretical distinction. These attacks have been of three sorts: (1) attempts to show that the analytic-synthetic distinction is untenable, and since the Received View embodies that distinction it is untenable in a way that reflects on its employment of the observational-theoretical distinction; (2) attempts to show that the observational-theoretical distinction can-

[134] See McKinsey, Sugar, and Suppes [1953]; McKinsey and Suppes [1953]; Rubin and Suppes [1954]; Birkhoff [1960]; Mulchkhuyse [1960]; and the articles by Rubin, Suppes, Walker, Ueno, Adams, and Landé in Henkin, Suppes, and Tarski [1959].

[135] The discussion just given leaves open the question whether the Received View's insistence on axiomatization leads to any philosophically interesting or fruitful results; this issue is taken up in Sec. F below.

not be drawn for scientific languages; and (3) attempts to establish accounts of observation which are incompatible with the observational-theoretical distinction. The first and second of these attempts will be considered respectively in the following two subsections; only passing reference will be made to the third approach here, as the more influential of those attempts are components of suggested alternatives to the Received View, which will be considered in Section V below.

1. Analytic-Synthetic Distinction

The analytic-synthetic distinction first was formulated explicitly by Kant in his *Critique of Pure Reason* where he defines a proposition as being analytic if the predicate concept is "contained in" the subject concept, and synthetic otherwise. The "contained in" metaphor is vague, and in recent times Kant's characterization has been replaced by more precise, but not necessarily equivalent, formulations.[136] Carnap [1966], for example, construes analytic ("A true or false") sentences as those sentences which, if true, are true in virtue of their logical forms and the meanings of the logical and descriptive terms occurring in them. On the other hand, "the truth or falsity of a synthetic sentence is not determined by the meanings of its terms, but by factual information about the physical world." [137] It is important to note that Carnap is *not* defining synthetic sentences as nonanalytic ones; he is giving an independent positive characterization for them—namely as those sentences whose truth or falsity can be *determined* by factual information about the world. This is not just to say that their truth or falsity *depends* upon the way the world is; this is required, but in addition it must be possible, in principle at least, to determine what that truth or falsity is. In advancing the analytic-synthetic distinction for sentences, Carnap clearly intends that every cognitively meaningful sentence is either analytic or synthetic, but not both. As such the analytic-synthetic distinction provides an alternative statement of the positivist's criterion of cognitive significance (see Section I): the claim that a sentence is cognitively significant if and only if it is either analytically true or false or else is empirically testable reduces to the claim that the cognitively

[136] For an example of such a nonequivalent reformulation, see Körner [1955], pp. 18ff. Such formulations are not necessarily equivalent to Kant's because they tend to equate synthetic with the a posteriori and analytic with the a priori—an equation Kant would deny. They also extend the analysis to propositions which are not in subject-predicate forms.

[137] Pp. 259–260; see also p. 267.

significant sentences are those which are analytically true or false or else synthetic.[138]

Under what circumstances can one determine the truth or falsity of a sentence by use of factual information? The Received View embodies an answer. For the language L in which a theory TC is formulated, there will be certain sentences which are analytic. For L_O, these will be those sentences which are logically true (that is, instances of tautologies) and those which are true in virtue of their logical form and the meanings of the logical and V_O terms occurring in them. The remaining L_O sentences will make singular assertions about connections occurring between, or properties of, the referents of V_O terms; these are synthetic since such assertions can be checked by direct observation. For L_O', the situation is not much different, the only difference being a result of the use of quantifiers and modalities in sentences; but since the only nonlogical terms in L_O' sentences are from V_O, all singular instances of L_O' sentences will be testable by direct observation, and so the truth or falsity of any such nonanalytic sentence can be determined inductively from factual information about the world. Thus all nonanalytic L_O' assertions will have L_O consequences sufficient to qualify them as synthetic. For L_T sentences and for mixed sentences (involving terms from both V_O and V_T), specifying analytic and synthetic sentences is more difficult. All such sentences which are instances of logical truths will be analytic. But what about the nonlogical truths which are analytic in virtue of their logical forms and the meanings of the logical and V_T terms occurring in them? Restricting attention to empirical meaning as Carnap does,[139] the meaning of the V_T terms is partially specified by TC, and analytic sentences will be those whose truth or falsity depends only on their logical form, the meanings of the logical terms occurring in them, and the meanings of the V_T terms partially interpreted by TC. However, TC cannot be construed *merely* as specifying the meaning of the V_T terms; for if that was all TC did, TC would be analytic. TC's being analytic is undesirable for several reasons: first, it would make TC not subject to empirical test; second, if one makes the natural assumption that the logical implications of analytic sentences are themselves analytic, all the L_O consequences of TC (the set T_O of L_O-

[138] Since the gradual loosening of the requirements imposed on correspondence rules (see Sec. II–A) parallels a loosening in the positivist's criterion of cognitive significance, one can thus view the various accounts given of admissible correspondence rules as different analyses of what it is to be synthetic; indeed, the discussion of the following paragraph can be viewed as showing how the final version of the Received View, through its account of correspondence rules, embodies the analytic-synthetic distinction.

[139] See, for example, Carnap [1966], Ch. 28.

predictions of *TC*) would be analytic; third, many of the sentences in *C* are descriptions of experimental procedures, and they would have to be analytic, rather than the synthetic descriptions of experimental procedures and the observable manifestations of systems of theoretical entities they clearly are.[140] Hence *TC* cannot be analytic even though it does supply the V_T terms with a partial specification of their empirical meaning. Similarly, *C* cannot be analytic without being subject to the third difficulty. Thus *TC* must have a factual component and a meaning component, and to specify the class of analytic nonlogical L_T and mixed sentences, the meaning component must be isolated. Carnap has suggested that this be done by specifying *meaning postulates* for *L*;[141] properly done, these will specify the meanings for sentences of L_T, L_O', L_O, and for the mixed sentences. Then the analytic sentences for *L* will be the logical truths together with those sentences which are logical consequences of the meaning postulates. Moreover, if properly done, these will be a subset of the logical consequences of the conjunction of *TC* and the meaning postulates for L_O. Having so specified the analytic sentences for *L*, hence for L_T and the class of mixed sentences, does it follow that the nonanalytic sentences all are synthetic? Given adequate meaning postulates, it will follow that every L_T and every mixed sentence has L_O consequences (when conjoined with the meaning postulates) which are subject to direct observation, and hence their truth or falsity can be inductively determined on the basis of direct observation.[142] Since the meaning postulates *M* for *L* and *TC* are just a restatement of the meaning component of *TC*, it follows from the Received View that every sentence of *L* is analytic or synthetic.

Since the Received View embodies the analytic-synthetic distinction, if that distinction is untenable for scientific languages the Received

[140] This is just another way of saying that making *TC* analytic confuses meaning with evidence.

[141] See the enlarged, 1956, edition of Carnap [1947], pp. 222–229 (this is a reprinting of Carnap [1952a]); [1966], Ch. 28. One of the earliest attempts to effect such a separation of the factual and meaning components of *TC* was in Reichenbach [1928].

[142] What counts as adequate meaning postulates is crucial. In order to make every nonanalytic L_T sentence *S* synthetic, it must be such that every such sentence has nonanalytic L_O consequences; the meaning postulates *M* must guarantee this, which is to say that '$M \cdot S$' must entail L_O sentences not entailed by *M* alone. Moreover, since *M* is supposed to be redundant of *TC*, *TC* must be such as to guarantee this. It is not clear how this adequacy condition is to be specified; but it seems probable that any plausible specification of it will require imposing further restrictive conditions on *TC*. Further, merely having some nonanalytic L_O consequences does not seem to guarantee the required inductive confirmability of the L_T or mixed nonanalytic sentences, so further restrictions probably must be imposed on *M*.

View also must be untenable. Accordingly, the recent attacks on the analytic-synthetic distinction bear directly on the adequacy of the Received View. I now want to consider those attacks, and then exploit considerations raised (especially by Putnam [1962a]) to show how the denial of the analytic-synthetic distinction reflects on the observational-theoretical distinction.

In his classic paper "Two Dogma's of Empiricism,"[143] W. V. Quine argues that the analytic-synthetic distinction is untenable. In barest outline, his argument goes as follows. First, he distinguishes two kinds of analytic sentences: the first class consists of logical truths; the second class of sentences which are not logical truths but are true in virtue of their meanings. He then observes that it is characteristic of the second class that they can be converted into sentences of the first class by replacing synonyms by synonyms. For example, the sentence

No bachelor is a married man

is of the second class; but 'bachelor' and 'unmarried man' being synonymous, can be converted into the sentence

No unmarried man is a married man

which is of the first class.[144] The first class is relatively nonproblematic as to its characterization, whereas the second is problematic since the notion of synonymy is as obscure as that of analyticity.[145] The problem of specifying the second class of analytic statements, then, is to do it without presupposing the notion of synonymy, or else by giving synonymy an independent characterization. Quine then proceeds to consider a number of ways either of these two approaches might be carried out. He considers the proposal that the second class of analytic statements consists of those sentences which can be reduced to the first class by definition. He then considers a number of notions of definition, and argues that those which are plausible candidates covertly presuppose the notion of synonymy; thus the notion of definition is of no help.[146] Next he considers the possibility that the synonymy of two linguistic forms consists in their interchangeability *salva veritate* (that is, without alteration of truth value in all contexts); if so, then the second class of analytic statements can be adequately characterized in terms of this notion of synonymy. However, he argues, interchange-

143 Reprinted with additions in Quine [1953]; all page references will be to this reprinting.

144 *Ibid.*, p. 23.

145 See the articles on synonymy in Linsky [1952] for a sample of the problems involved with the notion.

146 Quine [1953], pp. 24–27.

ability *salva veritate* provides a sufficient condition for synonymy only if the language is sufficiently rich that it can make assertions of the form 'Necessarily all and only *x*'s are *y*'s', where 'necessarily' is so narrowly construed as to apply only to analytic statements; the assertions of this form must be true of *x* and *y* if they are synonymous in this sense. This indicates that interchangeability *salva veritate* will not yield a sufficient condition for synonymy in extensional languages. For nonextensional languages it does provide a sufficient condition for synonymy; but to specify the relevant sense of 'necessarily' for such assertions, recourse will have to be made to the notion of analyticity, so the interchangeability *salva veritate* account of synonymy covertly presupposes the notion of analyticity which it is supposed to explain.[147] Abandoning the attempt to specify the relevant notion of synonymy, he goes back to the idea that analyticity is truth in virtue of meaning, and considers the possibility that, for artificial languages at least, the notion of analyticity can be made precise using the notion of *semantical rules* (meaning postulates) for the language. Considering various proposals, he argues either that they presuppose the notion of analyticity, define something else (*analyticity-for-L*) which tells us nothing about analyticity, or else involve equally problematic and unexplained notions. Thus, he concludes, the notion of semantical rules is of no help in defining the second class of analytic truths.[148] He then considers a proposal implicit in the verification theory of meaning (see Sec. I above), which says that the meaning of a statement is the method of empirically confirming or infirming it; then analytic statements could be defined as those which are confirmed no matter what. Thus, if the verification theory is an adequate account of statement synonymy, the notion of analyticity is saved. The verification theory's account in essence was that each statement was translatable into statements about immediate (for example, directly observable) experiences, and so the synonymy of two statements is their translatability into the same class of statements about immediate experience. Quine then traces the downfall of the verification theory and its doctrine of the *reducibility* of synthetic statements to statements about immediate experience,[149] and then concludes:

> But the dogma of reductionism has, in a subtler and more tenuous form, continued to influence the thought of empiricists. The notion lingers that to . . . each synthetic statement, there is associated a unique range of

[147] *Ibid.*, pp. 27–32.
[148] *Ibid.*, pp. 32–37.
[149] *Ibid.*, pp. 37–40.

> possible sensory events such that any of them would add to the likelihood of truth of the statement, and that there is also another unique range of sensory events whose occurrence would detract from that likelihood. . . . The dogma of reductionism survives in the supposition that each statement, taken in isolation from its fellows, can admit of confirmation or infirmation at all. My counter suggestion . . . is that our statements about the external world fact the tribunal of sense experience not individually, but only as a corporate body.
>
> The dogma of reductionism, even in its attenuated form, is intimately connected with the other dogma—that there is a cleavage between the analytic and the synthetic. . . . As long as it is taken to be significant in general to speak of the confirmation and infirmation of a statement, it seems significant to speak also of a limiting kind of statement which is vacuously confirmed, *ipso facto*, come what may; and such a statement is analytic.[150]

He then concludes the two dogmas are at root identical. The remainder of the article consists in sketching what sort of account one gets of scientific knowledge when these two dogmas are denied.

Even from this sketchy summary, some critical assessment can be made of Quine's article. First, he has not made his case. At best he has shown that a number of different attempts or ways of specifying analyticity will not work; this, of course, does not show that the dogma of the analytic-synthetic distinction is untenable—it only shows its tenability has not been shown. Second, concerning his "argument" against the dogma of reductionism, he is correct that the dogma is involved in Carnap's use of the analytic-synthetic distinction; indeed, in showing how the dogma is built into the Received View above, I in effect have had to employ the attenuated form of the reducibility dogma. But Quine has not shown the dogma untenable in its attenuated form; all he has done is make, and accept, a countersuggestion which entails its denial. That his arguments so obviously fail to establish his conclusion that the two dogmas are untenable leads one to suspect that Quine's motive in writing the paper was to throw down the gauntlet, to challenge those who hold the dogmas to give adequate defense of them.

A large number of papers were written in rebuttal to Quine, most of them arguing that there must be a distinction since we have examples of analytic and synthetic statements. Such rejoinders are irrelevant, however, since any distinction proposed, however untenable, has at least a few paradigm examples.[151] The first significant rejoinder was that of Grice and Strawson [1956]. In addition to making observations similar to those I have just made about Quine's arguments not making

[150] *Ibid.*, pp. 40–41.
[151] See Putnam [1962a], pp. 359–360.

his case, they proceed to show that there are theoretical reasons for supposing that the analytic-synthetic distinction does exist. Their argument, in essence, is that where there is agreement on the use of the expressions involved with respect to an open class, there necessarily must be some kind of distinction present. Since the expressions 'analytic' and 'synthetic' do enjoy such agreement (which is not to say there are not a number of cases where we are not sure which class to put a statement in),[152] they conclude there must be an analytic-synthetic distinction. While it does demonstrate the existence of a distinction, it does not display what the distinction is. More important, it does not show that the distinction is a strict bifurcation of statements or sentences into the analytically true or false and the synthetically true or false. In particular, it leaves open the possibility that, although some statements or sentences are analytically or synthetically true or false, there is a large class of statements or sentences which are neither.

Putnam [1962a] accepts Grice and Strawson's conclusion that there is a distinction, goes on to argue that the vast majority of statements cannot happily be construed as either analytic or synthetic, and attempts to characterize these classes. He begins by construing analytic statements as those which could not turn out false unless some change in the meanings of the constituent terms first occurred, and synthetic statements as those which could be confuted by isolated experimental test or verified by induction by simple enumeration.[153] In essence, Putnam's approach is to show that there is a large number of supposedly synthetic statements which qualify neither as analytic nor synthetic as these notions were just characterized, and that these include most of the so-called physical definitions, scientific laws, and so on, in science. Central to his argument is the notion of a lawlike cluster concept. The idea of a *cluster concept* is well known to philosophers, being a con-

[152] See Wang [1955] for a good selection of examples.

[153] It could be objected that Putnam had begged the question by so constructing 'analytic' and 'synthetic', the argument being that synthetic statements often are defined as being nonanalytic. Several replies are in order to this objection. If this is so, there is no problem whether there is an analytic-synthetic distinction. However, there will be a problem whether synthetic statements have the empirical properties usually attributed to them—the typical properties being those used by Putnam to specify the distinction. (For example, Carnap [1966], pp. 259–260, 267, defines synthetic as nonanalytic, but attributes to synthetic sentences the properties Putnam uses in his specification of synthetic.) Thus, whichever way one chooses to formulate the distinction, one has essentially the same problem about the distinction, though its formulation will be different. Furthermore, one can reply as Putnam himself does (in the abstract of his paper on p. x of Feigl and Maxwell [1962]) that this characterization of 'analytic' and 'synthetic' embodies "how philosophers, in large part, are actually using these terms today, regardless of how they may formally define them."

cept whose meaning is a cluster of properties, not all of which must be possessed by an individual to fall under the concept, although it must possess a goodly number of them.[154] In analogy to cluster concepts, Putnam introduces *law-cluster concepts* which are constituted not by a bundle of properties, but by a cluster of laws which determine the identity of the concept. In general, any one of these laws may be abandoned without destroying the identity of the law-cluster concept, just as an entity need not possess all the properties in a cluster concept in order to fall under the concept. A paradigm example of a law-cluster concept would be the concept 'energy' which plays a large number of law and inference roles which collectively constitute its meaning, rather than individually defining it.[155] What is most characteristic of law-cluster concepts is that if one or a few of the laws constituting the concept are abandoned, this does not alter the meaning of the concept. To be certain, the change in the kinetic energy laws occasioned by Einstein's relativity theory did alter the intension of 'energy' and 'kinetic energy', but it did not alter the extensions of the concepts.[156] After the change, the extension of 'kinetic energy' was literally the energy due to its motion, just as it was before. I think Putnam's point can be made more perspicuously in the following way: The laws constituting the identity of a law-cluster concept determine the extension of the concept, but they overdetermine it in several ways. First, the deletion of any one or a few of the laws does not alter the extension of the concept. Second, the laws do more than merely determine its extension; they also assert various factual connections purportedly holding between entities falling under the concept and other entities. These factual assertions are not part of the identity or extensional meaning of the concept. Thus the addition of laws to, or the removal of laws from, the cluster will alter the extension of the concept only if the factual connections require alterations in the concept's extension (as, for example, would be the case if the new law asserted factual connections which could not be true given the previous extension of the concept).

Consider now the laws and so-called definitions of science. By careful analysis, Putnam shows that the definition of kinetic energy ($e =$

[154] For an extremely lucid and careful formulation of cluster concepts, see Achinstein's [1968] discussion (Chs. 1 and 2) of definition in science; this account can be construed as including law-cluster concepts, and thus provides a fuller characterization of Putnam's key notion. (Related discussion also can be found in Suppe [1973c].)

[155] Putnam [1962a], pp. 378–379.

[156] *Ibid.*, p. 399; Putnam there raises doubts about the propriety of talking of the intensions of law-cluster concepts. The *intension* of a concept is roughly its sense, and its *extension* is roughly its range of reference.

$1/2\ mv^2$) and the principles of Euclidean geometry are principles formulated in terms of law-cluster concepts;[157] moreover he does so in a way which shows that "most of the terms in highly developed science are law-cluster concepts."[158] Since such principles do involve law-cluster concepts, they may be individually denied without altering the identity (extensional meaning) of the concepts. Since analytic principles are those which cannot turn out false unless some change in the meanings of the constituent terms just occurred, these principles cannot be analytic.[159]

Are such principles (including most of the laws of highly developed science) then synthetic since they are not analytic? Putnam's answer is that they are not, arguing these principles have "the characteristic of being so centrally employed as auxiliaries to make predictions without themselves being jeopardized by any possible experimental results."[160] Certainly the principle of kinetic energy, $e = 1/2\ mv^2$, and the principles of geometry are not the sort of principles which can be overthrown by any isolated experiment, nor are they the sorts of principles that can be verified by induction by simple enumeration. In order to test the principles of geometry these will have to be employed in conjunction with other principles—such as those from geometric optics. At best we can test their conjunction (the reason for this being the occurrence of law-cluster concepts in their formulation) and if the conjunction fails, it shows at most that their combination is in trouble; it does not show which is false. Thus, the principles do not admit of isolated experiments; similarly, they do not admit of individual inductive verification by simple enumeration. Accordingly, they are not synthetic.[161]

Thus, there is a large class of statements, including most principles,

[157] *Ibid.*, pp. 368–375.

[158] *Ibid.*, p. 379.

[159] One could object here that this is so only because one construes meaning extensionally. Putnam's consideration of 'kinetic energy' and concepts from geometry indicate that this is how meaning must be construed in such cases. More basically, however, if the law-cluster concepts are construed as specifying attributes of physical existents (as they clearly do), it can be shown that only the extensions of the concepts are relevant to the truth of the principles unless one maintains that the physical existents are intentional particulars; that this is so follows from results presented in Suppe [1973a]. Accordingly, it is legitimate for Putnam to construe meaning change here as change in extension, even though the extensions of the concepts do not exhaust their meaning.

[160] Putnam [1962a], p. 375; for related discussion of such auxiliary roles, see Putnam's contribution to Session V below.

[161] This is a restricted version of the so-called Duhemian hypothesis that scientific laws are not individually verifiable or falsifiable; see Duhem [1954], pp. 183–190; for a critique of Duhem's version, see Grünbaum [1963], Ch. 4, Sec. A.

definitions, and laws of highly developed science, which are neither analytic nor synthetic; the mark of these is that their constituents are law-cluster concepts. This is not to say, however, that there are no analytic or no synthetic statements, for there clearly are. On the analytic side, there are those statements such as 'All bachelors are unmarried' which do not involve law-cluster concepts. Since they do not, viewing them as false would require alteration of the meanings of their constituent terms. The concepts involved thus are "fixed points" in our language, strict synonymies which may be held just because they have a minimum degree of systematic import.[162] And there are synthetic principles, being low-level generalizations which *can* be overthrown by isolated experiments repeated often enough producing the same results. Putnam concludes his article by inquiring further into the nature of analytic statements and the rationale for introducing them,[163] presenting a criterion for analyticity,[164] and concluding that the rationale behind having them in a natural language is that there is no reason not to have them since they have no systematic consequences and they do have the advantage of allowing us to use pairs of expressions interchangeably.

Before considering what implications Putnam's findings have for the observational-theoretical distinction and the Received View, I want to consider one form or rejoinder which has been made to both Putnam and Quine—a reply relevant to our consideration of the role of the analytic-synthetic distinction in the Received View. Maxwell [1962a] maintains that analytic sentences are those which in a reasonable rational reconstruction would be unconditionally assertable; as such they are devoid of factual content. Maxwell makes it clear that this makes analyticity context-dependent in the sense that "a sentence which is analytic in one context may be synthetic in another." [165] As such, analytic sentences roughly correspond to Carnap's meaning postulates in a rational reconstruction, where the postulates chosen correspond to linguistic habits of speakers in the context being rationally reconstructed. With respect to Putnam's law-cluster concepts, Maxwell's doctrine becomes that, depending on context, some of the laws involved may be denied, and others may not; the former are analytic, while the latter are synthetic. Thus, the analytic-synthetic distinction still is useful and valuable, though which sentences are analytic will be context-dependent. Feigl [1956] presents a similar defense of the analytic-synthetic

162 Putnam [1962a], pp. 383–384.
163 *Ibid.*, pp. 381–397.
164 *Ibid.*, pp. 392–393.
165 Maxwell [1962a], p. 399.

distinction. The appropriate reply (which is implicit in Putnam's article)[166] to this "defense" of the analytic-synthetic distinction is, I think, the following: the distinction being defended is not the analytic-synthetic distinction, but rather one which is closely related to it. The notion of analyticity occurring in the analytic-synthetic distinction is such that analytic principles are those which *cannot* be given up without altering their meanings. Maxwell's analytic principles are those for which a decision has been made in the rational reconstruction that they *will not* be falsified or given up (the justification for the decision made being that in the context undergoing rational reconstruction, people give no indication they are willing to give them up). But, Putnam observes, "it is perfectly rational to make a rule that something is always to be done; and the rule is no less a rule that something is always done on account of the fact that the rule itself may be abandoned." [167] That is, the decision that the contextually analytic principle is not to be falsified does not mean that it cannot be falsified—hence Maxwell's contextually "analytic" meaning postulates are not analytic in the strict sense of the term. Moreover, their later abandonment need not involve changes in meanings of their terms, even though they are called meaning postulates. Maxwell certainly is correct that there are principles we are unwilling to reject in context (indeed, Putnam makes much the same point when he says that the law-cluster principles will be rejected only if there is an alternative theory accepted which holds them false); but it is totally misleading to call them analytic, as they are analytic in no strict sense of the term.

I think Putnam is quite correct in maintaining that there are a large number of statements and principles in physical theory whose constituent concepts are law-cluster concepts, and that such principles can, at least individually, be denied without altering the extensional meaning or content of the concepts; furthermore, I think he is correct in maintaining that the attempt to force these principles into either the analytic or the synthetic box unhappily obscures this characteristic of most principles or statements in physical theory. Moreover, Putnam's claims here have important consequence for the Received View and its reliance on the observational-theoretical distinction, which consequences I now want to explore.

It will be recalled that the Received View embodies the analytic-synthetic distinction by assuming that implicit in *TC* are various meaning stipulations which can be summarized into a set of meaning postu-

166 Putnam [1962a], pp. 381–389, and especially pp. 388–389.
167 *Ibid.*, pp. 388–389.

lates, where these meaning postulates in effect specify certain relationships between the nonlogical terms of the theory as being definitional. It is clear from Putnam's discussion that a large number of these terms will embody law-cluster concepts; moreover, not all of the laws or principles which contribute to the specification of these concepts will be from the theory; often a number of them will be from related theories or branches of science which the theory *TC* does not cover.[168] Any of these, either from within or without *TC*, may be given up without altering the theory. From our consideration of Maxwell's "defense" of the distinction, it becomes clear that the specification of certain of these as meaning postulates amounts to a decision not to give them up. In Carnap's specific use of these (see the beginning of this section), the ones not given up must include principles of the theory implicit in *TC* (otherwise the meaning postulates will not be redundant of *TC*). Thus the variability allowed is limited to the rejection of principles from outside *TC* together with *some* of the other principles of *TC* (those which specify factual rather than meaning components of *TC*). This is contrary to actual scientific practice where the principles assumed as undeniable often are from without the theory, not from within the theory—for example, in geophysics' use of classical mechanics, the principles from classical mechanics tend to be treated as definitional whereas those from geophysics are not. Thus, even if we allow principles to be analytic in Maxwell's weak sense, Carnap is mistaken in supposing that the "analytic" principles all are implicit in *TC*.[169] But even if we limit Carnap's account to cases where all the principles held undeniable (the "analytic" ones) are implicit in *TC*, the reply to Maxwell makes it clear that these principles are not analytic in any strict sense. Rather it is the case that Carnap's analytic sentences in *L* are nothing other than those sentences (together with their implications) which it has been *decided* will not be given up, come what may —though they may, in fact, later be given up. They in effect are the formulation of a rule to be followed in cleaning up any difficulties the theory may get into—namely, if the theory requires modification, no alterations are to be made which affect the "analytic" principles in *TC* if other modifications are possible.

Putnam's findings also show that insofar as Carnap's attempt to incorporate the analytic-synthetic distinction into the Received View is

[168] For related discussion of this point, see Nickles's contribution to Session VII below.

[169] This observation challenges the Received View more than one might suppose, since it indicates that V_T terms of *TC* often have empirical meaning components *not* supplied by *TC*.

an attempt to separate the factual content of TC from the meaning content, it fails. While it is the case that the principles which contribute to law-cluster concepts do aid in the specification of the extension ("definition") of the concept, none of the principles are analytic, none of them have definitional status; they each are factual assertions which are empirically true or false.[170] They are factual though they do contribute to the "definition" of the terms. Thus, in trying to divide the sentences of L into those which have meaning content and those which have factual content, Carnap is attempting the impossible. All his attempt succeeds in doing is to distinguish a set of sentences which, except as a last resort, are not to be modified in attempting to improve the observational fit of the theory.

The fact that Carnap's use of meaning postulates fails to show that each sentence of L is either analytic or synthetic in the strict sense should not be allowed to obscure the fact that this is what he was attempting to do. Moreover, the idea that the sentences are analytic or synthetic in this sense is central to the Received View, providing the rationale for its dependence on the observational-theoretical distinction.[171] The observational-theoretical distinction separates the nonlogical terms of a theory into V_O and V_T, where the terms in V_O refer to directly observables. Since L_O is restricted to V_O nonlogical terms and has a restricted logical structure, all sentences of L_O are analytic or synthetic in the strict sense. We saw above that the claimed payoff of Carnap's use of meaning postulates was to separate off the sentences of L having meaning content from those having factual content. Therefore, when conjoined with the meaning postulates M, any nonanalytic sentence of S of L which was not in L_O would be such that '$M \cdot S$' had L_O consequences which would enable S to be inductively confirmed or else disconfirmed in isolation. (Since M supposedly is analytic, having no factual content, the directly observable evidence reflects only on the truth of S, and not of M.) Thus S would be synthetic. Thus the function of the observational-theoretical distinction is to guarantee that every nonanalytic sentence of L will be synthetic: nonanalytic L_O sentences are synthetic; and any sentence of L involving V_T terms having testable observable consequences will be synthetic. However, we have seen that the sentences of L cannot be separated into those which have meaning content and those which have factual content; more specifically, the sentences in M do not exclusively have meaning content

[170] Putnam [1962a], p. 363.

[171] It is noteworthy here that once Hempel became convinced that the analytic-synthetic distinction was untenable, he abandoned the observational-theoretical distinction; see Hempel [1958] and [1963].

since they contain law-cluster concepts. Thus most of the sentences in *L* are neither analytic nor synthetic. It follows that the rationale for the observational-theoretical distinction is untenable.

Viewing the matter from another perspective will clarify the point. Originally the Received View's emphasis was not so much on the analytic-synthetic distinction, but rather on cognitive significance. Initially the rationale for introducing the observational-theoretical distinction was to guarantee that the sentences in *L*, hence *TC*, would be cognitive significant. But, however one specifies cognitive significance, it amounts to nothing more than the requirement that every sentence in *L* either be analytic or synthetic (in the strict sense) and not both. Thus, the analytic-synthetic distinction and cognitive significance come to the same thing. As Quine puts it, "The two dogmas are, indeed, at root identical." [172] And whichever way put, it is the rationale for the Received View's reliance on the observational-theoretical distinction. The upshot of the attack on the analytic-synthetic distinction thus is to show decisively what the failure to develop a satisfactory notion of cognitive significance hinted at—that the rationale underlying the observational-theoretical distinction was untenable.

2. Observational-Theoretical Term Distinction

Showing that the rationale underlying the observational-theoretical distinction is untenable does not, of course, demonstrate the distinction is untenable—though it does make a good presumptive case that it is. The *coup de grâce* for the observational-theoretical distinction was provided by a series of direct attacks on the distinction by Putnam and Achinstein, designed to show the distinction cannot satisfactorily be drawn.[173]

Paradigm examples of observational and theoretical terms include the following:

Observation Terms		*Theoretical Terms*	
red	volume	electric field	mass
warm	floats	electron	electric resistance
left of	wood	atom	temperature
touches	water	molecule	gene
longer than	iron	wave function	virus
hard	weight	charge	ego
stick	cell nucleus		

[172] Quine [1951], p. 41.

[173] Putnam [1962], Achinstein [1965]; Achinstein's paper is incorporated into a fuller treatment of the matter in Achinstein [1968].

What distinguishes the terms on these two lists, the Received View claims, is that observation terms refer to *directly observable* entities or attributes of entities whereas theoretical terms do not. The qualification that these entities and attributes be *directly* observable is crucial; merely being observable will not separate even the paradigm examples in this way. 'Observation', in the relevant sense, involves attending to something, and has the following characteristics noted by Achinstein [1968]: (1) how many aspects of an item, and which ones, I must attend to before I can be said to observe it will depend upon my concerns and knowledge; (2) observing involves paying attention to various aspects and features of the items observed, but does not always require recognizing the kind of item being observed; (3) it is possible to observe something even though it is in a certain sense hidden from view—for example, a forest ranger observes the fire even though he can only see smoke—so observing an item does not necessarily involve seeing or looking at it; (4) it is possible to observe something when seeing an intermediary image—for example, when looking at myself in a mirror; (5) it is possible to describe what I am observing in the sky as a moving speck or an airplane. These facts about observation indicate that observability does not separate the paradigm terms in the above lists in the indicated way. They allow me to report observing items such as electrons, fields, and temperature (points (3) and (4)), though by the above classification they are unobservable; furthermore, the distinction supposes that what is observable is describable in some unique way using a special vocabulary, whereas point (5) indicates this is not so—for example, I can describe movement through a bubble chamber either as a trace (observation term) or as an α-particle emission (theoretical term).[174] These considerations indicate that the notion of 'observable' involved in drawing the observational-theoretical distinction must be a special, technical sense if the distinction is tenable.

That a special sense of 'observable' is intended is made clear in Carnap [1936–37] where he requires that observational terms refer to *directly observables*, where the mark of being directly observable is that the truth of L_O sentences can be ascertained with the help of a relatively few observations involving at most simple instruments. Achinstein [1965][175] argues this does not suffice to mark the observational-theoretical term distinction. First, he observes, to say that something is not directly observable could mean that it cannot be observed

[174] Achinstein [1968], pp. 160–165.

[175] Sec. II; substantially the same points are made in Achinstein [1968], Ch. 5, Sec. 4. My discussion follows the fuller 1968 development.

without instruments or without observing something distinct from it. This certainly is part of what Carnap has in mind by direct observability (see the quotation from Carnap [1966] in Sec. II–D above). But it will not do. First, it is not sufficiently precise: does it count as unobservable an item (for example, a cell nucleus) observed only by the production of images and reflections? Second, what does '*X* is not observable without instruments' mean? If it means that *no* aspect of *X* is observable without instruments then 'temperature', 'kinetic energy', 'entropy', 'mass', 'charge', and so on, belong on the observational list, rather than on the theoretical list where they are placed, since we often can observe changes in them without recourse to instruments. If it means that instruments generally are required to detect the presence of *X*, this will be insufficient since one cannot appropriately talk about *the presence of* temperature, the wave function, or kinetic energy. If it means that instruments are generally required to measure *X* or its properties, then such terms on the observational list as 'volume', 'water', 'weight', and so forth, are on the wrong list. Achinstein thus concludes that the notion of direct observability as the observability of an object without recourse to instruments or the observation of something distinct from it fails to draw the observational-theoretical distinction in the required place.

Similarly, Achinstein argues that the requirement of deciding whether a predicate applies to an item on the basis of relatively few observations does not draw the distinction where desired. First, he asks whether the number of observations refers to the number of times the object must be observed, the number of times the experiment must be repeated, the number of different characteristics of the object that need to be observed, or the amount of preliminary investigation necessary before a final observation can be made. Whichever way this is intended, terms will end up on the wrong list! With sufficient background, a physicist can identify an α-particle emission in a cloud chamber on one or two observations, and such color terms as 'dark ultramarine' may require a number of observations to determine whether a thing is of exactly that color.

On the basis of these considerations Achinstein concludes that the observational-theoretical term distinction cannot be drawn in the ways Carnap and other proponents of the Received View have suggested and have even the paradigm terms show up on the lists they are supposed to. This of course does not show that the distinction cannot be drawn in some other way. Putnam [1962] does present arguments intended to show that the distinction cannot be satisfactorily drawn at all. He argues that if observation terms are terms which in principle only can be used to refer to observable things, then there are no observation terms at all. For there is no single term applicable to observables which *could not* be used in application to unobservables without altering its meaning—in the manner in which Newton used 'red' to postulate that red light consists of red corpuscles.[176] Thus, if there is a distinction between observation terms and theoretical terms, it must be such that observation terms are those which *sometimes* can be used with reference to observables; theoretical terms then must be those which *never* can refer to observables. But, then, many theoretical terms (for example, 'gravitational attraction', 'electrical charge', 'mass') will be observation terms since, for example, I can determine the presence of electrical charge by sticking my finger on a terminal. What these considerations indicate is that the meanings of most nonlogical terms in a natural scientific language are such that they can be used both with reference to what might plausibly be termed observables and also with reference to what plausibly might be construed as nonobservables. Accordingly there is no natural division of terms into the observable and the nonobservable.

I think the above considerations raised by Putnam and Achinstein collectively succeed in showing the following: first, they do show that the ways advocates of the Received View have attempted to specify the distinction fail to specify it precisely or in such a way that their paradigm examples of observation terms and theoretical terms clearly do qualify as such. Second, they make a strong (but not conclusive) case for the contention that the meanings of nonlogical terms in natural scientific languages generally are not such that they can be used exclusively with reference to just directly observables or just nondirectly observables—in any plausible sense of the term 'observable'.[177] It is important to note that these findings do not show the observational-theoretical distinction is untenable. For there is absolutely no reason why the Received View must be committed to the distinction being drawn on the basis of ordinary scientific usage of nonlogical terms. The Received View is advanced as a rational reconstruction (or explication) of scientific theories (see Sec. III), and there is absolutely no reason why the reconstruction of a theory cannot impose an

[176] This claim is argued more fully in Suppe [1972b]; the remainder of the argument is only implicit in Putnam's paper.

[177] While this is, I take it, the import of their arguments, the claims are not specifically made in their writings; nor do I think they make the strongest case possible for the conclusions. In Suppe [1972b] I have tried to present a tighter and stronger case for the claim; the assessment of their arguments which takes up the remainder of this paragraph is argued and developed much more fully in that article.

artificial division on the nonlogical terms. For example, assuming a plausible distinction can be drawn between entities and attribute-occurrences which are directly observable and those which are not, one could employ separate terms of *L* to refer to observable entities or attribute-occurrences and others to refer to nonobservable ones—for example, one might employ 'red$_o$' to refer to observable occurrences of the property *red* and 'red$_t$' to refer to nonobservables. Working out such a proposal certainly will involve many difficulties and complexities,[178] but none of the considerations raised by either Putnam or Achinstein do much to show this is unworkable. Since a satisfactory working out of such a distinction would be sufficient for the purposes of the Received View, I conclude that Putnam's and Achinstein's arguments fail to show the distinction untenable—even though they did succeed in convincing most philosophers of science that the distinction is untenable.

Such an artificial drawing of the observational-theoretical distinction certainly is going to make the Received View reconstruction of a theory very complex, introducing a degree and kind of complexity not found in theories as they are employed in actual scientific practice. Such increased complexity is justifiable only if the philosophical significance of the distinction warrants it; otherwise, drawing the distinction in such an artificial way can be construed as nothing other than an attempt to save the Received View analysis at any cost. What is supposed to be the philosophical significance of the distinction? Part of its intended significance was to guarantee that theoretical terms and statements will be cognitively significant. In the previous subsection we saw that this amounts to preserving the analytic-synthetic distinction for sentences of *L*, and that the distinction does not hold for *L*; thus the observational-theoretical distinction fails to guarantee the cognitive significance of theoretical terms and statements. A second claimed significance was indicated in Sections I and II, where it was held by many positivists to reflect the process whereby language was acquired and theories developed: by ostentation one learns the use of observation terms, then theoretical terms are introduced derivatively; the development of science proceeds "upward" from empirical generalizations about observables to progressively more abstract generalizations about nonobservables; in both cases the observational-theoretical distinction was supposed to mark these distinctions. Putnam [1962] rightly ob-

178 Some of these are indicated in Suppe [1972b] where the proposal is developed more fully.

serves that both these theses are false. That the observational-theoretical distinction cannot be drawn on the basis of ordinary usage indicates the language acquisition thesis is false. And it is not historically true that science proceeds upward from V_O to V_T generalizations. Indeed, the fact that V_T terms are not introduced separately by correspondence rules in the final version of the Received View (see Sec. II–B, E) indicates that even if these theses were tenable, the Received View no longer can claim to support either of them. What, then, is the philosophical significance of the observational-theoretical distinction? The only plausible answer is that there are significant differences in the epistemic properties of entities referred to by theoretical terms and nontheoretical terms, and that the observational-theoretical distinction captures that distinction. Putnam rightly claims the distinction between theoretical and nontheoretical terms is important, but denies that the observational-theoretical term distinction captures it. Under the observational-theoretical term distinction, theoretical terms are those which do not refer to directly observables. But theoretical terms, properly so-called, are terms which come from a scientific theory; and such terms can and often do refer to observables—for example, Darwin's theory of evolution, as originally put forward, referred exclusively to observables, but clearly employs theoretical terms. Moreover, observation reports, which are of epistemic significance, often do employ terms which do not refer to observables. Thus the observational-theoretical term distinction totally fails to capture the philosophical significance of theoretical terms in science.[179] Thus the observational-theoretical term distinction does not seem to mark any philosophically significant distinction.

The situation, then, concerning the observational-theoretical distinction is this. The primary rationale for the observational-theoretical distinction was to provide an empiricist methodology. Its approach to doing so was to show how the sentences of *L* were cognitively significant; doing so amounted to showing that the analytic-synthetic distinction held for all assertions in the language *L* a theory was formulated in. We have seen that the observational-theoretical distinction fails to do so. Furthermore, the distinction has not been successfully drawn, and what is more cannot be drawn in any plausible way on the basis of ordinary usage of terms in natural scientific languages. The only way the distinction could be drawn is artificially in a reconstructed lan-

[179] Putnam [1962], pp. 241–242; Achinstein [1965] and [1969], pp. 176, 197–198, makes similar observations.

guage, and doing so would introduce an unwarranted degree of complexity into the analysis. Furthermore, even if the distinction is drawn satisfactorily it will mark no philosophically significant or epistemically revealing distinction. Finally, the distinction fails to capture what is distinctive either of theoretical terms or observation reports in science. The observational-theoretical distinction obviously is untenable. As such most of the epistemological interest of the Received View is lost. Insofar as the observational-theoretical distinction is essential to the Received View, the Received View is inadequate.[180] Further arguments that the distinction is fundamentally untenable and philosophically confused are raised by Hanson and others in arguing for their alternatives to the Received View; these will be considered in Section V below.

C. Partial Interpretation

The observational-theoretical distinction plays an intimate role in the Received View's doctrine of *partial interpretation* for theoretical terms and assertions involving them. Clauses (4) and (5) of the final version of the Received View require that V_O terms and the sentences of L_O and L_O' be given a complete empirical semantic interpretation in terms of directly observables, but forbids that V_T terms (hence sentences of L involving them) be given any such direct observational interpretation. Thus a V_O term t might be interpreted as referring to the quality *red*, but it is expressly forbidden that an observational interpretation for a V_T term t' be given by specifying that t' refers to or designates anything. Rather, the only observational interpretation which may be given to V_T terms is what TC indirectly supplies them with. As Carnap [1956] puts it,

> All the interpretation (*in the strict sense of this term, i.e. observational interpretation*) that can be given for L_T is given in the C-rules, and their function is essentially the interpretation of certain sentences containing descriptive terms, and thereby the descriptive terms of V_T. . . .
>
> For L_T we do not claim to have a complete interpretation, but only the indirect and partial interpretation given by the correspondence rules. . . .
>
> Before the C-rules are given, L_T, with the postulates T and the rules of deduction is an uninterpreted calculus. . . . Then the C-rules are added.

[180] How essential it is to the Received View is not clear. Hempel's contribution to the symposium (Session I below) presents an analysis of theories very much like the Received View which does not employ the observational-theoretical distinction.

> All they do is, in effect, to permit the derivation of certain sentences of L_O from certain sentences of L_T or vice versa. They serve indirectly for derivations of conclusions in L_O, e.g., predictions of observable events, from given premises in L_O, e.g., reports of results found by observation, or the determination of the probability of a conclusion in L_O on the basis of given premises in L_O.[181]

In general, *TC* will not fully specify the observational content of V_T terms and assertions involving them, but will only provide them with a *partial interpretation.*

It should be clear from preceding discussion that the notion of partial interpretation occupies a central place in the Received View, being intimately involved in its incorporation of the analytic-synthetic distinction, employment of the observational-theoretical distinction, and doctrines about meaning. The notion of partial interpretation is, as Achinstein [1963], [1968], and Putnam [1962] have noted, notoriously unclear—the distinction having been introduced without definition in Carnap [1939], and "used subsequently by Carnap and other authors . . . with copious cross references, but no further explanation." [182] Moreover, according to Achinstein and Putnam, the notion cannot be formulated precisely in a way compatible with the requirements of the Received View; hence, in virtue of the Received View's reliance on the notion, its analysis of theories is untenable.

Achinstein [1963][183] and Putnam [1962] ask the question how the claim that *TC* provides V_T terms and assertions employing them with a partial interpretation is to be understood, and then suggest a number of interpretations they claim are inadequate. Achinstein's proposed interpretations are the following:

(1) A term *t* is partially interpreted means that the term has a meaning but only part of that meaning has been given.

(2) A term *t* is partially interpreted if there are no observational conditions all of which are logically necessary for *t* and whose conjunction is logically sufficient, but there are other sorts of analytic statements relating *t* to observation terms.

(3) A term *t* is partially interpreted if, among the sentences in which *t* appears in the theory, there are none of the form '$ta \equiv \phi a$', where ϕa is a sentence from L_O or L_O' and the sentence is not analytic.[184]

[181] Pp. 46–47; emphasis added.

[182] Putnam [1962], p. 245.

[183] This article is incorporated into Achinstein [1968]; my discussion follows the latter, more accessible, version which is found on pp. 85–91.

[184] Achinstein [1968], pp. 85–87.

Putnam's proposed interpretations are the following:

(4) To partially interpret V_T terms and sentences of L is to specify a nonempty class of intended models having more than one member.[185]

(5) To partially interpret a term t is to specify a verification-refutation procedure which does not apply to all individuals within the extension of t.

(6) To partially interpret a language L is to interpret part of the language (for example, to provide translations into common language for some terms and leave the others mere dummy symbols).[186]

It will be noted that these proposals variously define partial interpretation for terms, theories, and languages. This diversity is legitimate since advocates of the Received View apply the notion of partial interpretation to all three; presumably, specifying it for any one of these three would enable one to specify the notion for the other two.

Each of these proposals allegedly is inadequate. It will prove convenient to examine them as to adequacy in a different order. Against (2) Achinstein observes that if the correspondence rules C supply t with a partial interpretation, they will have to be analytic; clearly not all the rules in C may be analytic (see Sec. IV-B-1), so (2) must require that some C-rules are analytic while others are synthetic. Achinstein's entire objection to this interpretation is that it no longer will be possible to claim that semantical rules cannot be given for theoretical terms.[187] But this is no objection, since the only prohibition on semantic rules for V_T is that they cannot be independently given in terms of observables; allowing some C-rules to function as meaning postulates in the way proposed thus does not conflict with this prohibition.[188] This criticism probably would not bother Achinstein since he is of the opinion that Carnap and most other advocates of the Received View assert

185 A model for a theory is a semantic interpretation of the theory such that all the axioms are true; thus a model for TC would be an interpretation such that TC is true; see note 193 for related discussion.

186 Putnam [1962], pp. 245–246.

187 Achinstein [1968], pp. 86–87.

188 This can be seen more fully in terms of the final version of the Received View. The prohibition on specifying observational semantical rules for V_T and L_T is simply that you cannot directly give the sort of semantic interpretation clause (4) allows for L_O. This is a prohibition on the following sort of rule: "V_T term t designates observable property t"; the C rules do not provide *semantic rules* of this sort, their form being "Whenever '*Oa*' is true ('*O*' being in L_O), '*ta*' also must be true (where '*t*' is in V_T)." It thus becomes clear that the proposal Achinstein considers under (2) is not incompatible with the final version of the Received View; hence, contrary to Achinstein, the proposal requires no modification of it.

that *no* correspondence rules ever are analytic, and so the proposal is incompatible with their position. This, however, is just mistaken; for we have seen above (Sec. IV-B-1) that Carnap very clearly is committed to the position that some *C*-rules are analytic and others are not.[189] I conclude he has failed to show (2) incompatible with the purposes of the Received View. Achinstein observes that (3) seems closest to what Carnap and Hempel had in mind, that this is not a semantic rule in the sense of Carnap [1942], and so concludes it is misleading to talk of partial interpretation with respect to it. He concludes that the only plausible interpretations of 'partial interpretation' are (3) and possibly (2); he then asks what arguments could be given in support of the doctrine of partial interpretation (under either version), and argues that such arguments rest on two assumptions—(i) that the items referred to by V_T terms are unobservable and (ii) that if a term is interpreted as referring to something unobservable, it expresses a concept that is unintelligible or scientifically meaningless (p. 90). He certainly is correct that the doctrine is based on the first assumption, and that the assumption is untenable (see Sec. IV-B-2 above); as to the second assumption, we have seen that this is denied by those (including Carnap) who adhere to a realist version of the Received View.[190]

Thus his argument against (2) and (3) is directed against something of a straw man, since it attributes to advocates of the Received View a premise most of them clearly would deny. I do think Achinstein is on strong ground, however, when he urges that the partial interpretation notion's strong reliance on the observational-theoretical distinction renders it unsatisfactory. This does not show, however, that the notion would be unsatisfactory if it were tied to some other distinction (for example, Hempel's [1963] basic *vs.* nonbasic vocabulary distinction).

The arguments against (1), (5), and (6) are conveniently treated together since they all involve a denial that V_T terms, or sentences embodying them, can have meaning not supplied by *TC*. Achinstein

[189] The discussion of meaning postulates in IV–B–1 makes it clear that part of the content of *TC* is analytic in a way such that *TC* can be reformulated so that some sentences in *T* and *C* are analytic; see also Carnap [1966], pp. 267–268 and 270, for very definite commitments on this. In justification of his interpretation of Carnap, Achinstein refers to Carnap [1963c], p. 965. The only thing I can find there relevant to Achinstein's claim is an assertion that the Ramsey sentence for *TC*, TC^R, is a P-postulate, hence synthetic, and '$TC^R \supset TC$' is analytic. This is, of course, compatible with parts of *C* being analytic or *TC* having an analytic meaning component; so the passage does not support Achinstein's interpretation.

[190] See Sec. II–B. Carnap makes it very explicit that V_T terms do designate nonobservable entities in Carnap [1966], p. 256; he therefore must hold them to have some meaning.

rejects (1) on the grounds that it presupposes that the term *t* already has a meaning, which he says is denied for theoretical terms by the Received View. Against (5), Putnam observes that this proposal will result in many L_T sentences having undefined truth values. Furthermore, every time a new verification procedure involving V_T terms is adopted, the meanings of V_T terms will change, which clearly is absurd. Against (6), Putnam observes that this leads to the view that theoretical terms have *no meaning at all*, that they are mere computing devices. This, of course, is unsatisfactory under the realistic interpretation usually given the Received View. It is clear that each of these arguments shows its target unsatisfactory as an analysis of partial interpretation only if coupled with the assumption that V_T terms have no meaning other than what is supplied by partial interpretation—that is, by *TC*. Careful scrutiny of either the final version of the Received View or the quotation from Carnap [1956] at the beginning of this section will indicate that this assumption misinterprets the Received View; for it will be seen that the prohibition on supplying V_T terms with an independent semantic interpretation is limited to *observational interpretation* and does not prohibit supplying them with nonobservational meaning. Moreover, Carnap and Hempel do make it clear various places that independent nonobservational semantic interpretations are permissible.[191] I conclude, then, that the arguments against (1), (5), and (6) beg the question, and fail to make their case.

Before considering Putnam's reasons for rejecting (4), I want to develop a proposed account of partial interpretation which very closely resembles (4).[192] Assume that an observational interpretation has been given for L_O.[193] Consider now all the possible interpretations which could be given to *L*. Some of these will interpret L_O exactly in the same way as does the interpretation we have assumed given for L_O; and of

[191] See, for example, Hempel [1963], p. 695; Carnap [1939], p. 62; and Hempel's remarks on p. 260 below. It must be admitted, however, that they tended to do so begrudgingly and also to belittle the importance of giving such interpretations. The fact that by allowing such interpretations the notion of partial interpretation can be defended against criticisms (1), (5), and (6), coupled with the fact that it does enable a coherent account of partial interpretation to be given (see below), indicates that allowing independent semantic interpretations is far more important to the success of their program than they are willing to admit.

[192] The discussion which follows summarizes portions of Suppe [1971], where the claims are argued in full detail.

[193] An interpretation for a language *L* consists in specifying a domain of individuals, attributes holding for these individuals, and what entities or attributes are designated by what nonlogical terms of *L*. In terms of these, standard rules of truth are specified for the sentences of *L*.

these, some of these will be *models* of TC (that is, interpretations of L such that TC is true). Let M be the class of such *models* of TC which contain the interpretation given for L_O. M will have the following characteristics: (a) M is fully specified by the semantic interpretation given for L_O (clause (iv) of the initial version of the Received View), together with the assumed truth of TC. (b) If S is a sentence of L which is a theorem of TC, then S will be true in every model in M. (c) If S is a sentence of L containing V_T terms not explicitly defined in TC and S is not a theorem of TC, then S will be true in some models in M and false in others. It follows that if anyone asserts TC he is committing himself to one of these models M being correct.

It was mentioned above that it is consistent with the final version of the Received View to supply TC with an independent semantic interpretation. As Hempel [1963] puts it,

> Let T be interpreted by a system C which does not furnish every V_T-sentence an equivalent in terms of V_O. Then it is nevertheless quite possible to provide a necessary and sufficient condition of truth for every sentence expressible in terms of the theoretical vocabulary. All that is needed for the purposes is a suitable metalanguage. If we are willing to use a metalanguage which contains V_O, V_T, and C, or translations thereof, then indeed each L_T-sentence has a truth criterion in it, namely simply its restatement in, or its translation into, that metalanguage. . . .[194]

Suppose such a semantic interpretation is given for TC. Then V_T terms would be interpreted as referring to electrons, electron emissions, and so on, where 'electron', 'electron emission', and so forth, have their normal meanings in scientific language. If we look at theoretical terms such as 'electron', we find that while part of the conceptual content of the concepts these terms embody is observational (for example, electrons are entities which leave tracks in bubble chambers), much of the meaning concerns extra-observational associations—for example, for electrons there might include various features of the billiard-ball model, various classical intuitions about macroscopic point-masses, and so on. Such features contribute to the meaning of theoretical terms in ordinary scientific language, and it is quite likely that without them little scientific progress could be made. But despite their legitimate place as meaning constituents of such terms, such features need not, and usually do not, have observable or testable consequences.

[194] P. 695; Carnap makes essentially the same observation in Carnap [1939], p. 62.

Suppose then that a theory *TC* formulated in *L* is given an independent semantic interpretation in this way. What is added to the interpretation of *TC* that was not there before? In asserting *TC* I am claiming that one of the models in *M* is correct. In giving *L* (hence *TC*) a semantic interpretation, I am saying that the correct interpretation in *M* is one where, for example, term *t* refers to electrons, *t′* refers to electron emissions, and so forth. As such I am narrowing down the choice of correct interpretations in *M* to those which meet this condition. However, the terms in the ordinary scientific language such as 'electron' and 'electron emission' are not precise enough to narrow the choice down to just one of the models in *M*. However, in so interpreting *TC* I am committing myself to using the terms corresponding to V_T terms in such a way that, for example, electrons will have all of the observational manifestations specified by *TC*; that is, the assertion of *TC* together with its semantic interpretation does result in the observational meaning of the theoretical terms in the scientific language being compatible with that specified by *TC*. I am in effect saying that whatever else I mean by 'electron', electrons are things which have the observable manifestations determined by *TC*. Whenever I incorporate an experimental procedure into *TC* as a correspondence rule involving the V_T term corresponding to electrons and assert *TC* so interpreted, I am committing myself to using 'electron' in such a way that its observational content includes that specified by the correspondence rule.

At this point it begins to be clear that partial interpretation is not the same thing as definition in any strict sense of the term. When I give a semantic interpretation to *TC*, I am doing so relative to the meanings I already attach to terms in the scientific metalanguage. In asserting *TC* so interpreted, I am committing myself to the meaning of 'electron', and so on, being such that electrons have those observable manifestations specified by *TC*. That is *TC* demarcates (but does not define) the meaning of 'electron' and other V_T terms to the extent that their meanings are a function of observable consequences. If *TC* is such that all the models in *M* are extensionally equivalent (that is, if exactly the same sentences from *L* are true in each model in *M*), then *TC* would provide a complete specification (but not definition) of the observational content of V_T terms. In general, however, the models in *M* determined by *TC* will not be extensionally equivalent, and so *TC* only provides a partial specification of the observational content of V_T terms. It is in this sense that *TC* provides a partial observational interpretation of V_T and *L*. And it readily can be seen that this is version (1) of partial interpretation suggested by Achinstein.

At the same time, the mechanism of partial interpretation is very much like that proposed in (4) by Putnam. There Putnam proposed that partial interpretation consisted in the specification of a class of *intended models* for *TC*. The only difference between his proposal and mine is that *M* is the class of *all* models compatible with *TC*, whereas his proposed class would be that subclass of *M* consisting of those models in *M* which the realistically minded scientist would not reject as being flagrantly unintended interpretations which were not what he had in mind. Putnam argues, correctly I think, that any such specification of the class of intended models must employ "broad-spectrum" terms such as 'physical magnitude' which are not defined in advance, it being the job of the science to further specify their meaning. As such, there will be a large number of models in *M* for which we do not have any idea whether they are intended interpretations or not; hence the class of *intended models* cannot be well defined. Thus (4) is unacceptable.[195] Although these considerations show (4) unacceptable, they do not show the analysis I have proposed is inadequate for the simple reason that the models in *M* are *not* restricted to intended interpretations. However, Putnam's rejection of (4) does point out the following about partial interpretation. Under the Received View, all partial interpretation is supposed to do is specify the class of intended interpretations for *TC* only insofar as they can be specified in terms of observational consequences; and this amounts to specifying *M*. Fuller specification of the intended interpretations of *TC* will have to make recourse to extra-observational considerations including the extra-observational meaning of the terms in the scientific metalanguage corresponding to V_T terms. But even this is incapable of specifying fully which interpretations in *M* are intended since the terms used to specify the semantical interpretations for *TC* will include "broad-spectrum" terms (for example, 'physical magnitude') whose full specification constitute open questions for the science (for example, "What is a physical magnitude?"). In effect, then, when *TC* is partially interpreted and given a semantic interpretation, one is using the V_T terms so as to be committed to the existence of entities which have at least the observable manifestations indicated by *TC* and its consequences.

One last objection of Putnam's to (4) needs to be considered since, if correct, it counts against the account I have proposed. Under (4) he says that theories with false observational consequences will have no

195 Putnam's [1962] discussion of this (p. 246) is very elliptical, and it is not clear exactly what his argument is; the account attributed here to him is discussed at length and defended in Suppe [1971], pp. 70–72.

models in M; this is unacceptable since such a theory is false, not senseless. This objection, however, confuses empirical truth with semantical truth. The class M of models for TC in effect defines a set of worlds which are compatible with the assumed semantic truth of TC. All L_O consequences of TC are semantically true in each such world. Hence the definition of M is such that M is never empty unless TC is logically contradictory. Whether TC is empirically true or false is a matter of whether it truly describes conditions obtaining in the world; but this amounts to nothing more than the question whether the real world (or a portion thereof) is in M. Hence, if semantic truth and empirical truth are kept distinct, as they should be, Putnam's objection to (4) evaporates.

To conclude my consideration of the criticisms lodged against partial interpretation: in large part these criticisms are based on a misreading of the Received View's prohibition on supplying L_T with an independent observational interpretation, together with a confusion of partial interpretation with partial definition. As such, the objections to versions (1) to (3), (5), and (6) of partial interpretation misfire. Indeed, (1) does capture part of what is involved in the Received View's notion of partial interpretation. One of the objections to (4) is sound; the other (concerning empirical truth) is confused. But a closely related analysis of partial interpretation coupled with (1) yields a coherent analysis of partial interpretation which is adequate for the purposes of the Received View. The outlines of that analysis, which is developed in detail in Suppe [1971], have been sketched. This shows the notion of partial interpretation is a coherent one. However, it does not show that the Received View's notion of partial interpretation is adequate. For the doctrine of partial interpretation in the Received View presupposes the observational-theoretical distinction, and as such is unacceptable since that distinction is untenable. What is wrong with the doctrine of partial interpretation is its reliance on the observational-theoretical distinction; to the extent that the above analysis can be divorced from the observational-theoretical distinction (which, to my mind, it can), the analysis does reveal much that is correct about the interpretative relationships which do hold between scientific language and the theories and formulas formulated in terms of it.

In Section II-E I mentioned in passing that other versions of the Received View were propounded contemporaneously with the final version of the Received View. A number of these versions allow for partial interpretation of theoretical terms, and in most cases their authors do not explicitly sanction giving an independent semantic interpretation to sentences of L containing V_T terms via recourse to a richer metalanguage.[196] To the extent that such versions intend to prohibit the giving of such independent semantic interpretations to V_T terms and the sentences containing them, Achinstein's and Putnam's objections are more successful against them. For, then, their arguments do succeed in showing that partial interpretation cannot be construed in ways (1), (4), (5), and (6). Moreover, my suggested alternative account of partial interpretation will not work for such versions since it does presuppose an independent semantic interpretation has been given to V_T terms and the sentences containing them. A modification of it will work, however: the assumed truth of TC together with the observational semantic interpretation of L_O still determines M; as such it does partially certify (that is, imposes restrictions on or partially circumscribes) the referential meanings of the V_T terms. Because independent semantic interpretations are prohibited, one cannot further restrict M to that subset M' of M where, for example, t refers to electrons, and t' refers to electron emissions. Still, the determination of M is a kind of partial interpretation, and so a coherent notion of partial interpretation is possible; but these other versions' employment of the notion is unacceptable, as above, because of its intimate reliance on the observational-theoretical distinction.

D. Models

Under the account of partial interpretation just given for the final version of the Received View, L_T sentences are given an independent nonobservational interpretation by correlating V_T terms with terms of a natural scientific language. This interpretation does two things. First, it supplies the theoretical terms with the meanings attached to the words in the natural scientific language modulo whatever alterations

[196] Nagel's [1961] version of the Received View (pp. 90–117) is a case in point. He does, however, require that theories contain physical models as components, where these models are more or less familiar, concrete, and visualizable (for example, Bohr's billiard ball model of the atom) or else are mathematical structures; these models do qualify as semantic interpretations of the postulates T of the theory. But allowing this sort of independent semantic interpretation does not amount to allowing the sorts of semantic interpretations Carnap and Hempel do, wherein theoretical terms are referred to as designating electrons (as opposed to billiard balls or points in a mathematical space, and so on). As such, Nagel gives no indication that he would allow V_T terms to be interpreted by recourse to a richer metalanguage—which, in the current discussion, is what I mean by sanctioning an independent semantic interpretation.

are forced by the acceptance of *TC*. Second, it provides L_T with a semantic interpretation of the following sort: A "world" consisting of theoretical entities and their attributes is specified, and the terms in V_T are interpreted as referring to or designating various of these entities or attributes.[197] This interpretation is such that *T* presumably is true under it, and hence is a *model* for *T*.[198] Thus the doctrine of partial interpretation commits the final version of the Received View (interpreted realistically) to a model being supplied for the theoretical laws *T* of a theory.

As such, the Received View is committed to a position very similar to that advocated by Campbell [1920], Nagel [1961], and Hesse [1965], [1966], as a modification of the Received View. Nagel puts the position as follows:

> For the purposes of analysis it will be useful to distinguish three components in a theory: (1) an abstract calculus that is the logical skeleton of the explanatory system, and that "implicitly defines" the basic notions of the system; (2) a set of [correspondence] rules that in effect assign an empirical content to the abstract calculus by relating it to the concrete materials of observation and experimentation; and (3) an interpretation or model for the abstract calculus, which supplies some flesh for the skeletal structure in terms of more or less familiar conceptual or visualizable materials.[199]

In essence Nagel's analysis consists of a version of the Received View augmented by a requirement that *TC* be given a semantic interpretation in terms of more or less familiar visualizable or conceptual materials. The similarity of Nagel's view with the Received View when partial interpretation is construed as above should not be allowed to obscure the fact that his position differs significantly from the Received View. The difference lies in what he understands by a model.

A number of different senses can be attached to 'model'; one of these is the sense of a semantic interpretation for a theory such that the theorems of the theory are true under the interpretation. This is the

[197] This latter interpretation is what Carnap [1942] calls a language system.

[198] If the semantic interpretation for L_T is augmented by that for L_O, an interpretation for *L*, hence for *TC*, is obtained; if *TC* is assumed true this describes a possible world which may or may not be the real world—whether it is being the question of *TC*'s empirical truth (see the end of the previous section). Accordingly, we can construe the semantic interpretation for L_T as being such that it is a model for *T* without prejudicing the question whether *T* is true of the real world.

[199] Nagel [1961], p. 90; see pp. 95–97 and Ch. 6, Sec. I, for Nagel's elaboration of clause (3); the discussion which follows of Nagel's views is based on these passages.

sense in which we have been employing model' so far; I will refer to such models as *mathematical models.*[200] A second sense of model is that of a scale model, a model airplane, a wind tunnel model, and such. Central to this notion is the idea that a model is a model *of* some thing or kind of thing, and functions as an *icon* of what it models—that is, the model is structurally similar (isomorphic) to what it models.[201] I will refer to these as *iconic models.*

According to Nagel, the model supplied *TC* simultaneously will be *both* a mathematical model and an iconic model. For example, for the Bohr theory of the atom, the model would be the Bohr billiard ball model—a system of billiard balls moving in orbits around one billiard ball, with some of the orbiting balls jumping from one orbit to another at various times. This model is an iconic model since it is supposed to be an iconic representation of the structure and behavior of an atom; this is not to say that the atom *is* such a collection of billiard balls, but rather that it is *similar* to it in various respects. As Hesse puts it, where the system of billiard balls is known to be analogous to an atom, there is a *positive analogy* between them, where the atom is known to be disanalogous to the system of billiard balls, there is a *negative analogy,* and where it is not known whether they are similar there is a *neutral analogy.*[202] At the same time, according to Nagel, the Bohr billiard ball model is a mathematical model of *TC* in the sense that a semantic interpretation is given to *TC* in terms of such systems of billiard balls so that *TC* is true under the interpretation. This model is not, however, the mathematical model involved in partial interpretation under the Received View. For if *TC* is empirically true, the mathematical model of partial interpretation will be the world (or portion thereof); but the Bohr billiard ball model never will be the world (or a portion thereof). Furthermore, Nagel's requirement that this model be of "more or less familiar conceptual or visualizable material" disqualifies the actual atomic substratum of the world from qualifying as the model. Thus if

[200] This locution possibly is misleading for it may suggest that such models are mathematical structures; while mathematical structures (for example, vector spaces) may qualify as mathematical models, so too can other nonmathematical structures such as the students in a class who possess various properties and stand in various relationships to each other. For a readable general characterization of mathematical models, see Mates [1965], Ch. 4.

[201] This sense of model is discussed in a number of places, including Campbell [1920]; Hesse [1966]; Harré [1960], Ch. 4; Hutten [1953–54]; Black [1962]; Rosenbleuth and Wiener [1945]; Braithwaite [1953], Ch. 4; and Suppe [1967], Sec. 1.4. The notion of an iconic relation, which is central to this sense of model, is due to Peirce and discussed in Burks [1949].

[202] Hesse [1966], p. 8.

Nagel's proposal were accepted by the Received View, *TC* would be given two separate semantic interpretations, one in terms of the real world (if *TC* is empirically true), the other in terms of a visualizable system of entities, such that the latter would be a putative iconic model of the former if *TC* is empirically true. The difference between the two positions is indicated in the following diagrams for the Bohr theory (where *T* are the laws of the theory, *C* are the correspondence rules, *O* are observation sentences, and vertical or angular lines indicate semantic interpretations).

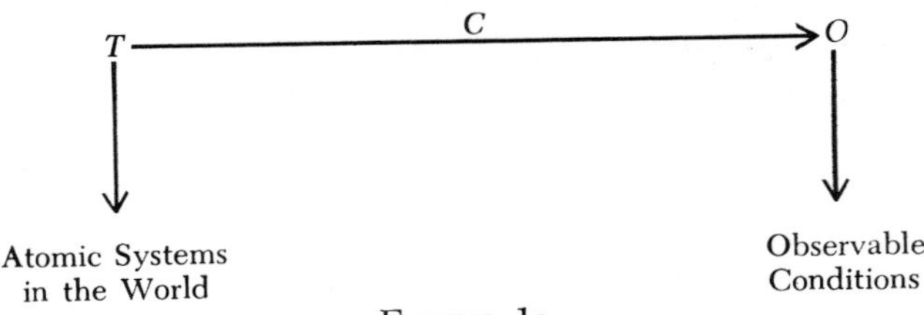

FIGURE 1a
(Interpretation of empirically true theories on Received View)

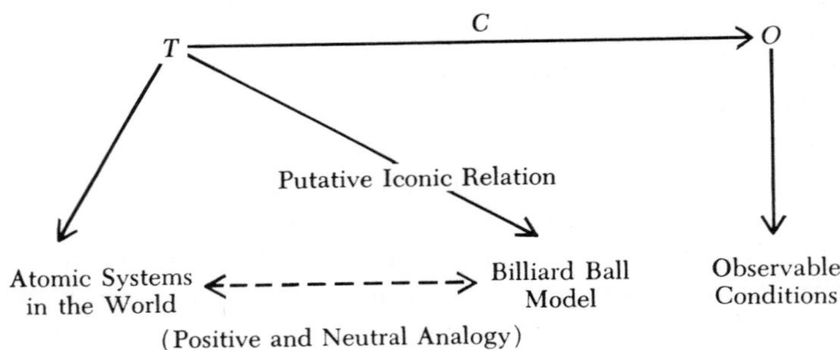

FIGURE 1b
(Interpretation of empirically true theories if Nagel's proposal were adopted by the Received View)

Nagel's claim is that every scientific theory must incorporate such an iconic model. If such iconic models must be in terms of familiar conceptual or visualizable materials, then Nagel surely is wrong. For it can be shown that quantum theory admits of no such model.[203] Being aware of this difficulty, Mary Hesse maintains a position essentially the same as Nagel's except that she allows the iconic model to be "any

203 See Bohm [1957], p. 93. The claim presupposes the Copenhagen interpretation of quantum theory.

system, whether buildable, picturable, imaginable, or none of these, which has the characteristic of making a theory predictive." [204] In particular, she is willing to allow mathematical structures specified by the formalism of the theory to be the iconic model.[205] Thus, apparently, the von Neumann mathematical model of the quantum theory formalism wherein the Schrödinger wave equation describes a viscous fluid flow through infinite-dimensional pre-Hilbert space would qualify as an iconic model.[206]

There is no doubt that the formalism of theories *can* be interpreted in terms of iconic models and that doing so often is heuristically fruitful in suggesting hypotheses, developing theories, and so on. Nagel's and Hesse's position, however, is not merely that such models *can* be given and are useful in such a way, but that they are *essential* and *integral* components of theories. Considerations of heuristic fruitfulness do not establish that they enjoy this status in theorizing since they can be heuristically fruitful without being essential and integral components of theories. Two sorts of reasons are given why such iconic models are essential components of theories. One reason is the claim that without them a theory cannot provide explanations.[207] Without considering this claim in detail, I think this argument can be rejected as inconclusive for several reasons. First, if prediction and explanation are essentially the same operation (as Hempel [1965a] and other advocates of the covering-law model claim), then the argument surely is unsound. Second, if explanation and prediction are not the same, then their claims are relative to an account of explanation which they have not provided or defended adequately. Third, if explanation is meant in any sense stronger than that which identifies explanation with prediction, it is not at all clear that scientific theories must provide explanations at all (it apparently being the case that quantum theory will not).[208] The second sort of argument claims that without such models theories will not be testable. Hesse presents such an argument:

[204] Hesse [1966], p. 19.

[205] Hesse [1965], pp. 23–24.

[206] It would be an iconic model since under it projection operators project "packets" in the flow onto linear Borel subspaces which are probability distributions over possible measured values for position and momentum coordinates of particles. These distributions are iconic representations of the actual probability distributions governing the measurement of position and momentum for particles.

[207] For example, Nagel [1961], Ch. 6, Sec. 1, and Campbell [1920], pp. 129–137, argue this way.

[208] Hesse [1966], esp. Ch. 1, also argues that considerations of explanation and prediction show the need for including iconic models in theories. Her concern is not so much with ordinary prediction and explanation, but rather with epistemically

> The major objection to the dictionary theory [that is, the Received View], however, arises from the assumption that phenomenal [that is, observational] statements can provide tests of hypotheses if the hypotheses have no meaning in themselves, or at least if phenomenal statements are independent of that meaning. Let us consider as a simple example the case of the straight stick apparently bent when placed in water. . . . Now the purely formal part of the theory of refraction consists of some postulates from which can be deduced the equation
>
> $$\frac{\sin \alpha}{\sin \beta} = \mu.$$
>
> According to the dictionary theory, the symbols α and β are now interpreted as certain angles which can be experimentally measured, and μ as a constant characteristic of air and water, and so this equation can be tested, and if it corresponds with the measurements, the hypothesis which led to it is said to be confirmed. According to the dictionary theory this is in principle all that can be said about the hypothesis which is normally called the wave-theory of light. But if this were really all, how would we know that this particular interpretation is relevant to the theory?
>
> If in the equation '$\sin\alpha/\sin\beta = \mu$', α and β were simply undetermined mathematical symbols, they might be interpreted in an indefinite number of different ways, some of which might be shown to be true of phenomena. They might, for example, be the angles between the Pole star and Mars and Venus respectively at midnight on certain given dates; why would not this be a confirmation of the formalism we have mistakenly called the wave theory of light? . . . The answer is of course that the possible interpretations of α and β are already circumscribed by the theory; the dictionary [correspondence rules] is not arbitrary, and the symbols of the hypothesis are already interpreted in terms of a model of light waves in such a way that we know what kinds of phenomena will be relevant to it.[209]

She makes it clear that these models will be iconic models of the phenomena the theory is about.[210]

---

novel explanations and predictions which lead to theoretical advances (for example, she is concerned with predictions such as Maxwell's prediction of radio waves, as opposed to the prediction of another eclipse of the moon). Like Kuhn and other advocates of alternatives to the Received View analysis of theories (see Sec. V–B–1), she views theories as things which grow and change in nonarbitrary, comprehensible, and predictable ways. She observes that such growth often (as with Maxwell) involves predicting phenomena that strictly speaking lies outside the current scope of the theory, and argues that this can be explained on the basis of iconic models. On this, she is certainly correct; but, as was indicated above in discussing heuristic uses of iconic models, this does not establish the necessity of including such iconic models as integral components of theories; and it certainly does not establish that such iconic models must exist for every possible theory.

[209] Hesse [1965], p. 17.

[210] *Ibid.*, pp. 21–28.

This argument clearly does not establish anything like Nagel's proposal. Rather the most it establishes is that theoretical terms must be given an independent semantic interpretation over and above that provided by the correspondence rules. In effect, then, her argument is nothing more than that partial interpretation for theoretical terms must be as outlined in the preceding section; it is an argument that the Received View must be in accord with Fig. 1a, something we have already argued as maintained (albeit not very clearly or emphatically) by Hempel and Carnap in their later writings. It does not demonstrate the need for models over and above what is provided in partial interpretation.[211] Out of fairness for both Hesse and Nagel, it should be emphasized that they have interpreted Carnap as denying that any independent interpretation can be given for V_T terms, and thus found a genuine difference between their position and Carnap's. Moreover, I think it fair to say that Carnap and Hempel attached insufficient importance to the semantic nonobservable interpretation allowed for V_T terms,[212] and Campbell, Nagel, and Hesse rightly have insisted that it is far more important than was thought. How important it is will be seen in the next section.

Hesse's emphasis on the role of models in interpreting V_T terms and L_T assertions do serve to point out some further aspects about partial interpretation. Typically the scientific languages used to interpret L_T assertions are extremely rich with associations from various branches of science, earlier theories, and so on. These associations include var-

211 Although their arguments fail to make their case, I think a case can be made for a variation on their position. In Secs. V–B–2–b and V–C it will be argued that theories are extralinguistic entities which cannot be identified with their linguistic formulations; this in effect means that *TC* is not a theory, but rather a *formulation* of the theory which designates or describes the theory. Thus if *TC* is empirically true, *TC* will describe the actual world and also will describe the theory; *TC* then will have two mathematical models. As there is some reason to suppose that the theory does stand in an iconic relation to the world if it is correct, these two models probably stand in an iconic relationship to each other. Viewed from this perspective, Campbell, Nagel, and Hesse are correct in insisting that the theory cannot be just the partially interpreted formalism, and must include a model—the model being the theory—which, if the theory is true, stands in an iconic relation to its phenomena.

212 As was indicated in the previous section, since Carnap [1939], Carnap and Hempel have allowed independent interpretations for V_T terms so long as the interpretation is nonobservational, but have treated it as being unimportant. Typically such interpretations have been allowed in asides to the argument, and its importance has been belittled—see, for example, Hempel [1963], p. 696, for an instance. At the same time they have emphasized that *C* rules provide all the observable interpretation allowed for V_T terms. It is no surprise that they have been mistakenly interpreted as denying the possibility of independent semantic interpretations for L_T assertions.

ious iconic models. Thus, for example, the term 'particle' as used in physical science contains associations with the classical notion of particle, the Bohr billiard-ball model, and so forth. Also, in introducing a theory, the terms used to interpret L_T often must be used with slightly different meanings than they had in previous theories, and sometimes models are used to specify the changes in the meanings (for example, the combined models of the wave and corpuscular models were used initially in quantum theory to indicate the changed meaning of 'particle'); gradually these models become assimilated into the meanings of the terms in the natural scientific language. Thus models do figure considerably in the semantic (nonobservable) interpretation of theories required by partial interpretation; to the extent she is claiming this, Hesse is correct.

Finally, it needs to be observed that for one sort of theory iconic models usually are supplied for *TC*. Whenever *T* is formulated mathematically, *T* admits of a mathematical interpretation as well as a physical one. Thus, the laws of classical particle mechanics admit of a mathematical interpretation which is a system of points in space together with various functions defined over points in that space. In asserting the theory one apparently is maintaining an isomorphism or structural similarity between the mathematical structure and the nonobservable portion of the world under consideration. In such cases, Fig. 1b applies with the iconic model being a mathematical structure.

To summarize: The Campbell-Nagel-Hesse criticisms of the Received View fail to establish the inadequacy of the Received View, but they do serve to shed additional light on the nature of the semantic interpretations given for *TC*.

E. Correspondence Rules

We observed above (Sec. II–A) that correspondence rules initially were thought to perform three main functions: (1) define theoretical terms; (2) guarantee the cognitive significance of theoretical terms; and (3) specify the admissible experimental procedures for applying a theory to phenomena. As the Received View evolved, the importance of the first two functions declined. Furthermore, criticisms raised against the Received View showed correspondence rules could not perform either of these functions. The untenability of the analytic-synthetic distinction (Sec. IV–B–1) shows that correspondence rules cannot guarantee cognitive significance for L_T assertions in the way claimed. The considerations raised in Section IV–C show that if the doctrine of partial interpretation is to be maintained, the *C*-rules cannot be construed as defining V_T terms.[213] Thus, the primary function of correspondence rules must be to specify the admissible experimental procedures for applying the theory to phenomena and/or the various sorts of correspondences asserted to hold between the theory and observable phenomena. Three different sorts of criticisms can be raised against the Received View's account of correspondence rules. First, it can be charged that the procedures for applying the theory to phenomena are not properly part of the theory. Second, it can be charged that its account of correspondence rules does not adequately represent the sorts of connections which hold between theories and phenomena. Third, it can be charged that the account of correspondence rules provides a misleading or inadequate account of the way theories experimentally are applied to phenomena. Each of these sorts of criticisms will be considered in turn.

According to the Received View a theory is a partially interpreted axiomatic system whose axioms are *TC*. Thus any change in *TC* will result in a new theory, as will any significant (that is, extensional) changes in *TC*'s interpretation. Thus, whenever a new experimental procedure is discovered for applying *T* to phenomena, *C* must be replaced by a new set *C′* of correspondence rules consisting of the rules in *C* together with a statement of the new procedure; so the incorporation of the new procedure into *TC* requires the replacement of *TC* by a new theory *TC′*. That this is a consequence of the Received View is at best misleading. For in such a situation the theory has not been changed at all. It is still the same theory; we just know more about how to apply it to phenomena. Thus it is misleading to construe the correspondence rules as being, strictly speaking, part of the theory; rather, the correspondence rules are *auxiliary hypotheses* of procedures for applying the theory to phenomena. In the initial version of the Received View, the inclusion of *C* as a component of the theory was justified; for these *C*-rules were explicit definitions, and no interpretation was given V_T terms other than what they provided. Thus any change in the *C*-rules did alter the (extensional) meanings of V_T terms, and so it was legitimate to view changes in *C* as changes in theory, and hence to incorporate *C* as a component of the theory. But once explicit definition was given up and the doctrine of partial interpretation was introduced, it no longer was defensible to construe correspondence rules as definitional of V_T terms, and hence no longer

[213] The most they can do is impose constraints on their meaning, being assertions that, as used in *TC*, the theoretical terms must admit of such and such observational manifestations of the systems described by *TC*.

defensible to include the C-rules as components of the theory. The Received View thus ought to identify the theory with T under its semantic interpretation, and construe the C-rules as auxiliary hypotheses which, when conjoined with T, do impose limitations on the observational content of L_T assertions.

A second consideration also leads to the same conclusion. The variety of legitimate possible ways of applying a theory to phenomena is potentially unlimited, and so the potential number of correspondence rules is unlimited. As the set C of correspondence rules is supposed to be finite, there is no guarantee that all of the legitimate ways of applying the theory to phenomena can ever be specified in any set of correspondence rules.[214] Accordingly it seems unreasonable to require that correspondence rules be a component of the theory. Reinforcing this point is the fact that in most presentations of theories only the theoretical postulates T and their interpretation generally are given; rarely does one find much in the way of a specification of the correspondence rules.

In a recent illuminating paper, Schaffner [1969] has argued that the Received View's treatment of correspondence rules misconstrues the ways in which theories are applied to phenomena. Schaffner holds that when a scientific theory is employed, the V_T terms have antecedent theoretical meaning, by which he means, roughly, that V_T terms are given an independent semantic interpretation. This does not mean, however, that correspondence rules do not function to specify the meanings of V_T terms. Of the three kinds of correspondence rules Schaffner recognizes, one sort functions to create meanings for V_T terms "drawing on antecedently understood notions and putting them together in a radically new way."[215] Although this often is done by drawing an analogy or presenting a model, in essence the process consists in specifying a rule connecting V_T terms with antecedently understood theoretical terms; thus, Lorentz's statement that electrons can be viewed as extremely small particles charged with electricity is an example of this first kind of correspondence rule. Such rules are involved in providing the independent semantic interpretation for V_T required in partial interpretation. Schaffner also distinguishes two species of correspondence rules which are involved in connecting a theory with phenomena. One type serves to coordinate V_T terms with laboratory English or laboratory measurement procedures, and thus specifies ways

[214] There may be cases where finite specification of all procedures is possible; the point being made here is that there is no guarantee that this is always possible.

[215] Schaffner [1969], p. 283.

in which theoretical parameters are measured, and so forth. These are the correspondence rules *C* of *TC*. There is a second way in which theories are applied to phenomena. Using various assumed or borrowed scientific theories, various "*causal sequences*" or chains are established as holding between states of affairs described by *T*, the borrowed theories, and observation reports. Such correspondence rules might, for example, establish a causal chain between the electron jump and, say, the appearance of a spectral line in a spectrometer photograph.[216] This latter sort of correspondence rule differs from the *C*-rules in *TC* in several essential respects. First, the *C*-rules merely specify procedures for measuring various parameters of the systems described by theories or correlating observations with theoretical states; they do not, and need not, specify the mechanism whereby the particular states of the systems cause the measurement apparatus to behave as it does; they do not explain why the instruments react as they do. On the other hand, the causal sequence correspondence rules specify causal links between states described by *TC* and by observation reports, and so provide theoretical explanations of the behavior reported in the observation reports.[217] In so doing the correspondence rules are scientific laws, generally being in the form of theories other than *TC*, used as auxiliary hypotheses in applying the theory *TC* to phenomena. The difference between the two kinds of correspondence rules is greater than it initially may seem. For, as was observed (Sec. IV–B–2) in actual practice, observation reports are not generally reports of congruences between, for example, pointer dials and needles; rather, they very often are couched in the language of other theories, and employ antecedently understood theoretical terms. Thus what is being explained by such correspondence rules might not be the causal mechanism underlying the experimental instrumentation, but rather the causal mechanism connecting, for example, the impact of gas molecules (theoretical description) with gas pressure (observation report). Second, Schaffner's distinction of these two sorts of correspondence rules emphasizes that the correspondence rules used to connect theories with phenomena often are not part of the theory, but rather involve the employment of theories borrowed from other areas of science. This is one further reason why the correspondence rules are not properly construed as integral parts of theories; rather they are various auxiliary hypotheses,

[216] Essentially the same function of correspondence rules is argued for, though from a different perspective, in Sellars [1961]; see also the comments by Hanson, Feyerabend, and Rudner which follow his paper.

[217] See Sellars [1961] for extensive discussion of this point.

procedures, and theories used to apply the theory to phenomena. To distinguish these two ways of applying theories to phenomena, let us refer to this causal sequence sort of correspondence rules as *auxiliary hypotheses*, and reserve 'correspondence rule' for the *C* of *TC* which are descriptions of various experimental procedures for connecting theories with phenomena.[218]

Not only does the Received View ignore the role of auxiliary hypotheses in applying theories to phenomena, but its account of correspondence rules presents a badly distorted picture of the experimental procedures for applying theories. As Patrick Suppes has argued in several papers (Suppes [1962], [1967]), what is wrong with the Received View is that it is too sketchy, that it is "far too simple," and that "its very sketchiness makes it possible to omit important properties of theories and significant distinctions that may be introduced between different theories." [219] In particular, Suppes thinks the Received View is especially oversimple in its treatment of correspondence rules. "The kind of coordinating definitions [that is, correspondence rules], often described by philosophers have their place in popular philosophical expositions of theories, but in actual scientific practice of testing scientific theories, a more elaborate and more sophisticated formal machinery for relating a theory to data is required." [220]

According to Suppes, "the concrete experience that scientists label as experience cannot be connected to a theory in any complete sense";[221] rather, mediating between a theory and the experimental situation is a hierarchy of theories, which consist of the following:[222] at the top of the hierarchy is the *physical theory* itself. In its typical formulation, the formalism of the theory includes continuous functions or infinite sequences. Of course, the results of experiments cannot be specified using such continuous functions, and so forth, without transcending the data; rather, experiments will yield discrete data. In order to con-

[218] The various functions of auxiliary hypotheses are discussed by Putnam in Session V below.

[219] Suppes [1967], p. 57.

[220] *Ibid.*, p. 62.

[221] *Ibid.*

[222] The general outline of the hierarchy is found in *ibid.*; a much more detailed treatment is in Suppes [1962]. My discussion essentially follows the latter treatment. There Suppes's examples are from linear response theory, but in my exposition I also provide what I take to be illustrations from classical physics. It is not clear to me whether Suppes's models of the experiment in Suppes [1967] are the same as in Suppes [1962]; in the former they seem to be more like the models of data in the latter. For related discussion, and for extensive further development of Suppes's ideas, see my [1973d] and Hooker [1975].

nect experimental data with the physical theory, it is necessary to determine, for a given type of experiment, the various possible combinations of finite and discrete data which are compatible with the theory. This is *the theory of the experiment.* Suppose, for example, that our theory were classical particle mechanics, and our experiment were an inclined plane experiment. The theory provides general continuous equations describing the behavior of any and all physically possible systems of n point-masses. Only certain of the systems these equations refer to, or correspond to, represent inclined plane systems. The theory of experiment's job is to say which of the systems described by the physical theory represent (if the theory is empirically true) inclined plane systems, and further which ones represent inclined plane systems of a given inclination angle α; it does so by specifying which discrete ordered sets of data (for example, position and momenta coordinates) correspond to sequences of states of inclined plane systems.[223] The theory of the experiment may employ other theories as auxiliary hypotheses. Thus the theory of experiment describes all possible sets of data obtainable from inclined plane experiments if the theory is empirically true. Turning now to the experimental data itself, in the laboratory an inclined plane is set up, a ball is weighed and released on it, and various position and time measurements made; in doing so, it is necessary to design the experimental setup, instrumentation, and so on. A statement of the general design principles of the experiment (for example, what one might ask a student to develop in an honors freshman physics lab) is the *theory of experimental design.* Not all considerations involved in the experiment are made explicit—for example, it will not be specified that if the ball is metal, the experiment should not be carried out on top of the electromagnets of a betatron. These various unstated control conditions in the design of the experiment are the *ceteris paribus* conditions, and are presumed by the theory of experimental design. Once the data has been collected in accordance with the theory of experimental design, the data is not yet in a form compatible with the various possible outcomes specified by the theory of the experiment. In the case of the inclined plane, the possible data specified by the theory of the experiment will be data about frictionless inclined planes; but the data yielded by applying the theory

[223] More precisely, special case solutions to the physical theory are obtained which characterize all possible inclined plane systems of inclination α. These solutions are continuous curves through a space (phase space); then the theory of experiment specifies which finite sequences of discrete points coincide with points along these curves.

of experimental design will be data (modulo experimental error) about frictional inclined planes. Before this latter data can be compared with the former possible data, it must be converted, shaped, and otherwise transformed into data representing what the behavior of the ball on the inclined plane would have been had the system been frictionless, and so on; also, the experimental data is in terms of distance traveled and elapsed time, whereas the possible data described by the theory of the experiment will be in terms of position and momenta coordinates at various elapsed times. The *theory of the data* specifies how the raw experimental data is to be converted into canonical-form data specified in terms of the experimental parameters of the physical theory (which, typically, are the parameters of the theory of the experiment). Various other physical theories may be employed here as auxiliary hypotheses; then this canonical data can be compared with the possible data specified by the theory of the experiment for agreement (typically by means of a statistical goodness-of-fit test). Thus the specification of the experimental hookup between the concrete experiment and the theory consists in the following hierarchy of theories: *ceteris paribus* conditions, theory of experimental design, theory of data, theory of the experiment, physical theory. Suppes suggests that the theory of the experiment, theory of data, and theory of experimental design respectively can be thought of in analogy to the characterization of a sample space, the characterization of a population, and the characterization of samples in the statistical hypothesis or theory.[224]

In the carrying-out of an experiment there will be putative realizations (models) of the various theories in this hierarchy.[225] For example, the actual experimental setup will be a putative realization of the theory of experimental design and the *ceteris paribus* conditions; the actual correction procedures used to put the raw data in canonical form will be putative realizations of the theory of data. And the predictions yielded from the theory will be putative realizations of the theory of the experiment. In experimentally testing or applying the physical theory, anomalous results may be obtained if any of these putative realizations fails to be a genuine realization of the theory. And (although Suppes does not emphasize this), in case of anomalous or disconfirming experimental results, the source of the anomaly may be the result of the experimental procedures failing to be realizations of any of these

[224] Suppes [1962], p. 260; for a related perspective, see Suppe [1973d].

[225] Suppes's exposition emphasizes the models rather than the theories; for reasons of expository clearness, I have presented his account primarily in terms of the theories of which his models are realizations.

theories or as a result of the theory's empirical falsity—which is another way of putting the Duhemian hypothesis (see Sec. IV–B–1 above). In case the physical theory is statistical, various statistics will be used to assess whether or not the experiments carried out are realizations of these theories.[226]

I do not think it is necessary to enter into a detailed consideration here how adequate are the details of Suppes's treatment or formulation of the hierarchy of theories connecting physical theory with concrete experience, for I think it is sufficiently clear that he is correct that things are at least as complex as his treatment indicates and also it is clear that something similar to what he suggests is characteristic of the hierarchy.[227] Thus, I think it can be concluded that Suppes has made his point that the Received View's treatment of correspondence rules oversimplifies things. Moreover, granting that Suppes's positive suggestion is essentially right-headed, then it is clear from the above that the Received View's oversimplification does obscure a number of epistemistically important and revealing features about experimental "hookup" between theory and concrete phenomena. Finally, I think Suppes's characterization of the "hookup" makes it patently obvious that it is a mistake to incorporate the correspondence rules into the theory as integral and individuating components.

To summarize, the Received View's treatment of correspondence rules is inadequate in three important respects: first, it mistakenly views them all as components of theories, rather than as auxiliary hypotheses;[228] second, the account ignores the fact that correspondence rules often constitute explanatory causal chains which employ other theories as auxiliary hypotheses; third, insofar as correspondence rules characterize the experimental connections between phenomena and theory, the account is oversimple and epistemologically misleading.[229] The Received View account of correspondence rules clearly is unsatisfactory.

[226] Suppes [1962] presents a detailed example of the employment of various statistics in such assessments.

[227] A related but somewhat similar account is given for a different class of theories in Suppe [1967], Ch. III. An abbreviated account of this treatment is found in Suppe [1972b], and a detailed generalization of it is given in Suppe [1973d]. My developments in these three works are reflected in the above interpretation and example of Suppes's analysis.

[228] For Schaffner's first sort of correspondence rules, their inclusion as components of theories may be legitimate. This sort of rule corresponds to Hempel's bridge principles (see his paper in Session I below).

[229] For further discussion of the third point from a different perspective, see Suppe [1972b].

F. Formalization Issues

According to the Received View every scientific theory is such that it can be given a canonical reformulation in accordance with the requirements of the final version of the Received View (Sec. III). This canonical reformulation is as an axiomatic system *TC*. In Section IV–A we argued that many theories, in their present states, do not admit of fruitful axiomatization, and so cannot be put in the canonical form required by the Received View. Thus, by insisting on axiomatic reformulation, the generality of the Received View analysis is restricted. Confining one's attention to theories where such axiomatic reformulations are possible, what is the point of insisting on axiomatic reformulations? What sort of understanding is gained by requiring axiomatization? On this issue there is considerable disagreement today. On the one hand, Suppes [1968] and Kyburg [1968] find axiomatization essential to solving virtually all problems in the philosophy of science, and on the other hand Hempel [1970] finds that the formalization or axiomatization of theories leaves most of the interesting philosophical problems untouched; in between we find authors such as Achinstein [1968] who find axiomatization of definite but limited usefulness. Depending which position one takes on this issue, the Received View's insistence on axiomatization is viewed as an asset, a liability, or legitimate if not overemphasized.

Is the Received View's insistence on axiomatization reasonable? No general consensus exists on this question today. I shall not attempt here to resolve this issue, but rather will content myself to raise some of the standard claims made in defense and criticism of the Received View's insistence on axiomatic reformulation. Further discussion of this issue is found in Hempel's paper below (Session I) and, implicitly, in Suppes's contribution to Session II below. To evaluate the Received View's reliance on axiomatization, we must recall something about the status of the canonical reformulation it provides. The Received View provides an explication of theories (see Sec. III), and so claims that theories at any stage must admit of its canonical reformulation; no claim is made that theories actually are so axiomatized or even that, in actual scientific practice, they should be.[230] Given this explicative nature of the Received View, how can one assess the reasonableness of its insistence on axiomatization? The point of explication is to reveal more closely the epistemological, ontological, and logical structure of the-

[230] Suppes [1968] does take the position that it would be better if they were.

ories; thus to insist on axiomatization is to claim that the axiomatic reformulation is epistemologically, ontologically, and logically more revealing of theories than nonaxiomatic reformulations. In light of the criticisms we have considered in preceding sections, it is clear that one cannot argue from the explicative success of the Received View to the legitimacy of its insistence on axiomatization, for its axiomatization clearly gives a very distorted and inadequate picture of the epistemological structure of theories. Thus if one is to defend the Received View's insistence on axiomatization (as opposed to its particular axiomatization), it will have to be done via more abstract considerations.

In arguing the merits of axiomatization and formalization,[231] Suppes [1968] mentions that in a number of cases recourse to axiomatization in science has solved various conceptual problems or resolved various controversies. Some obvious examples come to mind: Kolomogorov's axiomatization of probability which supplied the notion of probability with increased conceptual clarity, and von Neumann's formalization of quantum theory which proved the equivalence of wave and matrix mechanics. Suppes also gives examples from physics and psycholinguistics where scientists, by not adhering to the rigor of axiomatization, have been led to make indefensible claims and incorporate them into theories. While such considerations do show that axiomatization can be scientifically beneficial, on occasion, they do not show that axiomatization will be philosophically illuminating or revealing. Suppes does present further arguments for the philosophical advantages of formalization. He tells us that "the ultimate reason for formalization is that it provides the best objective way we know to convince an opponent of a conceptual claim." [232] Since "the role of philosophy in science is to clarify conceptual problems and to make explicit the foundational assumptions of each scientific discipline," [233] it follows that philosophy of science ought to proceed through formalization.[234] More specifically, Suppes sees formalization as having the following philosophical payoffs: (1) formalizing a connected family of concepts is one way to bring out their meaning in an explicit fashion; (2) formalization results in the standardization of terminology and the methods of conceptual analysis for various branches of science; (3) the generality provided by formalization enables us to determine the essential features of theories;

[231] Strictly speaking axiomatization and formalization are not equivalent notions, the former being contained in the latter. Their differences are discussed below.

[232] Suppes [1968], p. 663.

[233] *Ibid.*, p. 653.

[234] Kyburg [1968], Ch. 1, takes very much the same position.

(4) formalization provides a degree of objectivity which is impossible without formalization; (5) formalization makes clear exactly what is being assumed, and thus is a safeguard against ad hoc and post hoc verbalizations; (6) formalization enables one to determine what the minimal assumptions are which a theory requires.[235]

Against such claimed advantages to formalization, Hempel [1970] raises the following objections. He is willing to grant that axiomatization on occasion has shed light on philosophical problems concerning theories in empirical science,[236] but he denies that axiomatization is a primary method of philosophical analysis or significantly helps to clarify conceptual problems and make explicit the foundational problems of each scientific discipline; he denies that formalization of a connected family of concepts is an important way of bringing out their meaning in an explicit fashion.[237] Simply put, Hempel's reason for denying these alleged advantages of axiomatization or formalization are as follows. Axiomatization is basically an expository device which determines a set of sentences and exhibits their logical relationships. Since a wide variety of different axiomatizations of the theory are possible, no epistemological significance can be attached to features of the axiomatization; for example, that something has the status of a definition in an axiomatization tells nothing about whether it epistemically enjoys definitional status. Thus, "whatever philosophical illumination may be obtainable by presenting a theory in axiomatized form will come only from axiomatization of some particular and appropriate kind rather than just any axiomatization or even an especially economic and elegant one." [238] I think Hempel's point here is that in order to determine the appropriate kind of axiomatization, one already will have had to do extensive philosophical analysis to justify the appropriateness of the axiomatization, and that whatever philosophical insight is gained will be parasitic upon the informal analysis justifying the axiomatization. This is not to say that the justified axiomatization will not yield philosophical illumination beyond that supplied by the supporting informal analysis; but in most cases this illumination will be fairly minor compared to that provided by the supporting informal analysis, and in any case will be

[235] Suppes [1968], pp. 654–658; Kyburg [1968] and Feigl [1970] see similar advantages to axiomatization or formalization.

[236] He gives Reichenbach's analysis of relativity theory and von Neumann's arguments against the possibility of hidden variables in quantum theory as examples; see Reichenbach [1924] and von Neumann [1955], Ch. 4.

[237] Hempel [1970], pp. 150–152.

[238] *Ibid.*, p. 152; see Hempel's paper below (Session I) for expanded discussion of this issue.

no stronger than the informal analysis. I think Hempel's point here is sound insofar as it points out definite limitations on the philosophical benefits of axiomatization but allows that formalization does have its legitimate functions; I am aware, however, that many philosophers of science do not find Hempel's considerations compelling, taking the position that the informal analysis must be intimately tied to the formalization or axiomatization, and if done antecedent to the formalization will not result in the desired conceptual clarification.[239]

Even if one grants the importance of formalization for philosophical analysis of scientific theories, one may still reject the Received View's reliance on axiomatization. Throughout this discussion I have been talking of formalization and of axiomatization; the two are not the same. Axiomatization consists in the establishment of an axiomatic calculus, and thus consists in an essentially syntactical formalization.[240] Formalization encompasses both the syntactical techniques of axiomatization and the semantic techniques of model theory. A simple example will illustrate the difference. Suppose that I wish to provide a formal characterization of those sentences of propositional calculus which are tautologies. There are two ways to do this. First, I can present an axiomatic calculus and identify the class of tautologies with the class of theorems. Second, I can supply a semantic interpretation for the sentences of propositional calculus and define the class of tautologies in terms of this interpretation. The former approach provides a syntactical formalization, and the latter provides a semantic formalization. Analogously, I could formalize a theory by presenting an axiomatic calculus (such as the Received View does), or I could formalize the theory by semantically specifying a mathematical structure, interpreting a language L in terms of it, and stipulating that the theory is to be identified with the class of sentences of L true under this interpretation. There is one essential difference between the two approaches. To the extent that details of the formalization are epistemologically significant, under the axiomatic approach the epistemological distinctions must be presented syntactically. Under the semantic approach, the formalization can reflect those epistemologically significant distinctions which can be drawn syntactically as well as those which cannot. Accordingly, a philosopher committed to formalization in the characterization of theories still may reject the Received View's reliance on axiomatization on the grounds that the epistemologically

239 This apparently is Kyburg's position; see Kyburg [1968].

240 This is not to say, however, that the axiomatizations may not have intended semantical interpretations.

relevent distinctions cannot all be drawn syntactically.[241] I think it amply clear from the discussions of the observational-theoretical distinction and correspondence rules above that many of the epistemically relevant distinctions concerning theories cannot be drawn syntactically, and thus that the Received View's insistence on axiomatic canonical reformulation is untenable. Hence, if formalization is desirable in a philosophical analysis of theories, it must be of the semantic sort.

Finally, in passing, I want to make brief mention of an argument against formalization in the analysis of theories which is semiexplicit in the writings of Feyerabend, Hanson, Kuhn, and others. These writers view theories as deep conceptual systems which provide a *Weltanschauung*, or perspective, for viewing the world. As such, theories are viewed as essentially dynamic, growing entities,[242] and it is maintained that theories cannot be understood if divorced from the dynamics of their developments. These authors implicitly seem to take this as showing that formalization of theories is inappropriate in a philosophical analysis of theories. But such a conclusion is unwarrantedly strong. At best their position (if correct) shows that merely presenting a formalization will leave out much that is epistemologically significant about theories; in particular, it will ignore the "logic of discovery" dimensions. Even this may be too strong; all that need follow from their considerations is that formalizations, if legitimate, will have to be of a different sort—perhaps the formalization being in the form of an adaptive system specified in terms of automata theory.[243] In any case, it does not show that formalization of theories at any given stage in time is illegitimate or not philosophically revealing; at most it shows that such a formalization does not give the whole picture. At any given time a particular version of a theory is being employed, and formalization may provide a useful explication of significant characteristics of such stages of theories. Indeed, a possible approach to analyzing the dynamics of theory development is to consider the ways in which the versions of a theory change over time; and it has not been shown that formalized explications of theories at given times cannot contribute to the understanding of the development of theories.

To conclude, then, the cases for or against formalization in the anal-

241 This position is taken in Suppes [1967], pp. 57–59; and also in Beth [1963]. Beth's approach is discussed slightly in Sec. V–C below.

242 These views will be considered in detail in Sec. V–B below.

243 For examples of such an automata-theoretic treatment of adaptive systems, see John Holland's papers in Burks [1970]; for specific applications of such techniques to the evolution of scientific theories, see Suppe [1967], Ch. 4.

ysis of theories are inconclusive. This much is clear, however. If formalization has a place, it probably will be as semantic formalizations rather than axiomatizations; and whatever formalizations are employed must be buttressed by informal philosophical analysis. Many philosophers of science disagree with these conclusions, however.

G. Conclusions on the Adequacy of the Received View

Most aspects of the Received View have come under attack—its reliance on the analytic-synthetic distinction; the tenability of the observational-theoretical distinction; the notion of partial interpretation; its failure to include models as integral components; its analysis of correspondence rules; its reliance on axiomatization. In the face of all the criticisms we have considered, it seems hard to defend the Received View; and a general consensus that the Received View is inadequate now seems to hold among most philosophers of science. This consensus is, however, definitely quite limited: while there is agreement that the Received View is inadequate, there is no general consensus what the source of its inadequacy is. Different philosophers find different criticisms more telling than others, and what is viewed as the source of the Received View's inadequacy depends on which criticisms are thought most damaging. For example, some philosophers find the criticisms of the analytic-synthetic distinction unconvincing, at least to the extent that they feel such criticisms do not render a contextual necessary *vs.* contingent truth distinction untenable; feeling that the latter distinction contextually can yield much the same payoff as the analytic-synthetic distinction, they do not see the reliance on the analytic-synthetic distinction as being a serious defect of the Received View.[244] Others are of the opinion that even if an observational-theoretical term distinction is untenable, a similar distinction between basic and theoretical terms can be drawn on a different basis and will be adequate; thus the reliance on the observational-theoretical distinction does not require rejecting the Received View, but rather only requires a relatively minor modification.[245] As argued above, the criticisms of partial interpretation and the criticisms from models do not succeed in showing Carnap's and Hempel's final version of the Received View inadequate; however, as

[244] Maxwell [1962a] holds this position.

[245] Hempel [1958] takes this position. Later, however, Hempel abandoned it; see Hempel [1970] as well as his contribution below (Session I).

was mentioned above, other proponents of the Received View contemporaneously held less sophisticated versions of the Received View in which no independent semantic interpretation (as opposed to no independent *observational* semantic interpretation) may be given for V_T terms, and these criticisms do show these versions inadequate. As to the various criticisms of the Received View's treatment of correspondence rules, it is possible to maintain the Received View in face of them, arguing that, for some purposes, at least, the Received View's *TC* construal is epistemologically revealing while still admitting that full understanding of the connections between theory and phenomena requires a more detailed and sophisticated treatment. Finally, we have seen there is no general consensus on the tenability of the Received View's insistence on axiomatization, though there is reason to think semantic methods of formalization are superior to axiomatization. Thus it is possible to attach different strengths to the various criticisms leveled against the Received View, and depending how one views the various criticisms one may view various of the defects as reparable or irreparable. The ones viewed as irreparable will be taken as the source of the Received View's inadequacy. It is even possible to view all of the defects as reparable, and thus view the Received View as basically adequate, though in need of some cleaning up; anyone holding such a view probably would want to admit that the Received View's picture of scientific theories is incomplete, however, and that, for example, the construal of the correspondence rules does not tell the entire story of experimental design.[246]

Philosophy of science is not a monolithic enterprise, and there is wide diversity of opinion among philosophers of science as to the effect of these various criticisms on the Received View. There is a spectrum of opinion ranging from those who hold that each of the criticisms considered above show the Received View fundamentally inadequate, through those who hold that only some of the criticisms show it fundamentally inadequate, to those who hold that the criticisms show the need for modifications in the Received View but collectively do not show it basically untenable. The vast majority of working philosophers of science seem to fall on that portion of the spectrum which holds the Received View fundamentally inadequate and untenable, but with considerable disagreement why it is untenable. Where one finds the source of the Received View's inadequacy strongly influences what features

246 Feigl [1970] takes the position that the criticisms of the Received View do not show it untenable; he does grant, however, that it only gives one perspective on theories and does not tell the entire story.

one feels an adequate alternative analysis must incorporate; hence there is no consensus of opinion as to what would constitute an adequate account of theories. In the next section the extent of this disagreement will be seen when we consider the more important alternatives to the Received View which have been advanced; in doing so criticisms of the Received View's thesis of development by reduction also will be considered.

Although there is no consensus on exactly what is wrong with the Received View, some summary of the Received View's defects is in order. Perhaps the simplest way of doing so is to list the features required for an adequate analysis in the eyes of one who holds most of the above criticisms as reflecting fundamentally on the adequacy of the Received View. From such a perspective an adequate analysis of theories must possess the following characteristics:

1. The analytic-synthetic distinction must not be presumed.
2. No distinction between direct-observation and nondirect-observation terms may be assumed.
3. Theoretical terms must be construed as being antecedently meaningful, though their incorporation into a theory may alter their meanings to an extent.
4. The meaning of theoretical terms may incorporate, or be modified by recourse to analogies and iconic models.
5. The procedures for correlating theories with phenomena must not all be viewed as integral components of theories; at least some of them must involve auxiliary hypotheses and theories.
6. The procedures for correlating theories with phenomena must allow for causal sequence correlations and for experimental ones; the experimental correlations must be spelled out in full methodological detail.
7. The analysis cannot view the entire content of theories as being axiomatizable or formalizable.
8. Whatever formalization is involved must be semantic, not syntactical.
9. The analysis of theories must include the evolutionary or developmental aspects of scientific theorizing, and not limit itself to providing canonical formulations of theories at fixed stages of development.

Of course, those who find the Received View fundamentally inadequate, but not so pervasively so, will accept only some of these as being essential features of an adequate analysis; and there is considerable diversity of opinion which of these are essential features. Despite this diversity of opinion, there does seem to be a general consensus that enough of these features are essential that any analysis incorporating them will deviate significantly from the Received View and cannot be construed as another version of the Received View.

V. Alternatives to the Received View and Their Critics

At the same time the Received View was being subjected to direct criticism, alternative analyses of theories were being advanced; these alternatives were such that their acceptance required or presupposed the rejection of the Received View. A number of these have received serious attention and have been the subject of intensive criticism; today no single analysis of theories enjoys general acceptance among most philosophers of science. To understand the current state and range of philosophical thinking on theories, it is necessary to understand these alternatives. For what one views as essential to an adequate analysis of theories is conditioned by one's response to criticisms of both the Received View and these various alternatives. In this section I consider what seem to me the more influential and/or promising alternatives to the Received View and some of the criticisms which have been advanced against them.

Unlike the Received View, these various alternatives are current topics of debate among philosophers of science; that this is so requires that my approach to considering them be somewhat different than my consideration of the Received View. The Received View, being a view abandoned by most philosophers of science, now belongs to the history of philosophy, and my approach to it has been that of an analytical historian of philosophy who knows the ultimate fate of the movement. In dealing with the currently proposed alternatives I do not have the benefit of knowing how these views ultimately will fare, and so the historical approach is inappropriate. It would be out of place for me to attempt, in this introduction, anything approaching a comprehensive or definitive assessment of these various alternatives. Given the task of this introduction—providing the perspective and background for the symposium which follows—the most I can attempt to do is present summaries of these alternatives and some of the more important objections and criticisms raised against them. As the extent to which such objections are damaging to these proposals are matters of current debate, I cannot attempt to resolve these issues here. The most I can hope to do is to provide a perspective for viewing these controversies and, in a few cases, attempt to display and focus more sharply just what the issues are. The resolution of these issues is the task of the philosophy of science, and the symposium proceedings below indicate the various ways philosophers are attempting to resolve them.

The various proposed alternatives to the Received View I will consider can be conveniently grouped into three classes: (a) descriptive analyses of theories which are skeptical about there being any very deep features common to all theories; (b) analyses which view theories or scientific theorizing as being relative to a *Weltanschauung* or conceptual perspective upon which the meanings of terms are dependent; (c) semantical approaches. These three classes of analyses will be considered in detail in the next three subsections. In the last subsection brief consideration will be given to the possibility that recent work on the nature of scientific explanation may lead to other alternative analyses of the structure of scientific theories.

A. Skeptical Descriptive Analyses

Central to many of the proposed alternatives to the Received View is the idea that an adequate analysis of theories will not be a rational reconstruction. Rather than presenting an analysis how theories ideally should be formulated (an ideal that theories in practice fail to meet), it is held that an adequate analysis of theories should characterize theories as they actually are employed in science. Thus the analysis of theories should be descriptive of theories in actual scientific use. Upon looking at the theories actually employed in science, some authors have been so impressed by the diversity of theories encountered and the functions they perform that they despair of ever providing a comprehensive analysis of theories which displays deep properties common to all theories.

Achinstein [1968][247] provides a particularly good example of such a skeptical position. He begins his analysis by asking the question, "What does it mean to say someone has a theory?," and argues that the following answers can be given: (1) a person *A* has a theory *T* if he does not know *T* is true although he believes that *T* is true or that it is plausible to think it is and he cannot immediately and readily come to know the

[247] Ch. 4.

truth of *T* at the inception of his belief; (2) *A* does not know, nor does he believe, that *T* is false; he believes that *T* is true or it is plausible to think *T* is true, and he cannot immediately and readily come to know that *T* is true; (3) *A* believes that *T* provides, or will provide, some (or a better) understanding of something and that one of the main functions of *T* is to explain, interpret, remove puzzles, and so on; (4) *T* consists of propositions purporting to assert what is the case, where *A*'s having the theory does not require that he actually have formulated such propositions in language, and if he does formulate them in language, he could do so in several ways; (5) *A* does not know of any more fundamental theory *T′* from which he knows that the set of propositions comprising *T* can be simply and directly derived, where *A* satisfies all the other conditions with respect to *T′*; (6) *A* believes that the assumptions of the theory, together with others associated with the theory, jointly will be helpful in providing an understanding of those items for which *A* believes the theory may provide an understanding.[248] Achinstein regards only (4) as being logically necessary, but holds that whenever *A* satisfies a goodly number of the others as well, he may be said to have a theory. He then asks what it is to be a theory, and considers the thesis that *T* is a theory if it ever has been true of some *A* that he had the theory *T*. This is too stringent because it makes sense to talk of a theory nobody has had. If the thesis is weakened to the requirement that *T* is a theory if for some *A* it could be true that *A* has a theory *T*, it will be too weak in some contexts, whereas it will be adequate in others. He then concludes "*T* is a theory, relative to the context, if and only if *T* is a set of propositions that (depending on the context) is (was, might have been, and so forth) not known to be true or to be false but believed to be somewhat plausible, potentially explanatory, relatively fundamental, and somewhat integrated."[249] Whenever a theory makes a contribution to science itself, it is a scientific theory.[250]

Turning now to the presentation of a scientific theory, Achinstein considers four different ways in which a theory may be presented, where the choice of presentation can vary in its emphasis of these factors depending on the aims of the person presenting the theory and the intended audience. First, one may present the central and distinctive

[248] *Ibid.*, pp. 122–128; I have somewhat oversimplified the statements of these answers.

[249] *Ibid.*, p. 129; this is his truncated and rough statement; on the same page he gives a fuller statement in terms of conditions (1) to (6) above.

[250] *Ibid.*, p. 133.

assumptions of the theory, where different presentations of the same theory may take different propositions of the theory as central assumptions. Second, the underlying motivation for the theory may be given. Third, the development of the theory may be given; this may include introducing additional assumptions (for example, definitions), reformulating assumptions in a more manageable (usually mathematical) way, explaining the meanings of the assumptions by analogies or illustrations, introducing new concepts, deriving general principles as consequences of the central and distinctive assumptions, working out special-case solutions, using the assumptions to generate further developments and extensions of the theory, and so on. Fourth, consideration may be given to the confirming instances of the theory.[251] Achinstein appears to take the fact that theories can be presented in a variety of ways using various mixtures of these techniques as indicating that nothing significantly more detailed than his own positive account (above) can be given in the way of a general characterization of theories. This conclusion is implicit in his discussion, but he does not argue explicitly for it. The only way I can see it could be argued for on the basis of the above considerations is as follows: since theories are systems of propositions, any analysis of theories yielding deeper properties common to all theories will have to proceed in terms of some canonical form of presentation; but since alternative formulations are possible, the resulting additional common properties will not be features of theories, but rather of theory presentations or formulations. Hence nothing further in the way of a general characterization of theories is possible.[252] This argument does not seem to me conclusive, however, for several reasons. First, it is not that obvious to me that theories are merely possibly entertained systems of propositions. Rather, it would seem to me closer to the truth to say that theories are systems of propositions which specify structural systems which, if the theory is true, are idealized replicas of systems present in the world.[253] Thus, the propositions of classical mechanics describe idealized systems of point masses which, if the theory were true, would be idealized replicas of interacting systems of bodies in the world. If this is granted, then it follows that any presentation of a

[251] *Ibid.*, pp. 137–148.

[252] Something very much like this argument implicitly runs through Achinstein's discussion.

[253] It will be seen in Sec. V–C below that even this is not correct; I will argue there that scientific theories are not systems of propositions at all. In the present discussion I am granting, for sake of argument only, that theories include propositions.

given theory *T* will be a description (or partial description) of the idealized systems the theory specifies. The variety of possible modes of presentation for theories does not establish that there are not deep structural properties common to all the structures specified by theories. Indeed, some plausible candidates for such deep structural properties immediately come to mind: all structures apparently employ a notion of state or event characterized in terms of parameters, and involve relationships of state transition, state equivalence, or correlations with other states. If such candidates prove to be general structural properties of theories, then it would follow that there is much more in the way of characteristics common to scientific theories than Achinstein's analysis of theories suggests. I conclude, therefore, that the considerations Achinstein raises do not establish that nothing more detailed in the way of a general analysis of scientific theories can be given than the analysis he offers.

A stronger argument can be given against the possibility of there being a general deep structural analysis of theories. In an article which has attracted insufficient attention by philosophers, Anatol Rapoport presents an interesting taxonomy of theories.[254] The following sorts of theories can be distinguished: (i) theories which are intrinsically mathematical (in that mathematics can be avoided only by circumlocution) involve something analogous to the notion of a state, and describe a state-transition mechanism ("equations of motion"); examples include classical and quantum mechanics, quantitative analysis in chemistry, and the genetical theory of natural selection; (ii) the class of theories like the first except that they contain no state-transition mechanism; examples include most theories of equilibrium, classical thermodynamics, crystallography and classical optics; (iii) stochastic theories, which are mathematical and quantitized but the basis for quantitizing is counting rather than measuring; such theories generally do not involve a notion of state, rather employing the notion of an event; characteristic problems are sampling strategies and statistical validation; paradigm examples include theories in genetics, demography, epidemology, and ecology; (iv) qualitative theories, which concern themselves with such problems as recognition and meaningful classification, being concerned to answer such questions as "What is a social action?"; the success of the theory depends in large part on whether it so organizes our observations as to gain a heuristic and

[254] Rapoport [1958]; the classification which follows is rather freely adapted from this article, the adaptation being made in the light of developments on theories since the article was written.

predictive advantage; paradigm examples include qualitative analysis in chemistry, much of biology, and many portions of the behavioral sciences; (v) taxonomic theories, which, while often falling under other classifications given here, have as their central problems recognition and meaningful classification, and often include a stipulative or legislative feature; paradigm examples include kinship systems, classifications of natural languages, and biological classification; (vi) historical theories which are concerned to describe the occurrence of single events, rather than classes of events, and do so by attempting to give a genetic reconstruction of the single event being theorized about; paradigm examples include the continental-drift hypothesis in geology, migratory theories about the origin of the American Indian, and many anthropological and archeological theories; (vii) theories in the social sciences which have as their primary emphasis the imparting of an intuitive understanding of social behavior, institutions, political systems, cultures, and the like; paradigm examples include theories in depth psychology such as Freud's. That the entities commonly called scientific theories evidence such diversity does lend credence to the suggestion that there will not be any particularly deep or revealing characteristics common to *all* scientific theories other than what Achinstein incorporates into his analysis.

Even if it is concluded from a consideration of the diversity of theories that nothing more than Achinstein's account can be given in the way of a generalized account of theories, it does not seem to me that philosophers of science should rest content with doing just that. For a consideration of the above taxonomy reveals that each of the above classes of theories is relatively homogeneous, and so there is some reason to believe that the theories in a given class will evidence common deep structural properties. And if one accepts the suggestion that the propositions in a theory specify idealized structures, there is every reason to suppose that there will be deep structural similarities between the structures specified by theories in a given class. Indeed, for two of the cases ((i) and (v)) I have shown elsewhere that such deep structural properties are possessed by all theories in the class, where the properties do not depend on the mode of presentation of the theories.[255] I conclude, therefore, that an examination of the diversity of theories and their intended functions does lend some support to the

[255] For theories of type (i), see Suppe [1967], Ch. 2; for type (v), see Suppe [1973c]. Considerations raised in Sec. V–C below indicate that such deep structural properties will be found for classes (ii) and (iii). See also Suppe [1972b], Part II, [1973d], and [1973e], for related discussion.

contention that not much is possible in the way of a general structural analysis of all theories. However, theories each fall into one of a small number of fairly homogeneous classes of theories for which there is reason to suppose deep structural properties are common to all theories in a given class; and much in the way of increased understanding of theories could be gained by investigating the structural properties common to theories of a given class. Moreover, if all theories do have common deep structural properties, these properties are likely to be discovered by comparing the detailed structural analyses for these various classes. Given the centrality of theories in science, philosophy of science must look for such deep structural properties; to rest contented with Achinstein's sort of analysis would be tantamount to ceasing to do philosophy of science.

B. *Weltanschauungen* Analyses

Reichenbach [1938] introduced the phrases *context of discovery* and *context of justification* to mark the distinction between the way a scientific or mathematical result is discovered and the way in which it is presented, justified, defended, and so on, to the scientific or mathematical community. By this distinction he wishes to mark the difference between, for example, Kepler's working analogy that the solar system must be analogous to the Holy Trinity and the resulting empirically justified theory which Kepler ultimately presented. According to Reichenbach, problems in the context of discovery properly are the concern of psychology and history, not philosophy; epistemology is occupied only with the context of justification.[256] According to this view, which has been held by almost all adherents to the Received View, a philosophical analysis of theories may ignore factors in the genesis of theories, confining its attention to theories as finished products. Thus rational reconstruction is capable of dealing with problems in the context of justification, hence in epistemology. Long before the verdict was in on such issues as the observational-theoretical distinction, a small number of philosophers of science had come to the conclusion that Reichenbach's thesis that epistemology is concerned only with the context of justification was wrong; in particular, it was very wrong for science. Rather, science was viewed as an ongoing social enterprise with

[256] Reichenbach [1938], pp. 6–7.

common bonds of language, methodology, and so on. Full epistemic understanding of scientific theories could only be had by seeing the dynamics of theory development, the acceptance and rejection of theories, the choosing of which experiments to perform, and so on. To understand a theory was to understand its use and development.[257] Thus the positivistic treatment of the confirmation and disconfirmation of theories was misleading since it viewed the testing of theories as merely passing judgment on final versions of theories—if it passed the test, something was added to its degree of confirmation, and if it failed the test it was falsified—whereas, in fact, the failure of a theory to pass a test usually does not lead to its rejection, but rather to its modification; moreover, these modifications are not random, but rather governed by epistemic features of the scientific enterprise. Thus the context of discovery was held to be a legitimate and essential concern of epistemology. This, of course, requires rejection of Reichenbach's doctrine that philosophy of science only is concerned with the context of justification. With this rejection it no longer is plausible to maintain that an adequate analysis of theories will be a rational reconstruction of fully developed theories; for this reason, the Received View is inadequate and to be rejected. Rather, what is required is an analysis of theories which concerns itself with the epistemic factors governing the discovery, development, and acceptance or rejection of theories; such an analysis must give serious attention to the idea that science is done from within a conceptual perspective which determines in large part which questions are worth investigating and what sorts of answers are acceptable; the perspective provides a way of thinking about a class of phenomena which defines the class of legitimate problems and delimits the standards for their acceptable solution. Such a perspective is intimately tied to one's language which conceptually shapes the way one experiences the world. In short, science is done from within a *Weltanschauung* or *Lebenswelt*, and the job of philosophy of science is to analyze what is characteristic of scientific *Weltanschauungen*, what is characteristic of the linguistic-conceptual systems from within which science works. Theories are interpreted in terms of the *Weltanschauung;* hence to understand theories it is necessary to understand the *Weltanschauung*.[258] Such a *Weltanschauungen* approach to analyzing

[257] The later Wittgenstein work (see Wittgenstein [1953]) on language and philosophical psychology seems to have played a catalytic role in the origin of this view—especially for Toulmin and Hanson.

[258] As such, this approach to philosophy of science is heir to the philosophical tradition which includes Nietzsche (see Nietzsche [1967], esp. Bk. III), Charles Peirce (see Peirce [1931–58]), C. I. Lewis (see esp. Lewis [1929]), and Quine

the epistemology of science obviously must pay considerable attention to the history of science and the sociological factors influencing the development, articulation, employment, and acceptance or rejection of *Weltanschauungen* in science. As such, the concerns of the philosophers of science overlap those of the historian and the sociologist of science.

1. The Positions and Criticisms Specific to Them

A number of different *Weltanschauungen* analyses have been advanced. In this section I summarize the main features of the more important of these analyses and also consider objections specific to these particular analyses which have been raised. The positions presented here in the main share certain common doctrines and approaches, and in Section 2 below I consider more general criticisms which can be raised against these common elements.

(a) TOULMIN

Of the influential *Weltanschauungen* analyses offered in opposition to the Received View, the first was Toulmin [1953]; aspects of the position there were given further development in Toulmin [1961].[259] According to Toulmin, the function of science is to build up systems of ideas about nature which have some legitimate claim to "reality"; these systems provide explanatory techniques which not only must be consistent with data, but also must be acceptable, for the time being at any rate, as "absolute" and "pleasing to the mind."[260] By this Toulmin

---

(see, for example, Quine [1959], "Introduction"). Accordingly it conveniently can be viewed as a kind of neo-Kantian pragmatic position; unlike the nineteenth-century neo-Kantian philosophy of science (see Sec. I above), this approach does not claim there is a unique set of categories determining the *Weltanschauung*, but rather allows that significantly different ones are possible; it is committed, however, to there being certain distinctive features or characteristics of scientific *Weltanschauung*. It is also worthwhile to compare this approach with the linguistic relativity proposed by Benjamin Whorf; see Henle [1958], Ch. 1, for a lucid discussion of Whorf's thesis.

[259] I am presuming these two works are to be read together as a coherent whole. Actually, the two books deal with different but related matters with only slight overlap, and no mention of the first book is made in the second; so it is possible that Toulmin had rejected some of the doctrines in Toulmin [1953] when he wrote Toulmin [1961], though the latter gives no evidence that he did. In any case, the two works cohere sufficiently well that it seems reasonable to treat them as a piece, which is how I am interpreting them here. The summary of his views does not reflect his most recent developments in his [1972], which appeared after the symposium and thus did not come up for discussion there.

[260] Toulmin [1961], p. 115.

means that it is not sufficient for scientific usefulness or acceptability that a theory merely be able to predict data accurately. Although theories *inter alia* are used to predict,[261] the main function of theories is to provide explanations of recognized regularities.[262] Prediction or forecasting "is a craft or technology, an application of science rather than the kernel of science itself." [263]

How does science provide explanations? For a given domain, Toulmin tells us that the science proposes or assumes that certain behavior patterns are natural and expected; the expected does not require explanation—only the unexpected does. The job of a theory, then, is to specify these expected patterns of behavior and to explain deviations from them. All behavior within a given domain, then, is to be accounted for either by its conformity to expectations or by explaining its deviation from expectations. How does the theory do this? It presents an *ideal of natural order,* which specifies a certain "natural course of events" which does not require explanation. Thus, for Newton, his first law of nature (which describes the inertia of a body free from all forces including its own weight) would be an ideal of natural order; this principle specifies a dynamical ideal, the sole kind of motion which is self-explanatory, free of all complexity, calling for no further comment if it ever happened.[264] Of course, no phenomena ever realizes this ideal of natural order; phenomena always deviate from it in some way or another. To explain these deviations the theory presents various laws which specify forms of deviation from the ideal of natural order. To take a very simple example, in geometric optics the principle of rectilinear propagation of light ("light travels in straight lines") is the ideal of natural order. Refractory phenomena, however, are deviations from this ideal; these forms of refractory deviations from straight-line propagation are explained in terms of Snell's law, which accounts for, and thus explains, refractory phenomena.[265] Thus, a theory contains at least two distinct components: (1) ideals of natural order; and (2) other laws which are used to account for phenomenal deviations from the ideals.

What relationship does an ideal of natural order stand in to phenom-

[261] Toulmin [1953], p. 161.
[262] *Ibid.*, p. 44.
[263] Toulmin [1961], p. 36.
[264] *Ibid.*, pp. 55–56; Chs. 3, 4 *passim.*
[265] Toulmin [1953], Ch. 3, uses this example; there he refers to ideals of natural order as 'principles'; he does talk of principles as ideals however (for example, p. 61). Throughout this discussion I treat 'principle' in Toulmin [1953] as synonymous with 'ideal of natural order' in Toulmin [1961].

ena? It enables one to represent phenomena in a certain way. For example, the principle of rectilinear propagation of light enables one to represent light as straight lines; it provides a diagrammatic representation of optical phenomena in such a way that calculations can be performed on it and inferences drawn—for example, calculating the length of a shadow.[266] As such, the ideal of natural order provides fresh ways of looking at phenomena by providing a mode of representation for those phenomena.[267] Being methods of representation, they are neither true nor false; rather they are more or less "fruitful." [268] Laws of nature also provide ways of representing the ways phenomena deviate from the ideal of natural order. For example, Snell's law in geometric optics provides a way of representing the bending of light rays which occurs when light rays pass through a medium. In doing so the law presents the *form* of a regularity, stating that "whenever any ray of light is incident at the surface which separates two media, it is bent in such a way that the ratio of the sine of the angle of incidence to the sign of the angle of refraction is always a constant quantity for those two media." [269] One might get the impression from this statement of Snell's law that its form of representation holds for *all* cases of refraction; this is not so, as crystalline materials such as Iceland spar fail to conform to it. Snell's law has only a restricted *scope* or range of applicability, and Toulmin tells us that in science the practice is not to state the scope of the law in the formulation of the law itself; the scope of a law is stated separately, and often is not known until after the law has been accepted. The reason for this, Toulmin tells us, is that laws are neither true nor false. Laws are methods of representing regularities already recognized, being methods for representing phenomenal deviation from ideals of natural order. Representations, like diagrams and pictures, are not true or false, so laws cannot be true or false; statements of scope are true or false, being factual assertions that such and such phenomena can be represented by such and such law—[270] that is, that within measurement error, the phenomenon can be regarded as realizing the law, which is to say that the laws represent the phenomena.[271] But laws are not merely means of representing regularities in phenomena; they are representational devices which enable one to draw inferences about

[266] Toulmin [1953], pp. 26–28.
[267] *Ibid.*, p. 43.
[268] Toulmin [1961], p. 57.
[269] Toulmin [1953], p. 59; the foregoing discussion summarizes pp. 59–64.
[270] *Ibid.*, pp. 77–79.
[271] *Ibid.*, pp. 70–73.

phenomena; as such they are rules for drawing inferences; and like any other kinds of rules, they are not true or false, though statements about their range of application can be.[272]

Theories, according to Toulmin, consist of laws, hypotheses, and ideals of natural order;[273] statements of scope are no more part of theories than they are parts of the constituent laws or ideals. The laws, ideals, and hypotheses are organized hierarchically. On the top stratum there are the ideals of natural order which provide the whole orientation of the subject: to deny the principle of rectilinear propagation of light is to cease doing geometric optics.[274] Beneath the ideals are the various laws—those forms of regularity whose fruitfulness has been established.[275] Beneath these are the various hypotheses, which are putative forms of regularity whose fruitfulness is still in question. Although stratified in this way, a physical theory should not be viewed as being a logical pyramid in which lower strata constituents are deductively obtained from constituents of higher strata; for being neither true nor false, deductive relationships cannot hold between constituents of theories. Rather, the various laws, ideals, and hypotheses are such that in various combinations inferences about phenomena can be drawn in accordance with them.[276] This being so, in what sense are theories stratified? Primarily in terms of meaning. Statements of the various laws, ideals, and hypotheses in science are formulated in terms which usually are borrowed from ordinary or earlier scientific usage. In borrowing them, however, their meanings are altered to varying degrees; a *language shift* is involved.[277] This language shift comes from using the old words in conjunction with the statements of the laws, ideals of natural order, and so on. For example, in forming the principle of rectilinear propagation of light, old words—'light', 'ray', 'traveling', and such—are used in a new way whereby light travels in straight lines as rays. Thus the incorporation of these words into such a principle or law alters the meaning or uses of these old words. Sometimes new words are coined by their incorporation in laws. The incorporation of such terms into laws is such that the terms cannot be understood divorced from the laws incorporating them. As Toulmin says, "questions about refractive index will have a *meaning* only insofar as Snell's law holds,

[272] *Ibid.*, p. 79. Ryle [1949] maintains a similar position on laws of nature, though he does allow that lawlike sentences can be true or false.
[273] Toulmin [1953], p. 77.
[274] *Ibid.*, p. 83.
[275] *Ibid.*, pp. 79, 83.
[276] *Ibid.*, pp. 84–85.
[277] *Ibid.*, pp. 13ff.

so in talking about refractive index we have to take the applicability of Snell's law for granted."[278] Thus the meanings of the scientific terms occuring in theories are theory dependent. "In formalized sciences such as physics . . . the terminology is not fixed beforehand, least of all by the public. Theories, techniques of representation, and terminologies are introduced together, at one swoop."[279] The stratification of theories thus is with respect to meaning: "statements at one level have a meaning only within the scope of those in the level below."[280]

Like laws, theories are not true or false; rather they are ways of representing phenomena. In order to apply them to phenomena, they must be augmented with various directions for identifying constituents of phenomena as qualifying for the symbols or terms of the laws. For example, in the law '$2H_2 + O_2 \rightarrow 2H_2O$', directions must be given for identifying stuffs as qualifying for the chemical symbols 'H_2', 'O_2', and 'H_2O'.[281] Often this is done by recourse to models, the function of models being to enable the scientist to "see" phenomena in the way his theories require. The law is the skeletal formula, and the model provides the flesh or interpretation required to apply it to the phenomena.[282]

Toulmin's account of theories clearly is instrumentalistic—theories are rules for drawing inferences, and are neither true nor false. They are ways of looking at phenomena which work or do not work, are or are not fruitful. By what standards is a theory's fruitfulness judged? It is judged relative to various presumptions held by the science. The phenomena in question are presumed to evidence certain regularities, and the task of the theory is to determine forms for these regularities which will enable him to answer questions he counts as important. The theory embodies certain ideals of natural order, which are presumptions about phenomenal behavior which "carry their own understanding" in the sense of not requiring explanation. These presumptions constitute an intellectual frame of thought or *Weltanschauung* which determines the questions the scientist asks and the assumptions which underlie his theorizing. They even determine or influence what are counted as 'facts', and what significance is to be attached to them. If the discovered scope of the theory is such that the theory can explain a large variety of phenomena and answer a substantial proportion of the questions about the phenomena which are counted as important,

[278] *Ibid.*, p. 80.
[279] *Ibid.*, p. 146.
[280] *Ibid.*, p. 80.
[281] *Ibid.*, p. 157.
[282] *Ibid.*, p. 165.

then the theory is fruitful—for the meantime. Further investigations, changes in presumption, changes in intellectual climate, and so on may cause the fruitfulness of a theory to diminish in that further restrictions in scope are discovered or new questions are held important which the theory cannot answer. Fruitfulness of theories thus is judged relative to the presumptions and interests of the scientists; hence the acceptability of theories depends in part on these presumptions and interests.[283] Scientific theories thus are formulated, judged, maintained, and developed relative to a *Weltanschauung* which includes the changed meanings attached to terms after they undergo a language shift resulting from their incorporation into the theory, ideals of natural order, and presumptions which determine what are counted as significant facts, what questions the scientist asks, the assumptions which underlie his theorizing, and the standards by which he assesses the fruitfulness of the theory. This *Weltanschauung* is dynamically evolving, and may change as the theory undergoes development. The view that theories carry with them such a *Weltanschauung* clearly is incompatible with the assumptions of Nagel's account of theory-reduction, and so Toulmin's view entails a denial of the Received View's associated doctrine of development by theory reduction in science (see Sec. II–F above).

I think Toulmin is correct that theories *inter alia* provide methods for representing phenomena and that the acceptability of theories is judged in large part on how well theories cohere with a science's presumptions, interests, and conceptual orientation. I think he is wrong, however, in his insistence that theories are neither true nor false, but rather are rules for drawing inferences about phenomena. Toulmin's instrumentalism apparently is prompted by two sorts of considerations. First, he apparently thinks that the representational nature of phenomena and the relativity of criterion for their acceptance precludes theories being true or false. Second, the fact that scopes of theories are not stated in laws makes laws and theories statements of regularity with indeterminate scope, which prompts him to claim they are neither true nor false. This latter consideration seems to me unconvincing. By 'scope' he means range of correct application. Another meaning of 'scope' is range of intended application. In his sense of scope, the range of correct application sometimes is specified. For example, in most statements of Hooke's law something is included to the effect that the law holds only when the extension does not affect the coefficient of elasticity.[284] He is correct, however, that the scope in this sense often is not stated. However,

283 *Ibid.*, pp. 144–148; Toulmin [1961], Chs. 5, 6.
284 See, for example, Sears and Zemansky [1955], p. 120, for such a statement.

when a theory or law is advanced it is done so for an intended scope, and accepting it carries the commitment that the theory adequately represents all systems within that intended scope. The statement of the law almost without exception does incorporate that intended scope (even Toulmin's favorite example, Snell's law, does). As such, the law can be construed as true or false of the systems in its intended scope. If the law later is discovered to be false for that intended scope, the law still may continue to be used for those cases where it does hold, being a convenient approximation to the truth for cases where it works. Employment of the law in this latter way does require knowing the range of correct application—the reason it needs to be known being that the theory is false for its intended scope.[285]

Accordingly, if Toulmin is correct that theories are instrumentalistic in nature, it must be because of his first reason; for the considerations he raises there are sound. But they do not warrant his instrumentalist conclusion since the conclusion is untenable. Alexander [1958] presents considerations which, he argues, show Toulmin's instrumentalist conclusion unacceptable. In effect, what he tries to do is to establish that there are certain characteristics typical of laws which are inapplicable to rules of inference. First, it is possible to give evidence in support of laws, but it is impossible to do so for rules: the closest you can come to giving evidence for rules is to give evidence that they are obeyed or in support of the claim they should be accepted; but neither of these give evidence for the rules themselves in any manner analogous to the way one can give evidence for laws. Laws and rules thus stand in different relations to evidence. Second, it does make sense to say laws are true, but it does not make sense to say rules are true. Because of these two differences in the characteristics of laws and rules, they cannot be the same things.[286] Turning his attention to Toulmin's specific arguments, Alexander proceeds as follows: first, he observes that Toulmin is slightly narrowing normal scientific usage in confining the term 'law' to the mathematical statement; this he finds unexceptionable. However, he argues that Toulmin's parallel between laws (in this narrow sense) and rules or principles is positively misleading and mistaken. First, he observes, it is just false to say that the statement of the law *never* mentions its scope, though sometimes the scope is not mentioned (see the discussion of this point above). He then argues that even if Toulmin

[285] It is noteworthy that all Toulmin's examples of laws and theories in Toulmin [1953] are ones which have been shown false and superseded by better theories, but continue to be used as convenient approximations to these better theories.

[286] Popper raises similar objections to instrumentalism; see the discussion of Popper below (subsection V–B–1–d–i).

were correct that the scope was not included in the statement of the law, it would not follow that laws are rules or inference licenses. Toulmin claims laws are rules because their shortcomings do not lead us to abandon them altogether; rather, Toulmin claims, we just alter the scope statement; laws being rules thus enables one to account for this feature of laws. However, Alexander argues that this nonabandonment of laws because of shortcomings can be accounted for more naturally if laws are true or false. For laws are *multiply general*—that is, their representation by logical formula would require several quantifiers. Thus, for example, Snell's law gives us a formula which (1) sums the relations between the angles of refraction and the angles of incidence for *all* angles of incidence; (2) tells us that for *all* different specimens of the same two media, the formula holds and the constant of proportionality between the sines of the angles is the same;[287] (3) tells us that the formula holds for *all* or *almost all* transparent media but that the constant of proportionality is different for different pairs of media; (4) that the law is true at *all* times. Because of this multiple generality the law theoretically could be falsified in four different ways: (1) by finding, say, that refractive indexes of substances varied systematically with time; (2) by finding transparent media for which the law did not hold; (3) by finding that certain substances, although identical in all other respects, had different refractive indexes; or finding two normal specimens such that $\sin^2 i/\sin^2 r$ = constant; (4) by finding that all previous observations had been wildly mistaken, and the law which really held was $\sin^2 i/\sin^2 r$ = constant. Because of this multiple generality, a shortcoming in one respect should not lead us to abandon the law altogether. In particular, the fourth sort of falsification will be such that the falsified formula will be a valid first approximation to the more accurate formula or law; and there will be cases where the first approximation may be used; similarly, the second form of falsification frequently occurs, but does not necessitate complete abandonment of the law—rather we continue to employ it noting that its scope is restricted; the first and third forms of falsification do not seem to occur in the physical sciences. Moreover, such multiple generality is characteristic of laws in branches of science other than the physical sciences.[288] Finally, he argues it is a mistake to identify laws with the formulas in their statements, and when this is realized all plausibility to construing laws as rules disappears. Alexander's criticisms have considerable force. Since

[287] This requires construing the law to include both the formula and the statements of its scope; see Alexander [1958], p. 320.

[288] *Ibid.*, pp. 319–321.

we *do* speak of laws as true or false in science, an instrumentation is *prima facie* objectionable, and is to be accepted only in the face of compelling theoretical reasons showing that only an instrumentalism can make epistemological sense. Alexander has, I think, shown that Toulmin's arguments fail to establish the necessity of embracing an instrumentalism; for the considerations from multiple generality show that the nonabandonment of laws can be accounted for on realist grounds.[289]

What, then, do we make of Toulmin's position? Toulmin is correct, I think, in stressing that theoretical terms in laws and theories are theory-dependent, but also include part of their pretheoretic meaning; his notion of language shifts being involved in the incorporation of language into the formulation of a theory is sound. In Section V-B-2 we will raise various considerations which indicate that he is on basically sound ground in claiming that the adequacy of theories is relative to various presumptions held by scientists. He is also correct that theories do provide a mode of representation for phenomena. However, he has failed to show that these features of science and the theories it employs requires embracing an instrumentalism.

(b) KUHN

Kuhn [1962] presents an analysis of theories which resembles Toulmin's in several respects. Like Toulmin, Kuhn views science as working from within a perspective or *Weltanschauung* which shapes the interests of the science, how phenomena are viewed, the demands it makes on theories, and the criteria of acceptability it insists on for theories. Moreover both agree that this *Weltanschauung* is dynamically evolving. They do not agree, however, what the nature of this evolution is. Toulmin, on the one hand, maintains that science develops by augmenting the existing *Weltanschauung* with new ideals of natural order which supplement existing ones; the addition of these new ideals to the old *Weltanschauung* in no way occasions the rejection of older elements in the *Weltanschauung*, though it often results in a reduction in scope for the older ideals. As such, Toulmin seems to view the development of science as essentially cumulative. Kuhn, on the other hand, views the evolution of scientific *Weltanschauungen* as fundamentally discontinuous, with occasional extensive revisions of *Weltanschauungen* which amount to the rejection of one *Weltanschauung* in favor of another. He

[289] Hempel [1965a], pp. 354–359, presents further arguments against Toulmin's conception of laws as inference patterns, arguing that there are certain complex inference patterns in science which laws cannot reflect.

does allow, however, that prior to its rejection in favor of an alternative, a *Weltanschauung* may undergo certain kinds of evolution. With the change in *Weltanschauung* some of the old theories, laws, and results are rejected, and those which are not rejected are reinterpreted or modified when incorporated into the new *Waltanschauung*, and thereby have an altered empirical significance. In a word, then, Kuhn views major scientific advances as being revolutionary in nature whereas Toulmin denies there are scientific revolutions.[290]

In his most influential work, *The Structure of Scientific Revolutions*,[291] Kuhn has as his basic problem the nature of scientific change. His main thesis is that the thesis of development by reduction (see Sec. II-F) is incompatible with what actually has occurred in the history of science, and so must be rejected. Rather, the history of science indicates that scientific change fundamentally is revolutionary. Kuhn's book is devoted, in large part, to analyzing the nature or structure of scientific revolutions. In summary, his thesis is that "scientific revolutions are . . . those non-cumulative developmental episodes in which an older paradigm is replaced in whole or in part by an incompatible new one," [292] where paradigms are defined to be "accepted examples of actual scientific practice—examples which include law, theory, application, and instrumentation together—[which] provide models from which spring particular coherent traditions of scientific research." [293]

Unfortunately, in his development of this thesis, the central concept, 'paradigm', is used extremely loosely and becomes bloated to the point of being a philosophical analogue to phlogiston.[294] Masterman [1970] finds twenty-one different ways in which Kuhn employs 'paradigm', not all of which are compatible with each other; indeed, a careful look at the two passages quoted above will reveal that Kuhn is employing 'paradigm' in the first quotation to mean a *Weltanschauung*, whereas the definition of 'paradigm' in the second quotation above clearly does not qualify paradigms as being anything like *Weltanschauungen*. In a

290 That Toulmin and Kuhn disagree to this extent is made amply clear from Toulmin [1967a] and [1970], and Kuhn's reply to Toulmin in Kuhn [1970a], pp. 249ff. Although I will not attempt to argue it here, it seems to me that the root of their disagreement lies, to a large extent, in Toulmin's embracement of instrumentalism and Kuhn's (implicit) denial of it.

291 Kuhn [1962]; it has been reissued with minor changes and with the addition of a "Postscript" as Kuhn [1970b].

292 Kuhn [1962], p. 91.

293 *Ibid.*, p. 10.

294 Toward the end of the phlogistic theory of chemistry, phlogiston came to have whatever properties were required to explain a given reaction, and took on incompatible properties in different reactions.

particularly insightful review, Shapere [1964] observes that there is far more to the notion of the paradigm than the above quoted definition:

> These "accepted examples of scientific practice . . . include law, theory, application, and instrumentation together" (p. 10). A paradigm consists of a "strong network of commitments—conceptual, theoretical, instrumental, and metaphysical" (p. 42); among these commitments are "quasi-metaphysical" ones (p. 41). A paradigm is, or at least includes, "some implicit body of intertwined theoretical and methodological belief that permits selection, evaluation, and criticism" (pp. 16-17). If such a body of beliefs is not implied by the collection of facts . . . "it must be externally supplied, perhaps by a current metaphysic, by another science, or by personal and historical accident" (p. 17). Sometimes paradigms seem to be patterns (sometimes in the sense of archetypes and sometimes in the sense of criteria or standards) upon which we model our theories or other work ("from them as models spring particular coherent traditions"); at other times they seem to be themselves vague theories which are to be refined and articulated. Most fundamentally, though, Kuhn considers them as not being rules, theories, or the like, or a mere sum thereof, but something more "global" (p. 43), from which rules, theories, and so forth are abstracted, but to which no mere statement of rules or theories or the like can do justice. The term "paradigm" thus covers a range of factors in scientific development including or somehow involving laws and theories, models, standards, and methods (both theoretical and instrumental), vague intuitions, explicit or implicit metaphysical beliefs (or prejudices). In short, anything that allows science to accomplish anything can be a part of (or somehow involved in) a paradigm.[295]

Given this extremely broad notion of a paradigm, Shapere's thesis is that "the truth of the thesis that shared paradigms are (or are behind) the common factors guiding scientific research appears to be guaranteed . . . by the breadth of the term 'paradigm'," [296] and that Kuhn's view "is made to appear convincing only by inflating the definition of 'paradigm' until that term becomes so vague and ambiguous that it cannot easily be withheld, so general that it cannot easily be applied, and so misleading that it is a positive hindrance to the understanding of some central aspects of science." [297]

There is no doubt that Masterman's and Shapere's criticisms of the notion of paradigm are extremely telling, and that the loose use of 'paradigm' in his book has made *The Structure of Scientific Revolutions* amenable to a wide variety of incompatible interpretations. Indeed, in "Second Thoughts on Paradigms" (see Session VI below),

[295] Shapere [1964], pp. 384–385; all page references in this quotation are to Kuhn [1962].

[296] Shapere [1964], p. 385.

[297] *Ibid.*, p. 393.

Kuhn admits that his use of 'paradigm' confuses and identifies two quite distinct notions: *exemplars,* which are concrete problem solutions accepted by the scientific community as, in a quite usual sense, paradigmatic; and *disciplinary matrixes,* which are the shared elements which account for the relatively unproblematic character of professional communication and the relative unanimity of professional judgment in a scientific community, and have as components symbolic generalizations, shared commitments to beliefs in particular models, shared values, and shared exemplars.[298] Using this distinction, I will try to present the main feature of Kuhn's [1962] analysis employing the notions of exemplars and disciplinary matrixes; but in doing so I will try not to preempt the substance of Kuhn's paper below.[299]

If scientific change is fundamentally revolutionary, there must be nonrevolutionary periods as well,[300] and Kuhn's starting point is to characterize the nature of nonrevolutionary science or, as he calls it, *normal science*. What is characteristic of normal science is that it is carried out by a scientific community which shares "firm answers to questions like the following: What are the fundamental entities of which the universe is composed? How do these interact with each other and with the senses? What questions may be legitimately asked about such entities and what techniques employed in seeking solutions?" [301] In addition, the members of such a scientific community also share common values.[302] That is, what is characteristic of normal science is that it is carried out by scientific communities which share a common disciplinary matrix.[303]

Disciplinary matrixes, being a kind of scientific *Weltanschauungen,* are not amenable to a fully explicit characterization.[304] As such they

298 See "Second Thoughts on Paradigms" below (Session VI) for fuller details; additional related discussion can be found in Kuhn [1970a] and Kuhn [1970b], "Postscript."

299 I must confess that doing so has proved extremely difficult for me. On the one hand, I have found it impossible to write a summary of Kuhn's thesis using 'paradigm' instead of his two new notions which does not seem to me a flagrantly misleading interpretation of his position; on the other hand, in using the two new notions, I have found it extremely difficult to keep from stealing Kuhn's thunder. However, his most recent writings (including his paper below) will be discussed in my contribution to Session VI of the symposium and in the Afterword below.

300 This point is stressed quite emphatically in Kuhn [1970a]—much more so than in Kuhn [1962].

301 Kuhn [1962], pp. 4–5.

302 While implicit throughout Kuhn [1962], this feature is made much more explicit in Kuhn [1970b], "Postscript."

303 This appears to be a circular characterization of scientific communities and shared disciplinary matrixes; for discussion whether it really is, see Kuhn's paper in Session VI below.

304 Kuhn [1962], Secs. IV, V.

cannot be acquired by study of any explicit codification of them or catechism. Rather, disciplinary matrixes are acquired implicitly through the educational process whereby one comes to be a licensed practitioner of the scientific discipline. This implicit acquisition comes from the study of one portion of the disciplinary matrix which can be explicitly formulated, the exemplars. As a student one studies textbooks which include examples exemplifying the ways the science's symbolic generalizations (the so-called laws of theories) apply to phenomena; and in working textbook and laboratory exercises, he encounters still further examples exemplifying the ways the science applies or attaches its symbolic generalizations to nature. Later in his development he encounters still further examples while doing supervised research; and ultimately in his professional career, various journal articles, research reports, and so on, supply him with still further examples specific to his chosen area of specialization.[305] All of these examples are what Kuhn now calls *exemplars.* What is characteristic of exemplars is that they are archetypal applications of symbolic generalizations or theories to phenomena. As such they include various symbolic generalizations (for example, equations) in an experimental context together with descriptions of experimental setups for various kinds of phenomena, indications what the relevant parameters are, and a characterization of experimental design, the appropriate calculational procedures, and so forth, used in obtaining the data to be plugged into the symbolic generalizations and to solve those generalizations for the desired answers to various questions posed in the exercise.

No one denies that the study of such exemplars is part of a scientist's background and training; but according to Kuhn the scientist obtains his disciplinary matrix from the study of exemplars, and they in large part determine that matrix. For example, exemplars typically pose a question and then indicate how it is to be solved. By studying exemplars the novice scientist learns what kinds of questions to ask and the sorts of answers the science finds acceptable. In doing so he acquires a repertoire which includes experimental methods and procedures, ideas how to design experiments, and the sorts of parameters which are relevant and/or must be subjected to experimental controls. In doing so, he also begins to assimilate the various scientific values for evaluating scientific work shared by the scientific community into which he seeks admission. Kuhn's thesis, then, is that normal science is carried out by scientific communities bound together by a common disciplinary matrix which is acquired through an apprenticeship characterized by the

[305] *Ibid.*, Sec. II.

study of exemplars shared and accepted by the scientific community as being archetypal of good science. The only other way a disciplinary matrix conceivably could be acquired would be through the study of explicitly formulated methodological rules. But Kuhn rejects the idea that this is how a disciplinary matrix is acquired, since a consideration of both past and present science makes it clear that this is not how science is learned, and is not how theories are presented.[306]

Although it is only implicit in his original treatment, the central role Kuhn assigns to exemplars in the acquisition of disciplinary matrixes involves, and appears to stem from, a rejection of the Received View's correspondence rule account of the interpretation of a theory's formalism.[307] According to the Received View, the empirical or observational content of the symbolic generalizations in a theory is fully or partially specified by correspondence rules which explicitly state the allowed methods for attaching the generalizations to phenomena and also supply the various theoretical terms in the generalizations with their empirical interpretation or meaning. Kuhn rejects this account, arguing instead that "a new theory is always announced together with [exemplary] applications to some concrete range of natural phenomena." [308] That is, a theory always is advanced in conjunction with various exemplars which are presented as archetypal applications of the theory to phenomena. Nothing more is given in the way of correspondence rules than the stock or archetypal exemplars which one studies and later shares with the members of one's scientific community. These exemplars never exhaust the variety of acceptable applications of theory, and so never can be codified into methodological rules.[309] Rather, one applies a theory or symbolic generalization to new phenomena by modeling the application on those presented in the exemplars.[310] Thus Kuhn's thesis is that the symbolic generalizations of a theory are not explicitly interpreted, and that the acceptable methods for applying the theory's generalizations to phe-

306 *Ibid.*, Sec. V.

307 Both this claim and the interpretation given in the remainder of this paragraph are implicit in his discussion of paradigms not being reducible to rules (*ibid.*, Secs. IV, V), and his rejection of a neutral observation language (*ibid.*, Sec. X). That this is the point of these discussions is not made particularly clear, however, and most readers understandably have failed to see that this is the thrust of Kuhn's discussion (see, for example, Shapere's [1964] interpretation of rules); however, when these discussions are read in light of his later clarifications (Kuhn [1970a]; [1970b], "Postscript"; and his paper below) it becomes clear that the interpretation which follows must be what he has in mind.

308 Kuhn [1962], p. 46.

309 This is the point *ibid.*, Sec. V, attempts to establish.

310 *Ibid.*, p. 47.

nomena are not specified by anything as explicit as correspondence rules; rather, one implicitly acquires a skill in interpreting and applying symbolic generalizations by modeling the applications on studied archetypal exemplars.

This implicitly acquired skill in applying generalizations amounts to acquiring a view of the world, a *Weltanschauung*, and this world view is the disciplinary matrix. For in applying theories to situations not covered by any of one's exemplars, one must model the application on some similar exemplar; depending what exemplars one has studied and accepts, one will view different phenomena as being similar than will someone who possesses a significantly different stock of exemplars. As such, depending on the exemplars one holds, one will classify phenomena or nature differently: one will see the world differently, and will interpret data differently. Moreover, since the empirical content of the parameters or theoretical terms occurring in one's symbolic generalizations depends in large part on how one views the generalizations as correctly attaching to nature,[311] and since this depends upon the exemplars one accepts as archetypal and the way in which one models other applications on the exemplars, the meaning one attaches to the theoretical terms of one's generalizations will be a function of these. Furthermore, Kuhn finds the type of apprenticeship and training one undergoes before gaining full-fledged admission into a scientific community such that not only do all members of a scientific community share the same stock of exemplars but they also model the application of symbolic generalizations to new phenomena in essentially the same way. As such the members of a scientific community interpret their symbolic generalizations in the same way and thereby attach the same meaning to the theoretical terms they employ. It follows that two scientific communities whose symbolic generalizations are the same or employ some of the same theoretical terms, but possess significantly different exemplars, will attach different meanings to the theoretical terms and thereby interpret their generalizations differently. Thus, despite the commonness of vocabulary and symbolic generalizations, different scientific communities with different exemplars apparently will possess different theories, and will view the world differently. They will even classify data differently, since differences in exemplars lead to classifying phenomena differently—and data is relative to some classification. As such even the language of data is dependent upon the

311 In this respect, Kuhn apparently is accepting to a considerable extent the positivistic line on the meaning of theoretical terms, his main dispute with the positivists and the Received View being whether the meaning can be exhaustively specified by explicity formulated correspondence rules.

exemplar-induced disciplinary matrix and so there is no neutral observation language. Furthermore, since exemplars indicate the sorts of questions to be asked and the kinds of answers to be given, different communities with different stocks of shared exemplars will disagree on what questions ought to be asked and what count as solutions to these questions; in short, they disagree on what constitutes good science even if they are concerned with the same phenomena. That is, depending on one's exemplars, one has different scientific values. What is characteristic of a scientific community, then, is a commonly held disciplinary matrix which is acquired by the mastery of the scientific community's shared stock of exemplars and mastering the art of acceptably modeling new applications of its symbolic generalizations on the exemplars.[312]

Normal science, then, is the science practiced by a scientific community whose common possession is a disciplinary matrix based on a shared stock of exemplars. What sorts of things does normal science do? As was just indicated, symbolic generalizations are never explicitly interpreted, their only interpretation being that provided implicitly by the exemplars and the perspective for modeling new applications of the formalism on them. When a scientific community initially coalesces around a disciplinary matrix, the stock of exemplars may be relatively small, being relatively limited in scope and precision.[313] As such, the symbolic generalizations and their interpretations are amenable to further articulation and specification: new methods of applying the formalism to a wider variety of phenomena require development and investigation; the precision with which the generalizations apply in areas covered by exemplars can be improved, say by determining more precisely various physical coefficients such as that for gravitational attraction. Simply put, the exemplars leave a number of open-questions or "puzzles" how the symbolic generalizations apply to an ever increasing variety of phenomena, how new applications are to be modeled on the existing exemplars, and so on; there is ample scope for augmenting the number and variety of exemplars and thereby augmenting both the scope and the precision of both the symbolic generalizations and the disciplinary matrix which implicitly provides the empirical interpretation for the generalizations. The solving of these questions or puzzles from within the framework, confines, and perspective supplied by the disciplinary matrix—which in turn further articulates and extends that matrix—is the central task of normal science.[314] As Kuhn puts it, exem-

312 *Ibid.*, Sec. V, *et passim.*
313 *Ibid.*, p. 23.
314 *Ibid.*, Secs. II, III, IV.

plars "are achievements sufficiently unprecedented to attract an enduring group of adherents away from competing modes of scientific activity [which are] . . . sufficiently open-ended to leave all sorts of problems for the redefined group of practitioners to resolve." [315]

Normal science, then, is occupied with solving the open-ended problems or puzzles posed by the exemplars and the disciplinary matrix based on them.[316] As such it is a highly cumulative enterprise devoted to augmenting the initial successes of the exemplars in dealing with a problem area or class of phenomena—its task being the extension and the further articulation of the disciplinary matrix through the production of additional exemplars and the refinement of existing ones. It is the attempt to subsume an increasingly larger class of phenomena under the basic world view supplied by the evolving disciplinary matrix. It does not aim at the production of novelties of fact or theory; rather its aim is to show that nothing is novel, that everything is in accordance with its generalizations as interpreted by the disciplinary matrix via modeling on its exemplars.[317] Although normal science does not aim at producing novelties of fact, in its attempt to further articulate its disciplinary matrix and expand the scope of phenomena its interpreted generalizations can accommodate, normal science invariably stumbles upon anomalous phenomena which fail to accord with its expectations. When such anomalies are discovered the area of anomaly is subjected to more or less extended exploration in hopes that it ultimately can be squared with the world view provided by the disciplinary matrix. However, if such effort does not succeed in squaring a number of such anomalies with the disciplinary matrix, if the anomalies continue to resist dissolution, a scientific crisis results; such crisis sets the stage for a scientific revolution.[318] The role of the disciplinary matrix in this crisis needs to be emphasized. For the novelties which set the stage for crisis emerge "only for the man who, *knowing with precision* what he should expect, is able to recognize that something has gone wrong. Anomaly appears only against the background provided by the disciplinary matrix. The more precise and far-reaching that disciplinary matrix is, the more sensitive an indicator it provides of anomaly and hence of an occasion for disciplinary matrix change." [319]

When such anomalies are discovered which go against the scientific

[315] *Ibid.*, p. 10.
[316] *Ibid.*, Sec. IV.
[317] *Ibid.*, p. 52.
[318] *Ibid.*, Sec. VI.
[319] *Ibid.*, p. 65; in this quotation, wherever 'disciplinary matrix' occurs, the original text employs 'paradigm'.

community's expectations, and when repeated attempts to reconcile them with the world view supplied by the disciplinary matrix fail, this persistent failure to solve the normal science puzzles provided by the anomalies results in professional insecurity within the scientific community. The world view supplied by its shared disciplinary matrix no longer seems adequate to cope with all the phenomena. This results in attempts to alter the disciplinary matrix so as to accommodate the anomalies. These attempts to alter the disciplinary matrix typically take the form of changing the symbolic generalizations in such a way that some of the exemplars must be revised or replaced, or else so that radically new ones are required. As the anomalies continue to resist accommodation, one finds the alterations in the disciplinary matrix becoming increasingly ad hoc with less and less unanimity among the scientific community as to which alterations are legitimate and which are not. The situation at this point can be characterized in several ways. Since theories are interpreted symbolic generalizations, the different alterations of symbolic generalizations with different exemplars providing their empirical interpretations amounts to a proliferation of theories; different members of the scientific community are formulating and employing different but related theories, and so there is no longer one theory which is the common possession of the community. Since the disciplinary matrix is determined or induced by the stock of accepted exemplars, the proliferation of proffered exemplars has the result that different members of the scientific community no longer share the same stock of exemplars; thus different members of the scientific community come to possess different disciplinary matrixes. Indeed, since possession of a common disciplinary matrix is the mark of a scientific community, what once was a scientific community no longer is. And since it no longer is a scientific community with a shared disciplinary matrix, it no longer is doing normal science; it finds itself in a revolutionary crisis, the crisis being the breakdown of the scientific community through the loss of a shared disciplinary matrix.[320]

Such crisis is a necessary precondition for scientific revolution and the emergence of novel theories in an established area, but it is not itself sufficient for a scientific revolution. "Though they may begin to lose faith and then to consider alternatives, they do not renounce the theory that led them into crisis. They do not, that is, treat anomalies as counter-instances. . . . the decision to reject one theory for another is

[320] *Ibid.*, Sec. VII; admittedly, the interpretation just given involves a fair amount of reading between the lines on the basis of clues supplied in Kuhn's article below and in Kuhn [1970a] and the "Postscript" of Kuhn [1970b].

always simultaneously the decision to accept another." [321] Thus, before a disciplinary matrix is rejected, a replacement must emerge, and the scientific revolution consists in the switch of allegiance from the old to the replacement disciplinary matrix. This replacement will be the product of extraordinary research. What is most characteristic of extraordinary research is that it is individual, and not communal in the way normal science is. Different scientists work from within different ones of the proliferating disciplinary matrixes, each using different "rules for research"—which means that different scientists look at the field in different ways. Working from their different perspectives, the scientists often first will try to isolate the crisis-provoking anomalies, pushing the rules of normal science harder than ever to see the nature of the breakdown in theory and disciplinary matrix; concurrently they will try to generate speculative theories which, if successful, can accommodate the anomalies. Extraordinary research, not being constrained by a common disciplinary matrix shared by the scientific community, becomes more random research. That is, "confronted with crisis, scientists take a different attitude toward existing disciplinary matrices and their exemplars, and the nature of their research changes accordingly. The proliferation of competing articulations, the willingness to try anything, the expression of explicit discontent, the recourse to philosophy and the debate over fundamentals, all these are symptoms of a transition from normal to extraordinary research." [322]

Extraordinary research will resolve the crisis in one of three ways: (a) the precrisis theories, exemplars, and techniques ultimately prove

[321] *Ibid.*, p. 77, reading 'theory' for 'paradigm'. This reading of the last sentence quoted does not seem to me wholly appropriate since according to Kuhn a scientific revolution fundamentally involves the replacement of one disciplinary matrix by another. This suggests that it would be better to read 'disciplinary matrix' for 'paradigm'; such a reading would be misleading, however, since it suggests that disciplinary matrixes can be directly examined, adjusted, or rejected by the working scientist, whereas in fact Kuhn's view seems to be that such changes in disciplinary matrixes come only indirectly as a result of altering ones symbolic generalizations or exemplars. Accordingly, it does not seem that one really *decides* to reject a disciplinary matrix; rather one decides to reject one interpreted symbolic generalization for another, and this entails accepting a new set of exemplars, and hence a switch of disciplinary matrixes. I have not found any appropriately succinct reading for 'paradigm' which exactly captures this; 'theory', while not quite correct, seems the best approximation, and it does have the merit of emphasizing that the debate over competing disciplinary matrixes manifests itself as a debate over competing theories. Finally, it should be emphasized that any suggestions implicit in preceding paragraphs that disciplinary matrixes could be directly examined, adjusted, or replaced were unintentional.

[322] *Ibid.*, p. 90, reading 'disciplinary matrixes and their exemplars' for 'paradigms'. The foregoing paragraph is based on *ibid.*, Sec. VIII.

able to handle the crisis-provoking problems despite the despair of those who have seen it as the end of an existing theory or disciplinary matrix; (b) the problem continues to resist even radically new approaches and the problem is set aside for a future generation with more developed tools; (c) a new candidate for disciplinary matrix emerges with an ensuing battle over its acceptance.[323] This third form of resolving crisis constitutes a scientific revolution. The new candidate for disciplinary matrix largely, initially, consists of symbolic generalizations and proposed exemplars for attaching the generalizations to nature; in effect, then, it is a new theory.[324] This theory, unlike the one provided by or tied to the old disciplinary matrix, is able to render lawful the crisis-provoking anomalies.[325] As such, the new theory "must somewhere permit predictions that are different from those derived from its predecessors. That difference could not occur if the two were logically compatible."[326] The old theory and the candidate for replacement, thus, must be logically incompatible. To accept the new theory is to accept new symbolic generalizations and certain applications of these generalizations as archetypal exemplars. Of course, doing so requires accepting the sorts of questions these exemplars ask and the sorts of solutions they provide as being the sorts of questions and answers the science *ought* to ask. Since the exemplars implicitly interpret the symbolic generalizations and determine the meanings of the theoretical terms occurring in them, accepting the new theory requires accepting a new or altered vocabulary for viewing the world and engaging in theoretical science; and if the new theory employs some of the same terms as does the old theory, the acceptance of the new theory entails using these terms with different meanings than they had in the old theory. But all these changes constitute accepting or acquiring a new disciplinary matrix, and so acceptance of the new theory requires rejecting the old disciplinary matrix in favor of another which contains the new theory; thus the argument over competing disciplinary ma-

[323] Kuhn [1970b], p. 84; the first two alternatives are not considered in Kuhn [1962]. Again, it needs to be emphasized that the debate will not explicitly involve consideration of the disciplinary matrix; rather it will be carried out as a battle over competing theories. See note 321 above for fuller discussion of this point.

[324] Recall that for Kuhn a theory seems to be symbolic generalizations given an empirical interpretation which is only partially indicated by the exemplars. It should be noted, however, that Kuhn rejects this reading in his reply to me in Session VI below, suggesting instead that theories are to be identified with disciplinary matrixes; such a position seems to me incompatible both with the portions of his [1962] under discussion and his paper below.

[325] This is a minimal requirement for being a serious candidate for replacement; it need not be sufficient.

[326] Kuhn [1962], p. 96.

trixes is an argument over competing world views and competing ways of doing science.[327]

In the early stages of a scientific revolution the majority of the old prerevolutionary scientific community will be holding various of the proliferated versions of the old theory and disciplinary matrix, and a small minority will declare allegiance to the new candidate on the basis of its success in rendering lawful the crisis-provoking anomaly and its promise for dealing with other problems and the old theory's successes. Divided into opposing camps, debate ensues over the adequacy of the new candidate. For the success of the new candidate can only be measured relative to some standards of what are the problems the science ought to deal with, what sorts of answers are appropriate, and what sorts of experimental techniques and methodology legitimately are to be employed. But these are just the standards and values which are implicitly determined by one's exemplars; and since the old disciplinary matrix and the new candidate require the acceptance of different exemplars, the two camps do not share the same standards or values. Indeed, much of their dispute is over which standards and values are to be accepted. Although this fundamentally is their dispute, the ostensible topic of debate usually is which theory and which exemplars are to be accepted—that is, over which theory-cum-exemplars is most acceptable. As such the two camps argue at cross-purposes: each argues from within the values and standards of its own disciplinary matrix that its own theory is superior. As the two camps do not share common assumptions or values, no logical argument can prove the superiority of one theory over the other. Rather, the argument ultimately must be one of persuasion.[328] This is not to say that such arguments need be irrational, for there are rational means of persuasion. In particular, one reason why the arguments are at cross-purposes is that the same terminology is being used with different empirical meanings by the two camps. This is not limited just to the theoretical terms, but also to data terms; there is not even a neutral observation language since the exemplars, *inter alia,* involve interpreting and classifying the phenomena to which the symbolic generalizations are applied differently.[329] The problem here is partially one of translation: if the two camps can come to learn to translate each others' assertions (both theoretical and factual) into their own languages, some degree of understanding of each others' claims can be achieved—at least to the extent of being able to compare the relative abilities of the opposing theories to accommodate

[327] *Ibid.,* Sec. IX.
[328] *Ibid.,* Sec. IX.
[329] *Ibid.,* Sec. X.

the phenomena, anomalous or otherwise. In this way, some comparative assessment of the competing theories' merits is possible.[330] If the comparison does show the new theory better able to accommodate the phenomena than the old, then switch of allegiance to it and its associated disciplinary matrix by an increasing proportion of the scientific community *may* result. Merely doing a better job of fitting the phenomena is not sufficient, however. For accepting the new theory requires embracing the new disciplinary matrix—including its redefined values, its sense of which questions are significant, and its assessment of what count as acceptable solutions. There is no inconsistency in maintaining, with full understanding of the new theory, that while the new theory does fit the phenomena better, it does not yield answers to the significant questions and/or the answers it yields are not adequate or acceptable. This is better seen when one realizes that accepting the new theory and its attendant disciplinary matrix involves accepting the new theory as archetypal of how science ought to be done, that doing science this way will continue to be fruitful, and that productive normal science will result from working within the new disciplinary matrix; one rationally can admit the new theory does handle the anomalies and the old theory's successes and still deny that it yields a fruitful or desirable way of doing science. However, if sufficient numbers come to see the new theory as an achievement which can handle the anomalous cases and the old theory's successes while being "sufficiently open-ended to leave all sorts of problems for the redefined group of practitioners [that is, the holders of the new disciplinary matrix] to resolve,"[331] then they will switch their allegiances to the new theory and its accompanying disciplinary matrix, and will be willing to pursue normal science from within that matrix. The scientific revolution is completed when most of the scientific community has switched allegiance to the new disciplinary matrix; at this point the scientists once again belong to a scientific community bound together by a common disciplinary matrix and are engaged in doing normal science.[332]

How do the possessors of the new disciplinary matrix differ from the possessors of the old one? The new matrix may possess some of the old symbolic generalizations, but will do so with changed meanings attached to the theoretical terms. For example, relativity theory still employs classical equations of motion, but with different meanings, the equations being only approximations of limited scope to the general-

[330] This "translation" account is found not in Kuhn [1962], but rather in Kuhn [1970a], Sec. 6.

[331] Kuhn [1962], p. 10.

[332] *Ibid.*, Secs. X, XII, XIII, *et passim.*

izations of relativity theory; but they are not the old classical laws since the key terms such as 'mass' and 'force' now have the new meanings of relativity theory, not their old classical meanings. That this is so shows that the positivistic doctrine of theory reduction (see Sec. II–F) is wrong. Even though the formulas of Newton's Laws can be derived, subject to a few limiting conditions, "they are not Newton's Laws. Or at least they are not unless those laws are reinterpreted in a way that would have been impossible until after Einstein's work."[333] Thus, even if the old formulas are retained, they are retained as modified laws. Hence, when revolutions occur the scientific advancement which results is not cumulative; rather it is a fundamental reorientation of the science which requires rejecting the old science for new—even though some of the old generalizations are retained under a new interpretation. Scientific change thus is cumulative only within normal science; but not all scientific change is of this sort, the most significant scientific change being revolutionary and noncumulative.[334]

The conceptual changes which come from accepting a new disciplinary matrix are like a gestalt switch; two observers looking at the same things from within different disciplinary matrixes see different things. "Though the world does not change with a change of disciplinary matrix, the scientist afterwards works in a different world."[335] They see different things for several reasons. First, the data that the scientist collects are different under different disciplinary matrixes. For data are not pure sensory stimuli, they are not the sensory given; rather, data are the results of classifying phenomena, associating phenomena into similar groupings, performing measurements, and so on; different data will result from doing these operations from within different disciplinary matrixes. Second, data are expressed in the language of the science, and the meanings of the data expressions are different under different disciplinary matrixes. What is happening here is not that one sees the world and then interprets it from within one's disciplinary matrix; rather, one sees the world *through* one's disciplinary matrix, and although change in disciplinary matrix does not change the world, what is seen of it and how it is seen does change.

In summary, then, the above is Kuhn's account of the nature of scientific knowledge and change. Implicit in it is an account of theories: theories are symbolic generalizations empirically interpreted by exemplars and modeling of other applications on the exemplars. Science is done

333 *Ibid.*, p. 100; see also the related discussion of theory reduction on the following two pages.

334 *Ibid.*, Sec. X.

335 *Ibid.*, p. 120, reading 'disciplinary matrix' for paradigm.'

from within a disciplinary matrix or a *Weltanschauung*. This account of theories, like any other, obviously is intimately tied to an account of scientific knowledge and the nature of the scientific enterprise; and the account of theories is no more adequate than the epistemology it belongs to. The adequacy of Kuhn's analysis has been challenged in a number of ways. First, as mentioned above, Kuhn's notion of 'paradigm' has been severely criticized, and now Kuhn has abandoned it in favor of the twin notions of exemplars and disciplinary matrixes. How adequate that distinction is remains a subject of current debate, and is discussed in Session VI of the symposium below. Second, Kuhn's account of science fundamentally depends on the distinction between normal science and revolutionary science, and the claim that most of the time science is engaged in normal science carried out by scientific communities bound together by the common possession of a disciplinary matrix. A number of authors doubt whether the distinction between normal and revolutionary science can be drawn adequately; others doubt whether normal science actually occurs, and if it does, whether it is engaged in as pervasively as Kuhn's account requires.[336] Third, Kuhn's account of revolutions as involving conflict between incommensurable disciplinary matrixes, which conflict can only be resolved by persuasion and not logical argument, has led a number of authors to charge that science and scientific change become fundamentally irrational under Kuhn's account—that the acceptance of theories becomes a subjective enterprise which is fundamentally unempirical.[337] Fourth, and closely related to the previous point, on Kuhn's account data are relative to a disciplinary matrix as is all observation, and so one sees "different worlds" from within different disciplinary matrixes. Some authors (for example, Scheffler [1967]) have charged that this deprives science of an objective factual basis, and so "reality is gone as an independent factor; each view point creates its own reality." Thus, it is charged, disciplinary matrixes, "for Kuhn, are not only 'constitutive of science'; there is a sense, he argues, 'in which they are constitutive of nature as well'." [338] This charge, of course, misinterprets Kuhn, as he often makes it clear that the world does not change with a shift in disciplinary matrix—[339] although what we do

[336] See, for example, the articles in Lakatos and Musgrave [1970], esp. Toulmin's, and also Toulmin [1967a]; for a spirited defense of the distinction, see Kuhn [1970a].

[337] For such an attack, see Scheffler [1967], pp. 74–89. Kuhn's defense of this charge is to be found in Kuhn [1970a].

[338] Scheffler [1967], p. 19.

[339] For example, see Kuhn [1962], p. 120 (quoted above) and p. 128; the point is emphasized several times in Sec. X. Kuhn also does say that paradigms

see and the data and facts we do collect about it do change. Although Scheffler thus distorts Kuhn's position, there is lurking in his discussion an important question—namely, if one's only approach to the world is always through a disciplinary matrix which shapes and loads the data, how is it that the world, which does not depend on the matrix, exerts an objectifying and restraining influence on what science accepts? Put more flippantly, if science always views the world through a disciplinary matrix on Kuhn's view, then isn't Kuhn committed to some form of antiempirical idealism? [340] Finally, Kuhn's doctrine that switches in disciplinary matrixes or theory always result in changes in the meanings of the terms employed by a science has come under heavy attack. That is, his doctrine that meanings are so thoroughly disciplinary-matrix dependent is disputed.[341]

Space limitations preclude my giving any exhaustive account of the criticisms raised against Kuhn's position and the replies they have prompted. As these issues are current points of debate, they figure in some of the papers and the proceedings of the symposium below. The last two objections also have been made against the analyses offered by Hanson, Feyerabend, and Bohm, as well as against Kuhn's, and will be given more detailed consideration in Section V–B–2 below.

(c) HANSON

According to N. R. Hanson a major defect of the Received View account of theories is that it confines its attention to the finished product

---

(that is, disciplinary matrixes) are, in a sense, constitutive of the world (p. 109). The fact that his statements on the matter seem to be inconsistent indicates that one has a problem of exegesis in reading Kuhn. When contradictory claims suggest two possible interpretations of an author each of which enjoys some textual support, both interpretations are compatible with the remainder of his position, and one interpretation leads to a view far less defensible than the other, it seems to me that for purposes of fair criticism one must presume that the author intended the more defensible of the two interpretations. Thus, in charging that Scheffler misinterprets Kuhn on this point, I am not denying there is textual support for his reading of Kuhn as well as for mine. Moreover, it is not clear that all the relevant textual material can be squared with either Scheffler's reading or mine. However, by the exegetical principle just enunciated, charity toward Kuhn seems to be called for and so I have opted for a reading of Kuhn which does not fall prey to Scheffler's criticisms.

[340] Scheffler virtually charges that Kuhn is an idealist, Scheffler [1967], p. 19.

[341] See, for example, Achinstein [1965] and [1968], pp. 91–105; Shapere [1964], [1966]; and Scheffler [1967], Ch. 3. Kuhn's paper below (Session VI) is concerned in part with developing his doctrine of meaning dependence. These do not exhaust the criticisms raised against Kuhn's analysis; some of the one's I have omitted seem to evaporate given Kuhn's clarifications (or at least they do if the above interpretation is substantially correct). The criticisms listed seem to me the most important ones which remain given Kuhn's recent clarifications.

of scientific theorizing and gives no attention to the process of reasoning whereby laws, hypotheses, and theories receive their tentative first proposal.[342] Moreover, when one does look at how a scientist proposes or discovers these laws, theories, and hypotheses, one finds that he is not looking for anything like the physically interpreted deductive system of the Received View wherein his data are derivable consequences. Rather his initial search is for an explanation of the data—for a "conceptual pattern in terms of which his data will fit intelligibly along better-known data." [343] In *Patterns of Discovery* (Hanson [1958a]), he investigates this procedure of discovery; simultaneously he formulates an analysis of theories wherein "physical theories provide patterns within which data appear intelligible," [344] and thereby enable one to explain the phenomena which fall under them. Such theories are not discovered by inductively generalizing from data, but rather by retroductively inferring probable hypotheses from conceptually organized data. In developing this analysis Hanson first tries to show that observation and facts are heavily infused with conceptual organization—are "theory-laden"—and that our notions of causality concern a certain form of conceptual organization. Then, relying on these results, he partially develops a logic of discovery (*retroductive reasoning*) which attempts to display the "true logic" whereby laws are proposed. In doing so he develops his analysis of theories and makes further conceptual observations on scientific theorizing.[345] In some respects Hanson's analysis can be construed as supplementing or complementing Kuhn's analysis of scientific theorizing—his doctrine of the theory-laden nature of observation reinforcing and developing Kuhn's denial of a neutral observation language, and his analysis of retroductive reasoning analyzing further the logic of extraordinary scientific research.[346]

Hanson opens with a discussion of observation which has the twin goals of discrediting the Received View's doctrine of a neutral observation language and establishing the point that observation is "theory-laden." The Received View, it will be recalled, postulates the existence of an intersubjective observation language which can be given a direct

[342] Hanson [1958a], p. 71.

[343] *Ibid.*, p. 72.

[344] *Ibid.*, p. 90.

[345] In Hanson [1963] he works out a detailed case study of his analysis in terms of the discovery of the positron, making many of the same points in the process.

[346] Indeed, Kuhn [1962], Sec. X, acknowledges a debt to Hanson on the first point. In comparing the two, it is important to keep in mind that Hanson's book appeared four years before Kuhn's.

semantic interpretation independent of any consideration of any theories which employ it; as such the observation language is theory-neutral. Since the observation language is such that assertions made in it can be verified by direct observation, its intersubjective nature requires that all who employ the language see the same things when looking at the same objects. Hanson's opening question is whether it is actually true that two persons holding radically different theories about the same objects really do see the same thing. He asks us to consider Johannas Kepler and Tycho Brahe watching the dawn. Noting that Kepler regarded the sun as fixed with the earth moving around it whereas Tycho viewed the earth as being fixed with the sun revolving around it, Hanson raises the question whether Kepler and Tycho really do see the same thing in the east at dawn. One might claim they do see the same thing since they have a common visual experience—namely, they both are visually aware of the sun. If by this is meant that their eyes receive similar stimuli or retinal impressions, it does not follow that they see the same thing; for receiving a retinal impression is to be in a physical state, whereas to see is to have a visual experience—and the two are not the same thing. To this objection it often is replied that there is a sense in which they do have a common visual experience which entitles us to say that they do see the same thing: they both see a brilliant yellow-white disk centered between green and blue color patches. Thus they see the same sense datum[347] even though Tycho sees the sun rise and Kepler sees the earth moving so that the sun comes into view. On such a view whatever disparities result between their accounts of what they see is attributed to their giving different *ex post facto* interpretations to the same sense datum.[348]

It is this view, which I call the *sensory core theory*,[349] and its corollary of a neutral observation language that Hanson seeks to dethrone. To do so, he begins by a Wittgensteinean consideration of this view in light of various drawings such as duck rabbits, perspex cubes, and so on, which sometimes are seen to be one thing and other times seen to

347 A sense datum, roughly speaking, is a phenomenal image which can be directly perceived in such a way that its qualities are incorrigibly known. It is that residue of a perceptual experience which remains when all interpretative elements are removed. The content of a sense datum is what can be described using the locution "It looks . . . to me," where the blank is filled in with phrases describing shapes, colors, and so on. See Broad [1965] for a careful formulation of the sense-data theory of perception.

348 Hanson [1958a], pp. 5–8.

349 The terminology is that of Firth [1965], p. 216. There are two versions of the sense-data theory. One, the discursive inference theory, requires that the interpretation be temporally distinct from the perception of the sense datum; the

be a different thing by the same viewer. For example, the following figure

can be seen sometimes as an antelope, sometimes as a pelican. According to the sensory core theory one sees the same sense datum (a visual image having the shape, and so on, of the above diagram) and interprets it either as an antelope or as a pelican. If, while looking at it, what I see changes from an antelope to a pelican, I am still seeing the same thing, though my interpretation of it changes. Hanson counters this account with several arguments: (1) if seeing the figure first as an antelope and then as a pelican "involves interpreting the lines differently in each case, then having a different interpretation of [the] figure . . . just *is* for us to see something different. This does not mean we see the same thing and then interpret it differently." [350] The point Hanson is establishing here is that once it is admitted that interpretation does influence what you see, it must be granted that seeing the figure under the pelican interpretation and seeing it under the antelope interpretation amount to seeing two different things. Thus, on the sense data position one can see two different things while looking at the figure. Furthermore, from this fact alone it does not follow that there is anything common which one sees. (2) Having established that we do see different things when we see the figure as an antelope and as a pelican, he challenges the assertion that the difference in what is seen is a matter of interpretation, arguing that interpreting is a kind of thinking, an action, whereas seeing is an experiential state. When the antelope changes to a pelican, it does so spontaneously. One does not have to

---

other, the sensory core theory, allows that the perception and interpretation are simultaneous but analytically distinguishable. Since almost nobody holds the discursive inference theory today, I am interpreting Hanson as attacking the sensory core version on the assumption that he is not attacking a straw man. Firth's criticisms of the sense-data theory are particularly insightful. For a representative sample of arguments pro and con the theory, see the various articles in Swartz [1965].

[350] Hanson [1958a], p. 9. In the passage quoted, Hanson is referring to a different figure than the antelope-pelican, but the choice of figure does not affect his discussion; in general, I will confine my exposition to the one figure reproduced above rather than the plurality of optical examples Hanson employs.

think of anything special for the change to occur. One just sees now an antelope, now a pelican. And sometimes when told that a figure can be seen as a certain thing, no matter how hard one tries to think of it as such a thing, one cannot see it as that sort of thing. Thus no thinking is involved in seeing a pelican or an antelope when looking at the above figure; it follows that no interpretation is involved since interpreting is a form of thinking. Since the reversible perspective figures such as the antelope-pelican are examples of different things being seen in the same configuration, and since no interpretation is involved in what one sees, Hanson concludes that the difference in what is seen cannot be due either to differing visual images or to any interpretation superimposed on the sensation.[351] (3) Hanson then asks, if the difference in what is seen is not a matter of interpretation, what is it? His answer is that since nothing optical or sensational is changed when a reversible perspective figure changes perspective, the only change possible is in the organization of what one sees, where the organization cannot be anything in the figure which can be seen. Thus the organization is neither an element in the visual field nor anything that registers on the retina; rather it is the way in which elements in the visual field are appreciated.[352] (4) Next, he considers a number of examples where what one can see depends on context and the perceiver's knowledge, experience, and theories, and concludes that when one looks at *x*, seeing different things in *x* involves having different knowledge and theories about *x*. Thus, when Tycho and Kepler look at the sun, they see the same thing in the sense that they are visually aware of the same object, but they see different things in the sense that their conceptual organizations of their experiences are vastly different. Thus there is a sense in which "seeing is a 'theory-laden' undertaking. Observation of *x* is shaped by prior knowledge of *x*." [353] (5) Since seeing is shaped by knowledge, it is an epistemic achievement; but what is the nature of that epistemic achievement? Hanson's answer is that it is *seeing that*. Whatever else is involved, to see tables, chairs, oscilloscopes, wallabies, telephones, and so forth, is to have knowledge of certain sorts: "It is to see that, were certain things done to objects before our eyes, other things would result." [354] This is not to say, however, that seeing that is a psychological component of seeing; rather it is a logically distinguishable element in seeing-talk, in the concept of seeing: when we

[351] *Ibid.*, p. 11.
[352] *Ibid.*, p. 12.
[353] *Ibid.*, p. 19; the discussion summarized under (4) is found on pp. 13–19.
[354] *Ibid.*, p. 21.

see an object x, we see that it behaves in the way we know x's do behave, and if it fails to behave as we expect x's to we no longer may be able to see it as a straight-forward x. Thus, Hanson concludes that seeing that, hence knowledge about the behavior of objects, is involved in seeing.[355]

So far, Hanson has given arguments purporting to show the sensory core theory is false, and that seeing often involves the conceptual organization provided by the knowledge required to see that. He wants to establish something stronger, namely that these conceptual organizations are "logical features of the concept of seeing [which] are inextricable and indispensable to observation in research physics." [356] To this end he presents a final argument. (6) To see something is to be able to give some further information about what sort of thing we see —for example, that x would break if dropped, that x is hollow, et cetera, if we see a glass flask. Thus to see a flask is to see that certain things are the case. 'Seeing that', however, is always followed by a sentential clause, and so there is a linguistic or propositional component to seeing. Thus "there is a 'linguistic' factor in seeing, although there is nothing linguistic about what forms in the eye, or in the mind's eye." [357] Without this linguistic element, nothing we ever observed could have relevance to our knowledge. Hanson then contrasts picturing and linguistic assertions, arguing that whereas pictures stand for things in virtue of sharing certain features of the original, sentences do not. Sentences do not stand for anything at all; rather they are used to state what is or could be the case, to make assertions, to present descriptions, supply accounts, and so on. None of these uses require possessing properties in common with what is described, stated, asserted.[358] Thus, "the differences between representing and referring, between arranging and characterizing—these are the differences between picturing and language using." [359] This indicates what is wrong with the sense data position. For according to sense datists Tycho and Kepler see the same thing—a sense datum. But a sense datum is a kind of picture, and so represents rather than refers; as such, it is nonlinguistic; and since seeing has been shown necessarily to have a linguistic component, the sense data account must be incorrect.[360] Finally,

355 *Ibid.*, p. 19–24.
356 *Ibid.*, p. 24.
357 *Ibid.*, p. 25.
358 *Ibid.*, pp. 25–28.
359 *Ibid.* p. 28.
360 This, as I interpret it, is the argument which is embedded—none too clearly —into the discussion on *ibid.*, pp. 28–30.

since seeing has a linguistic component, if two persons truly assert 'I see an *x*' and mean different things by '*x*', they are seeing different things.[361]

As the doctrine that seeing and observation is theory-laden is crucial to Hanson's subsequent developments, some assessment of its merits seems in order. It should be clear from the above summary that Hanson's arguments are not conclusive. Indeed, I doubt that they are intended to be so; rather, they should be viewed as a set of persuasive considerations designed to convince one that the sensory core version of the sense data account is incorrect and that observation is theory-laden.[362] However convincing his discussion may be, there is considerable room for doubt about the correctness of his conclusions. For example, it is coherent to accept his claims that the kind of seeing relevant to scientific observation is seeing that, deny a sense-data account, and still maintain that there is a kind of seeing such that Kepler and Tycho do see the same thing even though they see it as different things. An analysis along these lines recently has been given in Dretske [1969].[363] However, as it stands, Dretske's analysis is not without its own problems;[364] for example, his analysis seems to embody the doctrine that there is a sensory given, a doctrine against which Sellars [1956] and Will [1973] have raised some very powerful objections.[365] So it is not clear whether the sorts of considerations Dretske raises do succeed in showing Hanson's conclusions incorrect. But even if Dretske does succeed in showing that not all seeing involves seeing that, Hanson's real point that all observation is seeing that seems to me sound.[366] And for most of his purposes this is sufficient. Thus, I think that Hanson has succeeded in making a plausible, but not conclusive, case for the assertion that all observation involves seeing that; moreover, considerations raised in Section V–B–2–a below strongly suggest that a fairly conclusive case can be made for the claim.

Having argued for his basic conclusion that seeing (or observation)

361 *Ibid.*, p. 23.

362 Hanson's mode of argument is patterned after that in Wittgenstein [1953], which further indicates that they are intended to have the status I have suggested.

363 Dretske's analysis is a development of a distinction which originates in Warnock [1965].

364 See, for example, Aldrich [1970].

365 There are certain twists in Dretske's arguments which make it somewhat unclear whether Sellars's and Will's arguments count against his position, though I think they probably do.

366 Indeed, the thrust of Dretske's book is to show that this is so. Also, if the alternative account proposed in Sellars [1956] is accepted, this conclusion follows. In Suppe [1973d] I argue for this conclusion.

involves seeing that, Hanson next attempts to obtain parallel conclusions about facts and causality. In analyzing facts he begins by establishing that facts are not picturable or observable entities, but rather are stated in language; his arguments are along the lines of Strawson's [1950] well-known arguments.[367] Having argued that facts can be stated, he tries to show that they are language-relative. He begins by asking whether there are facts expressible in some languages but inexpressible in others. He asks us to suppose that there were a language in which color words were verbs, and then observes that to speak or think in such a language would require conceiving of colors as activities and of things as coloring agents. This *suggests* at least that a person speaking such a language and a person speaking English would have difficulty apprehending the same facts. Similarly, since seeing is linguistic, the two speakers might have difficulty observing the same things. This, in turn, suggests that *given* the same world, the two speakers would have construed the world differently, spoken and thought of it differently, and perceived of it differently. This leads to the suggestion that the logical forms of one's language mold facts. Hanson argues this is so—at least to the extent that "the formulation of a concept x in a language not rich enough to express x (or in a language which explicitly rules out the expression of x), is always very difficult." [368] With the help of an argument due to Koyré [1939a], Hanson considers the difficulties experienced by Beeckman and Descartes in seeing the solution of a problem concerning the determination of the distance a body falls as a function of time; from this he claims to establish, in this case at least, that the two associated key terms with different concepts and that Beeckman, given his language, was able to see certain facts which escaped Descartes, given his language—the difference between the languages being the differences in the concepts attached to key terminology.[369] From this, Hanson concludes that facts, being asserted in language, hence tied to language, are such that, in physics at least, conceptual differences or differences in the meanings of terms employed in the language may facilitate or hinder the ability to determine or grasp certain facts. In particular, in physics the ability to see the facts often depends upon the concepts embodied in one's language. "This 'locking' of concept and language is fundamental in all physics." [370] As such, the ability to apprehend facts "is of a piece with

[367] Similar arguments also are presented in Herbst [1960].
[368] *Ibid.*, p. 36; the preceding discussion is a summary of pp. 31–36.
[369] Hanson [1958a], pp. 37–49.
[370] *Ibid.*, p. 35.

Tycho and Kepler seeing different things at dawn,"[371] which is to say that using language with different meanings results in their seeing different things and also determines which facts they easily can apprehend.

Turning to causality, Hanson tries to discredit the Laplacean view that if one knew the state of the universe at any one time and had a list of all causal laws, he could predict and retrodict every event in the world's history. This view implicitly involves the view that cause-effect relations are like geneological trees or the links of a chain. Hanson argues that the plausibility of such "causal chain" accounts is limited to fortuitous happenings or spectacular accidents; in other cases some other account is required. The reason why the causal chain analysis is generally unsatisfactory is that causal chain accounts are loaded with assumptions and theoretical presuppositions; these are such that without them the cause singled out would not be sufficient to produce the effect. Accordingly, the causal chain view distorts the notion of causality. Rather, the correct account of causality is as follows, "The primary reason for referring to the cause of *x* is to explain *x*,"[372] and we obtain an explanation of *x* only when *x* has been placed "into an interlocking pattern of concepts about other things, *y* and *z*."[373] Thus, in isolating something as the cause *x* of effect *y* in the context of various assumptions and theoretical presuppositions, we are incorporating *x* and *y* into the conceptual pattern of a theory which makes them intelligible and puts guarantees on inferences from *x* to *y*. "Causes certainly are connected with effects; but this is because our theories connect them, not because the world is held together by cosmic glue."[374] These various assumptions and theoretical presuppositions which implicitly figure in causal explanations are "built into" or part of the meaning of the terms we use to specify causes and effects. Diagnoses, analyses, and prognoses are built into the words. For example, to say that the moon is craterous is to say something about its origin—that it was quick, violent, and explosive. In particular, cause words carry with them a conceptual pattern, and the effect words are, as it were, parts of that pattern. Indeed, explanatory terms such as 'pressure', 'temperature', 'volume', 'conductor' are such that "to understand one of these ideas thoroughly is to understand the concept pattern of the discipline in

[371] *Ibid.*, p. 48.
[372] *Ibid.*, p. 54; the preceding is based on pp. 50–54.
[373] *Ibid.*, p. 54.
[374] *Ibid.*, p. 64.

which it figures."[375] As such these words are like game-jargon in that "the entire conceptual pattern of the game is implicit in each term: you cannot grasp one of the ideas properly while remaining in the dark about the rest."[376] In different contexts, 'cause' words enter into different conceptual patterns, and "they draw their explanatory force from conceptual patterns underlying the situations in which they are used."[377]

It is clear from this that Hanson is maintaining a doctrine of meaning dependence wherein the meanings of terms are a function of the conceptual patterns they enter into. It is less clear exactly what this doctrine of meaning dependence is, though he does give us some idea. First, Hanson makes it clear that his doctrine of meaning-dependence is not limited just to the terms employed in giving causal explanations. According to Hanson, a theory's function is to provide explanations by providing a conceptual pattern in which data appear intelligible. Causal theories are nothing other than a species of theory wherein the pattern of organization yields causal inferences; not all theories are causal theories. But all theories provide explanations, and so do provide a pattern of conceptual organization.[378] Hanson clearly intends that his discussion of meaning dependence for causal theories is archetypal of all theories. As such we can get a clearer idea of Hanson's doctrine of meaning dependence from various remarks he makes about classical and elementary particle mechanics.[379] To possess or understand a theory is to conceptually organize data; *inter alia* it involves having a system of concepts which interconnect in various ways. Not all these interconnections are provided by meanings, however. Although sometimes these interconnecting relations are a priori or analytic, other times they are contingent propositions, rules, recommendations, prescriptions, or conventions. Whatever their statuses or uses, to share a theory is to agree on a set of law sentences which specify these interconnections; but to share a theory is not to agree on the epistemic status of these propositions. Thus, in classical particle mechanics a group of scientists can agree that '$F = m(d^2s/dt^2)$' is part of the conceptual pattern of the theory, but can disagree on whether it is a definition, a contingent summary of a body of data, a rule of inference, a measurement technique, a convention for construing phenomena, or a criterion for demarking the phenomena we will count as macrophys-

375 *Ibid.*, p. 62.
376 *Ibid.*, p. 61.
377 *Ibid.*, p. 63; the preceding is based on pp. 54–65.
378 *Ibid.*, p. 90.
379 See *ibid.*, Chs. V, VI.

ical. Not only can different scientists differ on the status assigned to the law sentence, but any given scientist can employ the sentence with different statuses in different contexts. Thus, "once embedded in a theory, a law which originally was contingent joins a family of other assertions, all of which may be expressed by the same law sentence."[380] When these assertions are used to express propositions which will be maintained in the face of all experience, they express a priori propositions. Such assertions express meaning relations.[381] The situation, then, is this. There is a sense in which two persons who agree on a set of law-sentences share the same theory and hence conceptually organize phenomena the same way even though they accord different epistemic statuses to the sentences. At the same time, however, their patterns of thoughts are different in that the connections are viewed differently, as having different epistemic statuses: "The difference is not about what the facts are, but it may very well be about how the facts hang together. . . . Though they get the same answer to the problem, the difference in their conceptual organization guarantees that in their future research they will not continue to have the same problems."[382] So far Hanson has told us that only certain of the connections in the organizational pattern of a theory are connections of meaning; and his criterion of being a meaning relation is that they are context-dependent a priori—that is, they are meaning relations in a given content if, in that context (and perhaps some or even no other contexts), one is unwilling to give it up as a result of any experience which one might have.

Although Hanson maintains that all the terms which can bear any explanatory burden are theory-laden, he does not maintain that all terms are. He does acknowledge that there are nontheory-laden nouns and verbs such as the terms of a pure sense-datum language, but denies that such words can perform an explanatory function in a theory. Furthermore, whether a word is theory-laden is a matter of context; in some contexts it may function as a data word, and in other contexts it may function as a theory word.[383]

Hanson's doctrine of meaning dependence and the theory-ladenness of words can be summarized, namely: The meaning of a word is context-dependent.[384] Insofar as a word can bear any explanatory burden in a given context, that word must enter into a pattern of conceptual organization in that context; in some other context it may enter into

[380] *Ibid.*, p. 114.
[381] The account of meaning just given summarizes the import of *ibid.*, Ch. V.
[382] *Ibid.*, p. 118.
[383] *Ibid.*, p. 59.
[384] *Ibid.*, p. 61.

another pattern, or perhaps into none.[385] Some of the interconnections in the pattern will be relations of meaning, whereas others will be contingent relations, prescriptive relations, and so on. To see the term as applying in the context is to see all of these relations as holding, though depending on the statuses accorded to the relations, one will see them as holding in different ways. These conclusions enable us to give fuller specification to Hanson's conclusions about observation and facts. Since all observation in science is theory-laden in virtue of being linguistic, to see x in a given context is to see the referent of 'x' as entering into all of the relations determined by the conceptual pattern the term 'x' enters into in the context; some of these connections will be a matter of definition, others a matter of contingent fact, and still others a matter of methodological prescription or convention, and so on. Similarly, the facts and data about x yielded by observation will contain these connections. If it is a fact about the referent of 'x' that it is an x, then it is a fact about it that it enters into all of the (true) relations determined by the relations 'x' enters into in that conceptual organization. Thus the observations, facts, and data in a given explanatory context carry within them an organization determined by the conceptual pattern through which they are observed. Some aspects of this organization will be a matter of definition, others will be contingent lawlike correlations, and so on; and which they are may be a matter of context.

Although interesting in their own right, Hanson's purpose in establishing his conclusions on observation, facts, theories, and meaning dependence is to lay the basis for his central thesis: the positivists and other adherents to the Received View were wrong in insisting that the domain of philosophy of science is limited to the context of justification and that the context of discovery is the domain of psychology and history.[386] More positively, Hanson believes that the theory-laden nature of observation, facts, and theories is such that there does exist a logic of discovery—that there is a logic whereby one can conclude that certain hypotheses are reasonable for a given body in a given context, where what is reasonable is determined by the conceptual patterns infusing the data. That is, Hanson wishes to establish that

> Physical theories provide patterns within which data appear intelligible. They constitute a 'conceptual Gestalt'. A theory is not pieced together

[385] The latter possibility presumably is limited to functioning in a sense-datum language; there is reason to doubt that this possibility obtains; see the end of Suppe [1973b].

[386] For a summary of this doctrine, see the beginning of Sec. V–B above.

> from observed phenomena; it is rather what makes it possible to observe phenomena as being of a certain sort, and as related to other phenomena. Theories put phenomena into systems. They are built up in 'reverse'—retroductively. A theory is a cluster of conclusions in search of a premise. From the observed properties of phenomena the physicist reasons his way toward a keystone idea from which the properties are explicable as a matter of course.[387]

Hanson develops his logic of discovery or retroductive reasoning as follows:[388] following Peirce,[389] he distinguishes

(1) reasons for accepting a hypothesis, *H*

from

(2) reasons for suggesting *H* in the first place.

The former are reasons for thinking *H* true, whereas the latter are reasons which make *H* a plausible type of conjecture. This way of putting the question leaves it open whether the differences between the two kinds of reasons is one of logical type, degree, or of psychology or sociology. Since Hanson wishes to establish that it is a logical distinction, he reformulates the distinction as one between

(1′) reasons for accepting a particular, minutely specified hypothesis *H*

and

(2′) reasons for suggesting that whatever specific claim the successful *H* will make, it will nonetheless be a hypothesis of one *kind* rather than another.[390]

Hanson tries to show that these two kinds of reasons are logically distinct by showing the existence of reasons of the latter sort which could not function as reasons of the former sort. He does so by considering Kepler's reasons for supposing Jupiter's orbit was noncircular. In *De Motibus Stellae Martis* Kepler had established that Mars's orbit was an ellipse, inclined to the elliptic, and had the sun as one of the foci. Later

[387] Hanson [1958a], p. 90.

[388] Although Hanson presents a preliminary analysis of retroductive reasoning in *ibid.*, pp. 85–92, he subsequently developed it further in Hanson [1958]. This latter development was subjected to damaging criticism by Schon [1959], and a revised analysis was sketched in Hanson [1960] and more fully developed in Hanson [1961]. My account follows Hanson [1961].

[389] See Peirce [1931–58], Vol. I, Sec. 188; see also Vol. II, Bk. III, Ch. 2, Pt. III, where Peirce discusses retroductive reasoning which he calls abductive logic. Aristotle also recognized such a form of reasoning which he called ἀπαγωγή, which could sometimes be translated as 'reduction', but is better rendered as retroduction or abduction.

[390] Hanson [1961], p. 22.

(in *Harmonices Mundi*) he generalized this to Jupiter and other planets, employing such hypotheses as

H′: Jupiter's orbit is of the noncircular type.

One of his reasons for formulating *H′* was that Mars traditionally was regarded as the typical planet, and so if its orbit is ellipsoidal, it is reasonable to expect that, whatever the exact shape of the other orbits (for example, Jupiter's), they will be of the noncircular type. Commenting on this, Hanson observes, "But such reasons would not *establish H′*. Because what makes it reasonable to anticipate *H′* will be of a certain type is *analogical* in character. Analogies cannot establish hypotheses, even *kinds* of hypotheses. . . . *Logically*, Kepler's analogical reasons for proposing that *H′* would be of a certain type were good reasons. But logically, they would not then have been good reasons for asserting the truth of a specific value for H′. . . ."[391] Another sort of reason for concluding that a certain kind of hypothesis is needed would be the detection of formal symmetries in sets of equations or arguments.[392] In giving type (2′) reasons, the form of argument is different from the reasoning from observations of *A*'s as *B*'s to the proposal "All *A*'s are *B*'s," being the analogical inference from the fact that *C*'s are *D*'s to the proposal "The hypothesis relating *A*'s and *B*'s will be of the same type as that relating *C*'s and *D*'s." That these inferences are of logically different sorts is signaled by the following factors. First, since the former inference is an inductive inference, a challenge to "All *A*'s and *B*'s" here would be a challenge to justify induction, or to show that the particulars are correctly described; but such challenges are inappropriate when the arguments rest on analogies or on the recognition of formal symmetries. Second, the sorts of inductive reasons offered in the former type of inference are capable of establishing particular *H*'s, whereas the analogical reasons of the second sort cannot—only being able to make plausible the suggestion that *H* will be of a certain type.[393] Granting that (1′) and (2′) reasons are logically different kinds, the type of reasoning involved in giving type (1′) reasons is inductive reasoning whereas the type of reasoning involved in giving type (2′) reasons is retroductive reasoning, what is the nature of retro-

391 *Ibid.*, p. 25; italics Hanson's.

392 Campbell [1921], pp. 155ff., says Maxwell completed his electromagnetic equations in this way by inserting the term for displacement current. It is worth comparing this with Kuhn's notion that the application of theories is done on the basis of perceived symmetries between situations and exemplars. See the discussion of Kuhn above and especially his paper in Session VI below.

393 Hanson [1961], pp. 28–29.

ductive reasoning? Hanson says that it can be set out schematically as follows:

(1) Some surprising, astonishing phenomena p_1, p_2, p_3, . . . are encountered.

(2) But p_1, p_2, p_3 . . . would not be surprising were a hypothesis of *H*'s type to obtain. They would follow as a matter of course from something like *H* and would be explained by it.

(3) Therefore there is good reason for elaborating a hypothesis of the type of *H*; for proposing it as a possible hypothesis from whose assumption p_1, p_2, p_3 . . . might be explained.[394]

It is relatively easy to see how such retroductive reasoning relates to, indeed presupposes, Hanson's account of the theory-laden nature of observation and facts. In a given context one views a certain range of phenomena from within a conceptual pattern, and thus sees it as organized in a certain way. Then some phenomenon is observed which does not quite fit the pattern. On the one hand, the phenomenon and its observation is shaped by that conceptual organization. On the other hand, the conceptual organization does not completely organize the phenomenon, it does not render it completely intelligible. In order for it to fit more fully into that organization, the conceptual patterns must be augmented or altered. The choice of possible alterations is limited by the existing pattern in that whatever additions are made must be compatible with the existing patterns. If the conceptual pattern involves certain presumptions of symmetry, the range of allowable additions will be restricted further. As such the possible types of additional hypotheses are severely limited—the possible types of hypotheses falling within those limits being ones which will explain the surprising phenomenon. Alternatively, it could be that there is no plausible kind of hypothesis which will incorporate the phenomenon into the existing pattern without altering it. Which relations in the pattern are candidates for alteration will depend upon their epistemic statuses, and so the plausible types of additional hypotheses will be further constrained by the particular conceptual organization in the context.

To summarize: according to Hanson, one's scientific view of the world is theory-laden, viewed through a conceptual pattern. Part of this view is a function of the meanings one attaches to terms within a context; part of it is a function of the lawlike generalizations, hypotheses, and methodological presuppositions one holds in context. A

[394] *Ibid.*, p. 33.

theory is a pattern of conceptual organization which explains phenomena by rendering them intelligible. The theories one develops to handle unexplained phenomena are limited by one's pattern of conceptual organization, and the rational extension of a theory proceeds by means of retroductive reasoning.

How adequate is Hanson's analysis of scientific theorizing? First, it is clear that Hanson's analysis of retroductive reasoning depends heavily on his doctrines of theory-laden observation and meaning dependence, and is no more adequate than these doctrines. How adequate they are will be considered in Section V–B–2 below. Second, it is clear that Hanson has not really presented anything like a detailed analysis of scientific theorizing or observation. Such an analysis would give us a much more detailed picture of patterns of conceptual organization, criteria of meaning, and so on. And his account of retroductive reasoning certainly has not been developed to the position of being a "logic." Rather, Hanson is best viewed as presenting the programmatic outlines of a proposed analysis of scientific theorizing. Whether that program is satisfactory depends on its subsequent development, and is hard to assess in the absence of such development. This much is clear, however; the workability of the program depends on that of his basic notions of theory-laden observation and facts. Whether his basic position on these is tenable will be considered in Section V–B–2 below.

(d) FEYERABEND'S AND POPPER'S REALISMS

Paul Feyerabend has proposed an analysis of scientific theories which incorporates and pushes to the extreme a number of the ideas we have encountered in Toulmin's, Kuhn's, and Hanson's analyses. At the same time, Feyerabend's analysis draws very heavily from Sir Karl Popper's philosophy of science. Indeed, Feyerabend has written, "I for one am not aware of having produced a single idea that is not already contained in the realistic tradition and especially in Professor Popper's account of it." [395] As such, a brief summary of Popper's philosophy of science will provide a useful background for considering Feyerabend's views.

[395] Feyerabend [1965b], p. 251, n. 1; it should be noted, however, that in his most recent writings Feyerabend begins to criticize and deviate from a number of Popper's doctrines; see Feyerabend [1970], Secs. 12, 13.

Feyerabend is not the only contemporary philosopher who takes Popper's views as his starting point; especially important is Imre Lakatos's recent work on the growth of knowledge (see, for example, his [1968], [1970], and [1971]). Since his more important work appeared after the symposium, and thus did not come up for discussion there, it will not be discussed until Section III-B-1 of the Afterword.

i. *Popper*

Since the days of the Vienna Circle, Sir Karl Popper has presented a view of scientific theories which opposes a number of doctrines associated with the Received View. From the very beginning Popper rejected the verification criterion of cognitive significance, arguing that Hume's arguments against the possibility of logically justifying induction showed that scientific theories cannot be verified by any possible accumulation of observational evidence; however, scientific theories can be observationally falsified, and that empirical falsifiability is the criterion of the empirical and scientific character of theories.[396] Popper also differs with the Received View on the issue of whether theories should be analyzed in terms of artificial logical calculi. For he holds that the central problem of philosophy of science is the growth of scientific knowledge; and he does not think that the study of the growth of scientific knowledge can be reduced to a study of artificial languages or logical calculi formulated in terms of them.[397] Indeed, he is of the opinion that the solutions to problems in the philosophy of science offered by the Received View and other analyses which proceed in terms of artificial language systems work only because of the limitations in expressive power intrinsic to the artificial languages employed. As such the solutions they offer have no bearing on what actually happens in science; in particular they leave untouched the central problem in the philosophy of science—the growth of scientific knowledge.[398]

The most convenient account of Popper's views on theories is Popper [1956]. There he considers what he calls the instrumentalist and the essentialist views of theories. According to the instrumentalist view, theories are merely instruments which enable us to deduce phenomena from prior phenomena; a universal law or a theory is not a proper statement but rather a rule or a set of instructions for the derivation of singular statements from other singular statements. Popper rejects the instrumentalist view of theories arguing that the way in which computational rules are tried out is different from the way in which theories are tested, and the skill which the application of computation rules requires is quite different than that needed for the theoretical discussion and the theoretical determination of the limits of appli-

[396] The development of this doctrine is the central task of his *Logik der Forschung* published in 1935; the English translation is Popper [1959].

[397] Popper [1959], pp. 15–16.

[398] *Ibid.*, pp. 20–22.

cability of theories.[399] The essentialist view of theories has three basic premises: (1) the scientist aims at finding a true theory or description of the world (and especially of its regularities or "laws"), which shall also be an explanation of the observable facts; (2) the scientist can succeed in finally establishing the truth of such theories beyond all reasonable doubt; (3) the best, the truly scientific, theories describe the 'essences' or the 'essential natures' of things—the realities which lie beyond the appearances; such theories are *ultimate explanations*, and to find them is the ultimate aim of the scientist.[400] According to Popper the denial of instrumentalism requires acceptance of (1). He rejects (2) on the basis of his falsifiability doctrine discussed above. Although he does not deny that the essences postulated in (3) exist, he does not feel that belief in them helps us in any way—indeed he thinks that belief in them is likely to hamper us—so he rejects (3), claiming there is no reason why scientists should assume their existence. The reasons why belief in such essences is unnecessary or harmful are that belief in essences is likely to prevent fruitful questions being raised, and even if we should, by a lucky chance, hit upon a theory describing essences, we could never be sure of it. These criticisms do not, of course, show (3) wrong. At most they show that science would be better off if it ignored essences; but philosophy of science is not science, and if (1) is accepted and essences are acknowledged (a possibility Popper's argument leaves open), then it is hard to see how the truth of theories can be accounted for without recourse to essences: if the theory is true under such a position, it must be so because it correctly describes the essences—this being so even if it is granted that we can never determine whether a theory in fact does correctly describe the essences. So Popper has not shown (3) is untenable as a portion of an epistemological analysis of theories.[401] The primary counterargument to Popper's rejection of (2) is the Duhemian hypothesis that in every test it is not only the theory under investigation which is involved, but also the whole system of our theories and assumptions; so we can never be certain which of all these assumptions is refuted in a falsifying experiment (see Secs. IV–B–1 and also IV–E above). Popper optimistically replies to this that if we take each of two theories which differ with respect to the experimental outcome together with all this background knowledge, then we are deciding between two sys-

[399] Popper [1956], Sec. 5; recall from Sec. V–B–1–a that Alexander [1958] raised similar objections against Toulmin's instrumentalism.

[400] *Ibid.*, pp. 103–104 (all page references are to the Popper [1965] reprinting).

[401] I suspect that Popper's response to this objection would be to explicitly deny essences.

tems which differ only over the two theories which are at stake, and so we are testing just the theory.[402] It is not clear how successful this rejoinder is; for it is not clear whether such a procedure is always possible for a given experiment; if Hanson and others are correct that data are theory-laden, then Popper's procedure in general will be impossible.[403]

Popper's rejection of instrumentalism and principles (2) and (3) of essentialism, together with his acceptance of (1), leads him to present the following account of theories: Theories "are genuine conjectures —highly informative guesses about the world which although not verifiable (i.e., capable of being shown true) can be submitted to severe critical tests. They are serious attempts to discover the truth . . . even though we do not know, and may perhaps never know, whether it is true or not." [404] Theories do ascribe reality to the worlds described by them in the sense that, although hypothetical and conjectural, they *claim* to describe something real. Indeed, falsifications of theory indicate the points where reality has been touched. "Theories are our own inventions, our own ideas; they are not forced upon us, but are our self-made instruments of thought; this has been clearly seen by the idealist. But some of these theories of ours can clash with reality; and when they do, we know that there is a reality; that there is something to remind us of the fact that our ideas may be mistaken. And this is why the realist is right." [405] Moreover, according to Popper, our discoveries are guided by theory, rather than theories being discoveries due to observation—the reason for this being that all terms capable of describing observations are dispositional (for example, 'red' is a dispositional term referring to the ability of things to reflect a certain kind of light), and there are degrees of dispositional character which correspond fairly closely to those of the conjectural or hypothetical character of theories. This is not to say that dispositions are not real, for they are. But it is to say that there is no distinction between observation terms and theoretical terms; for all terms, being dispositional, attribute lawlike behavior to their referents; hence all terms are theoretical to some degree, though some are more theoretical than others.[406]

402 *Ibid.*, p. 112.

403 However, Feyerabend holds that data is theory-laden and at the same time accepts Popper's rejoinder; in the next subsection we will see that he gets into difficulty trying to maintain Popper's position while denying a neutral observation language—a fact which reinforces the point just made.

404 *Ibid.*, p. 115; this account is amplified in Sec. 6 of Popper [1956].

405 *Ibid.*, p. 117.

406 *Ibid.*, pp. 113–119; compare also Popper [1959], Sec. 25, and new appendix **, (1) to (4). Popper's view that all terms are dispositional is very similar to the pragmatic theory of meaning; see Lewis [1929].

Although the descriptive language of science is theory-laden, the terminology of science is not tied to associated theories in any monolithic way. A number of theories can be held simultaneously, and not all descriptive terms will obtain their dispositional or theoretical content from the same theory. This makes possible the comparison of theories and their falsifiability by crucial experiments. Furthermore, Popper does hold that there are basic observation statements which refer to publicly observable material objects, and thus are capable of being straightforwardly affirmed or denied as true or false. The existence of such a neutral observation language (whose terms presumably are dispositional) further facilitates the comparison of competing theories.

Finally, since theories can only be falsified and not confirmed, Popper views it as being unjustified for science to maintain one theory to the exclusion of all others. Rather, theories are conjectures, and science ought to proliferate theories as much as possible, subjecting a wide variety of theories to possible empirical falsification. Indeed, it is exactly this proliferation of a variety of theories which is responsible for the growth of scientific knowledge. Science should not be a closed society dogmatically tied to single theories or conjectures; it ought to be an open society.[407]

Having completed this brief summary of some of Popper's more important views on science, I now turn to a consideration of the analysis which results from Feyerabend's exploitation, modification, and development of them.

ii. *Feyerabend*

Although Feyerabend accepts Popper's doctrines that theories are falsifiable but not confirmable, that theoretical and observation terms are dispositional and theory-laden, that science ought to proliferate theories, and the growth of scientific knowledge comes via that proliferation of theories, he finds "an empirical 'core' . . . contained in Popper's point of view" which needs to be eliminated.[408] This "empirical core" is the doctrine that there is a neutral observation language which can be used to test theories. Feyerabend's philosophy of science is an attempt to develop a Popperian analysis of science in which the testability of theories does not presuppose a neutral observation language. His approach to doing so is to critically assess an empiricist view he finds widely held by adherents to the Received View, which he calls *radical*

[407] These views are made quite explicit in Popper's rejection of Kuhn's notion of normal science; see Popper [1970].

[408] Feyerabend [1965a], p. 153.

empiricism, and then use the results of his criticism to establish his own alternative account of scientific theorizing.[409]

By a radical empiricism Feyerabend means any doctrine containing the thesis that once a theory has been highly confirmed for a certain domain this theory must be retained until it is refuted or else its limitations are indicated by new facts; the retention of the theory carries with it a prohibition against the construction or development of alternative theories for that domain until such time that the theory is refuted or its limitations are known. Radical empiricism thus demands that science restrict itself to the employment of a single set of mutually consistent theories. In particular, it forbids the simultaneous employment of mutually inconsistent theories. Feyerabend terms the use of such mutually inconsistent theories a *theoretical pluralism*.[410] The empiricist philosophy associated with the Received View, the thesis of development by reduction (see Sec. II–F), and the covering law model of explanation[411] is, according to Feyerabend, "but a highly formalized version of radical empiricism." [412] Feyerabend claims it is characteristic of this version of radical empiricism that only two kinds of theory are admissible for a given domain—those which contain theories already employed in that domain and those which are consistent with them inside the domain. In order for this consistency condition to be met, terms in theories will have to be used with the same meanings when they occur in any of the admissible theories for the domain. Feyerabend tells us this meaning invariance condition has the effect that whenever these terms are employed in future theories for the domain they will have to be used with the same meaning.[413] This version of radical empiricism thus imposes two conditions on scientific theorizing,

[409] The core of Feyerabend's philosophy of science is developed in Feyerabend [1958], [1962], [1962a], [1963], and [1965a]. These papers are, for the most part, extremely lengthy and there is a great amount of overlap between them; for a brief introduction to Feyerabend's writings, see Feyerabend [1963] which is a relatively straightforward, short, and comprehensive presentation of the main features of his philosophy of science. Further development of, and modifications in, his basic view are made in his more recent writings—for example, Feyerabend [1965], [1970], and [1970b].

[410] Feyerabend [1965a], pp. 148–149.

[411] The covering-law model of explanation says that a theory *T′* or an event described by '*E*' is explained if it can be derived from some theory *T* augmented by appropriate auxiliary hypotheses—the appropriate ones in the case of explaining *T′* being essentially those allowed in theory reduction. Thus, whenever *T′* is reduced to *T*, *T* explains *T′* under the covering-law model. Compare Hempel and Oppenheim [1948] for the basic details of the covering-law model; for a thorough examination of the literature concerning this model, see Hempel [1965a].

[412] Feyerabend [1965a], p. 163.

[413] *Ibid.*, p. 164.

the first being the *consistency condition* and the second being the *condition of meaning invariance*.[414] Feyerabend sees these two conditions as being cornerstones of contemporary radical empiricism, and his attack on that view consists largely in trying to show the conditions untenable.

Feyerabend begins his attack by showing that contemporary radical empiricism is committed to these two conditions. That the two conditions are presuppositions of the thesis of development by reduction follows immediately since the conditions are, respectively, Nagel's requirements (a) and (b) for theory reduction (see Sec. II–F above). That the consistency condition is a presupposition of the covering law model of explanation follows from the fact that the explanation of a theory T' consists in deriving T' from a more comprehensive theory T; the meaning invariance condition follows from the covering law model by the fact that if it were not met the derivation of T' from T would involve an equivocation fallacy.[415] The condition of meaning invariance also is embodied in the Received View in virtue of its requirement that the observation language be given an independent interpretation which is theory-neutral.[416]

Having established the dependence of contemporary radical empiricism on these two conditions, he tries to show that in actual scientific practice advancement in science does not proceed in accordance with the thesis of development by reduction and that new successful theories do not explain old theories in the way alleged by the covering law model; the reason they do not is that the consistency and meaning invariance conditions typically are not satisfied by major scientific advances. Feyerabend is not trying to show that these conditions never are met, for he does concede that they do "fairly adequately represent the relations between sentences of the 'All-ravens-are-black' type, which abound in the more pedestrian parts of the scientific enterprise." [417] Where it fails is for general or noninstantiational theories—"such comprehensive structures of thought as the Aristotelian theory of motion, the impetus theory, Newton's celestial mechanics, Maxwell's electrodynamics, the theory of relativity, and the quantum theory." [418] That is, the conditions are not applicable to scientific advancements which involve theories that are more than mere empirical generaliza-

[414] In some of his other writings he calls the consistency condition the *derivability condition*; and the condition of meaning invariance the *stability thesis*.

[415] Compare Feyerabend [1962], pp. 32–34, and Feyerabend [1965a], pp. 163–164, for elaboration of these points.

[416] See Feyerabend [1962], pp. 34–36 and 40–43, for elaboration of this claim.

[417] *Ibid.*, p. 28.

[418] *Ibid.*

tions.[419] To show that the conditions are violated for such advancements in actual scientific practice, Feyerabend considers a number of cases of theory reduction and explanation taken as paradigmatic by advocates of radical empiricism. First, he tries to show that the consistency condition is violated for a number of cases which Nagel and others offer as paradigmatic of theory reduction or theoretical explanation.[420] For example, the incorporation of Galileo's law of free fall and Kepler's laws into Newton's theory often is cited as a paradigm example of theory reduction. But some of the consequences of Newton's theory are logically incompatible with some of the consequences of Galileo's and Kepler's laws in their domains of validity (for example, Galileo's law asserts that the acceleration of the free fall is a constant, whereas application of Newton's theory to the surface of the earth gives a decreasing acceleration), and so Galileo's and Kepler's laws cannot consistently be deduced from Newton's theory. Thus, in this paradigm example of theory reduction the consistency condition is violated, and so reduction cannot have occurred in accordance with Nagel's analysis.[421] Turning now to the condition of meaning invariance he considers various paradigmatic cases of reduction and tries to show that this condition fails. Taking a paradigmatic case of theory reduction, the reduction of classical mechanics to relativity theory, Feyerabend shows that the term 'mass' has different and incompatible meanings in the two theories, and hence that the condition of meaning invariance is violated. Underlying his analysis is the following account of meaning: "The meaning of every term we use depends upon the theoretical context in which it occurs. Words do not 'mean' something in isolation; they obtain their meanings by being part of a theoretical system. Hence if we consider two contexts with basic principles that either contradict each other or lead to inconsistent consequences in certain domains, it is to be expected that some terms of the first context will not occur in the second with exactly the same meaning." [422] Consider now a domain where both relativistic and classical mechanics are applicable. It follows from Feyerabend's account of meaning that if any

419 *Ibid.*, n. 1.

420 Depending on the article, Feyerabend shows the failures in terms of theory reduction or in terms of theoretical explanation; the choice is abitrary since whenever T' is reduced to T, T explains T' under the covering law model. In my exposition I will confine my attention to the reduction case.

421 Feyerabend [1965a], p. 168. In Feyerabend [1962], pp. 46–52, he presents a fuller treatment of this case; on pp. 52–62 of the same work he presents a similar detailed treatment of the reduction of the impetus theory to Newton's theory of motions. Much of Feyerabend [1962a] is concerned with the reduction of classical mechanics to quantum theory.

422 Feyerabend [1965a], p. 180.

statements from relativity theory involving 'mass' are inconsistent with any statements involving 'mass' from classical mechanics, then 'mass' must have a different meaning in relativity theory from what it has in classical mechanics. In this way Feyerabend proceeds to argue that 'mass' has a different meaning in relativity theory than it does in classical mechanics,[423] arguing that different and incompatible equations about mass hold in the two theories, that mass is a relation in relativity theory while it is a property in classical mechanics, that even if classical mass is construed as a relation the same transformation laws do not hold for classical mass as do for relativistic mass, and that relativistic mass is coordinate-system dependent whereas classical mass is not. It follows by his account of meaning that 'mass' has different meanings in relativity theory and classical mechanics. Thus the condition of meaning invariance fails for this case; hence this case of theory reduction fails to qualify as theory reduction under Nagel's analysis.[424] He concludes the condition of meaning invariance is incompatible with actual scientific practice.

The considerations raised thus far, if successful, show only that the thesis of development by reduction does not adequately characterize the sort of scientific development characteristic of scientific revolutions; to this extent, Feyerabend's argument can be construed as establishing a point similar to Kuhn's. Unlike Kuhn who seems to find the thesis of development by reduction acceptable for normal science, Feyerabend doubts whether any science is normal;[425] in any case he finds normal science undesirable. Specifically, he attempts to show that the radical empiricism is normatively unacceptable by establishing that the consistency and meaning invariance conditions are unreasonable.

He argues the consistency condition is undesirable as follows:

> Consider . . . a theory T' that successfully describes the situation in the domain D'. From this we can infer (1) that T' agrees with a *finite* number of observations (let their class be F); and (2) that it agrees with *these* observations inside a margin M of error only. Any alternative that contradicts T' outside F and inside M is supported by exactly the same observations and is therefore acceptable if T' is acceptable (we shall assume that F are the only observations available). The consistency condition is much less tolerant. It eliminates a theory not because it is in disagreement with the *facts*, but because it is in disagree-

[423] *Ibid.*, pp. 168–169.

[424] Feyerabend [1962] also develops this case (pp. 80–81) as well as a similar case for the reduction of phenomenological thermodynamics to the kinetic theory of gasses (pp. 76–80).

[425] See Feyerabend [1970a] where he argues that "normal or 'mature' science, as described by Kuhn, is not even a historical fact" (p. 207).

> ment with *another theory,* with a theory, moreover, whose confirming instances it shares. *It thereby makes the as yet untested part of that theory a measure of validity.* The only difference between such a measure and a more recent theory is age and familiarity. Had the younger theory been there first, then the consistency condition would have worked in its favor.[426]

This, however, does not get to the heart of the matter since it does not show why the alternative theory is acceptable or should be used. To show why alternatives should be used, and thereby why the consistency condition should be rejected, Feyerabend considers a possible defense of the consistency condition against the above charge: much investment has been put into the older theory, and it will be inefficient to introduce new theories unnecessarily. Since the new theory agrees with no more facts than the old theory and the old one does not disagree with any known facts, there is no real improvement gained by admitting the alternative theory; the only pressing reason for changing a theory or admitting alternatives is a disagreement between the old theory and the facts.[427] Feyerabend replies to this that the defense works only if coupled with an *autonomy principle for facts*—that facts exist and are available independent of whether or not one considers alternatives to the theory to be tested.[428] But the autonomy principle is unsatisfactory, for "the description of every single fact [is] dependent on some theory (which may, of course, be very different from the theory to be tested), but there also exist facts that cannot be unearthed except with the help of alternatives to the theory to be tested and that become unavailable as soon as such alternatives are excluded."[429] It follows that if a theory is to receive the fullest possible confrontation with the facts, if its adequacy is to be given a comprehensive test, then a whole set of partly overlapping, factually adequate, but mutually inconsistent theories must be entertained; for otherwise relevant facts will be suppressed. The resulting *theoretical pluralism* is, of course, incompatible with the consistency condition.

Two features of this argument for the inherent undesirability of the consistency condition require further comment. A key move in the argument is the claim that the description of every single fact is dependent upon some theory. That this is so follows from his account of meaning quoted above: as we have already seen above, it follows from this account that the meanings of theoretical terms in a given context

[426] Feyerabend [1965a], p. 173; italics in the original.
[427] *Ibid.*, pp. 173–174.
[428] *Ibid.*, p. 174.
[429] *Ibid.*, p. 175.

depend upon the theories they function in; it follows, then, that any theoretical language description of a fact in a given context will depend upon some theory (or theories). What about descriptions of facts in the observation language? In any test situation the meanings of observation terms occurring in predictions will be correlated with the theory by analogues to correspondence rules, and so, by the above meaning account, their meanings will depend upon the theories they are incorporated into. Thus descriptions of the theories' observable predictions depend upon some theory (or theories). These predictions are compared with descriptions of observed facts, and if any test of the theory is to occur, the descriptions of facts and the theory's predictions must use the observation terms with the same meaning. Hence all descriptions of observable facts depend upon some theory.[430] It follows from this discussion (if correct) that a neutral observation language usable for scientific testing is impossible. The second premise in Feyerabend's argument, that some facts relevant to testing a theory cannot be uncovered except by recourse to another theory, does not follow from the first premise. In support of it Feyerabend examines a case study concerning the Brownian particle whose existence refutes the second law of phenomenological thermodynamics, and argues that the relevant facts about the Brownian particle could not have been discovered except via recourse to the kinetic theory of gasses—which theory is inconsistent with the phenomenological theory.[431]

That the meaning invariance condition is inherently unreasonable is a straightforward corollary to Feyerabend's analysis of meaning. For any change in theory in a given context alters the meanings of terms, and thus accepting the meaning invariance condition would preclude theoretical advance in science. The price of the invariance condition is scientific stagnation.[432]

Granting for the sake of argument that Feyerabend has shown that the consistency and meaning invariance conditions are inherently undesirable, that a proliferation of incompatible theories is desirable, that descriptions of facts are theory-dependent, and that a neutral observa-

430 This argument does not occur explicity in Feyerabend's writings but is based on his discussions in Feyerabend [1965a], pp. 179–181; and Feyerabend [1962], pp. 34–39, 40–43, 83–88. It seems to me faithful to what he says in these passages and at the same time makes the strongest case I can see for his claim. It is worth noting that Feyerabend's view here comes as close as possible to a complete reversal of the Received View's picture of a one-way flow of meanings from the observation language to the theoretical language.

431 Feyerabend [1965a], pp. 175–176.

432 *Ibid.*, p. 179–181.

tion language is useless in testing scientific theories, what alternative view of science is possible? Feyerabend's answer is that it is possible to have a philosophy of science wherein theories are testable on the basis of observations, and he attempts to develop an account of how this is possible. His first step in doing so is to account for the role of observation reports in empirical testing without presupposing a neutral observation language. He does this by developing his *pragmatic theory of observation*. As does the Received View, this theory "admits that observation sentences assume a special position" in the testing of theories.[433] It disagrees, however, on the distinctive mark of observation sentences: "an observation sentence is distinguished from other sentences of the theory not, as was the case in earlier positivism, by its content." [434] To do so would require that they be about sense impressions, which renders them useless in the test of a theory; for theories are tested by determining how adequately they characterize the phenomena within their domain, and these phenomena are not sense impressions.[435] Rather, the pragmatic theory "puts the distinctive property where it belongs, viz., into the domain of psychology: observation sentences are distinguished from other statements not by their meaning, but by the circumstances of their production." [436] Sensations or perceptions are indicators of situations, and thus are on a par with the indications of meters and dials. To function in a test, they (like meter readings) must be given an interpretation which says something and is testable. The observation sentence is a causal or behavioral response to a sensation which interprets the situation of which the sensation is an indicator. The interpretation given by the observation sentence depends upon the theories it is incorporated into, being a function of the meanings attached to its terms by the theories. For example, an observation report that an object has such and such mass interprets the object as being one which behaves in accordance with the laws, theories, and other regularities characteristic of mass under the theories which give 'mass' its meaning in the context. Thus, under the pragmatic theory, observation statements extrapolate beyond "what is seen" (a sensation), the extrapolation interpreting the situation as an objective state of affairs behaving with characteristic regularities.[437] On this account observation reports which

[433] *Ibid.*, p. 212.

[434] Feyerabend [1962], p. 36.

[435] *Ibid.*, p. 35.

[436] Feyerabend [1965a], p. 212.

[437] *Ibid.*, pp. 151–152, 158, 160–163, 198, 212–214; see Feyerabend [1958] for more detailed treatment of the production of observation statements.

are theory dependent for their meanings are possible, and no neutral observation language need be assumed.

Since observation reports, as well as other factual descriptions, are theory-dependent, how one views the world will depend upon the theories one holds in a given context. As such general theories carry with them their own ontologies and are *Weltanschauungen*: "Scientific theories are ways of looking at the world; and their adoption affects our general beliefs and expectations, and thereby also our experiences and our conception of reality. We may even say that what is regarded as 'nature' at a particular time is *our own product* in the sense that all the features ascribed to it have first been invented by us and then used for bringing order into our surroundings." [438] When low-level or empirical generalizations are tested, it must be done so against the background of a general theory which interprets the observation reports or descriptions of fact pitted against the generalization. As such, the test of low-level generalizations must be done relative to a *Weltanschauung* supplied by the more general theories held. However, this background theory itself is an empirical theory and also needs to be subjected to criticism and empirical test. The test of it cannot be done in the same way as for low-level generalizations; for any data that could be relevant to testing the theory would presuppose the theory, and so the test would be viciously circular. The only way the general theory can be tested or criticized is by the use of alternative and incompatible theories. If the theory under test and the alternative share certain observation statements in common, then it is possible to perform a crucial experiment which will decide between the two—in the way advocated by Popper. At some stage, however, the alternatives may not share any observation reports with the theory under test. This will be the case when the theory tested concerns the nature of the basic elements of the universe. "To express it more radically, each theory will possess its own experience, and there will be no overlap between these experiences. Clearly a crucial experiment is now impossible . . . because there is no universally accepted *statement* capable of expressing whatever emerges from observation." [439] Such theories are *incommensurable* in the sense that the meanings of their main descriptive terms depend upon mutually inconsistent principles.[440] Three procedures are possible in such

[438] Feyerabend [1962], p. 29; italics in the original. It should be noted that it is consistent with this to maintain that there is a common world with which all theories are concerned; indeed, the pragmatic theory of observation tacitly assumes the existence of such a world.

[439] Feyerabend [1965a], p. 214.

[440] *Ibid.*, p. 227, n. 19.

cases. First, it may be possible to invent a still more general theory describing a common background that defines test statements acceptable to *both* theories; this allows the possibility of crucial experiments for choosing between the alternatives. "The second procedure is based on an internal examination of the two theories. The one theory might establish a more general connection to observation, and the interpretation of observational results might also be more direct. The third procedure . . . consists in taking the pragmatic theory of observation seriously. In this case we accept the theory whose observation sentences most successfully mimic our own behavior." [441] Thus for general theories empirical test and criticism are possible only in the face of alternatives, and so the doctrine of proliferation of theories is vindicated; in the process a Popperian philosophy of science has been developed which does not presuppose a neutral observation language.

Unfortunately, Feyerabend's account of the testing of general theories embodies a serious flaw which has been pointed out by a number of critics.[442] Feyerabend's first proposal requires that there be a common background theory for the two alternatives; such a theory presumably must be consistent with both alternatives, but this is impossible since the alternatives are incommensurable. The second and third proposals implicitly require that the two theories have common or at least compatible observation reports; this is impossible given that the alternatives have been assumed incommensurable. Thus none of these test procedures is possible if Feyerabend's general position is correct. Feyerabend admits that this line of criticism is damaging to his earlier account of how general theories can be tested, but he is of the opinion that his position can be modified so that these objections can be escaped while retaining the substance of his account. His attempts to modify his test account have led him in a Hegelian direction in which the criticism and development of general theories proceeds via a dialectical process of criticism.[443] A related problem can be raised about his doctrine of proliferation of theories and its role in the growth of scientific knowledge. On Feyerabend's view it is imperative that the

[441] *Ibid.*, p. 217.

[442] For example, Achinstein [1964], Putnam [1965], Shapere [1966], and Scheffler [1967], pp. 50–52.

[443] He acknowledges these criticisms and makes his first attempt to modify his doctrines in Feyerabend [1965b]. The Hegelian dialectic is introduced in Feyerabend [1970]. Certain aspects of that essay are developed further in a complementary paper, Feyerabend [1970b]. A brief account of these most recent developments, as well as a possible rejoinder to the criticism of his third proposal, is given below in Section II-B of the Afterword.

same scientists or scientific community be able to understand and compare many radically different theories or *Weltanschauungen*: it would not suffice to split science into a number of competing schools, each with its own single theory or *Weltanschauung*.[444] However, when the theories involved are general theories which function as *Weltanschauungen* for viewing the world, it becomes questionable whether there are any persons psychologically able either to alter world views when entertaining alternative theories or to switch from one *Weltanschauung* to another at will. Thus it is questionable whether his analysis is psychologically possible.

A number of other criticisms have been raised against Feyerabend's views. The most important of these have been directed at his analysis of meaning. Since virtually every one of Feyerabend's more important arguments depends crucially on this analysis of meaning,[445] it is the cornerstone of his position; and if this analysis is shown untenable, the entire development of his alternative position is refuted. In my opinion the attacks made by Shapere and others do succeed in showing his account of meaning untenable; as such there seems little reason to consider the other more specific criticisms which have been raised against other aspects of his position. As related, but generally less extreme, doctrines on meaning figure in the other *Weltanschauungen* analyses we are considering, and as the criticisms raised against Feyerabend's treatment of meaning have been raised against these other analyses, consideration of these criticisms will be postponed until Section V–B–2, below, where the more general criticisms of the *Weltanschauungen* analyses are discussed.

(e) BOHM

As an outgrowth of his attempts to provide quantum theory with an adequate physical interpretation, the physicist David Bohm has developed a philosophy of science which is similar in various respects to those advanced by Feyerabend, Hanson, and Kuhn. Before presenting his position, some background is needed on the problem of interpreting quantum theory.

The formalism of classical mechanics specifies a number of relations holding between measurable physical parameters such as mass, posi-

444 Feyerabend's rejection of normal science (see above) indicates that he would find this unacceptable.

445 Hopefully my exposition of his position has made this obvious.

tion, and momentum of particles. In its standard interpretation, these parameters are interpreted as objective measurable properties of bodies which, in theory, can be measured or determined with arbitrarily high precision; the laws of the theory specify deterministic or causal relations holding between these objective parameters. For several centuries this has been taken as paradigmatic of an adequate physical interpretation of a physical theory's formalism. *Prima facie* quantum theory does not admit of such an interpretation: rather than specifying determinate values for a body's position and momentum, it only yields probability distributions over possible measured values for position and momentum; the Heisenberg indeterminancy relation specifies that position and momentum for a body cannot simultaneously be determined with arbitrary accuracy—that if Δ_p and Δ_m are measures of the accuracy with which the position and momentum of a body simultaneously are determined that $\Delta_p \cdot \Delta_m \geq \hbar/m$, where $\hbar$ is Planck's constant and m is the mass of the body; quantum theory employs various hypothetical entities which are not amenable to experimental determination; electrons and protons sometimes act like corpuscles and other times like waves. These features seem to preclude giving quantum theory a physical interpretation anything like that given classical mechanics. At the Fifth Solvay Conference in 1927 an interpretation was proposed for quantum theory which has become the standard or "official" interpretation. For our purposes, the salient features of this interpretation—known as the *Copenhagen interpretation*—are as follows.[446] The basic hypotheses of quantum theory are assumed to be fundamentally correct, both mathematically and physically, and not susceptible to further modification. Exploiting the fact that microscopic particles sometimes act like corpuscles and sometimes like waves, the Heisenberg indeterminancy re-

[446] The account which follows is a mixture of Bohr's, Heisenberg's, and von Neumann's views on interpreting the formalism of quantum theory; this amalgamation of their views seems to capture what most working physicists understand as the Copenhagen interpretation. In any case, it suffices for my purposes here. Nonetheless, it should be pointed out that many careful students of quantum theory regard Bohr's approach as more coherent and successful than either Heisenberg's approach or the amalgamated account which follows; many persons of this persuasion prefer to reserve the name 'Copenhagen interpretation' for Bohr's approach, referring to the amalgamated view described in the text, for example, as the *orthodox interpretation.* The account which follows deviates from Bohr's view primarily in its treatment of Heisenberg's indeterminancy principle, giving Heisenberg's disturbance theory of measurement; this treatment deviates from Bohr's view which emphasizes the unity of the apparatus and the measured system. For good discussions of Bohr's analysis and the way it deviates from other versions of Copenhagen interpretation, compare Feyerabend [1968–69] and Hooker [1972a] and [1972b]; related discussion is found in Bub's paper, below, in Session IV.

lation is interpreted as showing the impossibility of measuring a physical quantity without causing a disturbance. Any attempt to improve the measurement of a parameter which characterizes a system will have the inevitable result of disturbing the value of another parameter of the system; unlike the macroscopic level, on the microscopic level these disturbances will be non-negligible; thus it is *impossible* to find the position and velocity of a subatomic particle at one moment with complete accuracy. This being so, the laws of quantum theory depend on chance; this, coupled with the assumption that the laws are fundamentally correct, means that the statistical laws describe an ultimate knowable reality which is noncausal and in which indeterminism is a fundamental fact; the Heisenberg relation puts a barrier to finding more about the workings of nature. Theories may contain only concepts which have a practical significance, and must keep to predictions which can be experimentally verified. Since the positions, momenta, velocities, and so on of microscopic bodies can be measured only by apparatus which disturbs the system, the measured values depend upon that interaction and do not represent objective properties of the body; thus before a measurement the body does not have, for example, a well-defined velocity, but rather has a whole series of velocities at the same time, each of which has a probability of being observed (the probability being determined in accordance with the theory and the Heisenberg relation); so there is no determinate velocity (or position or momentum) for the body, and an unequivocal description of nature is impossible. That is, we can only say a particle is the sum of the "potentialities of measurement" contained in its wave function. Since particles sometimes behave like waves and sometimes like corpuscles, both the wave and the corpuscle concepts are needed to cover all observations; the concepts of wave and corpuscle thus are *complementary* in that both are essential to any description of reality; both are potentially present to a greater or lesser degree, each appearing to the detriment of the other; similarly, position and momentum are complementary. Thus the description of microscopic systems is by couples of concepts or by complementary variables. This being so, a complete mechanical interpretation of the quantum formalism is impossible. Finally, since only experimentally determinable entities are to be acknowledged, there is nothing in reality corresponding to a number of the hypothetical entities employed in the theory's formalism; this precludes giving quantum theory a full realistic interpretation. On the Copenhagen interpretation, the theory's formalism is an instrument for predicting the results of possible measurements on particles which do not possess determinate properties, but rather only possess potential measured values.[447]

Although the Copenhagen interpretation enjoys the status of being the "official" interpretation of quantum theory, a number of physicists —including Einstein, Planck, Schrödinger, and de Broglie—have found it unacceptable. For example, Einstein rejected the conclusion that reality was fundamentally indeterministic, maintaining that the statistical nature of quantum phenomena could be attributed to a hidden variable which, when discovered, would result in a deterministic account. Schrödinger and de Broglie found unacceptable the principle that only experimentally discernible entities could be given ontological status, and thus found no support for the instrumentalist view adopted. Although Einstein and de Broglie devoted much effort to working out alternative interpretations for quantum theory which escaped these objections, formidable difficulties were encountered and no real progress was made until David Bohm's work in the early 1950s. Observing that the Copenhagen interpretation rested heavily on a number of philosophic assumptions,[448] Bohm launched a double-pronged attack on it. First, he attempted to isolate and show untenable a number of philosophical assumptions intrinsic to the interpretation; in the process he has developed an alternative philosophy of science. Second, he tried to show that when these assumptions are given up, it is possible to develop an alternative causal interpretation employing hidden variables.[449] In explicating Bohm's work, I shall confine my attention primarily to his philosophical developments.[450]

In opposition to attempts such as Einstein's and Bohm's to provide a causal interpretation of quantum theory in terms of hidden variables, proponents of the Copenhagen interpretation have adduced several

[447] For a fuller but readable characterization of what I am calling the Copenhagen interpretation, see Andrade e Silva and Lochak [1969], Ch. 3 and esp. Ch. 4; see also Bohr [1934], [1958], and [1963] for the original papers developing his version of the Copenhagen interpretation.

[448] For a careful and illuminating account of the philosophical seeds of the Copenhagen interpretation, see Peterson [1968].

[449] His original formulation of the alternative was presented in Bohm [1952]; since then the proposal has been modified to increase its generality and remove a number of artificialities; early modifications are discussed in Bohm [1957] and [1957a]. More recent developments of his alternative are discussed in Professor Bub's paper below (Session IV) and the references therein.

[450] My explication is based primarily on Bohm [1957] and the "Appendix" to Bohm [1965]. In doing so, I am compromising the intent of this introduction, which is to provide sufficient background to follow the papers and discussions in the symposium which follows; for the details of Bohm's alternative interpretation are discussed in Session IV below—both in Professor Bub's paper and in the discussion

arguments designed to show that such an attempt must fail. First, if quantum theory is correct, then the Heinsenberg indeterminancy relation specifies ultimate, absolute, and final limitations on the accuracy of measurements we could use to define the state of things by any possible means of measurements. Hence, even if a subquantum level containing the sorts of hidden variables required should exist, the inclusion of these variables could not increase the accuracy of any predictions beyond what quantum theory already obtains; thus it would not be possible to experimentally verify any causal theory that predicts the detailed behavior of an individual system at the atomic level.[451] Second, von Neumann has proved a theorem establishing that no conceivable distributions of motions of "hidden" parameters in the observed system could lead to precisely the same results as those of the Schrödinger equation when the wave function is interpreted probabilistically.[452] When coupled with the first argument, the von Neumann theorem is interpreted as leading to the conclusion that nothing even corresponds to a set of "hidden" parameters having a degree of precise definition going beyond the limits set by the Heisenberg relations; hence, a "hidden" variable causal account is impossible. Bohm subjects these arguments just sketched to a careful analysis from which he concludes that the conclusions concerning the need to renounce causality, continuity, and the objective nature of reality which are drawn from these arguments do not follow either from the experimental facts underlying quantum theory or from the mathematical formalism used to express the theory; for both arguments crucially depend on the assumption (often implicit) that certain features of the current formulation of quantum theory are absolute and final, that they never will be contradicted in the future or found to be approximations which hold only for a limited domain. Such assumptions in effect deny the possibility of there being any hidden variables or a subquantum level in which new kinds of motion occur for which new kinds of causal laws hold, and so they beg the question of the possibility of hidden variables. Thus the arguments against the hidden variable hypotheses depend essentially on extra-empirical or philosophical assumptions.[453]

---

of Professor Bohm's paper. I do not have sufficient space here to provide enough background in quantum theory to fully comprehend those discussions; fortunately they constitute only a minor portion of Session IV. The reader wishing to acquire the needed background for these portions of Session IV should consult the quite readable and manageable account of quantum theory given in Andrade e Silva and Lochak [1969].

451 For development of this argument, see Heisenberg [1930].

452 Von Neumann [1955], pp. 206–211, and Ch. 4, Sec. 2.

453 Bohm [1957], pp. 79–96.

The next step in his attack on the Copenhagen interpretation is to show that these philosophical assumptions central to it are untenable. To do so he presents an analysis of causality and chance. Although physical systems undergo complexities and transformations, various relationships remain effectively constant or invariant; when such invariances are *necessary* relationships, they are causal laws. A causal law is never absolute, however, for "one must conceive of the law of nature as necessary only if one abstracts from *contingencies,* representing essential independent factors which may exist outside the scope of things that can be treated by the laws under consideration, and which do not follow necessarily from anything that may be specified under the context of these laws. Such contingencies lead to *chance.* Hence we conceive of the necessity of a law of nature as *conditional,* since it applies only to the extent that these contingencies may be neglected." [454] If by the *significant causes* of a given effect we mean those conditions or events which, in the context of interest, have appreciable influence on the effects in question,[455] it becomes clear that many causal laws specify only *some* of the significant causes; such a law "represents an objectively necessary causal connection, but in this case, what is necessary is that the effect remain within certain bounds; and not, as in simpler types of causal laws, that the effect be determined uniquely." [456] To increase the precision of such laws, additional significant causes must be added which take into account "new and qualitatively different causal factors." [457] Contingencies have a relative independence of the properties of things within a context. Since "our general experience shows that all things are interconnected in some way and to some degree," [458] we see that, "like the notion of necessary connections, the notion of chance contingencies is . . . an approximation, which gives a partial treatment of certain aspects of the real process, but which eventually has to be corrected and completed by a consideration of the causal interconnections that always exist between the processes taking place in different contexts." [459] When the individual variations due to chance contingencies tend to cancel out, statistical laws are possible which permit the prediction of properties of the average behavior of aggregates or series of individuals.[460] Thus contingencies arising outside the context in which causal laws operate always limit

[454] *Ibid.*, p. 2; italics in the original.
[455] *Ibid.*, p. 8.
[456] *Ibid.*, p. 17.
[457] *Ibid.*
[458] *Ibid.*, p. 20.
[459] *Ibid.*
[460] *Ibid.*, p. 22.

and condition their necessity. These contingencies themselves satisfy statistical laws of chance which can be expressed using the theory of probability. This interconnection between causal relationships and chance contingencies shows that what are chance contingencies in a narrower context could be the result of necessary causal connections in a broader context. If so, these necessary causal connections in the broader context will themselves be subject to new contingencies since the context of these laws still is limited. Thus contingencies never can be eliminated completely. "Rather, the categories of necessary causal connection and chance contingencies are seen to represent two sides of all processes." [461] Any attempt to consider only one of these sides results in an approximation which can only be corrected by taking into account the other side.[462] Thus, "each particular theory or explanation of a given set of phenomena will then have a limited domain of validity and will be adequate only in a limited context and under limited conditions. This means that any theory extrapolated to an arbitrary context and to arbitrary conditions will . . . lead to erroneous predictions." [463] Such erroneous predictions do not show the theory invalid, but rather serve to define the conditions under which it is valid.[464]

It follows from this analysis of causality and chance that no causal or statistical law can be an ultimate law of nature which holds for all of reality; furthermore, any objectively valid or true scientific law, be it causal or statistical, is an abstraction giving an approximate and partial view of reality, and it is a mistake to "regard chance as reducible completely and perfectly to an approximate and purely passive reflection of determinate law," [465] or vice versa. Thus the philosophical assumptions of the Copenhagen interpretation's arguments against the possibility of a causal "hidden" variable explanation or interpretation of quantum theory are just as untenable as those which underlie a Laplacian determinism.[466] In particular, Heisenberg's indeterminancy principle at best shows that there are limits on the accuracy of measurement in the domain of quantum theory's validity. It does not show that a more comprehensive theory which employs entities at a subquantum level to explain the statistical regularities of quantum theory will be subject to the same restricted

[461] *Ibid.*, p. 29.
[462] *Ibid.*, pp. 29–30.
[463] *Ibid.*, p. 31.
[464] *Ibid.*, pp. 31–32; it is worth comparing this view with Toulmin's discussed above.
[465] *Ibid.*, p. 64.
[466] *Ibid.*, pp. 94–103, and esp. pp. 130–132.

accuracy; and it does not show that such subquantum entities are in principle not experimentally discernible. Hence the hypothetical entities which are not amenable to empirical determination according to quantum theory need not be intrinsically indeterminable; thus there is no reason why the present quantum theory should force us into an instrumentalist methodology; the success of quantum theory does not require the belief that all future theories whose domains include that of quantum theory must be instrumentalistic or non-causal. Thus there is no reason to rule out in principle the hypothesis of a subquantum mechanical level containing hidden variables wherein the statistical character of the current quantum theory originates in random fluctuations of new kinds of entities existing in the lower level. The tenability of such a hypothesis is not to be judged on a priori philosophic grounds, but rather is to be determined empirically the same as with any other scientific theory. Bohm's work in physics has concentrated on developing his hidden variable analysis to a state of precision such that its empirical adequacy can be determined.[467]

Although the above, if essentially correct, is sufficient to justify the *legitimacy* of Bohm's attempt to develop the hidden variable hypothesis, he has developed his philosophical account further. Implicit in his doctrine that laws are applicable only within limited contexts, over limited ranges of conditions, and to limited degrees of approximation is the possibility "that there may exist an unlimited variety of additional properties, qualities, entities, systems, levels, etc., to which apply correspondingly new kinds of laws of nature";[468] this leads to the notion that nature may have in it an infinity of different kinds of things. That is, we cannot justify a priori any assumptions denying that in different contexts there are inexhaustibly rich and diversified qualities and properties that exist in nature; accordingly Bohm assumes there is a *qualitative and quantitative infinity of nature.* "With regard to any given domain of phenomena, the specific form of the assumption of the qualitative infinity of nature . . . does not contradict the notion that these phenomena can be treated in terms of some finite set of qualities and laws, and indeed, in terms of a number much smaller than the number of items of empirical data that may be available."[469] Rather causal laws are possible in any

[467] As was indicated in an earlier footnote, the details of his theory will not be given here.

[468] *Ibid.*, p. 133.

[469] *Ibid.*, p. 135.

context where chance occurrences exert a negligible influence on events and statistical laws are possible in any context where causal occurrences exert negligible influence on events. Such laws abstract things and some of the relations they enter into from reality or nature.

> It is clear that we *must* utilize such abstractions and approximations if only because we cannot hope to deal with the qualitative and quantitative infinity of the universe. The task of science is, then, to find the right kind of things that should be abstracted from the world for the correct treatment of problems in various contexts and sets of conditions . . . we require [that] theories formulated in terms of these abstractions lead to correct predictions, and to the control of natural processes in accordance with the plans that are made on the basis of these theories.[470]

Such laws are approximations conditional on the assumption that causal or chance occurrences not considered by the theory exert a negligible influence on the events characterized; as such, laws and the theories incorporating them only have a limited domain of validity. Accordingly, laws and theories cannot represent absolute truths; theories are approximate, conditional, and relative truths.[471]

On this view what are the distinguishing marks of laws and theories? First, a genuine law or theory "affords correct knowledge going beyond the experimental facts which helped lead to its proposal" [472] and "has a fairly broad domain of validity." [473] The domain of a law or theory generally is unknown, and if applied beyond that domain the law will be falsified; indeed, it is only by the falsification of a law or theory that its domain of validity can be specified. Since every law or theory has a restricted domain of validity, all laws or theories are actually false if construed as general truths; they are only restricted truths.[474] Thus laws or theories describe what is *relatively invariant* in phenomena:

> A law of nature is, by our very way of conceiving of it, seen to express the fact that in a certain set of changes taking place in nature, as well as in a corresponding set of changes of points of view, reference frames, modes of investigation, etc., certain relationships can be discovered, which remain the same throughout all these changes. But this invariance is to be conceived of as only *relative,* in the sense that as the domain is broadened, we leave room in our minds to *entertain the notion that*

[470] *Ibid.*, p. 146.
[471] *Ibid.*, p. 165; Bohm [1965], pp. 123–126.
[472] Bohm [1965], p. 124.
[473] *Ibid.*, p. 127.
[474] *Ibid.*, p. 125–127.

> *the law may break down.* That is to say, it may be falsified in some future set of experiments. We do not commit ourselves as to when, where, and how it will be falsified but leave this to be shown by future developments themselves.[475]

This view of laws and theories leads naturally to Kuhn's view of scientific advancement resulting from an alternation between normal and revolutionary science. In normal science a great deal of research effort is aimed at extending a theory confirmed for a broad domain to ever new kinds of problems and improving its accuracy. However, since theories always have a limited domain of validity, this ultimately leads to the falsification of the theory, the result of which is a scientific revolution searching for a new theory embodying a new point of view whose domain of validity includes that of the old theory plus a wider range of phenomena. When such a new theory is found, normal science again prevails. Although this process results in a succession of theories with increasingly larger domains of validity, the qualitative and quantitative infinity of nature and the abstractive nature of laws and theories leaves no basis for assuming that these theories are converging on any absolute truths.[476]

Although theories are abstractions which enjoy only a conditional and relative truth, they do yield knowledge; for according to Bohm, "all knowledge is a structure of abstractions, the ultimate test of the validity of which is, however, in the process of coming into contact with the world that takes place in immediate perception."[477] Science, through its techniques of developing higher level abstractions which are tested against observations, thus is one way of obtaining knowledge about the world. And it is a method which requires an essentially perceptual process whereby the scientist is aware of contradictions between his hypothesis and what he observes; and the development of new conjectures or hypotheses requires that the scientist be sensitive to new relationships in what he observes.[478] According to Bohm, the connection between perception and scientific investigation is more intimate than these facts suggest: "Scientific investigation is basically a mode of extending our *perception* of the world, and not mainly a mode of obtaining *knowledge* about it."[479] That this is so follows, according to Bohm, from a consideration of the pervasive similarities between perception and scientific investigation. On the

[475] *Ibid.*, p. 127; italics in the original; see also p. 185.

[476] *Ibid.*, pp. 127–130; on p. 128, n. 1, Bohm expresses his acceptance of Kuhn's basic account of scientific development.

[477] *Ibid.*, p. 220.

[478] *Ibid.*, p. 226.

[479] *Ibid.*, p. 219.

basis of a lengthy review of various recent studies in the psychology and physiology of perception, he concludes the following about perception:

> We have discussed studies of the development of the process of perception in an individual human being from infancy, as well as direct studies of how this process takes place in adults. What comes out of these studies can be summed up in the statement that in the process of perception we learn about the world mainly by being sensitive to what is invariant in the relationships between our own movement, activities, probings, etc., and the resulting changes in what comes in through our sense organs. These invariant relationships are then presented immediately in our awareness as a kind of "construction" in an "inner show," embodying, in effect, a hypothesis that accounts for the invariant features that have been found in such experiences up to the moment in question. This hypothesis is, however, tentative in the sense that it will be replaced by another one, if in our subsequent movements, probings, etc., we encounter contradictions with the implications of our "constructions." [480]

This account of perception clearly bears strong resemblance to the above account of scientific theorizing; after detailing the similarities,[481] Bohm concludes, "through perception we are always in a process of coming into contact with the world, in such a way that we can be aware of the general structure of the segment with which we have been in contact. Science may then be regarded as a means of establishing new kinds of contacts with the world, in new domains, in new levels, with the aid of different instruments, etc." [482] As such, both perception and scientific investigation "can be regarded as limiting cases of one over-all process, of a generalized kind of perception, in which no absolute knowledge is to be encountered." [483]

Having concluded that science is a means of perceiving the world, the next step in the development of Bohm's position is to consider the role of language or communication in scientific theorizing. In his contribution to the symposium below (Session IV), Bohm does this, arguing that perception and communication are one whole, and thus that differences in theory, perception, and communication are of a part.[484] His development of this thesis results in a *Weltanschauungen*

[480] *Ibid.*, p. 217; pp. 187–216 are devoted to this survey, which includes work by Piaget, Gibson, Platt, Hubel, Held and Freedman, Held and Rekosh, and Hebb.

[481] Secs. A–4 and A–5 of the Appendix to *ibid.* are devoted to spelling them out.

[482] *Ibid.*, p. 230.

[483] *Ibid.*

[484] Portions of this thesis are given a preliminary development in Bohm [1971].

view of science strikingly similar to Feyerabend's. Since his view of science is subjected to extensive critical discussion and assessment in Professor Causey's commentary, Professor Bub's reply to Causey, and the discussion of his paper in Session IV below, I will not attempt any detailed criticisms here—except insofar as the general criticisms of *Weltanschauungen* views considered in the next section apply to his position; in virtue of the strong resemblance between his view and Feyerabend's, these latter criticisms constitute a strong challenge to his position.[485]

2. General Criticisms of *Weltanschauungen* Analyses

Despite substantive differences in position and development, the *Weltanschauungen* analyses surveyed above[486] present remarkably similar views of science. The analyses proposed by Bohm, Feyerabend, Hanson, Kuhn, and Toulmin each view science as proceeding from within a *Weltanschauung,* where different theories require or yield different *Weltanschauungen.* Furthermore, the accounts they give of how the *Weltanschauung* contributes to the scientific enterprise each centrally employ versions of the following three theses:

(1) Observation is theory-laden: The *Weltanschauung* determines or influences how one views, describes, or interprets the world; hence adherents to different theories will observe different things when they view the same phenomena.

(2) Meanings are theory-dependent: The descripitive terms (both observational and theoretical) used by a science undergo a shift in meaning when incorporated into, or used in conjunction with, a theory; thus the principles of a theory help determine the meanings of the terms occurring in them, and so the meanings of such terms will vary from theory to theory; hence changes in theory result in changes of meaning.

(3) Facts are theory-laden: What counts as a fact is determined by the *Weltanschauung* associated with a theory; as such there is no neutral set of facts for assessing the relative adequacy of two competing theories; rather, the adequacy of a theory must be assessed according to standards set by its associated *Weltanschauung.*

485 For other criticisms of Bohm's views—especially those developed in Bohm [1957]—see Feyerabend [1960].

486 Although his work was discussed in conjunction with Feyerabend's view, I do not consider Popper's position to be a *Weltanschauungen* analysis; the discussion which follows is not intended to apply particularly to his position.

Given the central role these theses play in *Weltanschauungen* analyses, the adequacy of the *Weltanschauungen* approach to understanding science and its theories depends largely on their tenability. Each has been the subject of critical attack. The more important attacks on these theses will be considered and assessed in subsections (a) to (c); some tentative conclusions about the adequacy of the *Weltanschauungen* approach will be drawn in subsection (d).

(a) OBSERVATION

According to thesis (1), observation is theory-laden: what one sees or observes is determined by the *Weltanschauung*. This is crucially vague, admitting of the following two interpretations:

(1′) The objects one observes, and the properties they possess, are constituted in part by the *Weltanschauung*.

(1″) Although the objects one observes, and the properties they possess, are as they are independent of the observer's *Weltanschauung*, what kind of objects they are observed to be and the properties they are observed to have are determined in part by the *Weltanschauung*.[487]

To assess thesis (1), it will be necessary to examine (1′) and (1″), both with respect to their tenability and their adequacy for the purposes of *Weltanschauungen* analyses.

On the basis of remarks such as Kuhn's that "disciplinary matrices . . . are constitutive of nature" [488] and Hanson's that Tycho and Kepler see different things while watching the dawn, Scheffler [1967] interprets advocates of *Weltanschauungen* analyses as maintaining (1′),[489] and then proceeds to show (1′) is untenable. The reason (1′) is untenable, he maintains, is that it embraces a subjective view of knowledge which is incompatible with the objectivity of scientific observation. The objectivity of science rests in the fact that its claims are "held subject to control by reference to independent checks." [490] Central to objectivity is "the ontological vision . . . of a universe of objects with independent existences and careers." [491] By its insistence

[487] In technical terms the difference between these two interpretations can be put clearly as follows: On thesis (1′) the particulars of observation are *intentional* entities, whereas they are not on thesis (1″); for discussions of intentional particulars, see Chisholm and Sellars [1958].

[488] Kuhn [1962], p. 109; reading 'disciplinary matrixes' for 'paradigms'.

[489] Pp. 14–15, and Ch. 2. Although Scheffler nowhere distinguishes or formulates (1′) and (1″), it is clear that he is attributing a position essentially similar to (1′) to advocates of *Weltanschauungen* analyses.

[490] Scheffler [1967], p. 2.

[491] *Ibid.*, p. 11.

that the objects science observes and their properties are constituted in part by the *Weltanschauung*, (1′) denies this ontological vision, hence denies the objectivity of science. In doing so it leads to a paradoxical view of science. If (1′) is correct, proponents of different theories cannot observe the same things in an effort to decide between the theories. This has "the effect of isolating each scientist within an observed world consonant with his theoretical beliefs,"[492] and leads to the position that "there is no scientific advance by standard criteria, only the rivalry of different theoretical viewpoints and the replacement of some by others. Reality is gone as an independent factor; each viewpoint creates its own reality."[493] The consequence, then, of accepting (1′) is "an extravagant idealism"; such a "bleak picture" of science, he says, is "a *reductio ad absurdum* of the reasonings from which it flows."[494] As such, (1′) is a self-refuting doctrine which ought to be rejected.[495]

This argument does not refute (1′), however; for the "bleak picture" of an extravagant idealism might just be true; the charge that (1′) leads to a bleak picture at best shows that the picture is bleak, not that it is an unacceptable misrepresentation. The only way to show (1′) is unacceptable is to produce an acceptable alternative which paints a less bleak picture. Scheffler is aware of this and attempts to present such an alternative. He begins by considering the evidence which lends support to (1′), and concludes that it does show that an adequate account of observation "will need to accept the continuity and interaction of observation and conceptualization, and it will further need to accept the continuity and interaction of observation reports."[496] This means that whatever independent observational control there is cannot involve any appeal to an uncategorized given (for example, a sense datum).[497] Scheffler then attempts to present an analysis of observation which grants an essential role to conceptualization in observation and still allows for an observational independence wherein reality can function as an independent factor in observation. Briefly, his alternative is as follows. He first distinguishes between categories for sorting objects and hypotheses as to which objects belong in which categories. Adopting a category system does not prejudge the actual distribution of items within the

[492] *Ibid.*, p. 15.
[493] *Ibid.*, p. 19.
[494] *Ibid.*, p. 19.
[495] *Ibid.*, pp. 21–22.
[496] *Ibid.*, p. 36; the discussion leading up to this conclusion is on pp. 21–36.
[497] *Ibid.*, pp. 35–36, 43.

categories; indeed conflicting hypotheses as to which items belong to what categories are possible for a given category system. All observation thus is relative to the category system one accepts; but accepting a category system does not prejudge which category an object is put in. This shows "that independent observational control over hypotheses is *possible* without an appeal to an uncategorized given, since the sort of determination effected by categorization falls short of a question-begging support of favored hypotheses."[498] Finding this alternative preferable to (1′), he rejects (1′).[499]

Although Scheffler tells us that his proposal allows for an "independent observational control" over hypotheses concerning the distribution of objects within the various categories of one's category system, he never indicates exactly what the nature of this control is or how it operates. The fact that adopting a category system does not prejudge the actual distribution of objects among one's categories yields significant "independent observational control" over hypotheses only if one further assumes that the truth of these hypotheses depends on the objective nature of things. That is, it must be the case that the "independent observational control" rests in the fact that the truth of hypotheses such as 'this is a rose' depends on the objective nature of things. Suppose I adopt a category system containing the category *rose* and I observe an item, call it '*b*'. Then Scheffler's "independent objective control" over the hypothesis 'Item *b* is a rose' must rest in the fact that whether his hypothesis is true depends on the objective nature of things—that is, depends on whether item *b* is in fact a rose, where its being or not being a rose does not depend on what category I observe it as falling under or on how I conceptualize things. But this raises a basic metaphysical problem. Presumably Scheffler is committed to the position that I have relatively free choice in setting up my category system. This means that I can set up my category *rose* pretty much as I see fit; in particular it seems to allow that I can specify my categories as interconnecting as I see fit. If so, then what it is to belong to the category *rose* is more or less my free decision; for example, I may decide that a necessary condition for belonging to category *rose* will be that it belongs to categories $c_1, \ldots, c_n$. Now if the hypothesis 'Item *b* is a rose' is true, it in effect says that item *b* does belong to category *rose,* hence that it also belongs to categories $c_1, \ldots, c_n$. But the "independent objective control" over hypothesis 'Item *b* is a rose' requires that the truth of the hypothesis depends on whether item *b*

498 *Ibid.*, p. 43.
499 This alternative is developed in *ibid.*, pp. 36–44.

has the property of being a rose, where being a rose does not depend in any way upon how I choose to conceptualize or categorize my experience. But then Scheffler's account leads to a set of demands which are *prima facie* contradictory: the truth of 'Item *b* is a rose' requires that item *b* actually belong to category *rose* where what it is to belong to category rose is within my control but where what it is to be a rose is totally beyond my control.

This *prima facie* contradiction evaporates only if there is some sort of correspondence between one's category system and the properties objects have independent of one's category system. Thus Scheffler's "independent objective control" over hypotheses is forthcoming only on the supposition of such a correspondence—a correspondence which is compatible with allowing alternative systems of categories which are relatively freely chosen. Scheffler has not given any indication what that correspondence would be like; he has not even given us any reason to believe that such a correspondence is possible. And in the absence of such a specification or such reasons, he has not demonstrated that his proposal leads to any significant "independent observational control" over hypotheses. Another way of putting the criticism is this: Scheffler's "solution" to the problem of "independent observational control" over hypotheses presupposes that it is possible to have the conceptual freedom typical of a coherence theory of truth while still enjoying the objectivity of a correspondence theory of truth. I am willing to grant that this is required if one is going to make the concessions he does about the pervasive influence of conceptualization in observation and still insist that there be his kind of objective control over observation. But the fact that his position requires this does not show that it is possible. The most his "solution" does is enable us to determine what is necessary if there is to be "independent observational control." To demonstrate that such control is possible, Scheffler would have to present the required analysis of truth, and he has not done so. Thus he has not demonstrated that his proposal leads to any "independent observational control." As such he has not made his case against (1′).[500]

Even if Scheffler had made his case against (1′), it would not make any difference; for in attributing (1′) to Hanson, Kuhn, and others,

[500] This is not to say that his case cannot be made, however. Wilfrid Sellars and I have recently developed analyses of facts which apparently will serve Scheffler's purposes. In Suppe [1973a] I argue that an adequate realistic account of facts and empirical truth must construe the intrinsic property of *being a rose* as being extensional in the sense that something is a rose if and only if it belongs to a class specifiable in an extensional language containing infinite disjunctions. On the other hand, the concept of being a rose is intensional. The intension of 'is a

Scheffler is attacking a straw man. To be sure, Hanson, Kuhn, and the others often speak carelessly in a way that gives license to attribute (1′) to them; but they also make a number of claims which disavow (1′)—for example, Hanson admits that there is a sense in which Tycho and Kepler do visually experience the same object, and Kuhn does acknowledge the existence of an independent world. Moreover, if the accounts I have given above of their various positions are essentially accurate, it is quite clear that nothing significant in Bohm's, Feyerabend's, Hanson's, Kuhn's, or Toulmin's positions depends upon accepting (1′). It is consistent with their positions to affirm that the objects, systems, and so on, they observe exist and have properties independent of conceptualization. All they need be committed to is the claim that which of these objects one observes, what kind of objects one observes them to be, and which properties one observes them to have are determined, in part at least, by the *Weltanschauung*. That is, (1″) is all that their positions commit them to.

To my knowledge no particularly damaging criticisms have been raised against (1″). On the other hand, it does not seem to me that it has been given sufficient development or argumentative support to justify accepting it. Of the proponents of *Weltanschauungen* analyses, only Hanson has attempted to develop and argue for it in detail; and as was indicated in Section V–B–1–c, his arguments do not succeed in making his case. Although an adequate case has not been made for (1″), I think a plausible case can be made. The best assessment I can make of (1″) is to sketch the outlines of that case.

Achinstein [1968] maintains, correctly I think, that in the relevant scientific sense observation involves attending to something in a way which (1) is influenced by my concerns and knowledge, (2) does not require recognizing what is observed, (3) allows one to observe what is hidden from view, (4) may involve seeing an intermediary image, and (5) allows what I am observing to be described correctly in

---

rose' determines an extension, and 'Item *b* is a rose'. will be empirically true if and only if the item designated by 'Item *b*' has a property whose extension is identical with that of 'is a rose'. It follows from this analysis that what it is to be a rose (belonging to the category *rose*) can be a conceptual free creation but the truth of 'Item *b* is a rose'. will depend on the objective nature of things; so there is reason to suppose that the analysis could be combined with Scheffler's to obtain an analysis wherein observation does yield significant independent observational control. My basic analysis of facts and empirical truth is developed into a general account of natural classification in Suppe [1973c]. Sellars' analysis is similar to mine, but has not yet been published.

different ways.[501] What is this "attending to something"? In visual observation it clearly involves seeing.[502] Merely seeing something is not sufficient for observation, however. For scientific observation must yield pieces of information which can be used to test theories, make predictions, and so on. That is, the end product of visual observation is an observation report whose warrant essentially involves seeing; the report is a record of what has been seen to be the case. This suggests that correct observation essentially involves seeing that: when I correctly observe that *P* I have seen that *P*, and *P* is the case.[503] Suppose that '*O*' designates an object which has property *P*. My ability to see that *O* is *P*, hence to observe that *O* is *P*, does not require that I actually see the object designated by '*O*'. For example, I can see that the gas tank is empty without looking in the tank if I can see that the gas gauge reads 'Empty'.[504] Recent work in perception theory indicates that an adequate analysis of what it is for a perceiver S to see that *O* is *P* must meet the following conditions: Whether S can see that *O* is *P* in a given situation depends upon S's background knowledge and belief; S can see that *O* is *P* even if he mistakenly identifies what he sees to be *P* as an *O*; one can see that *O* is *P* without seeing the referent of '*O*' at all or when only seeing an intermediary image of the referent of '*O*'; depending on vocabulary, special training, and background knowledge or belief, when S sees that *O* is *P*, S could have described differently what he saw that was the case; when it is true that S sees that *O* is *P*, S knows that *O* is *P*, and it must be true that *O* is *P*; thus S can only see that which

[501] Pp. 160–165; these claims were discussed more fully in Sec. IV–B–2 above.

[502] In sketching the case for (1″) I will confine myself to visual observation; analogous cases can be made for aural, tactile, and other kinds of observation.

[503] For a fuller and quite convincing case for the claim that (visual) observation essentially involves seeing that, see Dretske [1969], Ch. 6, Secs. 1 and 4. Although visual observation essentially involves that, the characterization just made in the body of the text oversimplifies things in several respects, as recent work by Shapere and myself indicates: First, under some circumstances it is possible to (visually) observe that *P* where *P* is inferred from *Q*, where one sees that *Q* but does not see that *P*; that is, observation may be inference-aided under certain circumstances. Second, in order for seeing that *P* to qualify as visually observing that *P*, certain conditions of relevance and reliability must be met. See Shapere [forthcoming a] and my [1973d], Sec. IV, for defense of these claims. Since the purpose of the present discussion is only to sketch the outlines of an adequate case for (1″), not to argue that case, the discussion which follows will ignore these complications and confine its attention to noninference-aided cases of observing that; the extension of what follows to accommodate inference-aided observation is found in my [1973d].

[504] For full arguments in support of this claim, see Dretske [1969], Ch. VI, Sec. 2.

independently is the case.[505] Thus an adequate analysis of seeing that shares all the characteristic features of observation indicated by Achinstein. This suggests that an adequate account of observation can be developed in terms of seeing that. Such an account will relativize one's ability to see that to one's knowledge or belief; hence which theories one accepts does influence what one is able to observe. If one grants that one's *Weltanschauung* is determined by the theories one believes, thesis (1″) follows as a corollary.

To summarize what we have discovered about thesis (1): the thesis is ambiguous, admitting of two interpretations. Interpretation (1′) leads to an extreme idealism; and although conclusive arguments have not been advanced to show (1′) untenable, *ceteris paribus* a less extreme account is preferable. However, none of the *Weltanschauungen* analyses we have considered need be committed to (1′);

[505] All of these points except the second are established in *ibid.*, especially Chs. III to V. Dretske seems to deny the second point, but its correctness follows from results I have presented in Suppe [1972a]. Although Dretske's arguments do establish that these conditions must be met by an adequate analysis, I do not find his analysis wholly adequate; in particular, his analysis of seeing that presupposes a notion of nonepistemic seeing which I find untenable for several reasons. First, whenever S hallucinates an object, Dretske's analysis commits him to giving ontological status to the hallucinatory object—for example, if S hallucinates a dragon, then on Dretske's analysis there must exist real hallucinatory dragons. Second, his notion of nonepistemic seeing requires that there be a nonconceptual given in perception, which claim seems to me unacceptable in the face of criticisms such as those raised by Sellars [1956] and Will [1973], Ch. 4. Additional problems with his analysis are discussed in Aldrich [1970]. Except for his reliance on nonepistemic seeing, I find Dretske's analysis of seeing that essentially sound. Moreover, if his recourse to nonepistemic seeing is replaced by an analysis of seeing along the lines of Sellars [1958a] (which seems to me basically correct), only minimal changes are required in his analysis of seeing that. When this is done, one obtains roughly the following analysis:

Let S be an observer. Then S sees that *O* is *P* if and only if

(i) S, as a result of being in a visual sensory state, uses '*O* is *P*' to predicate 'is *P*' of the object referred to by '*O*'.

(ii) The object referred to by '*O*' is P.

(iii) The circumstances S is in are such that he would not be in the visual sensory state he is in unless anything present having the characteristics he knows the referent of '*O*' to have would be *P*, and he doesn't have prior knowledge that the referent of '*O*' is P; this condition can be met without S knowing that it is met.

(iv) S, being in that visual sensory state, takes the referent of '*O*' to be *P* and wouldn't do so if he were in certain other visual sensory states.

Moreover, most of his arguments in favor of his four conditions for seeing that apply equally well to this modified analysis. As my purpose here is only to indicate that a plausible analysis of seeing that can be given which has the desired consequences indicated in the text, I do not intend to develop or justify the analysis here; they are developed in a manuscript currently in preparation.

interpretation (1″) is sufficient for their purposes. Interpretation (1″) has not been adequately developed or justified by those who accept it. Recent work in perception theory strongly suggests, however, that an adequate analysis of observation in terms of seeing that is possible, and that observation will be relative to the observer's knowledge and beliefs, hence will be relative to the theories one accepts; the outlines of such an analysis were sketched. That observation is theory-laden in this way does not establish thesis (1″), however. Only if the theory-ladenness of observation is coupled with the assumption that theories (partially) determine *Weltanschauungen* does (1″) follow. Thus to the extent that this latter assumption can be maintained, the *Weltanschauungen* analyses' reliance on (1″) is vindicated, though a full working-out of the analysis of observation probably would require some modifications of various claims made by proponents of such analyses. Whether the assumption that theories determine *Weltanschauungen* is plausible will be considered briefly in subsections (b) and (d) below.

(b) MEANING CHANGE

According to thesis (2) meanings are theory-dependent in the sense that the meanings of terms are determined, in part at least, by their incorporation into a theory; hence changes in theory result in changes in meaning. In his earlier writings Feyerabend held the following strong version of the thesis[506] which Bohm apparently also holds:[507]

(2′) All of the principles of the theory contribute to the meanings of the terms occurring in them; hence any change in theory alters the meanings of all the terms in the theory.

Toulmin, Hanson, and apparently Kuhn hold a weaker version of the thesis:

(2″) The meanings of terms in theories are determined partially by the principles of the theory in which they occur; only some of the principles may make such a contribution to

[506] He modified the thesis to allow that not all changes in theory are changes in meaning in Feyerabend [1965]; his modifications were in response to Achinstein [1964].

[507] That he does does not follow from anything presented in the previous summary of his position; rather it seems to follow from developments in his contribution to Session IV below.

> meaning, and it is even possible that their contribution will be context-dependent; hence some changes in theory will result in changes in meaning.[508]

Both versions of thesis (2) are intended to apply to the terms employed in reporting observations as well as to theoretical terms.

Version (2′) amounts to a reformulation of Feyerabend's analysis of meaning which, as we saw in Section V–B–1–d–i, is the keystone of his analysis. A number of devastating attacks have been made on this version of thesis (2).[509] First, according to (2′) any change in theory results in changed meanings for all the terms in the theory. Feyerabend understands theories to include "ordinary beliefs (for example, the belief in the existence of material objects), myths (for example, the myth of eternal recurrence), religious beliefs, etc. In short, any sufficiently general point of view concerning matter of fact will be termed a theory."[510] With such a broad conception of theory, it is not at all clear what would constitute a change in theory. Suppose my theory is a mythological system and my oracle informs me that one of the gods has just given birth to a child; as a result I add to the mythological system a new belief that a new god exists. Does the addition of this belief constitute a change in theory? Does it alter the meanings I attach to the terms in my mythology? The same questions can be raised if we restrict our attention to scientific theories. Suppose I hold a physical theory, redetermine the value of a physical constant, and then incorporate this revised value into my laws. To be sure, I have altered the theory; but have I changed the theory? Have I changed the theory in such a way that the meanings of the terms occurring in the theory have been changed? Version (2′) gives us no way to answer these questions as no specification has been given of what it is to be a change in theory or a change in meaning. In the absence of individuating principles for theories and meanings these questions cannot be answered; and without answers to these questions it is difficult if not impossible to assess (2′)—or for that matter (2″).[511] Second, according to (2′) the meaning of a term is determined by

[508] While Kuhn's account of normal science seems to demand that he accept (2″) rather than (2′), his account of the incommensurability of competing disciplinary matrixes and their theories seems to require that (2′) be approximated in such cases. In his most recent writings (for example, Kuhn [1970a] and [1970b]) he seems to be moving further away from (2′).

[509] Compare Achinstein [1964] and [1968], pp. 91–98; Putnam [1965]; Scheffler [1967], Ch. 3; and Shapere [1964] and esp. [1966].

[510] Feyerabend [1965a], p. 219, n. 3.

[511] See Shapere [1966], pp. 56–57, for this line of argument; Scheffler [1967] raises the problem for meaning on pp. 54ff. An attempt to meet this criticism is given in Feyerabend [1965].

the theory it occurs in. It follows that if the same term (word) is incorporated into two different theories, the term will have two different meanings in the two theories. This has the consequence that the two theories could never contradict each other. For example, on Bohr's theory of the atom, angular momentum and radiant energy of electrons cannot have continuous values, whereas they can have continuous values under classical electrodynamics. Although the two theories thus seem to contradict each other, they do not since 'angular momentum' and 'have continuous values' mean different things under the two theories. It is not even possible to express the disagreement between the two theories using the terms of some other theory; for in virtue of being another theory none of its terms will have the same meaning as they do in either of the two theories. Thesis (2′) thus has the consequence that the disagreement between two theories can never be expressed.[512] Third, essentially the same considerations show that there can be no agreement between different theories. As observation terms derive their meanings from the theories they are employed in conjunction with, there can be no neutral observation reports which can be employed to specify agreement between the theories. But if different theories can neither agree nor disagree, in what sense can they be viewed as alternatives between which a choice is to be made (as Feyerabend's testing methodology requires)?[513] Fourth, according to thesis (2′) each principle of the theory contributes to the meaning of the terms; presumably the rejection of a principle of the theory is a change in meaning, and so results in a change in the meanings of the terms used in formulating it.[514] But then the principle will be analytic.[515] Hence on (2′) every principle of every theory is analytically true; science now becomes a nonempirical discipline.[516] Fifth, the testing of theories is circular on (2′). If one attempts to test a theory by comparing its predictions with the results of observation, both the predictions and the observation report will have to be expressed in the same language, with the same meanings attached

[512] See Achinstein [1968], pp. 92–95, and Shapere [1966], p. 57, for this line of argument. Feyerabend has made several attempts to escape this criticism. In Feyerabend [1965b], he attempts to employ an isomorphism condition; Achinstein [1968], pp. 93–94, supplies a counterexample to this attempt.

[513] See Achinstein [1968], pp. 95–96.

[514] Presumably any rejection of a principle of a theory is a change in theory. However, in light of the first criticism, we cannot be entirely certain what it is to be a principle of a theory.

[515] Recall from the discussion of Putnam's work in Sec. IV–B–1 that the mark of a statement being analytic is that its denial requires alteration in the meanings of its terms.

[516] See Achinstein [1968], p. 96, for this line of argument.

to descriptive terms. Suppose now that the theory's prediction—say *P*—disagrees with the results of observation; then the observation report must entail not–*P*. The prediction, *P*, however is part of the theory and its denial presumably alters the theory and hence changes the meaning of the descriptive terms in *P*. It follows, then, from (2′) that the descriptive terms occurring in *P* and not–*P* cannot have the same meanings. Hence no observation report is possible which could possibly disconfirm or falsify the theory. That is, the only observation reports which are relevant to testing the theory will be those which are consistent with the theory. All testing of theories thus is circular.[517]

What is the force of these objections? The first could be answered by supplying criteria of meaning change and theory change. The second, third, and fifth objections conceivably could be circumvented by developing some new procedures for comparing theories, such as those discussed in Section II-B of the Afterword, although I doubt any such attempt will succeed. The fourth argument seems to me unanswerable. Moreover, Feyerabend has offered no convincing reasons for even the plausibility of (2′). Hence (2′) should be rejected as unacceptable.

Does version (2″) fare any better? Can it avoid the above objections to (2′)? The first objection can be met by supplying precise criteria for theory change and meaning change. Since (2″) requires that only some of the principles of a theory contribute to the meanings of terms, (2″) is able to escape the second, third, and fourth objections to (2′). However, in doing so the incommensurability between competing theories will have to be restricted; for the possibility now occurs that incompatible theories will employ the same terms with the same meanings (for example, if they share the same principles which contribute to meanings, but hold other incompatible theoretical principles). Hence, the incommensurability of theories must be demonstrated anew for particular pairs of theories. So long as some of the theory's predictions do not contribute to the meanings of terms employed in predictions, the fifth objection can be circumvented. Accordingly, if precise and acceptable criteria of theory change and meaning change are supplied, a version of (2″) might be possible which escapes the criticisms which undermined (2′); the price of that escape would be that the incom-

517 A number of different arguments for the circularity of testing have been advanced. The one just given is an amalgamation of considerations raised on pp. 93 and 96–97 of *ibid.*; other arguments are found in Scheffler [1967], pp. 49–53, and in Shapere [1966], pp. 57–62. Shapere's development also considers Feyerabend's three proposals for testing global theories where there are no common facts for assessing their relative merits, and he raises the sorts of objections we raised at the end of Sec. V–B–1–d–i.

mensurability of theories could at best be maintained in a restricted version.

The above discussion suggests, but does not establish, that some version of (2″) might be viable. No plausible candidates for such a version have been produced. Moreover, there is reason to suppose that the precise specification of a satisfactory version of (2″) will prove exceedingly difficult. For, as was indicated above, such a version must include a precise criterion of meaning change; the following considerations suggest that the formulation of such a criterion will require making significant progress in the solution of some of the most intractable problems in the philosophy of language. The question whether the meaning of a term T has changed can be reformulated equivalently as the question whether T as used at time t is synonymous with T as used at time t'; thus the problem of meaning change is intimately tied to the problem of synonymity. The fact that the latter problem has resisted solution despite intensive effort [518] strongly suggests that an adequate account of meaning change will be difficult or impossible to obtain. Furthermore, it is extremely unlikely that a precise criterion of meaning change can be obtained through an analysis of meaning; for the recent literature on meaning suggests that the latter will be extremely difficult or impossible to obtain.[519] As the formulation of a criterion of meaning change thus seems to require successfully attacking long-standing unsolved problems in the philosophy of language, the chances of developing a satisfactory criterion of meaning change, hence a satisfactory version of (2″), seem remote.[520]

Let us suppose, however, that these problems can be circumvented and a sufficiently precise version of (2″) has been produced. Even

[518] For the difficulties involved, see the discussion of Quine in Sec. IV–B–1 above, and also the various articles in Linsky [1952]; a good summary of the problems involved in obtaining a criterion of synonymity is found in Alston [1964], pp. 41–44.

[519] For a survey of the difficulties, see Alston [1964], Chs. 1 and 2. Austin [1961], Ch. 2, argues that the question, "What is the meaning of a word?," is incoherent, and so a clear analysis of the meanings of terms is impossible; related discussion is found in Austin [1962].

[520] Scheffler [1967] attempts to avoid these difficulties by construing scientific meaning as being *purely* referential—in the sense that only sameness of reference is of importance in science (Ch. 2, esp. p. 57). This move seems to me highly questionable for several reasons. First, differences in sense do seem to make a difference in science—at least to the extent of having a heuristic role in suggesting moves for extending, testing, and articulating theories. Second, when dealing with nonobservable or theoretical entities, the only way to determine that two persons are using a term with the same reference is to consider the senses they attach to them. Third, regardless whether science could in principle get along with purely

though we do not know the details of such a version, some general conclusions can be drawn about the viability of such a version of (2″) for the purpose of *Weltanschauungen* analyses. To do so an implicit feature of (2″) needs to be made explicit. As formulated above, (2″) requires that terms occur as constituents of a theory's principles; it also requires that meanings be attached to these terms. This in effect requires that the principles of theories be interpreted sentences of some particular language—that is, that they be propositions in the medieval sense of the term (however, they are not propositions in the modern sense of the term!).[521] In effect, then, the principles of a theory are propositions used to *formulate* the theory. The propositions of a theory collectively do not constitute the theory; for as 'theory' typically is employed when referring, for example, to the special theory of relativity or quantum theory,[522] theories are extralinguistic, hence are not collections of propositions. This can be seen from a consideration how theories are individuated. Suppose a theory first is formulated in English, and then is translated into French. The English formulation and the French formulations constitute different collections of propositions; if theories were collections of propositions, then the translation of the theory into French would produce a new theory; but, of course, it does not—it is the same theory reformulated in French. Similarly, quantum

---

extensional or referential languages, as a matter of fact they employ languages whose meaning includes sense as well as reference; and differences in sense do affect the ease with which scientists holding opposing theories or viewpoints can communicate and resolve their differences; thus to construe scientific meaning as being purely referential is to ignore much that is characteristic of scientific discourse. Still, as my [1973a] indicates, his suggestion embodies an important insight.

[521] The discussion which follows turns centrally on the fact that the principles of a theory, as construed by (2″), are propositions in the medieval sense but are not propositions in the modern sense of the term. As such the distinction must be made explicit or my line of argument may be missed. By the medieval sense of 'proposition', following Geach [1962], p. 25, I understand propositions to be things we propound or put forward, which may or may not be asserted. In this sense, propositions are linguistic entities which contain the sentences of a particular language; roughly speaking, propositions become statements when asserted. The modern sense of 'proposition' refers to a supposed kind of nonlinguistic entity which is signified by propositions in the medieval sense. In what follows 'proposition' always is used in the medieval sense. The reader who finds this use of 'proposition' confusing is advised to read 'statement' for 'proposition' in what follows; it is important to keep in mind that the principles of a theory need not all have been asserted, and so, strictly speaking, they are not statements; however whenever they are asserted they become statements.

[522] This is not the only use of 'theory' in science; in particular, 'theory' can be used to refer to an organized field of study or scientific tradition as in 'the theory of heat' or 'electromagnetic theory'; see Bromberger [1963], pp. 83–84, for a fuller discussion of the differences between these two uses of 'theory'.

theory can be formulated equivalently as wave mechanics or as matrix mechanics; whichever way it is formulated, it is the same theory, though its formulation as wave mechanics will constitute a collection of propositions which is different from the collection of propositions resulting from its formulation as matrix mechanics. Thus theories are extralinguistic and are not collections of propositions. In general a theory admits of a number of different formulations, each of which can be construed as a different collection of propositions. Under (2″) the principles of a theory are propositions. Accordingly, the principles of a theory are not, strictly speaking, constituents of the theory, but rather are constituents of a particular formulation of the theory; and different formulations of the same theory will employ different theoretical principles. We will assume that the theoretical principles of a formulation of a theory are all those propositions in the collection which constitute the formulation. These observations clearly indicate that (2″) is not about theories, but rather is about formulations of theories.

So clarified, (2″) asserts that some of the propositions (theoretical principles) in a particular formulation of a theory contribute to the meanings of terms occurring in them. While it is clear that this is true for some formulations of theories,[523] it is less clear whether this is so for all formulations of all theories. However, for the sake of argument we will assume (2″) true for all formulations of theories. Any alteration of the meanings attached to the terms occurring in a proposition results in a different proposition. Since formulations of theories are collections of propositions, any alteration in the meanings of the terms occurring in the theoretical principles of a formulation results in a new collection of propositions which may or may not be a formulation of the same theory.[524] More important, any change in a theory will require alteration in any full formulation of a theory.[525] Whenever the required al-

[523] That it is follows from the fact that in the initial formulation of a theory, theoretical terms sometimes are introduced definitionally; for example, in the initial formulations of thermodynamics 'entropy' was introduced definitionally. For a comprehensive discussion of the issues involved in determining when the introduction of terms is definitional, see Achinstein [1958], pp. 98–105; related discussion is found in Scheffler [1967], Ch. 3.

[524] There are three possibilities: the resulting collection of propositions may be a reformulation of the same theory, a formulation of a different theory, or else may fail to be a formulation of any theory at all.

[525] The qualification 'full formulation' is essential; in actual practice a science often employs partial formulations of theories which cover only aspects of the theory or else the theory with restricted scope; for example, elementary physics texts present partial formulations of classical mechanics which formulate only those portions of the theory which do not require recourse to differential equations. Depending on the partial formulation, various changes in theory may or may not require alteration in the partial formulation.

terations involve the replacement of theoretical principles which contribute to the meanings of terms by different principles which make inequivalent contributions to the meanings of terms, a change in the meanings of the terms will result.[526] These changes in meaning result in a new formulation of the theory. These observations indicate that a defensible version of (2″) will be no stronger than the following:

(2‴) In a particular formulation of a theory, some of the theoretical principles contribute (possibly in a context-dependent manner) to the meanings of some of the terms used in that formulation. Any changes in the theory which require alterations in that formulation involving the replacement of principles contributing to the meanings of terms by new principles making different contributions to the meanings of terms will result in a change in meaning.

We now turn to a consideration of how adequate (2‴) is for the purposes of *Weltanschauungen* analyses. First, (2‴) does not support the contention that accepting a theory determines the meanings of any terms; at best it shows that accepting a particular formulation of a theory determines the meanings of some of the terms. Second, it is fully compatible with (2‴) that a given person may employ a number of different formulations of the same theory in different situations for different purposes; and it is an open possibility that different meanings may be attached to the same terms in these different formulations. Third, (2‴) leaves open the possibility that two people who attach different meanings to the same sentences might be able to communicate freely about the theory; whether this possibility can be realized will depend on the solution of some general problems in the philosophy of language concerning the extent to which relatively full communication between individuals requires that they attach exactly the same meanings to terms. Thus, for example, Kuhn may be mistaken when he assumes that persons sharing a disciplinary matrix attach the same meanings to terms.[527] Fourth, (2‴) lends relatively little support to the contention that different and incompatible theories are noncomparable or incommensurable; by itself it certainly does not support any general incommensurability claims. Although (2‴) allows the possibility that two theories could be formulated in such a way that the meanings of the terms in the formulation of the one theory are inconsistent with theoretical principles in the formulation of the other, it also

[526] A more precise statement of this is impossible in the absence of a precise criterion of meaning change.

[527] For related discussion on this contention of Kuhn's, see his paper and my commentary on it in Session VI below.

allows that alternative formulations of theories are possible in general. This leaves open the possibility that one may be able to compare the two theories using different formulations phrased in a common language.[528] To demonstrate that two theories are incommensurable, it thus would be necessary to show that the two theories admit of no possible formulations which employ a common vocabulary. Fifth, for analogous reasons, (2‴) does not support the contention that a theory (for example, classical particle mechanics) cannot be reduced to another theory which is incompatible with it (for example, relativistic particle mechanics) in accordance with Nagel's account of theory reduction (see Sec. II–F above); for it is compatible with (2‴) that the two theories may be given formulations which satisfy the condition of meaning invariance—Feyerabend's and Kuhn's contentions to the contrary not withstanding. Sixth, part of the point of (2) was to establish that different theories carry with them their own *Weltanschauungen*, where different *Weltanschauungen* attach different meanings to terms. Thesis (2‴) is the strongest defensible version of (2), and it does not establish this conclusion; at best it supports (but does not establish) the contention that *Weltanschauungen* are determined by formulations of theories. From this it would follow that more than one *Weltanschauungen* is possible for a given theory.[529] Although (2‴) does not lend support to a number of the more extreme claims made on the basis of (2), it does support some of the more moderate ones. In particular, it does support Toulmin's contention that when a theory is learned or formulated, at least some of the terms used to formulate the theory undergo a language shift—that is, undergo alteration in meanings. For if (2‴) is correct, some of the principles of a theory's formulation do contribute to the meanings of some terms; so if they have pretheoretic meaning the incorporation of these terms into the formulation of the theory will alter their meaning.

To conclude our assessment: Two quite distinct forms of theses (2) are encountered in the *Weltanschauungen* analyses under consideration. The stronger form, (2′), proved untenable. Some version of the weaker form, (2″), may be defensible. A precise formulation of a de-

[528] Notice that what is being claimed here is that such common-language formulations may *in principle* be possible—not that it will be easy to find such a formulation in practice. Even if such common-language formulations are in principle possible, in practice it may prove exceedingly difficult or impossible to invent such a language and give them such formulations; if so the comparison of the two theories may prove a practical impossibility. Nothing in my argument depends on the practical possibilities of obtaining such common-language formulations.

[529] This follows only if it is assumed that a theory formulation carries with it a *Weltanschauung*; the reasonableness of this assumption is considered in subsection (d) below.

fensible version of (2″) faces formidable difficulties, will be about formulation of theories rather than theories, and will be no stronger than version (2‴). Such a version is incapable of supporting most of the contentions *Weltanschauungen* analyses have attempted to base on thesis (2), though it would support some of the more modest claims which have been made. As such, a defensible version of (2) does not seem to shed enough illumination on the nature of theories to justify the effort required to formulate it; that it sheds so little illumination is not surprising once it is realized that theories are not linguistic entities.[530]

(c) OBJECTIVITY OF SCIENCE

Some critics (especially Scheffler [1967]) charge that *Weltanschauungen* analyses present a subjective view of science in which the objective nature of things has no place in the acceptance or rejection of theories. Although this charge is based to a large extent on theses (1) and (2), thesis (3) also is viewed as contributing to the subjective view of science that emerges from such analyses. Thesis (3) maintains that (i) what counts as a fact is determined by the *Weltanschauung* associated with a theory, (ii) there is no neutral set of facts for assessing the relative adequacy of two competing theories, and (iii) the adequacy of a theory must be assessed according to standards set by its associated *Weltanschauung*. Does not thesis (3) thus maintain that there are different facts for different theories? If so, will not the testing of theories be circular, each theory being supported by its own facts? For those *Weltanschauungen* analyses which maintain (2′), the answers to these questions are affirmative; for as our fifth objection to (2′) indicated, the only evidence (facts?) relevant to the testing of a theory must be consistent with the theory, and so the testing of a theory will be circular. This leaves no place for the objective nature of things to exert any influence in determining the adequacy of a theory, and so it seems the acceptance or rejection of theories must be solely on the basis of "subjective factors"; such a view of science clearly is unacceptable. However, the fact that this unacceptable view of science follows from (2′) by itself (see the previous subsection) indicates that these arguments do nothing in the way of showing (3) unacceptable.

In order to determine whether thesis (3) is defensible when di-

[530] From a different set of considerations, Shapere [1966], pp. 67–70, comes to much the same conclusion—that considerations of meaning will be of little help in understanding the workings of scientific concepts and theories.

vorced from (2′), it will be necessary to become clear about certain features of facts. The recent literature on the nature of facts[531] makes it clear that facts are not some peculiar sort of entity; rather, as Strawson puts it, "facts are what [empirical] statements (when true) state." [532] This yields a number of important consequences. First, facts are expressed in language, being what is asserted or propounded by empirical propositions. Second, any statement of fact must be empirically true. Third, whenever it is true that *S* knows that *P*, and *P* is an empirical proposition, then it is a fact that *P*. Fourth, facts are the end-product of observation; for as was indicated in subsection (a) above, whenever *S* observes that *P*, *S* sees that *P* and *P* must be empirically true; hence, whenever *S* correctly observes that *P* it is a fact that *P*.[533] Fifth, to the extent that languages differ in what they are able to express, it follows from the first point that languages differ in the facts they can assert. Sixth, to the extent that conceptual differences are reflected in language, it follows from the fifth point that one's conceptual apparatus may limit the facts one can entertain. Seventh, as was indicated in subsection (a) above, one's prior knowledge and beliefs influence what one is able to correctly observe; hence it follows from the fourth point that differences in one's knowledge and beliefs affect the facts one can observe to be the case. Eighth, if it is assumed that all scientists are dealing with a common world and that an empirical proposition is empirically true if and only if it correctly describes that world, then it follows from the above points that there cannot be incompatible facts; hence, no matter how different two persons are linguistically or conceptually, no matter how much their knowledge and beliefs may differ, whatever facts they determine must be compatible. Ninth, to the extent that different languages are capable of stating the same things, those languages are capable of stating the same facts; and they can state the same facts in such cases even if it is impossible for speakers of the two languages ever to determine that they are asserting the same thing.[534]

[531] See especially Herbst [1960], Strawson [1950], and White [1970], esp. Ch. 4; see also Suppe [1973a].

[532] P. 38 in the 1964 reprinting of Strawson [1950].

[533] This does not imply that all facts are observable; in this respect I reject certain of Herbst's [1960] contentions about facts. Also, notice that here, as in subsection (a) above, the possibility of inference-aided observation is being ignored; see note 503 above. For arguments that the conclusion just drawn follows for inference-aided observation, see my [1973d]. The same comments apply to the seventh point, below.

[534] That is, it is possible that speakers of two languages who are in a radical translation situation with respect to each other may possess the same body of facts;

We now are ready to assess thesis (3). First one minor point needs to be clarified. Clauses (i) and (iii) make reference to the *Weltanschauung* associated with a theory; in virtue of the previous subsection's discussion this must be interpreted as referring to the *Weltanschauung* associated with a particular formulation of the theory. Clause (i) says that what counts as a fact is determined by the *Weltanschauung;* this is ambiguous. It could mean that the *Weltanschauung* determines what things are empirically true, hence determines what the facts are; thus every *Weltanschauung* creates its own world with its own facts.[535] This interpretation of (i) is unacceptable unless one is willing to embrace an idealism; furthermore it is incompatible with the working assumption that science deals with a common world. In the absence of any compelling reasons for accepting such an idealism or denying the existence of a common world, there seems no reason to accept (i) under this interpretation. Another reading of (i) is that the *Weltanschauung* determines which facts one is able to entertain. To the extent that the *Weltanschauung* incorporates a particular language with meanings attached to terms, one's conceptual apparatus, and one's prior knowledge and beliefs, it follows from the fifth, sixth, and seventh points above about facts that the *Weltanschauung* does determine which facts one can entertain. Another reading of (i) is that the *Weltanschauung* determines which of the facts one can entertain are to be taken as relevant to the adequacy or development of the theory; to the extent that the *Weltanschauung* incorporates standards for determining the relevance of information to the theory, this interpretation of (i) also is defensible.

Finding a defensible interpretation of (ii) is more problematic. According to (ii) there can be no neutral set of facts for assessing the relative adequacy of two competing theories; this admits of several interpretations. The first interpretation of (i) above construed the *Weltanschauung* as creating its own world with its own facts. Since two different theories cannot have the same formulation, hence cannot have the same associated *Weltanschauung,* it is a corollary to this interpretation of (i) that different theories cannot be about the same world and facts. This suggests that (ii) be interpreted as maintaining that facts

---

in such a situation they may not be able to determine that they do possess the same body of facts. For a fuller discussion of the relation between facts and their linguistic expression, and an analysis of facts which is compatible with the above observations, see Suppe [1973a].

[535] This is the interpretation of (i) which would be required if thesis (1′) were maintained; as the *Weltanschauungen* analyses under consideration need not be committed to (1′), there is no need for them to interpret (i) in this manner.

are specific to theories with different theories being concerned to accommodate different sets of facts, and so there is no single set of facts which can be used to judge the adequacy of two competing theories. If one assumes that the scientific enterprise is concerned to investigate a common world, this is an unacceptable interpretation; moreover, this interpretation is plausibly only as a corollary to the first interpretation of (i), which we saw to be defensible only if one embraces an idealism. Since none of the *Weltanschauungen* analyses need be committed to such an idealism, and since there are no compelling reasons for embracing such an idealism, it seems unreasonable to saddle *Weltanschauungen* analyses with this interpretation of (ii). Another way to interpret (ii) is as claiming that it is impossible to express facts in a language which is neutral with respect to two theories—in the sense that both theories could be formulated in the same language. The considerations raised in the previous subsection in assessing (2″) indicate that there is no reason to suppose this generally is so; in particular, (2‴) does not lend much support to the contention. Clause (ii) also can be interpreted as claiming that the proponents of two competing theories will be unable to agree which facts the competing theories must accommodate if they are to be adequate. The following considerations, which will be amplified and defended below, indicate that this is a wholly defensible claim.

Theories have as their subject matter a certain range of phenomena and they are developed for the purpose of providing answers to a variety of questions about the phenomena in that range. These questions may include requests for explanations, the nature of regularities among the phenomena, and so on. The range of questions the theory is intended to answer about the phenomena is quite selective; the theory is not expected to be able to answer all possible questions which could be asked about the phenomena in its range. (Consider, for example, the variety of questions one can ask about mechanical phenomena which classical mechanics or quantum theory is totally incapable of answering.) Theories provide the means for answering these questions by presenting generalized descriptions of aspects of the phenomena. For a theory to be adequate not only must these generalized descriptions be true, but also they must be capable of answering the questions the theory is committed to answering. Which facts are relevant to assessing the adequacy of the theory will be a function of which aspects of the phenomena the theory describes and which questions it is committed to answering. It is perfectly conceivable that the proponents of different competing theories may disagree on what sorts of questions ought to be answered by an adequate theory for a particular range of phenomena (as the Copernicans and the Ptolemaists did disagree), the two theories being introduced to deal with different sets of questions; in such a case different facts will be relevant to assessing the adequacy of the two competing theories.[536] Finally, (ii) can be interpreted as claiming that the theory one holds may limit the facts that one is able to determine observationally, and so proponents of competing theories who agree on what kinds of facts are to be accommodated may disagree on what the facts are which must be accommodated. The seventh point above about facts indicates that one's knowledge and beliefs may influence what facts one is able to determine observationally. Persons accepting different theories for a given range of phenomena thus may be able to observe different facts, and so may disagree on what the facts are which a theory must accommodate. The following, possibly apocryphal, story illustrates the point. After having discovered the moons of Jupiter through his telescope, Galileo is supposed to have tried to convince a group of Ptolemaist church fathers of the fact that Jupiter has moons by having them look through his telescope; the fathers looked through the telescope but denied that they saw that Jupiter had any moons. Although they saw the same light images Galileo did, their background beliefs (which, as Ptolemaic astronomers, included the belief that there was a single center of rotation in the universe) made it impossible for them to see that these light images were of satellites rotating around a second center of rotation, and so they failed to see that Jupiter has moons.[537] As such they failed to observe that Jupiter has moons, and so it was not an observational fact for them that Jupiter has moons.

Clause (iii), which says that the adequacy of a theory must be assessed according to standards set by its associated *Weltanschauungen*, has evoked the greatest controversy, prompting critics to charge that scientific change is fundamentally irrational under the *Weltanschauungen* analyses. If all the relevant standards for assessing the adequacy of a theory are determined by the *Weltanschauungen* associated with its formulations, then each theory carries with it its own standards of adequacy. If there are no higher adequacy standards against which all theories must be measured, there will be no rational way for choosing between two competing theories which are both adequate with respect

[536] The issues raised here involve the problem of scientific domains which Shapere and Nickles discuss in their contributions to Session VII.

[537] It is often claimed the fathers dogmatically refused to admit what they saw; however, on a plausible analysis of seeing that and observation, the account just given is more likely to be accurate. More important, on the sort of analysis of seeing that presented by Dretske [1969] or indicated in note 505 above, it can be shown that the fathers rationally could have failed to see that Jupiter had moons in the way just indicated.

to their own adequacy criteria. In such a case, one can only irrationally choose which standards to accept; to avoid such irrationality (iii) must be rejected.[538] It is important to realize what this criticism is and is not claiming. First, the criticism does not deny that the *Weltanschauungen* associated with formulations of a theory do impose adequacy standards for that theory, and it does not deny that these standards may vary from theory to theory. What it does deny is that these are the only adequacy standards involved in the assessment of a theory. In particular, the criticism claims there must be some general standards for assessing the relative adequacy of competing theories; these general standards could be common ingredients of all *Weltanschauungen* or they could be "higher order" standards for assessing the various adequacy claims made about competing theories on the basis of the standards supplied by their respective *Weltanschauungen*. A consideration of these latter claims provides a convenient means of evaluating (iii).

The following observations about theories will be useful in determining what is relevant to the assessment of a theory. Suppose a theory is proposed and given formulation *T*. The formulation *T* contains various generalized descriptions offered as characteristic of some class of phenomena.[539] This class of phenomena is the theory's *intended scope*. A necessary condition for the adequacy of the theory is that these generalized descriptions be empirically true for that intended scope. Like most descriptions, these generalized descriptions are selective as to which aspects of the phenomena are described. Typically certain aspects of the phenomena within the theory's intended scope are selected as parameters, and the theory attempts to describe the phenomena only insofar as it involves just these parameters. If the values of these parameters are independent of any factors which are not incorporated as parameters and the generalizations provided by *T* are empirically true, then these generalizations will describe the phenomena as they actually occur. However, it is a rare occasion when the selected parameters meet this independence condition; in most cases the selected parameters are influenced by factors not selected as parameters. In such cases the theory does not purport to describe the phenomena as it actually occurs. Rather, the generalizations afforded by *T* purport to describe the

[538] See Scheffler [1967], Ch. 4, for this line of criticism; Shapere [1964] also raises the charge of irrationality against the *Weltanschauungen* accounts of scientific change.

[539] If laws are construed as a species of theory, this may not be correct. There is some reason to suppose that historical explanations involve singular laws (see Donagan [1964]), in which case not all theories would contain general descriptions. Analogues to the following observations can be made for such singular theories, if any, and so this complication will be ignored here.

contribution of the interaction of these parameters to the phenomena within the theory's intended scope. That is, the generalizations provide descriptions of what the phenomena *would have been* had the systems involved been isolated from all influences except those which are incorporated as parameters of the theory; as such the generalized descriptions of the phenomena provided by *T* are counterfactual descriptions of what the phenomena would have been under idealized conditions. Thus, for example, classical particle mechanics does not purport to describe mechanical phenomena as they actually occur, but rather only describes what the phenomena would have been if only the position and momenta of a finite number of bodies were involved; it does so by construing the phenomena within its intended scope as if they were isolated systems of extensionless point masses in a frictionless vacuum. In such cases the adequacy of the theory requires that *T*'s generalizations be counterfactually true of the phenomena within the theory's intended scope.[540] Whenever *T*'s descriptions have this counterfactual status, the determination of their empirical truth is problematic. Not only does one have all the usual inductive problems of assessing truth, but there are methodological problems as well. Whatever assessment is made of the truth of *T*'s generalizations must be based on data obtained from experimental situations in which the idealized conditions of being isolated from outside influences are realized or approximated. In general, it cannot be directly ascertained that the systems involved are so isolated; rather, on the basis of often involved theories of experimental control and design, one determines which experimental setups approximate such isolation to within experimental error; such theories of experimental design and control may be underdetermined by available evidence, and there is room for legitimate disagreement over which experimental data represents such isolated systems and thus is relevant to the assessment of *T*'s generalizations.[541] In such cases it seems wishful thinking to suppose there is some agreed upon *summum bonum* of experimental methodology for assessing competing standards of experimental design and control.

Even if the proponents of two competing theories with the same intended scope could agree on appropriate canons of experimental de-

540 For further details and justification of these claims, see Suppe [1972b]; see also Sec. II–C above and Sec. V–C below for related discussion.

541 An example of such disagreement would be the controversy earlier in this century in psychology over whether introspective evidence was relevant in the assessment of behavioral theories, the charge leveled against such evidence by radical behaviorists being that their gathering did not involve sufficient experimental controls. For further discussion of the role of experimental design in the assessment of theories, see the discussion in Sec. IV–E above and my [1973d].

sign and control, it does not follow that they would agree in the assessment of the relative merits of their competing theories. For the factual truth of the generalized descriptions provided by formulations of their theories is only a necessary, and not a sufficient, condition of their adequacy.[542] Once it is granted that theories legitimately can limit their descriptions of phenomena within their intended scopes to counterfactual descriptions in terms of selected parameters, one allows the possibility of a variety of different empirically true theories for the same intended scope. If any choice is to be made between such "competing" theories it will have to be on some basis other than their factual adequacy. It is at this point that considerations of simplicity and theoretical fecundity come in. For in proposing the theory, one does not merely commit oneself to the counterfactual truth of *T*'s generalized descriptions; one also advances the theory as a fruitful source of answers to a number of questions viewed as important.[543] Whatever assessment one makes of the theory's fruitfulness, by however objective standards, must be parasitic on some assessment of which questions need to be answered. And even granting that the empirical truth of *T*'s generalized descriptions is not in question, different assessments of which questions the theory ought to answer lead to different assessments of its fruitfulness, hence its acceptability and adequacy. Furthermore, it is perfectly legitimate that different persons concerned with a given range of phenomena will be interested in it for different reasons, hence will view different questions as important, and thus will view different proposed theories as adequate. There seem to be no rational canons for determining which questions ought to be asked about a given range of phenomena, and so there seems to be no reason to suppose that there will be a *summum bonum* for assessing the fruitfulness of competing theories, for to do so would be to assume there was some objective criterion for deciding which questions ought to be asked.[544]

542 This is an idealized condition; in general factual confirmation of the theory is the most that can be determined and such confirmation is a necessary condition for being judged adequate.

543 See the related discussion above concerning clause (ii) which amplifies this point further.

544 Indeed, it seems relatively clear from the history of science that as a science develops there is a change in which questions the science wishes to answer. This opens the possibility that a theory which once was judged fruitful will cease to be so because the questions asked change, and although the theory could answer the questions originally held important, one's assessment of which questions are important changes and the theory becomes inadequate because it is incapable of answering the questions which later gain prominence.

These observations indicate that any attempt to analyze the "logic" of the acceptance of theories will become intimately involved with problems in erotetic logic (the logic of questions and answers); for a basic account of erotetic logic,

While the above observations in no way constitute a comprehensive treatment of the factors affecting the adequacy of theories,[545] they are sufficient to support the following conclusions adjudicating between the contentions of clause (iii) and those of its critics reported above. Clause (iii) is correct in asserting that the adequacy of theories depends essentially on standards held by its proponents (namely which questions the theory should address itself to and what methodology is to be used to determine the counterfactual truth of *T*'s generalized descriptions), and that there is no reason why the same standards should prevail for all theories. On the other hand, the critics of clause (iii) are correct to the extent that they claim that there should be certain common standards for assessing the adequacy of all theories—namely that an adequate theory must provide empirically true descriptions or at least be empirically confirmed by the facts. That adequate theories must be empirically true provides an objective basis for accepting or rejecting theories; but subjective factors (for example, which questions one wants answered) exert a legitimate influence as well, and they do so without undermining the objectiveness of the scientific enterprise. As such there seems little support for Scheffler's belief that a *summum bonum* for making neutral assessments between competing theories is possible.[546]

Although thesis (3) can be read as propounding an irrational view of theory acceptance, we have seen that clauses (i) to (iii) admit of straightforward interpretations which are defensible and illuminate how theories are rationally assessed. Combining these various interpretations together, we obtain the following defensible version of (3).

(3′) Assuming that an idealism is unacceptable, that science is concerned with a common world, and formulations of theories determine or carry with them *Weltanschauungen* containing a particular language with meanings attached to its terms, one's conceptual apparatus, prior knowledge and beliefs, and standards for assessing the adequacy of a theory including standards determining the relevance of information and which questions the theory is committed to answer, and canons of experimental control and design; then the *Weltanschauung* determines which facts one can entertain, which of those facts are

see Harrah [1963]; an attempt to analyze theories in terms of erotetic logic is considered, briefly, in Sec. V–D below. Shapere's contribution to Session VII below is also germane to the issues under discussion.

545 For a fuller treatment of the factors for a restricted class of theories, see Suppe [1967], Chs. 3 and 4.

546 See Scheffler [1967], pp. 82–86.

relevant to the adequacy or development of the theory, and which facts one is able to determine observationally. Hence different *Weltanschauungen* associated with theories dealing with the same range of phenomena may result in different assessments of which facts must be accommodated by a theory adequate for that range of phenomena. There seem to be no "higher level" rules for assessing the judgments of competing *Weltanschauungen.* At the same time, however, the adequacy of theories does depend on the objective nature of things; for an adequate theory must be empirically true for its intended scope.

(d) GENERAL CONCLUSIONS ON THE ADEQUACY OF THE *Weltanschauungen* APPROACH

In Section V–B–1 we sketched the main features of the more important *Weltanschauungen* analyses of the nature of scientific theorizing; at the same time we considered criticisms of specific features of these various analyses. Despite significant differences in these analyses, in Section V–B–2 we saw that there was a common core of agreement among them. Theories carry with them a *Weltanschauung* which exerts a determining influence on the nature of scientific theorizing; the most important of these influences were summarized in theses (1) to (3). We then turned to an examination of these theses and discovered that while they could be interpreted in such a way as to divorce science from a determination of the objective nature of things, they need not be so interpreted. In particular, we saw that versions (1″), (2‴), and (3′) of theses (1), (2), and (3) were defensible *provided that* formulations of theories determine or carry with them *Weltanschauungen* meeting certain conditions and it is assumed that science deals with a common world. While our findings thus vindicate moderate versions of some of the more controversial claims made by the *Weltanschauungen* analyses, they have not yet shown the *Weltanschauungen* approach satisfactory; for we have not yet considered whether it is reasonable to assume that formulations of theories do carry with them the required sorts of *Weltanschauungen.*

In analyzing theses (1) to (3), we have discovered that *Weltanschauungen inter alia* must include a particular language with meanings attached to its terms in such a way that some theoretical principles contribute to the meanings of terms; one's conceptual apparatus, prior knowledge and belief, canons of experimental design and control, and standards for assessing the adequacy of the theory and the relevance of information to the theory; and a determination of which questions the theory is committed to answer. As such the *Weltanschauung* is an exceedingly complex entity, being approximately the whole of one's background, training, experience, knowledge, beliefs, and intellectual profile which is of possible relevance to working with a theory. Once this is realized, it becomes exceedingly doubtful whether a *Weltanschauung* can be the joint possession of a group of scientists—as, for example, Kuhn's analysis requires. For there is every reason to suppose that there will be enough individual variation between individuals—even among individuals engaged in close cooperation in research—that no two persons will share exactly the same *Weltanschauung*. It thus seems unwarranted to postulate that a publicly shared or agreed-upon formulation of a theory determines or carries with it a unique *Weltanschauung*. The most one can plausibly assume is that each person working with a theory possesses his own *Weltanschauung* and that persons employing the same formulation of a theory who are in relatively full methodological agreement possess rather similar *Weltanschauungen*.[547] (This is the sort of view Bohm advocates in his contribution to Session IV of the symposium.) This being so, some alterations are required in those analyses of scientific change (such as Kuhn's) which require the joint possession of a *Weltanschauung* by the members of a scientific community.

How plausible is it to suppose that each person working with a theory possesses a *Weltanschauung*? It depends on what one means by 'possessing a *Weltanschauung*'. One gets the impression from reading some of the *Weltanschauungen* analyses we have considered that the *Weltanschauung* is postulated as a single entity incorporating all of the above-mentioned components. To do so is to view the *Weltanschauung* as some sort of new, irreducible, and larger unit in the philosophy of science. But short of a commitment to a doctrine of conceptual frameworks permeating and interconnecting all intelletual activity, there is no reason to suppose a single entity such as the postulated *Weltanschauung* exists. Furthermore, unless the *Weltanschauung* possesses a structure or properties over and above the properties possessed by its components nothing is gained by postulating its existence; for any defensible point which can be made via the invocation of the *Weltanschauung* can be made more economically by referring to the language, theory formulations, experimental canons, standards, and so on, which we have seen that the working scientist implicitly or explicitly must

547 The above criticisms are developed more explicitly with specific reference to Kuhn's analysis in my contribution to Session VI below.

possess. None of the advocates of *Weltanschauungen* analyses have given us any plausible accounts of what these additional properties or structures might be, and so considerations of parsimony suggest that it is unreasonable to postulate the existence of the *Weltanschauung* as a new basic unit in the philosophy of science. Moreover, even if such additional properties or structures could be specified, there is good reason to suppose that the postulation of *Weltanschauungen* for individual scientists will be of little value in the philosophy of science. For, as we have seen above, such *Weltanschauungen* will have to be such that different scientists working with the same theories in the same scientific communities or traditions may possess different *Weltanschauungen*; as such the *Weltanschauungen* serve to emphasize the differences among such scientists. But what is characteristic of scientists in a given scientific community is that, despite their individual differences in background, language, experience, and so on, they are able to employ the same theories, and come to general agreement on the testing, articulation, and employment of theories. The explanation how this is possible is a central task of the philosophy of science; and as these features cut across differences in the *Weltanschauungen* of the scientists, there is little reason to suppose that the postulation of *Weltanschauungen* can shed much illumination on how this is possible. I conclude, then, that there is no reason to suppose that there is anything like a *Weltanschauungen* having the status of a single entity possessed by working scientists; and even if there were good reason to postulate such an entity, doing so would contribute little to our understanding of the scientific enterprise.[548] It is possible to employ the notion of a *Weltanschauung* without postulating its existence as a new basic unit in the philosophy of science. For it certainly is the case that individual scientists do have languages they use to formulate their theories; and they do possess, implicitly at least, various canons of experimental design which they employ in testing theories and doing experimental work, standards according to which they assess the adequacy of theories, questions they wish answered, and so forth. If by saying that scientists possess *Weltanschauungen* one *merely* wishes to call attention to the central roles these languages, canons, standards, and so forth, play in the way the scientist approaches experience, and also to emphasize that these are not fixed but rather vary from scientist to scientist and from time to time, then it is reasonable to say that scientists do possess

[548] Shapere [1966], pp. 70–71, comes to essentially the same conclusion, though for somewhat different reasons.

Weltanschauungen; in this case '*Weltanschauung*' is nothing more than a collective term to refer to the scientist's language, experimental canons, standards, and so on, together. Although it is reasonable to say that individual scientists possess their own *Weltanschauungen* in this sense, doing so runs a certain danger, for it does tend to suggest that something more is being claimed about *Weltanschauungen*—namely that one is postulating their existence in the unacceptable manner just indicated. As such it would seem preferable to eschew *Weltanschauungen* talk and instead speak of languages, theory formulations, experimental canons, standards, and so on. There is a point to the *Weltanschauung* approach, but what is sound about that approach can be obtained less misleadingly if one refuses to talk of *Weltanschauungen*.[549]

In summary, I conclude that it is unreasonable to postulate *Weltanschauungen* as the joint possession of a community of scientists; it also is unwarranted to postulate that *Weltanschauungen* are single entities possessed by individual scientists which are a basic and important new unit in the philosophy of science. To the extent that the *Weltanschauungen* approach involves the postulation of such entities it leads to a metaphysically bloated and epistemologically unacceptable picture of scientific theorizing. To the extent that the *Weltanschauungen* approach can be divorced from the postulation of such entities, it does provide a valid perspective for viewing at least some aspects of the scientific enterprise, for it is correct in insisting that the varying languages, experimental canons, standards, and so on, of the individual scientists do figure centrally in the ongoing activity of the scientific enterprise. Despite their defects the *Weltanschauungen* analyses have cast considerable illumination on the nature of the scientific enterprise. For example, most of the substance of theses (1″), (2‴), and (3′) can be divorced from the postulation or mention of *Weltanschauungen*, and when reformulated accordingly they still will be largely defensible. As such *Weltanschauungen* analyses have added greatly to our understanding of the ways in which theories are adequate, the effects of changing interests in the scientific community, and the nature of scientific development. Despite these successes, none of the *Weltanschauungen* analyses we have considered can be viewed as satisfactory. Finally, it should be observed that while these analyses have led to an improved understanding of scientific theorizing, through their concentration on formulations of theories to the exclusion of theories they

549 Toulmin does roughly this, and as such his analysis is not misleading in this way.

have failed to reveal anything of significance about the structure of scientific theories.

Although the above conclusions about the general adequacy of *Weltanschauungen* theories do follow, in my opinion, from the considerations we have raised, there is no consensus today among philosophers either about the general adequacy of the *Weltanschauungen* approach or on the relative strengths and weaknesses of the particular analyses we have considered. These questions still are the subject of open debate among philosophers of science. We now turn to a consideration of another alternative approach to analyzing the structure of scientific theories—an approach for which there is some reason to suppose that it might prove fruitful.

C. Semantic Approaches

Both the Received View and the *Weltanschauungen* analyses attempt to discover the nature of scientific theories through an examination of their linguistic formulations, and on occasion even seem to assume that the theory *is* its linguistic formulation. We have seen, however, that theories are not collections of propositions or statements, but rather are extralinguistic entities which may be described or characterized by a number of different linguistic formulations (Sec. V–B–2–b). This observation does not show that an adequate understanding of theories cannot come from an examination of the linguistic formulations of theories, but it does suggest that such an approach is likely to result in a distorted picture of the nature of scientific theories. Such an approach can provide a detailed analysis of the characteristic features of theory formulations, but unless one assumes that analogues to these features are distinctive features of theories themselves;[550] such an analysis reveals nothing about what is characteristic of theories except that their formulations have certain characteristics; moreover as there is no particularly good reason to suppose that such an assumption is true, such an approach is likely to result in the attribution to theories of characteristics they do not possess. Even if all the distinctive features of theory formulations were reflections of characteristics of theories, there is no guarantee that the most distinctive or characteristic features of theories are mirrored in the formulations of theories. These considerations suggest that a direct examination of theories themselves is likely to result

[550] For example, as the early Wittgenstein assumed that the logical structure of reality was mirrored by the logical structure of a logically perfect language; see Wittgenstein [1922].

in a more detailed and accurate analysis of the structure of theories than is possible if one concentrates one's attention on theory formulations.

Theories are extralinguistic entities which can be described by their linguistic formulations. The propositions in a formulation of a theory thus provide true descriptions of the theory, and so the theory qualifies as a model for each of its formulations.[551] This suggests that the semantic techniques of model theory (in the sense of Tarski [1936]) will be useful in analyzing the structure of scientific theories. This suggestion gains further plausibility when it is noted that in actual practice the presentation of a scientific theory often takes the form of specifying an intended model for the sentences used to formulate the theory; this is especially so when more complicated theories of the sort encountered in the physical sciences are involved.[552] Various writers have experimented with such a semantic or model-theoretic approach to theories; von Neumann's proof that wave mechanics and matrix mechanics are equivalent formulations of quantum theory essentially involves this approach, though he never attempted to extend his techniques to any general semantic analysis of theories;[553] Suppes has argued that the semantic approach of model theory is likely to be more fruitful than axiomatic approaches in analyzing theories, and has made some progress in determining the general features of such models.[554] Beth has also developed semantic analyses for specific theories, argued that such an approach will be more fruitful than axiomatic analyses of theory formulations, and given some general indications what sort of general analysis he has in mind;[555] van Fraassen has extended Beth's approach into a general semantic analysis of theories.[556] And the author independently has developed an analysis which closely resembles Beth's and van Fraassen's.[557] The results obtained by Beth, van Fraassen, and myself collectively constitute a comprehensive analysis

[551] 'Model' here is being used in the sense of a mathematical model for a formal system; the theory also qualifies as an iconic model if they are understood in the extended sense of Hesse [1966]; see Sec. IV–D for a discussion of that sense. Recall also that 'proposition' is used in this essay in the medieval sense; see note 521 above.

[552] Suppes [1967], p. 61, and van Fraassen [1970], p. 337.

[553] See von Neumann [1955]; see also van Fraassen [1970], pp. 329–330; Birkhoff and von Neumann [1936] does contain a number of hints at what a general analysis would be like.

[554] See Suppes [1962], [1967], and [1967a].

[555] See Beth [1948], [1949], [1961]; although not directly concerned with the development of this approach, portions of his [1963] are relevant.

[556] van Fraassen [1970]; see also his [1968] and [1972].

[557] See Suppe [1967], Ch. 2, [1972b], [1973d], and [1973e].

of the structure of scientific theories which is heir to von Neumann's pioneering work; a number of Suppes's results complement this analysis.[558] The remainder of the section is devoted to sketching the main outlines of our analysis.

Scientific theories have as their subject matter a class of phenomena known as the *intended scope* of the theory. The task of a theory is to present a generalized description of the phenomena within that intended scope which will enable one to answer a variety of questions about the phenomena and their underlying mechanisms; these questions typically include requests for predictions, explanations, and descriptions of the phenomena.[559] The theory does not attempt to describe all aspects of the phenomena in its intended scope; rather it abstracts certain parameters from the phenomena and attempts to describe the phenomena in terms of just these abstracted parameters. In effect the theory assumes that only the selected parameters exert an influence on the phenomena and thus that these parameters are uninfluenced by any other parameters in the phenomena. As such the theory assumes that the phenomena are *isolated* systems under the influence of just the selected parameters. In actual fact, however, the phenomena in the theory's intended scope rarely are isolated systems —the selected parameters are influenced by factors not included in the selected parameters—although under appropriate conditions sufficient experimental controls can be introduced to approximate the fiction of being isolated to within measurement error. But the theory is intended to characterize all the phenomena within its intended scope regardless whether such experimental controls are realized or not. In such cases where the phenomena do not approximate isolated systems, the theory's characterization will not take into account the influence of factors

558 Although Suppes's approach shows important agreements with our approach, it is less clear how much he would accept of the analysis which follows. Closely related to his approach is that of Sneed [1971]. For a discussion how Suppes's views differ from ours, see van Fraassen [1972], Part I. Another philosopher following a semantic approach who should be mentioned is Bunge; his views differ in many respects from those of the other authors cited, however. For his views, see his [1959].

559 Philosophers of science tend to ignore the fact that the descriptions of phenomena often are in terms of their underlying structures (for example, in terms of theoretical language), and thus often problematic. An important task of the theory is to make possible such description, and often this task is at least as important as that of predicting or explaining the phenomena. Indeed, one of the central problems in the development of quantum theory was how quantum level phenomena were to be described, and much of the controversy over the adequacy of the Copenhagen interpretation of quantum theory (see Sec. V–B–1–e) concerns how such phenomena are to be described; the problem is intimately tied to the question of quantum logic (see the references in n. 570 below).

not included in its selected parameters, and so will not provide an accurate characterization of the *actual* phenomena. However, if the theory is adequate it will provide an accurate characterization of what the phenomenon *would have been* had it been an isolated system; in effect this idealized characterization is of the contribution of the theory's selected parameters to the resulting phenomena. This indicates that what the theory actually characterizes is not the phenomena in its intended scope, but rather idealized replicas of those phenomena. Such idealized replicas of phenomena are called *physical systems.*[560]

Physical systems are idealized behavioral replicas of phenomena which can be specified solely in terms of the theory's selected parameters. A particular configuration of the physical system is a *state.* If the parameters of the theory are measurable, then a set of simultaneously determined values for the parameters is a representation of that state; that is, states of physical systems can be represented as n-tuples of numbers. The behavior of a physical system is its change in state over time. When states are represented by n-tuples of numbers, these n-tuples can be viewed as the coordinates of points in an n-dimensional space, in which case the behavior of a physical system can be represented by a trajectory through the space which intersects the coordinates representing states the physical system assumes in the order in which the system assumes those states. An illustration will clarify this account. Consider how classical particle mechanics would characterize an object released in free fall through a viscous medium. Classical particle mechanics construes phenomena as if they were isolated systems of extensionless point masses in a vacuum whose behavior is influenced solely by the momenta and positions of the point masses. As such the object free-falling in a viscous medium would be characterized as two point masses (corresponding to the earth and the body) interacting in a vacuum where only the positions and momenta of the two particles influence the behavior of the system. The parameters of the theory thus are the twelve position and momentum coordinates of the two bodies, and the state of a system at a given time will be the values of these coordinates. The behavior of the physical system will be the change in these states over time, and thus can be viewed as a sequence of states. Since position and momentum coordinates are measurable parameters, their values may be represented numerically, being the values one could obtain by measuring the coordinates relative to some

[560] The above essentially is a restatement of various observations about theories which were made in Secs. II–C and V–B–2–C. More detailed discussion of these points can be found in Suppe [1967], Sec. 1.3.3 and Ch. 2 *passim*; [1972b], Pt. II; and [1973e], Sec. IX.

frame of reference. The values obtained by simultaneously measuring all twelve of the position and momentum coordinates at time t thus is a representation of the state of the physical system at time t. These twelve values may be construed as the coordinates of a twelve-dimensional space, and so the behavior of the system can be represented as a directed curve through that space which intersects the points representing the states the physical system assumes in the order in which they are assumed.

Understanding the nature of physical systems enables us to see more clearly what the role of experimental design and control is in scientific theorizing. Suppose one wanted to use classical particle mechanics to predict the position and momentum of a falling body through a viscous medium at a certain time t', where it is known experimentally what the position and momentum of the body was at an earlier time t. This falling body situation does not meet the idealized conditions of being an isolated system of extensionless point masses in a vacuum, so the theory does not present a straightforward characterization of the phenomenon. Rather the theory only characterizes abstract replicas of the phenomena within its intended scope; that is, it provides a generalized description of those physical systems which, if the theory is correct, are all and only those physical systems which are idealized replicas of the phenomena within its intended scope. Furthermore, the characterization is such that if the state of a physical system is known for any one time t, a unique subsequent state can be determined for the physical system at each subsequent time t'. In order to use the theory to predict, the following must be done. At time t we have experimentally determined the momentum and position of the falling body; we also know experimentally what the mass of the earth is, the density of the viscous medium, and so on. To use the theory to predict, these data must be converted into data about what the state of the phenomenon would have been had the idealized conditions presupposed by the theory been met; in doing so various auxiliary hypotheses, correction factors, and so forth, are employed. The resulting corrected data is a numerical representation of the state of the physical system which is an abstract replica of the phenomenon. Having determined this state, the theory now can be used to predict what state the physical system will assume at time t'; the phenomenon of course will not be in this state at t', but the numerical values obtained do represent the values measurement of position and momentum of the phenomenon would have yielded had the idealized conditions assumed by the theory been realized. Then, employing the same procedures used to determine the state of the physical system at time t from the phenomena, only this time in reverse, one determines the predicted values of the position and momenta for the actual phenomenon at time t'. If the theory is correct these predicted values should be in agreement (within the limits of experimental error) with the values which would be obtained if measurements were performed on the phenomenon at time t'. These considerations indicate that an important function of experimental design is to determine the representation of phenomena by physical systems. The details how this is done have been analyzed by Suppes [1962] and myself, and will not be given here.[561]

Scientific theories are introduced for the purpose of characterizing the behavior of all the physical systems which are idealized replicas of phenomena within the intended scope of the theory. The theory itself is a structure which represents the behavior of each of these physical systems. In case the parameters of the theory are measurable, this structure can be a *phase space*—which is an n-dimensional space where the n parameters of the theory are the coordinates of the space.[562] The behaviors of the physical systems are represented by various configurations imposed on the phase space in accordance with the laws of the theory. Laws may be classified as deterministic or as statistical; they also may be classified as laws of coexistence, laws of succession, and laws of interaction. Depending where the law falls in this two-fold classification, different characteristic configurations are employed to represent the behavior of the physical systems. As an example of a *deterministic law of coexistence,* consider the Boyle-Charles ideal gas law which is represented by the equation '$PV = RT$' and says that at any given time the pressure, volume, and temperature of a gas will satisfy this equation. This in effect says that only those points in phase space whose coordinates satisfy this equation will be physically possible, and thus picks out a subset of phase space as being physically possible. In general, deterministic laws of coexistence select the physically possible subsets of the phase space. The laws of motion in classical mechanics are examples of *deterministic laws of succession.* As our earlier example from classical particle mechanics suggests, laws of succession select the physically possible trajectories in the phase space. An example of a *statistical law of coexistence* is the Boltzmann hypothesis that each microstate of a gas has equal probability. Such laws in effect specify a probability measure over the phase space, which specifies the probability that each state will be physically realized. In

[561] Suppes's analysis is presented in Suppes [1962] and was sketched in Sec. IV–E. His sort of account is worked out in fuller detail in terms of the analysis of theories presented here in Suppe [1967], Ch. 3, and especially in my [1973d].

[562] van Fraassen [1970] uses 'state space' instead of 'phase space'.

the social sciences a number of phenomena are construed as finite Markov chains. The laws of such theories are examples of *statistical laws of succession.* Such laws describe a transition probability matrix over the phase space. Finally, *deterministic and statistical laws of interaction* describe the effects of several different systems (of the sorts characterized by the above kinds of laws); the configurations they impose on the phase space are composites of the configurations already mentioned.[563] Regardless what sort of law is involved, the laws of the theory impose configurations on the phase space, and each of these configurations specifies the behavior or configuration of a particular physical system (for example, in classical particle mechanics corresponding to the behavior of each physical system there will be a trajectory in phase space). If all of the configurations save one are removed from phase space, the result is a physical system.[564] Thus theories are structures, these structures being phase spaces with configurations imposed on them in accordance with the laws of the theory.[565] The variety of laws which can be handled under this analysis

[563] See van Fraassen [1970], pp. 330–334, for fuller details. For further discussion of deterministic and statistical laws of succession on this proposal, see Suppe [1967], Ch. 2, where they are referred to as representations of state-transition mechanisms.

[564] The above account does not enable one to handle deterministic statistical laws of the sort encountered in quantum theory. However, if the analysis is expanded to allow the possibility of infinite-dimensional phase spaces, such theories can be accommodated. In such a case the representation of quantum theory will be that presented in von Neumann [1955] where the configurations are roughly viscous flows through an infinite-dimensional Hilbert space with projections of packets in those flows onto linear subspaces which are Borel spaces. For detailed proposals how such theories are to be represented under the present account, see van Fraassen [1968] and Suppe [1967], Sec. 2.3.2. In the case of such deterministic statistical laws, the account how phase spaces relate to physical systems and the phenomena within the theory's intended scope must be complicated; following Birkhoff and von Neumann [1936] this can be accomplished through the introduction of observation spaces; see Suppe [1967], Sec. 2.4, for a detailed account.

[565] As just presented, the analysis of theories identifies theories with configurations imposed on phase space; in doing so I have been following van Fraassen's and Beth's version of the analysis—in part because it simplifies exposition. In point of fact, however, I tend toward the opinion that it is a mistake to make this identification. My reasons are as follows. First, in theories such as classical particle mechanics, the physical systems characterized are n-body systems, where n may take on any finite value. For each value of n, a different dimension phase space is required. If theories are identified with configurations imposed on phase spaces, there will be an infinite number of theories comprising the theory of classical particle mechanics. Second, for relativistic theories, such as the special theory of relativity, it is natural to construe each frame of reference as determining a different set of configurations on a phase space. The interconnections between these different configurations is a central part of the theory (being for the special theory of relativity the portion of the theory covered by the Lorentz

suggests that any theory whose parameters are measurable can be accommodated. Thus even the statistical correlation theories common in the social sciences can be accommodated. And it recently has been shown that the analysis can be extended to cover qualitative theories with nonmeasurable parameters.[566]

This analysis of theories also leads to a straightforward treatment of the relation between theories and their formulations. A formulation of a theory employs certain *elementary statements* about physical systems. These statements express propositions to the effect that a certain physical magnitude m has a certain value r at a certain time t. Of the elementary statements of this sort which can be employed in formulating the theory, some will be true and others will not. Since the theory is a model of any of its formulations, the semantic truth of an elementary statement depends on circumstances obtaining in the configurated phase space which is the theory.[567] Specifically, for each elementary statement U there is a region $h(U)$ of the phase space H such that U is true if and only if the physical system's actual state is represented by an element of $h(U)$. The function h which determines the region $h(U)$ of space is called the *satisfaction function*; if E is the set of elementary statements, then the combination $\langle E, H, h\rangle$ of E, H, and h is a simple kind of formal language known as a *semi-interpreted language*.[568] These elementary statements can be then combined together into com-

---

group of transformations between frames of reference). Thus, to identify the theory with the configurations imposed on phase space seems a mistake. (This objection is not decisive, however, for it does seem possible to construe the configurations for all frames of reference as being imposed on the same phase space, and then construe the Lorentz transformations as being a law of coexistence.) For these two reasons it seems preferable to view the configurations imposed on phase space as being canonical mathematical replicas of theories, theories being structures which are not so intimately tied to frames of reference. This is the position I maintained in Suppe [1967], Ch. 2. However, the possibility raised in connection with my second objection suggests to me that it is more plausible than I thought there to identify theories with collections of configurations of phase spaces. Nonetheless, there is one consideration which still seems to me to count decisively against making such an identification: Such an identification clearly precludes extension of the analysis to theories with nonmeasurable parameters; but if such an identification is not made, the extension is straightforward as I have shown in my [1973e].

566 See Suppe [1973d] and [1973e] for details; the extension presupposes theories are not identified with phase spaces (see note 565).

567 It is important here to distinguish the semantic truth of sentences from the empirical truth of theories; on the account being presented, empirical truth of theories will be construed along the lines presented at the end of Sec. IV–C; see also Suppe [1971] and especially [1973e] for further details of this account of empirical truth for theories.

568 See van Fraassen [1967] for a detailed characterization of semi-interpreted languages.

pound statements in accordance with some logic or another. Exactly what that logic is depends on the theory. The sets *h(U)* which satisfy elementary statements *U* are defined in terms of the mathematical (that is, topological) structure of the phase space, and the structure of phase space is a major factor in determining the ways in which elementary statements can be combined together to form compound statements which are true or false of the phase space. The topological structure of phase space in classical particle mechanics is such that any truth functional combination of elementary statements will be true or false of the phase space; the logic of the theory thus is a Boolean algebra. However, the topological structure of phase space in quantum theory is such that not all truth-functional combinations of elementary statements will be either true or false (that is, certain combinations will be without physical significance); in this case the logic of the theory will be a nondistributive lattice. Thus theories are formulated in semi-interpreted languages on which a logic has been imposed; the topological structure of the theory (configurated phase space) is a major factor determining the natures of both the semi-interpreted language and the logic. As such the theory imposes restrictions on the sorts of languages which can be used for its formulation. Since the same languages are used to describe the phenomena within the theory's intended scope,[569] the theory also imposes restrictions on the ways in which phenomena can be described. Incidentally, these results indicate a definite advantage of this analysis of theories over other analyses. The problem of presenting a physical interpretation for quantum theory can be viewed as the problem of determining the logic of quantum theory.[570] As such this analysis of theories is highly compatible with work going on in the foundations of quantum theory; this suggests the analysis is an accurate reflection of theories as actually formulated in the sciences.

[569] Exactly how semi-interpreted languages can be employed to do this is dealt with in Suppe [1973e]; Beth's [1963] distinction between strict and amplified usage of language occupies a prominent place in the solution. The question is intimately involved with a number of issues concerning the physical significance of theories under this analysis (for example, what sorts of structural relations hold between phase spaces and reality under realistic and instrumentalistic construals of theories); in Suppe [1973e], written after this introduction, I deal with these and related issues.

[570] For a readable account of this approach to interpreting quantum theory and the motivation behind it, see Hooker [1972a]; more detailed discussions of aspects of this approach are found in Hooker [1972b] and [1972c]. The quantum logic approach was first introduced by Birkhoff and von Neumann [1936]; significant recent developments concerning quantum logic are found in Heelan [1970] and van Fraassen [1968].

The analysis of theories just outlined is still in the process of development. Still, I would submit that its development has preceded sufficiently far to indicate that it is a promising approach to analyzing theories, and that it does reveal much that is significant about the nature of scientific theories. Whether it ultimately will lead to an adequate picture of the nature of scientific theorizing will not become clear until it has been developed further.[571] In any case, it does seem clear that semantic approaches to the analysis of theories are a promising alternative to the linguistic formulation approaches of the Received View and the *Weltanschauungen* analyses.

D. Explanation and Theories

In certain employments scientific theories provide explanations of phenomena. The covering law model of scientific explanation tacitly assumes the Received View analysis of theories and analyzes the explanation of an event described by '*E*' as the derivation of '*E*' from the theory augmented by the specification of various boundary conditions holding for the event.[572] As with the Received View, the covering law model of explanation has been subjected to severe criticism in the last decade, many philosophers of science now deny its adequacy, and a number of alternative accounts of scientific explanation have been advanced.[573] Because of the intimate connection between theories and explanation, it is reasonable to suppose that these proposed alternatives might lead to or suggest alternative conceptions of theories, and vice versa.

Of the proposed alternative accounts of explanation, one of them—Sylvain Bromberger's—embodies a conception of theories we have not yet considered. Briefly, Bromberger's approach to explanation is to assimilate explanations to answers to certain kinds of questions. He first

[571] Some further developments are found in Suppe [1967], Chs. 3 and 4, [1973d], and [1973e]. The results there indicate the analysis is compatible with the defensible versions of theses (1″), (2‴), and (3′) of *Weltanschauungen* analyses which result when they are reformulated so as to eliminate the postulation of *Weltanschauungen*.

[572] See Hempel and Oppenheim [1948] for details. In its usual formulation, the Received View is not explicitly acknowledged, but it can be shown that if the laws employed constitute a theory (or portion thereof) that theory must be in accord with the Received View.

[573] Indeed, Toulmin's, Kuhn's, and Feyerabend's proposed analyses have been offered, in part, as alternative analyses of explanation; in addition alternatives have been proposed by Bromberger [1965], Dray [1957], Scriven [1962], Salmon [1970], and others.

introduces two notions—*p*-predicaments and *b*-predicaments. "A is in a p-predicament with regard to [question] *Q* if and only if, on *A*'s views, *Q* admits of a right answer, but *A* can think of no answer to which, on *A*'s views, there are no decisive objections."[574] "A statement of the form '*A* is in a b-predicament with regard to [question] *Q*' (in which '*A*' must be replaced by an expression referring to some person or persons, and '*Q*' by one referring to some question) is true if and only if the question mentioned in it admits of a right answer, but that answer is beyond what the person mentioned can conceive, can think of, can imagine, that is, is something that persons cannot remember, cannot excogitate, cannot compose."[575] Explanations, roughly speaking, then are characterized as informed answers to the question *Q* which provide facts sufficient to remove *A*'s p-predicament or b-predicament with regard to *Q*.[576] A theory's typical function with respect to p- and b-predicaments is to provide answers which remove the predicament, and Bromberger has attempted to work out in some detail an account how theories do so.[577] For our purposes, the details of his account are not important; what is important is the account of theories he presupposes:

> Let *Q* be any question with regard to which it is in principle possible to be in a p-predicament; if *A* is a known proposition not known to be true, and not known to be false, but that contains an answer to *Q*, then *A* is a theory. If $A_1, \ldots, A_n$ each is a known proposition that contains an answer to *Q*, and each excludes the other, and each in the absence of the others would contain the only answer to *Q* not ruled out by the conditions, and each is neither known to be true nor known to be false, then each is a theory. If *X* is a proposition that is the contrary of some proposition of *Q*, and *X* is not known to be true, and is not known to be false, then *X* is a theory. Nothing else is a theory. Thus a theory is a hypothetical explanation, if my understanding of the natures of explanations is correct.[578]

He makes it clear that this account applies only to explanatory theories and does not apply for all uses of 'theory' in scientific contexts.[579]

Various criticisms of this account of theories can be made. It has been pointed out that on this account if something is known to be false it cannot be a theory; but this is unacceptable—for example, since the

[574] Bromberger [1965], p. 82. See Section I-A of the Afterword for further discussion of Bromberger's and others' work on explanation.

[575] *Ibid.*, p. 90.

[576] See *ibid.*, pp. 94–95, for an explicit statement of the relevant conditions alluded to.

[577] See Bromberger [1966] for details.

[578] Bromberger [1963], p. 102; various notational changes have been made in reproducing the passage.

[579] *Ibid.*

phlogiston theory is still a theory even though it is known to be false. It also follows from his proposal that any proposition not known to be false is a theory, which allows far too many propositions to qualify as theories.[580] While these criticisms do show that Bromberger's analysis does not adequately capture what is essential to being a scientific theory, it is not clear whether a modified version of it could be adequate. The latter possibility seems to depend largely on whether further development of Bromberger's approach to explanation provides an adequate analysis of scientific explanation. Evaluating the latter is beyond the scope of this essay.

Bromberger's approach is illustrative how work being done on the problem of explanation can influence thinking about theories and, if successful, could contribute to an improved understanding of scientific theories. The controversy over the nature of scientific explanation is an involved one, and the literature is nearly as extensive as that concerning the structure of theories. Any attempt to evaluate the thinking about theories contained in that literature would require a detailed summary and assessment of the literature as lengthy as the present essay. This obviously cannot be attempted here; as such I can do no more here than to point out its relevance, illustrating it as I have done by discussing Bromberger's approach.

580 See Achinstein [1968], pp. 135–137. In the above quotation, Bromberger apparently is using 'proposition' in the modern, and not the medieval, sense of the term; as such, propositions are extralinguistic entities and so Bromberger cannot be accused of identifying theories with their formulations.

VI. The Symposium: Main Issues Concerning the Structure of Theories—1969

In this essay I have concentrated my attention on two quite different approaches to understanding the nature of scientific theories. The first of these, the Received View, concentrates on trying to present a general logical or structural analysis of all theories which is epistemically revealing of theories and their connections with the evidence of experience and observation. The second approach is not so much concerned with presenting a structural account of the "logic" of theories as with presenting a general account of the nature of scientific theorizing which, derivatively, is revealing of the nature of scientific theories. Although a number of versions of the latter sort of analysis have been advanced, they all are in agreement that an adequate analysis of scientific theorizing must pay careful attention to, and be able to account for, the processes whereby scientific theories are introduced, evolve, changed, and so on; and each of these approaches attempts to make sense of such scientific development by means of some sort of *Weltanschauung* through which science works and approaches nature. Both the Received View and the various *Weltanschauungen* analyses we considered were shown to be unacceptable, at least in their current forms. Thus, at present philosophers of science still are searching for an analysis of theories which will provide an adequate philosophical understanding of theories.

What form is that search for understanding of theories taking today? Differently put, what are the burning philosophical issues concerning theories which philosophers of science today are grappling with in hopes of gaining a philosophic understanding of theories? No simple answer to the question is possible. For what are viewed as the crucial issues depends on how one reacts to the failures of the Received View and the difficulties the *Weltanschauungen* analyses have encountered; depending on what one views as the strengths and serious weaknesses of the approaches which have been tried, one looks for one's philosophical Rosetta stone in different places. Nonetheless, I think certain definite trends or approaches to the problem of understanding theories can be discerned in contemporary philosophy of science. It is convenient to summarize these trends by means of characteristic theses. The following is a list of the characteristic theses of the more obvious, apparent, or important trends today.

(1) Although the criticisms which have been raised against the Received View and the various alternatives to it that have been proposed do succeed in showing that these analyses are beset with serious difficulties, these criticisms do not reveal exactly where these various analyses are defective and where they are on sound ground. In order to see clearly what an adequate analysis must include and what it must exclude, it is necessary to re-evaluate those criticisms and raise new ones which pinpoint rather precisely the strengths and defects of these various analyses.[581]

(2) Although understanding the various roles or functions theories play and the processes whereby scientific theorizing is carried out is important to a full understanding of scientific theories, a satisfactory analysis of scientific theories and scientific theorizing centrally must involve a structural analysis of theories which reveals deep structural properties characteristic of all theories or else major classes of theories.

(3) In order to see clearly what the nature of theories is and what the nature of scientific theorizing is, it is essential that one understand in full detail the way in which theories, laws, and so on, attach to nature.

(4) Theories are not static entities, but rather are scientific artifacts undergoing development and use, and regularly are evaluated, judged, accepted, rejected, or modified. Only in the context of their employment, development, and so on, can one understand the nature of scientific theories, and so it is important to understand the dynamics of scientific theorizing, reasoning about theories, and such.

(5) Although known to have its shortcomings or defects, one or another of the *Weltanschauungen* analyses is headed in the right direction, and so the key to understanding theories lies in the repair and improvement of that analysis.

(6) Although the *Weltanschauungen* analyses have served a useful function in emphasizing the importance for an understanding of

581 To a large extent this introductory essay is attempting to do just this.

theories of the activity of scientific theorizing and the various presuppositions which condition that activity, they have made science too subjective, too mysterious, and too tied to metaphysical constructs; and their analyses require excessive reference to psychological and sociological factors. What is needed is a philosophical analysis of the activity of scientific theorizing which does not take recourse either to psychological or sociological factors or their reifications as *Weltanschauungen.*

(7) Scientific theories are invoked to explain phenomena or other theories, and so the key to understanding theories is an adequate understanding of the nature of scientific explanation and the employment of theories in providing scientific explanations.

(8) Scientific theorizing in essence is a means of obtaining empirical knowledge; as such an adequate analysis will provide partial solutions to the main epistemological problems concerning empirical knowledge—problems about perception and observation, problems about facts and empirical truth, problems about evidence and the justification of knowledge claims, and so on. As such, philosophers of science should concentrate directly on these central problems as they arise concerning the scientific enterprise.

Of course, it is possible for one to hold a number of these theses and combine the approaches they advocate. Moreover, exactly how one approaches the problem of scientific theories in accordance with these theses will be colored or influenced by the positions one takes on the following two questions:

(a) To what extent must an adequate analysis of scientific theories and scientific theorizing be an accurate description of what actually has transpired in the history of science or is happening in contemporary science?

(b) To what extent are formalizations an essential, or even a useful, ingredient in an adequate analysis of scientific theories and/or scientific theorizing, and to what extent are informal analyses desirable or acceptable?

For depending on what answers one gives to these two questions, one's attempts to analyze theories along the lines of the various theses listed above will result in quite different sorts of analyses.

Today philosophy of science thus evidences an intelligible diversity of approaches to a philosophic understanding of scientific theories, and that diversity is well represented in the proceedings of the 1969 Symposium on The Structure of Scientific Theories which follows.[582] In Session I, Carl G. Hempel presents an alternative analysis of theories which is very similar to the Received View but avoids its main defects; then using that alternative as a foil, he raises certain questions about the Received View and tries to pinpoint the source of its main defects. In the process of doing so, he sharply questions the desirability or usefulness of formalization as a technique for solving philosophical problems in the philosophy of science.

In Session II, Patrick Suppes continues his attempts to treat the connections between theories and experimental data with a realistic degree of complexity. He does so by concentrating on the different ways in which various theories handle errors in data, and in the process of doing so presents a preliminary two-fold taxonomy of theories on the basis of whether they are deterministic or probabilistic and whether or not they contain theories of error. He closes his paper with some philosophical conclusions about the chronological development of the types of theories in his taxonomy and the ways in which that development has involved the giving up of certain classical ideas about what theories are supposed to do and the sorts of justification required for theories. The commentary on Suppes's paper challenges the philosophical adequacy of his taxonomy and the tenability of his philosophical conclusions.

In Session III, I. Bernard Cohen and Peter Achinstein discuss the place of history of science in the philosophy of science, and the relevance of philosophy of science to history of science. In his paper Cohen asks the question whether the soundness and usefulness of the philosophy of science depends on its degree of historical authenticity. In an attempt to answer that question, he considers a number of historical examples designed to illustrate differences in the way historians and philosophers approach the history of science, the sorts of defects one finds in the use of history of science by philosophers, and the relevance of history of science to philosophy of science and of philosophy of science to history of science. From his consideration of these examples he draws some general conclusions about these questions. In the process he also develops an account of how concepts are transformed when a theory takes them over from older theories. In his reply to Cohen, Achinstein focuses his attention on four issues raised by Cohen—concerning whether philosophy of science must be historically based, why philosophers should get their historical facts straight, the

582 The discussions in Secs. V–B–2, V–C, and V–D above also illustrate some of these trends.

value of philosophy of science for the historian, and whether good philosophy can be based on bad history—and critically discusses Cohen's conclusions on these issues, suggesting what he thinks are better answers. In the process of doing so, he enters into a detailed discussion of Reichenbach's distinction between the context of discovery and the context of justification.

In Session IV, David Bohm further develops his analysis of scientific theorizing which was summarized in Section V–B–1–e above, arguing that communication and perception are one whole, hence that science is primarily a way of extending our perception-communication into new contexts and forms. In the process of doing so he discusses Kuhn's and Feyerabend's incommensurability claims, arguing that incommensurability is an irrelevant notion. Rather, he suggests, theories are "whole" and can not be analyzed into disjoint components; in particular, the terms in theories have meanings, factuality, and truth criteria only in the total context of the theory. He also considers normal science activity, arguing that during such periods theories are being changed steadily in certain deep and fundamental ways; these changes affect the appropriate descriptive forms for informal scientific description. He concludes with a sketch of certain consequences of the fact that theories are "wholes" intimately tied to the scientist's perception-communication. In his commentary on Bohm's paper, Robert Causey tries to point out various errors he sees in Bohm's paper, arguing that some of Bohm's examples are historically inaccurate and that his view leads to an untenable position of private science which enjoys all the defects of private language theses. As a means to assessing other of Bohm's claims, he sketches a dynamic picture of how theories are applied to phenomena and tries to use it as a foil for criticism. In his reply to Causey, Jeffrey Bub charges that Causey has missed the main thrust of Bohm's paper, and that Bohm's general philosophical claims can only be understood in the light of his discussions of quantum theory. Then, in an extremely illuminating and revealing manner, he proceeds to discuss Bohm's criticisms of the orthodox or Copenhagen interpretation of quantum mechanics, the rationale of Bohm's hidden variable thesis, and the relations between Bohm's and Bohr's approaches to the interpretation of quantum theory. In the process of doing so, he tries to state what he sees as correct on the issue of perception-communication.

In Session V, Hilary Putnam challenges the idea, common to the Received View and Popper's falsification analysis, that theories directly imply predictions. Rather, he maintains, many theories yield predictions only if augmented by auxiliary statements that are not a part of the theory. These auxiliary statements have different epistemological statuses than theories, and can be employed in conjunction with theories in at least three characteristic ways which he illustrates. He then uses one of the ways of employing auxiliary statements to illustrate, defend, and develop Kuhn's doctrine that normal science can be characterized as "puzzle solving" and that this accounts for the immunity of paradigm theories from falsification. In doing so he tries to illustrate wherein the explanatory power of a theory lies. He concludes by showing that his general conclusions reveal various shortcomings or defects in Popper's falsification analysis. In reply to Putnam, Bas van Fraassen argues that while much of what Putnam says is correct, he has overstated his case in one respect and understated it in another. First, van Fraassen argues that the historical cases Putnam uses to illustrate his main claims are historically false, and so they do not support his position. Second, he argues that Putnam's analysis suffers from an acceptance of the positivistic idea that one can draw a sharp distinction between the structure of theories and the methodology of scientific inquiry, charging that this has led Putnam erroneously to suppose that it is possible to have a worthwhile discussion of theories without exploring the internal structure of theories, without paying attention to their world pictures, and without characterizing theories in any way. As such he charges that Putnam's attempt to localize the explanatory power of theories in the deductive link between theories and consequences via auxiliary statements does not yield an adequate account.

In Session VI, Thomas Kuhn responds to the various criticisms which have been raised against his account of the scientific enterprise and scientific revolutions, admitting that his old notion of a paradigm was defective in that it refers ambiguously to two quite different notions. As a replacement for paradigms, he now distinguishes these two notions as exemplars and disciplinary matrixes. He then proceeds to develop these two notions in some detail, indicating how they relate to his old notion of a paradigm. Having thus illustrated how he would revise his earlier treatment by using these twin notions, he then turns to the task of further developing his thesis that it is through the study of exemplars that one learns how to apply symbolic generalizations to nature and to attach empirical content to those generalizations. After exposing various defects he finds in the correspondence-rule account of the Received View, he argues that the study of exemplars leads to the acquisition of a resemblance relation which, instead of being anything like correspondence rules, enables one to attach symbolic generalizations to nature without recourse to rules. In doing so, he briefly touches on the connections between this resemblance relation and perception. In my commentary on Kuhn, I explore various unclarities and inadequacies I find in Kuhn's treatment and draw certain consequences from his new analysis. I try to show that Kuhn's account of the application of symbolic generalizations to nature in terms of resemblance relations has various serious defects, and also that it is a consequence of his various revisions made in his basic analysis that members of a scientific community cannot be said to share either a disciplinary matrix or the same theory so long as Kuhn holds his previous doctrines on meaning. I conclude with a discussion whether he really needs to postulate shared disciplinary matrixes, resemblance relations, and the like to carry out his basic analysis of the activity of scientific theorizing, arguing that he does not.

Dudley Shapere's paper in Session VII introduces and develops the notion of a scientific domain as a replacement for the observational-theoretical distinction. According to him domains are bodies of information taken to be an object for investigation; characteristic of such bodies of information is that there are reasons for suspecting an underlying unity to them, where something is importantly problematic about the body of information and there is reason to suppose the science is capable of dealing with that problem in its current stage of development. Shapere is concerned to explore the patterns of reasoning employed in deciding what is a domain and in attempting to solve the problems associated with such domains. Understanding these patterns of reasoning, he urges, will help us to understand the nature and function of scientific theories, for theories can answer only certain sorts of problems about domains. To that end he raises six main questions about domains and the modes of reasoning associated with them, and the remainder of his paper is devoted to developing answers to these questions insofar as they are relevant to the concept of a scientific theory. In the process of answering these questions he demonstrates that different domains pose different types of problems which call for different sorts of theories as solutions. What Shapere is doing here can be viewed as an attempt to account for what Kuhn calls normal scientific activity in terms of reasoning patterns in such a way that no reference to psychological or sociological factors is required. In doing so, he contrasts these reasoning patterns with the notion of a logic of discovery. Shapere's discussion touches on the instrumentalist *vs.* realist controversy over the interpretation of theories, and in an editorial interpolation his treatment of that issue is summarized. His thesis there is that when the observational-theoretical distinction is replaced by the notion of a domain, one sees that some terms (both observational and theoretical according to the Received View) function in theories to make existence claims whereas others are used to express various idealizations, simplifications, approximations, and so on; and once these two uses of terms in theories and their interconnections are understood, one is able to see what is basically wrong with the instrumentalist and realistic views of theories. In his commentary on Shapere's paper, Thomas Nickles concentrates his attention on three of Shapere's main contentions on domains: (i) the domain approach reveals how significantly different various kinds of theories are; (ii) the concept of a domain replaces the old observational-theoretical distinction; and (iii) that identifying the heuristic and justificatory roles of the "principles of reasoning" which emerge in scientific attempts to handle domains of phenomena will help us to understand the rationale of scientific decisionmaking and the establishment of research priorities. He tries to throw into greater relief, and shed further illumination on, the first two contentions. Then, turning to the third issue, he considers it in the light of various problems concerning intertheoretic reduction, arguing that for advanced stages of research, theories and intertheoretic reduction provide answers to two of Shapere's six basic questions about domains, indicating what leads one to regard a body of information as a domain and how the description of items of the domain is achieved and modified at sophisticated stages of scientific development.

The symposium closes with a retrospective postscript by Stephen Toulmin which attempts to impose a perspective on what emerged during the symposium, and thereby focus what the key issues are in the search for a philosophic understanding of theories and suggest promising lines for further developments. He does so by considering when and how the Received View originated in the first place, and then asking whether the recent discontent with axiomatic models such as that of the Received View are genuine signs that such axiomatizations are more of a hindrance than a help to the philosophy of science. Using these two issues as foils, he contrasts the various positions taken on various issues by the different participants in the symposium and then proceeds to draw some general conclusions and make various recommendations about promising lines for future research.

Although necessarily brief, I do think the above summary of the various contributions to the symposium does indicate the ways in which different contributors to the symposium are following different combinations of theses (1) to (8) in the attempt to gain insight on the nature of scientific theories, or else are trying to answer questions (a) and (b) concerning the historical or formalistic character of an adequate analysis of theories. As such the symposium does present a representative picture of what philosophers today are doing in the search for philosophic understanding of theories. In addition, the summary of the symposium just given does, I think, display how, despite differences of emphasis and approach, philosophers of science today still are grappling with many of the main issues we have considered in the previous sections of this essay.[583] Indeed the current climate of philosophical thinking about theories cannot be understood if divorced from the philosophical heritage summarized in the first five sections of this essay. We now are in a position to explore the range of current philosophical thinking about theories as evidenced in the proceedings of the 1969 Symposium on the Structure of Scientific Theories.

Before we do, however, one clarifying remark is in order.[584] At the time of the 1969 symposium, philosophy of science had undergone a cataclysmic upheaval and was in a profound state of disarray—seeking a viable new approach to the philosophical analysis of scientific theories and theorizing. The symposium graphically displays that disarray and the varied attempts being made then to find a new direction for philosophy of science. The key issues outlined above were the focal issues of such attempts. However, since then philosophy of science has begun to find a new direction and is coalescing into a more directed perspective; thus, today in 1977 the key issues in philosophy of science no longer are precisely those just detailed; some progress has been made since 1969. After the symposium's proceedings provide us with a graphic display how philosophy of science—circa 1969—was attempting to find a new direction in the aftermath of positivism's collapse, in the Afterword I will detail how in the intervening eight years philosophy of science has found a new direction for its efforts and will attempt to discern what *now* are emerging as the focal issues. Hopefully the combination of this introduction, the symposium proceedings, and the Afterword will provide a particularly effective means of understanding where philosophy of science is today and the influences which led it there.

[583] In fact, those issues are being considered to an even greater extent than the above summary might suggest; for in the discussions following the papers in each session, the relations between what the authors are doing in their papers and the following issues or notions are discussed: the observational-theoretical distinction, whether methodologies are theory-specific, the instrumentalist-realist dispute over the status of theoretical terms, formalization issues, models, correspondence rules and auxiliary statements, language and the meaning of theoretical statements, the use of probabilisitic notions in theories, the nature of normal science, the incommensurability of competing theories, whether science is subjective and private, the extent to which psychological and sociological considerations have a place in philosophical analyses and the relation of this to the context of discovery *vs.* the context of justification issue, the acceptance and rejection of theories, whether scientific knowledge is relativistic, and so on. The exact locations of these discussions can be found by consulting the index.

[584] This paragraph was added in the 1977 revision to counteract a certain datedness in the foregoing characterization of the "current state of philosophy of science" circa 1969.

PROCEEDINGS OF THE SYMPOSIUM

Formulation and Formalization of Scientific Theories

A Summary-Abstract

CARL G. HEMPEL

Editor's Note: The paper read at this session by Carl G. Hempel was based, to a large extent, on his essay "On the 'Standard Conception' of Scientific Theories" (Hempel [1970]). To avoid extensive repetition, he preferred not to have the full text of his lecture included in the present volume. The discussion of the lecture, however, clearly warrants publication; and to provide a background for the reader, Mr. Hempel has written, at the editor's suggestion, a summary-abstract stating briefly those points of his lecture which are also set forth in the essay just mentioned, and presenting more fully some additional remarks, made in his lecture, on the subject of axiomatization. A few passages from Hempel [1970] are reprinted in the following summary by kind permission of Herbert Feigl and the University of Minnesota Press.

I

Theories are the key to the scientific understanding of empirical phenomena, and they are normally developed only when previous research has yielded a body of information, including empirical generalizations about the phenomena in question. A theory is then intended to provide deeper understanding by presenting those phenomena as manifestations of certain underlying processes, governed by characteristic laws which account for, and usually correct and refine, the previously established generalizations.

The formulation of a theory may therefore plausibly be conceived as requiring two kinds of statement, which I will call internal principles and bridge principles.

> The internal principles serve to characterize the theoretical setting or the "theoretical scenario": they specify the basic entities and processes

> posited by the theory, as well as the theoretical laws that are assumed to govern them. The bridge principles, on the other hand, indicate the ways in which the scenario is linked to the previously examined phenomena which the theory is intended to explain.[1]

If I and B are the sets of internal and bridge principles by which theory T is characterized, then the theory itself may be regarded as the set of all sentences which logically follow from the class sum of these two sets.

> The formulation of the internal principles will typically make use of a *theoretical vocabulary*, V_T, that is, a set of terms not employed in the earlier descriptions of, and generalizations about, the empirical phenomena which T is to explain, but rather introduced specifically to characterize the theoretical scenario and its laws. The bridge principles will evidently contain both the terms of V_T and those of the vocabulary used in formulating the original descriptions of, and generalizations about, the phenomena for which the theory is to account. This vocabulary will thus be available and understood prior to the introduction of the theory, and its use will be governed by principles which, at least initially, are independent of the theory. Let us refer to it as the *pretheoretical* or *antecedent vocabulary*, V_A, relative to the theory in question.[2]

The terms of the antecedent vocabulary are by no means assumed to be "observational" in the sense of the familiar theoretical-observational distinction; that is, they are not required to stand for entities or characteristics whose presence can be ascertained by direct observation, unaided by instruments and theoretical inference.[3] Indeed, the antecedent vocabulary of a scientific theory will often contain terms which were originally introduced in the context of an earlier theory, and which are not observational in the sense just mentioned.

Consider, for example, Bohr's early theory of the hydrogen atom. It served to explain certain previously established laws, such as that the light emitted by glowing hydrogen gas is limited to a set of discrete wave lengths which conform to certain mathematical formulas, among them Balmer's formula.

The internal principles of Bohr's theory specify that the hydrogen atom consists of a nucleus and an electron circling it in one or another

[1] Hempel [1970], p. 142.

[2] Hempel [1970], p. 143.

[3] The concept of observability, and the characterization of theoretical terms as nonobservational, has recently been subjected to serious criticism; see, for example, Putnam [1962] and Achinstein [1968], Ch. 5.

of a discrete set of orbits available to it, that the electron can jump from a narrower to a wider orbit, or vice versa, and that in this process the atom absorbs or emits an amount of energy that is uniquely determined by the two orbits involved. The bridge principles connect these intra-atomic processes with the optical phenomena to be explained; they specify, for example, that the transition of the electron from an outer to an inner orbit results in the emission of monochromatic light whose wave length is uniquely determined by the difference between the energies characteristic of the two orbits in question. These bridge principles include both theoretical terms such as 'electronic orbit' and 'electron jump', which are specifically introduced to describe the theoretical scenario, and antecedently available terms such as 'hydrogen gas', 'spectrum', 'wave length of light', 'velocity of light', and 'energy'. Clearly, at least some of these latter terms are not observational; in fact, they were originally introduced in the context of earlier theories, including wave optics. But when Bohr proposed his theory, they were well understood and served to describe the phenomena to be explained.

The conception of a theory T as characterized by a set I of internal principles and a set B of bridge principles may be briefly expressed by the schema

(I) $$T = \langle I, B \rangle$$

which identifies the theory with the ordered pair of the two sets.

II

The preceding characterization of theories bears some resemblance to a construal which has been widely adopted in the recent philosophy of science, and which has, in fact, been referred to as the standard, or the received, view.[4] This view, too, construes a theory as characterized by two sets of sentences. One of these, the so-called "calculus" C, is a deductively axiomatized system of uninterpreted sentences; its postulates correspond to certain fundamental assumptions of the theory, that is, they are obtainable from the latter by substituting variables or dummy constants for the theoretical terms. The second component is a set R of sentences, sometimes called rules of correspondence, which give empirical content to the calculus by interpreting some of its expressions in terms of an empirical vocabulary that is

[4] Thus, Putnam [1962], p. 240.

usually assumed to be observational.[5] This standard construal may be represented by the schema

(II) $$T = \langle C, R \rangle$$

While I have repeatedly relied on the standard construal in earlier writings, I have come to feel increasing doubts about its adequacy. I will now outline some of these doubts.

III

It would be missing the point to criticize the standard construal on the ground that it does not give an accurate account of how theories are in fact formulated in science. It is not meant to provide such a description; rather, it is intended as an explication that exhibits certain logical and epistemological characteristics of scientific theories. But what are those characteristics? What, to begin with, is the point of assuming the internal principles of the theory to be presented in the form of an axiomatized uninterpreted system?

An analysis of scientific theories that is informed by an axiomatic point of view can be philosophically illuminating. This is shown, for example, by Reichenbach's[6] axiomatically oriented examination of the basis and structure of relativity theory, which was aimed at exhibiting the roles of experience and of convention in physical theorizing about space, time, and motion. Again, an axiomatic presentation of the mathematical formalism of quantum mechanics served as the basis for von Neumann's argument[7] that this formalism cannot be turned into a deterministic theory by the introduction of additional, "hidden," variables.

But theories can be axiomatized in many different ways, and if philosophical illumination is obtainable, in a given case, by axiomatic analysis, it will require an axiomatization specifically suited to its purpose. For example, the problems which Reichenbach sought to clarify by his axiomatic study of relativity theory could not be tackled by means of the axiomatization of special relativity constructed by Suppes,[8] which is technically much more elegant and rigorous than Reichenbach's. Thus, the fact that certain philosophical issues may

[5] For some further details, see Secs. 2, 3, 4 of Hempel [1958].
[6] Reichenbach [1924], [1925].
[7] von Neumann [1955], Ch. 4.
[8] Suppes [1959].

be clarified by an appropriately chosen axiomatization of some particular theory surely does not suffice to justify the idea, embodied in the standard construal, that the internal principles of any scientific theory be conceived as being axiomatized in some unspecified way.

Axiomatization may be said, however, to provide a means of characterizing precisely the set of sentences a proposed theory is meant to assert: since the set is infinite, it cannot be specified by listing its members individually. This is true, but the argument would call for the assumption that the entire theory, and not just its calculus, is axiomatized.

The importance of axiomatically formalizing scientific theories, much in the manner of the calculus *C* envisaged by the standard construal, has recently been argued in a vigorous and provocative paper by Suppes,[9] one of the leading advocates and practitioners of this method. Let me comment briefly on some of his arguments.

One of Suppes's claims is that formalization and axiomatization of scientific concepts and theories constitutes "a primary method of philosophical analysis," and that to "formalize a connected family of concepts is one way of bringing out their meaning in an explicit fashion." [10] This view is closely akin to the idea that the postulates of a formalized theory serve as "implicit definitions" of the primitive terms, requiring the latter to stand for entities and attributes which jointly satisfy the postulates. But while this conception may be plausible for some theories in pure mathematics, it is quite problematic when applied to formalized scientific theories; for it implies that the basic principles of a theory—and hence, also their consequences—hold true by virtue of the meanings of the theoretical terms, since these must be understood so as to ensure the truth of the postulates. And this would make all scientific theories true a priori.

Besides, the constraints which, on this view, the postulates impose upon the primitives still allow for a vast variety of interpretations and thus do not suffice to specify their intended scientific meanings. Take one of Suppes's own examples, Kolmogorov's axiomatization of probability theory. The logical and mathematical characteristics of probability specified by this system are exhibited alike by quite different concepts of probability, among them Carnap's logical or inductive concept, the personalistic conception of de Finetti and Savage, and the construal in terms of relative frequencies. Moreover, many of the philosophical problems about "the meaning of probability" in science

[9] Suppes [1968].

[10] Suppes [1968], pp. 653 and 654.

concern the precise explication of these different conceptions: and on this subject, Kolmogorov's theory has nothing to say.

Another respect in which, I think, Suppes overrates the potential benefits of axiomatization for science is illustrated in his severe criticism of N. R. Campbell's theory of measurement.[11] Campbell held that all "fundamental measurement," that is, measurement that does not depend on the previous measurement of some other magnitude, has to be of the kind exemplified by the fundamental measurement of physical quantities such as weight or length, which relies on a suitable mode of physical combination or "addition" of two objects, the combined object then being assigned the sum of the weights or lengths, and so forth, of its components. Suppes argues that Campbell was mistaken, noting that methods are now known for the fundamental measurement of personal utility and of various sensory intensities, such as pitch, which presuppose no substantive mode of "addition." And he suggests that the standards imposed by axiomatic formalization might have kept Campbell from falling into his error: "Within a discipline that is formalized, claims like those of Campbell . . . are simply not made without formal proof." [12] But surely, a competent logician might well have produced an axiomatized theory of measurement incorporating Campbell's basic assumptions on fundamental measurement in its axioms. In such a theory, Campbell's claim would be capable of formal proof. Would such proof have conferred any additional warrant of soundness on the claim? Evidently not. From our present vantage point, we would have to say that the system permitting the proof represented a too narrow conception of the possibilities of measurement. But the new alternative methods of fundamental measurement were not produced by axiomatization: their discovery required logical resourcefulness and a good deal of psychological research. Those methods rely on individual judgments of human subjects concerning such matters as the equality of the differences between the elements of two pairs of sensory intensities. It required logical and methodological resourcefulness to recognize that such judgments could serve as a basis for fundamental measurement provided they satisfied certain relevant general conditions; and it required empirical research to determine in what sensory domains, and to what extent, those conditions are in fact satisfied by human dis-

[11] In Suppes [1968]; for Campbell's views being criticized, see his [1920], Pt. II; [1928].

[12] Suppes [1968], p. 659.

criminatory responses.[13] Here as elsewhere in empirical science, axiomatization can come only after a theory has been developed; it can serve as a means of precise exposition, but not as a guarantee of soundness for the conceptions incorporated in the axiomatized theory.

IV

I turn now to another difficulty of the standard view. The conception of an *uninterpreted* calculus *C* seems to me misleading because it suggests that the basic assumptions of a theory—those of which, broadly speaking, the postulates of *C* are disinterpreted versions—are expressed exclusively by means of the "new" theoretical terms introduced by the theory: for presumably it is these which in *C* are represented by dummy letters, and which are held to be "implicitly defined" by the postulates and empirically interpreted by the correspondence rules. Actually, however, the internal principles of most theories characterize the theoretical scenario at least in part by means of terms taken from the antecedent vocabulary. For example, the kinetic theory of gases ascribes to atoms and molecules such characteristics as mass, volume, velocity, momentum, and kinetic energy, which figure already in the antecedent studies of the motions of macroscopic bodies. Similarly, the undulatory theory of light uses such antecedently available concepts as those of wave length and frequency.

It might be replied that when antecedently available terms are thus used in the formulation of a theory they function in quite novel principles and accordingly acquire totally new meanings, and that they should therefore be reckoned among the theoretical terms. But this view is surely an exaggeration. If, in the absence of a satisfactory explicit analysis, we allow ourselves to speak of the "meanings" of scientific terms in an intuitive manner, it seems to be widely acknowledged that those meanings will be reflected, to a considerable extent, in the basic laws in which they are used. And then it is significant that in many—though not all—cases, the most basic laws in which the terms function at the pretheoretical level are carried over into their theoretical use. Thus, in the kinetic theory, the conservation laws for mass, energy, and momentum are applied also to atoms and molecules; in wave optics, the basic principles governing the propagation and

[13] Suppes mentions some of the empirical limitations in [1957], p. 270, footnote. Chapter 12 offers a lucid presentation, with various examples, of the axiomatic formalization of theoretical systems.

interaction of waves are carried over from the pretheoretical, macroscopic, level to the theoretical scenario of light waves. In fact, some such laws function not only as pretheoretical and as internal theoretical principles, but also as bridge principles. This is illustrated, for example, by the principle of additivity for mass, which, as a bridge principle of the kinetic theory, implies that the mass of a body of gas equals the sum of the masses of its constituent molecules.

This extensive theoretical use of antecedent terms appears to me to throw into question the conception of the internal principles of a theory as an axiomatized system whose postulates provide "implicit definitions" for its extralogical terms. For some of those terms normally are not "new" theoretical terms that somehow need to have their "meanings" specified: they are antecedently available and understood. Hence, the theoretical "calculus" of a theory of this kind cannot be regarded as a strictly formalized, uninterpreted system, and the concepts and methods of model theory cannot be applied to it without qualifications.

V

Some writers conceive a scientific theory as having a third component, in addition to the calculus and the rules of correspondence. Nagel refers to it as a "model for the abstract calculus, which supplies some flesh for the skeletal structure in terms of more or less familiar or conceptualizable materials."[14] Models in this sense, which will be considered presently, must be clearly distinguished from analogical models, such as the representation of an electric current in a network of wires of different resistance by the flow of a liquid through a network of pipes of different widths. The analogy here consists in an isomorphism between the laws governing the two processes:[15] in the relevant nomic respects, electric currents are shown to behave "as if" they consisted in the flow of a liquid. Analogical models can be of considerable didactic and heuristic value, but are not essential for the formulation and the application of a theory. The laws for electric currents, for example, can be stated without any reliance on the hydrodynamic model; and whatever electric phenomena can be explained by the theory in question are accounted for by the laws for

[14] Nagel [1961], p. 90.

[15] For some details, see Hempel [1965], pp. 435–436.

electric currents and not, of course, by their hydrodynamic counterparts.[16]

Models of the kind Nagel has in mind, however, seem to me to play an essential role in the formulation and application of many theories. The specification of such a model consists in an interpretation of terms in the calculus by means of empirical terms that belong to the antecedent vocabulary and, in this sense, are well understood. For example, the calculus associated with Bohr's theory of the hydrogen atom would contain mathematical formulas expressed in terms of uninterpreted functors, or quantitative variables. The model would characterize the hydrogen atom as consisting of a nucleus and an electron orbiting about it, and it would interpret the quantitative variables as standing for certain quantitative features of the scenario, such as the radii of the available discrete orbits, the energies of the atom in the corresponding states, and the frequencies of the emitted radiation. In this case, and similarly in the kinetic theory of gases, the gene theory for the transmission of hereditary traits, and the like, the specification of the model is not governed by a tacit "as if" clause:[17] gases are claimed actually to consist of rapidly moving molecules, and the complex composition and spatial structure ascribed to DNA molecules is claimed to represent the actual organization of those molecules. The specification of the model is here essential for the formulation of the theory and for its applications; it determines in part the experimental implications of the theory, such as certain characteristic x-ray diffraction patterns associated with substances of specified molecular structure. The specification of a model in this sense seems to me to be an especially important instance of the use of antecedent terms in the formulation of a theory.

VI

Next, some brief remarks on the concept of correspondence rules as constituents of a scientific theory. The customary designation of the sentences in question as "rules," or as coordinative or operational "definitions," strongly conveys the suggestion that they constitute truths guaranteed by terminological legislation or convention. But this idea is untenable for several reasons, among them the following.

16 Various conceptions of models and analogies, and their relevance to science, are illuminatingly discussed in Hesse [1966] and in Achinstein [1968], Chs. 7 and 8.

17 This conception is suggestively set forth by Spector [1965].

A theory will often provide us with several general principles that link, say, a theoretical quantity to different kinds of experimental finding; each of these might thus be said to represent a rule of correspondence for the theoretical term in question. But the theory providing these principles implies, briefly, that if one of the alternative experimental methods yields a certain value for the theoretical quantity, then the other methods will yield the same value. But it cannot be a matter of terminological convention whether matters in fact turn out that way.

And even if a sentence is initially introduced as true by stipulation, this is only an ephemeral trait, carrying no guarantee of immunity to revision in response to new empirical findings and further theoretical developments: "conventionality is a passing trait, significant at the moving front of science, but useless in classifying the sentences behind the lines." [18]

VII

One of the objectives of the standard conception was to explicate the ways in which theoretical terms are assigned specific "meanings" with the help of an observational vocabulary or, on a more liberal construal, with the help of a scientific vocabulary that is antecedently understood. The explication proposed by the standard construal proved to be open to serious question: we noted difficulties both with the conception that the theoretical terms are implicitly defined by the postulates of the calculus and with the idea that they are empirically interpreted by means of correspondence rules.

But I have suggested no alternative solution to the problem. And indeed, I think the problem as just stated is spurious because it rests on an erroneous presupposition. It presupposes that if theoretical terms have definite meanings, then it must be possible to construe those terms as introduced by specifiable logical procedures, which assign them meanings with the help of terms that are antecedently understood.

This presupposition, which I once thought quite sound, seems to me mistaken for several reasons, among them the erroneous belief that significant new terms cannot be introduced and come to be understood except by means of linguistic devices relating them to a set of previously understood terms. As Putnam[19] has argued convincingly,

[18] Quine [1963], p. 395.
[19] Putnam [1962].

theoretical terms are introduced, and come to be understood, much in the way most words are introduced and understood; there is no reason to believe that the process can always be explicated or rationally reconstructed in accordance with the presupposition just mentiond.

Discussion

Professor Suppes:

It is a pleasure to engage in discussion again with Professor Hempel. We had a debate on some of these topics a few months ago.[1]

I would like to comment briefly on some of the issues he raises. I think they are difficult issues to sharpen, but I will not spend long since it is not my purpose to reach for equal time. In dealing with these issues I would like to try to bring one or two specific arguments to bear on the usefulness of formalization in science. Rather than deal with the broad issues, let me take a try at one or two very specific ones. First, a passing remark on the matter of implicit definitions and the meaning of concepts. The matter was probably first made explicit in a classical exchange between Frege and Hilbert. The purpose of formalization is primarily to give an explicit definition of the overall concept, not an implicit definition of the subsidiary concepts.

Second, there are issues in the philosophy of science and also of scientific interest that require formalization for settling or clarifying the issues. Let me mention two rather distinct matters that are very lively issues among some philosophers of science and some scientists. First, a very large body of current literature on the status of probability in quantum mechanics has been developed by physicists, philosophers, and mathematicians. Without formalization it simply is impossible to resolve the issues that have now become very complex regarding the role and the position of classical probability in quantum mechanics. We cannot make any further progress in pinning down the complex set of issues that are now in front of us simply by informal remarks and by intuitive interpretations. Also related to these problems is the argument about the status of classical and nonclassical logic in quantum mechanics; and here again I think we are beyond the stage at which further progress can be made by any other means than very careful, explicit, and adequate formalization.

[1] At the Eastern Division Meetings of the American Philosophical Association, December, 1968, where Hempel served as a commentator on Suppes [1968].

The second example, which is from a different domain but shows that formalization has the same role to play, is the issue between the behavioral psychologists on the one hand and cognitive and linguistically oriented psychologists on the other regarding whether behavioral psychologists' concepts are rich enough to account for language learning and for language behavior. A great many words have been said and a great many debates[2] have taken place about this, and it seems to me that further clarification of the substantive scientific issue, which is also an interesting philosophical issue, will depend partly upon formalization. In this case clarification may very well depend ultimately upon further empirical work as well, but at the very least progress can be made on certain parts of the argument only with further formalization.

Finally, regarding the view that formalization is restricted primarily to the internal principles (what Professor Hempel calls the set *I* of principles) I would claim that, from the standpoint of scientific methodology, this very much is *not* the case. One of the most elaborate, sophisticated, and extensive efforts at formalization in the methodology of science takes place in the context of bridging rules—the entire effort of the last thirty years in mathematical statistics can be thought of as an attempt to put in very explicit and very formal terms the problems of methodology that are involved in the testing of hypotheses, the designing of experiments, and all the other similar questions that we are concerned with in any kind of complicated science. The thing that is very characteristic of this statistical literature is that it has been written in a very firm and very definite atmosphere of formalization exactly as a part of contemporary mathematics.

Professor Hempel:

Professor Suppes's first remarks touched on an interesting difficulty in the conception of a postulate system as providing implicit definitions for the primitives: by these "definitions," all of the primitives are characterized jointly, so that, in a manner of speaking, each primitive is "defined" in terms of the others. Thus, what meanings or what extensions may be assigned to one of the primitives always depends on what interpretations are given to the others. It may be preferable, therefore, to say that the constraints which the postulates impose on permissible interpretations concern, not the primitives individually, but the entire ordered set of them. This idea is implemented by a mode of axiomatization that Professor Suppes and his associates have ingeniously

[2] See, for example, Skinner [1957] and Chomsky's [1959] review of it.

applied to a variety of theories, namely, axiomatization by explicit definition of one set-theoretical predicate.[3] In the case of an axiomatized theory with *n* primitives, the predicate is defined so as to apply to an *n*-tuple of set-theoretical entities (sets, functions, and so on) just in case the interpretation of the primitives by those set-theoretical entities turns the postulates into true sentences. This procedure has certain logical attractions, but these do not invalidate any of the reservations I expressed concerning some of Professor Suppes's arguments for the desirability of axiomatization in science, for those arguments were essentially independent of the particular mode of axiomatic formalization. Let me acknowledge again, however, that axiomatization of theories can be of value for certain philosophical or scientific purposes; Professor Suppes has mentioned some pertinent examples in his remarks today.

As for axiomatizing the sentences that provide the interpretation of a formalized theoretical system, this is certainly possible, and in some cases, as in the theory of measurement, has yielded illuminating results. But the procedure again eventuates in a formal system, which must be given a specific interpretation if the intended specific content of the theory is to be captured. Thus, at some point, there will have to be an interpretation in terms already understood that does not in turn rely on formalization. Here is one context in our discussions where I think Professor Kuhn's paper is highly relevant, for it explores ways in which the requisite agreement in the understanding and the use of scientific terms may be attained by the members of a scientific community without reliance on, or even availability of, explicitly formulated criteria of application.

Professor Causey:

I would just like to ask Professor Hempel a couple of questions. The first is mainly a terminological one. If I am not mistaken you defined a theory, or at least the set of sentences of a theory, to be the set of all logical consequences of the union of the internal principles *I* and the bridge principles *B*. Although I do not think it is a terribly crucial matter, it seems to me that if we are going to talk about theories and use the term in any sense at all like it is used by working scientists, then this notion or this definition of a theory as a set of sentences is much too broad, because it will include in those sets of consequences all kinds of pretheoretical sentences which I would think the average scientist would not want to consider part of *his* theory.

[3] The method is explained and illustrated in Suppes [1957], Ch. 12.

Now a deeper question, and one which is rather general, is the following: You raised a number of good objections against the Received View. But so far as I understand your view of a theory in terms of internal principles *I* and bridge principles *B*, and to the extent that I understand at least most of your objections against the Received View, it seems to me that these objections also will apply to your own view —though perhaps in a slightly altered form.

Professor Hempel:

A scientist will formulate a theory by specifying only a finite subset, say S, of its intended assertions. He will not know all of the logical consequences of this set; and while affirming the theory, he might possibly doubt or even deny certain sentences which, without his knowing it, are consequences of S. Would this make it more appropriate to construe a theory as a set of sentences each of which its adherents would clearly feel themselves committed to assert?

For the purposes of a logical and methodological analysis, this would be unacceptable; for—to mention one reason—a careful experimental disconfirmation of certain logical consequences of *S* would count as disconfirming the theory even if some of its adherents did not feel themselves committed to give assent to those consequences. Hence, if a theory is at all represented by a set of sentences, then it must be construed as containing all consequences of any of its subsets. This in turn makes it necessary to reckon among the assertions of a theory also such consequences of *S* as would generally be regarded uninteresting or trivial, as well as those containing only antecedent terms. That a theory should yield consequences of this latter kind is, in fact, an essential requirement if theories are assumed to yield predictions couched in the antecedent vocabulary by deduction from sentences describing prior occurrences in antecedently available terms.

As for Professor Causey's second point, I do not think the conception of a theory as represented by internal principles and bridge principles, as in schema I, is open to essentially the same objections as the standard construal represented by schema II. In particular, the internal principles are not claimed to provide implicit definitions for the theoretical terms, nor are they assumed to be couched exclusively in the "new" theoretical vocabulary; similarly, the bridge principles are not regarded as assigning empirical content to the theoretical terms, nor are they held to be established by convention or by rules; they are taken to be statements on a par with the internal principles and subject to possible revocation if the theory should be found to conflict with well-established empirical findings.

However, as I acknowledged in my lecture,[4] I have offered no precise criteria for delimiting the two sets. In particular, the dividing line cannot be drawn by reference to the constituent nonlogical terms since both sets normally contain antecedent as well as theoretical terms; nor is there a distinguishing difference in epistemic status, such as acceptance by terminological convention *vs.* acceptance on empirical grounds. It is thus assuredly a vague distinction, but I hope it may be sufficiently clear and suggestive in the context in which I have used it, namely, as a background for a discussion of the standard conception.

Professor Achinstein:

You have given up one distinction and are advocating another one; you have given up the observational-theoretical distinction and you are advocating a distinction between theoretical terms and antecedently available terms, and now I am wondering whether this distinction does not introduce as many problems as the old one.

One preliminary point: you mentioned the Bohr theory as your first example; now each term that Bohr actually used was available prior to the Bohr theory. Some of the terms were used by Rutherford, and even before Rutherford, terms like "electron" and "nucleus." Indeed, I would venture the claim that with respect to most theories most of the terms in that theory that Positivists and others traditionally have called theoretical were available before that theory was formulated.

Second, when you speak of the "antecedently available vocabulary" do you have in mind simply words or do you mean the concepts behind them? For example, if in their theory of mechanics physicists had used the term "energy of motion" first and then someone came along and used the term "kinetic energy" instead with the same meaning, would the latter then be a theoretical term in the theory? One would be tempted to say here that no new concept has been introduced even though a new term has. On the other hand, Clausius introduced the term "entropy" which he defined explicitly by reference to the antecedently available terms "heat" and "temperature" and the notion of the mathematical integral. In this case one is tempted to say that a new concept has been introduced even though the term "entropy" is explicitly defined by means of the antecedently available vocabulary. So when you speak of the theoretical terms of the theory are you referring simply to the terms or to the concepts they express? If the latter, what criteria do you use to decide whether a concept is a new one or is antecedently available?

[4] See Hempel [1970], end of Sec. 6; the point is not mentioned in the summary-abstract above.

Professor Hempel:

The two vocabularies are assumed to consist of scientific terms in their specific scientific modes of use, or with their specific scientific meanings or interpretations. Even the representation, in the standard conception, of theoretical terms by uninterpreted constants is not meant, of course, to characterize those terms as devoid of meaning: it is an analytic device intended to explicate the logical means by which, and the extent to which, the theory may be said to specify the meanings—or the extensions—of the theoretical terms within a conceptual and linguistic framework antecedently available. The two principal logical devices envisaged by the standard construal, as I have mentioned, are implicit definition by theoretical postulates and empirical interpretation by rules of correspondence.

The standard construal often assumes that the empirical interpretation is effected by means of an observational vocabulary. To avoid the difficulties of this latter notion and of the construal of all theoretical terms as nonobservational, I suggested that the basis for the empirical interpretation could more simply be taken to be a set of previously understood terms, no matter whether they stand for items which, in some plausible sense, might qualify as observable.

Professor Achinstein is right in what I take him to be suggesting, namely, that in the sense here intended, the theoretical terms of a given theory cannot be characterized simply as those extralogical words or symbols which occur in the formulation of the theory, but not in the antecedent vocabulary. For an old term might acquire a new interpretation when used in the theory; and in this case, the question of how its new meaning or its new extension is specified arises for the old terms no less than for the new ones. The sorting out of the theoretical terms would therefore require criteria determining whether a given antecedently available term as used in a theory has the same meaning—or the same reference—as in its pretheoretical use.

I do not know of any satisfactory explication of sameness of meaning, and I agree with Quine and other critics in regarding the idea as intrinsically unclear. But even if we ask only about changes of extension, I see considerable difficulties, for it is not clear how the extension of a term as used in a given theory is to be characterized in a nontrivial way.[5]

But the principal purpose of my paper was to raise certain questions about the standard construal of theories; and the questions I did

[5] Professor Hempel's reply to Professor Putnam, below, contains a slight amplification of this remark.

raise do not depend on exactly where the dividing line between the antecedent and the theoretical vocabulary is drawn.

Professor Bromberger:

I would like to ask a very simple-minded question: Exactly what is the status of this analysis of a theory? What function does it fulfill and how does it clarify? As an analysis of the concept of a theory, that is, the concept that is embodied in our use of the word 'theory' in English or equivalent ones in other languages, I think it is demonstratively false. Now I take it that there is some kind of a program associated with this general sketch. The view that a theory consists of an uninterpreted calculus and rules of interpretation had one great virtue as a program, namely that it was a program which, if successful, would have made explicit the rules that govern or that ought to govern acceptance and rejection of theories. It failed as a program and therefore it failed to fulfill this task, which I think is an important task of the philosophy of science. Now do you envisage your new distinction as entailing a program that will show how the theories that we in fact have might ultimately be analyzed? And would such an analysis then make explicit why they are accepted, how they are accepted, and whether their acceptance is based on principles that are philosophically kosher?

Professor Hempel:

Professor Bromberger is right in stressing the programmatic side of the standard conception. One of its objectives was to explicate, and appraise from the point of view of an analytic-philosophical conscience, the principles governing concept formation in scientific theories. Another objective was similarly to exhibit and appraise the principles governing the testing of scientific theories. On the standard view, the testing of a theory depends essentially on the deductive connections which the theory is taken to establish between empirical sentences couched in observational—or, more generally—in antecedent terms.[6]

My paper was intended principally as a criticism of the basic assumptions by means of which the standard construal tackles its tasks; I did not put forward a properly developed alternative. Let me just add that the standard construal of the connection between new theoretical concepts and antecedent ones seems to me overly restrictive, and that it appears to be prompted by an assumption which

[6] For details, see, for example, Hempel [1958], pp. 46–48, 75–76.

impressed me as quite reasonable when I wrote "The Theoretician's Dilemma," [7] but which I now regard as unwarranted, namely that, to be "philosophically kosher" as Professor Bromberger calls it, the introduction of theoretical terms must somehow provide an explanation, in formally reconstructible ways, of the new concepts by means of the antecedent ones. The considerations that militate against this view also throw into doubt the conception of theories as establishing deductive transitions among sentences couched in terms of the antecedent vocabulary. But these are issues about which I am just trying to form clearer ideas, and thus, to my regret, I cannot be more specific about them now.

Professor Putnam:

I agree with almost all of the things you said. However, there are still I think two points where I think our views are in disagreement and I would like to get your reaction to one of them. You said something to the effect that if a term introduced into a theory had no exact meaning then it makes no sense to ask whether it is true or false. Now I think that is wrong—I think first of all that very few terms have what one could call an exact meaning, and anyway I suspect that scientists are not interested in the exact meaning, in the linguistic sense, of the terms they use; they would be very bored. And I suspect that is one mistake that really mattered. If meaning is an issue then it hangs over all the way because I want to get into problems about concepts and how I would know it is the same concept. This all gets cut short if one says at the outset that the question is not whether the terms of a theory have meaning, or what they mean in the sense of linguistic usage or anything like that—or whether they refer to anything. Of course, Quine would say this because he is pessimistic about the notion of meaning. I am not as pessimistic, but I do think that the notion of meaning is fairly irrelevant to this part of philosophy of science, and that one can proceed in a purely extensionalistic way. That would be the first thing on which I want to get your reaction. Then I think we would see that many of the questions are somewhat easier; they are still hard but at least they are a little different. For example, I do not face the question, when should I say a term in an older theory is the same concept as the term I am now using. I do face the question, when should I say it refers to something that I now recognize. Should I say that Bohr's term 'electron' referred to what I called electrons? And there I would say "yes" because I advocate a

[7] Hempel [1958].

principle of charity with respect to such questions: a lot of his beliefs are still true judging from the standpoint of my present theory, so rather than say that the poor man was not talking about anything at all, that it was like witches or phlogiston, I charitably say "Yes, he was talking about electrons although some of his sentences were false." And here I would say the great insight for me contained in Tarski's theory of truth is that anyone who grants me this mild thing that I can say what Bohr's terms were referring to has granted me the concept of truth for all of Bohr's sentences. You know, Donald Davidson has recently been emphasizing that it is one of the main ways one can look at Tarski: if you give me the reference, I have got truth.[8]

Put in another way to anticipate future polemics, if you are not convinced by Kuhn's talk about scientists being in different worlds, if you do not buy that as far as reference is concerned, if it is not true enough to lead me to say that I do not know what Bohr was referring to, then you cannot buy it as far as truth is concerned either.

Professor Hempel:

I feel quite dubious about the concept of meaning—in fact, I share what Professor Putnam calls Quine's pessimism on that score. I spoke about the meanings of scientific terms principally in order to reflect one of the philosophical assumptions that seem to me to have informed the standard conception. This is the idea that (*i*) a philosophical analysis of scientific theories should seek to explicate, among other things, by what logical means theoretical terms are assigned—or may be conceived as being assigned—specific meanings, given the linguistic and terminological apparatus available prior to the construction of the theory; and that (*ii*) unless a philosophically satisfactory explication of those means can be given, the sentences of the theory, insofar as they contain theoretical terms, would have to be regarded as lacking clearly determined meanings and, consequently, as being neither true nor false.

Professor Putnam is right in saying that to ensure truth or falsity for those sentences, it would suffice that their constituent nonlogical terms each have a definite reference; that the question of meanings or intensions may be disregarded in this context. But this still leaves the question whether the formulation of a theory does assign determinate extensions to the theoretical terms, and if so, whether this assignment is achieved or achievable in philosophically satisfactory ways by

[8] See Davidson [1967].

means of the conceptual and linguistic apparatus of science available when the theory is being constructed.

The answer would clearly be in the affirmative if it could be shown that a theory implies, for each of its theoretical terms, a biconditional sentence linking the term to an expression containing only antecedent terms, for the theory would then assign to the theoretical terms the same extension as to that expression. But this condition is rarely, if ever, met; and the standard conception may be regarded as suggesting a more modest answer, to the effect that the extensions of the theoretical terms are fixed in part by the postulates of the calculus and in part by the rules of correspondence. And in so far as my critical observations concerning the standard view carry weight, they raise questions also about its adequacy for the extensional characterization of theoretical terms.

Let me add some further thoughts on Professor Putnam's suggestion. Even though, as Quine has often stressed, the theory of reference is in philosophically much more satisfactory shape than the theory of meaning, there are special problems concerning the reference of theoretical terms which the general theory of reference does not automatically answer. In fact, these problems exhibit distinct analogies to those concerning the "meanings" of theoretical terms. Take Putnam's example about the references of the term 'electron' as used, say, in Bohr's first theory of the hydrogen atom and the term 'electron' as used in contemporary physics; let us abbreviate these as 'e_B' and 'e_C', respectively. To say, with Putnam, that the two terms have the same reference comes to asserting that

$$(x)(e_B x \equiv e_C x).$$

But to prove this, or even to make it plausible, we would need specifications of the two extensions. What sentences of each of the relevant theories should count as determining those extensions? (This is strongly reminiscent of the question: what sentences of a given theory are to count as determining the meaning of one of its theoretical terms?) Surely not all the sentences of each theory, for the two theories may well be incompatible. Besides, by asserting that the two terms have the same reference, Professor Putnam presumably wants to say that the two theories refer to the same set of objects but make different—perhaps incompatible—assertions about them. Hence it seems that the two extensions would have to be specified by two logically compatible characterizations of electrons that are implied by, but not logically equivalent to, the respective theories. But how are these characterizations to be chosen?

And—supposing this question were answered satisfactorily—how is the coextensiveness of the two characterizations to be established? It would hardly amount to a purely logical truth: but then, are we to use certain principles of Bohr's theory or of the contemporary theory, or perhaps some combination of the two kinds, in arguing for coextensiveness?

Thus, even if we concentrate our analytic efforts exclusively on the extensions of theoretical terms and the truth of theoretical sentences, some difficult problems remain.

SESSION II

The Structure of Theories and the Analysis of Data

PATRICK SUPPES

On at least two previous occasions (Suppes [1962], [1967]), I have tried to set forth my views on the complicated nature of the relation between theories and relevant experimental data. What I have especially objected to is the unrealistic simplicity of the standard sketch that goes like this. A theory consists of two parts, one of which is an abstract or logical calculus and the other of which is a set of rules that assign an empirical content to the logical calculus by giving empirical interpretations of at least some of the primitive or defined symbols of the calculus. The purpose of the present paper is to give a taxonomy of theories with respect to the way they handle data, and especially errors of measurement. The standard sketch's lack of a theory of error is one of its most glaring omissions, but I do not want to suggest that what I have to say is complete or definitive. The subject is much too undeveloped and as yet much too unstructured to aim at any final results.

I begin by discussing deterministic theories with incorrigible data. By *incorrigible data* I mean data to which no theory of error is applied in measuring, recording, or analyzing them.[1] Later on I shall say something about the relations of incorrigible data to earlier concepts of incorrigible data and to earlier concepts of incorrigible elementary sensations or perceptions.

1. Deterministic Theories with Incorrigible Data

I shall not attempt a formal definition of theories of the kind described by the heading. Roughly speaking, by *deterministic theories* I mean

[1] What I want to mean by *incorrigible data* is clarified further in my response to Fred Suppe in the discussion following the paper (see pp. 303–304).

theories that do not embody in their own theoretical concepts any use of probabilistic notions, and I would like to discuss three examples of such theories; the first one is deterministic but seems to need no theory of error, just because of its qualitative character and its conceptual simplicity. The second example already raises problems of a more subtle kind, and the third is a historical example drawn from ancient astronomy that illustrates more a failure of ancient science than anything else.

Before formulating the first example, I should state that I shall move back and forth between two ways of talking about theories. For the simple examples I shall adopt a relatively formal, set-theoretical idiom, but with the more complicated examples I shall leave matters in a rather sketchy state and try to concentrate on the conceptual point without using any very precise apparatus to do so.

The first example is meant to be a simple minor one familiar to everyone and blest with an almost complete lack of subtlety. This is the theory of biological parenthood in the human species. To avoid difficulties about an infinite regress or the claim that every human has had only human ancestors, we can restrict the theory in terms of parenthood to parenthood of humans now living. We thus base the theory on the set A of humans, the subset L of humans now living, the subset M of males, and the relation P of parenthood, that is, xPy when x is the parent of y.

A formal statement of the theory is embodied in the following set-theoretical definition.

DEFINITION 1. *A structure* $\mathfrak{A} = \langle A, L, M, P \rangle$ *is a human-parent structure if and only if the following axioms are satisfied for every* x, y, *and* z *in* A:

Axiom 1. *If* xPy *then not* yPx.
Axiom 2. *If* x *is in* L *then there is a unique* y *such that* y *is in* M *and* yPx.
Axiom 3. *If* x *is in* L *then there is a unique* z *such that* z *is not in* M *and* zPx.

It is deterministic and incorrigible from the standpoint of ordinary or normal data about any collection of human beings to determine whether or not a possible realization of the theory is actually a human-parent structure. This does not mean that no aberrant medical cases exist. It does mean that for normal data no theory of error would be introduced in checking whether the axioms of Definition 1 were satisfied. In the case of a collection of human beings that did not satisfy the axioms, it is easy enough to state how to enlarge the basic set A so as to obtain a model of the theory. We simply add the parents of all humans in the set L. The point is that the theory is sufficiently qualitative in its checks and sufficiently unelaborate so that no theory of data analysis with special attention to problems of error is needed.

It is perhaps wise to elaborate somewhat more at this point on the notion of incorrigible data used in this paper. One of the theses back of the analysis given here is that the classical demand for certainty in perception is replaced methodologically in science by the concept of incorrigible data. The notion of incorrigible data in scientific methodology does not have the same epistemological status as the notion of incorrigible sense data in philosophical theories of perception. For me, the important insight is that the absolute demands of classical theories of perception are replaced by relativistic demands of scientific methodology. With respect to a given theory and given collections of data or experiments, incorrigibility is accepted as normal, but no deeper status, in particular, no ontological status, is assigned to the incorrigible data. I shall expand upon this point later in the paper.

I turn now to a second example of a deterministic theory with incorrigible data. This example is a good deal more subtle and is meant to be taken more seriously as a theory than the first example. The theory I consider is one of the simplest examples of fundamental measurement in which we pass from qualitative observations to quantitative claims.

We may develop the axioms of extensive measurement with at least three specific interpretations in mind. One is for the measurement of mass by means of an equal-arm balance, one is for the measurement of length of rigid rods, and one is for the measurement of subjective probability. Other interpretations are certainly possible, but I shall restrict detailed remarks to these three.

From a formal standpoint the basic structures are triples $\langle X, \mathfrak{F}, \geq \rangle$ where X is a nonempty set, $\mathfrak{F}$ is a family of subsets of X and the relation $\geq$ is a binary relation on $\mathfrak{F}$. By using subsets of X as objects, we avoid the need for a separate primitive concept of concatenation. As a general structural condition, it shall be required that $\mathfrak{F}$ be an *algebra of sets* on X, which is just to require that $\mathfrak{F}$ be nonempty and closed under union and complementation of sets; that is, if A and B are in $\mathfrak{F}$ then $A \cup B$ and $\sim A$ are also in $\mathfrak{F}$.

The intended interpretation of the primitive concepts for the three cases mentioned is fairly obvious. In the case of mass, X is a set of physical objects, and for two subsets A and B, $A \geq B$ if and only if the set A of objects is judged at least as heavy as the set B.

In the case of the rigid rods, the set X is just the collection of rods, and $A \geq B$ if and only if the set A of rods, when laid end to end in a straight line, is judged longer than the set B of rods also so laid out. Variations on exactly how this qualitative comparison of length is to be made can easily be supplied by the reader.

In the case of subjective probability, the set X is the set of possible outcomes of the experiment or empirical situation being considered. The subsets of X in $\mathfrak{F}$ are just events in the ordinary sense of probability concepts, and $A \geq B$ if and only if A is judged at least as probable as B.

Axioms for extensive measurement, subject to the two restrictions of finitude and equal spacing, are given in the following definition. In Axiom 5, $\approx$ is the equivalence relation defined in the standard fashion in terms of $\geq$; namely, $A \approx B$ if and only if $A \geq B$ and $B \geq A$.

DEFINITION 2. *A structure* $\chi = \langle X, \mathfrak{F}, \geq \rangle$ *is a finite, equally spaced extensive structure if and only if* X *is a finite set,* $\mathfrak{F}$ *is an algebra of sets on* X, *and the following axioms are satisfied for every* A, B, *and* C *in* $\mathfrak{F}$:

1. *The relation* $\geq$ *is a weak ordering of* $\mathfrak{F}$;
2. *If* $A \cap C = \emptyset$ *and* $B \cap C = \emptyset$, *then* $A \geq B$ *if and only if* $A \cup C \geq B \cup C$;
3. $A \geq \emptyset$;
4. *Not* $\emptyset \geq X$;
5. *If* $A \geq B$ *then there is a* C *in* $\mathfrak{F}$ *such that* $A \approx B \cup C$.

From the standpoint of the standard ideas about the measurement of mass or length, it would be natural to strengthen Axiom 3 to assert that if $A \neq \emptyset$, then $A > \emptyset$, but because this is not required for the representation theorem and is unduly restrictive in the case of subjective probability, the weaker axiom seems more appropriate.

In stating the representation and uniqueness theorem, we use the notion of an additive measure μ from $\mathfrak{F}$ to the real numbers, that is, a function μ such that for any A and B in $\mathfrak{F}$

(i) $\mu(\emptyset) = 0$
(ii) $\mu(A) \geq 0$
(iii) if $A \cap B = \emptyset$ then $\mu(A \cup B) = \mu(A) + \mu(B)$,

where $\emptyset$ is the empty set; it is also required for the applications intended here that $\mu(X) > 0$. A surprisingly strong representation theorem can be proved to the effect that there are only two nonequivalent sorts of atoms.

THEOREM. *Let* $\chi = \langle X, \mathfrak{F}, \geq \rangle$ *be a finite, equally spaced extensive structure. Then there exists an additive measure* μ *such that for every* A *and* B *in* $\mathfrak{F}$

$$\mu(A) \geq \mu(B) \text{ if and only if } A \geq B,$$

and the measure μ *is unique up to a positive similarity transformation. Moreover, there are at most two equivalence classes of atomic events in* $\mathfrak{F}$*; and if there are two rather than one, one of these contains the empty event.*

For proof of this theorem, see Suppes [1969a], Pt. I.

The "nice" question about this theory of extensive measurement, which is surely one of the simplest theories of fundamental measurement in its formal statement, is this. Without introducing a theory of error, can we realistically apply this theory to the construction of fundamental scales as, for example, in the construction of fundamental standards of weight or length? If we cannot, how are we to introduce the difficult and troublesome problem of error just at the point when we are making the transformation from qualitative to quantitative concepts? It is my belief that at the first stage of crude analysis we can forego any such explicit theory of error. More refined laboratory analysis is performed in terms of a recursive procedure of one system or set of standards being used to serve as the basis for the next stage. I am interested here only in the first stage of the institution of such procedures of quantitative measurement. At this stage, objects are constructed—for example, a fundamental set of weights—that seem to satisfy the axioms exactly. The next step of estimating the error of measurement to indicate the accuracy of the set of standards is a step beyond the first institution of fundamental measurement procedures. This additional step is needed for any sophisticated laboratory or field work. Nevertheless, a good case can be made for the claim that it is even necessary not to require it initially in order to get the transformation from the qualitative to the quantitative underway. In summary, I am claiming that many basic theories of fundamental measurement can be regarded as examples of deterministic theories with incorrigible data.

My third example, which is one of the most beautiful and important examples in the entire history of science, I shall only sketch, because of its complexity. The absence of an explicit theory of error is one of the great surprises about it. The example I have in mind is the development of ancient mathematical and observational astronomy leading up to the theory embodied in Ptolemy's *Almagest*. In spite of the closeness of fit achieved between theory and data in Ptolemaic astronomy, and the level of analysis that was thoroughly quantitative and mathematical in character, no explicit theory of error for the adjustment of discrepant observations is used anywhere in the corpus of ancient astronomy. It seems to be assumed, without being made explicit, that all normal observations must fit the theory exactly. At the very least, no systematic concept of error in the measurement of observations is introduced. This is especially surprising in certain respects because of the relatively crude observation methods available.

As I review the situation, the theory of human parenthood is an appropriate although overly simple case of deterministic formulation with incorrigible data. The second example of fundamental measurement is on the borderline of difficulties, and difficulties are indeed encountered once a more refined analysis is required. The Ptolemaic theory is in explicit terms a deterministic theory with incorrigible data, but the absence of a systematic theory of error is perhaps the greatest methodological failing of Ptolemaic astronomy.

2. Deterministic Theories with Corrigible Data

The great classical example of a theory of the type described by the heading of this section is classical mechanics. It needs to be mentioned at once that the corrigibility of the data does not follow from the structure of the theory as such, and in this respect all deterministic theories basically have the same structure. It does follow from the methodology of testing the theory. What has been fundamental about classical mechanics is that a very elaborate theory of error has been developed and applied extensively in the important applications of the theory. In other words, I am considering under this heading deterministic theories that incorporate within their own structure no theory of error, but that are applied to data recognized to contain errors, and therefore require some theory to handle the corrigibility of the data. In many respects, the impetus given to the theory of probability by Laplace's deep analysis of errors, especially in astronomical observations, has been one of the most important methodological features of modern science. It is above all a characteristic that distinguishes modern from ancient science.

If we distinguish modern quantitative science from premodern science by the presence or absence of a systematic theory of error, then Newton must be counted as premodern. The quantitative and systematic consideration of data in the *Principia* is almost entirely confined to Book III, and it is worth noting that in the Rules of Reasoning in Philosophy, with which Newton begins Book III, there is no mention of the problem of error or the rectification of unreasonable observations. It is true that in discussing both important phenomena and also the related propositions that follow in Book III, Newton does mention occasionally the neglect of errors and makes various qualitative remarks about errors of observation. For example, consider Phenomenon VI which is that the motion of the moon in relation to the earth's center describes an area proportional to the time of description. Following this description, Newton asserts "this we gather from the apparent motion of the moon, compared with its apparent diameter. It is true that the motion of the moon is a little disturbed by the action of the sun: But in laying down these Phenomena, I neglect those small and inconsiderable errors." Newton is also noted for his contributions to the theory of interpolation of data which, in itself, is an effort at reducing the magnitude of errors.

However, it was not until the eighteenth century that there appeared any systematic treatments of the theory of error. The earliest memoir on the application of probability theory to the analysis of error mentioned by Todhunter [1949] is a work published by William Simpson in 1757 under the title of *Miscellaneous Tracts on Some Curious, and Very Interesting Subjects in Mechanics, Physical-Astronomy, and Speculative Mathematics.* Again following Todhunter, the next systematic treatise on the topic was published by Lagrange in the fifth volume of the *Miscellanea Taurinensia,* which was issued for the years 1770 to 1773.

Granted the analytical difficulties that are quickly encountered in any general treatment of the theory of errors, it is not surprising that the first problem treated by Lagrange is described by Todhunter in the following words: "The first problem is as follows: It is supposed that at every observation there are A cases in which no error is made, B cases in which an error equal to 1 is made, and D cases in which an error equal to −1 is made; it is required to find the probability that in taking the mean of n observations, the results should be exact" (pp. 301–302). In subsequent problems treated in the memoir, Lagrange passes from the discrete to the continuous case. He finds thereby an expression for the probability that the error in the mean result will lie between assigned results on reasonably general hypotheses about the occurrence of single errors.

The entire subject of the analysis of errors of observation was brought to maturity by subsequent memoirs of Laplace, and it is really in Laplace's application of the apparatus of probability theory to errors in astronomical observation that the probabilistic analysis of incorrigible data reached a mature and sophisticated state.

As a result of the efforts of Simpson, Lagrange, Laplace, Gauss, and others, classical physics in the nineteenth century included a systematic theory of error analysis, and at least the elementary results were used in subjects as diverse as astronomy and electromagnetic theory.

On the other hand, it would be a mistake to exaggerate the extent to which the systematic theory of errors was actually used in nineteenth-century physics. A treatise as fundamental and as important as Maxwell's on electricity and magnetism scarcely includes anywhere in its entire two volumes quantitative analysis of errors of measurement. In fact, one of the disappointments of Maxwell's treatise, and an indication of the relative newness of his subject, is the absence of the often tedious and highly refined error-analyses of data in astronomy, where very small discrepancies between observation and theory are given great attention. It is a disappointment also that there is no real summary anywhere in the treatise of the discrepancy between theory and observation, and no attempt to assign these discrepancies to theory on the one hand and errors of measurement on the other. In the long history of astronomy such analysis has been of fundamental importance, and for that reason, in the twentieth century perhaps the best example of a deterministic theory with corrigible data is the theory of relativity. In this instance great attention has been given to the accuracy of the measuring apparatus. In assessing the success of the general theory of relativity it has been important to ask whether discrepancies that remain between theory and observation lie within the limits of error of observational measurement.

3. Probabilistic Theories with Incorrigible Data

As an example of the theory of the type discussed in this section, I have selected linear-learning theory from mathematical psychology. I choose this example not because of its conceptual depth or empirical adequacy, but because it can be formulated in a fairly simple way and will be understandable to someone not familiar with the general field of mathematical psychology. More adequate theories would require considerably more space and time to state explicity. For a general formulation of stimulus-response theory in axiomatic terms see Suppes [1969].

To simplify the presentation of the theory in an inessential way, let us assume that on every trial the organism in the experimental situation can make exactly one of two responses, A_1 or A_2, and after each response receives a reinforcement, E_1 or E_2, of one of the two possible responses. A possible experimental outcome in the sense of the theory is an infinite sequence of ordered pairs $\langle i, j \rangle$, where $i, j = 1, 2$ and i represents the observed response and j the reinforcement on a given trial of the experiment.

A possible realization of the theory is an ordered triple $\chi = \langle X, P, \theta \rangle$ of the following sort. The set X is the set of all sequences of ordered pairs $\langle i, j \rangle$ with $i, j = 1, 2$. The function P is a probability measure on the smallest σ-algebra containing the algebra of cylinder sets of X; and θ, a real number in the interval $0 < \theta \leq 1$, is the learning parameter.

To state the axioms of the theory, we need a certain amount of notation. Let $A_{i,n}$ be the event of response A_i on trial n, $E_{j,n}$ the event of reinforcement E_j on trial n, where $i, j = 1, 2$, and for x in X, let x_n be the equivalence class of all sequences in X which are identical with x through trial n.

DEFINITION 3. *A structure* $\chi = \langle X, P, \theta \rangle$ *is a linear-learning structure if and only if the following two axioms are satisfied for every* n *and for* $i, i', j = 1, 2$.

Axiom 1. If $P(E_{i,n}A_{i',n}x_{n-1}) > 0$, then

$$P(A_{i,n+1}|E_{i,n}A_{i',n}x_{n-1}) = (1-\theta)\, P(A_{i,n}|x_{n-1}) + \theta.$$

Axiom 2. *If* $P(E_{j,n}A_{i',n}x_{n-1}) > 0$ *and* $i \neq j$, *then*

$$P(A_{i,n+1}|E_{j,n}A_{i',n}x_{n-1}) = (1-\theta)\, P(A_{i,n}|x_{n-1}).$$

The first axiom asserts that when a response is reinforced, the probability of making that response on the next trial is increased by a simple linear transformation. The second axiom asserts that when a different response is reinforced, the probability of making the response is decreased by a second linear transformation. From a psychological standpoint, it is evident that this is what might be called a pure reinforcement theory of learning. The theory has been used extensively in analyzing experimental data. I shall not enter here into its strengths and weaknesses in the analysis of experiments, but concentrate on the general point of how such a probabilistic theory stands with respect to the data of any experiments to which it is applied.

To indicate how linear-learning structures are used in the analysis of experimental data, we may consider one of the simplest sorts of experiments, a probability-learning experiment with noncontingent reinforcement. We shall denote the probability of an E_1 reinforcement by π and the probability of an E_2 reinforcement by $1 - \pi$. The reinforcement schedule is such that exactly one reinforcement occurs on each trial.

The term *noncontingent* means that the probability of a particular reinforcement occurring is independent of the response of the subject and indeed of any previous pattern of responses and reinforcements. In a typical experiment with human subjects, the subjects are asked to respond for several hundred trials. The data for these trials are then analyzed in terms of their comparison between observed relative frequencies in the data and the predicted probabilities of the theory. The first problem to be faced, and a typical problem in all theories of any sophistication, is the estimation of parameters whose values cannot be determined independently. In the present situation the learning parameter θ has this status. It must be estimated itself from the data, and the predictions can only be made after this estimation has been obtained. In fact, for complete analysis of the data, an additional parameter must be estimated, namely, the initial probability of an A_1 response, but we shall ignore that problem here, looking only at asymptotic predictions.

The experimental data that we consider, to give this discussion concreteness, are drawn from Suppes and Atkinson [1960], Ch. 10. In this experiment, subjects sat at a table on which two keys were placed with two lights on a vertical board, one light directly above each key. The problem for the subject was to predict which light would flash on each trial. The flashing of the lights, of course, were the reinforcements E_1 and E_2 for the predictive key responses A_1 and A_2. Details of the experimental procedure and description of the apparatus are given in the book just referred to, and will not be repeated here. In the particular experiment we shall consider, each subject was run for 200 trials, and there were thirty subjects in the experiment. The subjects were all undergraduate students at Stanford. The probability of reinforcing E_1 was set at $\pi = 0.6$.

Let us first consider the problem of estimating the parameter θ at asymptote. We use a pseudomaximum-likelihood procedure based on the conditional probabilities

$$\lim_{n \to \infty} P(A_{i,n+1} | E_{j,n} A_{k,n}) = P(A_{i,n+1} | E_{j,n} A_{k,n}).$$

The derivation of these conditional probabilities as a function of θ and π is given in Estes and Suppes [1959]. For the case at hand the results are as follows:

$$\begin{aligned}
P_\infty(A_{1,n+1} | E_{1,n} A_{1,n}) &= (1 - \theta)a + \theta, \\
P_\infty(A_{1,n+1} | E_{2,n} A_{1,n}) &= (1 - \theta)a, \\
P_\infty(A_{2,n+1} | E_{1,n} A_{2,n}) &= (1 - \theta)b, \\
P_\infty(A_{2,n+1} | E_{2,n} A_{2,n}) &= (1 - \theta)b + \theta.
\end{aligned}$$

where

$$a = [2\pi(1-\theta) + \theta]/(2-\theta)$$

and

$$b = [2(1-\pi)(1-\theta) + \theta]/(2-\theta).$$

The function to be maximized is defined in terms of these conditional probabilities and the observed asymptotic transition frequencies. Specifically,

$$\begin{aligned} L^*(\theta) = {} & 748 \log [(1-\theta)\,a + \theta] \\ & + 298 \log [1 - (1-\theta)a - \theta] \\ & + 394 \log [(1-\theta)a] \\ & + 342 \log [1 - (1-\theta)a] \\ & + 462 \log [1 - (1-\theta)b] + 306 \log [(1-\theta)b] \\ & + 186 \log [1 - (1-\theta)b - \theta] \\ & + 264 \log [(1-\theta)b + b]. \end{aligned}$$

It is straightforward to solve this equation numerically and show that the maximum to two decimals is obtained with $\theta^* = .19$. It should be remarked immediately that this pseudomaximum-likelihood estimate is set up formally to look like a maximum-likelihood estimate, but it does not have the desirable statistical properties of a maximum-likelihood estimate. The pseudomaximum-likelihood rather than the maximum-likelihood estimate is used because of the difficulty of obtaining an analytical expression for the maximum-likelihood estimate itself. It is not appropriate here to enter into statistical details of the problem, but it is perhaps worth remarking that even for a theory of the simplicity of linear-learning structures, it is impossible to apply a good many of the standard statistical methods and criteria of excellence in estimators, and we must resort to less satisfactory methods. In the present case, as the pseudomaximum-likelihood estimator is changed by increasing the conditionalization through the inclusion of further pieces of the past, the full maximum-likelihood estimate is approached closer and closer. (Even this guarantee of approaching the maximum-likelihood estimator is itself dependent upon the process being ergodic.)

TABLE 1. Comparison of Asymptotic Sequential Predictions of Linear Model with Observed Data

	Observed	Predicted
$P(A_1 \mid E_1A_1)$	.715	.710
$P(A_1 \mid E_2A_1)$	.535	.520
$P(A_1 \mid E_1A_2)$	.602	.625
$P(A_1 \mid E_2A_2)$	.413	.435

For the estimated value of θ, comparison of the predicted frequencies and the observed relative frequencies is given in Table 1. The χ^2 test for goodness of fit between the predicted and observed values yields a χ^2 of 3.49. There are four degrees of freedom, but one parameter has been estimated from the data, and so the χ^2 is to be interpreted with the degrees of freedom equal to 3 and, as would be expected from inspection of Table 1, there is not a statistically significant difference between the predicted and the observed data. There are other theoretical relationships in the data that are predicted by the theory, and for which the fit is not as good. We shall not pursue these matters here; they are discussed in detail in the reference already cited.

Even in Table 1 there is some evidence of discrepancy, and it is interesting to see how one may think about these discrepancies within the framework of a probabilistic theory.

From an a priori standpoint we might wish to say that some of the data were wrongly recorded, and in unusual situations, where peculiar and difficult-to-understand aspects of the data turned up, we might indeed challenge the veracity of the data. However, in all normal cases, when we claim the data are incorrigible, we mean that the data are accepted without challenge, and there is no systematic attempt to estimate error in the measurements or in the recording of the data. It is evident why this is so in the present case. All that is recorded on each trial is the occurrence of a left or right response and the occurrence of a left or right reinforcement immediately following. Under ordinary circumstances no errors will be made, and in particular, the theory of observational errors as developed in physics is not required for the assessment of errors in this type of observation. Consequently we would be unlikely to attribute discrepancies between data and theory to errors of observation. We would treat the data as incorrigible in all normal cases, and this is exactly the situation in the present instance. In other words, in testing probabilistic theories, data that involve classification are treated as incorrigible. There is a deeper reason also why the data are treated as incorrigible; the theory itself provides slack, so to speak, to take up the small discrepancies between theory and experiment, and there is a natural tendency always to use this slack, rather than presumed errors in recording, in analyzing any discrepancies that do exist. In the present case, the natural explanation of small discrepancies between the observed and predicted values is to be found in the statistical theory of sampling. It is exactly why we have applied a χ^2 test. What the χ^2 test says is that for the number of observations being considered here, sampling fluctuations of the order obtained do not indicate a significant discrepancy between theoretical predictions and experimental data. It is to be emphasized that the way in which this comparison is built into probabilistic theories is much more natural and direct than in the case of deterministic theories. In the case of deterministic theories, the comparison cannot be made within the theory itself but must be pushed outside to the theory of errors of measurement and errors of observation, and then the best estimates obtained by applying the theory of errors of measurement are used to test the deterministic predictions of the theory. Even then, we must append an additional discussion to ask whether or not the small discrepancies still existing between theory and experiment are to be regarded as significant, and once again the discussion is not wholly natural as it is in the case of probabilistic theories.

4. Probabilistic Theories with Corrigible Data

Undoubtedly the most significant scientific example of a theory of this type is quantum mechanics. The theory itself is thoroughly probabilistic in character, and at the same time, the data are corrigible in the sense being used in this paper. The standard theory of errors is used in many cases to analyze observations and is reported in a high percentage of experimental papers. However, even in the case of quantum mechanics, in spite of the fact that many of the variables are continuous in character and therefore naturally subject to a systematic theory of error of observation, many analyses of the fit between data and theory are inadequate from a statistical standpoint. This is all the more surprising in the case of quantum mechanics, in contradistinction to a typical sort of theory I shall describe in a moment, because in quantum mechanics there has been a tendency for physicists to sweep the probabilistic aspects of theory under the rug. I mean by this that they will look at expectations, for example, in terms of such large samples that the slack introduced by probabilistic theories, as discussed above, is totally eliminated.

In the case of theories that are tested in terms of full distributions of random variables and not simply in terms of expectations, a standard theory of error is often not applied, even though it is evident that errors in measurement are definitely present. Reasons for this have already been given. It is because the slack introduced by the probabilistic formulation of the theory and the sampling assumptions involved in considering the fit of a finite body of data to a predicted distribution do in themselves account for any minor discrepancies between theory and experiment.

It may be useful to examine one such theory of a simple character in some detail. The natural generalization of linear-learning structures to a continuum of responses provides an easy case to consider. The discussion here follows Suppes [1959a].

For either the finite or the continuous case an experiment may be represented by a sequence $(A_1, E_1, A_2, E_2, \ldots, A_n, E_n, \ldots)$ of random variables, where the choice of letters follows conventions established in the literature: the value of the random variable A_n is the number representing the actual response on trial n, and the value of E_n is the number representing the reinforcing event which occurred on trial n. Any sequence of values of these random variables represents a possible experimental outcome. Hereafter, we write down only finite sequences of these random variables, and it is convenient to write them in reverse order: $(E_n, A_n, E_{n-1}, A_{n-1}, \ldots, E_1, A_1)$.

For both the finite and continuous models, the theory is formulated for the probability of a response on trial $n + 1$ given the entire preceding sequence of responses and reinforcements. For this preceding sequence we use the notation s_n. Thus, more formally, s_n is a finite sequence of length 2n of possible values of the sequence of random variables $(E_n, A_n, E_{n-1}, A_{n-1}, \ldots, E_1, A_1)$. The (cumulative) joint distribution of the first n responses and n reinforcements is denoted by J_n; that is, if

$$s_n = (y_n, x_n, \ldots, y_1, x_1),$$

then

$$\begin{aligned} J_n(s_n) &= J_n(y_n, x_n, \ldots, y_1, x_1) \\ &= P(E_n \leq y_n, A_n \leq x_n, \ldots, E_1 \leq y_1, A_1 \leq x_1), \end{aligned}$$

where P is the measure on the underlying sample space. For notational clarity we use variables $x_1, x_2, \ldots, x_n, \ldots$ for values of the response random variables and $y_1, y_2, \ldots, y_n \ldots$ for the reinforcement random variables.

In the continuous case we have a learning parameter θ, which serves much the same function as the corresponding parameter of the finite model. However, it does not seem reasonable for the full effect of reinforcement to be concentrated at a point as it is for the finite case. Consequently we add a *smearing distribution* $K(x;y)$ which spreads the effect of reinforcement around the point of reinforcement. For each reinforcement y, $K(x;y)$ is a distribution on responses; that is, $K(a;y) = 0$ and $K(b;y) = 1$, and if $x \leq x'$, then $K(x;y) \leq K(x';y)$ for every y in [a,b].

The first two axioms below are simply directed at making explicit assumptions of smoothing properties which seem highly justified empirically. The third axiom asserts the analogue of the two axioms for the finite case.

Axiom C1. *The distribution* J_n *is continuous and piecewise twice differentiable in both variables.*

Axiom C2. *The distribution* $K(x;y)$ *is continuous and piecewise twice differentiable in both variables.*

Axiom C3. $J_{n+1}(x|y_n, x_n, s_{n-1}) = (1-\theta)\, J_n(x|s_{n-1}) + \theta K(x; y_n)$.

Axiom C3 says that given the sequence (y_n, x_n, s_{n-1}), the conditional distribution of the response random variable on trial $n+1$ is $(1-\theta)$ times the conditional distribution of the response random variable on trial n given the sequence s_{n-1}, plus θ times the smearing distribution $K(x;y_n)$. The parameter of the smearing distribution is the point of reinforcement y_n in the sequence (y_n, x_n, s_{n-1}).

In experiments used to test this theory extensively over several years, we used an apparatus consisting of a large circular disc which, for measuring purposes, was divided uniformly into 400 arcs of equal length. When a subject made a response, or when a reinforcement was given, data were recorded in terms of one of these 400 numbers. The circular disc itself had a diameter of approximately six feet, and so it was easy to determine more accurately the exact point of reinforcement or response, but from the standpoint of testing the theory there was no need for a more accurate observation. The fit between data and theory could be satisfactorily tested by histograms that in fact did not even use the 400-scale, but aggregated observations into divisions of a still coarser scale in order to have a sufficient number of observations in each cell to meet the theoretical requirements of standard statistical tests like that of χ^2.

Continuous linear-learning structures exemplify an early stage in the development of probabilistic theories with corrigible data. There is no question about the corrigibility of the data. The observations are not accurate and a systematic theory of error is appropriate, but it is simply not needed. This is because the theory has not yet been very thoroughly developed, and the phenomena under investigation are being studied at a relatively crude quantitative level compared to the kind of quantitative results that dominate ancient and thoroughly developed disciplines like classical astronomy.

On the other hand, as I have already emphasized, one of the most important characteristics of probabilistic theories is to provide apparatus to derive very exact quantitative conclusions from what appear to be rather weak probabilistic assumptions. One of the important areas of investigation in terms of the structure of probabilistic theories has been the pursuit of asymptotic results, or more generally, results that hold with probability 1. Once results that depend upon very large samples and invoke thereby some one of the laws of large numbers are applied, the slack between theory and experiment is eliminated, and errors of measurement must once again come into play and be given their proper place.

I have provided a natural fourfold classification of theories, and it might be thought that I intend for this classification to be exhaustive and definitive. However, it is apparent that it is a fairly crude classification, and as I suggested at the beginning, it should only be regarded as a preliminary taxonomy. Quantum mechanics provides one of the best examples of how the classification given here needs further elaboration and refinement. From a philosophical standpoint, one of the most important topics in quantum mechanics is the discussion at the end of von Neumann's treatise of the quantum mechanical treatment of the interaction between experimental phenomena and the measuring apparatus used to observe the phenomena. In this case of interaction, which is important in microscopic phenomena, additional and subtle things are to be said about the relations between theory and data, and I have not begun to touch upon these topics here.

5. Some Philosophical Conclusions

The order in which the four types of theories have been discussed here represents in a fairly accurate way the chronological order of development. Ancient astronomy is the paradigm case of a deterministic theory with incorrigible data, and as I have indicated, even Newton's work can fairly be put under this heading. The sophisticated development of a theory of errors in combination with celestial mechanics by Laplace is the paradigm example of a deterministic theory with corrigible data. The many investigations in the behavioral sciences, in biology and in medicine of qualitative phenomena, represent paradigm cases of probabilistic theories with incorrigible data. Finally, stochastic processes with continuous random variables, the sorts of theories that have only recently come into their own in various parts of science, are the natural examples of probabilistic theories with corrigible data.

It seems to me that the first and oldest type of theory represents a naive way of thinking about the world that is still very much present in large parts of philosophy. It is a way of thinking about the world that demands two general characteristics of its theories and its evidence. First, the theories should be absolute; the causal analysis given in the theories should be final and ultimate. Second, the data of the experiments should rest ultimately on something that is perceptually certain and without any component of error. In actual scientific work, even in ancient times, it of course had to be recognized that these objectives could not be fully met and some account had to be given of error, although the central tendency was to accept the theories as ultimate. Aristotle's physics and his account of the motion of the heavens very much fit into this framework, but this belief in ultimate concepts and incorrigible data has existed far into modern times. Descartes' *Principia* is one of the best examples in the first half of the seventeenth century. Descartes reduces all causes of motion to simple impact, and he seems firmly to believe that this is an ultimate account of the cause of motion, or more exactly, change in motion. His efforts to find a rockbed of perceptual certainty are too familiar to recount here. Descartes had enough good sense to realize that a program of absolutism and certainty could not be carried through in detail to explain all physical phenomena, and consequently, he was willing to introduce hypotheses that were clearly admitted to be hypotheses in the latter part of the *Principia*. It is here that he used his theory of vortices to account for major physical phenomena. (The incorrectness of most of the account he gives is not an issue here.)

This same search for absolutism of concepts and certainty of knowledge finds perhaps its most sophisticated expression in Kant. Not only *The Critique of Pure Reason,* but also in greater detail, *The Metaphysical Foundations of Natural Science* attempts to argue that a genuinely ultimate account of causes in nature can be given. This is kept at a fairly general level in the discussion of causation in the *Critique,* but it becomes much more particular and definite in the *Metaphysical Foundations* where Kant attempts to give an account in terms only of forces of attraction and repulsion. What is important from a philosophical standpoint is that the general propositions alleged to be true of these causes of motion are known a priori and are not based in any fashion upon experiment. It is often remarked that Kant attempted to convert classical mechanics into a systematic metaphysics, but it seems to me at least as important to remark that in his search for an ultimate basis of knowledge he was working in an absolutistic tradition as old as Plato and one that has been extremely difficult to escape from.

Even so empirical and cautious a philosopher as John Stuart Mill believed that by the processes of careful scientific investigation we should reach ultimate laws, and ultimate laws for him were laws that are deterministic and not probabilistic in character. Here is a useful summarizing statement of his view (Mill [1936], p. 318):

> The preceding considerations have led us to recognise a distinction between two kinds of laws or observed uniformities in nature—ultimate laws and what may be termed derivative laws. Derivative laws are such as are deducible from, and may, in any of the modes which we have pointed out, be resolved into other and more general ones. Ultimate laws are those which cannot. We are not sure that any of the uniformities with which we are yet acquainted are ultimate laws; but we know that there must be ultimate laws, and that every resolution of a derivative law into more general laws brings us nearer to them.

The general philosophical thrust of this paper should now be evident. The doctrine that I want to preach is this. Consider the classical philosophical theses that an absolute causal account can be given of phenomena, that ultimate laws of a deterministic sort can be gleaned from natural phenomena, and that some rockbed of perceptual certainty is necessary to gain a firm knowledge of the world. All three of these theses are false and hopelessly out of date in terms of the kinds of theories now coming to dominate science. In ordinary talk and ordinary affairs, such certainty and absolutism are not necessary and are in fact deleterious to the exercise of good sense. It is from ancient antecedents in religion and philosophy, not from ordinary experience, that these fallacious doctrines have been drawn and have received sanction for so long a time.

There is somewhere a beautiful quotation from deFinetti in which as part of defending the Bayesian use of far-from-certain prior information in making decisions, he says that it is better to build on sand than on a void. I believe we can rephrase this remark and say something that is important for philosophy. When it comes to matters of knowledge, real houses are always built on sand and never on rock.

Commentary on Suppes's "The Structure of Theories and the Analysis of Data"

Editor's note: The commentary on Professor Suppes's paper at the symposium was given by Professor Sylvain Bromberger; he received Patrick Suppes's paper only a few hours prior to the Second Session of the Symposium, and so the commentary he presented was a somewhat impressionistic and off-the-cuff informal presentation given without the benefit of a prepared text. Unfortunately circumstances have prevented Professor Bromberger from preparing a more formal commentary subsequent to the symposium for inclusion here. Nevertheless, the commentary he gave figures in the discussion which follows and also in the discussion of Session V; accordingly, it is necessary to include a commentary which makes those points Professor Bromberger made which came up in discussion. What follows is an attempt by the Editor to develop some of the main points raised by Professor Bromberger in his commentary. It has been prepared without the benefit of a full transcript of Professor Bromberger's commentary, and so there is no guarantee that what follows is either what he presented or would wish to present; however, to the best of the Editor's ability, it attempts to make the strongest case he can for what, so far as he can reconstruct, were the main points of Professor Bromberger's commentary. Accordingly, nothing which follows is Professor Bromberger's responsibility. Although he has been forced to play the Devil's advocate in preparing it, the Editor accepts full responsibility for what follows.

Professor Suppes's paper consists largely of an attempt to develop a philosophically illuminating taxonomy of theories. It is the contention of this commentary that he has failed to do so. As this is a strong charge, let me attempt to substantiate it.

Professor Suppes's taxonomy of theories is a four-fold one drawn on the basis whether theories are deterministic or not and whether they apply to corrigible or incorrigible data. By a deterministic theory, he understands a theory which contains no probabilistic notions. By incorrigible data, he understands data to which no theory of error is applied in measuring, recording, or analyzing them. Although he does not make it explicit, he apparently is identifying theories of error with statistical theories or analyses of error.

This taxonomy is rather curious, for it is a taxonomy which attempts to classify theories partially on the basis of extratheoretical considerations. Whether a theory is deterministic depends upon features of the theory; but whether data is incorrigible or not is independent of the theory's structure, being rather a matter how the theory is applied to phenomena. Suppose a theory were applied sometimes to corrigible data (that is, data to which a theory of error has been applied) and other times to incorrigible data (that is, data to which a theory of error has not been applied). According to Professor Suppes's taxonomy, we have got two different kinds of theories, hence two different theories, depending on which kind of data we apply it to. But this is absurd—it is the same theory in both cases, the only difference being how it is applied to phenomena. Or, perhaps, Professor Suppes would want to say it is the same theory, but that in such a case, the theory falls under two different classes. In either case, it is an inadequate classification for theories: for it either proliferates theories or else classifies them in an ambiguous and not very helpful or illuminating way. That is, the reason for its inadequacy as a classification is that it tries to classify theories on the basis of extratheoretical considerations.

The taxonomy also is too crude to be philosophically illuminating. This is so for two reasons. First, the distinctions between deterministic and indeterministic (or probabilistic) theories, and between corrigible and incorrigible data, do not satisfactorily separate out the various philosophically significant ways in which theories are or are not deterministic, and the ways in which data are or are not incorrigible. Second, the taxonomy is too misleading to be philosophically useful. I say it is misleading because we do not normally mean by saying a theory is deterministic that it does not contain probabilistic notions. Quantum theory is deterministic in a very straightforward way, even though it is fundamentally statistical. And we certainly do not usually mean that data is incorrigible whenever it does not make recourse to a probabilistic theory of error. Thus the divisions between kinds of theories seem to be drawn at the wrong places. More important, however, is the fact that the taxonomy is excessively crude. It is excessively crude because neither Professor Suppes's distinction between deterministic and indeterministic theories, nor his distinction between corrigible and incorrigible data, divide theories or data into groupings which are similar or dissimilar in any philosophically significant way. Take his division of data into the corrigible and the incorrigible: It is true that the data to which theories are applied differ in how errors are handled, and that these differences sometimes are philosophically significant, affecting the way in which theories are confirmed, the sorts of predictions they can make, and so on. But surely the significant differences are not whether a *probabilistic* or statistical theory of error has been applied to the data. To treat this as the significant difference, as Professor Suppes does, is to lump together most of the interesting cases under incorrigible data. To say that a statistical theory of error has not been applied to data is not very revealing about how errors are handled, for it treats those cases where no error corrections were made on a par with those cases where significant error corrections were made without recourse to statistics. It lumps Galileo's and Kepler's work, which involved widespread error correction, together with the Babylonians and Greeks who apparently were unconcerned with errors. A useful classification of data on the basis of how errors are handled would enable us to distinguish the ways in which errors are handled, whether the means were statistical or not. Professor Suppes's taxonomy fails to do so. Moreover, his classification is positively pernicious and misleading here since it suggests that the only desirable way to handle errors is by recourse to statistical theories of errors. Not only is this suggestion unsubstantiated, but there seem to be cases where all the evidence suggests errors should not be handled in this way. I have in mind the lack of success in using statistical means of handling errors in data to be applied to theories of grammar and psycholinguistics. Not only have the attempts to do so been very unsatisfactory, but also there is every reason to suppose they should fail. For such theories are intended to be theories of linguistic competence, whereas the data is collected from fallible humans who only approximate competence to varying degrees. And there is no reason to suppose that a statistical theory of error will be of any use. For here the error correction involves converting the data gathered about the fallible semicompetent linguistic behavior of humans into data about how a linguistically competent human would behave; and there is no statistical theory of error known or anticipated which can do that. Similarly, a statistical theory of error can not handle Galileo's error problems which involved error corrections which consisted of converting data about how bodies acted in the atmosphere into data about how they *would* act in a vacuum. Often how errors are handled seems to be largely a matter of which relevant parameters we are ignorant of, not whether we apply statistical error routines. My point, then, which these examples have tried to illustrate, is that there are a number of different philosophically significant ways errors in data can be handled other than by recourse to statistical theories of error. Professor Suppes's division of data into the corrigible and the incorrigible glosses over most of them, and thus is too crude—too crude in such a way that his division appears to be philosophically unilluminating.

His division of theories into the deterministic and the indeterministic also is too crude. Theories which contain probabilistic notions can employ them in different ways; and theories which do not make recourse to them can be invoked to do a number of different things—to make different sorts of predictions or explanations. For example, classical particle mechanics and the theory of ideal gases both do not contain probabilistic notions in their formulations and are used to make predictions. But the former enables us to predict unique subsequent states in a "deterministic" fashion, whereas the latter only enables us to predict equivalent equilibrium states. In particular, the theory of ideal gases can yield predictions of unique subsequent states only if certain additional external constraints are assumed; no such constraints are required in the classical case. Or consider the difference between quantum theory and a finite Markov process. Both theories utilize probabilistic notions in their formulations. In the former, the notion of a state is statistical, and the theory can be used to make "deterministic" predictions (for example, via the Schrödinger wave equation) what statistically specified states the system subsequently will assume. On the other hand, in the Markov process the states are not statistically specified; rather the transition between states occurs in a statistical manner. The point I am trying to illustrate with these examples is that the philosophically significant differences between kinds of theories are not whether they make recourse to probabilistic notions. Rather, insofar as the inclusion of probabilistic notions is significant it is a question of how they function in the theory, not whether they do. And more generally, the philosophically significant differences which ought to be displayed by an adequate taxonomy have to do with what sorts of predictions, and so forth, the theory can make; and this is not primarily a matter whether the theory takes recourse to probabilistic notions.

There is one further difficulty in Professor Suppes's distinction between deterministic and indeterministic theories. He draws the distinction on the basis whether they involve probabilistic notions. It is by no means clear what it means to "involve" probabilistic notions. Presumably he means that a probabilistic operator figures in the statement of the theory. If this is what he means, then presumably Darwin's formulation of the theory of evolution is deterministic—which seems an absurd thing to say. If we allow more informal analogues to probability operators, we can handle Darwin. But what about the ideal gas laws? No probabilistic notions occur in the formulation of these laws, but the formalism is usually interpreted as describing determinate relations between pressure, volume, and temperature which occur as a result of large-scale random movements of gas particles. Are we to say that the ideal gas laws involve probabilistic notions or not? Are we to classify this theory as deterministic or not? Again, Professor Suppes's taxonomy seems too crude.

To summarize the connected series of points I have been making: There are a number of philosophically significant different ways in which errors can be handled and there are a number of philosophically significant different ways in which theories can characterize the phenomena within their scopes. Taxonomies of either which display these differences are philosophically desirable and would be useful. Professor Suppes's taxonomy is excessively crude and obliterates these philosophically significant differences by drawing the wrong distinctions. His distinctions do not display the philosophically significant cuts. Moreover, his taxonomy fails by trying to classify theories in terms of the extratheoretical issue how the theory is applied to the phenomena.

As a final note I want to reject the conclusion Professor Suppes draws at the end of his paper. There he seems to be implying that the emergence of probabilistic theories in science shows the outmodedness of the idea that scientific theories (1) should give an absolute casual account; (2) should yield ultimate deterministic laws; and (3) must rest on some rockbed of perceptual certainty. Although I accept his conclusion I want to strongly deny that his argument shows these theses false. All that follows from the present-day use of probabilistic theories in science is that science today accepts theories which do not meet these standards. It certainly does not follow that these standards are undesirable; all that follows is that these standards are out-of-date in the sense that they are not fashionable today. To show they are out-of-date in the stronger sense of being naive desires which ought to be rejected would require philosophical arguments of a sort not found in Professor Suppes's paper.

Discussion

Professor Suppes:

It is fun to have this opportunity to reply to Sylvain. I should mention that Sylvain and I have known each other for many years so we do not have to hold the punches; we have been arguing since the 1940s when we were graduate students together at Columbia. My first response to Sylvain is this. He says that nothing happens in my paper. I say of his commentary, "Lots of smoke but no fire." More seriously, let me deal with some of the issues that he raised that I think are pertinent and necessary to bear down on. First, on his point about the distinction between a theory being deterministic and my distinction about the corrigibility of data, I certainly do agree—and I said as much in the paper—that determinism in a theory is intrinsic to the formal statement or the intrinsic statement in the theory, whereas the corrigibility of the data will vary with the way in which a theory is applied. But if we go back to the kind of account that Professor Hempel was giving us yesterday[1] and that most people tend to give, we do not identify the theory just with the statement of principles. We also have some bridging to the experiments and the data. And so I have included that within my conception of theory while still agreeing that there is a distinction between what we formally call the statement of principles—or in my terms the axiomatic statement—and the theory. I concur about this and I do not see the point of arguing about something I state already in my paper. I cannot agree, and do not think that Sylvain's arguments have established that a different theory of error is at work in the examples he cites from Galileo and the grammarians and psycholinguists. He bases this claim on the fact that Galileo was really interested in the vacuum but had to do business in the atmosphere, and that the grammarians and psycholinguists are interested in a theory of competence but have to do business with fallible human beings. But I consider it a

[1] See Hempel's contribution to this volume in Session I, above.

mistake to put matters this way, and would claim that it is just an expedient simplification on the part of Galileo, the grammarians, and the psycholinguists. It is not that there is any interest in the vacuum as opposed to the atmosphere, it is just that the theory would be difficult to formulate if proper attention were given to the atmosphere. I am not willing to concede that there is a different kind of theory of error—a different sort of beast, so to speak.

To turn to the next point, there is a confusion in Sylvain's reading of my paper. I certainly do not argue in my paper that the outmodedness of the absolutism and certainty I mentioned at the end follows from or is implied by the existence of probabilistic theories. What I think is important is the change in the atmosphere both in science and in philosophy. I would not want to say that the existence of probabilistic theories argues for the outmodedness of doctrines of absolute or ultimate casuality or of certainty in perception. What I would say if I wanted to make that point (which I did not make) is that the nonexistence of deterministic theories for certain important and fundamental phenomena argues for the outmodedness. In this respect it is important to recall Laplace's position on determinism. Paradoxically enough, Laplace formulated his great thesis about determinism not in his treatise on celestial mechanics[2] but in his treatise on probability,[3] because for him probability was subjective. According to him probability was operative due to ignorance of causes. An important thing has happened to Laplace's deterministic viewpoint about scientific theories. It is this. Other than when scientists are in church, Laplace's deterministic viewpoint is neither seriously accepted nor a serious matter of doctrine in science today. And it seems to me that the nonexistence of successful deterministic theories has led to the outmodedness of the Laplacean—or, if you will, Kantian—doctrine.

Sylvain says that the classification I have entered into is not of any interest, and mentions issues that he says are of interest. Since I have already read a long paper, I do not think I will recapitulate why I think the classification I have given is of some interest. There is, however, one point in his comments with which I certainly would agree—namely, that my classification is crude. It is preliminary and meant to be crude. Many additional distinctions of importance and significance about problems of error exist; in this I can concur with him. But, I do not think that he has offered us any serious alternative for a beginning point. I think his rhetorical reference to ignorance is fine but it is just

[2] Laplace [1882].
[3] Laplace [1814] and [1951].

that, a rhetorical reference; it does not offer any classification of theories as an alternative to what I have been proposing. Admitting, I emphasize, the crudity of the distinctions I have made, let me close these comments with one final remark. The development of probabilistic theories and the recognition that the deterministic theories which formerly dominated classical physics apparently are not going to dominate science from this point onward are important and fundamental facts about science with very considerable implications for philosophy. The historical course of development from deterministic theories with ultimate casual analysis and incorrigible data to probabilistic theories with corrigible data is a development of both scientific and philosophical significance of the first order.

Professor Causey:

I would just like to ask Pat Suppes a very general question which may help to inform me a little. Suppose a scientist is studying certain phenomena and is trying to develop a theory of this phenomena and has had "partial success" with a deterministic theory in the following way: He has been able to get reasonable agreement with the predictions from his deterministic theory only by assuming that very large experimental errors are involved. Thus, he becomes interested in the possibility of constructing a probabilistic theory, and perhaps using a theory of errors along with it. To what extent can the presently existing theory of statistics give him any guidance as to whether he should try to develop a probabilistic theory or not? In other words, to what extent can this theory be a methodological aid to him in the actual construction of theories—or can it?

Professor Suppes:

In many classical cases it seems to me that the evidence is quite clear. Radiation decay is a good case in point. Let us take a very common, ordinary phenomenon that is related to a radiation-type phenomenon, the prediction when a light bulb will go out; this displays probabilistically all the distributional phenomena of radiation in a very ordinary example. The differences in measurement of duration of homogeneously prepared light bulbs is too large to be due to errors of measurement. What is fundamental for my thesis is that there do exist many obvious cases in which a probabilistic theory is called for because the discrepancies clearly cannot be accounted for by errors of observation or any known deterministic theories.

Professor Putnam:

I am bothered by your attack on deterministic theories. Of course, as you use the term 'deterministic', it is not the usual issue of determinism. Your attack on deterministic theories at the end of the paper seems to me to be not really well supported either by the internal argumentation of the paper or by what you now bring in about the external development of science. It seems to me that your classification is that theories may be divided into those which contain the term 'probability' and those which do not. This is true, but is important only insofar as probability is a notion that we still have not succeeded in successfully explicating. I mean here that I think it is interesting to divide theories into those which contain explicitly some such notions as 'random', or, 'at random', or 'by chance', or explicitly the mathematics of probability and those that do not, for the simple reason that we still do not know how to restate the former kinds of theories in some other way. But it is also important now that we also do not know that in principle it cannot be done; and of course both in statistical mechanics and in quantum mechanics that is a very hot issue. Second, you are dividing data into data which uses your favorite mathematics—that is the mathematics of error—and that which does not. While both cuts may be interesting from the standpoint of a probability theorist or a statistician, I do not think that either cut can be a major philosophical cut. I doubt whether the division of theories into those which use the notion of probability and those which do not is even as important as that between theories that use the calculus and those that do not. And I would be the last to say that as philosophers of science that this is the major way in which we should chop up theories. Now remembering that by 'deterministic theory' you mean a theory that does not use this mathematics of probability, I think that your statement that science is moving away from deterministic theories toward probabilistic theories is very weakly supported by the evidence. Maxwell's theory is the only theory that really has held up, that may for all we know really be true from the very small to the very large. That is an amazing fact: the one theory which really has had an enormous and unprecedented survival value is the theory of the electromagnetic tensor which is not a probabilistic theory. And in spite of your criticism of Maxwell for not being very interested in measurement error, it is a theory in which we have great confidence today. Take gravitational theory; we have no totally successful gravitational theory, but there are lots of statements which we can make without using the concept of probability which are true, at least if you are willing to quantify over potentials and fields which spread out from every single massive body in the universe. This happens to be a retarded potential and not a noninstantaneous potential, but Newton was not totally wrong in the "deterministic", if you like, statement, that every single body in the universe emanates a field or potential, which spreads out indefinitely and can keep spreading out. That is a very important deterministic statement. I do not see the fact that we may want to use the notion of probability in some statements is any reason to think that we will ever want to stop making statements in science which do not contain the notion of probability at all. Finally to come to quantum mechanics, I think myself by the way that it can be reformulated as a deterministic theory—but that, of course, is a very lively issue of controversy. On the light-bulb example, suppose you say that one cannot have a deterministic theory of when the light bulb will stop burning—and support that by reference to quantum mechanics—saying that it depends on certain quantum events which are in principle unpredictable. But the trouble with that is that quantum mechanics—even in its standard form and its von Neumann form—does not say of a single observable that its future values in principle are unpredictable. In fact one of the criticisms of the von Neumann axiomatization is that it implies precisely the reverse: for any observer at any time t, if you want to know the value of that observable at a future time t' there exists some observable such that if you measured it right now you could predict that value of that observable at the future time t'. In other words, if the light bulb stops burning right now there is, in principle, some measurement I could have made this morning which would have told me that fact. Now probably I did not measure that observable this morning, so the unpredictability of when the light bulb will stop burning reduces to the truism that if you did not make the appropriate measurement at the appropriate time then you cannot predict the appropriate observable at the appropriate later time. Accordingly, I think that in fact this one theory, quantum mechanics, which is itself one for which we have no generally agreed upon interpretation, is a very poor thing on which to stake a general claim with respect to scientific theories. I think it is something like "human beings cannot really know the laws," an attitude typical of advanced capitalism.

Professor Suppes:

Hilary Putnam has brought up a number of issues that I think are important. Let me deal with some of the particular questions first. I am sorry that I did not bring any empirical data on this question, but if we look at the current literature of science—that is, contemporary literature of what is being published now as new science—I think I could muster some pretty good support for some of my claims about probabilistic theories. We could look at the change in frequency over time of probabilistic theories in major scientific publications in various areas and see if what I am saying is true. I mean that I think that my claim regarding the change in types of theories is an empirical claim that I have not supported with any serious data. Still, I think we would all agree that if you looked at the physical literature before 1850, let us say, there would not be any probabilistic theories in physics; and charting that change from 1850 to 1969 I think would be an interesting task.

Regarding Maxwell's theory, I do have to take exception to the universality that Hilary Putnam mentions in the following sense: it is standard in modern textbooks on electromagnetic theory to state very carefully what are the dimensions at which it is claimed the theory holds. For example, it is standard to say that electromagnetic theory in its classical presentation is not meant to hold below measurements of the order of 10^{-6} centimeters, and a number of standard current texts will give a very careful and very explicit statement of the limitation of the theory regarding the microscopic. I am not sure that Hilary's remark was in that direction, but I think it is important to note that is exactly the kind of thing and the sort of qualification we find missing in Maxwell. But in addition to that point, I would like to return to what I said about Maxwell's theory in my paper. I think, for example, that though Newton does not have an explicit theory of error there is much greater attention to error in Book III of Newton's *Principia*[4] than there is in Maxwell's treatise on electricity and magnetism.[5] When one reads Maxwell's treatise, one cannot come away from it with a clear sense of what are the problems that are not understood: What are things that are probably problems of measurement error? Where is the fit not too good because our measuring setup is not too good? What are the things that the theory does not treat in satisfactory form? It is disappointing that Maxwell's treatise is indeed not better on exactly that kind of separation. I completely agree with your remarks about Newton; my point about Newton simply is that there is no systematic system of error. As to Hilary's remarks about quantum mechanics as a deterministic theory, I think I will pass by that one; that is a rather elaborate and special argument which would take us too far afield. I do not agree

[4] Newton [1968].
[5] Maxwell [1892].

with Hilary's analysis of the light-bulb case, and I think I would like to stick by my comments. The claims he makes are large and the proof is in the pudding of detailed analysis, which he does not offer. I am skeptical that even theoretically it can be done.

Regarding his general doubt that the distinction between deterministic and probabilistic theories is philosophically important, I would like to expand briefly on the remarks made in the paper. Both the notion of the contrast between deterministic and probabilistic theories and the contrast between corrigible and incorrigible data are very much tied up with our notions of error, our notions of cause, and our notions of randomness. It seems to me that one of the great intellectual surprises is the extreme lateness of any theory of randomness, any systematic theory of probability, and any systematic theory of error. In view of the close connections between philosophy and theology, and their joint thrust for certainty and absolutism, the intertwining of science and philosophy in ways of thinking about randomness and the increasing intrusion of these ideas into the mainstream of science is philosophically important. It is the source—not entirely, but to some extent—of secular ways of looking at the world today. These ways are more skeptical (in a proper sense) and are more relativistic and more modest. In this connection, I quite agree that the status of probability still is a very open problem. The conceptual foundations of probability continue to be a major source of analysis and controversy in philosophy and related disciplines. The issues concerning the tendency to move from the Laplacean position that there are true or ultimate causes, that probability is merely an expression of ignorance, and that randomness is an expression of ignorance on the part of the observer and not something *in natura*, are very related to the distinction between deterministic and probabilistic theories. The placing of randomness, whether entirely in the observer or also in nature, continues to be of fundamental philosophical importance.

Professor Kuhn:

I am not perfectly certain whether the remark I would like to make is any more than a slight extension or even just a recapitulation of what Sylvain Bromberger has already said, but the point seems to me important enough to risk repetition. Its importance is underscored by what Pat Suppes has just said, so that even if it is a recapitulation I would like to try to make it. What bothers me is the range of implications that sneak into Pat's paper with the phrase "incorrigible data." I take it that one of the primary points of philosophical interest in his paper is the suggestion that having had increasing difficulties recapturing any firm bedrock notion corresponding to what used to be the certainty of perception (for example, of a sense-datum language), there is real hope that we can find at least sand to stand on if we talk about something that is locally (at this time and place) incorrigible data. I think this is a promising notion, but what happens next in Pat's paper is that the difference between corrigible and incorrigible data becomes dependent upon whether there is an error theory to go with the manipulation of data and to some extent upon whether the theories that we apply to data are themselves probabilistic theories. What strikes me is that, although Pat's approach has real interest, his paper passes right by the central question about the corrigibility of data. And I think one must discuss that question before one can get to what seem to me to be the higher level issues of error theory and probabilistic theory.

Pat's own example of biological parentage relationship provides an immediate instance of what I have in mind. He says that the data is incorrigible in the sense that one does not have an error theory. But what would an error theory be in this case? Certainly none is called for. And Pat seems to recognize this, for he immediately proceeds to say, "Suppose we apply this to a given population of human beings and the theory doesn't work. Then we know how to fix that: we go and find the parents of the other living people and now increase the size of the set *A* so that the theory works." Now, in any sense that I know about, that is correcting the data to make the theory work, and it is a perfectly typical procedure that goes on in the sciences. But it is not clear to me how one is going to subsume it as a special case of the development of a probabilistic theory. The corrigibility of data does not seem to depend on error theory or probability theory.

Pat also says that to the best of his knowledge (and mine for that matter) there is no indication that there was any theory of error in connection with ancient astronomy. It would be terribly surprising if there were. However, with respect to the problem of precession, for example, it is quite clear that, looking at his data and doing his computations, astronomer after astronomer said, "Oh! The observer must have been asleep that night because that is just totally out of line," and he then set the datum aside as one that he simply could not draw a curve through. Examples of selecting data, of deciding which data are good data and which data are bad data, run through ancient astronomy to a very considerable extent. Corrigibility does not require error theory.

There are many cases of this sort. To me they suggest that the real question is, "Up to what point is it all right to throw out data because they do not fit the theory?"; just how far can you go responsibly, and what are the regulations? That is a question I cannot answer, but one which seems to me one must start by asking if one is committed to the very approach that Pat is advocating. So I think it is a mistake to act as though one were getting at this sort of problem—which is I think *the* problem of incorrigible data if one is looking for sand—by plugging in probabilistic error theories at once. This is merely to grab onto some apparatus that we happen to have, and to pass over all that is philosophically interesting about incorrigible data.

Professor Suppes:

I see I am in clear disagreement with Tom Kuhn as well. Maybe one of the problems is that I live mainly in the twentieth century—and not in an earlier century—in my thinking about science. In other words, I agree with Tom's remarks that we want to discuss and think about these various anecdotal methods of dealing with sleeping astronomers and left-handed observations and what have you; they are important in science. But what I consider methodologically important is that there also has been a very competent and a very deep-running theory developed for handling them, and that if one deals with more sophisticated science and not merely with simple-minded examples, then the importance of that theory comes very much into evidence. Let me give one classical example that is twentieth century—the example of D. C. Miller's experimental repetition of the Michelson-Morley experiments.[6] It is a very interesting example because D. C. Miller repeated the Michelson-Morley experiments on the motion of the earth through the

[6] Prerelativistic electromagnetic theory postulated a rarefied, liquidlike, all pervasive (for example, space-filling) medium through which electromagnetic waves were propagated. This *ether* was assumed to be so rarefied that planets could pass through it without appreciable friction. Electromagnetic fields were construed as a kind of stress in the ether, which could transmit waves through the ether. For a long time it was known in principle how to test the hypothesis of the ether: Since the Earth moves in its orbit at some unknown velocity and that velocity differs in summer and winter by about 36 miles/sec., if the ether did exist then there should be a difference of the order of 10^{-8} in the observed speed of light at the two seasons. For a long time physicists lacked apparatus capable of making reliable measurements of that magnitude. Toward the end of the nineteenth century inferometers capable of high precision had been developed. Around 1880 A. A. Michelson designed an apparatus involving a high precision inferometer with three mirrors, one of them half-silvered, separated by some distance, placed on a quite stable mount which was sufficiently accurate in measurement that the predicted difference in the observed speed of light could be detected and measured as a fringe shift. (For a detailed account of the physics of the experiment, see Bohm [1965], Chs. 3 and 4.) In his initial experiments, Michelson failed to observe the predicted shift (see Michelson [1881]); later, with E. W. Morley, he improved the precision of his apparatus and again detected no shift (see Michelson and Morley [1887]). This obviously was a crucial experiment whose negative results

ether and came out with a non-negative result; the experimental results seem at variance with the Michelson-Morley experiments and all of the consequences for the special theory of relativity that had been drawn from those and related experiments. (Actually, of course, in real fact Tom Kuhn knows a lot of twentieth-century science and a lot more about this problem than I do; he will probably be correcting my account of the D. C. Miller case in a minute.) The facts as I remember them about the debate over Miller's experiment are roughly this: A committee was established to investigate the Miller experiments and particularly the accuracy of the apparatus. The report of this committee did not consist of saying such things as "Miller had beer one night and got erratic in his laboratory," or "Another night Miller went to sleep," or various other anecdotal accounts of how mistakes were made in the data. That is not at all the character of the report on Miller's experiments. The report consisted of a detailed quantitative analysis of the accuracy of the experimental apparatus and a detailed argument to show that the accuracy of the apparatus was not sufficient to substantiate the claims that Miller made. It seems to me that the main thrust of the methodology that began so gloriously with Laplace is reflected in this example, and not in the example of the Babylonian asleep some evening. Not that the Babylonian asleep is not important —but the deep thrust, the methodologically important thrust, and the move beyond naive views is this development that began with Simpson, Lagrange, and Laplace and which has been so important subsequently. I think I will stop with this one detailed example. Of course, I do want

---

seriously undercut the ether theory of electricity. In response to the Michelson-Morley experiment, a number of unsuccessful efforts were made to save the ether theory (an interesting discussion of some of the more celebrated of these attempts is found in an appendix to Michelson and Morley [1887]). The Michelson-Morley experiment thus triggered a crisis which was only resolved by Einstein's development of relativity theory and its subsequent acceptance by physicists. In 1925, well after relativity theory had been accepted and the ether theory rejected, a physicist, D. C. Miller, duplicated the Michelson-Morley experiment and obtained positive results smaller than the predicted shift in the speed of light due to the postulated ether. Miller's results were discussed inconclusively at a conference held in 1927 or 1928, and H. A. Lorentz studied his results and work for many years without finding any defects in it. It was only in 1955 that a satisfactory explanation of what was wrong with Miller's results was found. Nonetheless, despite the consternation it caused it never was seriously proposed that relativity theory be scrapped and the ether theory resurrected—even though it had been Michelson's and Morley's negative results which had led to the replacement of the ether theory by relativity theory. For discussions of Miller's results, see Shankland [1955] and also the report of the conference mentioned above in the *Astrophysical Journal*, 68 (1928), pp. 341ff.

to build the theory on sand—but only with proper structural considerations.

Professor Cohen:

May I begin by saying that I am happy that in my scholarly pursuits I *do not* live in the twentieth century. It is not surprising, therefore, that I was a little astonished to find Patrick Suppes, an old friend with whom I have joyfully argued on many occasions, giving a contemporary paper in which the only example taken from the twentieth century is an experiment of his own, although there were references enough to Ptolemy, Maxwell, Newton, Mill, Kant, Bayes, Simpson, Laplace.

I should like to make two comments, one of which reinforces what Professor Kuhn has just said and another which takes a different tack. The first point invokes two examples: Newton and Maxwell. It is related directly to Professor Kuhn's remarks, because I do not really believe that the problem with which we are concerned is based entirely upon anecdotal discrepancies.

I have never made a detailed study of the history of the theory of errors, but I do know the writings of Simpson. Although I am willing to believe that his is a pioneering work, I suppose that there must have been significant predecessors, if only because I cannot conceive of him as having been quite so original as to be the starting point of a new discipline—but this is conjecture. But there can be no doubt that there existed a tradition among major scientists in the seventeenth century, all of whom had a serious concern for observations or measurements where the data did not agree. In Book III of the *Principia,* which has been cited, Newton frequently gives sets of data with different values, originating with different observers, and even brings in new numerical data from edition to edition; for example, in the "Phenomena" at the beginning of Book III, relating to the motions of the satellites of Jupiter, and their distances from Jupiter's center, or in the Scholium to Proposition IV, in which he points out the existence of a whole series of slightly different values for the distance from the Earth to the Moon. Concerned as Newton was with the theory of the Moon, he sought the most accurate data possible, and his correspondence with the astronomer Flamsteed reveals the strategic importance of getting the best observations he could. Whether or not Newton actually systematized his views on the accuracy of observation, or the discrepancies between different observations, there can be no doubt that the subject was of major concern to him.

The Islamic astronomers certainly introduced refinement of data, new methods of observation, and built new and larger and improved instruments and observatories. Why did they do so if they were not motivated by making the data more accurate? In his major work on astronomy, the *Almagest,* Ptolemy himself did not make corrections for atmospheric refractions, a topic which was discussed in his book on optics, presumably written after his great work on astronomy. But, thereafter, astronomers were aware of an error factor introduced by the refraction of light entering the earth's atmosphere, and there was much concern as to how to make corrections for it. In short, we must realize that over many centuries there has been a serious concern for the accuracy of data.

The name of J. Clerk Maxwell has been introduced, and our speaker is certainly correct in his statement that Maxwell's great treatise on electricity and magnetism does not give the reader a sense of concern for systematic discussion of error in measurement. And this may seem even more surprising in the light of the fact that Maxwell saw the importance of making measurements, which became a feature of the new Cavendish Laboratory, of which he was the inaugural director. In his introductory lecture, he referred to the importance of measurement in the strongest possible terms, saying that we must find out which features of phenomena are "capable of measurement, and what measurements are required in order to make a complete specification of the phenomena." It was in this famous lecture, in stating that the characteristic of modern experiments is "that they consist principally of measurements," that he referred to the "opinion" which "seems to have got abroad" that before long "all the great physical constants will have been approximately estimated, and that the only occupation which will then be left to men of science will be to carry on these measurements to another place of decimals."

Now for point number two. Let me put this in the form of a question to the speaker. May it not be the case that we are often guilty of concentrating too much on data, numerical data, and the exactness of data? History shows us examples of scientists who were able to make a great leap forward specifically because they were not limited by the data. One of the most dramatic examples occurs at the beginning of the nineteenth century, when we may find a scientist willing to ignore the limitations of numerical facts for the sake of a correct idea or theory, even to the extent of saying that certain numbers probably should be made a little bit bigger, others a little smaller, and so on. It was precisely in this way that Dalton proceeded in developing his atomic theory. Some scientists do not like examples of this sort, because they imply a special virtue "fudging" the evidence or "cooking" the data, and they warn us that we must not ever tell our science students that discoveries have been made in this way. Such examples do not illustrate truth derived from error, but rather the force of a deep perception or intuition transcending the limitations of mere numbers in the known data.

In the long run, which has been the most potent force in the advancement of science: good ideas or accurate numbers? Dalton once remarked to his critics, in words which I shall paraphrase in closing, that if men had tried to discover the law of the gravitational attraction of the earth by digging toward its center, they would still be digging today, and we would know nothing about the subject.

Professor Suppes:

It is a pleasure to comment on Bernard Cohen's remarks. First let me state very clearly that the experiments of my own I mentioned are meant to be rather simple-minded experiments and not at all great moments of twentieth-century science. The great example I am pushing for the twentieth century is that of quantum mechanics which is very much in the tradition of Laplace and Newton. The experiments I mentioned of my own were mentioned because I controlled the data in detail, not because of their scientific significance, and they are very much a transient thing. Working in these areas, I have reflected on some of these rather simple experiments and I am very much aware of their transience. I have a sense of the transient character of current scientific work and the fast pace at which theory changes and data go out the window and new data come in; it is important that we keep this in mind since it is a point which can be lost in some of our concerns. Because of the current tempo of science and the rapid pace of development, a leisurely discussion of Ptolemy or Laplace can be misleading. So let me emphasize very strongly that I do not think the experiments I mentioned are of any serious scientific significance; they are already a matter of very minor history on the subject from which they are drawn, a subject which has already changed a great deal in the ten years since those experiments were performed.

In returning to the problems of error, I think I am in agreement with much of what you say and what other people have said here; and yet I return to the fact that I think there are some intellectual puzzles of very considerable interest. To see what I mean, let us take another example from the Ancients. Take the linear methods of the Babylonians, a very numerical kind of method for making astronomical predictions.[7] Linear methods which are in spirit very similar to the Babylonians are now used in parts of science today that have about that degree of development that Babylonian astronomy did. Such linear methods are very common in economics, in biology, and in psychology. In fact, the whole tradition of using linear regression methods is not too far removed in intellectual spirit from the linear methods of the Babylonians. But a very important difference has occurred. In reporting such linear regression data (and the current scientific literature in various domains that are being developed are full of such reports), one now gives a very clear report from a probabilistic standpoint of the status of the relation between the rather simple linear theory that is used—perhaps in an exploratory way—and the data. In view of this very long history, what I find surprising is why some of these things did not begin earlier. For example, given the relative simplicity conceptually and mathematically of the beginning ideas, and the corresponding very great sophistication of many parts of the analysis to be found in ancient astronomy, it is surprising that these elementary things did not get going. And I would continue to wish to emphasize that for me the point of conceptual and philosophical interest is that an explicit theory of error or probability comes so very late.

Regarding the remarks about Maxwell, I think you will find remarks in the treatise[8] which are very much in the spirit of the remarks you are referring to in Maxwell's inaugural lecture. That is, Maxwell gives careful attention (specifically of the kind that is important for experimenters) as to how a particular measurement should be made, and he has a lot of wise and important things to say on the matter. What is missing is the systematic theory of error that already was present in Laplace.

Finally, the question about whether we think too much about data in science. I continue to be impressed by the beautiful traditions in astronomy where one simply does not get a hearing really without being very responsible to data. Distinctions on the role and importance of data are easily made for different parts of science. In the social sciences, for example, it is already a contrast that is commonly remarked between economics and psychology; from a formal standpoint, theory in economics is very much more sophisticated than in psychology; from a data standpoint it is very much less sophisticated. That is, in psychology—roughly speaking in what is called experimental (that is, nonclinical) psychology—theory is not given much of a hearing unless

[7] See Neugebauer [1969], Chs. 2 and 5 for details.
[8] Maxwell [1892].

it is put in intimate relation with data; but the theory itself is not as sophisticated. The contrast is a rather opposite one in economics, and it seems to me that that type of difference in emphasis exists across other domains of science. I guess it is part of my skeptical temperament to want to insist on "Let's see some data!"

Professor Suppe:

I am somewhat bothered by this notion of incorrigible data you have got running around here, and I think what bothers me relates to Tom Kuhn's worries. I think you are quite right that there is an interesting and important question how the theories of error, and so on, do have a place and how they fit into the problem of data. But I think that that is only a special case of the real problem of incorrigible data. As a way of getting at it let us look at your stimulus-response example of the experimental theory. In your experimental apparatus you have got lights and keys and you make recordings of key hits, light flashes, and so on. But that is not your data. Your data are the subject's predictions, and responses, which are obtained from your recordings by throwing-out a lot of key hits, and so forth, on the grounds that these really are not responses—"the person *really* didn't predict this, he just bumped the key lighting his cigarette." In the fundamental sense of corrigibility, the data has already been made corrigible just at that move there. It is corrigible in the basic sense that it can be called into question, that in the case of divergence between theory and data, the data can be rejected. Now if you set up the experimental design correctly, then sometimes it is corrigible in a way such that the theory of measurement applies; but that probably is a special case of this more basic form of corrigibility. The point of this is that the basic sense in which data is corrigible is that it can be called into question and rejected, and that I do not think your notion of incorrigibility has very much to do with the real problem of data being corrigible or incorrigible; and that in the really fundamental sense of being corrigible or incorrigible, the data you call incorrigible is corrigible data. So I do not understand what you mean by incorrigible data.

Professor Suppes:

Fred Suppe's discussion has been a very useful one to me in seeing that I want to extend or make more explicit certain notions in the paper. There is a deliberate risk involved in using a term such as "corrigible," given its history in philosophy, especially in the philosophy of perception. Perhaps the distinction I am pushing for here and that ought to be made the explicit distinction in the paper can be made more precise and that this hopefully will take care of some of what I have been calling, perhaps semipejoratively (in the spirit of Sylvain's remarks), the anecdotal correction of data—(you know, the assistant was drunk last night, or had his mind on something else, or some other topic, and so on). After we have what is sometimes called prequestions, questions that precede questions of systematic analysis, we put the data in canonical form: we put the data in the form that we record for other scientists to scrutinize. In some parts of science the full record of data is published. In these records we do not put in, "I have the lousiest assistant in the world," or "His bifocals never really work very accurately"; we put the data into some form that we like to stand by. I think some of the examples Professor Cohen mentioned are of this sort. From recent science it is easy to find many such examples. Once we put the data in canonical form we stand by those data in some clear methodological sense. We can now make the distinction between corrigible and incorrigible data at the level of the canonical form of the data. In the case of incorrigible data, no systematic theory of error is applied to the analysis of those data in canonical form. This is what I mean in a more exact way by "incorrigible data." In the case of corrigible data (of which astronomy furnishes a very good example) we do apply such a systematic analysis after the data are in canonical form. In fact, the systematic analysis of error that grows out of the work of Laplace depends upon the data being in canonical form. The anecdotal corrections must precede that systematic analysis, and it is at the systematic level that I am introducing this distinction. I think that one thing I have learned from the discussion here is that my own distinction needs to be sharpened, and I hope that the remarks I have just made will clarify what I intended but did not say clearly and exactly enough.

Professor Bromberger:

I have a question—perhaps it is also a comment—about what Pat says is the underlying motivation for bringing out the distinction: he is particularly concerned with the influence of philosophy on the practice of scientists, and that influence can obviously be nefarious. Peirce said a long time ago that philosophers should not block the path of inquiry but allegiance to certain ideal models of scientific theories (that is, to certain ideal structures, or, as some people would call these things, "paradigms") can block or inhibit the development of theories with different structures, regardless of what other merits such theories might have. But I think that there is a similar danger at this point in the history of certain disciplines, in taking too seriously the success of theories that are essentially statistical in nature. I have psychology in mind. I think that in spite of the time constant which Pat mentioned and his remarks about the outdatedness of his stimulus-response experiments, these experiments are still fairly typical of the sorts of phenomena that psychologists in many places now investigate: phenomena that are intrinsically uninteresting and trivial, but which have the one great virtue of being amenable to statistical analysis. On the other hand, in areas like psycholinguistics, or for that matter linguistics itself, we find widespread ideological resistance to certain kinds of non-statistical conceptions—for example, the conception of competence and this because it appears that the theories that will eventually rest on such conception and admit the interesting phenomena they point to, these theories will not meet the fashionable patterns set by statistical theory. When I speak of such phenomena as intrinsically interesting, I mean interesting insofar as one finds human beings interesting and insofar as one really wants to know, for example, how it is possible for them, on the basis of a very small corpus, to acquire and internalize such complex structures as grammars. I wonder whether Pat has any comments on this and whether he will not admit that what he himself is doing is psychology and that the kind of phenomena that he is working on is not to a large extent the result of his allegiance to a certain fashionable form of theory.

Professor Suppes:

Not a bit! I am totally imperialistic in my thrust for probabilistic theories and I think that Sylvain brings up a very good topic—one which I would be quite happy to go into in quite substantial detail, but I do not think we have time here, especially since both of us have rather strong views about the relation between psychology and theories of language-learning, so let me just try to sweep with a broad broom.

First, I would agree with him about the simple character of the experiments that I have mentioned here and I would disagree—and I think it is a misunderstanding on his part—about calling these theories simply a matter of statistics. I think that is a misunderstanding of the way in which probability is used in a theoretical context; and that misunderstanding is, I think, still widespread. The use of a stochastic process—to say that you are going to use a stochastic process and, therefore, to use probabilistic ideas and to test the notions statistically

—is of course only to begin. What is important in such a theory is what are, in this case, the psychological concepts that are imbedded in this formal or probabilistic framework. That, it seems to me, is where we would differ regarding the status of these theories.

The second point concerns language learning and the MIT brand of dogma about language-learning.[9] I do not for a minute concede that the case has been devastatingly put. I do think that Chomsky did do a good job of putting down Skinner,[10] but that is a pretty simple thing to do. Serious scientific analysis is quite another matter. Regarding whether or not probabilistic and statistical ideas will be used or be of use in treating language-learning and the analysis of the acquisition of language, my thesis would be a resounding "indeed they will be." When it comes to MIT doctrine, in terms of data it is at the pre-analysis stage. The MIT linguists have not tangled yet in a serious way with data or with a serious test of their theories. Although it is fun to be pejorative in these discussions—and it is one of the pleasures of philosophy that one can be—I want to be careful in saying to Sylvain that I think that what has been done by Chomsky and philosophers like Sylvain who have been associated with him is important work, but in any empirical sense it is yet primarily prescientific. As it becomes scientific, probabilistic questions will be ever present and probabilistic theories will be fundamental. I could, if we had the time, sketch in detail my own ideas of how one writes probabilistic grammars for the talk of two year olds and choose between grammars by using a standard goodness-of-fit test.

Professor Dulany:

Since Fred Suppe said that he was not asking me to be moderator in order to shut me up, I would like to ask Pat Suppes a brief question. It has something to do with the argument for the usefulness of probabilistic theories and the implications of this for probabilistic rather than deterministic conceptions in learning experiments. It happens that in nearly all of these experiments the individual differences in performance among subjects are enormous. The probabilistic theories that are used are very unsuccessful in predicting individual behavior and they are highly successful in predicting the mean expectation of those random variables that are defined over the individual behaviors of subjects. Now, I wonder, then, if the success of the theory in that area follows more from the inherent nature of the process as probabilistic

[9] For details, see Chomsky [1968], as well as position papers in Fodor and Katz [1969].

[10] See Chomsky [1959].

than from an unrealistic or unreasonable reluctance on the part of psychologists to measure some of those individual parameters—namely, what the subject is thinking?

Professor Suppes:

I do not agree for a moment that the experiments show what Don Dulany is saying. In fact, to put it in probabilistic terms, one of the scandals of those who claim there are individual differences is that the rather difficult problem of pushing through a complete analysis has not been accomplished. Now, I cannot charge Don with this scandal. It is a weakness of the work on stochastic learning theories that such an analysis has not been carried through. Consider, for example, the linear-learning theory with a finite number of responses described earlier. There are two parameters to be estimated from the data, the initial guessing probability $P(A_{1,1})$ and the learning parameter θ. Ordinarily these estimates are made from group data on the assumption that the subjects used in the experiment are homogeneous. A more adequate and more sophisticated approach is to assume there is a bivariate distribution of these two parameters in the population of subjects and to estimate this distribution rather than two single numbers from the data. Unfortunately the purely mathematical aspects of this approach are surprisingly difficult. In most purely empirical studies of individual differences a multivariate normal distribution is used. If the random variables measured take their values on a finite interval, say, (0, 1), then a transformation is used, for example, $\log (x/(1-x))$, to distribute the values on the whole real line. Unfortunately when such transformations are introduced on $P(A_{1,1})$ or θ, it then becomes impossible to obtain in closed form even the simplest quantities, like the mean learning curve, that need to be compared with data. If, on the other hand, we try to use some general parametric form of a bivariate distribution on the unit square (since both $P(A_{1,1})$ and θ must always lie between 0 and 1), we find the subject as yet very badly developed.

The moral of this simple but intractable example is that probabilistic theories and the relevant mathematics are still in their infancy. But the future is theirs and philosophical views of the structure of scientific theories must recognize this fact in order to be relevant to one of the mainstreams of contemporary science.

History and the Philosopher of Science

I. Bernard Cohen

1. Introduction

Many writers on philosophy of science today draw so heavily on historical examples that a first glance may often fail to reveal whether a given publication is primarily a philosophical essay taking its source materials from the history of science or a historical inquiry guided by philosophical considerations or by some special aspect of the philosophy of science.[1] The tradition of philosophical-historical writing about science is centuries old, a major early instance being Joseph Priestley's critical studies of the "history" and "present state" of electricity and of optics (and vision).[2] Notable examples occur in the nineteenth century, in the writings of William Whewell, Charles Sanders Peirce, Ernst Mach, Pierre Duhem, and Arthur Hannequin.[3] Only the passage of time may make it possible to discern which of the philosophical-historical writings on science of our own era will be especially noteworthy for their contributions to history and which for their contributions to philosophy.[4]

Of course, a distinction must be made between a historical inquiry written by a critical philosopher and a study of philosophy of science

[1] I shall not even consider the question as to whether there might exist in any single given work so perfect a unity of history and philosophy that my distinction would not apply.

[2] See Joseph Priestley, *Priestley's Writings on Philosophy, Science and Politics*, ed. with an introduction by John A. Passmore (New York: Collier Books, 1965).

[3] While the writings of Whewell, Peirce, Mach, and Duhem are widely read and discussed today, Hannequin's name is scarcely known. A major work of his is *Essai critique sur l'hypothèse des atomes dans la science contemporaine* (2nd ed., Paris: Félix Alcan, 1899, Bibliothèque de Philosophie Contemporaine). I was introduced to Hannequin's writings by Alexandre Koyré.

[4] Ernst Mach's *Science of Mechanics* (see Section 2 below) is just such a work; in our own time, T. S. Kuhn's *Structure of Scientific Revolutions* may be another.

drawing on (but not necessarily drawn from) historical examples.[5] The French have been particularly notable for historical studies of science made by philosophers: at once such names leap to mind as Gaston Bachelard, Léon Brunschvicg, Georges Canguilhem, Pierre Duhem, Arthur Hannequin, Alexandre Koyré, Hélène Metzger, Emile Meyerson,[6] Gaston Milhaud, Abel Rey.[7] Pierre Duhem differs from the others in that he was a practicing scientist and a major philosopher of science *sensu stricto*, and in addition was a notable founder of the modern discipline of history of science.[8] The others (Meyerson excepted) came to the subject of history of science from professional philosophy, in particular from the study of the *history* of philosophy, and as such they differ from those present-day specialists in philosophy of science who may turn to the history of science for their major examples or who write on historical subjects. And it is this latter group of philosophers of science, rather than the historians of philosophy, whose work I shall discuss below.

The philosophers of science who are concerned to a major degree with aspects of the history of science include a great company of writers in English,[9] among them Joseph Agassi, Gerd Buchdahl, Joseph Clark, Paul Feyerabend, Adolf Grünbaum, Mary Hesse, N. R. Hanson, Ernan McMullin, Imre Lakatos, Ernest Nagel, Dudley Shapere, Karl Popper, Hans Reichenbach, Stephen Toulmin, and others. But I must note, even at the expense of belaboring the obvious, that not all philosophers of science make use of historical materials or are generally concerned with (nay, are even genuinely interested

[5] It is important to keep in mind that not every philosopher of science makes use of historical scientific examples, or even of examples from contemporary science treated as 'current history'. A recent instance of such a work, almost entirely innocent of any specific event or utterance in history (past or present) is Nicholas Rescher, *Scientific Explanation* (New York: Free Press, 1970).

[6] Meyerson belongs to the 'French school', even though he was not trained primarily as a philosopher (but as a chemist) and even though he emigrated to France only when he had reached maturity.

[7] Of course there were philosophers from other nations who made contributions to the history of science, for example, Ernst Cassirer; but nowhere was there so large and influential a group of philosophers writing history of science as in France.

[8] Because Duhem's contributions to history of science and philosophy of science are so important today, we may tend to forget that he was also a creative scientist. For instance, he was influential as a thermodynamicist in recognizing and applying the work of J. Willard Gibbs.

[9] I leave out of consideration the degree (if any) to which these and other philosophers of science may have forged their own views and concepts while studying the history of science, rather than turning to history for illustrative material to use in expounding views and concepts developed outside of any historically oriented framework.

in) the history of science. Two outstanding members of the profession, R. Carnap and W. V. Quine, have not based their philosophies on the analysis of the history of science, nor have they tended even to buttress their arguments by the accumulated case histories of historians of science,[10] or even by extensive use of examples drawn from current scientific practice.

Moreover, there exists a considerable body of writing of a philosophical kind by scientists, much of which tends to be analytical rather than historical, or to treat as history only those episodes in which the authors themselves may have actively participated. But, needless to say, some philosophically minded scientists have produced admirable philosophical-historical writings.[11]

Of course, whenever a philosopher of science uses a specific example, even if drawn from contemporary or near-contemporary science, he is entering the domain of history. The study of even a single historical event is subject to all the pitfalls of any statement

10 In what follows, I do not want to appear to be criticizing philosophers in general, and philosophers of science in particular, merely because their point of view may be ahistorical. As proof that I am able to view ahistorical philosophers with the utmost admiration, let me cite the following two personal experiences relating to R. Carnap and to W. V. Quine.

Some thirty years ago, when Carnap was spending a term in Cambridge, Massachusetts, I gathered up my courage and asked him whether he would speak to our graduate-student history of science club. He was polite enough not to refuse at once; before giving me his answer, he asked me to walk home with him and to tell him why I found the history of science interesting and worthy of study. We spent a good bit of the afternoon together; in the end, he thanked me, and remarked that he felt he could *not* speak to our group. I had convinced him, he said, that he really was as unhistorically minded a person as one could imagine. He had nothing whatever to say, he concluded, about the study of the *history* of scientific ideas that could possibly be of interest to historians!

My second encounter, with an old friend and colleague, W. V. Quine, occurred twenty-odd years ago, when I met him just after he had completed a lecture in a course on Hume. How wonderful it must be, I said, to deal with such interesting ideas as Hume's. He replied quite bluntly that he was not at all drawn to ideas solely because they were expressed by even the greatest of men; he was only concerned with statements that are true. When I verified this encounter with Quine, not too long ago, he told me of a remark about history which is generally attributed to him. He said that he does not remember making it, but he would not disown it. The statement is: "There are two reasons why a person is attracted to philosophy: one is because he is interested in *philosophy*—and the other is because he is interested in the *history* of philosophy."

Carnap's display of integrity obviously did not diminish my personal regard for him. And I gladly admit that I regard Quine as the foremost living philosopher.

11 They include such scientists as David Anderson, E. N. da C. Andrade, Salomon Bochner, Max Born, Louis de Broglie, René Dubos, Gerald Holton, L. K. Nash, George Thomson, Clifford Truesdell, B. L. Van der Waerden, E. T. Whittaker, and many others.

of history and does not differ in this regard from an extended treatment of a whole episode in the history of science.[12] Nor are the presentations by philosophers of science any the less immune from historical criticism because they are concerned with a restricted rather than an extended subject.

It is a common experience for historians of science to be dismayed on encountering their own subject in the writings of philosophers.[13] Philosophers of science may be equally disturbed when they find historians of scientific ideas exhibiting what may seem an appalling ignorance of current philosophy of science, to say nothing of philosophy in general. My assignment here, however, is strictly limited to

[12] For example, many philosophers of science and scientists write of 'Galileo's principle of inertia' and then make a pseudo-Galilean, post-Newtonian statement that could never have originated with Galileo, and could not even be a paraphrase. For instance, such allegedly Galilean presentations will begin with a condition that a body in inertial motion is far removed from other bodies; this assumes that such other bodies might have influenced the body in question, whereas Galileo explicitly rejected the possibility of such attraction and even criticized Kepler (in the *Dialogo*, on the two great world systems) for supposing that the moon might draw the seas so as to produce tides.

[13] The question is often raised as to whether historians of science may not be too myopic or pedantic in their reaction to the way historical episodes or incidents may appear in scientific textbooks, treatises, or explanatory works, or in articles and books on the philosophy of science. Is it, in proven fact, better to have such historical material appear in a historically acceptable form? In raising this question, I use the word 'better' in the sense of 'more useful' for the purpose of the writer. It is not up to a historian to judge the value of inaccurate statements in teaching or in making a philosophical point. But surely a historian's hackles will rise when he finds a prominent display of a quotation from the "*Principia* (1686)" and is aware that there was no edition in 1686, but rather 1687, and that the quotation is taken from Rule IV, written by Newton for the third edition of the *Principia* (1726). He will be equally puzzled in a presentation of "a philosopher's door into natural philosophy" to see the gratuitous addition of the phrase "ad infinitum" to an alleged quotation of Newton's first law, plus the expression "free of impressed forces" for Newton's "unless it is compelled to change that state by forces impressed thereon." These are questions of simple verifiable fact. But of far greater concern is the lack of distinction between historical situations and philosophical analysis, as in a conflation of (1) the way Newton advanced from Galileo's laws of falling bodies and Kepler's laws of planetary motion to a system of general dynamics and celestial mechanics (= Newton's physics) and (2) an alleged logical incompatibility between what is presented as "Galileo's theory" or "Kepler's theory" and "Newton's theory"—when what is intended is not 'Galileo's' or 'Kepler's' or 'Newton's' but rather some anachronistic 'Galilean' or 'Keplerian' or 'Newtonian', where these names do not necessarily designate what may be found in the writings of Galileo or Kepler or Newton. On this point, see Sections 5 and 6 below and the writer's article on " 'Galileo's theory' and 'Kepler's theory' vs. 'Newton's theory'," to appear in *Some Aspects of the Interaction Between Science and Philosophy*, to be published for the Van Leer Jerusalem Foundation by the Humanities Press, New York, in 1973.

the use of history (or historical examples) by philosophers,[14] and I shall leave it to others to draw attention to the philosophical failings of historians.[15]

I believe that a greater sensitivity to the canons of history could readily produce a dramatic rise in the historical level of accuracy and authenticity of philosophical discourse. At some time or other, almost every philosopher of science discusses some aspect of the work of Galileo or Newton.[16] Is it unreasonable to expect that he will read at least a portion of the actual writings of Galileo or Newton, and even find out whether there is a recent or current scholarly account of the topic under discussion? [17] In most cases, the philosopher in question will have no difficulty in obtaining the original writings he wishes to study, either in the original language or in translation,[18] and thus he will be able to find out what Galileo and Newton actually have written. Additionally, a philosopher of science or a scientist can usually find out what the current state of discussion may be concerning historical questions: as, for instance, the nature of Galileo's concept of inertia. In short, it is usually not very difficult for a philosopher or a scientist to base his historical statements on primary rather than on secondary sources and to take cognizance of recent and current research in the history of science.

Let me now contrast so simple an assignment with the situation of a historian of science studying conceptual history, say the formation or 'transformation' [19] of some set of scientific ideas, and who may wish to ascertain whether there is any aspect of philosophy of science which may be relevant to his inquiries. I personally find great difficulty in ascertaining which books or articles dealing with the philosophy of science may be useful for historical inquiries. It often seems as if a

14 I must keep stressing the fact that I am not counseling philosophers of science as to how they should work, nor is it up to me to prove that there is a definite *philosophical* advantage to a different manner of referring to or using history of science than is now current. I can only express the feelings of many historians with regard to much of the philosophical literature, *insofar* as the treatment of history is concerned.

15 Of course, sound and constructive criticism by philosophers of science would be most instructive, especially if illustrated by examples.

16 I cite Galileo and Newton because their names occur so often in discussions that show no evidence that the authors in question had ever so much as consulted any of their writings.

17 An annual critical bibliography of the history of science is published as part of *Isis* by the History of Science Society. Attention may also be called to the *ISIS Cumulative Bibliography*, ed. Magda Whitrow, Pt. I, Personalities (London: Mansell, 1971), and to the new *Dictionary of Scientific Biography*, ed. Charles C. Gillispie, currently being published by Charles Scribner's Sons, New York.

18 Needless to say, all works that might be of interest do not exist in translations, and all translations are not fully reliable. See, further, Section 5 below.

19 On 'transformation' see Section 3 below.

historian would have to become aware of all the major developments in philosophy of science before he could make a valid judgment as to the possible ways in which any or all parts of the philosophy of science might be useful for his problems. This task seems well beyond the philosophical capacities of almost all historians. Whereas the philosopher of science can very easily improve the historical level of his discussions, a similar change (and even "improvement") of the level of philosophy of science used by historians seems to me far more difficult to achieve. Indeed, for this latter problem, the only possible solution that I can envisage is a much closer contact between historians of science and philosophers of science, and an attempt to draw philosophers of science more and more into the study of historical questions in a partnership with historians of science. By joint effort, and by demonstrations in which philosophical techniques are shown to improve historical inquiries, I believe that philosophers of science might help historians immeasurably. But surely it is not the historian's task to study whether or not a more accurate use of history would necessarily produce a better philosophy of science.[20]

In my presentation, I shall focus attention primarily on two major topics: (1) I shall examine some of the ways in which I find historical material treated in a misleading fashion and (2) I shall try to indicate what I conceive to be the role of historians in relation to the creative processes of philosophers. In my conclusion I shall make a few remarks about the reverse process, that is, the importance of philosophical studies to the practicing historian of science. The examples I shall use derive from my personal reading and research and certain chance encounters, and should not therefore be taken as indices of my general agreement or disagreement with the points of view of those philosophers or scientists who may happen to be cited. Nor, accordingly, should any special significance be attached to a specific reference to (or the omission altogether of) the name of any particular philosopher.

Since I shall be displaying examples of either the misuse of history or the use of false history, I must first defend the very existence of a true history or the concept of a correct use of history. I need not discuss here the truism that there is no absolute historical truth, that all attempts to re-create the past are imperfect and necessarily personal. This is one reason why historians disagree among themselves and constantly criticize each other's work. It may be argued that we need not explore any failure of philosophers or scientists to find the

[20] I suppose, of course, that any reasonable philosopher of science ought to want to avoid false history.

alleged historical truth, when even historians fail to do so. But such discussions may be applied with validity only to certain precisely definable parts of history: for instance, to any interpretations of trends in science, or of the thought of a single man. To take an example: there is no way of making an absolute judgment on the importance of Platonism in the science of the Renaissance and of the seventeenth century, nor of the relative significance of empirical and of purely intellectual elements in the scientific thought of Galileo. Nor is it always clear what influence one man may have had on another. There are also debatable questions such as the importance of artisans in the creation of modern science, the significance of social and economic factors in the growth of science,[21] and the creative function of the individual scientific personality. But there is usually no such doubt, for example, as to what a man may have written, according to the texts presently available, even though there may be a considerable discussion or debate as to what he meant. As we shall see below, a conspicuous failing of many philosophers and scientists who write about history derives primarily from their neglect of (or ignorance of) historical documents, and is not at all a direct function of doubt and uncertainty or disagreement on the part of historians. Even more fundamental, perhaps, is the fact that when philosophers of science examine historical topics, they usually do not tend to do so in the manner of historians: which may only be another way of saying that historians all too often find that in dealing with historical matters philosophers do not appear to be asking historically significant questions.[22]

The examples that follow are taken primarily from the foundations of dynamics in the seventeenth century. I shall, accordingly, discuss aspects of the physical science of Galileo, Kepler, Descartes, and Newton, but I shall try to do so within a context of a general framework of the history of ideas, and of the concerns expressed by scientists and philosophers relating to this founding period of the pioneer-science of dynamics. Indeed, the vast literature that has accumulated about these men and this period is enormous. The mere

21 The doctrine, so dear to Marxists, of the importance of artisans in the formulation of the new science appears to have found one of its first unambiguous expressions in Mach, who wrote that Galileo "began his investigations with the notions familiar to his time—notions developed mainly in the practical arts. One notion of this kind was that of velocity. . . ." See Ernst Mach, *The Science of Mechanics,* trans. Thomas J. McCormack (4th ed., Chicago, London: Open Court Publishing Co., 1919; and later editions and printings).

22 For an example of the difference in the type of question that may be asked by philosophers and by historians, see Section 5 below.

mention of such names as William Whewell, Ernst Mach, Pierre Duhem, Henri Poincaré, Gaston Bachelard, Ernst Cassirer, Alexandre Koyré, Alfred North Whitehead, Ernest Nagel, Karl Popper, Hans Reichenbach, Paul Feyerabend, N. Russell Hanson, Karl Pearson, and E. T. Whittaker, among a host of others,[23] reminds us that the science of the seventeenth century, and the founding of the conceptual system of modern dynamics, has been a central concern of major writers on the philosophy of science for well over a century.

2. Galileo and the Science of Motion

Today's historians of scientific ideas have been greatly concerned to understand the formation of a science of motion in the seventeenth century: as the old saying puts it, *Ignorato motu, ignoratur natura.* Galileo has particularly attracted the attention of historians because of the great influence of Alexandre Koyré's *Etudes galiléennes*,[24] the founding document from which so many of us have learned how to analyze scientific concepts historically and to study the growth of scientific ideas.

Galileo has long been a central figure because of a rather general belief that he is the first among moderns to espouse and to practice an experimental physical science. Who has not been thrilled by reading of the famous experiment in which he ascended the Leaning Tower with a 100-pound and a 10-pound weight, which he then let fall from the top, with a result that confuted all Aristotelians! [25] Galileo is commonly described as the founder of the modern science of motion, for did he not 'discover' the law of freely falling bodies, the principle or

[23] In the foregoing text of Section 1 and the notes, I have not referred to the many scientists who have written in significant fashion about the philosophy of science, but who have not notably pursued historical questions or who have not made extensive use of historical examples, for example, Niels Bohr, Max Born, Albert Einstein, Philipp Frank, Peter Medawar, Richard v. Mises, Hermann Weyl.

[24] A Koyré, *Etudes galiléennes* (Paris: Hermann & Cie, 1939, Actualités Scientifiques et Industrielles 852–853–854; reprinted in 1966). A convenient volume of essays in the conceptual analysis of historical problems in science is A. Koyré, *Metaphysics and Measurement: Essays in Scientific Revolution* (London: Chapman & Hall; Cambridge: Harvard University Press, 1968).

[25] See Lane Cooper, *Aristotle, Galileo, and the Tower of Pisa* (Ithaca, N.Y.: Cornell University Press, 1935); also Alexandre Koyré, "Galilée et l'expérience de Pise: à propos d'une légende," *Annales de l'Université de Paris* (1937), pp. 441–453, reprinted in A. Koyré, *Etudes d'histoire de la penseé scientifique* (Paris: Presses Universitaires de France, 1966, Bibliothèque de Philosophie Contemporaine), pp. 192–201.

law of inertia, the independence of vectorial components of motion (and the general principles of resolution and composition of vectors), the analysis of the trajectory of projectiles to show their parabolic path, and even a relation between force and motion that is either the 'root' or a 'near approach' to what we know as Newton's 'second law'? And, using experimentation as his means of discovery, is Galileo not the founder of modern experimental science in general, as well as the originator of dynamics? So bold are such assertions that they have challenged our foremost investigators, especially those who cannot believe that science proceeds by gross discontinuities. For about three-quarters of a century, there has been intense research into the medieval and Renaissance precursors of Galileo,[26] and we are now aware that the gap between Galileo and his predecessors, however great, was not quite so incredibly great[27] as had once been alleged. At the same time, intense analysis of Galileo's own writings has revealed that the Galilean science of motion has marked aspects of distinction from the 'accepted', or 'classical', Newtonian form of the subject.[28]

Galileo stands in a rather uncertain position among today's historians. We are not in universal agreement as to whether he should be regarded as the first of the moderns or the last of a line that begins in either the twelfth or the fourteenth century.[29] Ernst Mach taught that "Dynamics [which he held to be "entirely a modern science"] was founded by Galileo." I add one or two further 'Machisms': Galileo discovered "the so-called law of inertia, according to which a body not under the influence of forces, i.e., of special circumstances that change motion, will retain forever its velocity (and direction)." The "notion of force as we hold it to-day was first created by Galileo." What Galileo "*perceived* in the natural phenomena" is that "it is *accelerations* which are the immediate effects of the circumstances that determine motion, that is, of the forces." Again, "An entirely new no-

[26] An admirable review of Galilean problems and of recent Galilean scholarship is given in the editor's introduction (pp. 3–51), Ernan McMullin, ed., *Galileo, Man of Science* (New York: Basic Books, 1967). See, further, Stillman Drake, *Galileo Studies: Personality, Tradition, and Revolution* (Ann Arbor: University of Michigan Press, 1970).

[27] See Marshall Clagett, *The Science of Mechanics in the Middle Ages* (Madison: University of Wisconsin Press, 1959), Ch. 6 (§5), Ch. 9 (§5), Ch. 12; E. J. Dijksterhuis, *The Mechanization of the World Picture*, trans. C. Dikshoorn (Oxford: Clarendon Press, 1961), Ch. IV. 2 (Pt. C); Ernest A. Moody, "Laws of Motion in Mediaeval Physics," *Scientific Monthly*, Vol. 72 (1951), pp. 18–23, and "Galileo and Avempace," *Journal of the History of Ideas*, Vol. 12 (1951), pp. 163–193, 375–422.

[28] See, notably, A. Koyré, *Etudes galiléennes*.

[29] See E. McMullin, *Galileo*.

tion to which Galileo was led is the idea of *acceleration*."[30] I have always found it curious that Mach, who had so many profound insights into the creative process of science, should have allowed himself to be thus so hoodwinked as to conceive that a single man, even a Galileo, could have been so completely the *fons et origo* of modern science or even of modern dynamics.[31]

Step by step, the statements of Mach which I have just quoted can easily be proved false. Galileo was certainly *not* the first person to have had the concept of acceleration, which was well developed by the end of the fourteenth century. The links between Galileo and the late medieval writers on motion have been established beyond any question of doubt; even the form of the Galilean argument, for instance, that in defining uniform motion one must stress the fact that the same distance is traveled in *any* equal time intervals, is a prominent feature in the medieval writers.[32] We know definitely that Galileo had read the medieval works since his notes refer to individual authors by name.[33]

Many scientists and philosophers believe that the search for links between great scientific advances and the preceding ages, or for predecessors (I detest the word "precursors"), stamps the historian as one who takes the greatest pleasure (or, perhaps, finds his chief satisfaction) in reducing the creative giants of our science to the status of pygmies. I hold a very different point of view. The Galileo presented by Mach and so many others seems to me to deny all the qualities by which we identify creative scientists in any recent historical period. The Galileo revealed to us by historical research, many of whose ideas can be found in a more primitive state in writers of his own time and of earlier centuries, seems to me to be a great creative man. In fact,

30 Ernst Mach, *Science of Mechanics*, pp. 128, 141, 141–142, 142, 145. In the sixth American edition, based on the ninth German edition (La Salle, Ill.: Open Court Publishing Co., 1910), some of these remarks are altered: "In the former editions of this book, the exposition of Galileo's researches was based on his final work, *Discorsi e dimostrazioni matematiche* of 1638. However, his original notes, which have become known later, lead to different views on the course of his development" (p. 155). For his revised views, Mach relied heavily on the researches of Emil Wohlwill, chiefly the latter's history of the principle of inertia and his two-volume study of Galileo and his fight for the Copernican system.

31 Do we not have here a primary example of a scientist-philosopher writing about the past as if it were essentially different from the present? For surely Mach must have known from the advances in science in his own time that "It is not in the nature of things for any one man to make a sudden violent discovery; science goes step by step, and every man depends on the work of his predecessors." I am now quoting Rutherford, not Mach!

32 See A. Koyré, *Etudes galiléennes*; also M. Clagett, *Science of Mechanics in the Middle Ages*.

33 But see, further, S. Drake, *Galileo Studies*, Ch. 11, esp. pp. 214–223.

in the Wiles Lectures, which I gave in 1966 in Belfast,[34] I argue that this information actually aggrandizes rather than belittles the creative greatness of Galileo. The enormity of his indebtedness to his predecessors indicates that his greatness did not consist in the mere good luck of living before the science of dynamics had been created by anyone else, but rather in being alone among his contemporaries to see how certain traditional concepts could be transformed or reinvented and then used to give a new direction to scientific thought about motion. It is in this sense that we may define his insight and his incredible creative powers.

I have proposed that we conceive of this process, in a term actually used by Mach himself, as a revolution by 'transformation'.[35] Galileo did not merely pick up ideas which were in the air, and produce what is sometimes called a 'synthesis' of them—whatever that may mean! Far from it! Whatever ideas, concepts, doctrines, and methods Galileo encountered and put to use were imbued with new meanings and were then applied in new circumstances that inspirited them with new senses and a significance perhaps far beyond any vision of their former exponents. The very number of such points of contact with contemporaries and predecessors seems to me to prove Galileo's greatness, rather than denigrate his creative ability.[36] We can gauge the quality of Galileo's creative abilities by the very fact that he alone of all his contemporaries saw exactly how these elements might be put together fruitfully, to become transformed and used for the advancement of science. The same information was available to Kepler, to Isaac Beeckman, to Descartes, to Cavalieri, and to a host of other brilliant men; but there was only one Galileo! (I shall say more about this concept of 'transformation' below, in Section 3.)

I shall analyze here one single aspect of Galileo's doctrines of motion, the 'law of inertia', so often attributed to Galileo by well-meaning philosophers, scientists, and even historians, who wish to do him honor. The question of inertia is most fascinating to the historian of scientific ideas—and, I would suppose, to the philosopher—because it shows us that the new physics of the seventeenth century, which replaced the

[34] These are to be published in 1974 by Cambridge University Press under the title *Transformations of Scientific Ideas: Newtonian Themes in the Development of Science*. A preliminary exposition of this point of view has been given in my article "Dynamics: The Key to the 'New Science' of the Seventeenth Century," *Acta historiae rerum naturalium necnon technicarum* (Czechslovak Studies in the History of Science), Prague (1967, Special Issue 3), pp. 79–114.

[35] See the preceding footnote, and Section 3 below.

[36] This is the sense in which a measure of Galileo's originality and creative genius is found in his discernment of which of the many then-current concepts and principles might be susceptible of 'transformation' in a fruitful way.

older concepts of motion, rest, and change, involved a radical reorientation of the view of the cosmos and the possibilities of infinite void space,[37] thus yielding an almost entirely new philosophy of nature and a wholly different physics that contradicted ordinary intuition and common sense. Alexandre Koyré has taught us that, as a result of such factors as these, the 'inertial' revolution was difficult to accept and more difficult to achieve, and thus required the creative energies of more than a single individual, even a Galileo.[38] Let me direct your attention to some statements from Galileo's last published work, his *Dialogues on the New Sciences,* published as *Discourses and Mathematical Demonstrations Concerning Two New Sciences Pertaining to Mechanics and Local Motions*, usually referred to nowadays as the *Discorsi.*[39] (1) "Furthermore we may remark that any velocity once imparted to a moving body will be rigidly maintained as long as the external causes of acceleration or retardation are removed, a condition which is found only on horizontal planes. . . ." (2) "Imagine any particle projecting along a horizontal plane without friction; then we know, from what has been more fully explained in the preceding pages, that this particle will move along this same plane with a motion which is uniform and perpetual, provided the plane has no limits." [40] Is this the Newtonian law of inertia? Not quite! For in the Newtonian concept of inertia, a body need not be so supported on a "horizontal

[37] In a postil to a speech of Salviati, Galileo writes: "Two things [are] required for motion to be perpetual; unbounded space and an indestructible movable body"; Galileo Galilei, *Dialogue Concerning the Two Chief World Systems—Ptolemaic and Copernican,* trans. Stillman Drake (Berkeley and Los Angeles: University of California Press, 1953), p. 135.

[38] Today's scientists, and all too often philosophers, tend to look into writers of the past to see the extent to which they may have anticipated the science of the present age. I argue throughout this paper for a different view, namely, that we should try to see a man in his own time and to understand what it was that *he* thought he was doing. Galileo's achievements, I believe, can only be described by such adjectives as 'stupendous'. But by this I mean that what he achieved was 'Galilean physics', and not 'Newtonian physics', and certainly not 'post-Newtonian physics'. Indeed, to get from 'Galilean physics' to 'Newtonian physics', as I have shown in the Wiles Lectures (referred to in footnote 34 above), there were required not only a Galileo and a Newton, but also a Kepler, a Descartes, a Gassendi, a Wallis, a Wren, a Huygens, a Hooke, and yet others.

[39] The title under which Galileo's last treatise on mechanics and the accompanying dialogues had been published was one to which he objected; it was certainly not his own choice.

[40] It is to be observed that the motion in this case is described as "uniform," and is said to be "horizontal." Galileo, as we shall see in a moment, further specifies (in this work) that he does not really distinguish between the "horizontal" and a small portion of an arc of a great circle, say the circumference of the earth. True horizontal inertial motion (for instance, unsupported by a plane on which an object may be rolling) occurs in Galileo's thought only in very limited circumstances at or near the surface of the earth.

plane." In the world of physics, in the universe of the physical reality with which Galileo was concerned, as opposed to the mathematical world of pure thought, there can be no infinitely extended horizontal plane, and hence no infinite inertial (that is, uniform rectilinear unbounded) motion—in Galileo's sense.

The limitation of a supporting plane, and Galileo's implied imposition of conditions of spatial finitude in the real world, help us in part to specify the barrier between the Galilean views on motion and the Newtonian (or, more properly, Cartesian-Gassendian-Huygenian-Hookian-Wrennian-Wallisian-Newtonian) analysis of planetary motion as compounded of a linear inertial component and a descent toward the center. In the second quotation, above, Galileo makes it clear at once that he is thinking of a physical plane, "limited and elevated." He says that the moving ("heavy") particle will pass "over the edge of the plane," so as to acquire "in addition to its previous uniform and perpetual motion, a downward propensity due to its own weight; so that the resulting motion which I call projection [*projectio*], is compounded of one which is uniform and horizontal and of another which is vertical and naturally accelerated."

Let me turn now to a third quotation, in which Galileo further qualifies what he means. He observes that with respect to the Earth's surface, we may consider a "minute of arc on a great circle as a straight line." Citing the authority of the great Archimedes,[41] Galileo explains that what has appeared to the reader to be possibly an example of motion along a straight line may prove to be only motion along a small arc of a very large circle. It is probably a mistake to say that Galileo ever believed in a 'circular inertia', although his form of 'inertia' did

[41] According to Galileo, Archimedes "takes for granted that the beam of a balance or steelyard is a straight line, every point of which is equidistant from the common center of all heavy bodies, and that the cords by which heavy bodies are suspended are parallel to each other." The reason is that in practice our instruments and the usual distances which we discuss "are so small in comparison with the enormous distance from the center of the earth that we may consider a minute of arc on a great circle as a straight line, and may regard the perpendiculars let fall from its two extremities as parallel." Additionally, Galileo points out "that, in all their discussions, Archimedes and the others considered themselves as located at an infinite distance from the center of the earth, in which case their assumptions were not false, and therefore their conclusions were absolutely correct. When we wish to apply our proven conclusions to distances which, though finite, are very large, it is necessary for us to infer, on the basis of demonstrated truth, what correction is to be made for the fact that our distance from the center of the earth is not really infinite, but merely very great in comparison with the small dimensions of our apparatus." All quotations are taken from Galileo Galilei, *Dialogues Concerning Two New Sciences*, trans. Henry Crew and Alfonso de Salvio (New York: Macmillan, 1914, and later reprints). See footnote 90 below.

maintain bodies in motion along arcs of very large circles:[42] circles which were so large as not to be easily distinguished from straight lines. In fact, Galileo never asked the question of whether *unsupported* motion could ever really continue for very long in a linear mode. At least one Galileist, John Wallis, writing just before Newton's *Principia*, stated again and again a principle of 'inertia', in which the 'straight line' was understood to be part of a very large "circle concentric with the Earth."

And thus it is clear that the new inertial physics was so revolutionary as actually to require (in the sense I have used earlier) several stages of 'transformation' for its creation, one stage of which (a major one) was contributed by Galileo, and others by Kepler (who introduced the expression "inertia" or "natural inertia" into the science of motion[43]), by Descartes and Gassendi, by Huygens, and by Newton.

3. 'Transformations' in the Development of Science: the Concepts of 'Inertia' and 'State of Motion'

The development of an 'intertial' physics demonstrates how a scientist, in 'creating' a 'new theory' of 'his own', is apt to borrow or use or adapt a definition or a law or an axiom or a principle, or even a whole theory, from one of his predecessors; the degree of 'transformation' may be (or may later prove to be) so great that the scientist is in effect producing a 'wholly original' creative contribution. This 'transformation' may be overt and conscious, or it may be unconscious—as an implied result of introducing a new field of application, or some new connotation, unintended (or unimagined) by the original inventor. From this point of view, the scholarly endeavor of seeking out and identifying the elements in the past that are present in the creative efforts of any given scientist affords a means of gauging the true degree

42 Galileo's clearly expressed preference for a kind of circular (rather than purely linear) natural inertia was probably conditioned to some degree by his Copernicanism and his instinctive sense for 'conservation'. No doubt, such a preference for the circle, which Professor Koyré quite properly called the "hantise" of circularity, came from a traditional idea of circles as the only uniform, or continuing, or perpetually unchanging, motion. As to Copernicanism: Galileo had to account for the fact that bodies behave on a rotating and revolving earth just as on an earth standing still, a result which seems to imply that they have a natural 'circular' (or, perhaps, circulating) motion. As to conservation: Galileo indicates in his writings his concern that if a body moved by itself on a straight line along a tangent of the earth, it would be rising up—in the sense of getting further away from the center—without any outside force of exertion.

43 See Section 3.

of originality, as measured by the profundity and variety of the 'transformations' that will prove to have been made. This is the sense in which an examination of the origins of Newton's concepts and principles could not possibly constitute a reduction of his magisterial creative achievement to some kind of 'synthesis', some sort of mere patching-together of what everybody could have been supposed to have known. From the point of view of 'transformations', the discovery of precursors to Galileo's concepts or principles becomes a means of reckoning his true greatness, and need no longer be considered a step in the whittling away or diminution of his genius. If, as I have said in Section 2, only Galileo, of all his contemporaries, actually discerned in the science and philosophy and mathematics of his age those elements that could undergo 'transformation' so as to become joined into a part of 'the new science' of dynamics, then the creative effort of a Galileo has a double sense: first, to find what may be possibly 'transformed' and, second, to make the 'transformation'. One is the potentiality, the other the actuality.[44]

Furthermore, I believe that an emphasis on this process of 'transformation' will make our historical reconstructions of the growth of science more in harmony with the actual experience of scientists.[45] And by stressing differences between successive generations of concepts (through 'transformation'), rather than emphasizing their apparent and undifferentiated similarities, the point of view I am advocating will reveal the fine structure of the creative enterprise of science where today we may tend to see only the gross features of scientific change.

As an example of a simple kind of 'transformation', let me turn at once to the name 'inertia' (or 'natural inertia'), introduced into the discourse of physical science by Kepler, which became a commonly used expression after Newton's *Principia*. What is interesting from the point of view of creativity is, first of all, the novelty of the Keplerian concept and its applications. Kepler conceived that matter is characterized by an "inertness," an "inactivity," a "laziness," an "inclinatio ad quietem." Thus any sample of matter will stay at rest or come to rest if it is not actually being moved by a 'mover' or 'motor'. Several rather remarkable consequences follow at once. For instance, if a body will come to rest *whenever* a motive force stops acting on it, that same body will

[44] It may seem that my point of view is extreme, for are not some ideas in science (for example, concepts, laws, principles) wholly new, and thus independent of any predecessor? A positive answer would presuppose a creative effort wholly in divorce from any predecessor, or any contact whatsoever with the scientific and cultural stream of history. I know of none such.

[45] See Rutherford's statement, quoted in footnote 31 above, and I. B. Cohen, *Transformations*, Chs. 1, 2.

come to rest *wherever* it happens to be when the motive force ceases to act; thus Kepler could and did discard the Aristotelian doctrine of 'natural places'. Furthermore, the existence of a continuous motion of the planets will now imply a continually acting motive force, for otherwise the 'inertia' of the planets would bring them into a state of rest. Kepler showed that this force must originate from the Sun itself.[46]

Newton's inertia, or "force of inertia," went a step further and was not limited to keeping nonmoving bodies at rest, or to bringing moving bodies to rest when the motive force ceases to act. For him inertia tends also to keep bodies moving uniformly in a straight line. In short, Newton's inertia tends to maintain a body in whatever 'state' it may happen to be in, whether that be a 'state' of rest or a 'state' of motion, it being understood that motion is a 'state' when and only when uniform and rectilinear.[47]

The 'transformation' from Kepler's inertia to Newton's inertia thus requires the introduction of a non-Keplerian concept: the 'state of motion'. This too was a radical innovation, since motion had traditionally been considered (in its Aristotelian sense) as a process—in fact, the process of a potentiality becoming actual. Newton did not invent the concept of a 'state' of motion, nor the determining feature of such a 'state', namely, that it can continue of and by itself in the absence of a motive force; but, so far as I know, he was the first person to attribute this *state of motion* to the "inertia" or the "force of inertia" inherent in any material body, thus radically 'transforming' and extending Kepler's original concept.[48]

Newton encountered the concept of a 'state' of motion in reading

[46] On Kepler's science of motion see A. Koyré, *La révolution astronomique* (Paris: Hermann, 1961), Pt. II, Kepler; Max Jammer, *Concepts of Force* (Cambridge: Harvard University Press, 1957), Ch. 5, and *Concepts of Mass* (Cambridge: Harvard University Press, 1961), Ch. 5; Edward Rosen, "Kepler's *Harmonics* and His Concept of Inertia," *Amer. J. Physics*, Vol. 34 (1966), pp. 610–613; Edward Rosen, trans. and commentator, *Kepler's Sommium* (Madison: University of Wisconsin Press, 1967), Appendix I, "Kepler's Concept of Inertia"; Emile Meyerson, *Identity & Reality*, trans. K. Loewenberg (London: Allen & Unwin, 1930; reprinted by Dover Publications, New York, 1962), Appendix III, "The Copernicans and the Principal of Inertia."

[47] Newton, in fact, entered a manuscript note in his own copy of the second edition of the *Principia*, explaining this difference between Kepler's "force of inertia" and his own; see I. B. Cohen, *Introduction to Newton's 'Principia'* (Cambridge: Harvard University Press; Cambridge, Eng.: Cambridge University Press, 1972), Ch. II, Section 4.

[48] On Newton's concept of inertia, see I. B. Cohen, "The Concept and Definition of Mass and Inertia as a Key to the Science of Motion: Galileo—Kepler—Newton—Einstein," a symposium paper contributed to the XIIIth International Congress of the History of Science (Moscow, August, 1971); Section 2 of that paper is equivalent to Section 3 of the present communication.

Descartes' *Principia philosophiae*, where it is the subject of Descartes' first "law of nature." [49] Incidentally, the title of Newton's own treatise is no doubt a simple but profound 'transformation' of Descartes' "philosophiae principia" into *Philosophiae naturalis principia mathematica.* Furthermore, Newton's laws of motion are presented as the axioms on which the whole edifice is erected, a transformation of the Cartesian "regulae quaedam sive leges naturae" into Newtonian "axiomata sive leges motus." [50] There are many other similarities between the two *Principias*, such as Newton's use of the phrase "perseverare in statu suo" for Descartes' "in eodem statu perseveret," and the use by both Newton and Descartes of the Lucretian expression, "quantum in se est." [51]

There are fundamental differences between Descartes' "leges naturae" and Newton's first "lex motus" that go far beyond mere vocabulary (such as Newton's use of "vis inertiae"). First of all, Descartes did not clearly understand that the conservation (or continuation) of motion depends on a vector concept of motion. Again, having stated his "prima lex naturae" (that a body will "persevere" in any given "state" of motion), he found it necessary to introduce a second and distinct law ("altera lex naturae") stating that all motion in and of itself is rectilinear. Finally, Descartes believed that the conservation of "motion in matter" depends on and is derived from "the immutability of God." Clearly, a real 'transformation' was required to get to a single law of inertia (as in the *prima lex motus* in Newton's *Principia*), and to have the law follow from the nature of matter and not to be a consequence of the attributes of God; furthermore, motion had to be 'transformed' into a vector quantity, and the law of inertia had to become an axiom based on experience rather than on first principles. Newton added yet another major transformation by his concept of "vis insita" or "vis inertiae."

Our point of view that highly original scientific creative thought may be a kind of 'transformation' leads at once to a second stage of

[49] See Descartes' *Principia philosophiae*, Pt. 2, Secs. 95–98; cf. A. Koyré, *Newtonian Studies* (Cambridge: Harvard University Press, 1965; London: Chapman & Hall, 1965), esp. III, "Newton and Descartes."

[50] See, for further details, I. B. Cohen's *Transformations*; and also "Dynamics: The Key to the 'New Science'," with the corrections and emendations by the author which appear in Special Issue 4, Prague (1968), pp. 35–41, along with important commentaries by E. J. Aiton, pp. 67–70, and J. B. Pogrebyski, pp. 43–50.

[51] See, further, I. B. Cohen, " 'Quantum in se est': Newton's Concept of Inertia in Relation to Descartes and Lucretius," *Notes and Records of the Royal Society of London*, Vol. 19 (1964), pp. 131–155.

inquiry: where Descartes himself may have found the concept of a 'state' of motion. His source was almost certainly Galileo, who had written of a 'state' of motion in his book on sun spots (1613).[52] Galileo was arguing that "physical bodies" have a "physical inclination" to some motions, a "repugnance to others," and an indifference to yet others. He concluded that "all external impediments removed, a heavy body on a spherical surface concentric with the earth will be indifferent to rest and to movements toward any part of the horizon. And it will maintain itself in that state to which it has once been placed: that is, if placed in a state of rest, it will conserve that: and if placed in movement toward the west (for example), it will maintain itself in that movement."[53]

What I find particularly astonishing about this passage is not so much that Galileo flies in the face of tradition by considering motion as a 'state', but that this revolutionary concept of a 'state' of motion was introduced without any fanfare. We may wonder, furthermore, why this concept was not again a feature of Galileo's discussion of the subject: I have not found it in either the *Dialogo* or the *Discorsi*. Mentioned once, *en passant*, as it were, this bold use of a word drops wholly out of sight until it is revived (and, as I believe I have shown, not reinvented) by Descartes. But Descartes would have had to introduce two 'transformations', both of conceptual profundity. First, there was the task of making of Galileo's passing remark a general principle of nature (the "prima lex naturae" of the Cartesian *Principia*). Second, Descartes had to insist (in an "altera lex naturae") that for motion to be a 'state', it must necessarily be not only uniform but also rectilinear. I believe that Descartes' introduction of this second and separate law of rectilinearity emerged from a 'transformation' of Galileo's own example of what he conceived to be a "state of motion": "Thus a ship, for instance, having once received some impetus through the tranquil

[52] For the evidence, see I. B. Cohen, *Transformations*, Ch. 2.

[53] Translation by Stillman Drake, *Discoveries and Opinions of Galileo* (Garden City, N.Y.: Doubleday Anchor Books, 1957), "Letters on Sunspots," p. 113; *Le opere di Galileo Galilei*, ed. naz., Vol. 5 (3rd printing, Florence: G. Barbèra Editore, 1965), pp. 134–135, *Istoria e dimostrazioni intorno alle macchie solari. . . .*

The reader should be aware that Drake differs from almost all of his colleagues with respect to Galileo's concept of inertia. See his contribution "The Concept of Inertia," *Saggi su Galileo Galilei*, being published by the Comitario Nazionale per le Manifestazioni Celebrative del IV Centenario della Nascitá di Galileo Galilei (preprint, Florence: G. Barbèra Editore, 1967). Also, his article "Galileo Gleanings-XVII. The Question of Circular Inertia," *Physis: Rivista Internazionale di Storia della Scienza*, Vol. 10 (1968), pp. 282–298. A revised version of these and other articles may be found in his *Galileo Studies*.

sea, would move continually around our globe without ever stopping . . . if . . . all extrinsic impediments could be removed. . . ." If this example be not an instance of circular inertia, the reason is surely that Galileo is not making a distinction between a plane and a portion of an enormous spherical surface, say as large as the Earth.[54] In this, I remind the reader he was not alone; for John Wallis, in his *Mechanica*, more than once introduced apparently *linear* terrestrial inertial motion, specifying "so long as it is understood that the horizontal plane is coincident with the surface of a sphere concentric with the Earth."

Galileo, in his several writings, presents a variety of inertial concepts. Some appear to be of circular motion (as in the extract just quoted), many are of horizontal motion, most are of motion on a supporting plane (in one notable case, brought to my attention by Père Costabel, an inclined plane[55]). One example is of a falling body; the downward force of weight is eventually compensated by the resistance, and the motion is thereafter uniform downward. When Galileo most nearly expresses a principle of inertia that is formally like Descartes', and when there is no supporting plane for the motion, it then turns out that the motion is very limited, as in the case of the horizontal component of a projectile's motion, and does not endure either perpetually or even for a significantly long time. It does no good to our historical understanding, therefore, to demand from Galileo's mute lips an answer to a question such as whether he expressly believed in a distinction (on some level of post-Newtonian reality) between limited large-scale circular inertia or purely linear inertia, or whether he thought the latter could 'really' continue infinitely or even indefinitely in the universe around us.

The variety (or, if you like, the ambiguity) of the Galilean concepts of (or expressions of) what we call inertia are a measure of the degree to which the Cartesian concept of the principle of inertia was itself a

[54] The debate on Galileo's theory or principle of inertia seems never ending, and I cite only a few of many studies on this topic: Emil Wohlwill, "Die Entdeckung des Beharrungsgesetzes," *Zeitschrift für Völkerpsychologie*, Vol. 14 (1883), pp. 365–410, and Vol. 15 (1884), pp. 70–135, 337–387; Ernst Mach, *Die Mechanik in ihrer Entwicklung historisch-kritisch dargestellt*, of which seven German editions appeared from 1883 to 1912, during the author's lifetime (1838–1916), and which has been translated into many languages (six English editions have been published by the Open Court Publishing Co., Chicago, 1893–1960); A. Koyré, *Etudes Galiléenes*, Pt. 3, "Galilée et la loi d'inertie"; Drake, *Galileo Studies*, Chs. 12 and 13, "Galileo and the Concept of Inertia" and "The Case against 'Circular Inertia' "; Maurice Clavelin, *La philosophie naturelle de Galilée, essai sur les origines et la formation de la mécanique classique* (Paris: Armand Colin, 1968).

[55] *Discorsi e dimostrazioni* . . . ("two new sciences"), "third day," scholium following Proposition XXIII (*Opere*, ed. naz., p. 244).

mighty transformation[56] of the versions or pre-versions of this concept that occur in Galileo's writings. If I declare Galileo the founder of inertial physics, therefore, it is because I find a series of dramatic 'transformations' that begin with Galileo and eventually lead to Newton. But I certainly do not believe, and would hold it a travesty of both science and history to assert, that Galileo should be credited with either having discovered (or having formulated or invented) Newtonian inertia, or having made use of Newton's first law of motion. Let us be amazed at how close Galileo may have come to the Newtonian concept and principle of inertia, and rejoice that others were stimulated to begin the set of 'transformations' that led up to Newton. And we must not forget that the Galilean revolution itself was the final 'transformation' in an earlier sequence of 'transformations' that had produced medieval impetus physics.

Let me now list some of the major 'transformations' required to convert Galileo's concepts into Newton's first law of motion: (1) precision as to inertia being only rectilinear, (2) extension from motions along planes near the Earth (or along spherical surfaces concentric with the Earth) to any rectilinear, and generally to any unsupported, motion, (3) the physical intuition that inertial motions may actually continue in the real external world of nature for a very long time, (4) the formulation as a primary axiom that inertial motion is a 'state', (5) the association of inertia, and hence of inertial motion, with mass as quantity of matter.

The first of the 'transformations' was made by Descartes, the second and fourth by Descartes and by Newton, and the fifth was made by Newton alone. The first two are perhaps the most interesting since they may indicate to us the real difference between reading Galileo before 1687 and after that date. For once Newton had published the *Principia* in 1687 with its plain (though perhaps not wholly unambiguous) statement of the principle of inertia as his first law of motion, and had declared that Galileo had known and used this law, no one could ever again read Galileo without seeing Newtonian implications or at least Newtonian potentialities.

4. Newtonian Dynamics: the Second Law of Motion

Galileo's example shows us the inherent difficulty in the concept of a proper (or linear) inertia: how far from 'obvious' or 'self-evident' the

[56] We must keep in mind that the transition to a Newtonian (or even a Cartesian) law of inertia was a tremendous intellectual step. See footnote 57 below.

law of inertia actually is.[57] And so we are prepared to find that the Newtonian first law of motion was achieved only after a number of 'transformations', beginning at least with Galileo's formulation and going on to the innovations made by Descartes and Gassendi, with an admixture of Kepler's concepts, before being 'transformed' yet again by Newton.[58] And we are, then, led to question any statement about an easy and absolute identification of 'Newton's physics' and 'Galileo's physics'.

Newton's physics—and I refer here specifically to the doctrine of definitions, laws, principles, and methods found in the *Principia*—rests on two definite but related concepts of mass, two kinds of force,[59] a pseudo-force (or "force of inertia"), a specific doctrine of space and time, and three laws of motion. The laws of motion are called "axiomata" but they are (at least the first two of them) already stated or at least fully implied in the prior definitions. A determining or defining aspect of Newton's physics is his concept of mass (*quantitas materiae*), which (Definition III) is its 'inertia' or "force of inertia" or resistance to a change of state.[60] At any given place, the "force of inertia" of any body is proportional to its weight.[61] This specification was notably absent from physics prior to the *Principia*, although in part implicit in the work of Huygens.

The second law is stated expressly by Newton as follows: *Mutationem motus proportionalem esse vi motrici impressae, & fieri secundum lineam rectam qua vis illa imprimitur.*[62] There should be no doubt

[57] We may, therefore, agree with Ernst Mach, who very wisely pointed out that the law of inertia could hardly be "obvious" or "self-evident" since throughout most of recorded history men believed in a quite different law and would have denied the Cartesian-Newtonian inertial principle.

[58] Gassendi was the first person to publish a law of inertia, not Descartes; see A. Koyré, *Newtonian Studies*, esp. Appendixes I and J to Ch. III, "Newton and Descartes."

[59] One is a blow or impulse, acting instantaneously; the other is a continuously acting force.

[60] This "force of inertia" (*vis inertiae*) or "inherent force" (*vis insita*) resists a change in state, but cannot of and by itself cause a change in state. For this reason it was called by Newton a "passive" force, as contrasted with "active" forces, which do produce changes in state. See I. B. Cohen, "Newton's Second Law and the Concept of Force in the *Principia*," *The Texas Quarterly*, Vol. 10 (1967), pp. 127–157. The whole issue of this journal for Autumn, 1967 (Vol. 10, No. 3) is devoted to Newtonian studies. A revised version of my paper has been included in an expanded reprint of this issue, published by the M.I.T. Press (Cambridge, Mass.), ed. Robert Palter.

[61] No doubt, one of the most significant novelties in the *Principia* was Newton's proof by *experiment* that the "force of inertia" (or "quantity of matter") is proportional to weight. One is a measure of resistance to change in state (or resistance to acceleration), and the other is a measure of the force it gives rise to when placed in a gravitational field.

[62] The statement of this law is unaltered in the three editions of the *Principia* (1687, 1713, 1726). See footnote 66 below.

as to what Newton meant. In the translation of Andrew Motte: "The alteration of motion is ever proportional to the motive force impress'd; and is made in the direction of the right line in which that force is impress'd." [63] By "force" Newton here has in mind what we would call an 'impulse'—and he tells us that the "alteration" of "motion" (that is, of "quantity of motion," measured by the product of mass and velocity) is proportional to such an 'impulse' or "force." He then explains that: "If any force generates a motion, a double force will generate double the motion, a triple force triple the motion, whether that force be impress'd altogether and at once, or gradually and successively." [64] How shall we reconcile this statement, so apparently simple, straightforward, and direct, with the attempts made by commentators on the foundations of dynamics, to have this be the familiar second law of our textbooks, "$F = mA$"? The answer is given by Newton himself.[65]

Observe that in the discussion of the Second Law which I have just quoted, Newton has said that a "force" (or 'impulse') will produce the same alteration in momentum whether "simul & semel" or "gradatim & successive"—whether "impress'd altogether and at once, or gradually [that is, by degrees] and successively." The end result will be the same whether we apply a single impulse or blow or whether we break up that single impulse into a succession of lesser ones. This is obviously true for the total change in momentum (that is, in the speed and direction of motion) according to the impulse-momentum form of the second law. For, if three impulses Φ_1, Φ_2, Φ_3, applied to a body of mass m, produce changes of momentum Δmv_1, Δmv_2, Δmv_3, respectively, then a single impulse Φ, the vector sum $\Phi_1 + \Phi_2 + \Phi_3$, will produce a change in momentum Δmv where

$$\Delta mv = \Delta mv_1 + \Delta mv_2 + \Delta mv_3$$

that is, in the one case there will be a polygonal trajectory, in the other a straight line; but the final momentum will be the same in both cases because the total change in momentum is the same in both cases. In the limit, as the interval between blows becomes less and less, *ultimately* we will have a continuous force acting. And the same would be

[63] *Mathematical Principles of Natural Philosophy*, by Sir Isaac Newton, trans. Andrew Motte, 1729, with an introduction by I. Bernard Cohen, 2 vols. (London: Dawsons of Pall Mall, 1968).

[64] There thus can be no doubt that it is an impulse, a blow, a thrust, that Newton has in mind.

[65] In what follows I shall not cite the many authors who have written about Newton's second law—including many historically minded philosophers of recent years. Most of these articles do not introduce any new textual material, and they tend to ignore the important factor of Newton's concept of time and the nature of Newtonian infinitesimals.

true for a series of infinitesimally small impulses whose sum was a 'finite' force. In this limiting case, of a continuous force, Newton presents to us a second law that includes a factor of time, in just that form that Newton has proposed (in Definition VII or Definition VIII) when presenting the "accelerative" or "motive" quantity (or "measure") of a centripetal force—that measure of it which is "proportional to the velocity [or quantity of "motion"] which it generates in a given time." I believe that Newton's two types of accelerative forces—discrete impulses and continuous forces—did not lead him to two forms of the second law of motion, probably because of his concept of mathematical time.

Some light on this topic, long discussed by almost every major philosopher of science, may be shed by alternative versions of the second law which Newton wrote out in manuscript in the years 1692/1693. I shall give but one of the new forms: "Law II. That a motion arising [in a space either immobile or mobile *del.*] is proportional to the motive force impressed and occurs along the right line in which that force is impressed." [66] In the commentary he explains: "And this motion, if the body was at rest before the impressed force, must be computed in an immobile space according to the determination of the impressed force, but, if the body was moving before, must be computed in its own mobile space, in which the body without the impressed force would be relatively at rest." [67] This is a novel way of conceiving Law II. In the *Principia*, in all printed versions, a body that receives a blow (or "impulsive" force) may be either at rest or in uniform motion, presumably because it has received such a blow at some anterior time. Then the new motion is to be added to the pre-existing motion; or, if two blows are given simultaneously, the two motions may be added together. Examples are to be found in Corollary 1 to the Laws of Motion and Proposition I, Book I.[68]

[66] The many variations of the second law are given in the Introduction and Apparatus Criticus of the edition with variant readings of Newton's *Principia*, prepared by the late Alexandre Koyré and me, jointly by Cambridge University Press and Harvard University Press in 1972. In all the different ways Newton wrote out the second law, there is *no variation* with regard to the definite and clear statement of a law relating an impulsive force to the production or alteration of "motion," by which Newton means "quantity of motion" or momentum. In no case is the second law expressed as a relation between a continuously acting force and the rate at which momentum is reduced or altered. See also my article "Newton's Second Law."

[67] I give these texts in translation; for the Latin versions, see my article "Newton's Second Law." See, further, footnote 72 below.

[68] In Corollary 1 to the Laws of Motion, an impulse is given to a body that is already moving; this impulse produces an alteration in the existing motion or causes a new motion. Then says Newton, the new motion will—according to Law

But now Newton asks us to think in a new way about the situation in which a body in motion may receive a blow and gain a new component of motion to be added to the original motion. The body, says Newton, is to be considered at rest within a uniformly moving space. Then it gains a motion from the blow according to the principles of bodies at rest, that is, the ordinary form of Law II. To an observer at true rest, the motion of the body is then composed of the motion within the space of reference, resulting from the blow, and the motion of the space of reference itself. This way of looking at the second law does not add (or require) any new physical concept or principle, since Newton had already established that physical events (notably the actions of forces and the motions they produce) occur in exactly the same manner in a system of reference at rest and in a system of reference in uniform rectilinear motion. But what is of major interest about this new way of casting the second law is that the eventual trajectory shown by Newton in a diagram is a curve looking much like a parabola, as if it were the product of a continuously acting force; this is so even though the context of the second law puts it beyond any doubt that Newton was conceiving of an impulsive (quasi-instantaneous) force and the change in motion (or change in momentum) it may produce. We would have supposed that the effect of such a 'force' (impulse) on a uniformly moving body would be to produce a linear path according to the diagonal construction, and not a parabola-like curve. But clearly Newton must have had in mind a "continuously acting" force, since only such a force may produce a continuous curve. Hence we conclude that the impulse in the new form of Law II will produce its effect "successive & gradatim" (and not "simul & semel"), and thus by an infinite series of infinitesimal impulses. Or, this curve represents the limit of a finite sequence as the time between successive blows becomes zero (or "infinitesimally small").[69]

In the *Principia,* Newton evidently regarded the impulse-momentum

---

I—continue of and by itself (*quantum in se est,* to quote the phrase from Lucretius used by both Descartes and Newton in presenting the law of inertia).

This aspect of the Laws of Motion is particularly fascinating, because it represents a situation in which a body is at first in motion, inertial motion (uniform and rectilinear), and is given a blow; Newton then computes the resulting motion. This situation comes directly from Descartes' explanation of refraction, a work which is referred to specifically by Newton in lectures which he gave on light long before he wrote the *Principia.* See my article "Newton's Second Law."

[69] In the original printing of my article on Newton's second law of motion this particular point is stated erroneously. I regret that owing to my having been abroad, the slowness of mail delivery caused some proof corrections to be received too late to be included.

form of Law II as fundamental; at least, this is the form in which the law is stated in the "Axiomata sive Leges Motus," and this is the form in which Newton states that the same effect is produced whether the "force" act (or "be impressed") "simul & semel" or "gradatim & successive." In Proposition I, it seems that Newton considered the continuous form of the law to be derivable, in the limit, from a series of blows, that is, an action "gradatim & successive." Hence, in Newtonian practice, there need be no real distinction made between the forms of the Second Law which we would write today as:

(1) $\Phi \alpha \Delta V$

(2) $f \alpha dV$

(3) $f \alpha \frac{dV}{dt}$

(4) $fdt \alpha dV$

(where **f** stands for a continuously acting rather than an instantaneous force).

The equivalence of these alternative forms of the 'second law' is due to a feature of Newton's fluxional conception of force: that time is always a uniformly fluent variable. In other words, the infinitesimal increments of time (dt) are always constant and so need not be specified by Newton.[70] Thus, Newton would not conceive of equation (1), and its limit, equation (2), as absolutely separate and distinct from equation (3) and equation (4). Today we are concerned that **Φ** in equation (1) and **f** in equations (2), (3), and (4) have a different dimensionality, so that the continuous 'force' **f** cannot strictly be the limit of a series of impulsive 'forces' **Φ**. Hence, we make a distinction between force and impulse, and define an impulse (**Φ**) in terms of a 'force' (**F**),[71]

(5) $\Phi = F \cdot \Delta t$

so that we can make explicit the time Δt in which the 'force' acts; but we do so because for us **Φ** is not a force at all, but a different type of

[70] Newton's views on time, in relation to these problems, and many others, have been illuminated by the texts and interpretive comments in *The Mathematical Papers of Isaac Newton*, ed. D. T. Whiteside, currently being published by Cambridge University Press. The present discussion owes much to Dr. Whiteside's suggestions.

[71] A distinction is made between **F** and f, since f may vary during the time Δt; in the case of a varying force, **F** would be the average value during the interval. This would not be a question during an infinitesimal time interval dt.

physicomathematical quantity. *We now* substitute $\mathbf{F}\cdot\Delta t$ for $\mathbf{\Phi}$ in equation (1) to get

$$(6)\quad \mathbf{F}\cdot\Delta t \,\alpha\, \mathbf{V}$$

and then take the limit either directly,

$$(7)\quad \lim_{\Delta t\to 0} \mathbf{F}\cdot\Delta t = \mathbf{f}dt \,\alpha\, \lim_{\Delta t\to 0} \Delta\mathbf{V} = d\mathbf{V}$$

or after dividing equation (6) by Δt,

$$(8)\quad \mathbf{F} \,\alpha\, \frac{\Delta\mathbf{V}}{\Delta t}$$

$$(9)\quad \lim_{\Delta t\to 0} \mathbf{F} = \mathbf{f} \,\alpha\, \lim_{\Delta t\to 0} \frac{\Delta\mathbf{V}}{\Delta t} = \frac{d\mathbf{V}}{dt}.$$

But such a procedure is *ours* and *not* Newton's. For he did *not* conceive a continuous force as primary, and an impulse as a derived concept obtained by multiplying the force by the time interval in which it acts, whether finite or infinitesimal. Clearly, in Newton's view, the same constant infinitesimal increment of uniformly flowing time was built into the concept of $\mathbf{\Phi}$ in equation (1), and in the limit form, when $\mathbf{\Phi} \to \mathbf{f}$, in equation (2) and (3). Newton's undifferentiated use of 'force' for what I have called $\mathbf{\Phi}$ in equation (1), $\mathbf{f}$ in equation (2), and $\mathbf{f}$ in equations (3) and (4) is the source of many difficulties to today's reader.[72]

The problem of understanding Newton's production of a curved trajectory thus depends on keeping distinct the two ways in which a 'force' may act: "simul & semel," in which the orbit is constructed as the result of a sequence of infinitesimal discrete force-impulses; and "gradatim & successive," in which a series of 'infinitesimal arcs' is generated by a continuous force (of second-order, infinitesimal, discrete force-impulses). Both of course lead to exactly the same theory of central forces. Confusion on this point, and failure to read the actual text

[72] It would be ungracious to make a parade of all the authors who have quoted Newton's second law, sometimes even in the original Latin, and then have assumed that Newton's 'second law' must involve "rate of change of momentum" or "change of momentum per unit time" (because they could not conceive that Newton would have written a statement which was dimensionally unsound or physically meaningless). This may be an example of the sort to which I refer later, toward the end of my paper, in which philosophical analysis or scientific knowledge may get in the way of true historical inquiry: in this case preventing the philosopher or scientist from seeing that the problem must lie in the meaning of 'force' for Newton.

A somewhat different view may be found in R. S. Westfall, *Force in Newton's Physics: The Science of Dynamics in the Seventeenth Century* (London: Macdonald; New York: American Elsevier, 1971).

of the *Principia* (apart from the Definition and Laws), has caused many writers to assert incorrectly that Newton did not "know" the continuous form of the second law. Of course, he did not ever write

$$\mathbf{F} = \mathrm{km}\mathbf{A}$$

or

$$\mathbf{F} = \mathrm{km}\frac{\mathrm{d}\mathbf{V}}{\mathrm{dt}} = \mathrm{km}\frac{\mathrm{d}^2\mathbf{s}}{\mathrm{dt}^2}$$

as we would. Nor did he even write out a 'fluxional' equation, such as

$$\mathrm{F} = \mathrm{kms} = \mathrm{km}\mathbf{V}.$$ [73]

But anyone who studies carefully Proposition XLI of Book I (or many others, such as Proposition XXIV, Theory XIX, Book II) will see at once that the mere absence of an equation or a differential or fluxional algorithm cannot mask the fact that Newton was perfectly aware of the second law in the form in which we know it—that is, for continuous forces.[74]

[73] The first person to write Newton's second law using differentials was J. Hermann in his *Phoronomia.* So far as I know, the first person to express Newton's second law in the language of fluxions (but not necessarily using the symbols of fluxions) was Colin Maclaurin. On the relation of Newton's second law to the history of dynamics in the eighteenth century, see Thomas Hankins, "The Reception of Newton's Second Law of Motion in the Eighteenth Century," *Archives Internationales d'Histoire des Sciences* (1967), XX_e année, pp. 43–65. See also Hankins's *Jean d'Alembert, Science and the Enlightenment* (Oxford: Clarendon Press, 1970), Ch. 8, "The Laws of Motion and d'Alembert's Principle."

[74] Again and again throughout the *Principia,* Newton assumes the truth of (or merely uses) the second law for continuous forces, introducing time as an explicit factor.

Thus, in the Definitions, at the beginning of the *Principia,* Newton shows that for any one and the same body, the ratio of its "weight" to its acceleration of free fall is a constant, even as we move out into space away from the earth. The constant in question is, of course, the body's 'inertia' or (to use Newton's expression) its "force of inertia." This is a constant of a body, and does not vary as the weight does.

Again, in Book II, Section VI, Newton deals with pendulums, in which case the force which acts is the continuous force of weight. He says (Proposition XXIV): "For the velocity, which a given force can generate in a given [quantity of] matter in a given time, is as the force and the time directly, and the matter inversely. The greater the force or the time is, or the less the matter, the greater velocity will be generated. This is manifest from the second law of motion." Incidentally, this is the famous theorem which leads Newton to show that pendulums may be used to test the proportionality (at any one and the same place) of mass and weight, or of 'inertia' and weight.

The foregoing result is, no doubt, one of the most striking in the whole *Principia,* from the point of view of physical principles, but it is generally misunderstood. Newton says explicitly, in describing the experiments that he made, that these experiments merely show with a greater degree of accuracy what had been known by observing freely falling bodies, which are seen to descend to the

5. Ambiguous History: Texts and References

A careful analysis of the historical record discloses no simple or universally applicable rules for making discoveries, no automatic path from experience to concepts, no unambiguous formation of theories or devising of experiments. Rather, we find scientists groping in the dark, with an occasional illumination from a sudden flash of intuition or inspiration, and slow stages of development by 'transformation'—in short, a science truly worthy of our philosophizing.

Karl Popper has called attention to this aspect of science in a succinct discussion of the relation of "Newton's theory" to "Galileo's or Kepler's," pointing out that "Newton's theory" was "far from being a mere conjunction of these two theories." [75] His conclusion reads: "Only after we are in possession of Newton's theory can we find out in which sense the older theories were approximations to it." Popper demonstrates that "logic, whether deductive or inductive, cannot possibly make the step from these theories [of Galileo and Kepler] to Newton's dynamics. It is only ingenuity which can make this step." No historian could express this point of view more admirably, with the possible exception of the substitution of some other expression like 'the exercise of the creative imagination' or even 'intuition', for Popper's word 'ingenuity'.

---

earth from equal heights in equal times (Book III, Proposition VI). Indeed, this leads to another greatly misunderstood aspect of Newton's dynamics. Throughout the *Principia,* "mass" is the resistance the body has to having a change in its "state" of motion or of rest, or its resistance to being accelerated. The confusion arises because of Definition I, in which it is generally alleged that Newton 'defined' the "quantity of matter" as a 'product of volume and density'. Newton did nothing of the sort. What he introduced in Definition I was a "measure" and in order to explain what he had in mind he said that *this particular measure* is the one "arising from the bulk and density conjunctly." The significance of Newton's procedure is that in this Definition I he attempts to give the reader some feeling for what "mass" or "quantity of matter" is, allying himself with an older tradition; but in Definition III, and in the *Principia* as such, he uses 'inertia' or "force of inertia." On the significance of the concept of "measure" (which turns out to be a feature of five of the eight definitions), see I. B. Cohen, "Isaac Newton's *Principia,* the Scriptures, and the Divine Providence," Appendix I, "New Light on the Form of Definitions I–II and VI–VIII," pp. 523–548, esp. pp. 537–542, of Sidney Morgenbesser, Patrick Suppes, and Morton White, eds., *Essays in Honor of Ernest Nagel: Philosophy, Science, and Method* (New York: St. Martin's Press, 1969). This aspect of Newton's conceptual framework of dynamics is displayed in further detail in the communication to the XIIIth International Congress of the History of Science; see footnote 48 above.

[75] See K. R. Popper, "The Aim of Science," *Ratio,* Vol. 1 (1957), pp. 29ff.

But the examples cited by Popper, and used by others, introduce a level of ambiguity of a type which historians find particularly troublesome in the writings of philosophers. Popper quite correctly shows that a system which *he* calls "Newton's theory" or "Newton's dynamics" cannot "be induced from Galileo's and Kepler's Laws," or "be strictly deduced from them." From these statements, however, it is far from clear as to whether Popper is citing a real or a fictitious Galileo, Kepler, and Newton. Using quotations from these authors, and even a diagram from one of Newton's works,[76] he gives the otherwise uninformed reader the impression that he is talking of a real (that is, empirically verifiable) Galileo and Newton.

"Galileo's theory" as presented by Popper, however, does not take account of the limitations imposed by Galileo, and of Galileo's conclusion that in the earth's atmosphere the paths of projectiles are not truly parabolas.[77] And as to the alleged inconsistency between "Newton's theory" and "Kepler's theory" or "Kepler's third law," there was no need of philosopher-critics to show that "we can derive from Newton's theory" the relation

$$(1)\ A^3/T^2 = M_0 + M_1$$

and that this is contradicted by "Kepler's third law"

$$(2)\ A^3/T^2 = \text{constant}.$$

It was, in fact, Newton himself who showed that for a system of two attracting bodies the relation (1) holds, and that the relation (2) is true only of a system of bodies that do not affect each other's motion, a system in which all the bodies circulate about a center of force which is unaffected by them or their motions.[78]

This example is very instructive in that it illustrates how the acute insights of philosophers of science pose fruitful questions for historians; and yet this very same example shows that we should not suppose philosophers of science to be writing history so much as history-based or history-oriented analyses. Popper directs our attention in a forceful way to the impossibility of any strict logical con-

[76] This particular diagram is taken from a posthumous work, and is not a faithful rendition of the diagram that appears in Newton's manuscript.

[77] For Galileo's own recognition of the difference between the simplified results, such as the pure parabolic path and the actual trajectories or projectiles in the real world, see footnote 41. According to Galileo, the "horizontal motion" of a projectile will not in actual fact "be uniform," nor will "the natural acceleration [downward] be in the ratio assumed, nor the path of the projectile be a parabola. . . ."

[78] This occurs in the *Principia*. I discuss this topic in the article cited at the end of footnote 13 above.

nection between "Newton's theory" and "Kepler's theory." He is not a historian, and so he stops at that point; his job is completed. The historian must then go on to the next stage of investigation. Since the corrected form of 'Kepler's third law' was known to Newton, what role did the original 'third law' of Kepler's play in the development of Newton's 'theory' of dynamics? How is this topic treated in the *Principia*? Since Newton, in his advance upon the subject, began by using both Kepler's law of elliptical orbits and the original 'third law', and then later learned of (and used) the law of areas, the historian—his sensibilities now sharpened by Popper's analysis—must ask whether Newton erred in his 'deductions'. And he must fully face up to the problem of how Newton actually obtained a 'theory' that contradicts its apparent base. A related problem which is aroused by Popper's analysis is the treatment of Kepler's laws in the *Principia*.[79] If Newton knew they were not 'true' statements, and supposing his own dynamics and celestial mechanics to be valid, how could he have stated these laws as valid propositions, with proofs? In short, Popper has not performed the historian's analysis of finding how Newton made use of Kepler's laws in either the development of his own 'theory' or the presentation of that 'theory' in the *Principia*. But he has posed a basic problem that the historian cannot ignore if his own account of Newton is to be sound and complete.

Newton's actual presentation (in the *Principia*) is fully worthy of the attention of a philosopher interested in problems of method. For Newton's procedure is to add complexities, one after the other, to an original simple mathematical model, so as to have it approach closer and closer to the realities of the physical situation revealed by observations. Newton begins with a point mass or unit mass subject to the action of a force originating from a fixed center, and shows the meaning of Kepler's laws under such circumstances. Then Newton advances to real bodies, discussing first an immovable central attracting body; next, two bodies attracting one another, each free to move with a resulting motion about the center of gravity of the system, which itself may be either at rest or in uniform motion. Next, Newton introduces the action of a third perturbing body, and discusses two notable examples: the motion of the Moon about the Earth under the perturbing

[79] In point of fact, it is often the case that the advance of science does not occur in a simple deductive way from one set of laws to another set of laws or theory, but rather through an intermediate step of making such a deduction for a greatly oversimplified model, to which are then added those features of the real world system which actually invalidate (or show the limitations of) the original set of laws which started the train of discovery or invention.

action of the Sun; and the motion of Saturn about the Sun, under the perturbing action of Jupiter, which Newton says should be most notable at a close approach of the two planets. Indeed, far from stating that his 'theory' enables him to deduce Kepler's law, or vice versa, Newton may be said to have shown the validity of his system by indicating how it may predict (in a *quantitative* manner) the observable deviation from Kepler's laws.[80] And so we are led squarely to a question that has been implicit since the start of this paper: is philosophy valid when derived from, or based upon, history that does not come up to the highest critical standards?

In this example, as in the examples above, the reader may see how important it is to refer to (and to read) the primary sources and to base statements on textual analysis. Clearly we do Newton a great injustice by correcting his second law, adding the phrase "per unit of time," instead of trying to find out what *he* meant.

But texts are very dangerous, especially translations. The current English version of Galileo's *Discorsi* (on the "two new sciences") would have Galileo say that he has "discovered *by experiment* some properties of it [motion] which are worth knowing and which have not hitherto been either observed or demonstrated." The words "by experiment"—as Alexandre Koyré pointed out—are conspicuously absent in the printed Latin text, and were added by Crew and De Salvio in an attempt to make of our Galileo an empiricist, in contradiction of fact.[81]

Curiously enough, the attempt—conscious or unconscious—to empiricize Galileo began in his own century. This may be seen in a most fascinating passage in the *Dialogo*, where the question arises as to the path of an object let fall from the mast of a moving ship. In the "second day," Galileo has an Aristotelian refer to the "experiment of the stone dropped from the top of the mast of a ship, which falls to the foot of the mast when the ship is standing still, but falls as far from that same point when the ship is sailing as the ship is perceived to

[80] A mature historical analysis of the *Principia* shows, therefore, that Newton demonstrated three separate aspects of Kepler's laws of planetary motion (as he did of Galileo's law of falling bodies): he showed under what very restricted and artificial circumstances Kepler's laws are valid; then he showed why they are not actually valid in the real world of experience; and finally, he derived a new law (or a modified version of the older law) that could be used without error in the world of phenomena.

[81] See the edition cited in footnote 41, p. 153. Cf. A. Koyré, "Traduttore-traditore, a propos de Copernic et de Galilée," *Isis*, Vol. 34 (1943), pp. 209–210. Happily, a new and more accurate English version of the *Discorsi* (prepared by Stillman Drake) will be published soon.

have advanced during the time of the fall, this being several yards when the ship's course is rapid." *Salviati* (more or less speaking for Galileo) leads *Simplicio* to argue that this 'experiment' may be used to indicate whether the ship is moving or at rest, since "when the ship stands still the rock falls to the foot of the mast, and when the ship is in motion it falls apart from there," so that "from the falling of the rock at the foot it is inferred that the ship stands still, and from its falling away it may be deduced that the ship is moving." The significance of this alleged experiment is that "what happens on the ship must likewise happen on the land," so that "from the falling of the rock at the foot of the tower one necessarily infers the immobility of the terrestrial globe." [82]

Salviati then asks *Simplicio,* "Now, have you ever made this experiment of the ship?" *Simplicio* replies that he has never performed the experiment, but he certainly believes "that the authorities who adduced it had carefully observed it." *Salviati,* in rebuttal, says that *Simplicio's* opinion is "sufficient evidence that those authorities may have offered it [the experiment] without having performed it, for you take it as certain without having done it, and commit yourself to the good faith of their dictum." Then he goes on to say that maybe they also "put faith in their predecessors, right on back without ever arriving at anyone who had performed it." And the reason for this assertion is rather simple, namely, "the experiment shows exactly the opposite of what is written; that is, it will show that the stone always falls in the same place on the ship, whether the ship is standing still or moving with any speed you please." Hence, *Salviati* asserts, experiments of dropping weights from towers, to find out whether they will fall at the foot of the tower or at some distance from the tower, can never tell whether the earth is at rest or in motion.[83]

But, of course, Galileo is not only a great scientist; he is ever a consummate artist. He does not make a fool of *Simplicio* by having him be completely absurd. And so, a few lines later, there is a reference to the experiment once again. *Simplicio* asks whether *Salviati* has or has not made the experiment. He admits he has not done so. "How is this?" asks *Simplicio*: "You have not made an hundred, no nor one proof thereof, and do you so confidently affirm it for true? I for my part will return to my incredulity, and to the confidence I had that the Experiment hath been tried by the principle Authors who made use thereof, and that the event succeeded as they affirm." Then, *Salviati*

[82] *Dialogo*, Drake edition cited in footnote 37, pp. 141–144.

[83] Simplicio and Salviati are discussing a major pre-Copernican 'test' of whether the earth is at rest or in motion.

replies, in a sentence that was a favorite of Alexandre Koyré's, for in it Koyré read the pride of a Platonist.[84] *Salviati* says (and I am now quoting the translation of Thomas Salusbury, published in London in 1661, within two decades of Galileo's death):

> I am assured that the effect will ensue as I tell you; for so it is necessary that it should. . . .[85]

The same text, translated recently by Professor Stillman Drake, reads:

> Without experiment, I am sure that the effect will happen as I tell you, because it must happen that way. . . .[86]

Note that Salusbury, consciously or unconsciously, dropped the simple words *senza sperienza,* without "experiment" or without "recourse to experience."

When I discovered that Salusbury had left out these two words, thus finding a complete confirmation of Koyré's interpretation, I could hardly believe my eyes. And I was all the more astonished in that I was already quite aware that Galileo, according to a letter he had written to Ingoli, had actually made such an experiment, and could therefore very easily have based his reply upon the evidence of experience.[87] Galileo quite consciously chose *not* to base his argument upon experience or experiment, but Salusbury—way back in the seventeenth century—obviously could not resist the temptation to make of Galileo an empiricist, in the great tradition of the 'new science' in England, at the time of the founding of the Royal Society, and its motto: *Nullius in verba,* On the word of no man, no authority, only experience!

These two examples of the falsification of Galileo's texts, one in the seventeenth century and the other in the twentieth, both reflect a philosophical aspect of the distortion of history. For in each of these two passages, the translator would have the great Galileo appear to us as an outstanding empiricist, thus to personify a particular concep-

[84] See A. Koyré, "Galileo and Plato," *Journal of the History of Ideas*, Vol. 4 (1943), pp. 400–428; reprinted in A. Koyré, *Metaphysics and Measurement: Essays in Scientific Revolution* (London: Chapman & Hall; Cambridge University Press, 1968), pp. 16–43.

[85] This translation has been reprinted (1962) in a facsimile edition, with an introduction by Stillman Drake (issued by Dawsons of Pall Mall in London, and by Zeitlin and Ver Brugge in Los Angeles).

[86] *Op. cit.*, p. 145.

[87] See I. B. Cohen, "A Sense of History in Science," *American Journal of Physics*, Vol. 18 (1950), pp. 343–359. On Galileo's correspondence with Ingoli, a lawyer from Ravenna, see the *Opere,* ed. naz., Vol. 5, pp. 403ff.

tion of the scientist: proceeding happily by the exercise of 'method' (the "soul of science") from experiment to theory. This characterization of scientists is especially cherished by writers of textbooks; it has infected so much of the current literature of science that it is now extremely difficult to rescue scientific discovery from this particular philosophical straightjacket. We do not dare to tell our students that Dalton's magnificent construction of the atomic theory was made possible by his deliberate adjustment of certain experimental results to fit his theory, since this would impugn the alleged empirical foundation of his atomic theory.[88] And in recent science, as my colleague Gerald Holton has pointed out, there has been a similar attempt to impose an empiricist philosophy on Albert Einstein by declaring the special theory of relativity to have been an attempt to explain the Michelson-Morley experiment. Einstein's famous paper of 1905, however, does not explicitly mention this experiment and is based primarily on puzzles arising from purely theoretical considerations of the classical electromagnetic theory.[89]

These falsifications are features of interpretive textbook writers, philosophers, and of scientists. And they are aggravated by the reliance on translations. Galileo's *Two New Sciences* is rendered poorly in the current version,[90] and Newton's *Principia* fares equally badly.[91] I would caution any philosopher or scientist (or historian of science,

[88] On Dalton, see Arnold Thackray, *John Dalton* (Cambridge: Harvard University Press, 1972). In a debate of not too long ago, a scientific colleague argued that it was for this very reason that teachers of science would be well advised not to use accurate history. He also asked whether it would be an "edifying example" for our students to learn that Pauli discovered one of the most important principles of modern physics (the exclusion principle) while relaxing at a "girly show" in Copenhagen. The answer should be, of course, that we must decide whether we wish our students to become perfect models of what textbook writers envisage science and scientists to be, or whether we wish them to be Daltons or Paulis.

[89] See Gerald Holton, "Einstein, Michelson, and the 'Crucial' Experiment," *Isis*, Vol. 60 (1969), pp. 133–197.

[90] There are many errors in the Crew and De Salvio translation of this work. For instance, in the "third day," Theorem I, Proposition I reads: "The time in which any space is traversed by a body starting from rest and uniformly accelerated is equal to the time in which that same space would be traversed by the same body moving at a uniform speed whose value is the mean of the highest speed and the speed just before acceleration began." One does not even need to consult the original to see that something is wrong in this English version; surely Galileo would not have referred to a body's "speed just before acceleration began" when the opening statement is that the body is "starting from rest."

[91] On the current translation of the *Principia*, see I. B. Cohen, "Pemberton's Translation of Newton's *Principia*, with Notes on Motte's Translation," *Isis*, Vol. 54 (1963), pp. 319–351; an appendix discusses some faults in Cajori's revision of Motte's translation.

for that matter) who uses historical material to be aware that translations are always apt to be faulty and even downright misleading.

Let me give you two examples which show how a minimum amount of historical caution may save an author from a maximum degree of error. In the Scholium to the Laws of Motion, the Cajori version of the *Principia* contains the following sentence: "When a body is falling, the uniform force of its gravity acting equally, impresses, in equal intervals of time, equal forces upon that body, and therefore generates equal velocities. . . ." [92] How fascinating, we are told, to find Newton using such "contrasting" meanings of the word "force" in the same sentence. Such is the kind of analysis to which this passage has been subjected. Anyone who looks at the Latin original will quickly see that in Newton's sentence the word force (*vis*) occurs only once, and so without contrast.

Let me refer to another misleading and curious passage in the Cajori volume, in the presentation of Newton's *System of the World*. This tract is based on Newton's original manuscript version of Book III of the *Principia*, which he discarded when he prepared the final copy for the printer. In this text (p. 550) there occurs a pair of paragraphs of great philosophical significance, which are presented in English in the Cajori versions as follows:

> But our purpose is only to trace out the quantity and properties of this force from the phenomena, and to apply what we discover in some simple cases as principles, by which, in a mathematical way, we may estimate the effects thereof in more involved cases; for it would be endless and impossible to bring every particular to direct and immediate observation.
>
> We said, *in a mathematical way,* to avoid all questions about the nature or quality of this force, which we would not be understood to determine by any hypothesis; and therefore call it by the general name of a centripetal force, as it is a force which is directed towards some centre; and as it regards more particularly a body in that centre, we call it circumsolar, circumterrestrial, circumjovial; and so in respect of other central bodies.[93]

Clearly, this is an important statement of a philosophical position, and

[92] This sentence occurs in the Scholium to the "Axioms, or Laws of Motion," Sir Isaac Newton's *Mathematical Principles of Natural Philosophy* and *His System of the World*, trans. by Andrew Motte in 1729. The translation revised and supplied with an historical and explanatory appendix by Florian Cajori (Berkeley and Los Angeles: University of California Press, 1934 [6th printing, paperbound edition, 1966]). Concerning this passage, see I. B. Cohen, "Newton's Use of 'Force,' or, Cajori versus Newton: A Note on Translations of the *Principia*," *Isis*, Vol. 58 (1967), pp. 226–230.

[93] *Op. cit.*, p. 550–551.

has fairly recently served to give the title to an article on Newton's method, published in a very learned journal.[94] Interestingly enough, in the original Latin manuscript of Newton's, and in all the known copies of it (of which I have located five in all), this particular passage reads very differently.[95] In a rather literal version, we find Newton saying:

> Our purpose is to bring out its quantity and properties and to investigate mathematically its effects in moving bodies; further, in order not to determine its type hypothetically, we have called by the general name 'centripetal' that [force] which tends toward some centre—or in particular (with the name taken from the centre) [we call] circumsolar [that] which tends toward the sun, circumterrestrial [that] which [tends] toward the earth; circumjovial [that] which [tends] toward Jupiter; and so in the others.

This discrepancy is most fascinating, and was uncovered quite naturally in the course of investigations of the translations and original texts (both published in 1728) of this work. The English translation was published before the Latin original, and from another manuscript version or copy than the one in the hands of Newton's executors. Whether (as may be possible) this manuscript contained another version of this passage or not, we cannot at present say, since no such manuscript is known to exist. We have no warrant whatever for assuming—as of now—that this interesting expression of Newton's point of view, however Newtonian it may sound, is an authentic statement by the author of the *Principia.*

This section shows the pitfalls that await the user of incomplete texts, or translations, and may very properly be interpreted as a criticism of historians of science, and not of philosophers of science, scientists, or the writers of scientific textbooks. For the fact of the matter is that it is up to historians of science to provide readable and reliable texts and translations, and the monographs needed for sound interpretation of them. It is not sufficient for historians of science to plead that the profession is a young one, and that the number of historians is small. Historians of science have a sacred obligation to produce trustworthy texts and translations, but I greatly fear that today many historians of science are not willing to take on this responsibility. In this circumstance, it would be unseemly for any historian of science

[94] See Stanislaus J. Dundon, "Newton's 'Mathematical Way' in the *De mundi systemate*," *Physis*, Vol. 11 (1969), pp. 195–204, esp. n. 2 (p. 195).

[95] See I. B. Cohen, "Newton's *System of the World*: Some Textual and Bibliographical Notes," *Physis*, Vol. 11 (1969), pp. 152–166. See also Sir Isaac Newton, *A Treatise of the System of the World*, trans. into English [1731] with an introduction by I. B. Cohen (London: Dawsons of Pall Mall, 1969).

to criticize a philosopher of science or a scientist unduly, when the fault may lie with the historians. On the other hand, this set of circumstances does not absolve philosophers or scientists of responsibility. All too often, errors or misinterpretations are not caused so much by the want of available texts or translations as by the failure to consult such original sources or to use these sources improperly.

6. Conclusion: The Philosopher *vs.* the Historian

On several occasions in this paper, I have indicated a difference between the points of view of the analytic or critical philosopher of science[96] and of the historian of scientific ideas who seeks to understand the creative experience of a scientist. An example has already appeared in my discussion of Karl Popper's brilliant paper. The difference between a historian's point of view and a philosopher's occurs in the questions they ask. Popper is concerned to inquire into whether a 'Newtonian theory' stripped down to its bare essentials is or is not consistent with (and so 'derivable' from) a 'Keplerian theory' or a 'Galilean theory'.[97] But the historian has a very different assignment: to find whether there may be documentary information as to whether Newton did discover his 'theory' by a series of logical steps starting from Galileo's and Kepler's results. Did he believe that his own 'theory' was deducible from Galileo's and Kepler's laws? In short, the historian must be wary lest the quite proper logical analysis of the philosopher blind him to the significant aspects of the thought-processes of a Newton, a Kepler, a Galileo, a Darwin, or an Einstein.

We have, in fact, good evidence that in 1684, presumably in August, Edmond Halley came to Cambridge to ask Isaac Newton what path the planets would describe if they were continually attracted by the sun with a force varying inversely as the square of the distance. Newton immediately replied: an ellipse! Hence, whatever restrictions Newton later stated in the *Principia* (*ed. princeps* 1687), or already knew about truly elliptical orbits, his answer to Halley's question is different from the results of the logical argument introduced by Karl Popper. Psychologically, from the point of view of understanding how Newton made his 'discoveries', Popper's argument is irrelevant, save insofar as it may show us the extralogical aspects of scientific creativity. Newton's encounter with Halley set in train the sequence of events

[96] I am using the adjectives 'analytic' and 'critical' in their general signification, and not in the sense of particular philosophies.

[97] See Sec. 5 above.

that led to the writing of the *Principia*, and its importance therefore cannot be minimized.[98]

We may see in this episode why the historian feels strongly that our modern methods of mathematical or logical analysis should never place a screen between us as observers and the historical conditions of discovery. Indeed, to many historians, the major danger in the writing of history by nonhistorians (and even by some members of the profession) is the anachronistic application of our present canons of logic and mathematics and of scientific knowledge[99] to prior experiments, laws, and theories. To view the concepts, laws, and theories of a Galileo, a Kepler, and a Newton as 'approximations' to some later ideal creations of critical or philosophically minded scientists will block us from a meaningful understanding of the creative processes of any scientist we may be studying, including the interaction of the individual and his social and intellectual environment.

It is surely a peril to our understanding of the course of history, and not only of the creative process, to see a Galileo and a Kepler through the eyes of Newton, or to read a Newton through the eyes of Mach or of Einstein. To search through Galileo's writings for extracts that may sound like samples of Newtonian (or inertial) dynamics is to discard the historical Galileo, and is not to do proper

[98] See I. B. Cohen, *Introduction to Newton's 'Principia'* (cited in n. 66 above). In Supplement I to that *Introduction*, I have gathered together a number of autobiographical statements of Newton's. One reads: "I began to think of gravity extending to the orb of the Moon, [having deduced *del.*] having found out how to estimate the force with which ⟨a⟩ globe revolving within a sphere presses the surface of the sphere: from Keplers rule of the periodical times of the Planets being in a sesquialterate proportion of their distances from the centers of their Orbs, I deduced that the forces which keep the Planets in their Orbs must ⟨be⟩ reciprocally as the squares of their distances from the centers about which they revolve: & thereby compared the force requisite to keep the Moon in her Orb with the force of gravity at the surface of the earth, and found them answer pretty nearly." Also, "At length in the winter between the years 1676 & 1677 I found the Proposition that by a centrifugal force reciprocally as the square of the distance a Planet must revolve in an Ellipsis about the center of the force placed in the lower umbilicus of the Ellipsis & with a radius drawn to that center describe areas proportional to the times."

[99] There are two almost conflicting aspects of the history of science, one of which is related to the times in which a particular aspect of science was developed or practiced and the other to the state of knowledge today. The latter is, of course, transitory, and an overemphasis on interpreting older physics in the light of present-day physics (or astronomy or mathematics or biology or geology) would require that all history be revised and completely rewritten every several decades at the least. Of course, if Newton 'proved' (or thought he had so proved) a particular theorem, it is clearly of great interest if the historian is aware that this particular theorem is false; and especially if a knowledge of that falsity were to lead to an understanding of the limitation of Newton's method of proof. A famous instance of this type is the alleged proof by Fermat of what is known as

history at all. It is part of our understanding of the creative faculties of Isaac Newton for us to be able to recognize both the degree to which he may have held that his theory could—at least in part—arise from Kepler's laws and of his possible later recognition that his own theory requires a major modification of Kepler's laws. However helpful philosophical hindsight may be in clarifying certain logical, methodological, or conceptual aspects of science, these very factors may well prove to be inimical to the best historical scholarship, especially if they are applied anachronistically rather than being used only to sharpen the historian's wits and critical awareness *ab initio*.

The critical philosopher tends to use the 'superiority' of his present position to show the limitations and errors in the scientific writings of the past, or in the scientific thought which he alleges to have occurred in the past. But the historian's job is rather to immerse himself in the writings of scientists of previous ages, to immerse himself so totally that he becomes familiar with the atmosphere and problems of that past age. Only in this way, and not by anachronistic logical or philosophical analysis, can the historian become fully aware of the nature of the scientific thought of that past age and can he really feel secure in his interpretation of what that scientist may have thought he was doing. The goal of the historian of science, unlike that of the philosopher, must be to see whether he can make precise the circumstances of some past age, together with the idiosyncratic qualities of thought of an individual whom he is studying. His success may be seen in the degree to which he can correctly apply the words Alexandre Koyré used to delight in using about a scientist of the past, "And he was right!"

---

his 'last theorem', which we may doubt his having proved. But it is certainly irrelevant to our understanding and evaluation of Joseph Priestley's work in chemistry that later chemists rejected the concept of 'phlogiston'. Nor is it of any particular consequence, save as an antiquarian curiosity, that we reject Dalton's postulate that all atoms of any given chemical element have the same weight (or mass) and a different weight (or mass) from the atoms of any other chemical element. Nor is it notably relevant to our understanding of the significance of John Dalton that we today no longer believe that the chemical 'atom' is indivisible.

To look at the problem somewhat differently, I hold that our present judgment about the validity or invalidity of any type of astrology is irrelevant to the work of a student of astronomy and astrology in medieval Islam, Persia, or Europe. Furthermore, such a scholar might find that the time required to become a master of present-day astronomy would be largely wasted insofar as his historical research was concerned; & that he would do better to become an expert in the science of *that* time rather than of *our* time. Indeed, I think it fair to say that there is a tremendous danger to historians of science in (again consciously or unconsciously) being biased in their approach to the science of any earlier period by a knowledge of the science of the twentieth century.

Historians and philosophers have written almost endlessly on Newton's famous slogan, *Hypotheses non fingo*. The historian must consider this phrase not only as one of Newton's statements about hypotheses, and as part of his general philosophy, but also as a timebound document. He must keep in mind that this declaration of Newton's about not feigning or framing hypotheses is dated: it appeared for the first time in the second edition of the *Principia* of 1713, in the celebrated General Scholium which Newton wrote as a conclusion for that edition. The point Newton is making is that he has explained "the phenomena of the heavens and of our sea by the power of gravity," but that he has not yet "assigned the cause of this power." Then he says that he will not *feign* or *frame* (Newton himself uses both words in English[100]) any hypotheses, and so will not discuss the "cause of those properties of gravity" because he has not been able "to deduce" the cause "from phenomena." He then explains that "whatever is not deduced from phenomena is to be called a hypothesis," and hypotheses of all sorts ("whether metaphysical or physical, whether of occult qualities or mechanical") have "no place in experimental philosophy."

I shall use this passage to illustrate a major difference between two extremes: the way in which philosophers attack a problem and the way in which a critical historian should approach the same problem. Philosophers are concerned very properly with the analysis of scientific thought, whereas historians deal with particular instances of the scientific thinking of individuals. The contrast is thus between science as abstraction, or system, and science as a living process of discovery and growth—it is a contrast, to use the phrase so happily introduced by Alfred North Whitehead, between the "logic of the discovered" and the "logic of discovery." [101] Let me illustrate the philosophical point of view, in relation to this passage, by quoting from a most acute analysis by Professor William Kneale. Kneale quite correctly refers to this as a "strange passage," and—in particular—would have us notice "that Newton speaks in a very curious way of *deducing* propositions from phenomena. This expression occurs in other places, and we must assume that Newton used it deliberately; but it obviously cannot mean what is ordinarily called 'deduction', and I can only conclude that Newton meant that the propositions which interested him were derived from observations in a very strict way." [102]

[100] On this subject, see I. B. Cohen, "The First English Version of Newton's *Hypotheses non fingo*," *Isis*, Vol. 53 (1962), pp. 379–388.

[101] Whitehead used these phrases in his *The Aims of Education* (New York: Macmillan, 1929), p. 80.

[102] William Kneale, *Probability and Induction* (Oxford: Clarendon Press, 1949), pp. 98–99.

I commend to the critical reader the whole chapter in which Professor Kneale discusses this topic as constituting a most valuable key for our understanding of the general subject of Newton's thought. As an analysis of a text presented to us *as it stands,* Kneale's discussion exemplifies the traditional role of the philosopher-analyst at its best. The historian approaches the topic in a slightly different fashion. He observes, in the first place, that whatever Newton says about "hypotheses" in this General Scholium must be taken with great caution, since Book II of the *Principia* contains a plainly labeled "Hypothesis" in every edition. Furthermore, the second edition (1713), Book III, to which the General Scholium is appended, contains two hypotheses ("Hypothesis I" and "Hypothesis II"). Furthermore, the careful historian will have found out that in the first edition (1687), in which there was no General Scholium as a conclusion, there had been a whole series of hypotheses, labeled "Hypothesis I," "Hypothesis II," and so on. In the second edition, 1713, in which the General Scholium with its slogan *Hypotheses non fingo* was first published, some of these hypotheses became the "Regulae Philosophandi" while others became "Phaenomena." If now, in the second edition, Newton is making a distinction between hypotheses and phenomena, he has obviously changed his mind, or at least his usage, since what had previously been called "Hypotheses" are now to be called "Phaenomena." [103]

The philosopher, trained in logic and critical analysis, at once notices in Newton's phrase the word "deduction," employed in a fashion which is not familiar, and he cannot help addressing himself to Newton's apparently unusual logical procedure. But in doing so, he closes his eyes to the historical problem. For the fact of the matter is that there are two novel features (among many) that are particularly striking about Book III in the second edition. One is the General Scholium, in which Newton talks about hypotheses as being neither phenomena nor 'deductions' from phenomena. The other is the grouping together of a set of propositions or statements under the new general heading of "Phaenomena." It would seem, therefore, that in our attempt to understand what Newton had in mind, we should look carefully at his usage of this new category of "Phaenomena," which he introduced into the *Principia* in 1713 at the same time as the statement about phenomena in the General Scholium.[104]

[103] See I. B. Cohen, "Hypotheses in Newton's Philosophy," *Physis*, Vol. 8 (1966), pp. 163–184.

[104] This topic is discussed at greater length, together with documentary information, in Ch. III of *Transformations of Scientific Ideas* (cited in footnote 34 above).

But enough of examples! Surely it should now be clear as to the grounds on which historians often find a difference between the approach to history in the writings of philosophers and the methodology which characterizes the books and articles by the best critical historians of science. Furthermore, as I have expressed earlier in declaring my admiration for the precepts of Karl Popper, the philosophical writings of philosophers of science are of an obvious and crucial importance to the practicing historian of scientific ideas, who certainly cannot hope to deal adequately with the birth, growth, application, or transformation of scientific concepts without some training in philosophy. I am very aware of my personal indebtedness to Duhem, Poincaré, Hannequin, Meyerson, Cassirer, and Brunschvicg; and, on a more immediate and personal level, to Philipp Frank, Alfred North Whitehead, and Ernest Nagel, and to R. Carnap, Hans Reichenbach, W. V. Quine, and Karl Popper, and—above all—Alexandre Koyré and Harry A. Wolfson. I continually wish that my own training and background in philosophy were deeper, just as I wish it were also deeper in psychoanalysis and sociology, but I certainly do not propose to give up the profession of historian altogether to become a philosopher. Similar considerations surely apply to philosophers of science, who cannot be expected to give up their professional careers in order to become historians.

Philosophers use history to provide an empirical base for their statements, or at least to find examples in the real world of science (as it has actually been practiced) which may illustrate a thesis of their own or confute a thesis of their opponents. Surely this goal is always better served by true than by false history, or—at the very least—by discovered rather than imagined history. Imagined history is of no use at all, since it only projects into the past of the limits of our understanding of what 'we already know'. It thus denies its own existence, the reason for studying history in the first place. As Ernest Nagel once expressed the matter, the chief value in studying the history of science is that it adds a new dimension to our experience of science, one that we would not have known had we not made historical investigations. In this sense, I advocate a more critical attitude toward the use of historical materials, not merely from a moral or aesthetic standpoint. I am firmly and fully committed to a belief in the mutual benefits of a continual dialogue between historians of science and philosophers. But I do not see how any fruitful dialogue can take place if the types of 'history' conceived by these two groups have no close correspondence.

History and Philosophy of Science: A Reply to Cohen

PETER ACHINSTEIN

Professor Cohen's paper raises some rather intriguing issues. I want to discuss the following four because I think they are important for philosophers of science and because I feel that it is of value to consider what arguments might be given in defense of, or in opposition to, some of the stands Cohen takes on these issues. The first issue is whether philosophy of science must be historically based. The second is why philosophers of science should get their facts straight. The third is the value of philosophy of science for the historian. The fourth is whether good philosophy of science can be based on bad history.

Near the beginning of his paper Cohen points out that not all philosophers of science have "based their philosophies on the analysis of the history of science" (p. 310), and he cites as examples of great "ahistoricalists" Carnap and Quine. A philosopher is developing a historically based philosophy of science, we might say, if, or to the extent that, he satisfies either or both of the following conditions: (a) he arrives at his philosophical conclusions by considering, among other things, past and present scientific activities and results, (b) he defends or justifies his conclusions by appeal, among other things, to past and present scientific activities and results. The ahistorical philosopher of science, then, is one who arrives at and defends his conclusions without appeal to past or present scientific activities or results.

Speaking very roughly we might categorize quite a few contemporary philosophers of science as being in one of two camps. In one camp are philosophers such as Hanson, Toulmin, and Shapere who by examining historical cases in the sciences proceed to describe science as it is and was actually practiced and to describe concepts that are or were actually in use. These philosophers would accept both condition (a) and condition (b). They are historicalists in the fullest sense. In the other camp I would place philosophers like Hempel, Suppes, Carnap, and Quine. In their writings one finds not a case history approach but rational reconstruction, or what Carnap calls "explication." The aim is to replace a faulty concept, set of ideas, or scientific system by another one which is clearer, more exact, free of inconsistencies, and more fruitful. Concepts such as theory, probability, model, and explanation —concepts actually in use in the sciences—are to be explicated, that is, replaced by ones that bear some similarity to the old concepts but have the advantages noted above. And formulations of particular theories, such as Newton's formulation of mechanics, are to be replaced by more precise and more elegant axiomatic systems of the sort that Professor Suppes has developed. Let me call this view Reconstructionism, and the former view Constructionism. The Constructionist wants to "tell it like it is." The Reconstructionist wants to "tell it like it should be."

On this occasion I do not wish to discuss the merits of these approaches; I have done so elsewhere.[1] I do want to point out, however, that despite appearances the Reconstructionist, like the Constructionist, is committed in theory to a historically based philosophy of science, although his actual practice does not generally illustrate this. The Reconstructionist advocates replacing a concept or system in use on the ground that, as Carnap puts it, there are certain "critical contexts" in which its use "involves confusions or even inconsistencies" and leads to unanswerable questions and paradoxes.[2] But unless we know what is wrong with the present concept or system we will not know whether the Reconstructionist's explication avoids the difficulties and thus is superior. Until we know this we have no justification for abandoning the original concept or system and adopting the new one. But to know what is wrong with the present concept involves knowing something about it. At the outset, as Carnap puts it, we must "clarify the explicandum," something he advocates but unfortunately rarely pursues. Knowing something about the concept or concepts of *model* actually in use in the sciences involves knowing what items are classified as models by scientists, past and present, what attitude scientists take with respect to them, for what purposes they actually use them. It may turn out that there are several different concepts of model in use. It may turn out that all or some of these are vague or internally incoherent in some way. But unless an examination is made of actual cases we will never know. *A fortiori*, we will never know whether the Reconstructionist's replacement—for example, Braithwaite's concept of a

[1] Achinstein [1968] and [1969].
[2] Schilpp [1963], p. 933.

model as another interpretation of a theory's calculus, or Suppes's concept of a model as a set in which the axioms of a theory are satisfied—avoids the difficulties. Accordingly, to sell his *new* concept the Reconstructionist must at some point examine the old one, and this will involve what I have called an historically based analysis. I conclude that a completely ahistorical philosophy of science is a myth. For the Constructionist it is a myth in practice as well as in theory; for the Reconstructionist it is a myth in theory, though unfortunately less so in practice.

Now for the second issue. Why should philosophers of science get their historical facts straight? One answer historians of science sometimes give—an answer implicit in several remarks Cohen makes—is this. Philosophers of science insofar as they utilize historical facts are engaging in the history of science, and this if done at all is worthy of being done accurately for its own sake since the subject is so interesting and basic. I reject this answer for the philosopher of science, since he is not, or need not be, pursuing the subject of history of science for its own sake, as interesting or basic as this subject is. Why the philosopher of science should get his historical facts straight can be answered quite simply by reference to the previous point concerning historically based philosophy of science. (Cohen does finally grant this, though a bit belatedly at the end of his paper.) If, as I believe he should, the philosopher arrives at and defends his conclusions by considering, among other things, past and present scientific activities, then his philosophical conclusions are acceptable only to the extent that the historical facts from which he drew them or by reference to which he defends them are accurate. In this respect the philosopher of science is no different from anyone else who draws conclusions in the light of what he takes to be the facts. As far as I can see this is the only reason why the philosopher of science, quâ philosopher, should get his historical facts straight.

The third issue I want to consider—and this in more depth—is the value of philosophy of science for the historian of science. Toward the end of his paper Cohen states that "the philosophical writings of philosophers of science are of an obvious and crucial importance to the practicing historian of scientific ideas" (p. 349). Given other things he says I am not really clear why Cohen believes this. Near the beginning he complains that the literature of philosophy of science itself does not usually contain the slightest clue as to whether any part "may be useful for historical inquiries" (p. 312). And he seems to think that the number of major developments in the philosophy of science, the time and effort required to understand them, and the distinct possibility that they will turn out to be useless to the historian, make a study of philosophy of science on the part of historians an impossible task, at least as philosophy of science is now practiced (p. 313). On pp. 336-337 Cohen does commend Popper for directing the historian's attention to the absence of a logical connection between Newton's laws and Kepler's laws, which he thinks is a valuable service to the historian. Yet on pp. 344-355 he seems to be suggesting that what Popper does here is not particularly relevant to the historian's task. What, then, is the value of philosophy of science for history of science? As with any issue pertaining to philosophy, one is bound to find varying viewpoints.

One is that the historian should approach his problem from a given point of view, with a framework in hand, with a bias—if you will—something that the philosopher is supposed to be good at explicating if not furnishing. This might be a world view, for example, rationalism of the sort found in Koyré. It might be a philosophical view about paradigms, normal science, and revolutions, of the sort found in Kuhn. Or it might be a view about scientific "transformations" of the sort Cohen himself advocates. But whatever it is it suggests the sorts of inquiries the historian of science ought to make. And as many philosophers of science I believe rightly complain, too often historians employ such frameworks without sufficient philosophical clarification.

There is a second view due to the late Russ Hanson. It emphasizes the analysis of scientific arguments.[3] The philosopher of science is able to aid the historian by assessing the cogency of scientific reasoning of the present and the past. The philosopher of science, Hanson wrote, "ought to be able cooly to reconsider the experimental evidence available to microphysicists in 1931 and determine therefrom who had the best arguments—those who quickly opted for the existence of antiparticles (like the positron), or those (like Bohr and Rutherford) who sought to reinterpret the shocking cloud-chamber tracks of Anderson, Blackett and Occhialini . . . in terms of more familiar ideas well known in the 1920s." Hanson's point is that a real understanding of a scientific argument of the past cannot be achieved solely by determining what premises were employed. One needs to know also whether the premises entail the conclusion or make it probable in the light of the known evidence. The philosopher of science, in view of his logical training and historical knowledge, is eminently qualified to examine premises, conclusions, and the relationship between them.

No one, I think, will deny that it is of intrinsic interest to discover whether an argument actually employed by a scientist of the past is

[3] Hanson [1958].

cogent, and if this is "your thing" then by all means you ought to be allowed to do it. Some might deny that this is history of science. The historian, it might be said, should worry only over what the argument is, not over whether it is any good. Be that as it may, the task Hanson sets for himself, if not that of the historian, at least beautifully complements the task of the historian.

No doubt other philosophers will say that they can furnish aid and comfort in other ways. Let me mention one which I believe is particularly important. This is the analysis of concepts employed by both the scientist and the historian of science. I have in mind concepts such as theory, explanation, model, and law. There is a passage in his paper in which Cohen states that the job of the historian of science is to "immerse himself in the writings of scientists of previous ages" (p. 346. In the same passage there is the suggestion that *philosophical* analysis is often inimical to historical scholarship because it is frequently applied anachronistically. Perhaps this is a danger, but before we follow Cohen's plan of total immersion we might consider one or two of the benefits of philosophical analysis, even if this is applied somewhat anachronistically.

Suppose you want to learn something about nineteenth-century models of the ether and the electromagnetic field. Nowhere in the pages of history can one find more total immersion on this subject than in those of Sir Edmund Whittaker. Chapters from his *History of the Theories of Aether and Electricity* are replete with descriptions of and comparisons between models of Maxwell, Kelvin, FitzGerald, Larmor, Helmholtz, *et al.* The danger of the sort of immersion exhibited by Whittaker is that certain very interesting questions just do not get asked. In 1861 Maxwell published a paper entitled "On Physical Lines of Force," in which he presented a model of the electromagnetic field. The model contains certain assumptions, for example, that electromagnetic phenomena are due to the existence of matter under certain conditions of motion or pressure in every part of the magnetic field and not to action at a distance; that there is inequality of pressure in a magnetic field which is produced by the existence of vortices; that these vortices are separated from each other by a single layer of round particles which are in rolling contact with the vortices which they separate and which, as Maxwell puts it, "play the part of electricity." All of this is dutifully recorded by Whittaker who even gives reasons for the various assumptions and compares them with earlier assumptions of Bernoulli and Faraday.

What does not emerge clearly from Whittaker's discussion is how

Maxwell treated his assumptions. Was he saying that the electromagnetic field is actually composed of the mechanical system he described? Was he simply drawing an analogy between the electromagnetic field and that mechanical system—in the way in which he drew an analogy some years earlier between the electric field and an imaginary incompressible fluid? Or was he doing something quite different from either of these? Was he showing simply what the electromagnetic field *could* be like if it operated entirely on mechanical principles without committing himself to the claim that it does operate on mechanical principles or even that if it does it has the structure he imputed to it? These are important questions that must be answered if we are to understand what Maxwell was doing when he proposed his assumptions and if we are to compare Maxwell's model with those of other physicists whose aims may have been quite different.

By contrast, suppose that before total immersion in history you had received preliminary purification in philosophy. Of course you must know how to pick your Guide to Purification, but suppose by good fortune you chanced upon one that insisted on the following: The term "model" is applied to various quite different sorts of conceptions in the sciences. One use of the term is to refer to a three-dimensional physical representation of an object—the representation being such that by studying it one can ascertain facts about the original. This class includes tinkertoy models of molecules, models of solar systems found in museums, as well as so-called analogue models, such as an electric circuit model of an acoustical system. In another use the term "model" refers to a set of idealized assumptions about the inner structure, composition, or mechanism of an object or system. Examples would be the Bohr model of the atom and the free electron model of metals. In still a third use, it refers to a set of assumptions about a system which are supposed to show what the system could be like if it were to satisfy certain conditions but which are not intended to be taken as assumptions any system actually satisfies. An example is Poincaré's model of a non-Euclidean world which is supposed to show what a physical world could be like if it were to satisfy Lobachevsky's geometry. The philosopher of science will go on to clarify each use of the term "model," that is, each of these types of models. He will do this by considering their characteristics and also perhaps by contrasting them with analogies with which they are sometimes identified but from which they ought to be distinguished.[4]

[4] For more purification, see Achinstein [1968].

Armed with a reasonably clear set of concepts the historian will more readily be able to raise certain important questions about nineteenth-century models of the ether and the electromagnetic field. He will be much more likely to consider what status Maxwell's mechanical assumptions had. Until this is known, by the way, it will be impossible to engage in Hanson's task of critically appraising arguments. Unless you know whether Maxwell was actually attributing the mechanical structure he described to the electromagnetic field or whether this was simply intended as a description of an analogue or as a description of a possible mechanism if the field were purely mechanical, you have little basis for assessing Maxwell's reasoning. To be sure, there may be some anachronism in the set of concepts the philosopher develops, especially if in developing them he considered twentieth-century science only. Or, it may be that nineteenth-century physicists did not think in such terms. They certainly did not explicitly make the distinctions to which I have referred. Even if this were so I think it would be of value to have a set of concepts and in the course of the discussion to say how, if at all, nineteenth-century concepts differed from them or to say that in certain cases at least it is unclear what type of model the nineteenth-century physicist was proposing. There would be some enlightenment in following such a procedure. But have no fear. I think that the concepts to which I alluded do have application in nineteenth-century physics and that in many cases, though not all, it is reasonably clear from the writings of the physicist what sort of model he was proposing, even if the physicist himself lacked a philosophical system of classification.

For example, I think it is reasonably clear that in his 1861 paper Maxwell was proposing what I call an imaginary model of the electromagnetic field. He was saying what this field could be like if it were purely mechanical, but he was not claiming that it is actually like this or even that it is purely mechanical. I think it is reasonably clear that when in 1899 FitzGerald proposed a model according to which the ether is a fluid full of vortical motion he was proposing what I call a theoretical model. He was saying what the structure of the ether is actually like, if only approximately. I think it is reasonably clear that when Kelvin gave the Baltimore Lectures at Johns Hopkins and placed on the lecture table various mechanical contraptions these were intended as representational models of the ether—as three-dimensional objects in which are reproduced certain mechanical characteristics Kelvin attributed to the ether.

Let me turn to one final example, and this will bring us back to Hanson's emphasis on reasoning and argumentation. For Hanson the primary role of the philosopher of science is to investigate the cogency of particular scientific arguments. But I think there is another role as well, which may be of even greater value to the historian of science. This is the investigation and clarification of various modes or patterns of reasoning actually employed in the sciences. Hanson himself described one such pattern, retroduction. This consists in arguing from the existence of observed phenomena that are puzzling to a hypothesis which if true would explain these phenomena. I do not believe that Hanson describes this type of inference in a way that is free of difficulties, but I do believe there is an explanatory type of inference often used in science and that it can be correctly described.[5] Moreover, contrary to what Hanson sometimes suggests and to what has more recently been stated by Gilbert Harman, I believe there are certain nonexplanatory, nondeductive patterns of inference actually employed in the sciences. They are inductive and analogical forms of reasoning, but I believe these also have not been adequately characterized. I do not have time here to say how I think these modes of reasoning should be formulated. Let me suppose for the moment that this has been done. Before considering how this is relevant to the historian of science, a distinction must be noted that has become somewhat notorious in the philosophy of science.

This is the distinction between the context of discovery and the context of justification. According to Positivists and others, questions pertaining to the discovery of a hypothesis are empirical questions best left to the psychologist, or to the historian of science. The philosopher of science, on this view, is and should be concerned only with the justification of hypotheses. It is in this context that the scientist's reasoning can be appraised. There is no logic of discovery, only a logic of justification. To this Russ Hanson strenuously objected. There is, he insisted, a logic of discovery; on the whole it is different from the logic of justification, and it is and should be of interest to the philosopher of science. The logic of discovery is concerned with reasons for *suggesting* a hypothesis in the first place, the logic of justification with reasons for *accepting* a hypothesis. Retroductive or explanatory reasoning, Hanson claimed, is reasoning falling under the logic of discovery, whereas deductive reasoning from established theories is reasoning falling under the logic of justification.

Now I think that it is misleading for Hanson to suggest as he does that there are two "logics" that on the whole are distinct. I reject the view that there are reasons for suggesting hypotheses in the first place

[5] See Achinstein [1971], Ch. 6.

and reasons for accepting hypotheses which by and large are different. Any of the reasons Hanson mentions for suggesting a hypothesis can also be, and often are, reasons for accepting it. Take Hanson's retroductive reasoning. The fact that a hypothesis offers a plausible explanation of the data can be a reason for suggesting it, but it can also be a reason for accepting it once it has been suggested. Or take deductive reasoning from an established theory, which, according to Hanson, falls under the logic of justification. The fact that a proposition follows deductively from such a theory may be a reason for accepting it; but it can also be a reason for suggesting it in the first place. There is no such thing as a *logic* of discovery as opposed to a *logic* of justification.

There is, however, a distinction worth making here. If a scientist first came to be acquainted with a hypothesis in the course of reasoning to its truth or plausibility, we might say that his reasoning occurred in a context of discovery. If the scientist had been acquainted with the hypothesis before his reasoning occurred and had engaged in the reasoning in the course of attempting to defend the hypothesis, we might say that his reasoning took place in a context of justification. But the reasoning involved, the inference that is made, can be of the same type in both cases. The present distinction is by no means exhaustive. A scientist might have known about hypothesis H before inferring on the basis of the data that H is true or plausible; and he might not have inferred that H is true or plausible in the course of attempting to defend H. He might simply have considered the data and inferred that H is true. If so his inference would not fall into a context of discovery or a context of justification.

What is the relevance of all this for the historian of science? I am supposing now that the philosopher has provided an adequate characterization of various modes of reasoning and that the distinction between reasoning occurring in a context of discovery and reasoning occurring in a context of justification is sufficiently clear. I believe the historian of science can use all of this to raise and answer certain questions.

Suppose the historian is concerned with the origin of Gay-Lussac's law of combining volumes and wants to determine, among other things, what reasoning Gay-Lussac employed. Given the categories and distinction introduced by the philosopher, the historian might consider questions such as these: Was Gay-Lussac's reasoning entirely inductive? Did he simply generalize from experiments with various gases such as hydrogen and oxygen, fluoboric acid gas and ammonia? Was there in addition a theoretical assumption in virtue of which such generalizations from particular gases seemed plausible? Or was this really a retroductive inference to a law that would explain the many regularities Gay-Lussac observed. Was Gay-Lussac's inference from his observations to his law made in a context of discovery, justification, both, or neither? Did he have the idea first and then conduct the experiments to corroborate it or did the idea emerge from the experiments?

The historian of science M. P. Crosland in his generally informative paper entitled "The Origins of Gay-Lussac's Law of Combining Volumes of Gases" [6] considers, as he puts it, "factors guiding Gay-Lussac to his law." He mentions experiments that had been performed relating to the composition of the atmosphere, a theoretical interest on Gay-Lussac's part in questions of chemical affinity, certain experiments with boron trifluoride, and so on. But in this discussion (and this is not an isolated phenomenon among historians) there is, I feel, a little too much general talk of ideas in the air, or, to use Crosland's term, of ideas that "converged" in Gay-Lussac's work (p. 8). Did Gay-Lussac actually reason from these ideas? If so what form or forms did his reasoning take? And did his reasoning proceed in a context of discovery, justification, or neither? The historian who has the concepts and distinction of which I have been speaking can more readily devote attention to these rather specific questions, the answers to which are surely important for the more general question of the origin of Gay-Lussac's law.

These concepts and this distinction would also be important for specific tasks of the historian which Cohen emphasizes in his paper. For example, on p. 344 he claims that the philosopher of science—and here he has Popper in mind—is concerned with what logical relationships actually exist between Newtonian and Keplerian theory, whereas the historian of science is concerned with what relationships Newton *believed* obtained, and more generally, with the question of what thought processes actually occurred to Newton in arriving at his theory. In saying this there is the suggestion that for the historian's task the philosopher's investigation is not particularly relevant. My own view is that a philosophical investigation of various modes of reasoning is quite important for the historian's task. If we have clarified such modes we can ask which if any did Newton actually use in reasoning to his theory. We can consider whether he used these in a context of discovery or in a context of justification. And we can consider ways in which he might have deviated from them. Doing these things is bound to be of some help in describing the thought processes that led Newton

[6] Crosland [1961].

to his theory, since I believe it is fair to say that such processes involved some measure of reasoning.[7]

Now, very briefly, to the final issue. Can good philosophy of science be based on bad history? If by "bad history" you mean history that is not complete and detailed—history that is not the result of total immersion—then my answer is yes. The philosopher of science need not go into all the details the historian would. Which is not to say that he need not even get his feet wet. If by "bad history" you mean history riddled with false statements, then my answer is: It is possible but unlikely. If you start with nonfacts or appeal to them in defending your philosophical conclusions, it is possible that these conclusions will turn out to be correct and illuminating when the real facts are brought to light. Possible—but as with any theory based on falsehoods—unlikely. Of course if by "good philosophy" you mean philosophy that not only reaches true conclusions but reaches and defends them legitimately, then the answer must be no. Good philosophy cannot be based on bad history. At least not if historicalism is true.

[7] The opposing view that scientific discovery is a matter of intuition and conjecture which involves no reasoning the philosopher can investigate is critically examined in Achinstein [1971], Ch. 6.

Discussion

Professor Putnam:

I agreed with Professor Cohen's talk, and I had one small disagreement with Peter Achinstein's talk: I did not think you did full justice to what Hanson and others may have had in mind by the distinction between a logic of discovery and a logic of justification. If a logic of discovery has to consist of reasons for suggesting *H* where *H* is an hypothesis then I agree with you that it is hard to think of anything that would be a good reason for suggesting *H* but not a good reason for accepting *H*; but even there I am not wholly sure because there might be a good reason for suggesting *H* as something one ought to look at, which might be a very bad reason for accepting *H* without further evidence. So one would need some clarification of the notion of a good reason for accepting. If a good reason for accepting is something that by itself is a good reason for accepting *H* then even in that sense of 'logical discovery' (that is, a logic of discovery as something that certifies reasons as good reasons for suggesting *H*), there could be a good reason for *suggesting H* which was not a good reason for *accepting H*. But the main thing, it seems to me, is that that is not what people have been looking for. I think what they have been looking for are heuristics for arriving at an hypothesis, and I think that an heuristic for arriving at an hypothesis may not even have the form of a reason for suggesting a sentence. Such an heuristic might be an algorithm where you do not have anything that even looks like a sentence until the end of it. Then, perhaps, you might say that corresponding to the algorithm there would be a reason for suggesting *H*—namely, that it is the output of this algorithm. Of course, the standard move against the suggestion that there could be a logic of discovery is that no one has ever produced one. I presume, however, that does not mean that no one has ever produced any maxims; I think one can in fact find a large number of maxims starting with Aristotle. Rather, to say that nobody has produced one seems to mean that no one has ever given a mechanical procedure for arriving at a hypothesis. I have always been astounded by the fact that most of those who raise this objection also claim that there is a logic of justification, since exactly the same objection would apply to the alleged inductive logic or the logic of confirmation.

Professor Achinstein:

The people who claim that there is no logic of discovery seem to be saying what Hilary just said—namely that there is no heuristic for arriving at an hypothesis. But from this they seem to draw the wrong conclusion—namely that there are no inferences to hypotheses other than inferences in the context of justifying them. In my commentary, I mentioned the example of Gay-Lussac. It seems reasonably clear that at some point in his career Gay-Lussac made an inference in a context of discovery not to the definite truth of his hypothesis but at least to its plausibility, on the basis of certain data. My interest would be in what sort of an inference this was. Did Gay-Lussac simply reason inductively or was this an inference based on the fact that his law would explain the observed data?

Hanson's point, I take it, was not simply that reasons for suggesting an hypothesis in the first place are extremely interesting and that these comprise the logic of discovery; he held this, but he also seemed to be saying that reasons for suggesting an hypothesis are of a logically different type from reasons for accepting an hypothesis. It is this reaction that I reject. Of course, you might have a reason which is a very good reason for suggesting an hypothesis which is not as strong a reason for accepting it. But it could be indeed one reason for accepting it. Take Hanson's example of Kepler's first law. According to Hanson, the reasoning that Kepler employed was retroductive reasoning: The proposition that the Martian orbit is elliptical would explain Brahe's data. This, it seems to me, is a perfectly good reason for proposing the proposition in the first place, but also a good reason for accepting it.

Professor Cohen:

May I speak to that? I hesitate to get into a purely philosophical problem, but from the historical point of view the question seems to me to have a number of very different aspects from that of the purely philosophical one, and perhaps the use of the word 'logic' in the sense that I quoted from Whitehead may be misleading with regard to what I intended. But if I may, I would like to speak about this as a historical problem, illustrating it with regard to the principle of inertia. The justification given for the principle of inertia as an axiom, hypothesis, law, or whatever you want to call it, has been, since the seventeenth century, very different at different times. For example, both Descartes and Gassendi conceived it as being justified in terms of the fact for Descartes that it was related to a conservation principle in the way in which God had created the world. Gassendi tried to base it on the fact that since space is isotropic, if anything was moving it would just have to stay moving, since there was no part of space different from any other. It then became, according to much of the literature of the nineteenth century, to be considered self-evident. Hence Mach very wisely pointed out that this was absurd historically because in most of man's recorded history he had believed in quite a different kind of principle. Clearly, then, in at least what you find people doing, the treatment they give to a given hypothesis is not a constant; but what would be a constant, it would seem to me, would be the conditions under which it had first suggested itself to the man who had proposed it—if there was a first time when it gets out. And in this I believe in the antiphilosophical position a little bit. It seems to me we are dealing here with a very important problem which does involve psychology, the analysis of the pressure of cultural factors, and things which are not in any sense logical, but in which one would hope there would be some way of applying logical procedures to sort out all things applicable. The main trouble is that the evidence is very difficult to obtain. And in many cases I think it is difficult to obtain because of philosophical bias. It is, I think, rather significant that in both the untrue and the true anecdote there is an over-reliance on empirical factors and the so-called induction problem —or at least dependence on them. For example, we are told that Galileo—in what must be ridiculous fashion if anyone would stop to think of it—discovered the laws of falling bodies by dropping weights from the tower. This is a very nice empirical story, but if you think about how he would have got his results you cannot figure out how he would do it. The story that Newton discovered the law of gravitation by an apple falling is of the same kind—the only trouble being that whereas later poor historians or antedoters invented the story of Galileo, Newton apparently invented the story of the apple. Whether he did it simply because it was true, or because it was a good story, or whether he too felt somehow or other he had better give a little bit of empirical basis we do not know; but even if it did happen, I think one then has to ask in psychological terms, "Was it really the cause or was it the occasion?" If some sort of experience that occurs sets off an inspiration because of a prior conditioning, there are problems not only about how to make hypotheses but how they occur —how chance favors the prepared mind. I always used to think this was very valuable until I wondered how you knew the mind was prepared except after the events. You really have not said any more than that chance occurs better apparently in some people than others. But I think there are historically two very different questions here concerning how the thing actually arises; and it seems to me a mistake when we simply dismiss the first one by saying it is the latter. I argued about it many times with Russ Hanson. It seems to me that although he often tried to say that they were different, that in his retroduction—it was a word of Peirce's he told me—which he applied what he really was doing was using a principle of justification for his principle of discovery. Would you like to say what he really was doing was to reconstruct a thought process whereby you would start with certain principles and get to the hypothesis—which is a way of justifying it, but which really is not dealing with the inspirational quality of how Kepler's mind might have worked. How, to use another phrase, one really makes the great leap?

Professor Achinstein:

As you may recall, Hanson's retroductive mode of inference is this: Some surprising phenomenon *P* has been observed; *P* would be explicable as a matter of course if hypothesis *H* were true; hence there is reason to think that *H* is true. Now you can say, "Well, look where did *H* come from?" and then you bring in psychological factors, training, and so forth. Hanson really does not answer the question of where the hypothesis came from—yet it seems to me that if this is the objection, it misses the point. Of course there are causal factors that determine what ideas a scientist has. Kepler might not have discovered his laws if he had not had the training and personality that he did have. But this is in no way incompatible with the claim that he made a retroductive inference from Brahe's data to his hypothesis. Many people seem to think that if there is a causal explanation of how a scientist came to formulate a law then the scientist could not have engaged in a process of reasoning to that law. This is a non sequitur. When you ask the question "Where did *H* come from?," if you want to know what psychological or other causal factors were involved, Hanson provides no answer. On the other hand, he does provide an answer to this question that is relevant when he says that Kepler arrived at *H* by considering what hypothesis would explain Brahe's data.

Professor Shapere:

I agree with both the speaker and the commentator that the history of science is important for the philosopher of science, and that the philosophy of science is important for the history of science, though myself, I think that the relationship goes a little deeper than the speakers may have brought out. For instance, Professor Achinstein tells us that what he calls the constructionist approach to the philosophy of science wants to "tell it like it is"; and then in your following remarks you seem to suggest that the major reason for wanting to "tell it like it is" is to test the reconstructionists' thesis about science. Although I am not sure whether you meant to say this, I would certainly like to emphasize that that kind of approach would be intended not just to test hypotheses about science, but also to try to dig up certain positive general principles that might be ignored by attempts that do not pay as much attention to the historical details of science—because it seems to me that the real point is that the history of science, including contemporary science, constitutes the data which the philosopher of science tries to observe and on the basis of which he draws his conclusions about science. As far as the importance of the philosophy of science for the historian, my own feeling is that the awareness of difficulties in the tools with which the historian approaches his subject is necessary. For instance, with respect to concepts like *theory* or *hypothesis,* it seems to me that in writings by historians of science concerning the relation between theory and evidence there is very often terrible naiveté that distorts the pictures painted by the historian about what the man did—say in discussing the work of Galileo or the work of Newton. And, to take another example, Newton's discussion of hypotheses in the passage that you discussed: here it seems to me that it is certainly important and fruitful for the historian of science to be well aware of the alternative interpretation given by various philosophers of hypotheses that might be relevant to that particular point and what is wrong with these various alternatives. This brings me to one remark that Professor Cohen made that disturbed me. In the first place it disturbed me that the only philosopher whom he discussed in any detail with regard to his interpretation of history was Popper—who did not think that an examination of history was particularly relevant in any way to his philosophical conclusions; but Professor Cohen says that he finds Popper's general philosophical position most congenial! Well, I hope myself that that does not interfere with his interpretation, say, of Newton's discussion of hypotheses, because Popper wrote his major works quite some time ago, and there has been a lot of water under the bridge since then, including a lot of objections against Popper's own views. I would hope that any use Professor Cohen makes of Popper's general philosophical position in the interpretation of science would be approached with a critical awareness of philosophical difficulties that have been pointed out in that position. Finally, about your remark that you might want to supplement Popper's views by something like "intuition" or "creative imagination" —I shudder too much at the dangers of that to make any comments about it.

Professor Cohen:

First of all, let me address myself to Dudley Shapere's comments about Karl Popper. I do not want to have my statement read out of context, and the context was not to Popper's early work, but to a rather recent article which appeared in the journal *Ratio,* in its very first issue (Popper [1957]). In this article Popper does not exhibit any disdain for history, although I believe it fair to say that he does not investigate his subject in the manner of a good historian. I shall not go into this subject further, since I have written a separate article concerning it.

I am perfectly familiar, of course, with other writings of Popper, and what I have quoted from him was not to summarize a general philosophical position, but rather the position that he adopted in the above-mentioned article. He insists there, as he does elsewhere, that there is no automatic process for enabling you to conceive ideas simply from looking at bald facts; in short, that there is is no mechanical process of induction that can be applied. I find Popper's position with regard to induction extremely helpful, and I think it is especially helpful to any historian concerned with the genesis and development of scientific ideas. The reason is that a belief in induction, like a mindless applicable scientific method, diverts the attention of the historian from the creative factors.

I am sorry that it is necessary to shudder at the introduction of terms like "intuition" or "creative imagination," but shudder we must —I do it all the time. And I shudder especially whenever I have to deal with the problems of the creative imagination on the part of any thinking scientist. As to intuition, many philosophers do not like to use the term, although many scientists do use it. And yet how else can one explain the process whereby certain rather incredible scientific men have been able to see results long before they could prove them, and in some cases even when they could not ever find such a proof. Again, what other expression can we use to make precise the fact that certain scientists again and again seem to know which are the most fruitful questions to ask in the course of experimental inquiries?

Now let me turn to the comments of Peter Achinstein. Certainly I would agree that historians may (and often must) learn from philosophers. High on the list of what may be so learned I would put the method of analyzing ideas and the ways in which ideas may be used; also, the classification of different sorts of ideas, and the provision of some insight into the technique of breaking down a theory into its component parts. Nevertheless, I would assert as strongly as possible that I can think of no greater danger for a historian of ideas than to tie himself so closely to a particular variety of philosophy, or a particular and current stage of philosophical thought, that his history becomes merely a time-bound exercise in a particular philosophy, and one whose value would lie chiefly in illustrating that philosophy, and so not have much permanent value as a historical contribution. Is not this really the point about E. T. Whittaker? But I find that this example is being used *against me,* as an instance of a historian immersing himself fully in a given period. Whittaker was never truly a historian of science, never trained, never giving himself to this job full time. He was a scientist turned philosopher, who wrote a kind of history, and bad history at that—even for its kind. So, if you like, Whittaker may be an example of how a philosopher—however immersed he may be in a period—may yet be a bad historian.

The record of history is strewn with the wreckage of works by historians who were so wedded to a then current philosophy that it is difficult, if not impossible, for us to read their writings profitably today. This is unfortunately true to some degree of many of the otherwise valuable writings of Ernst Cassirer, of Ernst Mach, of León Brunschvicg, of Pierre Duhem, and of countless others. I find it very doubtful, in conclusion, to suppose that a good working knowledge of the state of *our* understanding of models in theory building *as of 1970* may be the best ground for understanding *Maxwell's theories.* Rather, I would think there is a far greater danger of our becoming blind to what Maxwell intended, because we are so immersed in our philosophy that we cannot any longer discern his.

Professor Bromberger:

It seems to me that Peter Achinstein has made one very interesting suggestion about which you said something but not enough, that is, that a good understanding of the philosophy of science should lead historians to ask questions which they might otherwise not ask because they might not have the concepts that give rise to these questions; they might thus not be curious about certain things, expressed by questions and issues that would not occur to them for lack of philosophic perspectives. In the light of this, I am surprised that neither of you mentioned one respect in which one might expect the philosophy of science to be useful or relevant to what the historian of science does. It is a fact, I think, that most scientists—at least most great or important scientists—held philosophical views, and in fact held "philosophies of science." But, an explicit useful formulation of these views and a critical analysis and an insight into how it affected what these scientists did is probably best obtained through a study of the most advanced forms of philosophy, or at least the more recent ones. Yet neither of you even considered this possible contribution. I wonder whether either or both of you would comment on this?

Professor Cohen:

I am asked to discuss whether or not a good understanding of the philosophy of science would lead historians to ask questions which they would not ask if they did not have available the concepts that go into the formulations of such questions. In short, whether or not the philosophy of science is directly relevant to the historian.

I just do not know the answer to that question, but I must say that I have thought about it for a long, long time. The question is very similar to another one, often asked, as to whether the best method of preparing to understand the science of an earlier period is to obtain the most advanced knowledge possible of that same subject today. I just do not know. For instance, living as we do after Faraday and Maxwell and their heirs, it is all too easy for us to read into Newton's physics the concept of field, allegedly anticipated (even if unconsciously). I hold this type of history to be invalid. And there are many other examples.

Of course, if we are merely insisting on a certain philosophical awareness, and a philosophically critical faculty, then I am all for it—and even as a necessary qualification for every historian of scientific ideas. And so I have often thought that the best training for a historian of science would be not so much the current philosophy of science as the *history* of the philosophy of science, and even the history of philosophy. Indeed, I am committed to the view that to understand Newton's thought it is far more essential to be fully conversant with the philosophy and the philosophy of science current in his day than it is to be familiar with, say, logical positivism. Or, to take another example, there are many scientists who have stated an explicit philosophy of science; Ampère is one such. I take it that the problem is whether we should first analyze Ampère's philosophy of science in terms of *our* current philosophy of science and then and only then analyze the science of Ampère. Or, possibly, what is being suggested is that to analyze the science of Ampère, it is more important to be well schooled in the philosophy of science of the mid-twentieth century than in the philosophy current in Ampère's day. But I cannot possibly agree that to analyze Ampère's science we would do better to be well schooled in today's philosophy of science than to be expert in Ampère's philosophy of science.

Professor Bromberger:

It seems to me that the clearest description of what his philosophic views were and how they affected his science cannot be given by paraphrasing them either in only everyday concepts or by paraphrasing in the terms he would have used. It seems to me that using the analytic notions of contemporary philosophers of science might provide a much greater insight into those views.

Professor Cohen:

My example may indicate that I really do not know the answer to this question. Life is short, and the growth of philosophy (like art) is long. I do not see how any historian of science can keep up with the work in his own field, do original research in the primary sources of the science of the past, and—additionally—keep up with all the latest work of philosophers of science. Certainly, the current developments in pure mathematical logic do not seem to me to have any obvious relation to an understanding of the science of the past. But perhaps I should turn the question over to Tom Kuhn, the other practicing historian of science on the panel, who has always been very closely concerned with questions of philosophy. Won't you say a word on this subject now? Or do you want to wait for your own presentation?

Professor Kuhn:

Let me comment at the moment only on the very last point. I worry ex-officio as Director of Princeton's Program in History and Philosophy of Science about what philosophy the historian should have; my colleague Peter Hempel will tell you that this issue has been the subject of much staff discussion. After it all, I come almost exactly to your conclusion. As to requirements, we do not in fact insist that historians of science take any philosophy, but if they do not, they must take science. Most of them choose the philosophy option and they tend to take courses in the history of philosophy or the history of the philosophy of science. They get interested in these topics rather than in substantive issues in the philosophy of science. I think they are selecting properly if their object is to be better historians of science.

My main reason for feeling that way comes back to the point Sylvain Bromberger has just made. I am all for being trained by a philosopher in the subtle handling of ideas, the perceptions, distinctions, and critical techniques which the philosopher has to offer. I cannot doubt that a more perceptive historian of ideas is produced by such training. But, if one's concerns are historical, it does not seem to me necessarily a good idea to get very deeply involved with all the available alternatives provided by contemporary philosophy, because I think from experience that when this happens the historian often winds up trying to fit an author into a contemporary philosophical school or analyzing an author's views in terms of current alternatives. The result is a figure who is extraordinarily far from representing the historical figure.

Given more time, I would try to illustrate by comparing the historian's Descartes with the philosopher's, for it provides a classic example. Let me instead try to pinpoint the source of the difficulty. The philosopher reading an older author is trying to find a position that makes contemporary sense, either by criticizing his subject or by isolating the kernel of truth. The historian could not care less whether the ideas which emerge make contemporary sense; he wants to discover how they ever could have made sense to an intelligent man. The result is that his reconstruction of what his subject believed is often very different from the philosopher's.

Professor Putnam:

I think the danger is real but that the danger should be taken. I think that the risk is even greater if you do not take it. In fact, if you look at history of philosophy today you see that in fact that histories of philosophies written by people not competent in philosophical analyses have been systematically worse—just as history of the past—than histories written by people competent in philosophical analysis. G. E. L. Owen is a very good example of someone who is first-rate in classical philosophy and whose work is deeply informed by correct conceptual analysis. Gregory Vlastos at Princeton would be another similar example. Certainly there is the danger of seeing the past through present ideological lenses in the bad sense of saying you know which of the current ideologies you should make Newton turn out to subscribe to. Should I make him a Popperian—heaven forbid—or Carnapian or whatever? Why should the risk be taken if there is this danger that you might see the past through ideological lenses? The answer is this—that what the clash of ideologies in general does (or at least one of the things it does perhaps as a byproduct but as an important byproduct) is to bring out ambiguities in what were previously taken as unambiguous formulations which make us see conceptual alternatives and conceptual questions that we did not see before. Take Plato on predication for example. While it would be very bad to anachronistically project current questions on predication back onto Plato's work, it is very good to approach what Plato said with some understanding of the complexities of the logic of predication. What has happened with the historians of philosophy who did not do that shows that that is no protection from seeing the past through ideological lenses. For example, narrow nominalistic lenses very often have been worn by historians of Aristotle who completely failed to see the sort of subtleties in the Aristotle-Plato debate partly because they themselves were very confused on the logical issues involved and on what is tenable and what is not tenable. Or, to take another example from pure logic: In mathematical logic we discovered very recently (in fact, in the last five years) that you can rigorously do the calculus in the way that Leibniz wanted to—which is to say with infinitesimals.[1] While one should be wary of the danger of anachronistically projecting back ultraproducts or ultrafilters into Leibniz, on the other hand it seems to me that, as Abraham Robinson has suggested, some rewriting of the history of mathematics is now called for because a lot of the history that has been written has been based on a mathematically false assumption—namely, that the epsilon-delta method is the only way of meeting Berkeley's objections.

Professor Cohen:

May I make one further remark? Even though I said before that there is a great danger of history getting into a straitjacket of philosophy, and becoming bound to a particular time and a particular philosophy, there are some works of such interest to the reader today that they may transcend the particular philosophy of the author, or even may be interesting because they are an expression of that philosophy. An example is Ernst Mach's great book on mechanics (Mach [1919]). From the point of view of the historian, this book has all the errors that derive from the narrow confines of a single philosophy, and we can show these errors to our students one by one. But there is also no

[1] See Robinson [1963], Ch. 9, Secs. 4–6, and Robinson [1966] for details.

question of the fact that Mach's book is one of the most interesting in the whole field of the history of science, and one from which a student can learn an enormous amount once he is warned at the beginning of the errors and limitations. In this case, the truth about this book being time-bound by its philosophy does not imply that the book is valueless, even for one who will not accept completely the philosophy of Mach, which of itself is important and worthy of study.

Professor Suppes:

I would like to continue on this point about what is useful for the historian to know in dealing with the past in the history of science, and I would like to argue that as the particular scientific issues or problems become more technical then the more desirable it is not simply to have a plain man's approach. I think particularly good examples of this can be found in the history of mathematics. There the first task is simply to get straight just what is the mathematics that has been developed, which is often a rather difficult matter, even if it is done in modern notation. The conceptual problems of handling mathematics from remote times are difficult. Ordinarily most of the published texts are already modernized in notation; they are seldom presented in original form. One of the reasons for this is the conceptual problem of getting straight in a serious way as to what has been said, and I think the historian inevitably must rely on the best knowledge of his time. Hilary Putnam's example is a case in point. As an historian he simply cannot study ancient mathematics as a plain man looking at it from a common-sense standpoint; there is not a common-sense standpoint for reading Appolonius, for example, or reading Ptolemy. Similarly, there are topics of importance in the history of science where it seems to me that the standard of philosophical discussion requires the discussion historically to be at quite a different level than in the past; a good example of this would be in the foundations of probability. We do not for a moment have to agree about what is the proper way to formulate the foundations of probability; but certainly contemporary discussion of the kind of foundations offered by Laplace or those given a good deal later by Bertrand or by other major figures in the nineteenth century is aided by more recent work that has been done in the foundations of probability. This work gives us a great deal more insight into what the problems were and the way they were thinking about probability concepts. This is so not because we have adopted any straitjacket regarding a particular viewpoint, but just because the intellectual level of discussion of these matters is now at a very different level than it was in the nineteenth century.

Professor Achinstein:

Maybe the intellectual straitjacket will turn out to be the right one to be bound by; then it will not be so bad. But even if it is not, it may provide answers to the sorts of questions I would like. I mentioned models as one example. If you ask what conceptions of model were employed in nineteenth-century studies of the electric field, you can turn to Whittaker.[2] You just do not get very much clarification. On having read a number of things that have been written on Gay-Lussac and Avogadro by historians of science I do not get my questions answered—questions concerning the modes of reasoning these scientists actually employed. And my feeling is that this would have been clarified if a philosopher had proposed even some idealized modes of inference; perhaps these will be modes which are never and ought never to be used, but at least they will be modes of inference with which we can compare the reasoning that actually took place. It seems to me that one could advance in the history of science by asking not simply what ideas "converged" on Gay-Lussac (that was the expression that Crosland[3] used) or what ideas were "in the air," or something like this, but what ideas did he actually use and how did he use them? What sort of reasoning did he actually employ?

Professor Kuhn:

I do not want merely to repeat what I said before, but at least I would like to illustrate the difficulty of the problem. In principle I would like to say that the historian of science needs any techniques, any insights, and any sources of additional distinctions he can get. To the extent that he can get them from the philosopher, he should do so as well as from any other place he can. And I agree that philosophy is a particularly relevant source. But against the course being advocated, there is a good deal of experience with what more than a little involvement with philosophical problems *for their sake* can do to the historian as well as of the sort of work that comes out. And without trying to illustrate, I would just say I do not know what Peter Achinstein means when he said "take off one straitjacket and put on another and try them." If that were possible, my reservations would disappear, but it is the nature of a straitjacket that trying one on and taking it off and putting on another tells you they were not straitjackets in the first place. But they often are.

[2] Whittaker [1951].
[3] Crosland [1961].

SESSION IV

Science as Perception-Communication

David Bohm

The general theme of this symposium is to inquire into the adequacy of traditional ways of talking about scientific research and, if possible, to indicate new modes of discourse that may be more suitable or relevant in this context.

Let me begin by saying that, in my view, science is *primarily* an activity of extending perception into new contexts and into new forms, and only secondarily a means of obtaining what may be called reliable knowledge. I have discussed this view fairly extensively in the Appendix of my book, *Special Theory of Relativity*,[1] and will therefore not go into this in great detail here. What I want to call attention to in the present talk is a further development of these notions, that is, that science involves *communication* in an equally fundamental way. However, in saying this, I want to emphasize that scientific research does not consist of *first* looking at something and *then* communicating it. Rather, the very act of perception is shaped and formed by the intention to communicate, as well as by a general awareness of what has been communicated in the past, by oneself and by others. Even more, it is generally only in communication that we deeply understand, that is, perceive the whole meaning of, what has been observed. So there is no point to considering any kind of separation of perception and communication. Perception and communication are one *whole*, in which analysis into potentially disjoint elements is not relevant. To indicate this, I use the hyphenated form, perception-communication.

I feel that a number of people, including Kuhn, Feyerabend, and others have already seen the need to develop such a view, and have in certain implicit and tacit ways actually begun to do so. However, it seems to me that their explicit communications are not in full harmony with what I take to be their implicit intentions, and that this dishar-

[1] Bohm [1965].

mony can lead to a certain kind of difficulty in the further development of such views.

Just by way of example, we can discuss Kuhn's notion[2] that scientific theories are mainly paradigms that serve as "media" for communication and as tacit notions that infuse and guide the essentially perceptual day-to-day activities of scientists in all sorts of undefinable and unspecifiable ways. As part of this view, it is implied that successive theories are in some sense "incommensurable" (and this way of putting it is supported in certain ways by several authors, for example, Feyerabend[3]). This further implies, of course, that successive theories cannot furnish some kind of "accumulation of true knowledge about nature" since, in general, there is no way for two such theories to bear significantly on what could be identified as the "same content."

While I do not wish to disagree with what is very probably the intended meaning of the notion of "incommensurability" of theories, I would like to point out that the use of the word in the present context is itself a *form* of confusion, and that this confusion will (at least subliminally) interfere with full communication on these questions, even if we all feel that "we know what the term really means." For the word "incommensurability" begins tacitly by admitting the *relevance* of the notion of "commensurability" of theories, and then denying only the content of this notion by adding the prefix "in." This would mean, for example, that it is in principle possible for successive theories to be "commensurable," but that as a matter of contingent fact, it happens that such commensurability does not actually obtain in the particular cases studied in the history of science. What I would like to suggest instead is that as *a form of discourse* the notion of commensurability of different theories is irrelevant from the very outset, so that even to use the word "incommensurable" and thus to imply the relevance of commensurability is confused and can be a source of serious further confusion. A similar kind of confusion would arise, for example, if we used a form of discourse involving a term such as "nonquadrangular triangle," which would imply that the "nonquadrangularity" of certain triangles is a contingent fact (or perhaps contingent on theorems proved in mathematics), rather than a meaningless irrelevancy.

The reason why the term "incommensurable" involves difficulties of the kind described above is that each theory is itself a whole, in which analysis into disjoint components or elements is not relevant (just as in the case of perception-communication). This is because all the terms in such a theory can have their meanings and their criteria of factuality

[2] Kuhn [1962].
[3] P. Feyerabend; private communication.

and truth only in the total context given by *that* theory. There is therefore actually no way to "measure" or "evaluate" the basic concepts and notions of any one theory in terms that are common to those of another theory, so that one could meaningfully compare the theories and thus establish whether they are commensurable or incommensurable.

As an example of the irrelevance of the notion of commensurability of theories, one can consider research into malaria. Now, the word "malaria" means "bad air," and this indicates the early theory that the disease was caused by damp night air. If this theory had been accepted in modern times, it could have contained its own tacit criteria for what is a relevant fact or a relevant test. For example, one could have developed very sensitive hygrometers, making possible careful and exhaustive methods of measuring the humidity everywhere. With the aid of statistical studies, one could have clearly demonstrated that high humidity and malaria were correlated. By removing the pools of water that are very often responsible for the dampness, one could have in many cases significantly decreased the incidence of malaria. This would have been a very convincing confirmation of the whole structure of pure and applied science which could have been built up around the notion that it is relevant to consider damp night air as a direct cause of malaria.

Of course, a later theory was that malaria was caused by microorganisms carried by mosquitoes. Here, the damp night air was a factor that was basically irrelevant. In many cases, it was merely an incidental consequence of the presence of pools of water, in which could grow mosquitoes capable of carrying the direct cause of the disease, that is, microorganisms. This theory thus implied new notions of what is relevant causally, along with new modes and criteria of testing (involving, for example, observations in microscopes, growths of cultures of microorganisms, and so on), as well as new forms of application of the resulting biological science (that is, killing mosquitoes with pesticides and killing microorganisms with drugs).

But then one can ask why only *some* people who are exposed to malarial microorganisms in this way actually fall ill. It has been suggested that, potentially, everyone may be naturally resistant to such diseases but that, because of unhealthy modes of living, the body becomes weakened and thus cannot respond properly when microorganisms enter the bloodstream. The relevance of this view is strongly suggested by considering the fact that we are always being "invaded" by microorganisms of all kinds, and that if we tried to kill them *all* with drugs and antibiotics the probable result would be that the treatment would kill *us* much more rapidly than it would kill the microorganisms.

So what is indicated is the possible fruitfulness of inquiring into how our mode of living decreases resistance to disease. In such an inquiry, microorganisms are not in themselves very relevant. The kinds of facts that one has to observe in order to test this theory now involve an inquiry into the *psychological* and *social* factors that lead us to live generally unhealthy lives. Hygrometers, microscopes, and chemical laboratories have little or no place in such an inquiry. The application of the results of discoveries in such an investigation would involve psychological and social changes that cannot be produced, for example, by pharmaceutical means.

It should be clear that there is little or no "commensurability" between these different "theories" of malaria. What are regarded as basic and essential notions in one point of view are regarded as irrelevant side issues, or even trivialities, in another. What is regarded as strong confirmatory evidence in one is tacitly or explicity dismissed in another as having no bearing on the point that is really at issue. That is to say, while successive theories may have certain aspects that are similar (for example, they may all deal with something that is *called* malaria), it is being suggested that these similarities are generally superficial. What is needed is therefore to begin by focusing attention on the *differences* between such theories. These differences are generally so radical that there is little or no place for either asserting or denying the notion of commensurability in a relevant manner. Instead, what has to be emphasized is the *wholeness* of the content of a theory and its basic forms of description, criteria of factuality and truth, modes of being tested and applied, and so forth. Each new theory *is* a new whole, and it is therefore a source of confusion to bring the notion of incommensurability into a context in which this theory is discussed as if there were some way in which this notion could coherently be applied. (But because the word *has* been brought into such context, I shall, from time to time, use it with quotation marks to indicate that its *intended meaning or content* is relevant, but that *as a form of discourse*, it is not.)

The issue of "commensurability" of successive theories is particularly significant in Kuhn's description of the history of science as a succession of revolutions and quiet periods of consolidation (called normal science by Kuhn), which are in turn followed by new revolutions. I wish to suggest here that the key to understanding this form of development is in the careful scrutiny of the quiet periods of "normal science." During these periods, the theory is actually being changed steadily in certain deep and fundamental ways. However, these changes are hardly noticed because it is widely believed that "nothing essential has changed." If the situation is actually different in the sense that something novel and not coherent with past theories has been brought into the discussion, while scientists generally believe that the situation is essentially unchanged, the result must be an ever growing confusion in *what is done with theories.* Eventually, this confusion is found to be intolerable and people are thus ready to recognize the need for change. By now, the trouble is so widespread and so deep that the change is described as a "radical and fundamental revolution." But this "revolution" is merely the natural and inevitable result of the quiet period of "normal science" in which scientists are failing to see the relevance of continual change that is *always* bringing in what is new and "incommensurable" with past notions and ideas.

The fact that progress in what is called a quiet period of normal science often involves such fundamental change, the relevance of which is overlooked, can be illustrated by considering certain features of the development of the quantum theory. Now, along with the development of the *formalism* of this theory by Heisenberg, Born, Jordan, Pauli, Dirac, and others, there was at least equally important development of new modes of *informal description,* that is, a kind of new language for discussing the overall experimental situation, including the experimental conditions and the experimental results. In this development Bohr and Heisenberg played a key part. In this short talk, I shall only attempt to indicate the whole context of informal use of language in quantum theory by discussing Heisenberg's famous microscope experiment in a somewhat different way from that which has generally been adopted.

One can begin by asking in terms of *classical physics* what it means to make measurements of position and momentum. For this purpose, it is convenient to start, not with a *light* microscope, but rather with an *electron* microscope.

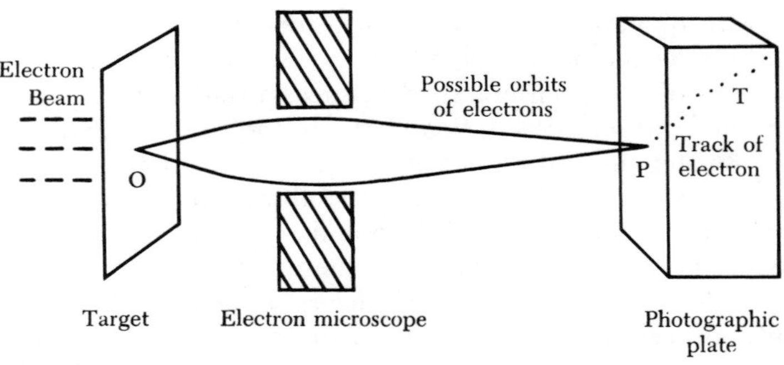

FIGURE 1

In the above diagram, there is in the target an "observed particle" at O, assumed to have initially a known momentum (for example, it may be at rest, with zero momentum). Electrons of known energy are incident on the target and one of these is deflected from the particle at O. It goes into the electron microscope, following an orbit that leads it to the focus at P. From here, the particle leaves a track, T, in a certain direction, as it penetrates the photographic plate.

Now, the *directly observable results* of this experiment are the position P, and the direction of the track, T. But, of course, these in *themselves* are of no interest. It is only by knowing the *experimental conditions* (that is, the structure of the microscope, the target, the energy of the incident beam of electrons), that the experimental results can become relevant in the context of a physical inquiry. With the aid of an adequate description of these conditions, one can use the experimental results described above to make *inferences* about the position of the "observed particle" at O, and about the momentum transferred to it in the process of deflecting the incident electron. As a result, one "knows" both the position and the momentum of this particle at the time of deflection of the incident electron.

All this is quite straightforward in *classical* physics. Heisenberg's novel step was to consider the implications of the "quantum" character of the electron that provides the "link" between the *experimental results* and *what is to be inferred from these results.* The electron can no longer be described as being just a classical particle. Rather, it also has to be described in terms of a "wave" as shown below.

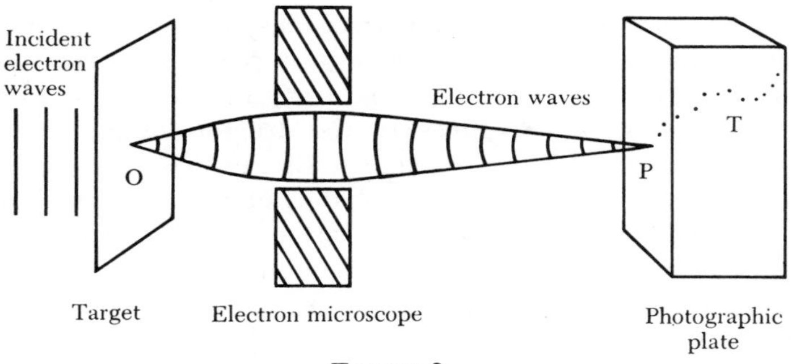

FIGURE 2

Electron waves incident on the target are said to be diffracted by the atom at O, then pass through the microscope, where they are also diffracted, and are focused at the photographic plate. Here, they are said to determine only the "probability" that a track T begins at P and goes in a certain direction.

However, as was implicit in Heisenberg's discussion (and as was later brought out more explicitly by Bohr), this whole situation involves something radically new and "incommensurable" with classical notions. Heisenberg tried to express this novelty by saying that both the position X and momentum P of the "electron link" between O and PT are "uncertain," the extent of this uncertainty being measured by the "uncertainty relationship" $\Delta X \Delta P \geq h$. But this involves a very significant kind of disharmony between the form of the language and the content to which Heisenberg implicitly intended to call attention.[4] The form of the language implies that the "link" electron actually has a definite orbit that is, however, not precisely known to us. Bohr[5] gave a thorough and consistent discussion of this whole situation, which made it clear that the orbit of the electron is not "uncertain" but, rather, that it is what he called *ambiguous*. Unfortunately, even this word does not give a very clear notion of what is meant here. Perhaps one could say instead that both the notion of a particle following a well-defined orbit (whether known or unknown) and of a wave following a similarly well-defined wave equation are *irrelevant*. What we have to deal with here is a radically new form of description, not "commensurable" with either of the old forms.[6]

Now, because of the irrelevance of the description of the "electron link" in terms of well-defined particle orbits or in terms of well-defined wave motions, it followed that from the observed results of an experiment, one could no longer make inferences of unlimited precision about the observed object. But something more also followed the very deep and far-reaching significance of which most physicists tended to overlook. To see what this is, we note that from a particular set of experimental conditions, as determined by the structure of the microscope, and so on, one could in some rough sense say that the limits of relevance of the classical description of the "observed object" are indicated by a certain cell in the phase space of this object, which we denote by A in Figure 3. If, however, we had different experimental conditions (for example, a microscope of another aperture, electrons of different energy, and so forth), then these limits would be indicated by *another* cell in this phase space, indicated by B in the diagram. Both cells would have the same area, h, but their "shapes" would be different.

4 Bohm [1971].
5 Bohr [1934] and [1958].
6 See the work cited in note 4 above.

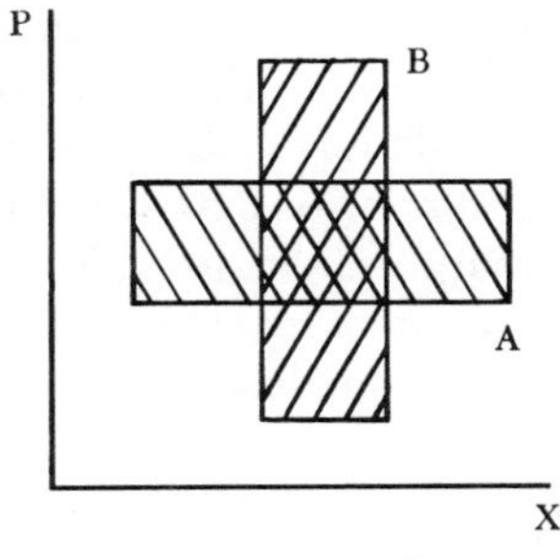

FIGURE 3

Now, in the corresponding discussion of the classical situation, it is possible to say that the experimental results do nothing more than permit inferences about an observed object, which exists separately and independently, in the sense that it can consistently be said to "have" these properties whether it interacts with anything else (such as in observing apparatus) or not. A description of the experimental conditions is needed to permit these inferences to be carried out properly, but this description is in no way needed for saying what is meant by the properties of the observed object, that is, position and momentum.

However, in the "quantum" context the situation is very different. Here, certain relevant features of what is called the observed particle, that is, the "shapes" of the cells in phase space, cannot properly be described except in conjunction with a description of the experimental conditions. Nor can one say the "shapes" correspond only to our lack of knowledge about the precise position and momentum of the observed object, considered as separate and disjoint from the overall experimental arrangement. Indeed, as a more extensive discussion of the mathematical formalism shows, the region in which "the wave function of the observed object" (and its Fourier coefficients) are appreciable corresponds to the "shape" of the cell, as discussed above. But this wave function is coordinated, or "correlated," to that of the "link electron" in such a way that one has no meaning without the other. As a result, "the wave function of the observed object," which gives the fullest possible formal means of determining averages of physical properties, cannot be discussed relevantly, apart from the experimental conditions, which provide a necessary context for a treatment of the wave function of the "link electron."

Thus, the mathematical formalism contains a reflection of the general situation with regard to "shapes" of cells in phase space that has been described here in informal terms. Therefore, the description of the experimental conditions does not drop out as a mere intermediary link of inference, but remains amalgamated with the description (both formal and informal) of what is called the observed object. This means that the "quantum" context calls for a new kind of description, which does not make use of the potential or actual separability of "observed object" and "observing apparatus." Instead, the form of the experimental conditions and the content of the experimental results have now to be one whole, in which analysis into disjoint elements is not relevant.

The irrelevance of such an analysis (for example, in terms of the notion that the "observed object is disturbed by the observing apparatus") is brought out in a very forceful way in the famous discussion between Einstein, Podolsky, and Rosen,[7] and Bohr.[8] This showed that such wholeness of description was needed even when observations are carried out very far from each other in space and under conditions in which one would have said in terms of classical physics that no mechanical or dynamical contact or interaction between these observations is possible.[9]

In a context in which the detailed description of the "observed object" is not relevant, so that the "cells" in phase space could be replaced by points, however, the "shapes" of the cells would not matter. Thus, in such a context, all significant aspects of the "observed object" could meaningfully be described without bringing in a description of the experimental conditions. Thus, one could consistently use the traditional notion that the object can be discussed in terms of a "state" or of properties, that need not refer in any essential way to anything else at all. Therefore, the description in terms of a potential or actual disjunction between observed object and observing apparatus is a relevant simplification, in a context in which the fine details of the "quantum" description do not matter. But where the details are significant, this simplification cannot properly be carried out, and one has to return to a consideration of the wholeness of the total experimental situation.

What is meant here by wholeness could be indicated in a somewhat informal and metaphoric way by calling attention to a pattern (for example, in a carpet). Insofar as what is relevant *is* the pattern, it has no meaning to say that different parts of such a pattern (for example, various flowers or trees that are to be seen in the carpet) are disjoint objects in interaction. Similarly, in the "quantum" situation, terms like "observed object," "observed instrument," "experimental conditions," and "experimental results" are just aspects of a single overall "pattern"

[7] Einstein, Podolsky, and Rosen [1935].
[8] Bohr [1935].
[9] See the work cited in note 4 above.

that are, in effect, abstracted and "pointed out" or "made relevant" by our mode of discourse. Thus, it has no meaning to say, for example, that there is an "observed object" that interacts with the "observing instrument."

We see, then, that something quite new had come into the language of physics, in the sense that where a detailed description is required, the traditional notion of analysis of the world into a union of disjoint parts ceases to be relevant. What is relevant instead is the wholeness of the description. However, very few physicists seem to have been able to see the full significance of this new mode of *informal discourse.* Instead, there arose a tendency to focus attention extremely heavily on the *mathematical formalism,* and tacitly to dismiss informal notions of the kind described above as not very relevant.

Among those who gave a great impetus to the tendency was von Neumann, who wrote a treatise on the quantum theory that very strongly emphasized the *mathematical logic and coherence of the formalism.*[10] Very probably, von Neumann was motivated in part by the fact that various physicists, such as Heisenberg, Schrödinger, Pauli, Jordan, Dirac, and so on, had each presented somewhat different formalisms that did not fully cohere with each other, and that may not even have been entirely coherent internally. To meet this situation, von Neumann developed a set of axioms, from which he attempted to derive the whole subject systematically, logically, and coherently. By his mode of presentation, one can gather that he did not feel that he was proposing *changes* in the quantum theory, but, rather, that his axioms contained the *essence* of a theory that was already well established.

If one looks carefully, however, one can see that there are certain significant *formal differences* between what von Neumann does and what the earlier physicists did. It is clear that while von Neumann may have been aware of these differences in some way, he was in effect judging them to be *irrelevant.* But, of course, this judgment is purely a private and personal one, since there is no way to be sure that a certain formal difference between these theories may not be a relevant one, whose significance reveals itself in further developments.

For example, it was widely believed in the nineteenth century that Newtonian dynamics and Hamilton-Jacobi wave theory of dynamics were "essentially the same." Nevertheless, we can now see that the difference between "wave dynamics" and "particle dynamics" was potentially of very great relevance in the sense that the former can lead in a

[10] von Neumann [1955].

natural way to quantum theory, while the latter cannot. Indeed, as a simple discussion shows (which I give in my elementary classes), the possibility of the whole set of Einstein-de Broglie relations for "matter waves" could have been anticipated in the nineteenth century if physicists had not believed that wave and particle formalisms were "essentially the same." In other words, what was overlooked was that Hamilton-Jacobi theory was in some ways novel and "incommensurable" with what Newton had done. So, the "quantum revolution" had to wait until it was forced on physicists by the irresistible pressure of events.

Von Neumann not only developed a novel formalism, but he also developed what was in certain ways an even more novel way of discussing the informal "quantum" situation (that is, the form of the experimental conditions and the content of the experimental results). What he did in this connection was to propose a sharp separation between observed object and observing apparatus. The former was assumed to obey "quantum" laws and the latter to obey "classical" laws. Between the two, there was a certain kind of conceptual "cut." It was somewhat arbitrary just where the "cut" was to be placed, but von Neumann gave arguments tending to suggest that the net results of the theory do not depend critically on just where it is placed.

Von Neumann's notion of a "cut" between classical and quantum domains can be illustrated by drawing a line in the diagram as shown below.

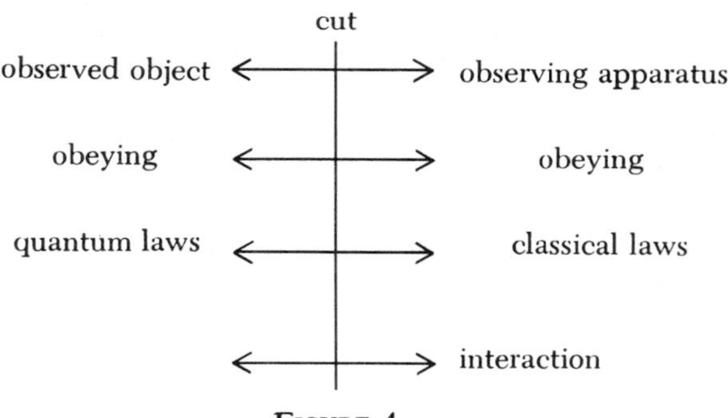

FIGURE 4

Since both the quantum mechanical observed object and the classical observing apparatus are treated as "disjoint parts of the world," it seemed natural to him to suppose that they were capable of entering into a certain kind of dynamical interaction (somewhat similar to that taking place between disjoint particles of a classical mechanical system).

Now, what von Neumann did not seem to notice was that the terms of his informal description tacitly ruled out the whole general approach of Bohr and Heisenberg as irrelevant. Indeed, in von Neumann's theory, the experimental conditions, which were so heavily emphasized in the work of Bohr and Heisenberg, are not described at all. In effect, what appears in their place is the notion of a "cut" across which interaction is supposed to be taking place. But, of course, Heisenberg and Bohr treated the experimental situation as a whole, in which it would have no meaning to say that quantum laws applied in one part, while classical laws applied in another. These two informal descriptions were thus radically different and completely "incommensurable." Yet, von Neumann and those who followed on lines initiated by him tacitly treated their work as a kind of essence of the very same "quantum" situation that was discussed by Bohr and Heisenberg. This kind of action of tacitly ignoring relevant differences *is*, of course, just what is meant by the term "confusion."

Whenever one inquires into something new and unknown, a certain kind of confusion is inevitable. Such confusion tends naturally to clear itself up as further work is carried out. However, if one has made a *fixed* judgment of the irrelevance of certain differences that are actually relevant, this kind of confusion tends to persist, to "stabilize itself," and to entangle and spread as one (largely tacitly and subliminally) applies this judgment in all sorts of different contexts. For these differences that are being ignored will, of course, nevertheless manifest themselves and when this happens, they will be ascribed to something else that is not actually relevant. Such a process can go on without limit, so that *what we do* with our theories may become so mixed up that we may no longer be able "to find our way out of the maze."

Consider, for example, the fact that most physicists have absorbed the language of Bohr and Heisenberg so that both tacitly and explicitly it is almost impossible for them to talk about the quantum theory without incorporating these language forms at almost every moment. But then, they have also similarly absorbed terms such as "quantum state," which are relevant in von Neumann's language, that strongly distinguish the "classical observing apparatus" from the "quantum mechanical observed object, which exists separately and disjointly in a certain quantum state." However, in the language of Bohr and Heisenberg, the term "quantum state," with all that it implies, can have no place at all because they talk in terms of wholeness of observing apparatus and observed object, in which the analysis or disjunction that is needed to give meaning to the term "the quantum state of the object" has no relevance. Nevertheless, physicists are freely mixing these two mutually irrelevant (or "incommensurable") theories all the time because of the general belief that they are "essentially the same." Such a mixture will inevitably give rise to spreading confusion.

This confusion becomes especially noticeable in what has been called the theory of measurement. Now, when von Neumann came to consider measurements, he discussed the subject in terms of certain extremely idealized and formalized descriptions, in which the fact that there was no room for a specification of the experimental conditions apparently created no serious difficulties. However, when one tries to apply von Neumann's theory to an actual experimental situation, one finds that without a proper description of the experimental conditions, it is not possible to understand the relevance and significance of the experimental results. Therefore, even those who work in terms of von Neumann's theory are compelled, somehow or other, to try to take the experimental conditions into account. This is usually done in each separate case by assigning what is in effect a form of interaction across the "cut" between classical and quantum parts of the world that depends, in a certain tacit way, on the experimental conditions. Thus, in a rather roundabout and implicit manner, a certain kind of "wholeness" reenters the discussion. For it turns out that, after all, one cannot apply the theory to an actual experimental arrangement unless the description of the behavior of the various "parts" of the world is inseparably amalgamated with a description of the overall experimental conditions. (It is rather as if in classical dynamics the basic mathematical form of the interaction of one particle with another depended crucially on the arrangements of instruments used in a particular experiment.) This way of bringing in a kind of wholeness "by the back door," so to speak, is, however, not in harmony with the explicit form of the mathematical theory which, as has been seen, adopts a description of the world in terms of disjoint dynamical components as its basic form of discourse.

Such a lack of harmony has serious consequences in attempts to carry the theory further. For because the experimental conditions are not described explicitly and nevertheless play a key role tacitly, the way in which they are taken into account will depend on largely subliminal and fortuitous choices, which will in general be somewhat different for each person who uses the theory. Therefore, different investigators, beginning in this way with different premises that are not fully relevant to each other, cannot properly communicate. This is actually the situation in the field, which contains a number of sharply separated schools who do not seem to be able even to decide in what ways they agree and in what ways they disagree.

This sort of ambiguity is intensified because each physicist mixes in the views of von Neumann with those of Heisenberg and Bohr, according to what most suits his taste. In addition, the original formal notions of von Neumann have by now been replaced by others, involving non-Boolean algebras and nondistributive lattices. These new notions open up a wide range of novel questions that are relevant within their language forms so that, basically, they involve new possibilities that are "commensurable" neither with those of older formalisms that were *called* quantum theory, nor with those of von Neumann's original formalism. Nevertheless, they are all treated as if they were "essentially the same."

Of course, there are certain similarities between all these theories (for example, they may all use a term such as "Hilbert space" or something more or less equivalent in meaning). But, as I suggested earlier, those similarities are not nearly as relevant as is implied in the way physicists generally treat them, while the differences are far more relevant than is implied by the way in which they are almost entirely ignored. In this regard, one may also consider the further development of what has been *called* "quantum theory" over the past thirty years or so. The first new step was the emergence of quantum field theory, which is full of unresolvable problems, such as infinities. Then came renormalized field theories, then S-matrixes, then group theories (for example, SU(3)), then current algebras. And since none of these was fully coherent or satisfactory we may expect that this kaleidoscopic succession of formalisms will very probably continue. But we can well ask whether it is relevant, either tacitly or explicitly, to treat them all as mere variations of what is in essence the same thing—which is "quantum theory."

For example, even in quantum field theory, with its nondenumerable set of degrees of freedom, it has been shown that there is something quite novel, that is, inequivalent Hilbert spaces" [11] (not capable of being made equivalent through a unitary transformation). Such novelties are generally tacitly dismissed as irrelevant, merely by saying that this is in essence still the same thing as we had before, that is, quantum theory. It may well be that the difference between renormalized field theories and the original particle theories is potentially as significant as is the difference between Newton's theory and the Hamilton-Jacobi theory. Generally, all these different formalisms very probably contain potentially relevant novelty.

A principal barrier to progress may, therefore, be just our habitual

[11] Gårding and Wightman [1954].

way of using language, in which something new and "incommensurable" emerges, while we say: "In essence, nothing has changed." The result of this habit is an ever growing confusion, which eventually leads to an intolerable situation, calling for a revolution.

I hope it is clear that it is not my intention to *blame* or *criticize* people for going on with this habitual form of communication. Actually, this form is the heritage of thousands of years of civilization, so that it is not the unique responsibility of any individual. What is called for is simply to see the whole meaning of this form, that is, how it eventually leads to confusion. If one sees this, then one will cease to use such forms. One will realize that theories are changing all the time; that each new step may introduce something novel and "incommensurable" with what came before. Indeed, even to read an article and to understand it is, in general, to change it significantly. For understanding something is assimilation, that is, making it a whole with oneself. When this happens, what is thus assimilated takes on a form that is in certain ways unique, being different from the form of another person's understanding, or from that of one's own understanding at another time. Of course, we are all aware of these differences, but we tend to say that they are inessential, that is, irrelevant.

What I am saying here is that this relevance judgment is a purely personal one, based not on perception of the fact, or on logical reasoning, but on a rather mechanical habit of thinking and communication that has been built up over the ages and passed down to us. When we deeply perceive the irrelevance of this habit, we cease to be affected by it significantly and we are free to be sensitive and alert to what is new and different, even in a momentary "flash of understanding" in one's response to learning what someone else has done. So the basic action of science is seen to involve *perception of what is new and different* from moment to moment. In this regard, it is similar to the relevant activity in everyday life, which is also such a kind of perception. The notion that we are accumulating "permanently valid knowledge" is, however, not very relevant. Indeed, because different theories are not "commensurable" with each other, this notion can be maintained only if we ignore relevant differences by rather arbitrarily asserting that the development of new theories (at least in periods of "normal science") does not lead to essential changes.

As an example of what this kind of perception would mean in science, one could suggest that those who are continuing along lines initiated by von Neumann could usefully explore the possible relevance of new and different features of their formalisms. In addition, of course, it would be necessary to go carefully into the question of how the experimental conditions are to be described in terms of their theories (or perhaps to do something else that would make such a description irrelevant in a coherent and consistent way). Similarly, those who work with renormalization or S-matrixes or current algebras could usefully begin to give serious attention to studying what is qualitatively different from earlier quantum theories in these formalisms, as well as the development of ways of giving an adequate informal account of the experimental conditions in terms of the language of their theories (which questions have thus far been largely ignored).

But even this is hardly a beginning. Because of the heritage of the past, we tend to treat mathematical formalisms as fixed truths that we already have, or else, we search for new formalisms that would fulfill some kind of ideal of fixed and ultimate truth. I suggest that mathematical formalisms are systematic modes of relatively precise description and inference, rather than truths. Thus, they are mainly an extension of our overall language forms, so they can be changed as freely as we can change the meanings of words in informal discussions. To emphasize what I mean here, I would suggest that it is useful to regard formalisms as similar to the ephemeral "shapes" that we can see in the clouds (that is, horses, mountains, and so on). We can use any "shape" that appears in mathematics, as long as it is relevant to the context under investigation, and then we can abandon it freely in favor of another "shape," which may indicate a new order of relevance and therefore a new context.

In all this action, results of previous work are in the "back of the mind," having been assimilated, that is, understood. But, for example, it is not relevant to regard one's work as a "contribution to Bohr's work," aimed perhaps at "explaining or interpreting Bohr" or "putting his notions on a more clear and solid logical foundation." Rather, as indicated earlier, it is impossible to talk "about" Bohr without changing what he did in various ways, and it is impossible to know the full potential relevance of such changes. So it may as well be admitted from the very outset that as Bohr introduced what was novel and not "commensurable" with classical physics, so each physicist may, at any moment, bring in what is novel and "incommensurable" with what Bohr did. (But, of course, it is necessary for him to be ready to *say* that his notions are no longer "essentially the same as Bohr's," or else he will be initiating a new form of confusion.)

It can thus be seen that it is not the physicist who tries to apply or extend the content of Bohr's work who most partakes of what is characteristic of Bohr, that is, the capacity for original perception and for coherent communication of this perception. Rather, it is the one who is ready to consider *new forms* that go beyond the context in which Bohr's work is relevant.

All this means, of course, that there is no point to the effort to get closer to ultimate truth, mathematical or otherwise. What is needed at each stage is just that one's thinking and communication be in harmony with the whole context, experimental and theoretical, to which it is relevant. And the key to such harmony is sensitivity to *disharmony* in what has already been done. This sensitivity tends to be dulled when one perceives something that is in some ways novel, and says: "It is essentially the same as what came before."

As has been pointed out here, things are seldom, if ever, the same as they were before. Indeed, even a new account of a certain situation in scientific research, such as was given by Bohr, actually *changes* that situation fundamentally, because it leads to new kinds of action and new kinds of inquiry, not "commensurable" with those carried out before this new account was given. Since the situation *is* different, this in turn calls sooner or later for yet another account, which will not be fully "commensurable" with the one Bohr gave.

It is an arbitrary judgment based on our heritage from the past that leads us to give great value to what is thought to be permanent. This judgment is mainly what leads us to believe that we need a certain minimum period of "normal science" before we are ready for further novelty that is "incommensurable" with past science. When one sees the irrelevance of this judgment, one can see also that it is unpredictable just when it will be appropriate to have a radically new idea—perhaps in the next moment, the next week, or the next year. The main point is that this cannot be known beforehand. What is called for is, therefore, just the alertness which is *at any moment* ready to spring into action with a basically different idea or approach, as soon as a suitable cue is sensed or perceived. When the new idea or approach turns out to be wrong or irrelevant, then it is just dropped.

What has been said here is just as significant for society as a whole as it is for science. Thus, fundamental social changes are *always* taking place and there is, in general, no way to prevent this from happening. However, those who are attached to past social forms have always said: "Nothing has changed in essence." By trying to live as if this were, in fact, the case, they actually produced a situation of ever growing confusion which meant, of course, a tendency toward failure of communication. When this situation became critical, others who saw the need to change socially called for a revolution. But when the revolution was over, these in turn failed to notice that the very "success" of the revolution had changed things fundamentally. Rather, they too said: "Nothing has changed in essence since the revolution." So what they did was to try to "conserve or protect the revolution" and, thus, the revolutionaries became conservatives. On the other hand, the former conservatives tried to reestablish the old order. But since this had changed in a way that could not be reversed, what they were actually doing was to try to establish yet another order. Thus, in a certain way, the conservatives became revolutionaries. Therefore, in the long run there has been little basic difference between conservatives and revolutionaries, while there has been a deep basic similarity in that both have tended to respond to the *fact* of change in what they regarded as precious or valuable by saying: "Nothing is changed in essence."

What is called for in the whole of society (as in science) is to perceive that fundamental change is always taking place and to allow this perception freely to be communicated in one's discourse, as the change takes place. Then, action can be in harmony with the fact of change, so that there is no need for mounting confusion and the resulting crises that lead to the call for revolution. Conservatism and revolution will then be seen to be equally irrelevant. What is relevant is the creation of harmony in action rather than the creation of confusion and disharmony.

Finally, let us recall that perception-communication is one whole. So the confusion that means a failure of communication also means a failure of perception. Therefore, to be sensitive to the fact of unceasing change and to allow ourselves freely to communicate this fact is the only way for perception to be clear and for action to be creative of harmony.

Professor Bohm's View of the Structure and Development of Theories

ROBERT L. CAUSEY

I

Professor Bohm tells us in his paper, "Indeed, even to read an article and to understand it is, in general, to change it significantly. For understanding something is assimilation, that is, making it a whole with oneself." Now, I certainly doubt whether I have succeeded in making Professor Bohm's paper whole with myself, but I am sure that I have changed it. Since I do not want to raise captious objections, I will restrict my criticisms to what I think is a collection of related, major errors in Professor Bohm's paper. Then I will very roughly sketch a picture of the structure of theories which I think Professor Bohm and I would agree is reasonably accurate and methodologically prudent. This picture is probably not exactly what Bohm has in mind, but, as he says, "things are seldom, if ever, the same as they were before."

However, before we start changing things, it will be useful to note some general aspects of the symposium topic. First of all, the symposium is about the structure of theories, and to describe the structure of a thing one needs to determine its component parts as well as certain relations between these parts. Of course, it is usually possible to analyze a thing into parts in more than one way; thus it usually will not have a unique, correct structural description. Furthermore, if the thing's structure, under a given type of analysis, changes with time, then a structural description might be a dynamic rather than a static picture. We might make a moving picture of it over a period of time, or we might take a still shot of it at a particular time. Until recently, most philosophers of science have been primarily concerned with taking still shots of a theory at a particular time. Sometimes these still shots are subjected to a great deal of retouching; this is called "logical reconstruction." To a large extent these still pictures are made because philosophers are interested in investigating what is, or ought to be, satisfied when a theory, as it is at a certain time, is tested or is used to explain certain data. Such still pictures of theories can be very illuminating.

However, in recent years, several historians and philosophers have examined scientific development and, more generally, have tried to analyze the nature of scientific progress. Also, some of them have criticized the still pictures of theories and their companion analyses of explanation and testing. They apparently believe that their descriptions of how theories change somehow show that the still pictures are not correct. If suitable details could be filled in, then this type of reasoning would certainly be valid. By observing how a thing changes, we can sometimes discover that we have mistakenly described its structure. A wonderful example of this occurred a few years ago in studies of crystal growth.

A theory of crystal growth was developed on the basis of the assumption that molecules gradually collect on a flat crystal side until the entire side collects an entire new layer of molecules which produce a new flat surface. Then more molecules must collect on this surface until it in turn is entirely covered by a new layer of molecules. Unfortunately, this theory predicts crystal growth rates (for instance, the rate of growth of iodine crystals from supersaturated vapor) which are enormously slower than the measured rates. Around the early fifties, F. C. Frank showed that growth rates in good agreement with measured rates could be predicted from a theory which assumes a different growth structure. His theory assumes that many crystals are not perfectly formed, but rather have screw dislocations (like miniature spiral staircases) which grow continuously at a fast rate. Large growth spirals have since been observed and had been reported earlier (see, for instance, van Bueren [1960], pp. 500–505).

This example from the theory of crystal growth illustrates that observations of how a thing changes can sometimes indicate that we have misdescribed its structure. However, Frank did not just criticize a theory of structure; he produced a moving picture of the structure of a growing crystal. This moving picture also led to improved still pictures of static crystals. In my opinion, much of the recent so-called "nontraditional" work in the philosophy of science has not gone much beyond the critical stage, for it has not produced reasonably detailed dynamic analyses of the structure of theories. I will return to these matters later. Right now we must consider certain points of Professor Bohm's paper.

II

Professor Bohm is very concerned with problems of communication. This leads him to discuss the issue of commensurability of theories. I believe that this discussion contains some serious errors.

Bohm believes that it is in principle impossible for theories to be commensurable. He thinks that each theory is a "whole" and "all the terms in such a theory can have their meanings and their criteria of factuality and truth only in the total context given by *that* theory."

Unfortunately, he does not give us an "in principle" argument for this; instead he tries to illustrate it with the historical example of malaria research and with other examples from physics. (I wish his malaria example *were* an argument, because then we could call it "The Argument from Malaria"! At any rate, it is hardly convincing.)

Professor Bohm mentions the "early theory" that the diseases now called "malaria" are caused by bad air, *mal-aria*. He correctly points out that such a theory could be (and indeed it was) confirmed by various observations and various attempts to irradicate or avoid the fevers. He then points out that other kinds of data, experimentation, and technology are relevant to the "later theory" that malarial fevers are caused by microorganisms *(Plasmodium falciparum, P. malariae, P. vivas, P. ovale)* transmitted by certain kinds of mosquitoes *(Anopheles gambiae, A. funestus,* and so on). Finally, he mentions complications in the epidemiology of malaria which might require *psychological* and *social* (and he should have added *genetic*[1]) studies. He concludes that "It should be clear that there is little or no 'commensurability' between these different 'theories' of malaria." He even suggests that they have little in common other than that they all deal with something that is called "malaria."

Now the history of malaria is long and interesting, and it does not seem to match Bohm's interpretation well. A few points should make this clear.

The symptoms of malarial fevers are quite distinct and have been rather well described since before the time of Hippocrates. Hippocrates himself taught that malaria is not caused by demons or gods, and, moreover, he described correlations between malaria and marshes, stagnant water, and so on (Russell [1955], p. 8). Since his time there have been many "theories" of malaria; people have attributed it to such things as bad air, drinking bad water, bad foods, various chem-

[1] Persons with the genetically determined sickle-cell trait have higher resistance to malaria than those with "normal" hemoglobin (see, for instance, Beadle and Beadle [1967], pp. 148–150).

icals, parasites, moisture, spores, changes of temperature, and bacilli (Russell [1955], Ch. 1). Some of these theories competed with each other at the same time and tried to account for some of the same data. In fact, the bad air theories were often considered vague and were refined in various ways by assuming different things to be in the bad air.

Now Bohm is partly right—each of these theories was confirmed by some data, and it was often possible to rule out other data as irrelevant. However, the *Plasmodia-Anopheles* theory is able to account for far more long-accepted observations than the bad air theories. It is *not* incommensurable with these theories. Both theories deal with many of the same observations (some of which have been known for thousands of years), and both have been confronted with many of the same problems. Moreover, the *Plasmodia-Anopheles* theory is even able to explain why the bad air theory was confirmed by certain kinds of data. Of course, it also explains such things as the cyclic recurrence of the fever and chills, which the bad air theory is not able to handle well. In addition, understanding the role of mosquitoes has led to DDT spraying with fantastic effects on the incidence of malaria.[2] Finally, the more recent epidemiological studies to which Bohm refers do not ignore the *Plasmodia-Anopheles* theory, but rather add to it (Macdonald [1957]).

Thus, a detailed study of the history of malaria does not show that successive theories are incommensurable; instead it shows that theories are sometimes easy to confirm and hard to falsify. If the various theories of malaria had been confronted with completely disjoint sets of problems, then one might be justified in saying that they are incommensurable (of course, in such a case we would probably also say that they are theories dealing with different classes of phenomena). But history shows that they *did* face many of the same problems, and that they were commensurable.

Furthermore, notice that this conclusion follows solely from a literal reading of history. It does not require assuming the existence of some kind of absolute observation language. Indeed, in order to show that the various malaria theories are incommensurable, one would have to show that history is deceptive. In particular, one would have to show that what I have called "the same problems" only *appear* to be the same problems, but that they are really different problems. This would

[2] To take one example, DDT spraying on a nationwide basis was begun in Ceylon in 1946 to 1947. The malaria morbidity rates have fallen from 574 per 1,000 in 1940 to 413 in 1946, fifty-eight in 1951, thirty-four in 1952, and eleven in 1953 (Russell [1955], p. 167).

require showing that the bad-air theorist and the *Plasmodia-Anopheles* theorist use many of the same terms with different meanings, and that, moreover, these meanings are different in such a way as to make what appear to be the same problems really different problems. Bohm has given no such argument. Indeed, I have never seen such an argument that was at all convincing.

Moreover, such an argument would lead to an extremely skeptical position. It would imply that the bad-air theorist and the *Plasmodia-Anopheles* theorist each have their own "private theoretical language." This situation is reminiscent of skeptical arguments in the philosophy of mind which lead to questions such as, "How can I be sure that you see the same *red* as I see?" Instead of private languages, we end up with something which might be called "private science."

III

Professor Bohm is really primarily concerned with the various kinds of changes which theories can undergo, especially when these changes are likely to lead to confusion. Of course, we have just seen how difficult it would be to show that *theories* are incommensurable. It is therefore unfortunate that he introduced the talk of "incommensurability," even in quotes, because this led him to talk of incommensurabilities produced by changes in *a* theory. For instance, he tells us that the "Hamilton-Jacobi theory was in some ways novel and 'incommensurable' with what Newton had done." He also tells us that the informal descriptions of von Neumann are "radically different and completely 'incommensurable' " with those of Bohr and Heisenberg.

First consider the Hamilton-Jacobi theory. If it were really incommensurable with Newton's theory, then these two theories should handle completely disjoint sets of problems. But of course, any problem which can be solved by the Hamilton-Jacobi theory can also be solved by Newton's theory. I think that all Bohm really means to say here is that nineteenth-century physicists did not take full advantage of the wave interpretation of mechanics suggested by the Hamilton-Jacobi theory, but it is hard to see why they should have.

The case of Bohr and Heisenberg versus von Neumann is more subtle, and I do not wish to become involved in all of its complexities. However, we should note how this example differs from the malarial and mechanical cases. Here Bohm is not simply saying that two *theories* are incommensurable, or that two *formalisms* of *a* theory are incommensurable. He is saying that the *informal descriptions* of von

Neumann are incommensurable with those of Bohr and Heisenberg. However, I am not sure that I understand very well what an informal description is supposed to be. Apparently an informal description provides one with an interpretation of the formalism of a theory; it thus allows one at least to describe a set of models of this formalism. But at the same time these models can be assumed to mirror certain aspects of experimental situations to which the theory is applied. Thus, an informal description also provides one with a way of talking informally about experiments. However, if I have understood Professor Bohm's discussion correctly, it appears that all he has really shown is that there are *some* terms of the von Neumann description which are not interpretable in the Bohr-Heisenberg description, and vice versa. Of course, this could, by itself, be sufficient to cause serious confusion. Bohm does not even need the stronger claim that these descriptions are "completely incommensurable."

IV

This brings us back to Bohm's major concern: to examine the kinds of changes which theories undergo and to consider confusions which can arise from these changes. Now, it would be irrelevant and hazardous for us to dwell on confusion. Therefore, let us consider changes in theories.

As was said earlier, the so-called "traditional" view of theories was largely developed in studies of the logic of explanation and theory testing. Quite properly, some philosophers were very concerned with the falsifiability of theories. However, much earlier, Duhem had already pointed out that most tests of theories are really simultaneous tests of several hypotheses. Thus, an experimental result which disagreed with a theoretical prediction would usually not falsify a particular hypothesis. Moreover, by suitable adjustments in certain secondary or auxiliary hypotheses, it is usually possible to prevent, or at least delay, the experimental falsification of the main hypotheses of a theory.

On the other hand, a successful theory, such as the *Plasmodia-Anopheles* theory of malaria, is confirmed by its successful applications. These successful applications include instances of its ability to explain puzzling phenomena, its ability to predict certain phenomena (especially things previously unexpected), and its applications in the development of technology. Quite clearly, if a scientist attempts to apply a *successful* theory to a particular problem and fails, he is not going to reject the theory on the spot. Because of the Duhemian argument, he is not forced to consider the theory as falsified by its failure to solve a particular problem. Of course, some theories are so unsuccessful that they hardly get off the ground. In these cases the scientist might indeed say that these theories have been falsified and reject them for that reason. But a *successful* theory is not usually considered to have been falsified unless an *even more successful* theory has been developed which contradicts it.

For instance, nineteenth-century organic chemists did not consider the atomic-molecular theory to be falsified every time they were unable to explain why a certain compound has certain derivatives. Instead they went back to their drawing boards and tried to dream up another molecular structure for the compound. Each proposed molecular structure for a given compound can be considered a mini-theory pertaining to that particular compound. But such structural hypotheses are also auxiliary hypotheses of the much more general atomic-molecular theory of matter. Indeed, as Bohm would say, the problem of inventing structural formulas for compounds is made relevant by the more general atomic-molecular theory.

With suitable auxiliary hypotheses, a good, general theory can have many successful applications. The theory can be likened to the torso of an octopus, while the auxiliary hypotheses are like tentacles reaching out to apply the theory to various problems. However, the theory does not have only eight arms; it is not just an octopus. It is, would you believe, a *myriapus*, for many new applications will involve postulating new auxiliary hypotheses. These new hypotheses will be like new arms growing on an octopus, and a very general theory could sprout an unlimited number of such arms. Moreover, if some attempted applications fail, then the corresponding arms are chopped off. But as long as it has some arms left, it continues to live; it will only die if its central torso is killed (that is, if a more successful theory is developed which contradicts it). Since the theory can be applied to a wide variety of problems, and since a few failures of application do not kill it, we can say that it has an *elasticity of application.*

What is the nature of its arms, its auxiliary hypotheses, which contribute to its variety of applications? This is difficult to say in general. In the case of physical theories formulated in terms of a few general laws, some of the important auxiliary hypotheses are usually hypothesized initial and boundary conditions which help to define a particular possible system obeying the general laws. These "possible systems" may still be quite abstract; they may be little more than a *possible realization,* or *model,* in the sense that logicians use these terms. Nevertheless, initial and boundary conditions often are the arms, or at least an important part of the arms, of a theory, including theories like the *Plasmodia-Anopheles* theory. Some philosophers may prefer not to consider these arms part of the original theory. Perhaps they are better described as subtheories, or side theories. At any rate, the fact that a theory can grow them, and can also afford to lose a few, accounts for much of its elasticity of application.

Yet there is still another important feature of a theory, with which Bohm is particularly concerned. To a large extent a theory determines the type of applications we will make of it. For instance, the *Plasmodia-Anopheles* theory leads to DDT spraying to eradicate mosquitoes for the purpose of eradicating malaria (and it can also lead to poisonous pollution). Thus a theory can help us to discover previously undreamed-of relations between phenomena. But, of course, this is well known.

On the other hand, it has perhaps not been sufficiently appreciated that this *relevance-determining* aspect of theories can also be detrimental. For instance, suppose that it is believed that chromosomes are nothing but carriers of genetic traits. Suppose someone measures a chromosome in a way that would normally be considered a molecular weight measurement. A certain numerical result is obtained, but this result would have little or no relevance to what is believed to be the nature of chromosomes. Thus, this measurement would probably be considered to have little or no significance. On the other hand, if it is believed (or hypothesized) that a chromosome is a DNA molecule, then the measurement has indeed a great deal of significance.

In recent years philosophers have begun to pay more attention to the relevance-determining aspect of theories. I believe that some writers, including Bohm, have vastly overemphasized its importance, for they have been led to conclude that theories are incommensurable. Nevertheless, a theory's elasticity of application and its relevance-determining ability must both be reckoned with, if we are adequately to understand theoretical explanation, theory testing, and the nature of theory growth and change.

Can our picture of a theory with arms do all this? I think not, and Bohm thinks not. In particular, he realizes that the models at the ends of the arms are often still quite abstract; they may be nothing more than mathematical structures satisfying the laws of the theory plus certain initial and boundary conditions. Bohm claims that, in addition to all of this, a theory is usually used in association with an informal mode of description. This informal descriptive language is used both to describe models of the theory and experimental situations. It thereby helps to interpret whatever formalism the theory might have. With practice, such an informal descriptive language can be used to describe experimental or observational situations in such a way that they can be considered models of the theory plus suitable auxiliary conditions. This is quite important. For instance, a major part of learning how to *use* classical mechanics is learning how to describe a wide variety of different kinds of systems in mechanical language which interprets the formalisms of classical mechanics.

If I understand him correctly, Professor Bohm believes that an informal descriptive language is an integral part of a theory. Thus our myriapus is, as it were, enveloped in an informal descriptive language. Bohm also believes that such modes of description contribute very largely to the relevance-determining aspect of theories.

This picture of theories is much too vague and general. It introduces descriptive language in an ad hoc way and thus begs the classical problem about the meanings of theoretical terms. However, if we just assume, as Bohm apparently does, that informal descriptions can just be invented, then this picture of a theory can be extended into a moving picture. It enables us to see different ways a theory can change.

First of all, a theory can grow by sprouting more arms to new applications. If the arms are not considered part of the theory, at least we can say that it spawns subtheories. In addition, Bohm points out that the theory can also change by gradual changes in the formalism, or by changes in the informal language of description. If one of these changes without appropriate, corresponding changes in the other, then, according to Bohm, confusion is likely to result. Even if confusion does not result, the scientist may fail to see possible advantages of new ways of looking at things, for example, the possible advantages of the Hamilton-Jacobi formulation of classical mechanics.

How does all of this complicated and fuzzy moving picture of theories compare with the so-called "traditional" picture of the structure of theories? Of course, there is not just one "traditional picture," but at least the pictures used for discussing explanation and theory testing are fairly well known. At best these pictures are *still* pictures of theories taken through very narrow angle lenses with a filter. They usually do not show theory growth and change. They usually filter out the informal language of description, and they tend to focus, through their narrow angle lens, on only one arm of the theory. This gives the impression that, if this arm were chopped off, then the theory would be falsified.

However, our moving picture does not imply that "successive" theories are "incommensurable," nor does it imply that theories have unlimited elasticity of application, or that theories completely determine the relevance of experiments. Moreover, although our moving picture does not filter out informal languages of theories, it also does not focus sharply on them. This is a very serious shortcoming.

Reply to Professor Causey[1]

JEFFREY BUB[2]

Professor Causey has missed the main thrust of Bohm's paper. To understand what Bohm is saying, it is essential not to separate his discussion of the quantum theory from his more general philosophical or methodological remarks. Professor Causey has not come to grips at all with Bohm's remarks on the quantum theory, and they are intimately related to his notion of science as perception-communication. I shall not attempt to explain or defend Bohm here, or to speak for him in any way at all. Rather, I shall simply state what seems to me to be right on this issue, with the hope that my thoughts reflect something of what Bohm is trying to say.

Bohm has usually (and mistakenly) been regarded by philosophers of science and physicists as the advocate of a naive realistic interpretation or reformulation of the quantum theory, for this is how the "hidden variable" approach is understood as being opposed to the Copenhagen interpretation (which is variously seen as subjectivistic, or idealistic, or positivistic, or nonsensical). To my mind, what most philosophers of science should find remarkable about Bohm's paper is that it is very much in harmony with the spirit of Bohr's ideas. Let me explain how this can be so.

One commonly held (and quite confused) view about the significance of the change from classical to quantum mechanics, is that this has something to do with the impossibility of simultaneously measuring or observing certain physical attributes of microobjects—there is no similar measurability restriction for the corresponding properties

[1] In writing these comments, I have freely used several ideas which arose in conversation with Mr. William Demopoulos, of the Philosophy Department, University of Pittsburgh.

Editor's note: Professor Bohm's paper was presented *in absentia* and his place in discussion was taken by Professor Jeffrey Bub, who is a former student and collaborator of his. His formal reply to Professor Causey's commentary has been included as the present article.

[2] Research supported by the National Science Foundation.

of macroobjects. On this view, then, classical mechanics is applicable to the macrolevel, because the properties of macroobjects are represented in the theory by real-valued functions on the points (classical states) of a suitable vector space (phase space). Quantum mechanics is applicable to the microlevel, because the properties of microobjects are represented in the theory by (the eigenvalues of self-adjoint) operators on a suitable vector space (Hilbert space). The noncommutativity of some operators then reflects the impossibility of simultaneously measuring the corresponding properties. This is proposed as the meaning of the uncertainty principle, or the feature of complementarity, and the reason for the essentially statistical character of the quantum theory.

On this view, Bohm's approach—the hidden variable approach—seems to involve nothing more than the reactionary program to reinstate classical mechanics as the fundamental description of the microlevel and the rejection of all that is novel in the quantum theory. So, to the question: "What is a hidden variable theory?," the standard answer is: "Hidden variables are introduced in order to characterize a phase space of microstates on which real-valued functions can be defined to represent the properties of microobjects, in the manner of classical mechanics, so that the peculiar statistical relations of quantum mechanics are simply explained by the incompleteness of the quantum theory." (This way of putting it shows the irrelevance of the controversy over determinism. It is a further question—and one not generally considered—whether a suitable deterministic equation of motion can be found for the phase space points, which would be consistent with the time transformations of the quantum theory.)

Now, von Neumann and others have shown that the algebraic structure of self-adjoint Hilbert space operators cannot be embedded into the algebraic structure of real-valued phase space functions, so that the statistical relations of the quantum theory cannot be recovered in this "cheap" way simply by introducing additional hypothetical variables to "complete" the quantum theory. But, what no one seems to have noticed, in all the sound and fury about hidden variables, is that there is not one single example of a hidden variable theory that has ever actually been seriously proposed, that is, published in the literature, that conforms to this von Neumann conception of a hidden variable theory. If you want to relate hidden variable theories which have *actually* been proposed—call these HV theories to avoid confusion—or if you want to relate these to the idea of a statistical mechanical phase space reconstruction of the quantum statistics, then you would have to say that HV theories in effect introduce *different phase spaces and associated probability measures for each complete commuting set of self-adjoint operators.*[3] This is one way of formalizing the idea—referred to in Bohm's paper—that the shapes of the phase space cells defining the quantum mechanical "uncertainty relationships" are significant, as well as their finite size.

Here we begin to approach Bohr's idea of complementarity and "wholeness." Part of what Bohr meant to say, I think, was that the quantum statistics cannot be understood in an analogous way to the statistics of classical statistical mechanics, in terms of a distribution of properties over an ensemble of systems represented as points in a phase space, because different phase spaces and associated probability measures would then have to be introduced for "incompatible observables." These different phase space descriptions are reducible to one single description in the classical case; in the quantum mechanical case they may therefore be said to be "complementary," insofar as they are understood as being about what classically would be considered as "the same object." Because the ensemble, or the distribution, is stipulated relative to a set of relevant experimental or background conditions, the quantum description is often characterized by saying that "the individual system cannot in principle be separated from the experimental conditions." This is the idea of "wholeness" in the loose sense.

Having rejected the usual answer to the question concerning the significance of the hidden variable approach, I should now propose a different answer. Instead, I shall first consider another question: "Is there a nontrivial sense in which the quantum theory, or rather, the theoretical transition from classical to quantum mechanics, is *unique* in the history of physics?"

Aage Petersen has described a conversation[4] in which Bohr made the intriguing remark: "Ultimately, we human beings depend on our words. We are hanging in language." When Petersen objected that reality "lies beneath" language, Bohr replied: "We are suspended in language in such a way that we cannot say what is up and what is down." In the context of Bohr's writings on correspondence and complementarity (Bohr [1934], [1958], [1963]), I find a very close parallel between this comment and certain aspects of Wittgenstein's thought, particularly as expressed in the *Tractatus*. What is it that *we cannot say?* Wittgenstein [1963] writes: "4.12 Propositions can represent the whole of reality, but they cannot represent what they must have

[3] This point is discussed at length in Bub [1969].
[4] This conversation is described in Petersen [1963] and Petersen [1968], p. 188.

in common with reality in order to be able to represent it—logical form. In order to be able to represent logical form, we should have to be able to station ourselves with propositions somewhere outside logic, that is to say outside the world." We cannot say "what is up and what is down" with respect to language and reality, because to do so would mean representing the logical form of reality in just that sense which Wittgenstein found objectionable. For a proposition can represent a situation, the existence of certain states of affairs and the nonexistence of other states of affairs, only by determining a place in "logical space." And in order to be able to use propositions to represent that in virtue of which propositions are able to represent in any way at all—the possibility of representing—we should have to be able to make logical space itself an object of discourse from outside.

The "quantum jump" from classical to quantum mechanics involves a change in the logical form displayed in the propositions of mechanics. Since propositions cannot represent logical form, the only way in which a change in logical form can be mirrored in language is "from the inside." Bohr used to compare the quantum situation with the first crisis in arithmetic: the problem of defining the irrationals in terms of the rationals.[5] The logical status of the "quantum object," relative to the objects of classical physics, is analogous to the status of $\sqrt{2}$ relative to the rationals. The significance of Bohr's concept of a quantum *phenomenon,* and his insistence on retaining "plain language, suitably refined by the usual physical terminology," [6] that is, classical concepts, for the characterization of phenomena, should be understood in the light of this analogy. The change in logical form shows itself in the language of (classical) physics through the logic of "indivisible, closed phenomena," in which the experimental conditions and results are described classically. These are the new states of affairs in the sense of atomic facts (Wittgenstein's *sachverhalte*), and *this* is the meaning of the "feature of wholeness." The quantum algorithm—the Hilbert space formalism or equivalent—amounts to a *definition of the quantum object,*[7] in determining a logical space of phenomena. Bohr's statement—so obviously absurd that it must be true—that "the language of Newton and Maxwell will remain the

[5] See Petersen [1963]. Bohr seems to have been much less obscure in informal discussion than he is in print.

[6] The quotation is from the first essay in Bohr [1963].

[7] To avoid an apparent inconsistency, notice that the phrase "quantum object" is used in an entirely different sense in my article Bub [1969] with no connotation of a change in logical form.

language of physicists for all time" (Bohr [1931]), is surely the assertion that the language of classical physics is the language of physics, and that the transition from classical to quantum mechanics is to be interpreted as a change in logical form "from the inside," not as the introduction of a new physical language.

This is the sense in which the quantum situation is unique. It is unfortunate that the logical issue has been buried in the polemics of the measurement problem—a trend which has probably been influenced by the intuitive appeal of Heisenberg's microscope *gedanken* experiment, which Bohr saw as quite irrelevant. A similar confusion was initiated by von Neumann's discussion of the measurement process as an interaction between two quantum mechanical systems (von Neumann [1955]). This theory has recently been extended to a so-called quantum ergodic theory of macrosystems, as an attempt to show that quantum mechanics can "stand on its own feet" as a theory of the microlevel to which the macrolevel can be reduced in the usual sense.[8]

Von Neumann did publish a paper with Birkhoff entitled "The Logic of Quantum Mechanics" (Birkhoff and von Neumann [1936]), which has been revived as the basis of a "lattice-theoretic" approach to quantum mechanics.[9] The Birkhoff-von Neumann paper presents the essential difference between a classical mechanical phase-space description and a quantum mechanical Hilbert-space description as a difference in the lattice structure of propositions. The lattice associated with phase space is distributive, whereas the lattice associated with Hilbert space is nondistributive. The lattice—represented as a Hasse diagram—can evidently be regarded as a convenient device for displaying logical form, or the features of logical space. Thus, the Birkhoff-von Neumann paper can be understood as showing in what way the logical form of reality, mirrored in propositions constructed according to the rules implicit in Hilbert space, differs from the logical form implicit in phase space. What the nondistributive quantum lattice indicates is the logic of *phenomena*.

[8] The attempt to solve von Neumann's measurement problem in this way has a long history. See Bub [1968] for a discussion.

[9] J. M. Jauch and D. Finkelstein are perhaps to be credited with this revival. See Jauch [1968] and Varadarajan [1968] for general references. With few exceptions, the lattice theoreticians seem to be more interested in the new manipulative techniques suggested by this approach than in the logical question, which is emphasized by Hilary Putnam in an article entitled "Is Logic Empirical?," in Cohen and Wartofsky [1969], and by David Finkelstein in "The Physics of Logic", International Centre for Theoretical Physics, Trieste, March 1968.

In an orthocomplemented lattice, there is a unique orthocomplement a' to every element a, defined by:

$$(a')' = a$$
$$a \leq b \text{ implies } b' \leq a'$$
$$a \wedge a' = 0$$
$$a \vee a' = 1$$

The complement of an element a is defined by the last two conditions and is not necessarily unique. There is a well-known theorem that complementation is unique and is orthocomplementation in a distributive lattice. It is also a theorem that the existence of a unique complement implies distributivity in an orthocomplemented lattice.[10] Hence, a nondistributive orthocomplemented lattice L is essentially a lattice in which complementation is not unique. This means that L is simply a family of complemented distributive lattices (D_1, D_2, . . .) pasted together in a certain way. That is to say, combinations of elements from different distributive lattices are defined so that an element of the lattice D_i in general has additional complements outside D_i.

This is immediately obvious for the lattice of closed subspaces of Hilbert space, the quantum lattice. In this case, the distributive sublattices D_1, D_2, . . . correspond to different sets of subspaces, each determined by a complete commuting set of self-adjoint operators (through an associated set of commuting projection operators). The different complete commuting sets of operators are usually said to correspond to "incompatible observables." But this terminology obscures the significance of nondistributivity. One should rather say that each distributive sublattice corresponds to a certain kind of phenomenon. This makes it clear that the Hilbert space, insofar as it incorporates a nondistributive lattice, amounts to a definition of the quantum object in just such a way as to engender descriptions which are logically incoherent but complementary, in the sense that descriptions associated with different ("incompatible") distributive sublattices nevertheless refer to the same object.

The significance of nondistributivity lies in the fragmented description induced by the logical indivisibility of the phenomenon as a means of showing a change in logical form. This can be seen most clearly through the logical operation of negation, which is represented by the complement in a Boolean algebra, a complemented distributive lattice. Within a distributive sublattice of L (in which complementation is not unique), the complement of an element is unique and

[10] See Birkhoff [1940], Theorems 6.1 and 6.11.

coincides with the orthocomplement. So, the nondistributivity of the quantum lattice signifies that the logical operation of negation is in each case to be applied relative to a given phenomenon, that is, within a given distributive sublattice.

I can now propose an answer to the question concerning the significance of the hidden variable approach. HV theories are preliminary outlines for the development of a *theory of quantum objects.* Quantum mechanics, as originally formulated and articulated through the Hilbert space formalism or equivalent, is a *definition of the quantum object.* As it has since been extended to include new experimental results, quantum mechanics is a patchwork of contradictory formalisms, because the uniqueness of the quantum situation has not been generally realized. In addition, the failure to understand the true meaning of quantum mechanics has led to the complete corruption of the original Copenhagen interpretation, which has been replaced by a vague and amorphous "orthodox interpretation" (including elements of von Neumann's analysis of measurement), involving confused assumptions about the ultimate character of the quantum statistics and the impossibility of certain kinds of theoretical change. HV theories reveal the irrelevance and untenability of these assumptions by developing concepts and postulates appropriate to quantum objects. Thus, HV theories display a logical form different from that displayed by the phase space of classical mechanics. This is apparent if one considers that the lattice of propositions involving different phase spaces associated with different complete commuting sets of self-adjoint operators will not be distributive.

Bohm's concern with the structure of scientific theories should be understood in the context of his view of the quantum theory. By implying that each theory involves its own methodology (and history), that is, that every theoretical change introduces new criteria of factuality and truth, Bohm suggests that the quiet periods of "normal science" are really very noisy indeed; in other words, that insofar as the evolution of physics involves changes of "conceptual frame," this kind of change is virtually continuous. What is not generally recognized is the difference between a change of conceptual frame and the kind of change implicit in the theoretical transition from classical to quantum mechanics. It is this kind of change which necessitates a radically new approach to the problem of scientific explanation, the logical structure and epistemological status of scientific theories. I understand Bohm's idea of science as "perception-communication" as an attempt to capture the sense of a possibility of a change in logical form, echoing Bohr's remark that we are hanging in language.

Discussion

Professor Causey:

Professor Bub suggested that I either did not fully understand Bohm's paper or at least was not sympathetic enough toward it. I was not very sympathetic, although the latter part of my commentary was indeed an effort to develop (in my own way) what I think are some of Bohm's important points. I do think that I understand Professor Bohm's paper.

Professor Bub has told us that Professor Bohm's philosophical views have their origin in what he believes about quantum mechanics. I am quite willing to agree with that, for this has always been the impression I have had. But whatever the origin of his philosophical views, I think that he has also been influenced by Kuhn and Feyerabend and others. Furthermore, Professor Bub has not pointed out one specific place where I have allegedly misunderstood Professor Bohm's paper, and he has not defended its philosophical theses against my criticisms.

Professor Kuhn:

I am not sure whether I can illuminate the issue, but my name has been invoked enough so that I feel I must try. I am going to say very little about the term 'incommensurability'. It is a term I have used, although it is not one I have been very fond of. I am entirely sympathetic with Dr. Bohm's critique of the problems it raises, but I am also totally unsympathetic with the conclusions he then draws. Having recognized these problems, what he does is banish them by concluding that incommensurability is not appropriate because there in fact is not any possibility of communication; every view has to be taken in isolation all by itself and be a sort of private science. And that, I think, makes it impossible even to work on, much less to resolve, what I see as very real and unresolved problems. Some sort of communication goes on, and we must learn to understand it by making something out of phrases like 'partial communication,' or 'preservation of reference for certain terms, although some of the referential apparatus has itself changed.' I do not want to act as though presently I know what to do with these problems, but it is clear to me that one can hope to work on them. By making every theory totally a thing in itself, fully incomparable with all others, Bohm obscures the real problems.

By the same token, although I am totally in agreement with what Professor Causey has said in criticizing Bohm, I think he is wrong to suppose that one can merely discard what the people who introduced the term incommensurability were getting at. The evidence he produces in the case of malaria is terribly important: what it tells us is that when different views are held by different groups of people, you generally discover historically that there were many words that they had in common and that they could explore these words together. They could find arguments which both groups up to a point would at least partially accept. But to say that is not to suggest that their theories became one-to-one comparable through-and-through in a language that both would accept. Rather they had techniques for beginning to explore differences, and we need to know more about them. I therefore would not take either the private-box view of incommensurability or the nonexistence view of it, and I regret that these two approaches leave what seems to me genuinely worthwhile lost in the middle.

There is another whole aspect of Dr. Bohm's paper that nobody has pointed to and that also related to the private-science view that emerges, particularly at the end of his paper. I have in mind his description—throughout the paper but most explicitly at the start—of what goes on during the quiet periods of normal science. As I understand it, Bohm is suggesting that what looks like a quiet period is really only quiet because people do not quite observe what is going on but instead develop their private scientific worlds. In fact, however, step-by-step their deep divergences and incoherences emerge increasingly within the scientific community, but people do not see them until finally the confusion becomes so great that the situation breaks down. He illustrates this by talking about the development of quantum mechanics since, let us say, 1926, the date of the invention of the Schrödinger equation. But his description does not, I think, fit at all well what I take it actually happened in the development of quantum mechanics. Two quite different sets of development are being identified in order to make a special point.

It is certainly true that, together with the change in formalism with the coming of the Schrödinger equation, there was an absolutely fundamental change, which Bohm describes extraordinarily well, in the informal language which people deployed in making use of that equation. One cannot for a minute ignore the fact that quantum mechanics is not just the formalism of the Schrödinger equation but includes the informal language of application. On the other hand, excluding some later subtleties, the developments of which Bohm speaks took place almost entirely in the two years after the development of the Schrödinger equation. It was a major development being part of the revolution which brought wave mechanics. But for the purposes of almost all physicists, it was finished at the meeting in Brussels of the Solvay Congress very early in 1928. Indeed, one of the things I discovered when talking to physicists about the development of quantum mechanics is that even people who studied with Heisenberg, the author of the uncertainty principle, at Leipzig from 1928 on never heard of these problems unless they visited Copenhagen and were exposed to Bohr. They simply did quantum mechanics in the new vocabulary, without any concern for the fact that there were problems that could be raised by people who were bothered about the consistency of the vocabulary, and so on. The development Bohm speaks of did occur, and it was terribly important, but it was all over before 1930. Since then, the problems he refers to have been more-or-less "read out of" physics.

This is not to say that physics is problem-free or even that it is not at the moment breaking down. There is a whole other set of problems to which Professor Bohm's paper also points which are the problems that have arisen out of the attempts to understand the interactions of field and matter as well as the proliferation of elementary particles. Everybody knows there are gigantic unsolved problems in physics and in the relation of theory to nature at this time. They have been growing ever since the late 1940s, and the result is a group of schools—such as symmetry schools, field-theoretic schools, and analytic-continuation schools—which do have real difficulty communicating with each other. The situation Bohm describes does exist. But I think it has nothing to do, either historically or, at this time, logically, with the problems of the interpretation of the Schrödinger equation. Although I may stand to be corrected, it is my impression that one of the greatest difficulties faced by people who are concerned to revise the Bohr interpretation is that none of the problems that emerge for them makes any contact whatsoever with the technical problems that physics has faced in recent years, and that has created a profound crisis for the profession.

In short, though both ends of Bohm's description are very apt, I think there is no justification for laying them end to end and making them a single story. But it is apparently only by doing that manipulation that we are going to get evidence for Bohm's picture of the quiet periods which are really not quiet at all. I do not think that version of normal science will do at all.

This brings me to my last point which I shall try to make very brief because it reintroduces the whole question of each physicist doing things a little bit differently, therefore having his own theory, and therefore not being able to communicate with other theorists. That is Bohm's final picture of what has been going on, and it is the situation which he urges scientists to avoid by being more tolerant of each other's views. I do not, however, see how talk about science as perception-communication can be made compatible with any such solipsistic view. If each individual holds his own theory, then he cannot talk to other people; then it is not perception-communication or at least it is not communication any longer. It becomes a private science, which is exactly what I am going to urge it cannot possibly be. I have also confessed that I am not altogether clear about the way out of this box, but the way I should try (you also will see this at the beginning of my paper tomorrow[1]) is to suggest that when we talk about the various groups now doing, say, field theory, S-matrix theory, and so on, we are talking about recognizable and identifiable *collections* of people within the physics community. There are schools within the physics community and you can pretty well pick out their membership at any given time: individuals communicate relatively fully within the schools but with much more difficulty across school lines. The perception-communication approach can be applied within each school but not equally well across schools. I think that is the way it is supposed to behave, but it does not leave you wanting to say "each man his own theory." One wants instead to say "each school its own theory," a remark which does not drive one to the sort of solopsism that Professor Causey pointed to and does not make the problem equivalent to "Do you see the same red that I see." That we must not let it become.

Professor Bub:

Something about what Professor Kuhn just said really disturbed me: it seemed to me that he was suggesting that one should really only care about what most physicists are concerned about today. Now I really find this very puzzling! What significance for philosophy of science is it that today or in the last thirty years most physicists have been concerned with the particular sorts of problems and that certain problems

[1] See Session VI below.

have been dropped as irrelevant—namely, the problem of the interpretation of the quantum theory or the problem of the vocabulary (as I think he referred to it)? I think this is really a very peculiar sort of way to look at the history of physics or the way physics is carried out and then to take what most physicists are doing as some sort of standard on which to base a methodology in the prescriptive sense.

Professor Causey:

I would also like to comment on Professor Kuhn's comments. He mentioned many things. First of all he implied that he does not agree with the extent to which Bohm would carry certain ideas. Nevertheless, he feels that Bohm is pointing out important things about scientific methodology and about the communication of theories. To some extent I agree with this. My myriapus model of a theory, my discussion of the relevance-determining aspects of theories, and my brief mention of the elasticity of application of theories were attempts to try to account for some aspects of the nature of scientific work which I believe the old "still pictures" of theories are not fully able to account for. Yet I was attempting to account for these aspects in a reasonably clear way that does not involve us in talking about incommensurabilities and radical differences in language, and so on.

Professor Kuhn also pointed out that nobody had mentioned Bohm's remarks about the changes that take place in normal science. When I wrote my commentary, I asked myself whether I should discuss this, and I decided not to because there were many other things I wanted to discuss. Furthermore, I predicted to myself that Professor Kuhn would have something to say about this anyway.

Professor Kuhn does not think that we should talk in terms of private science on an individual level. But I am anxious to learn in his paper what he has to say about that private science on a level of small research groups, because maybe there is something of great importance there.

Professor Achinstein:

It seems to me that there are at least three things involved here in the use of the term "incommensurability": one is that if two theories are incommensurable they just do not talk about the same problems, so one might say that Newtonian theory is incommensurable with Freudian theory, since they are just not dealing with the same issues. That seems to be the sense, or at least the main sense, in which Causey was using the term. Now Bohm may have been using the term 'incommensurable' in a somewhat different sense, in such a way that incommensurability involves different meanings—that is, that two theories are incommensurable insofar as they use terms in common but do not mean the same things by them. At first it seems this is what Bohm has in mind, but then in the latter part of his paper it turns out that perhaps he does not mean this at all, but simply that two theories are incommensurable if they are just two theories, that is if they are different; and this, it seems to me, is a very uninteresting sense of incommensurability. So I think that there are at least these three notions which are independent in certain ways. For example, merely because two theories do not talk about the same problems does not mean that they use terms with different meanings, and even if they use terms with the same meanings it does not mean they are talking about the same problems. So I find this whole talk of incommensurability quite complex and confusing.

Professor Causey:

Professor Achinstein mentioned that Bohm was rather vague about exactly what he meant by 'incommensurability'—whether he was talking about differences in meanings, differences in problems, differences in facts, differences in methodology, and so on. I am quite aware of this; I found it extremely difficult to try to see what he meant. In fact, I think that he has different notions of incommensurability which he somehow thinks are all tied together. In the examples that I particularly discussed—the malaria example, the Hamilton Jacobi example, and the Bohr-Heisenberg *vs.* von Neumann example—I mentioned at least three different kinds of incommensurability which Bohm discusses.

Now, I think that much of the recent discussion about incommensurability has centered around the claim that scientists holding incommensurability theories are dealing with different problems and different worlds, and of course this claim is also connected with meanings and facts. In particular, I wanted to point out that especially in the case of malaria, history does not seem to indicate that the problems are all that different. At least there were many problems common to the various theories. To show that these problems were really different one would have to give a very subtle linguistic argument (which I mentioned in the commentary) and Bohm has not given any. At least, if it could be made to go through, a linguistic argument probably would be sufficient to show that there were different problems. There may also be other ways to show that there are different problems. In addition, there are other senses in which theories can have different problems. But I think that most people have had this linguistic argument in mind. However, I have never seen this argument developed convincingly. I quite agree with Achinstein that *different meanings* and *different problems* are not equivalent notions—but they are related.

Professor Putnam:

I found the exchange between Jeffrey Bub and Causey very interesting in that at the very end Bub suggested that Bohm's notion of incommensurability might be understood in the idea that scientific theories carry their own methodology. Now I think that that is too strong. I think one would not want to say that every new scientific theory brings in with it a new methodology, and I agree with Causey that the case of the two different theories of malaria is probably an especially bad example in that respect. On the other hand, it does seem to me that in the case of the most exciting theories of the twentieth century that part of the excitement has been generated precisely by the sense that the new theory involved a challenge not only to what were previously taken to be laws of nature, but also a challenge to what were previously taken to be canons of methodology. Quantum mechanics, for instance, was certainly thought to involve a violation of the principles of determinism, and there is still a lot of argument going as to whether it ultimately does. It was certainly thought to. In that respect accepting quantum mechanics with a standard indeterministic plus no hidden variables interpretation seems to be saying, "The devil with Kant and the canons of methodology that have been generally accepted by scientists and philosophers of science since Kant." The acceptance of general relativity involved the giving up of the idea that Euclidean geometry is a part of mathematics or alternatively giving up the idea that mathematics is immune from revision. Take your choice—either one is giving up something that has the status of a methodological principle. Although I do not want to stick my neck out at this point and say what I think about this, I do think it would be worthwhile in our discussion if we look at the question of the extent to which new scientific theories may involve new methodologies. Perhaps I should direct this question to Professor Causey.

Professor Bub:

I like Professor Putnam's way of putting the problem very much. In fact, I am a little surprised at myself—I was almost sure I would not.

Here, perhaps, my own view may differ somewhat from Bohm's, because it does seem to me worthwhile to distinguish between theoretical changes which involve giving up methodological principles, and theoretical changes which do not.

Professor Causey:

Professor Putnam, I quite agree with you. I think that in Bub's commentary, and implicit in Bohm's paper, is the idea that different theories have their own distinct methodologies.

Offhand I do not know what I would want to say about this. I think that you are right in that theories involving a "scientific revolution" seem to involve new methodologies. Probably Professor Suppes would agree with this. Certainly there are different methods involved in the use of probabilistic theories versus deterministic theories. Some people say that facts are "theory-laden." Perhaps we could say that theories are "methodology-laden." This is another aspect of theories which hopefully we may someday be able to describe systematically.

Professor van Fraassen:

I would like to ask Professor Bub to clarify part of Professor Bohm's paper if he can. Professor Bohm apparently endorsed the standard Bohr move against the Einstein-Podolsky-Rosen paradox,[2] the move of saying that in a *measurement* the system cannot be considered separately from the experimental conditions. And then he argues that those following von Neumann who ignored this are going wrong and would bring it back in through the back door. Let me read a sentence that I found puzzling: "For it turns out that after all one cannot apply

[2] The paradox is a criticism of the standard (Copenhagen) interpretation of quantum theory. The paradox is generated by a hypothetical experiment in terms of a molecule containing two atoms whose spins point in opposite directions insofar as they have any direction at all. The molecule is then disintegrated by a process which does not alter angular momentum of the particles. Einstein, Podolsky, and Rosen [1935] then introduce various criteria for being a complete physical theory, the most important of which is that if, without in any way disturbing the system, we can predict with certainty (that is, with probability equal to one) the value of a physical quantity, then there exists an element of reality corresponding to this physical quantity. Using this criterion, Einstein, Podolsky and Rosen then argue that under the conditions of the above hypothetical experiment, it can be shown that there are precisely defined elements of reality which must exist in the second atom which correspond to the simultaneous definition of all three components of its spin. But, the Schrödinger wave function can describe at most one of these components at a time with complete precision, and so they conclude that the wave description does not provide a complete description of all elements of reality existing in the second atom (see Einstein,

this theory to an actual experimental arrangement unless the description of the behavior of the various 'parts' of the world is inseparably amalgamated with the description of the overall experimental conditions" (p. 386 above). I think that what he is referring to here in von Neumann's treatment is the fact that if you have two interacting systems (for example, a system in a measuring apparatus) and you know the density matrix for each component, then in general you cannot deduce the density matrix for the whole. But it seems to me that this just does not justify his conclusion that this is a way of bringing in a kind of wholeness and inseparability of experimental conditions in the system "by the back door" because this is a feature of any interaction, not just of measurement; it has nothing to do with experimental conditions if the emphasis is on *experimental* as it was apparently for Bohr. It is simply the fact that measurement is considered here as one kind of interaction. So, unless I misunderstand him, I think the conclusion is not justified.

Professor Bub:

With respect to van Fraassen's question, I feel there is a misunderstanding here. Let me read the passage from Bohm's address which van Fraassen quoted: "For it turns out that after all one cannot apply this theory to an actual experimental arrangement unless the description of the behavior of the various 'parts' of the world is inseparably amalgamated with the description of the overall experimental conditions" (p. 386 above). Now this remark occurs in the context of a general discussion on the measurement problem, and does not refer directly to the Einstein-Podolsky-Rosen experiment, which Bohm memtioned earlier. I think what Bohm has in mind here are certain current attempts to provide a solution to the measurement problem as posed by von Neumann—for example, the theory recently proposed by the Italian physicists Daneri, Loinger, and Prosperi in *Nuclear Physics*, and in *Il Nuovo Cimento*. This theory (and other such theories, which

Podolsky, and Rosen [1935] or Bohm [1951], pp. 611–622, for details). This is a paradox since, under the Copenhagen interpretation, quantum theory is inconsistent with hidden variables. The Bohr resolution of the paradox is, roughly speaking, that the Einstein-Podolsky-Rosen criteria of a complete theory involve in an integral way the implicit assumption that the world is actually made up of separately existing and precisely defined "elements of reality," whereas quantum theory implies quite a different picture of the structure of the world at the microscopic level—a picture in which the system being measured cannot be separated from the experimental situation. See Bohr [1935] and Bohm [1951], for details.

take the problem as von Neumann posed it) brings in by the back door, so to speak, the very feature it has been designed to avoid, namely, "the Observer," or the "wholeness of experimental conditions and experimental results."

Professor Suppes:

I will make a comment very briefly, which is directed to Dr. Bub. It seems to me that reference has been made to the use that can be made of some of the work that has been done in philosophy and in logic in recent decades. One of the things that I find generally disturbing about Bohm's paper is the lack of intellectual clarity and precision. That is, Dr. Bub has alluded to the fact that one should be concerned not with the malaria example which Bohm did introduce, but with the quantum mechanical case; but, of course, if you want to take Bohm's ideas as broad generalizations for the analysis of science, quantum mechanics is a particularly bad case in the sense of the degree of precision and clarity with which matters are discussed. If we take analogies from other parts of science and mathematics that have been important historically, one example I would take is the clarification of geometry in the nineteenth century. We now have developed a very clear picture of the relationships between various geometries and how these geometries apply to the world. We have some very sharp formal results about various geometries and it is considered a responsibility of anybody who talks about these problems to deal with these results. What I would like Dr. Bub to comment on is the following: Isn't it the case that we need the same kind of deepening of the intellectual results and discussion of quantum mechanics and not to continue to discuss it at the very vague and general level of Bohm's paper?

Professor Bub:

Professor Suppes suggests that we should try to get away from the vague and sloppy way of discussing the problems of the quantum theory which has become typical, and really be hard-headed about things and talk precisely and axiomatically about what we are doing. I do not have any sympathy with this at all. I would certainly agree that there has been a tremendous amount of very vague and very confusing discussion on the quantum theory which should just be dropped. On the other hand, there is a certain kind of discussion (via axiomatics) which claims to be very clear and very lucid because it is presented mathematically, but actually misses a lot of the problems originally expressed in informal terms. For to be very precise about a certain way of looking at the quantum theory is to pursue one particular direction in one particular framework, but to ignore certain other aspects of the problem which, if taken into account, might very well lead to something which goes quite *beyond the quantum theory*. So I agree that there has been a tremendous amount of very loose talk on the foundations of the quantum theory, but I do not know that the actual discussions which have claimed to be very lucid have really gone any further.

Reply to Discussion

DAVID BOHM

Editor's note: As was mentioned in an earlier note, Professor Bohm was unable to attend the session in which his paper was read, and his place in discussion was taken by Professor Jeffrey Bub. Although Professors Bohm and Bub share similar philosophical views, there are differences in their positions, and so it is only fair that Professor Bohm be given an opportunity to reply himself to the various comments and criticisms made in the discussion of his paper. On the basis of transcriptions of the preceding discussion he has written this reply.

I would like to begin by raising the question of whether it was wise for me to give such a talk without the possibility of my being present to answer questions. Although Dr. Bub did a very good job of "standing in" for me, it must be pointed out that he was not familiar with my recent views, and that (as comes out in the discussion) he is not completely in agreement with them. I must therefore apologize to Dr. Bub for unwittingly putting him into a very difficult position, while at the same time, I wish to thank him for doing as well as he did.

I shall not answer in detail individual comments, but will aim merely at giving a reply to what I felt were the main points raised in the discussion.

My talk seems to have given people the impression that I favor a "solipsist" view that could be called "private science" as opposed to "public science." Let me first say that this is not the case. What I wanted to suggest was that physics is actually fragmenting into a great many "relatively private" views (that is, restricted to small groups) and that this has largely escaped notice, because communications tend to focus attention very heavily on certain formal mathematical modes of expression which are, in some measure at least, shared by most of the groups in question. With regard to more subtle but not less important questions of "philosophy" and general language form, however, these groups have radically different views, implying different methodologies, different basic questions, different modes of testing, and so on.

Thus, a large range of "relatively private" sciences is developing and this fact is responsible for the growing confusion to which I referred in my talk.

My suggestion was that such fragmentation originates mainly in the effort of each group to hold fast to its own views, and that this in turn originates, at least in part, in the belief that there are "quiet" periods of "normal science" in which such views are not changing significantly. I suggested that during such periods, significant changes do take place and that because they are not recognized as such they lead to fragmentation and confusion. I meant further to imply that when there is a general understanding that such changes are always taking place, then fragmentation of science into a large number of "relatively private" views will cease, because scientists will remain in communication with each other with regard to the fact of continual fundamental change of scientific theories.

With regard to Professor Causey, I feel that he did put more emphasis on technical questions (for example, such as those raised in connection with the malaria example) than I wished to give in my talk. If I were to do the talk over, I would not emphasize these details so much. Rather, I would point out, first of all, that changes are continually taking place in scientific theories, and that assessment of the significance of these changes depends on certain relevance judgments. For example, if one regards the calculation of planetary orbits as *centrally relevant,* then the replacement of Newtonian theory by Hamilton-Jacobi theory is only *peripherally relevant.* On the other hand, if one regards the centrally relevant issue as the appearance of a new concept of matter (that is, waves or fields instead of particles) then the Hamilton-Jacobi theory is, in principle at least, a "germ" of a radically different approach to the subject as a whole, while the agreement of the two methods in a certain limited context of calculating planetary orbits is only a secondary feature, of peripheral relevance. Which of these relevance judgments is adopted may depend, to a considerable extent, on accidental and fortuitous preferences of the people concerned. Thus, it may happen that one individual (or a few individuals) make a certain relevance judgment of this kind and that other physicists, influenced by this individual (or individuals), accept this judgment without deeply understanding what is behind it. What is needed is a widespread understanding of the important role of such relevance judgments. This will make it possible for each physicist to judge for himself whether he can accept the relevance judgments of other physicists. As a result, it will be possible to arrive at a genuine public understanding of the subject, rather than at a situation in which most physicists accept the "private" judgments of a few leaders in the field because they do not feel competent to question such judgments deeply.

Rather than go into the "malaria example" in further detail, let me try to say in a few words what I had in mind. This can perhaps be brought out by noting that the root of the word "health" is the Anglo-Saxon "hale," meaning "whole." Thus, when a doctor "heals" a patient, he is "making him whole." The essence of medical science is therefore determined by whatever is meant by the current notion of "health" or "wholeness." Different notions of "wholeness" imply correspondingly different forms of medicine, with different judgments as to what is centrally relevant, different methodologies, methods of testing and application, and so forth.

In ancient times, there was a general notion that things that are similar or analogical are aspects or indications of universally pervasive forces, that are "wholes." Such a way of thinking was common not only to medicine, but also to physics, astrology, alchemy, magic, and so on. In more modern times, this approach was largely dropped and replaced by mechanical notions of "wholeness." That is to say, central relevance was given to analysis of a system into parts, while "wholeness" was understood in terms of phrases such as "the whole is the sum of its parts" (when the parts do not interact) or, "the whole is more than the sum of its parts" (when the parts interact and give rise to "collective properties"). In such an approach, the analysis into parts is always of crucial significance, whereas in the older view, what are now called "parts" were not viewed as such, but rather as "indications or manifestations of an unseen but all-pervasive force, which is not analyzable into parts."

The modern analytical view of "wholeness" spread into every aspect of human knowledge. In physics, it appeared in the notion that matter could be reduced to its atomic constituents, while in medicine and biology it appeared in the notion that particles such as cells, viruses, DNA molecules, and such, are of a correspondingly fundamental significance. More recently, however, this mechanical approach to "wholeness" has been questioned in science. Thus, in medicine, it has been noted that a disharmonious way of life favors disharmony of every kind. For example, one may consider the notion that, ultimately, there is no real division between the social disharmony that leads to war and the destruction and pollution of natural resources and the disharmony that leads to susceptibility to infection, cancerous growths, and psychological disturbances. Similarly, in physics, Einstein suggested a "unified field theory" which implied that there is no division or separation between various aspects of the universe (that is, they all merge as aspects of a single unified field). Bohr suggested that the form of the experimental conditions and the content of the experimental results are also a "whole," in which analysis into parts is not relevant.

In many cases, what are judged to be "small" changes in a theory (for example, "small" with regard to immediate experimental content) may be "germs" of radical changes in the general notion of "wholeness" along lines such as those indicated above. Basically, the nature of civilization is characterized by its approach to "wholeness" and this will come out in countless ways, among which are subtle but crucially important changes in the forms of scientific theories.

Finally, let me say that Dr. Bub overemphasizes the similarity of my views on the quantum theory to those of Bohr. Actually, my views differ in many very important ways from Bohr's. However, in the talk, it was my intention to try to give Bohr's views as clearly as possible in order to indicate certain aspects of modern scientific development. My own view is that I want to see a movement in physics which embodies Bohr's insights, but breaks away from his static adherence to classical language as the basis of the description of the experimental situation. This view will be further developed in later publications.

SESSION V

Hilary Putnam's 'Scientific Explanation'

An Editorial Summary-Abstract

Editor's note: As presented at the symposium Professor Putnam's paper was not in a form which could be published here. He has changed his views on a number of the issues he discussed, and when he sat down to prepare his paper for publication he found that he could not produce a version which satisfied him, for such a version would have to argue a position he no longer fully agreed with. This posed a problem, since without his paper the discussion of it during Session V could not intelligibly be included in this volume; also Professor van Fraassen's extremely fine commentary would have to be omitted. Since both the commentary and the discussion deserve publication here, I posed the problem to Professor Putnam and suggested that the difficulty could be assuaged by including an editor's summary-abstract of what he presented at the symposium. Professor Putnam very kindly agreed to the suggestion. What follows is the *editor's* summary-abstract of what Professor Putnam presented at the symposium. Although I have tried to make this summary-abstract as accurate an account as possible of what Professor Putnam presented, there is the possibility that I may have inadvertently distorted his views at places. As a check against this I urge the reader to consult Putnam [1971] which considerably overlaps what Professor Putnam presented. To further minimize the possibility of such distortions creeping in, I have tried to confine the summary-abstract to a coherent presentation of those points which came up for consideration in Professor van Fraassen's commentary or in discussion.

The standard "inductivist" account of the confirmation of theories is as follows: Theories imply predictions which are basic sentences or observation sentences; if any of these predictions are false, the theory is falsified; if sufficiently many of these predictions are true, the theory is confirmed. Sir Karl Popper denies that theories can be confirmed, but he does maintain that they can be falsified; the process of falsification is the deduction of predictions from the theory which are false. He does allow, however, that the testing of theories can *corroborate* them—by which he means that a theory has been subjected to severe tests and has withstood them.[1] Despite their differences both the standard "inductivist" account of confirmation and Popper's falsifiability analysis share the same common doctrine: basic sentences or predictions are *deducible* from theories. Both schemes say: Look at the predictions a theory implies and see if they are true. It is the purpose of this paper to challenge this deductive link. Its central claim is that in a great many important cases, scientific theories do not imply predictions at all. The paper also illustrates the significance of this fact for the philosophy of science by showing how it supports and enables one to improve on Kuhn's thesis that the activity of normal science is "puzzle solving."

I

A consideration of Newton's *theory of universal gravitation (UG)* illustrates the claim that predictions are not always deducible from theories. The theory *UG* consists of Newton's three laws together with the following law:

> Every body a exerts on every other body b a force F_{ab} whose direction is toward a and whose magnitude is $g \cdot (M_a M_b / d^2)$, where g is a universal constant, M_a and M_b are the respective masses of a and b, and d is the distance between a and b.[2]

Since the theory says nothing about what forces other than gravitation may be present, any motions whatsoever are compatible with the theory. And as the forces F_{ab} are not themselves directly measurable, not a single *prediction* is deducible from the theory.

In order to obtain predictions from *UG* it needs to be augmented by further assumptions. For example, to obtain Kepler's laws as predictions we might employ the following simplifying assumptions:

(1) No bodies exist except the Sun and the Earth.
(2) The Sun and the Earth exist in a hard vacuum.
(3) The Sun and the Earth are subject to no forces except mutually induced gravitational forces.

Notice that the prediction of Kepler's law cannot be deduced from *UG* alone; they are obtained only by deducing them from the conjunction

[1] For arguments that Popper's doctrine commits him, *contre lui*, to a theory at induction, see Putnam [1971], Secs. 1–3. Popper's doctrines are found in Popper [1959].

[2] The choice of this theory is not essential to the case; any of a number of other theories could have been used.

of *UG* and the above three *auxiliary statements (AS)*; of course other auxiliary statements could have been used. The *AS* are not part of the theory, as the following considerations show. As scientists actually employ the term 'theory', (1) to (3) are not part of the theory of universal gravitation. As the term 'theory' actually is used, theories are sets of laws; and (1) to (3) are not laws. Moreover, theories are supposed to be true by the nature of things, but none of (1) to (3) have this character. Indeed. they are known to be false. To construe the *AS* as part of the theory is to blur the distinction between the laws the scientist wishes to establish as true and the statements he already knows to be false.

The following features of *AS* should be noted. Although (1) to (3) could have been worded so as not to be known false, in practice they are not. Indeed, a striking difference between *AS* and theories is that scientists state theories with great care whereas they introduce *AS* quite carelessly. The *AS* also are far more subject to revision than theories. For over 200 years *UG* was accepted as unquestionably true. And if the standard *AS* had not resulted in successful predictions in that period, they would have been modified—not the theory. For example, when predictions about the orbit of Uranus made on the basis of *UG* turned out to be wrong, the theory *UG* was not questioned. Rather the *AS* to the effect that all the known planets were there was rejected, and Adams and Leverrier predicted there must be another planet; that auxiliary assumption (or *AS*) enabled correct predictions to be made. And if it had not, other *AS* would have been attempted until something worked. One might object here that the success of the new *AS* depended crucially on the discovery of the new planet, Neptune, and without that discovery the new *AS* could not have been maintained. This is not so. One often maintains *AS* in the absence of any observational support for them. For example, in astronomy one often explains the irregular behavior of stars by postulating companion stars, and when these companions cannot be seen through a telescope, one postulates *dark companions* which cannot be seen.

Thus, theories such as *UG* lead to predictions only when augmented by *AS* which are not part of the theory. These *AS* are far more subject to revision than theories. Indeed, if the theory is accepted as a paradigm and no better alternative theory exists, the theory will be maintained even if there are known phenomena for which no *AS* that have been tried lead to successful predictions. For example, the orbit of Mercury is not quite successfully explained by Newton's theory. In the presence of an alternative theory, such as general theory of relativity, it shows the theory wrong; but in the absence of such an alternative, Mercury's irregular behavior is just a slight anomaly for which we have not yet discovered the cause. The point here is that, given the fact that *UG* has had overwhelming success in virtually all cases, given that the *AS* may be false and probably are false as stated, it is more *likely* that the *AS* are false than that the theory is—at least when no serious alternative theory has been advanced.

So far it has been argued that (a) theories do not imply predictions; only the conjunction of a theory with certain *AS* does that; (*b*) the *AS* frequently are highly risky, being assumptions about boundary conditions or initial conditions; and (c) since we are very unsure about the *AS*, we cannot regard a false prediction as definitively falsifying a theory. Thus theories such as *UG* are not falsifiable by deriving predictions from it. The standard "inductivist" account of confirmation and Popper's falsifiability doctrine thus are wrong.[3] For over 200 years scientists did not derive predictions from *UG* in order to falsify it; rather they devised predictions from *UG* to explain astronomical facts, and when their attempts failed (as in the case of Mercury) the facts were put aside as anomalies.

These conclusions do not deny that scientists sometimes derive predictions from theories and *AS* in order to test the theories. If Newton had not been able to derive Kepler's laws from *UG* he would not have put forward *UG*. Even if his predictions had been way off and "knocked out" the theory, their falsity could have been due to the *AS* being false, and upon the discovery that the *AS* were false at a later date, *UG* could then be reinstated. Falsification thus is not conclusive.

II

It has been shown that theories such as *UG* can be employed in different ways in dealing with scientific problems—for example, to yield predictions and to explain facts. Consider the following three schemata for employing theories to deal with scientific problems:

Schema I	Theory
	Auxiliary Statements
	Prediction—True or False?

[3] These arguments only show the falsifiability and prediction portions of the standard "inductivist" account wrong; it does not show that they are wrong in claiming that scientists try to confirm theories *and AS* by deriving predictions from them and verifying the predictions.

Schema II	Theory
	????????????
	Fact to be explained
Schema III	Theory
	Auxiliary Statements
	????????????

Schema I, which is emphasized by standard philosophy of science, applies to the type of problem where we have some *AS*, we have derived a prediction, and the problem is to see if the prediction is true or false. Schema II applies to the case where we have a fact to be explained, the *AS* are missing, and the problem is to find *AS* which are true or approximately true which can be conjoined to the theory to obtain an explanation of the fact. This schema embodies the kind of reasoning which, according to the argument of the previous section, was typical of the use of *UG* in the 200 years following Newton. Schema III applies to cases where we have a theory and some *AS*, and the problem is to find out what consequences we can derive. The problems fitting Schema III are not always trivial, for knowing what the testable consequences of a theory are often is extremely difficult—for example, the mathematical difficulties in deriving consequences from Einstein's "unified field theory" are such that very little is known today of its physical consequences.

An illustration of the use of these schemata is in order. Recall the problem of explaining Uranus's orbit prior to the discovery of Neptune. The problem there was that *UG* augmented by the *AS*

> S_1: Bodies are moving in a hard vacuum, subject only to mutual gravitational forces, and so on; and the solar system consists of at least Mercury, Venus, Earth, Mars, Jupiter, Saturn, and Uranus.

could not predict accurately the orbit of Uranus. The problem, then, was a Schema II problem:

Theory:	*UG*
AS:	S_1
Further *AS*:	????
Explanadum:	The orbit of Uranus.

The problem here is not to find further explanatory laws (though it could be under Schema II), but rather to find additional assumptions about the initial and boundary conditions governing the solar system which will, together with *UG* and S_1, enable the explanation of Uranus's orbit. Since approximately true *AS* are allowed, any number of *AS* could solve the problem (the solution to the problem is underdetermined); but first one tries the simplest assumption.

S_2: There is one and only one planet in the solar system in addition to those mentioned in S_1, and all the planets in the solar system are subject only to mutual gravitational forces.

This then leaves us with the following Schema III problem:

Theory: *UG*
AS: S_1, S_2

Consequence ?

The solution to this turns out to be an orbit *O*. This leaves us with the following Schema I problem:

Theory: *UG*
AS: S_1, S_2

Prediction: A planet exists moving
in orbit *O*—true or false?

If the solution to this problem turns out to be that the prediction is true, then the prediction is precisely the statement S_3 we need to solve our original problem; we thus get the following deduction as the solution:

Theory: *UG*
AS: S_1, S_2, S_3

Explanadum: The orbit of Uranus.

III

The standard view in the philosophy of science construes scientific activity as being done in accordance with Schema I. Recently a number of philosophers, including Thomas Kuhn, have put forward a new view of scientific activity.[4] Although Kuhn commits errors, the tendency he represents is a needed corrective to the deductivism of standard philosophy of science and of Popper.

[4] This view was anticipated in Hanson [1958a], and in Putnam [1962a] where it was suggested that some scientific theories cannot be overthrown by experiments and observations alone; the view reaches its sharpest expression in Kuhn [1962] and the writings of Louis Althusser.

Central to Kuhn's account is the notion of a *paradigm*. Although he has been legitimately criticized for inconsistencies and unclarities in his use of the notion, at least one of his explanations of the notion is suitable for his purpose. A paradigm is a scientific theory together with an example of a successful and *striking* application. That it be striking is essential, and means that the success is sufficiently impressive that scientists are led to try to emulate that success by seeking further explanations, predictions, and so on, on the same model. *UG* together with the derivation of Kepler's laws and the derivation, say, of one or two planetary orbits was such a paradigm. The more important paradigms generate scientific fields—as the *UG* paradigm generates the field of celestial mechanics. According to Kuhn, paradigms that structure a field are highly immune to falsification and can be overthrown only by a new paradigm. This probably is an exaggeration, but it is true that in the absence of drastic and unprecedented change in the world and in the absence of it turning out that the paradigmatic successes were phoney (for example, the data were faked), a theory which is not paradigmatic is not given up because of observational and experimental results by themselves, but only because and when a better theory is available. Once a paradigm has been set up and a scientific field has developed around it, an interval occurs which Kuhn calls "normal science." Kuhn describes the activity of scientists during a normal science interval as "puzzle solving." Such a period terminates with the introduction of a new paradigm which manages to supersede the old one. Kuhn's account of how one paradigm is replaced by another ("scientific revolutions") is controversial and is overly subjectivist and relativistic as well as being tied to a number of incorrect doctrines about meaning and truth. But a discussion of this part of Kuhn's analysis is not the subject of this paper; the concern here is with normal science and its "puzzle-solving" character.

Kuhn's characterization of "normal science" as "puzzle solving" is intended to convey the idea that normal science is neither an activity of trying to falsify one's paradigm nor an activity of trying to confirm it; rather it is something else. It is the contention of this paper that Schema II exhibits the logical form of what Kuhn calls a "puzzle," and that the kind of solution to Schema II problems illustrated in the preceding section for the problem of explaining Uranus's orbit is typical of the "puzzle solving" activity of normal science. This illustrates why Kuhn's term "puzzle" is appropriate; one is looking for an *AS* to plug a hole, and that is a kind of puzzle.

The realization that Schema II is the logical form of the "puzzles" of normal science explains a number of facts. The whole problem of solving a Schema II type of problem is to find the *AS* which will explain the fact; there is no question of deriving a prediction from *UG* plus given *AS*. As such the theory is not up for confirmation or falsification in the context; it is not functioning in a hypothetical role and so is unfalsifiable in the context. Failures are not false predictions but rather the failure to find *AS*; as such, failures do not falsify the theory. Indeed, during normal science paradigmatic theories are highly immune from falsification; their tenures as paradigms end only with the appearance of a better theory on the science. And they are not confirmed, either, during that tenure because they are not hypotheses in the need of confirmation; rather, during their tenure as paradigms they are the basis of a whole explanatory and predictive technique, and possibly even a technology. That is, the "puzzles" of normal science exhibit the pattern of Schema II; in such cases the theory is taken as fixed, and one seeks further facts which are not physically necessary that enable us to fill out the explanations of particular facts on the basis of the theory.

Not everything going on in normal science between the introduction of a paradigm and its eventual replacement is described by Schema II. Normal science exhibits a dialectic between the desire to solve Schema II problems, such as explaining the orbit of Uranus, and the testing of new hypotheses. In the example given in the previous section, there was a dialectic between the discovery of S_2 and the testing of it by deriving S_3 from it and testing S_3. The tendency to test hypotheses is the *critical* tendency, and is represented by Schema I; the tendency to explain facts is the *explanatory* tendency, and is represented by Schema II. The two tendencies are in conflict because in a Schema II situation one tends to regard the given theory as *known*, whereas in the Schema I situation one tends to regard the theory as *problematic*. But the two tendencies are interdependent, as the example from the previous section shows, and the conflict or tension between the attitudes of explanation and criticism is what drives science to progress.

IV

The above account stresses the way in which a theory may be immune from falsification. Popper, on the other hand, views falsifiability as the sine qua non of a scientific theory; as might be expected, Popper has an answer to the view just presented. He recognizes that "auxiliary hypotheses" may be required in the derivation of predictions, but he regards these as part of the total "system" under test. As such the attempt to save a theory from a contrary experimental result by making an ad hoc change in the auxiliary hypotheses is, for Popper, an illegitimate "conventionalist stratagem."

That Popper's account is not satisfactory as a reply to the Kuhnian view can be seen by the following considerations: First, in the case of *UG* the auxiliary hypotheses *AS* are not fixed, but depend on context. *UG* simply is not a part of a fixed "system" whose other part is a fixed set of auxiliary hypotheses whose function is to render *UG* highly testable. Second, it is possible to make ad hoc alterations in one's beliefs without being unreasonable. In the example of dark companions to stars mentioned above, the assumption that stars have dark companions is ad hoc in the literal sense (meaning "to this specific purpose")—the assumption being made for the purpose of accounting for the fact that no companion is visible. The assumption is also highly reasonable. In cases such as that of *UG*, the *AS* are not only context-dependent but highly uncertain, and in such cases changing them or even admitting in a context that we do not know what the right *AS* are may be ad hoc in the literal sense, but it is not ad hoc in the extended sense of being unreasonable.

Popper's view that a theory becomes corroborated by passing severe tests, which consist in deriving predictions from the theory whose truth is unknown and then experimentally determining their truth or falsity, presents an equally unsuccessful challenge to the account proposed here. This can be seen by considering how *UG* came to be accepted. Newton first derived Kepler's laws from *UG* and the *AS* (1) to (3); this was not a test in Popper's sense as Kepler's laws were already known to be true. Newton also showed that *UG* could account for the tides on the basis of the gravitational pull of the moon and that *UG* could accommodate small perturbations in the orbits of planets; for the same reason, these were not "tests" in Popper's sense. By this time the whole civilized world has accepted —and indeed acclaimed—*UG*; but it had not been "corroborated" at all in Popper's sense. In fact it was not until the Cavendish experiment—roughly a hundred years after *UG* had been introduced—that *UG* underwent a Popperian "test" involving the derivation of a new prediction which was risky relative to background knowledge.[5]

[5] *Editor's note*: Although the claim made in this sentence occurs in the manuscript from which Professor van Fraassen prepared his commentary, the evidence available to me strongly suggests that it was not a part of Professor Putnam's

The point here is that a theory should not be accepted unless it has real explanatory success, and these successes must not be ad hoc. Popper tries to rule out ad hoc "successes" by requiring that the predictions not be known true antecedently; the consideration of *UG* indicates his condition is too strong. The Popperian position thus fails to contravene the account of scientific reasoning advocated in the previous sections of this paper.

---

presentation at the symposium, apparently having been deleted sometime previously. Accordingly, there is some question whether it should be included in this summary-abstract. I have decided to include it here, with appropriate reservations about doing so, since it does figure somewhat centrally in Professor van Fraassen's commentary.

Putnam on the Corroboration of Theories[1]

BAS C. VAN FRAASSEN

Professor Putnam has challenged a number of familiar tenets concerning scientific theories—tenets characterizing what he calls the *positivistic* philosophy of science. He challenges the view that theories are tested by their predictions, that they are accepted because they survive these tests better than their rivals, denies that in periods of "normal" science the paradigm is still implicitly being tested in this manner, and denies that a paradigm is discarded because what it predicts turns out not to be so. (All this is qualified in some ways, but at least the central importance given to these theses by the positivists is denied.) In much of this I think that he is right, but I also think that in one respect he has overstated his case, and that in another respect he does not go far enough.

Happily Professor Putnam acknowledges that his claims should be tested against history, and he chooses Newton's theory of gravitation as the touching stone. With the right auxiliary hypotheses, this theory explained all manner of known phenomena. Putnam claims that this is what led to its acceptance as a paradigm. He claims that Newton spent his years explaining known facts concerning tides, planetary orbits, and such. "By this time [1700] the whole civilized world had accepted [the theory]; but it had not been 'corroborated' at all in Popper's sense!" (p. 432). No such test was, he claims, performed till the Cavendish experiments of 1781 roughly a hundred years after the theory's introduction. And the theory was not the survivor among rivals of predictive testing.

Now these claims seem to me historically false. Newton's theories did have a great rival, namely the Cartesian theories. And on the Continent, especially in France, Newton's theories were not accepted and acclaimed by the time to which Putnam refers. Perhaps Professor

1 The author wishes to thank the historians of science at Indiana University for their gracious guidance, and NSF grant GS-1566 for financial support.

Putnam is not including France in the civilized world, a not uncommon failing in Anglo-Saxon philosophers. Newton derived from his theory that the earth was flattened at the poles, *oblate in figure,* and used his theory of gravitation to deduce an ellipticity of 1-230th. The Cartesians however deduced from their theory that the earth was not oblate but oblong. In 1701, Dominic Cassini measured 7 degrees of latitude from Amiens to Perpignon and confirmed the Cartesian theory. The Newtonians objected that the measured part was too small to count as a test. The French rose gallantly to this challenge and in 1733 sent out scientific expeditions to Peru and Lapland, and also repeated Cassini's measurements, at national expense. This time all three efforts clearly confirmed the Newtonian predictions.

This seems to me to refute at once the claims that the theory was accepted before its predictions had been tested, and that it was not the survivor of several rival theories subjected to the same tests. In addition, Newton himself reports experiments testing the underlying mechanics, for example, in the Scholium to Section VI of Book II of the *Principia.* And third, the period of normal science in the century following the *Principia* has as its most famous accomplishments examples of predictions tested and confirmed. The experiments by Cavendish mentioned by Professor Putnam were in this period, and certainly tested predictions. Halley hypothesized that a certain comet traveling in an elliptical orbit about the sun would reach its perihelion in 1758 or 1759, and posed the problem of calculating the gravitational effect of the planets on this comet. This was done by Clairault who predicted that the comet would reach its perihelion on April 13, 1759, give or take a month—and it did, on March 13, 1759. Finally, the Newtonian work on Lunar theory, which begins in the *Principia,* was not a matter of puzzle-solving and academic attempts at explaining known phenomena. Lunar tables were needed to *predict* positions of the moon, so that navigators would be able to use these to calculate their longitude. The extant tables were very inaccurate in these predictions, and the Dutch and English governments announced substantial prizes for their improvement. Finally, the Michelson-Morley experiment, instrumental in the downfall of the old paradigm, is clearly a case of predictive testing going wrong.

Against this, Putnam would surely argue that in the absence of a better theory, classical physics would have survived Michelson and Morley. As certainly it would, for Lorentz's theories clearly account for it, and not in what I would call an ad hoc manner. But if the old theory saves the phenomena so well, and so strikingly well as in this case, how can Professor Putnam possibly hold that all that is needed to establish a new theory as a new paradigm is that it allow us to save the phenomena?

I use the terminology "save the phenomena" with all due respect. When Putnam replaces Schema I by Schema II, in the role of the most basic feature of normal scientific progress, he is arguing that not *predictive testing*, but *saving the phenomena* is the typical mode of normal scientific advance. And there seems to me to be a great deal in that: much scientific work seems to be correctly characterized by Putnam's Schema II. But Schema I seems to me more important for just the purposes held dear by the positivists. And also, equally unimportant —which brings me to my second difference with Professor Putnam. What Schemas I, II, and III have in common is that to provide an instance, the scientist has only to show a deductive link between *ingeniously* chosen components. This, I think, is Putnam's heritage from the tradition he attacks. In the usual, facile, positivistic manner, he draws a sharp distinction between structure of theories and the methodology of scientific inquiry. He makes the familiar assumption that we can have a worthwhile discussion of scientific theories without exploring the internal structure of the theories, without attention to their world picture, indeed, without characterizing scientific theories in any way except as theories, theories *überhaupt*. The explanatory power of theories is, within the positivistic tradition, localized entirely in the deductive link to their consequences. This debt can only be obscured by Putnam's insistence that scientific theories have no observational consequences. For this only amounts, for him, to a shift of emphasis to hypothetical consequences ($AS \rightarrow O$) which the theory does have. As commentator it is not my place to start elaborating alternatives to Professor Putnam's approach, but perhaps I am allowed to express my deep conviction that the fruitful approach for philosophy of science will consist in not remaining on this level of generality.

Discussion

Professor Putnam:

So van Fraassen, we meet again! On the first part of van Fraassen's criticisms, I think he is right. The history of science is rather putrid, and as the talk came closer and closer I became more aware of that myself. I think that perhaps I will become convinced after all that the history of science is irrelevant; it is the easiest way out. I gather from a quick talk with Professor Cohen that the fact that the orbits were not all known in Newton's day, although some of the perturbations were known, does not really help Popper because Popper would have to argue that that was essential—that is say, that we would have not been justified in accepting Newton's theory if, instead of calculating the orbits and looking through a telescope to see whether we were right, we had calculated the orbits then looked them up in a book to see if we were right. For that would be to say that in the second of these two cases corroboration would have been absent, and my own feeling is that this is wrong; it really makes no methodological difference with respect to the justification for accepting theories whether you have to look through a telescope or whether you use someone else's data. I agree, however, that it makes a lot of difference to the value of a theory as a tool for guiding various kinds of practice. I mean, if you already knew all the orbits and had them in a book then Newton's theory would not be useful as a tool for guiding practice until you got to the stage where you could really do something new; but I would still think that you would be justified in accepting the theory—at least I advanced that as a counter-Popper criticism. How central that is to Popper's account I do not know. He has always insisted that the prediction be new and that it not be risky relative to background knowledge. Of course what he wants to rule out is the case where the scientist knows that the thing is true and makes up the theory with malice of forethought so it will lead to just that prediction. He is quite right in saying if that is what went on then the fact that a theory implied that prediction probably does not confirm the theory; although, even then, if the theory turns out to be strikingly simple and it is very surprising that a theory that simple could explain such a large number of predictions, then I would again think that one might have an overwhelming reason for accepting the theory. So again it seems to me that in this respect I am more in agreement with standard philosophy of science than I am with Popper's account. Nevertheless, I do not want to minimize my historical failing here; it seems to be very bad. I think that you are right that, in fact of course, Newton's theory was used historically both to explain facts which were already known and to predict facts which were not already known. Its success in both kinds of contexts justified accepting it. Of course in the case where the fact was not already known, the conjunction of the theory with the standard kind of auxiliary hypotheses was running the risk of falsification. However, and against Popper's account of what falsification is, I would urge this is equally running a risk of falsification when you try to deduce a fact that is already in a book. Perhaps I am putting too much emphasis on that because Popper was my target. I think most philosophers of science would in fact say that the question whether the prediction at the bottom of Schema I is true or false could be checked either by making a new observation or by looking it up in a book. So if you understand Schema I more generously than Popper does (that is, if you understand the notion of prediction and of seeing whether a prediction is true or false in order to test a theory as encompassing both of the above possibilities), then in this widened sense I would agree that Schema I-type successes seem to me to be essential if a theory is to get off the ground at all. On the other hand, I would say that once we have had enough of those successes to take a theory as a paradigm, then we will in fact preserve the dark companions case, and so forth; we will preserve the theory in a variety of ways rather than give it up without any idea of what should replace it or what should be true rather than that. This is shown by the examples I cited, such as the one of Mercury; and there are many examples which could be cited concerning still unexplained secular variations in the case of the moon and Venus. In fact, one could give one other striking example. Let us suppose that an astronomical body wanders to the solar system with the trajectory shown on p. 439. Now I think it is quite clear that the trajectory of that wanderer is not successfully going to be predicted by *UG* (universal gravitational theory) plus the type of *AS* (auxiliary statements) I mentioned; and I think it is quite clear that in the face of the failure of Newton's theory to predict it, we would decide not that Newton's theory was falsified but rather that that object was under the influence of a lot of funny forces.

Now let me consider van Fraassen's second criticism which seems to me more important—namely, that I failed to go into the structure of theories, that that is where progress lies in the philosophy of science, and that it is essential to do since one cannot say anything interesting taking theories as unanalyzed wholes. First of all, I think I have gone partly into the structural properties of theories—I probably should say into the structural properties of a certain type of theory. The type of theory for which I am using the term 'theory' simpliciter in this paper is a theory that consists of a set of proposed or putative laws. That does not say a great deal, to be sure, but it already singles out a certain very special type of theory for consideration. It excludes, for example, theories about how a particular mountain got formed and theories some of whose statements are not laws. I agree that it will be desirable to say more about the structure of laws and that that is extremely important. I think it is important also to say more about heuristics for discovering laws—about the so-called problem of logic of discovery—in which I think real progress can be made and has not been made largely because people have thought that if you give some descriptions of how to go about trying to discover a scientific theory which are not an algorithm and so do not lead to an unique result, then you have done nothing. Perhaps that is an unfortunate legacy from Baconianism. Bacon pretended to have set forth a logic of induction—which of course really does not work. But the fact that in almost every century or every generation since Bacon there has been some philosopher making fantastic claims about an inductive logic he has discovered has led to our failure to see that we are in the same boat today and probably will be in the same boat for a long time with respect to the problems of discovery and the problems of justification. So I certainly agree with Bas that we want to go deeper into a whole lot of things. But for my purposes here there is a principle of relevant precision—to discuss the issue of falsifiability and unrevisability—and for that it has seemed to me more fruitful to proceed in terms of examples rather than in terms of attempting to do some kind of taxonomy or some kind of analysis of the general structures of those examples. Contrary to what many people think, my view is that philosophy is not something related to logic, but rather is the most empirical of the sciences, and I think we are still making the outer approaches to the phenomena in the philosophy of science. I mean that we have got physics in an almost a priori state compared to philosophy, where we have got data with virtually no theories. So, given this view about philosophy, I feel some legitimacy in proceeding as I did.

Professor Cohen:

I would like to address a comment to Hilary Putnam, in relation to Schema I. If I am not mistaken, in Schema I we are presented with a theory and auxiliary statements and true or false predictions. These predictions are to be interpreted in two different ways, one of which we might term structural, and the other we might term something more sociological (or, at least, nonstructural). The sociological element arises because, while it is true that verifiable predictions are of paramount importance, especially for those scientists who approve of the form or basis of a theory, those very same predictions will not produce an acceptance of that theory by scientists who may be opposed to some aspect of the theory, for example, the use of "action-at-a-distance" or "vortices" or "aether." A typical example is provided by Christiaan Huygens, perhaps the greatest of the mathematical physical scientists in Newton's day. Huygens accepted the mathematics of Newton's *Principia*,[1] and even the results or applications or predictions; and yet he so abhorred the concept of action-at-a-distance that he could not accept the Newtonian theory of universal gravitation or attraction. This example shows that the reaction to a proposed theory, by even the greatest scientists, may not be limited to the degree of verifiability of predictions, but may reflect personal prejudices or predilections about the nature of science and of theories in general, all of which are nonstructural.

The correspondence of Christiaan Huygens shows another aspect of the Newtonian presentation in relation to the life of theories. At the end of Book II of the *Principia*, Newton had shown that the hypothesis of Cartesian vortices had to be cast out of physics. He was delighted

[1] Newton [1968].

to reject this hypothesis because of his general antipathy to all such hypotheses. But he went further than that, to show that this particular hypothesis led to a prediction which was grossly inconsistent with Kepler's laws, and thus (as he said) "the hypothesis of vortices is utterly irreconcilable with astronomical phenomena, and rather serves to perplex than explain the heavenly motions." As a result of Newton's demonstration, Huygens, who had hitherto believed in a kind of Cartesian vortex, was convinced that he could do so no longer. Huygens thus accepted this Newtonian result, even though he rejected its basis in action-at-a-distance or attraction. Convinced by Newton's conclusion that celestial physics could not be based on Cartesian vortices, but unwilling to go along with Newton's doctrine of "attraction," he sought a new or modified basis of celestial physics which would simultaneously accommodate the Newtonian dynamics and his own standards of philosophy. This example may show that when one talks about Schema I, the situation is not quite so simple as was made out in the critique of Putnam's paper.

Furthermore, the question of the acceptance or rejection of the Newtonian theory cannot be understood unless due consideration be given to the use of a new mathematics, and of an extensive reliance on mathematics. This was an important factor which held back the spread of Newtonian physics. In France, one of the major reasons for not accepting the Newtonian philosophy of gravitation was the Cartesian bias, but no doubt there was also a natural reluctance to having to learn a certain amount of mathematics. We have a statement by Newton's friend and disciple, J. T. Desaguliers, to the effect that some people in France had said they would rather continue in their Cartesian error than have to learn enough mathematics to read Newton's *Principia.* I believe this to have been especially true for many French astronomers, although Clairault, a Frenchman, took the next major step in celestial mechanics after Newton, in developing the theory of perturbations. The mathematically minded scientists in France had to disassociate the concept of action-at-a-distance, which they could not accept, in part because of their Cartesian prejudice, from the splendid array of mathematical results which they esteemed. If you read the reviews of Newton's *Principia,* this point becomes clear.

What kind of really convincing evidence could Newton offer that would be sufficient to convince his contemporaries to learn more mathematics if necessary, and to accept his system which seemed based on a concept of action-at-a-distance? This question may give us an important point for our discussion. I think Newton's contemporaries were willing to go along with his presentation to the degree that he had demonstrated the kind of world system in which Kepler's laws are valid; he had also shown why Kepler's laws do not hold exactly in the real universe. Furthermore, he had shown the physical significance of each law, as—for instance—that the law of areas is a necessary and sufficient condition for a force to be directed toward a central point. Newton had shown how the tides could be predicted by invoking the very same principle he had applied to the motion of the moon, and so on.

Professor van Fraassen has told us about the important Newtonian predictions of the shape of the earth which, as he rightly pointed out, became a very, very crucial argument in the eighteenth century. But he neglected to call our attention to one aspect of this prediction which was considered to be stupendous by those scientists who could understand it, and which was a very important argument for the Newtonian theory. Newton had not merely predicted the shape of the earth as a derived result from his general theory, that a spinning body tends to flatten at the poles and bulge at the equator. Rather, he had shown that a consequence of this particular shape, an oblate spheriod of given proportions, would be—according to his system of celestial mechanics—an annual precession in the very amount that occurs in the world of observation. The result of a bulge would be that the moon would exert a different force of gravitational attraction on the near bulge and the far bulge, thus exerting a pull that would tend to alter the inclination of the earth's axis to the plane of its orbit, thereby producing precession. The facts of precession had been known for centuries, but the general cause of the phenomenon and the reason for its particular numerical value had been a mystery until Newton's *Principia*. It was certainly a spectacular result of Newtonian physics to be able to predict the phenomenon of precession, and its quantitative value! In this case, we can see how it may be of as much significance to predict something already known, like precession, as to predict something not yet known which then may be found.

Professor Putnam:

I agree with all of Professor Cohen's remarks. I hope that my putting Schema I down did not give the impression that I think that Schema I as it stands is a schema for confirmation any more than for falsification. Those of you who know my views know I do not for one minute believe that; nor do I think that very much progress has yet been made on just what is involved in verification. Popper's scheme is that you take the theory in what he calls a theoretical system (which includes the *AS*), then you derive the predictions and see whether they are true or false; and if they are false you know you are out and if they are true you are still in the game and you try again. The problem with this picture, of course, is that what happens in every one of the interesting cases is that you get some false predictions—you get some false predictions even after you take account of a theory of error. But in fact some false predictions do knock out a theory and some do not; and that fact is the main reason why all accounts to date of the verification of theories (whether they are accounts that take Bayes's theorem as the central idea or accounts that take eliminative induction as the central idea) are presently in deep trouble. I wish I had the solution to that; if I did, I would know where my Nobel prize in philosophy was coming from, if there was such a Nobel prize. So I agree that things like the metaphysics of the times—prejudices if you like—scientific ideas, general world views, and so on, certainly influence the acceptance or rejection of theories, and I certainly agree with the point Professor Cohen made with the precession example where predicting the already known precession was just as important a success of confirmation as predicting something that you had to look and see if it was true. And, indeed, that was one of the points that I was trying to make in my paper, and Professor Cohen's example is a very good one.

Professor Suppe:

My comments are addressed to Hilary Putnam and they relate to his reply to Bas's second point. While I think that Hilary's paper makes an important contribution to our understanding of theories, his reply to Bas's charge that he did not go enough into the structure of theories was that for what he was doing he did not have to. I am not at all sure this is true, and I would like to illustrate why by suggesting a possible line of argument against the claim. I am not sure whether the line of argument will work, but in any case it is one the answer to which, or the evaluation of which, may tell us something about the adequacy of Putnam's analysis. The reason that I do not find obviously correct the assumption that a scientific theory of the sort we are talking about basically is a bundle of laws is that there seem to be components of theories which do not obviously qualify as laws. That is, there clearly are laws in a theory, but it is not clear that everything one finds in a theory is either a lawlike statement or a putative law. For example, is it the case that Lorentz transformations in relativity theory are laws? They clearly are components of the theory, but it is not obvious to me that they have the status of being laws. Second, in theories such as the ideal gas laws, and in fact in most exact scientific theories, you have something like a physical system (for example, ideal gasses, systems of mass points, and so on), playing around in there. Now is a physical system a law? It is probably a component of a theory, or at least there probably is something about a theory that makes it a necessary part of an exact theory; but it is not clear to me that saying that a theory is a bundle of laws will accommodate that. Although I could not really argue for it at this point, I also suspect that every scientific theory—regardless of whether it is exact or not—has a taxonomy floating around (either implicitly or explicity) as an important defining component of the theory, and I fail to see how they can be construed as laws. And in something like classical particle mechanics, I would think the notion of a state is an absolute crucial structural feature of a theory, and it is not clear to me the extent to which this will show up in any characterization of theories that proceeds on the assumption that we are fundamentally talking about collections of laws when we talk about theories. If I am right in doubting that scientific theories are basically collections of laws, but rather are laws with a lot of other components like physical systems, taxonomies, states, transformation groups, and so on, then maybe the other components are where the deep structural properties lie; or at least their investigation may be crucial to understanding what the structure of theories is. Given these considerations it is not at all clear that theories can be reasonably construed as collections of laws. But, more immediately, this raises questions about the adequacy of your analysis of theories. In your analysis, Schema II purports to tell us how auxiliary hypotheses are used to relate theories to facts. If the sort of consideration I have just raised convinces one that theories are more than just laws, and if one also accepts your Schema II analysis, then it would follow that in applying the theory to facts, the auxiliary statements may ignore every component of the theory except the laws. But it is not clear that this is how the auxiliary statements do in fact operate. If they are statements of boundary conditions, it very well may be the case that they are used in conjunction with the laws to characterize the class of physical systems (or something like this). Or it may be that the theory is applied to phenomena or nature, or used to explain facts, by solving the general equations of motion to get a special version of it (or, as a special case, the characterization of some particular physical system), and the role of the auxiliary statements is to provide the boundary conditions needed for that solution. If such things happen, then the auxiliary statements are employed in conjunction with components of theories other than just laws. Furthermore, laws generally are about physical quantities which are not dependent upon frames-of-reference or measurement parameters, whereas the facts theories are applied to are about measured quantities which are dependent on frame-of-reference. And it would seem that one of the functions of auxiliary statements would be to mediate these differences and tie the two together. That is, in specifying the facts you generally assume fixed measurement parameters and use values which depend upon these, whereas the laws of the theory are about physical quantities which presumably are invariant under change of frame-of-reference. And the auxiliary statements are used to tie the physical quantities to the measured qualities, for example, by providing what is needed to obtain a special solution to the laws which is in terms of the appropriate frame-of-reference (for example, a phase space), or by converting the frame-of-reference dependent data into frame-of-reference invariant data (that is, physical quantities). So it may be that auxiliary statements often may be about phase spaces, frames-of-reference, transformation groups, and so forth, and not laws. But to understand these roles of auxiliary statements, theories need more structure than Schema II provides. That is, in applying the theory to phenomena or facts, the laws and the auxiliary statements are in there somewhere, but it is not clear that they show up in quite the way Schema II suggests, or that the laws (your theory) are that central to the operation of the auxiliary statements—as opposed to some associated mechanism such as physical systems, and so on. So my point, simply put, is that it is not obvious that your characterization of theories as a bundle of laws really is tenable, and if it is not it may influence the adequacy of the analysis that you have given of the relation between theories and auxiliary statements. That is, until we give theories more structure, we do not really have a hold on the auxiliary statements.

Professor Putnam:

I am not altogether clear as to the thrust of your criticism. When I say I want to think of theories or at least certain theories as groups of laws, that seems to be an important class of theories. Certainly in physics it is a very important class of theories. I do myself think of the statement that all physical laws of a theory are Lorentz invariant as itself a physical law. I am perfectly willing to go up several levels of language in order to state physical laws. I certainly think that physical laws can refer to Hilbert spaces or phase spaces, and so on. To say, however, that I think a theory is a set of laws is not to deny anything that you said—that a full account of any particular physical theory involves talking about what you called its taxonomy, talking about the new mathematical apparatus it may or may not have brought in, how different it is from older theories conceptually, and so forth. In Schema II, I want to emphasize that the solution to the puzzle may not be an auxiliary statement—it may be a new law, it may be a whole new theory, it may be a mixture of theories in boundary conditions. That is why I said in the paper that the nature of the solution is very underdetermined. If, for example, a theory you were given happened to be quantum mechanics without the Pauley exclusion principle and the explanadum was liquidity of water at ordinary temperatures, then part of the solution would be the Pauley exclusion principle; you might well know that.

Professor Achinstein:

Hilary, I would like to ask you whether you are really more of a positivist than you make out. I take it that Schema II, which contains the theory plus the question marks and the facts to be explained, is a deduction; and to explain the facts then is simply to deduce them from the theory and the auxiliary hypotheses that you are going to discover. This is what you call puzzle solving, but so far at least it seems compatible with the positivist's conception.

Professor Bromberger:

My question is to Hilary Putnam. I also like to invent my own history of science. In fact I go beyond you—I even like to invent my own science. And in the light of my fantasies I would like to make three points. One is about Schema II which is so central and which you present as characterizing what is involved in exhibiting the explanatory power of a theory. Now it seems to me first that there are counter examples to this (and you know my counter examples); but furthermore there is another objection to the claim that this kind of schema exhibits explanatory power, namely, the objection that it fails to account for the variety of things alluded to by talk about the explanatory power of a theory. This sort of schema does not enable one to distinguish when a theory explains *why* from when it explains *how*, from when it explains *precisely what are the causes* or *what are the circumstances responsible* for a phenomenon. Yet it seems that these sorts of explanations—or their absence—are not all always of equal importance when one seeks out, or when one tries to exhibit the explanatory power of a theory—in order for instance to determine whether it ought to be accepted or not. Now my second point: it seems to me that the topic of problem-solving potential (or ability) of a theory is somewhat more complicated in relevant ways than you suggest. The complexity arises from the fact that in some cases one can talk about a specific individuated problem which a particular theory enables one to solve, but in other cases one has to consider the *types* of problems, instances of which the theory helps one to solve. I think this is particularly true in the case of Newton, since Newton's theory is part of a whole mechanics, that is, a science that addresses itself to families of problems taken wholesale rather than one at a time. It is not just Newton's gravitational theory after all, but all of the things that go with it—its relevance and connection with the theory of projectiles, free-falling bodies, and so on. When one talks about the problems that such a theory solves, one very often must talk about or consider not merely individuated problems or a finite list of problems, but types of problem—that is, classes of problems which are specified by specifying types of data and types of questions to which solutions should be obtainable from the data. Yet your schemata take only individual problems as instances and convey nothing about problem types or the power to deal with them. The third point that I would like to make concerns your very good point that being ad hoc is not necessarily being unreasonable. I think that one can be a little bit clearer about the circumstances under which an ad hoc hypothesis or an ad hoc assumption (such as the invisible stars—the dark companion stars hypothesis) is reasonable. The circumstances are like the circumstances under which it is reasonable to continue to hold on to a theory in the face of counterevidence, that is, the absence of an alternative theory. I think, similarly, any hypothesis for which there is no evidence but to which no alternative is known is an ad hoc hypothesis that is nevertheless a reasonable hypothesis.

Professor Putnam:

In answer to Sylvain's questions, and also to Peter Achinstein's, I did not mean to suggest that I think that anything that satisfied the form of Schema II taken simply as a deductive form is an explanation. I did not want to be guilty of Hempelianism, and I thought that what I wrote avoided that. It crossed my mind that someone might misunderstand me in that way, but I hoped they would not. What I say is that in the second type of problem we have a theory, we have a fact to be explained, that the *AS* are missing, and that the problem is to find a set of *AS*, if we can, which are true or approximately true that have to be conjoined to the theory to get an explanation of the fact. That is to say that what is being searched for in Schema II is not a deduction but an explanation—whatever that is. It may be that the problem-solving power of a theory cannot be adequately measured by just the amount of previously known facts that it is able to explain—either by itself or in conjunction with further laws, boundary conditions, and so forth (the number of phenomena it is able to save in Bas van Fraassen's phraseology). But I certainly think that is one important aspect of its problem-solving power. I agree that further progress could be made—perhaps along lines you suggest, Sylvain—on saying when ad hoc is reasonable.

Professor Suppes:

I found very attractive your remarks a moment ago at the last of your reply to van Fraassen about the empirical nature of the philosophy of science. I think in your paper you properly take Popper to task at one point for not discussing the application of theories in any detail. It seems to me that what you have given us here very naturally suggests as a first step that we take it seriously empirically—to take it seriously not in the sense of examining a single case, universal gravitation, but to look at various disciplines. For example, we could look at the publications in science to see how well you can classify what is done actually by scientists under the headings of these schemes. Certainly I think that one would want to add to Schema I and Schema II a scheme in which we replace the theory by a question mark, and I do not think we necessarily have to be involved in the classification of that as normal or non-normal science. My own conjecture is that we would find that pretty normal if we looked at a lot of journals, normal in the sense of having high frequency. My question to you is: If we take seriously your remark about the philosophy of science being empirical would it be a meaningful empirical study for you to attempt to classify (for example, in physics or in chemistry or in economics, and so on) papers under the headings of these schemes? Are they meant to be taken seriously in the sense that published pieces of work and the activities of scientists that lie back of those published pieces of work could indeed be classified according to these schemes (perhaps augmented by some additional ones), even though there were difficulties around the edges and certain vaguenesses of classification?

Professor Putnam:

With respect to Pat Suppes's question of whether, in view of my idea that philosophy of science is empirical, I am therefore committed to the idea that you should be able to classify scientific papers along the lines of the schemata, let me say two things: When I say that philosophy of science is empirical what I mean is (to use a happy phrase of Dick Boyd's) that what we are looking for are regularities of methodological significance. That is, I think on the one hand we are looking for regularities in what scientists do because I think that is what we have. I do not think we have algorithms and I certainly do not think we have a priori truths—certainly not a priori truths of the form "You're irrational unless you do *x*"; but we are not looking for just any regularities. We are looking for regularities which we think are good regularities—which is of course where the peculiar exercise of philosophical judgment comes in. For example, I may observe, and Popper might agree, that scientists frequently save a theory by modifying the *AS*; and it is very likely that Popper will say in his reply to me that then insofar as they do that they are being bad scientists. And I would say, "No. Most of the time they are being good scientists." So this would be an example of a case in which we both agree that a regularity exists but disagree as to its methodological significance. Now I do think that in many but not all cases, a scientist can say which schema his work falls into. Whether it is evident just from his paper or whether you have to ask him, I do not know. A scientist often can say, "Here I started out with a problem explaining why *x*, where *x* is an already known fact; here I was trying to test such and such a theory; here I was trying to solve a mathematical problem," and so forth. I am not committed to the view that he always can say this or that anyone always can say it, but I think that it is quite clear to anyone who has done any empirical science that very often one could say which he was doing. I suppose one could actually use the classification, but how useful that would be empirically would be to go into the Suppes-Bromberger controversy over how much classification and statistics and so forth are useful in empirical science;[2] and I am going to keep my neck out of that one today in a cheap and cowardly way.

Professor Shapere:

My question (or rather questions) is addressed to Professor Putnam. It seems to me, Hilary, that you have oversimplified the situation both with regard to auxiliary statements and to theories and that in your oversimplification you have presented something of a distorted picture

[2] For the controversy, see Suppes's paper and the commentary on it in Session II above.

of the acceptance or rejection of theories. Let me first say something about auxiliary statements. There are a lot of different kinds of statements that you have locked together under this heading, and it seems to me that the different kinds and the different statuses of these statements might have a very important impact on what we will do when we have a choice between rejecting the auxiliary statements or rejecting a theory. For instance, the way you make it sound the theory is perfectly straightforward and it is clear why, once we have had a lot of predictive success, we do not reject the theory. On the other hand, you speak of the auxiliary statements in rather a derogatory way as 'simplifications.' They are uncertain; there are always lots of alternatives to them, so they may be wrong. In at least some of the later stages of normal science once we have decided on that particular theory as a paradigm we do not reject it unless there is an alternative theory. You say that these auxiliary hypotheses are uncertain: sometimes they are and sometimes they are not. Sometimes they can be, well to put it briefly, so certain that it will be more likely that the theory is wrong than that the auxiliary statement is wrong. Take another one of your claims: that there always are lots of alternatives. Well, take one of your own historical cases, the case of Leverrier, but not this time with regard to the peculiarities of the motion of Uranus but rather with respect to the peculiarities of the motion of Mercury. After his success with Uranus, Leverrier tried to take account of the motion of Mercury. Well, what happened? He tried all of the reasonable alternatives that might be tried—that there was a planet in there, that there were clouds of dust, and so on. Finally, after all of these auxilary statements did not seem to work out, he came to the conclusion that maybe the law of gravitation was wrong and that it would have to be modified. As a matter of fact, there is a long history of attempts to modify or of the feeling that the law of gravitation had to be modified or replaced. And this shows an oversimplification in your attitude toward the concept of the theory—namely, the way you have painted the picture, the theory is always fairly sure once it has had predictive successes; and you seem to imply that these predictive successes were clear-cut. But, of course, this is not the case. Newton and his successors did not have complete success with regard to all of the predictions that you attribute to him as being clear; there were very grave difficulties here that made the theory not quite as sure as you have painted it. And this finally brings me to the point! I think that there is an ambiguity in your statement that a theory will not be rejected until there is a better theory to replace it. I think it is ambiguous because there might be good reason to suspect or even in some cases to be pretty sure that a theory is wrong even though at the same time you will not reject it—in the sense that you will not use it any more—because it might be perfectly usable in a great many contexts. You may even know what contexts, so that in one sense you will have rejected a theory as false but not have rejected it as far as using it goes because you do not have an alternative theory. So you may very well know or strongly believe that the theory is incomplete or incorrect even though you have no alternative theory to replace it with.

Professor Hempel:

A brief remark by way of a footnote to Professor Shapere's comments. As you will recall, he took exception to Professor Putnam's characterization of auxiliary statements as being always vague, tentative, open to doubt, and indeed, often known to be false. As a consequence, when a prediction derived from a theory in conjunction with certain auxiliary statements turns out to be false, the theory need not be regarded as falsified. I think that in order to dramatize his opposition to Popper's falsificationism, Professor Putnam sounded sometimes almost as if he were a verificationist. But clearly, on his view of auxiliary statements, one could not speak of the predictive "successes" of a theory any more than of its predictive failures, for the truth of a prediction can count as marking a success of the theory only if the auxiliary statements used in deriving the prediction can with some confidence be regarded as true.

Professor Putnam:

Dudley Shapere's comment impressed me very much because, like Bas van Fraassen, he touched on some of my secret fears about this paper. Another respect in which philosophy is an empirical science is that everything you say is wrong, but if we say we are doing empirical science we do not have to be so ashamed about that; if we say what we are doing is logic then we are in trouble. Some of the things he said I think were misunderstandings, due partly to the way I wrote the paper and partly to the pace at which I read it. I certainly did not want to say that auxiliary statements could never be certain; I did not want to say in the definition of auxiliary statements that they are uncertain. I think what I said in the paper is that they frequently are statements of boundary conditions and frequently are very risky suppositions about boundary conditions. That is not to exclude the possibility that an auxiliary statement could be a law, and not to exclude the possibility that no matter what type of statement it is that it could be certain. I chose the term 'auxiliary statement' for the purpose of lumping together different kinds of statements. That is, I want to say that in the sense in which a physicist uses the term when he says 'Maxwell's theory,' 'the theory of gravitation,' or as other scientists use the term when they say 'Mendel's theory' or 'Darwin's theory,' I think it is not natural to take the auxiliary statements as part of those theories. And I want to say, therefore, that it seems to me methodologically important that the theory, in that sense, does not imply predictions in antecedent vocabulary, but rather to get them you have to join on other statements. In fact, I think that in the actual cases there is almost always at least one statement which is quite risky—at least risky until it has some predictive success, of course. To answer Hempel, I would say that of course it does not need to remain risky once you have found that you get correct predictions with respect to the orbits in a number of cases. You are confirming not only the law of universal gravitation, but also that electrical and more generally nongravitational forces can be neglected and that interplanetary space is pretty much a hard vacuum.

Now to come back to the things in Shapere's comments which I found troubling—particularly his criticism of my assertion that a theory can only be overcome by a better theory.[3] First of all, I do not believe I have ever said in my life that *no* theory can be overthrown save by a better theory; the closest I have come to making such a statement was about 1957 in "The Analytic and the Synthetic,"[4] where I made it with respect to geometry. I said there only that the account held for some theories. Yes, in that account I used the somewhat criticized idea of a paradigm to try to speciate a class of theories. I think there are mistakes in that idea, but I think there is also an important truth in it which I would still defend. To see that truth, let us take gravitation as an example (which I now think may not be the best example but is a partial example). Once you have found that the theory seems to be pretty exactly right in a fair range of situations, both small and large, there obviously is, say, a $1/r^2$ force at work. Then the mere experimental discovery that in some other situations you cannot find it is not going to lead you to say that the theory is false. Now I do think it is true that it will do something to the theory; it may lead you to say the theory *may* be false. And I think we have to distinguish between falsifying a theory and saying, "This theory *may* be false; we had better start looking for another theory." If the process of falsification could not be discontinuous in that way, then it becomes hard to account why people

[3] *Editor's note*: The remainder of this answer was given as part of a comment made by Professor Putnam in Session VII. In light of the fact that Putnam's comments there explicitly were a further reply to Shapere's comments above, it seemed preferable to interpolate them here.

[4] Putnam [1962a].

should start looking for a new paradigm. And I think this sort of weak falsification discovery—"Look, this theory may be false; we cannot account for these cases, so maybe we should start looking for a new theory"—perhaps may have something to do with that. So that is one correction that has to be made. Although I still want to maintain that my claims about the unrefutability of paradigm theories contain an important truth, I think that I overstated the case (partially on purpose) with respect to how unrefutable such theories are.

Professor Shapere:

I just want to say that it is very important that you overstated that case for the nonrejectability of theories because it is exactly that that makes you attribute great significance to the views of Tom Kuhn and your interpretation of them.

Professor Putnam:

You are getting worse and worse, you know. Whose side are you on? However, let me say two things: It seems to me now—or it had seemed, since actually I thought of this objection before you stated it—that there are two things that have to be said. First of all, different types of theories (and this is where going into the nature of theories is important) differ significantly in their degree of unfalsifiability. I think that with respect to geometry, which is the example I used in "The Analytic and the Synthetic," [5] that it is quite true that Euclidean geometry could not have been falsified by observations alone but it required the conceptual possibility of non-Euclidean geometry before one could falsify it. Today the status of the conservation of energy would seem to me an interesting paradigm for philosophy of science to consider with respect to just that question—whether observations alone could show today that energy or mass-energy is not conserved. I am actually skeptical. With respect to the theory of gravitation, I think probably that could have been falsified or at least restricted in scope by a number of negative results along the way. I think, however, that very often what can happen to a paradigm is not that it may be clearly falsified, but it may lose the status of a paradigm. That is to say that after some things go wrong we may not say, "Well, we know it is false," but rather we may say that we do not know for sure whether it is true and start looking for alternatives. And so I am inclined to introduce an intermediate notion between verification and falsification—namely, the intermediate notion of being dethroned or downgraded.

[5] Putnam [1962a].

Professor Kuhn:

This is really a remark to Hilary, though there is one aspect to which Bas may want to respond. After what has already been said I am left with very little, but I would like to associate myself with a few points that have been made and then add one other to them. May I say, Hilary, that I am basically in entire sympathy—and I ought to be—with what you are trying to do. But, I distrust your schemas for a lot of the reasons that have been put here, and particularly because, as I think Bas's commentary suggests and has already been pointed out by others, it is very hard to tell just where you would want to put any particular problem that actual people are working with. You leave yourself, for example, in a position which almost demands that the computations of the moon's motion to which Bas was referring go in Schema I. But what in fact happened with those computations? The fit was bad, but the problem was widely—though not everywhere—thought to be due to the approximations and the difficulties of the mathematics. Clairault did say, "Maybe we should conclude that gravity is not exactly an inverse-square law." But that was not followed up, and the mathematical approximations worked out better and things came back together. Where among your schemas does that go?

I would therefore say that if we are after a schema here, the best thing I can see at the moment is to say, "All right, let us write 'Theory' and put a question mark behind it," remembering that we are really not quite sure whether adjusting the inverse-square law a little bit would be a new theory or would be within the permissible flexibility of Newton's theory. Then, let us write 'auxiliary statements,' which are certainly also in this game, and put a question mark after them because we certainly have room for adjustment of the auxiliary statements in trying to bring things together. Are they new auxiliary statements or adjustments? Then draw your horizontal line and put a question mark at the end of it, because in the deductive and mathematical processes involved there are almost always approximations that have to be made so that the mathematics will not be unmanageable. So there again it is not clear when deduction involving approximation should count as rigorous with respect to the theory plus auxiliary statements and when not. And finally one needs a question mark after the "determined facts" which are not themselves always all easy to come by and which sometimes must be measured again a little bit more accurately. All of which leads me to say that the normal scientific game has varying "gives" at varying points, but basically is always an effort to bring all of these aspects of the schema at once as closely as possible into line. You may have to look in extraordinary detail at a particular historical case in order to decide whether the "give" has turned out to be at one of these levels or at another level. And that is found out by trying, not by the logic of the situation.

My reason for saying all this—which I realize does largely repeat what has already been said—is that there is one thing you do that I really disagree with, and the reason for my disagreement becomes clearer when I reformulate the schema in this way. It seems to me a great pity to attach the notion of puzzle-solving, as a characterization of normal science, to a particular one of these schemas. Clearly, if the problem in your Schema III is that the mathematics is difficult, then there is clearly also again a puzzle-solving enterprise. How do we get the solution? Or, in Schema II, if Newtonian theory is adjustable a little by slightly changing the inverse-square law, then adjusting the theory to find a deviation from the inverse-square which will take care of the moon's motion is again a puzzle to be solved in the sense indicated by drawing the question marks at the level of the auxiliary hypotheses. And so on for all the schemas.

I therefore do not think that the term 'puzzle' trivializes the enterprise of normal science, for what I had in mind in introducing it is a point common to all your schemas and one that I think that you are missing at the moment. Who is at fault if you do not succeed in bringing the elements of the schema together finally; if you have to give up? The general answer—to which Bas's case and others really fit very well—is that you decide, "I wasn't good enough to do it." That is the force of 'puzzle.' "I could not do the crossword puzzle. I am not bright enough, but when somebody brighter comes along he will be able to get it." Now, clearly, one does not always feel that way when things break down, but it is the first response in the normal scientific game. That is the central aspect of the term 'puzzle,' and I think the attempt to adapt the game to pick it out by distinguishing between Schema I and Schemas II and III does miss the point in important ways.

Professor Putnam:

With respect to Kuhn's remarks, I did have in mind precisely the thing that is the force of the term 'puzzle'—namely, that whereas in the standard schema the outcome is supposed to be that I was right or that I was wrong or, if you are the enemy of the scientist's theory that you are testing, that he was right or he was wrong, the outcome of the puzzle-solving is neither. I guess that is not where I (or we) am going to get my Nobel prize. And I have used precisely that example. I agree that Schema III is also an example of puzzle-solving. Both Schema II and Schema III have precisely that character. In case of failure you simply go away and try something else. Now I agree that there are probably other kinds of puzzles. Since I was bothered by the lack of examples in your writing, perhaps this is a step in the right direction. Now when I say that 'puzzle' is trivializing, what I meant was that the use of 'puzzle' falls into the general tradition of "We scientists are only playing intellectual games," a tradition that especially with the world situation the way it is and the world of science being what it is we might as well give up once and for all. Scientists are not solving puzzles; they are discovering laws of nature, trying to explain things, creating whole technologies, blowing us all up, and so forth; but they are not merely solving puzzles.

Professor Causey:

Basically I agree with Hilary on a great number of points, and I would like to make a couple of comments. I agree with the other questioners here, and particularly with Professor Kuhn, that these schemas may not be the easiest or most direct way to characterize puzzles—particularly not one particular schema. I sketched in Session IV what I thought was a moving-picture analogy to a theory which I think is in the spirit of what you are trying to do here in many ways. It does not go much further, but I think that rather than thinking in terms of schemas you might think of my monstrous myriapus and ask yourself just what are all the possible ways of fiddling around with these things which are enveloped, as Bohm would have it, in an interpretative language rather than an informal descriptive language. You have some ways represented by these schemas, and other people have suggested other ways just now; and I think that when you get a broader picture of what is going on you might be able to generate twenty-five schemas. I really do not know, but I think at least this might be a small beginning in this direction. And because of the complexity of the situation, I am extremely skeptical about attempts to characterize what a given scientist is trying to do at a given time—particularly if he is doing an experiment or working out some problem in theory. It is too easy to say that he is trying to make a prediction, that he is trying to explain, that he is trying to solve a puzzle, that he is just trying to gather data. He may be doing all of these things at the same time it seems to me. I still am extremely skeptical of the value of trying to speak of puzzle-solving in normal science because I think it may very well be, for instance, that a man goes out in the experimental laboratory and spends a whole lifetime doing a perfectly standard type of experiment; and relative to the kinds of things that are done in his lifetime, some of them might be more ingenious or original than others; but basically I think that all the time that the scientist is doing this he has a secret dream—particularly if he is an experimentalist—that he is somehow really going to discover something absolutely unexpected and, by luck and perhaps a little bit of ingenuity, very surprising. It reminds me of a little principle that the great biochemist Max Pobrook calls his principle of limited sloppiness. The principle of limited sloppiness says that when you are doing an experiment, you should be sloppy enough that something unexpected is likely to occur but not so sloppy that you cannot repeat it later on. And I think this certainly is the spirit of a great many of the better scientists, particularly the experimentalists. And I think there is an analogous kind of thing that the theoretician tries to do in inventing the theories, in inventing ingenious auxiliary statements, and deriving ingenious unexpected experimentally testable consequences. And even though I say this right after Professor Kuhn's remarks, I still think that simply to call this puzzle-solving is a kind of trivialization of what is going on.

Professor Buck [Moderator]:

We are just about out of time, so rather than entertain further questions, I will ask Professor van Fraassen if he would like to make any comments on the discussion.

Professor van Fraassen:

I just want to make two short comments on the remarks made here. First of all, about auxiliary statements I have just the same queasy feelings as some of you and I think that this must all sound very familiar to Professor Putnam from his protracted battle with Professor Grünbaum on similar things.[6] If the auxiliary statements really are so risky and so flexible, then the schema seems to lose its value. Roughly the situation seems to be this: There are these various planets going around in various orbits, and you have a theory and you want to know whether your theory is a good one so then you introduce some auxiliary hypotheses to the effect that there are no other forces operative and that the gravitational forces exerted, say, by asteroids and so on are negligible; and then, lo and behold, the consequences are in agreement with the observations. So after that you say the theory must be alright, and if anybody remembers the riskiness of your auxiliary hypotheses you say,

[6] See Grünbaum [1963a] and Putnam [1963].

"Well, that's all right, you see, because the picture that the theory gives us is such that these other factors are negligible so the auxiliary hypotheses are OK"—which reminds me of an observation that used to console me in my hungrier days that if we had bacon we could make bacon and eggs for breakfast if we had eggs. It does not seem to go to the point of confirming anything in that case, so I think really a lot of work would have to be done on the bounds of flexibility of the *AS*. Second, I think that Professor Cohen is exactly right about the basic motivations that are operative in the case of rival theories. They tend to be much in the direction of metaphysics. He talked of Cartesian prejudices about action-at-a-distance. (I would not use the word "prejudice"; I would say "philosophical sensibility" in this regard.) I do think that the explanatory power of the theory does not lie so much in the deductive consequences as in the fact that it gives us a certain picture whose coherence and articulateness yields understanding. I have exactly Professor Suppe's qualms about talking about such vague things in such vague terms; and I think the only good cash value would be a mathematical and a metamathematical approach to the formal structure of theories.

SESSION VI

Second Thoughts on Paradigms

Thomas S. Kuhn

It has now been several years since a book of mine, *The Structure of Scientific Revolutions,* was published. Reactions to it have been varied and occasionally strident, but the book continues to be widely read and much discussed. By and large I take great satisfaction from the interest it has aroused, including much of the criticism. One aspect of the response does, however, from time to time dismay me. Monitoring conversations, particularly among the book's enthusiasts, I have sometimes found it hard to believe that all parties to the discussion had been engaged with the same volume. Part of the reason for its success is, I regretfully conclude, that it can be too nearly all things to all people.

For that excessive plasticity, no aspect of the book is so much responsible as its introduction of the term 'paradigm,'[1] a word which figures more often than any other, excepting the grammatical particles, in its pages. Challenged to explain the absence of an index, I regularly point out that its most frequently consulted entry would be: "paradigm, 1-172, *passim.*" Critics, whether sympathetic or not, have been unanimous in underscoring the large number of different senses in which the term is used.[2] One commentator, who thought the matter

[1] Other problems and sources of misunderstanding are discussed in my essay, "Logic of Discovery or Psychology of Research," in I. Lakatos and A. Musgrave, eds., *Criticism and the Growth of Knowledge* (Cambridge: Cambridge University Press, 1970). That book, which also includes an extended "Response to Critics," constitutes the fourth volume of the proceedings of the International Colloquium in the Philosophy of Science held at Bedford College, London, during July, 1965. A briefer but more balanced discussion of critical reactions to *The Structure of Scientific Revolutions* (Chicago: University of Chicago Press, 1962) has been prepared for the Japanese translation of that book. An English version has been included in subsequent American printings. Parts of these papers carry on from where this one leaves off and thus clarify the relations of the ideas developed here to such notions as incommensurability and revolutions.

[2] The most thoughtful and thorough negative account of this problem is Dudley Shapere's "The Structure of Scientific Revolutions," *Philosophical Review,* Vol. 73 (1964), pp. 383–394.

worth systematic scrutiny, prepared a partial subject index and found at least twenty-two different usages, ranging from "a concrete scientific achievement" (p. 11) to a "characteristic set of beliefs and preconceptions" (p. 17), the latter including instrumental, theoretical, and metaphysical commitments together (pp. 39-42).[3] Though neither the compiler of that index nor I think the situation so desperate as those divergences suggest, clarification is obviously called for. Nor will clarification by itself suffice. Whatever their number, the usages of 'paradigm' in the book divide into two sets which require both different names and separate discussion. One sense of 'paradigm' is global, embracing all the shared commitments of a scientific group; the other isolates a particularly important sort of commitment and is thus a subset of the first. In what follows I shall try initially to disentangle them and then to scrutinize the one which I believe most urgently needs philosophical attention. However imperfectly I understood paradigms when I wrote the book, I still think them worth much attention.

I

In the book the term 'paradigm' enters in close proximity, both physical and logical, to the phrase 'scientific community' (pp. 10-11). A paradigm is what the members of a scientific community, and they alone, share. Conversely, it is their possession of a common paradigm that constitutes a scientific community of a group of otherwise disparate men. As empirical generalizations, both those statements can be defended. But in the book they function at least partly as definitions, and the result is a circularity with at least a few vicious consequences.[4] If the term 'paradigm' is to be successfully explicated, scientific communities must first be recognized as having an independent existence.

[3] Margaret Masterman, "The Nature of a Paradigm," in the volume cited in note 1, above. Parenthetical page references in the text are to my *The Structure of Scientific Revolutions.*

[4] The most damaging of these consequences grows out of my use of the term 'paradigm' when distinguishing an earlier from a later period in the development of an individual science. During what is called, in *Structure of Scientific Revolutions*, the "pre-paradigm period," the practitioners of a science are split into a number of competing schools, each claiming competence for the same subject matter but approaching it in quite different ways. This developmental stage is followed by a relatively rapid transition, usually in the aftermath of some notable scientific achievement, to a so-called "post-paradigm period" characterized by the disappearance of all or most schools, a change which permits far more powerful

In fact, the identification and study of scientific communities has recently emerged as a significant research subject among sociologists. Preliminary results, many of them still unpublished, suggest that the requisite empirical techniques are nontrivial, but some are already in hand, and others are sure to be developed.[5] Most practicing scientists respond at once to questions about their community affiliations, taking it for granted that responsibility for the various current specialties and research techniques is distributed among groups of at least roughly determinate membership. I shall therefore assume that more systematic means for their identification will be forthcoming, and content myself here with a brief articulation of an intuitive notion of community, one widely shared by scientists, sociologists, and a number of historians of science.

A scientific community consists, in this view, of the practitioners of a scientific specialty. Bound together by common elements in their education and apprenticeship, they see themselves and are seen by others as the men responsible for the pursuit of a set of shared goals, including the training of their successors. Such communities are characterized by the relative fullness of communication within the group and by the relative unanimity of the group's judgment in professional matters. To a remarkable extent the members of a given community will have absorbed the same literature and drawn similar lessons from it.[6] Because the attention of different communities is focused on different matters, professional communication across group lines is likely

---

professional behavior to the members of the remaining community. I still think that pattern both typical and important, but it can be discussed without reference to the first achievement of a paradigm. Whatever paradigms may be, they are possessed by any scientific community, including the schools of the so-called "preparadigm period." My failure to see that point clearly has helped make a paradigm seem a quasi-mystical entity or property which, like charisma, transforms those infected by it. There is a transformation, but it is not induced by the acquisition of a paradigm.

[5] W. O. Hagstrom, *The Scientific Community* (New York: Basic Books, 1965), Chs. IV and V; D. J. Price and D. de B. Beaver, "Collaboration in an Invisible College," *American Psychologist*, Vol. 21 (1966), pp. 1011–18; Diana Crane, "Social Structure in a Group of Scientists: A Test of the 'Invisible College' Hypothesis," *American Sociological Review*, Vol. 34 (1969), pp. 335–352; N. C. Mullins, "*Social* Networks among Biological Scientists," Harvard Ph.D. thesis, 1966, and "The Development of a Scientific Specialty," *Minerva*, Vol. 10 (1972), pp. 51–82.

[6] For the historian, to whom interview and questionnaire techniques are ordinarily unavailable, shared source materials often provide the most significant clues to community structure. That is one of the reasons why widely read works like Newton's *Principia* are, in *Structure of Scientific Revolutions*, so often referred to as paradigms. I should now describe them as particularly important sources of the elements in a community's disciplinary matrix.

to be arduous, often gives rise to misunderstanding, and may, if pursued, isolate significant disagreement.

Clearly, communities in this sense exist at numerous levels. Perhaps all natural scientists form a community. (We ought not, I think, allow the storm surrounding C. P. Snow to obscure those points about which he has said the obvious.) At an only slightly lower level, the main scientific professional groups provide examples of communities: physicists, chemists, astronomers, zoologists, and the like. For these major communities group membership is readily established, except at the fringes. Subject of highest degree, membership in professional societies and journals read are ordinarily more than sufficient. Similar techniques will also isolate the major subgroups: organic chemists and perhaps protein chemists among them, solid state and high energy physicists, radio astronomers, and so on. It is only at the next lower level that empirical difficulties emerge. How, prior to its public acclaim, would an outsider have isolated the phage group? For this, one must have recourse to attendance at summer institutes and special conferences, to preprint distribution lists, and above all to formal and informal communication networks, including the linkages among citations.[7] I take it that the job can and will be done, and that it will typically yield communities of perhaps 100 members, sometimes significantly fewer. Individual scientists, particularly the ablest, will belong to several such groups, either simultaneously or in succession. Though it is not yet clear just how far empirical analysis can take us, there is excellent reason to suppose that the scientific enterprise is distributed among and carried forward by communities of this sort.

II

Let me now suppose that we have, by whatever techniques, identified one such community. What shared elements account for the relatively unproblematic character of professional communication and for the relative unanimity of professional judgment? To this question *The Structure of Scientific Revolutions* licences the answer "a paradigm" or "a set of paradigms." That is one of the two main senses in which the term occurs in the book. For it I might now adopt the notation

[7] E. Garfield, *The Use of Citation Data in Writing the History of Science* (Philadelphia: Institute for Scientific Information, 1964); M. M. Kessler, "Comparison of the Results of Bibliographic Coupling and Analytic Subject Indexing," *American Documentation*, Vol. 16 (1965), pp. 223–233; D. J. Price, "Networks of Scientific Papers," *Science*, Vol. 149 (1965), pp. 510–515.

'paradigm$_1$', but less confusion will result if I instead replace it with the phrase 'disciplinary matrix.' 'Disciplinary' because it is the common possession of the practitioners of a professional discipline; 'matrix' because it is composed of ordered elements of various sorts, each requiring further specification. Constituents of the disciplinary matrix include most or all of the objects of group commitment described in the book as paradigms, parts of paradigms, or paradigmatic.[8] I shall not at this time even attempt an exhaustive list but will instead briefly identify three of these which, because central to the cognitive operation of the group, must particularly concern philosophers of science. Let me refer to them as symbolic generalizations, models, and exemplars.

The first two are already familiar objects of philosophical attention. Symbolic generalizations, in particular, are those expressions, deployed without question by the group, which can readily be cast in some logical form like $(x)(y)(z)\phi(x, y, z)$. They are the formal, or the readily formalizable, components of the disciplinary matrix. Models, about which I shall have nothing further to say in this paper, are what provide the group with preferred analogies or, when deeply held, with an ontology. At one extreme they are heuristic: the electric circuit may fruitfully be regarded as a steady-state hydrodynamic system, or a gas behaves like a collection of microscopic billiard balls in random motion. At the other, they are the objects of metaphysical commitment: the heat of a body *is* the kinetic energy of its constituent particles, or, more obviously metaphysical, all perceptible phenomena are due to the motion and interaction of qualitatively neutral atoms in the void.[9] Exemplars, finally, are concrete problem solutions, accepted by the group as, in a quite usual sense, paradigmatic. Many of you will already have guessed that the term 'exemplar' provides a new name for the second, and more fundamental, sense of 'paradigm' in the book.

To understand how a scientific community functions as a producer and validator of sound knowledge, we must ultimately, I think, understand the operation of at least these three components of the disciplinary matrix. Alterations in any one can result in changes of scientific behavior affecting both the locus of a group's research and its standards of verification. Here I shall not attempt to defend a quite so

[8] See *Structure of Scientific Revolutions*, pp. 38–42.

[9] It is not usual to include, say, atoms, fields, or forces acting at a distance under the rubric of models, but I presently see no harm in the broadened usage. Obviously the degree of a community's commitment varies as one goes from heuristic to metaphysical models, but the nature of the models' cognitive functions seems to remain the same.

general thesis. My primary concern is now with exemplars. To make room for them, however, I must first say something about symbolic generalizations.

III

In the sciences, particularly in physics, generalizations are often found already in symbolic form: $f = ma$, $I = V/R$, or $\nabla^2\psi + 8\pi^2 m/h^2(E - V)\psi = 0$. Others are ordinarily expressed in words: "action equals reaction," "chemical composition is in fixed proportions by weight," or "all cells come from cells." No one will question that the members of a scientific community do routinely deploy expressions like these in their work, that they ordinarily do so without felt need for special justification, and that they are seldom challenged at such points by other members of their group. That behavior is important, for without a shared commitment to a set of symbolic generalizations, logic and mathematics could not routinely be applied in the community's work. The example of taxonomy suggests that a science can exist with few, perhaps with no, such generalizations. I shall later suggest how this could be the case. But I see no reason to doubt the widespread impression that the power of a science increases with the number of symbolic generalizations its practitioners have at their disposal.

Note, however, how small a measure of agreement we have yet attributed to the members of our community. When I say they share a commitment to, say, the symbolic generalization $f = ma$, I mean only that they will raise no difficulties for the man who inscribes the four symbols f, $=$, m, and a in succession on a line, who manipulates the resulting expression by logic and mathematics, and who exhibits a still symbolic result. For us at this point in the discussion, though not for the scientists who use them, these symbols and the expressions formed by compounding them are uninterpreted, still empty of empirical meaning or application. A shared commitment to a set of generalizations justifies logical and mathematical manipulation and induces commitment to the result. It need not, however, imply agreement about the manner in which the symbols, individually and collectively, are to be correlated with the results of experiment and observation. To this extent the shared symbolic generalizations function as yet like expressions in a pure mathematical system.

The analogy between a scientific theory and a pure mathematical system has been widely exploited in twentieth-century philosophy of science and has been responsible for some extremely interesting results. But it is only an analogy and can therefore be misleading. I believe that in several respects we have been victimized by it. One of them has immediate relevance to my argument.

When an expression like $f = ma$ appears in a pure mathematical system, it is, so to speak, there once and for all. If, that is, it enters into the solution of a mathematical problem posed within the system, it always enters in the form $f = ma$ or in a form reducible to that one by the substitutivity of identities or by some other syntactic substitution rule. In the sciences symbolic generalizations ordinarily behave very differently. They are not so much generalizations as generalization-sketches, schematic forms whose detailed symbolic expression varies from one application to the next. For the problem of free fall, $f = ma$ becomes $mg = md^2/sdt^2$. For the simple pendulum, it becomes $mg\mathrm{Sin}\theta = - m\mathrm{d}^2/\mathrm{sdt}^2$. For coupled harmonic oscillators it becomes two equations, the first of which may be written $m_1\mathrm{d}^2\mathrm{s}_1/\mathrm{dt}^2 + \mathrm{k}_1\mathrm{s}_1 = \mathrm{k}_2(\mathrm{d} + \mathrm{s}_2 - \mathrm{s}_1)$. More interesting mechanical problems, for example the motion of a gyroscope, would display still greater disparity between $f = ma$ and the actual symbolic generalization to which logic and mathematics are applied; but the point should already be clear. Though uninterpreted symbolic expressions are the common possession of the members of a scientific community, and though it is such expressions which provide the group with an entry point for logic and mathematics, it is not to the shared generalization that these tools are applied but to one or another special version of it. In a sense, each such class requires a new formalism.[10]

An interesting conclusion follows, one with likely relevance to the status of theoretical terms. Those philosophers who exhibit scientific theories as uninterpreted formal systems often remark that empirical reference enters such theories from the bottom up, moving from an empirically meaningful basic vocabulary into the theoretical terms. Despite the well-known difficulties that cluster about the notion of a basic vocabulary, I cannot doubt the importance of that route in the

[10] This difficulty cannot be evaded by stating the laws of Newtonian mechanics in, say, a Lagrangian or Hamiltonian form. On the contrary, the latter formulations are explicitly law sketches rather than laws, as Newton's formulation of mechanics is not. Starting with Hamilton's equations or Lagrange's, one must still write down a particular Hamiltonian or Lagrangian for the particular problem at hand. Notice, however, that a crucial advantage of these formulations is that they make it far easier to identify the particular formalism suitable to a particular problem. Contrasted with Newton's formulation, they thus illustrate a typical direction of normal scientific development.

transformation of an uninterpreted symbol into the sign for a particular physical concept. But it is not the only route. Formalisms in science also attach to nature at the top, without intervening deduction which eliminates theoretical terms. Before he can begin the logical and mathematical manipulations which eventuate with the prediction of meter readings, the scientist must inscribe the particular form of $f = ma$ that applies to, say, the vibrating string or the particular form of the Schrödinger equation which applies to, say, the helium atom in a magnetic field. Whatever procedure he employs in doing so, it cannot be purely syntactic. Empirical content must enter formalized theories from the top as well as the bottom.

One cannot, I think, escape this conclusion by suggesting that the Schrödinger equation or $f = ma$ be construed as an abbreviation for a conjunction of the numerous particular symbolic forms which these expressions take for application to particular physical problems. In the first place, scientists would still require criteria to tell them which particular symbolic version should be applied to which problem, and these criteria, like the correlation rules that are said to transport meaning from a basic vocabulary to theoretical terms, would be a vehicle for empirical content. Besides, no conjunction of particular symbolic forms would exhaust what the members of a scientific community can properly be said to know about how to apply symbolic generalizations. Confronted with a new problem, they can often agree on the particular symbolic expression appropriate to it, even though none of them has seen that particular expression before.

Any account of the cognitive apparatus of a scientific community may reasonably be asked to tell us something about the way in which the group's members, in advance of *directly* relevant empirical evidence, identify the special formalism appropriate to a particular problem, especially to a new problem. That clearly is one of the functions which scientific knowledge does serve. It does not, of course, always do so correctly; there is room, indeed need, for empirical checks on a special formalism proposed for a new problem. The deductive steps and the comparison of their end products with experiment remain prerequisites of science. But special formalisms are regularly accepted as plausible or rejected as implausible in advance of experiment. With remarkable frequency, furthermore, the community's judgments prove to be correct. Designing a special formalism, a new version of the formalization, cannot therefore be quite like inventing a new theory. Among other things, the former can be taught as theory invention cannot. That is what the problems at the ends of chapters in science texts are principally for. What can it be that students learn while solving them?

IV

To that question most of the remainder of this paper is devoted, but I shall approach it indirectly, asking at first a more usual one: How do scientists attach symbolic expressions to nature? That is, in fact, two questions in one, for it may be asked either about a special symbolic generalization designed for a particular experimental situation or about a singular symbolic consequence of that generalization deduced for comparison with experiment. For present purposes, however, we may treat these two questions as one. In scientific practice, also, they are ordinarily answered together.

Since the abandonment of hope for a sense-datum language, the usual answer to this question has been in terms of correspondence rules. These have ordinarily been taken to be either operational definitions of scientific terms or else a set of necessary and sufficient conditions for the terms' applicability.[11] I do not myself doubt that the examination of a given scientific community would disclose a number of such rules shared by its members. Probably a few others could legitimately be induced from close observation of their behavior. But, for reasons I have given elsewhere and shall advert to briefly below, I do doubt that the

[11] Since this paper was read, I have realized that eliding the two questions mentioned in the preceding paragraph introduces a possible source of confusion at this point and below. In normal philosophical usage, correspondence rules connect words only to other words, not to nature. Thus theoretical terms acquire meaning via the correspondence rules that attach them to a previously meaningful basic vocabulary. Only the latter attach directly to nature. Part of my argument is directed to this standard view and should therefore create no problems. The distinction between a theoretical and a basic vocabulary will not do in its present form because many theoretical terms can be shown to attach to nature in the same way, whatever it may be, as basic terms. But I am in addition concerned to inquire how "direct attachment" may work, whether of a theoretical or basic vocabulary. In the process I attack the often implicit assumption that anyone who knows how to use a basic term correctly has access, conscious or unconscious, to a set of criteria which define that term or provide necessary and sufficient conditions governing its application. For that mode of attachment-by-criteria I am also here using the term 'correspondence rule', and that does violate normal usage. My excuse for the extension is my belief that explicit reliance on correspondence rules and implicit reliance on criteria introduce the same procedure and misdirect attention in the same ways. Both make the deployment of language seem more a matter of convention than it is. As a result they disguise the extent to which a man who acquires either an everyday or a scientific language simultaneously learns things about nature which are not themselves embodied in verbal generalizations.

correspondence rules discovered in this way would be nearly sufficient in number or force to account for the actual correlations between formalism and experiment made regularly and unproblematically by members of the group.[12] If the philosopher wants an adequate body of correspondence rules, he will have to supply most of them for himself.[13]

Almost surely that is a job he can do. Examining the collected examples of past community practice, the philosopher may reasonably expect to construct a set of correspondence rules adequate, in conjunction with known symbolic generalizations, to account for them all. Very likely he would be able to construct several alternate sets. Nevertheless, he ought to be extraordinarily wary about describing any one of them as a reconstruction of the rules held by the community under study. Though each of his sets of rules would be equivalent with respect to the community's past practice, they need not be equivalent when applied to the very next problem faced by the discipline. In that sense they would be reconstructions of slightly different theories, none of which need be the one held by the group. The philosopher might well, by behaving as a scientist, have improved the group's theory, but he would not, as a philosopher, have analyzed it.

Suppose, for example, that the philosopher is concerned with Ohm's law, $I = V/R$, and that he knows that the members of the group he studies measure voltage with an electrometer and current with a galvanometer. Seeking a correspondence rule for resistance, he may choose the quotient of voltage divided by current, in which case Ohm's law becomes a tautology. Or he may instead choose to correlate the value

[12] See *Structure of Scientific Revolutions*, pp. 43–51.

[13] It is, I think, remarkable how little attention philosophers of science have payed to the language-nature link. Surely, the epistemic force of the formalists' enterprise depends upon the possibility of making it unproblematic. One reason for this neglect is, I suspect, a failure to notice how much has been lost, from an epistemological standpoint, in the transition from a sense-datum language to a basic vocabulary. While the former seemed viable, definitions and correspondence rules required no special attention. "Green patch there" scarcely needed further operational specification; "Benzene boils at 80° Centigrade" is, however, a very different sort of statement. In addition, as I shall suggest below, formalists have frequently conflated the task of *improving* the clarity and structure of the formal elements of a scientific theory with the quite different job of *analyzing* scientific knowledge, and only the latter raises the problems of present concern. Hamilton produced a better formulation of Newtonian mechanics than had Newton, and the philosopher may hope to affect further improvements by further formalization. But he may not take for granted that he emerges with the same theory with which he began nor that the formal elements of either version of the theory are coextensive with the theory itself. For a typical example of the assumption that a perfected formalism is ipso facto an account of the knowledge deployed by the community which uses the formalism to be improved, see Patrick Suppes, "The Desirability of Formalization in Science," *Journal of Philosophy*, Vol. 65 (1968), pp. 651–664.

of resistance with the results of measurements made on a Wheatstone Bridge, in which case Ohm's law provides information about nature. For past practice the two reconstructions may be equivalent, but they will not dictate the same future behavior. Imagine, in particular, that an especially adept experimentalist in the community applies higher voltages than any realized before and discovers that the voltage-to-current ratio changes gradually at high voltage. According to the second, the Wheatstone Bridge, reconstruction, he has discovered that there are deviations from Ohm's law at high voltage. On the first reconstruction, however, Ohm's law is a tautology and deviations from it are unimaginable. The experimentalist has discovered, not a deviation from the law, but rather that resistance changes with voltage. The two reconstructions lead to different localizations of the difficulty and to different patterns of follow-up research.[14]

Nothing in the preceding discussion proves that there is no set of correspondence rules adequate to explain the behavior of the community under study. A negative of that sort scarcely can be proven. But the discussion may lead us to take a bit more seriously some aspects of scientific training and behavior that philosophers have often managed to look right through. Very few correspondence rules are to be found in science texts or science teaching. How can the members of a scientific community have acquired a sufficient set? It is also noteworthy that if asked by a philosopher to provide such rules, scientists regularly deny their relevance and thereafter sometimes grow uncommonly inarticulate. When they cooperate at all, the rules they

[14] A less artificial example would require the simultaneous manipulation of several symbolic generalizations and would thus demand more space than is presently available. But historical examples which display the differential effects of generalizations held as laws and as definitions are not hard to find (see the discussion of Dalton and the Proust-Berthollet controversy in *Structure of Scientific Revolutions*, pp. 129–134), nor is the present example without historical foundation. Ohm did measure resistance by dividing current into voltage. His law thus provided a part of a definition of resistance. One of the reasons it proved so notably difficult to accept (neglect of Ohm is one of the most famous examples of resistance to innovation offered by history of science) is that it was incompatible with the concept of resistance accepted prior to Ohm's work. Just because it demanded redefinition of electrical concepts, the assimilation of Ohm's law produced a revolution in electrical theory. (For parts of this story see, T. M. Brown, "The Electric Current in Early Nineteenth-Century Electricity," *Historical Studies in the Physical Sciences*, Vol. 1 (1969), pp. 61–103, and M. L. Schagrin, "Resistance to Ohm's Law," *American Journal of Physics*, Vol. 31 (1963), pp. 536–547.) I suspect that, quite generally, scientific revolutions can be distinguished from normal scientific developments in that the former require, as the latter do not, the modification of generalizations which had previously been regarded as quasi-analytic. Did Einstein discover the relativity of simultaneity or did he destroy a previously tautologous implication of that term?

produce may vary from one member of the community to another, and all may be defective. One begins to wonder whether more than a few such rules are deployed in community practice, whether there is not some alternate way in which scientists correlate their symbolic expressions with nature.

A phenomenon familiar both to students of science and to historians of science provides a clue. Having been both I shall speak from experience. Students of physics regularly report that they have read through a chapter of their text, understood it perfectly, but nonetheless had difficulty solving the problems at the chapter's end. Almost invariably their difficulty is in setting up the appropriate equations, in relating the words and examples given in the text to the particular problems they are asked to solve. Ordinarily, also, those difficulties dissolve in the same way. The student discovers a way to see his problem as like a problem he has already encountered. Once that likeness or analogy has been seen, only manipulative difficulties remain.

The same pattern shows clearly in the history of science. Scientists model one problem solution on another, often with only a minimal recourse to symbolic generalizations. Galileo found that a ball rolling down an incline acquires just enough velocity to return it to the same vertical height on a second incline of any slope, and he learned to see that experimental situation as like the pendulum with a point-mass for a bob. Huyghens then solved the problem of the center of oscillation of a physical pendulum by imagining that the extended body of the latter was composed of Galilean point-pendula, the bonds between which could be instantaneously released at any point in the swing. After the bonds were released, the individual point-pendula would swing freely, but their collective center of gravity, like that of Galileo's pendulum, would rise only to the height from which the center of gravity of the extended pendulum had begun to fall. Finally, Daniel Bernoulli, still with no aid from Newton's laws, discovered how to make the flow of water from an orifice in a storage tank resemble Huyghens's pendulum. Determine the descent of the center of gravity of the water in tank and jet during an infinitesimal interval of time. Next imagine that each particle of water afterwards moves separately upward to the maximum height obtainable with the velocity it possessed at the end of the interval of descent. The ascent of the center of gravity of the separate particles must then equal the descent of the center of gravity of the water in tank and jet. From that view of the problem, the long sought speed of efflux followed at once.[15]

[15] For the example, see, René Dugas, *A History of Mechanics*, trans. J. R. Maddox (Neûchatel: Éditiones du Triffon and New York: Central Book Co., 1955),

Lacking time to multiply examples, I suggest that an acquired ability to see resemblances between apparently disparate problems plays in the sciences a significant part of the role usually attributed to correspondence rules. Once a new problem is seen to be analogous to a problem previously solved, both an appropriate formalism and a new way of attaching its symbolic consequences to nature follow. Having seen the resemblance, one simply uses the attachments that have proved effective before. That ability to recognize group-licensed resemblances is, I think, the main thing students acquire by doing problems, whether with pencil and paper or in a well-designed laboratory. In the course of their training a vast number of such exercises are set for them, and students entering the same specialty regularly do very nearly the same ones, for example, the inclined plane, the conical pendulum, Kepler ellipses, and so on. These concrete problems with their solutions are what I previously referred to as exemplars, a community's standard examples. They constitute the third main sort of cognitive component of the disciplinary matrix, and they illustrate the second main function of the term 'paradigm' in *The Structure of Scientific Revolutions*.[16] Acquiring an arsenal of exemplars, just as much as learning symbolic generalizations, is integral to the process by which a student gains access to the cognitive achievements of his disciplinary group.[17] Without exemplars he would never learn much of what the group knows about such fundamental concepts as force and field, element and compound, or nucleus and cell.

I shall shortly attempt, by means of a simple example, to explicate

---

pp. 135–136, 186–193, and Daniel Bernoulli, *Hydrodynamica, sive de viribus et motibus fluidorum, commentarii opus academicum* (Strasbourg: J. R. Dulseckeri, 1738), Sec. III. For the extent to which mechanics progressed during the first half of the eighteenth century by modeling one problem solution on another, see, Clifford Truesdell, "Reactions of Late Baroque Mechanics to Success, Conjecture, Error, and Failure in Newton's *Principia*," *Texas Quarterly*, Vol. 10 (1967), pp. 238–258.

[16] It is, of course, the sense of 'paradigm' as standard example that led originally to my choice of that term. Unfortunately, most readers of *The Structure of Scientific Revolutions* have missed what was for me its central function and use 'paradigm' in a sense close to that for which I now suggest 'disciplinary matrix.' I see little chance of recapturing 'paradigm' for its original use, the only one that is philologically at all appropriate.

[17] Note that exemplars (and also models) are far more effective determinants of community substructure than are symbolic generalizations. Many scientific communities share, for example, the Schrödinger equation, and their members encounter that formula correspondingly early in their scientific education. But, as that training continues, say toward solid state physics on the one hand and field theory on the other, the exemplars they encounter diverge. Thereafter it is only the uninterpreted, not the interpreted, Schrödinger equation they can unequivocally be said to share.

the notion of a learned similarity relationship, an acquired perception of analogy. Let me first, however, sharpen the problem at which that explication will be aimed. It is a truism that anything is similar to, and also different from, anything else. It depends, we usually say, on the criteria. To the man who speaks of similarity or of analogy, we therefore at once pose the question: similar with respect to what? In this case, however, that is just the question that must not be asked, for an answer would at once provide us with correspondence rules. Acquiring exemplars would teach the student nothing that such rules, in the form of criteria of resemblance, could not equally well have supplied. Doing problems would then be mere practice in the application of rules, and there would be no need for talk of similarity.

Doing problems, however, I have already argued, is not like that. Much more nearly it resembles the child's puzzle in which one is asked to find the animal shapes or faces hidden in the drawing of shrubbery or clouds. The child seeks forms that are like those of the animals or faces he knows. Once they are found, they do not again retreat into the background, for the child's way of seeing the picture has been changed. In the same way, the science student, confronted with a problem, seeks to see it as like one or more of the exemplary problems he has encountered before. Where rules exist to guide him, he, of course, deploys them. But his basic criterion is a perception of similarity that is both logically and psychologically prior to any of the numerous criteria by which that same identification of similarity might have been made. After the similarity has been seen, one may ask for criteria, and it is then often worth doing so. But one need not. The mental or visual set acquired while learning to see two problems as similar can be applied directly. Under appropriate circumstances, I now want to argue, there is a means of processing data into similarity sets which does not depend on a prior answer to the question, similar with respect to what?

V

My argument begins with a brief digression on the term 'data.' Philologically it derives from 'the given.' Philosophically, for reasons deeply engrained in the history of epistemology, it isolates the minimal stable elements provided by our senses. Though we no longer hope for a sense-datum language, phrases like 'green there,' 'triangle here,' or 'hot down there' continue to connote our paradigms for a datum, the given in experience. In several respects, they should play this role. We have no access to elements of experience more minimal than these. Whenever we consciously process data, whether to identify an object, to discover a law, or to invent a theory, we necessarily manipulate sensations of this sort or compounds of them. Nevertheless, from another point of view, sensations and their elements are not the given. Viewed theoretically rather than experientially, that title belongs rather to stimuli. Though we have access to them only indirectly, via scientific theory, it is stimuli, not sensations, that impinge on us as organisms. A vast amount of neural processing takes place between our receipt of a stimulus and the sensory response which is our datum.

None of this would be worth saying if Descartes had been right in positing a one-to-one correspondence between stimuli and sensations. But we know that nothing of the sort exists. The perception of a given color can be evoked by an infinite number of differently combined wavelengths. Conversely, a given stimulus can evoke a variety of sensations, the image of a duck in one recipient, the image of a rabbit in another. Nor are responses like these entirely innate. One can learn to discriminate colors or patterns which were indistinguishable prior to training. To an extent still unknown, the production of data from stimuli is a learned procedure. After the learning process, the same stimulus evokes a different datum. I conclude that, though data are the minimal elements of our individual experience, they need be shared responses to a given stimulus only within the membership of a relatively homogeneous community, educational, scientific, or linguistic.[18]

Return now to my main argument, but not to scientific examples. Inevitably the latter prove excessively complex. Instead I ask that you imagine a small child on a walk with his father in a zoological garden. The child has previously learned to recognize birds and to discriminate robin redbreasts. During the afternoon now at hand, he will learn for the first time to identify swans, geese, and ducks. Anyone who has taught a child under such circumstances knows that the primary pedagogic tool is ostension. Phrases like 'all swans are white' may play a role, but they need not. I shall for the moment omit them from consideration, my object being to isolate a different mode of learning in its purest form. Johnny's education then proceeds as follows. Father points

[18] In *The Structure of Scientific Revolutions*, particularly Chapter X, I repeatedly insist that members of different scientific communities live in different worlds and that scientific revolutions change the world in which a scientist works. I would now want to say that members of different communities are presented with different data by the same stimuli. Notice, however, that that change does not make phrases like 'a different world' inappropriate. The given world, whether everyday or scientific, is not a world of stimuli.

to a bird, saying, "Look, Johnny, there's a swan." A short time later Johnny himself points to a bird, saying, "Daddy, another swan." He has not yet, however, learned what swans are and must be corrected: "No, Johnny, that's a goose." Johnny's next identification of a swan proves to be correct, but his next "goose" is, in fact, a duck, and he is again set straight. After a few more such encounters, however, each with its appropriate correction or reinforcement, Johnny's ability to identify these waterfowl is as great as his father's. Instruction has been quickly completed.

I ask now what has happened to Johnny, and I urge the plausibility of the following answer. During the afternoon, part of the neural mechanism by which he processes visual stimuli has been reprogrammed, and the data he receives from stimuli which would all earlier have evoked 'bird' have changed. When he began his walk, the neural program highlighted the differences between individual swans as much as those between swans and geese. By the walk's end, features like the length and curvature of the swan's neck have been highlighted and others have been suppressed so that swan data match each other and differ from goose and duck data as they had not before. Birds that had previously all looked alike (and also different) are now grouped in discrete clusters in perceptual space.

A process of this sort can readily be modeled on a computer; I am in the early stages of such an experiment myself. A stimulus, in the form of a string of n ordered digits, is fed to the machine. There it is transformed to a datum by the application of a preselected transformation to each of the n digits, a different transformation being applied to each position in the string. Every datum thus obtained is a string of n numbers, a position in what I shall call an n-dimensional quality space. In this space the distance between two data, measured with a Euclidean or a suitable non-Euclidean metric, represents their similarity. Which stimuli transform to similar or nearby data depends, of course, on the choice of transformation functions. Different sets of functions produce different clusters of data, different patterns of similarity and difference, in perceptual space. But the transformation functions need not be manmade. If the machine is given stimuli which can be grouped in clusters and if it is informed which stimuli must be placed in the same and which in different clusters, it can design an appropriate set of transformation functions for itself. Note that both conditions are essential. Not all stimuli can be transformed to form data clusters. Even when they can, the machine, like the child, must be told at first which ones belong together and which apart. Johnny did not discover for himself that there were swans, geese, and ducks. Rather he was taught it.

If we now represent Johnny's perceptual space in a two-dimensional diagram, the process he has undergone is rather like the transition from Figure 1 to Figure 2.[19] In the first, ducks, geese, and swans are mixed together. In the second, they have clustered in discrete sets with appreciable distances between them.[20] Since Johnny's father has, in effect, told him that ducks, geese, and swans are members of discrete natural families, Johnny has every right to expect that all future ducks, geese, and swans will fall naturally into or at the edge of one of these families, and that he will encounter no datum that falls in the region midway between them. That expectation may be violated, perhaps during a visit to Australia. But it will serve him well while he remains a member of the community that has discovered from experience the utility and viability of these particular perceptual discriminations and which has transmitted the ability to make them from one generation to the next.

By being programmed to recognize what his prospective community already knows, Johnny has acquired consequential information. He has learned that geese, ducks, and swans form discrete natural families and that nature offers no swan-geese or goose-ducks. Some quality constellations go together; others are not found at all. If the qualities in his clusters include aggressiveness, his afternoon in the park may have had behavioral as well as everyday zoological functions. Geese, unlike swans and ducks, hiss and bite. What Johnny has learned is thus worth knowing. But does he know what the terms 'goose,' 'duck,' and 'swan' mean? In any useful sense, yes, for he can apply these labels unequivocally and without effort, drawing behavioral conclusions from their application, either directly or via general statements. On the other hand, he has learned all this without acquiring, or at least without needing to acquire, even one criterion for identifying swans, geese, or ducks. He can point to a swan and tell you there must be water nearby, but he may well be unable to tell you what a swan is.

Johnny, in short, has learned to apply symbolic labels to nature without anything like definitions or correspondence rules. In their absence he employs a learned but nonetheless primitive perception of

19 For the drawings I am indebted to both the pen and patience of Sarah Kuhn.

20 It will become apparent below that everything which is special about this method of processing stimuli depends upon the possibility of grouping data in clusters with empty space between them. In the absence of empty space, there is no alternative to the processing strategy that, designed for a world of all-possible-data, relies upon definitions and rules.

FIGURE 1

FIGURE 2

similarity and difference. While acquiring the perception, he has learned something about nature. This knowledge can thereafter be embedded, not in generalizations or rules, but in the similarity relationship itself. I do not, let me emphasize, at all suppose Johnny's technique is the only one by which knowledge is acquired and stored. Nor do I think it likely that very much human knowledge is acquired and stored with so little recourse to verbal generalizations. But I do urge the recognition of the integrity of a cognitive process like the one just outlined. In combination with more familiar processes, like symbolic generalization and modeling, it is, I think, essential to an adequate reconstruction of scientific knowledge.

Need I now say that the swans, geese, and ducks which Johnny encountered during his walk with father were what I have been calling exemplars? Presented to Johnny with their labels attached, they were solutions to a problem that the members of his prospective community had already resolved. Assimilating them is part of the socialization procedure by which Johnny is made part of that community and, in the process, learns about the world which the community inhabits. Johnny is, of course, no scientist, nor is what he has learned yet science. But he may well become a scientist, and the technique employed on his walk will still be viable. That he does, in fact, use them will be most obvious if he becomes a taxonomist. The herbaria, without which no botanist can function, are storehouses for professional exemplars, and their history is coextensive with that of the discipline they support. But the same technique, if in a less pure form, is essential to the more abstract sciences as well. I have already argued that assimilating solutions to such problems as the inclined plane and the conical pendulum is part of learning what Newtonian physics is. Only after a number of such problems have been assimilated, can a student or a professional proceed to identify other Newtonian problems for himself. That assimilation of examples is, furthermore, part of what enables him to isolate the forces, masses, and constraints within a new problem and to write down a formalism suitable for its solution. Despite its excessive simplicity, Johnny's case should suggest why I continue to insist that shared examples have essential cognitive functions prior to a specification of criteria with respect to which they are exemplary.

VI

I conclude my argument by returning to a crucial question discussed earlier in connection with symbolic generalizations. Suppose scientists do assimilate and store knowledge in shared examples, need the philosopher concern himself with the process? May he not instead study the examples and derive correspondence rules which, together with the formal elements of the theory, would make the examples superfluous? To that question I have already suggested the following answer. The philosopher is at liberty to substitute rules for examples and, at least in principle, he can expect to succeed in doing so. In the process, however, he will alter the nature of the knowledge possessed by the community from which his examples were drawn. What he will be doing, in effect, is to substitute one means of data processing for another. Unless he is extraordinarily careful he will weaken the community's cognition by doing so. Even with care, he will change the nature of the community's future responses to some experimental stimuli.

Johnny's education, though not in science, provides a new sort of evidence for these claims. To identify swans, geese, and ducks by correspondence rules rather than by perceived similarity is to draw closed nonintersecting curves around each of the clusters in Figure 2. What results is a simple Venn diagram, displaying three nonoverlapping classes. All swans lie in one, all geese in another, and so on. Where, however, should the curves be drawn? There are infinite possibilities. One of them is illustrated in Figure 3, where boundaries are drawn very close to the bird figures in the three clusters. Given such boundaries, Johnny now can say what the criteria are for membership in the class of swans, geese, or ducks. On the other hand, he may be troubled by the very next waterfowl he sees. The outlined shape in the diagram is obviously a swan by the perceived distance criterion, but it is neither swan, goose, nor duck by the newly introduced correspondence rules for class membership.

Boundaries ought not, therefore, be drawn too near the edges of a cluster of exemplars. Let us therefore go to the other extreme, Figure 4, and draw boundaries which exhaust most of the relevant parts of Johnny's perceptual space. With this choice, no bird that appears near one of the existing clusters will present a problem, but in avoiding that difficulty we have created another. Johnny used to know that there are no swan-geese. The new reconstruction of his knowledge deprives him of that information. Instead it supplies something he is extremely unlikely to need, the name that applies to a bird datum deep in the unoccupied space between swans and geese. To replace what has been lost we may imagine adding to John's cognitive apparatus a density function that describes the likelihood of his encountering a swan at various positions within the swan boundary, together with similar functions for geese and ducks. But the original similarity criterion supplied

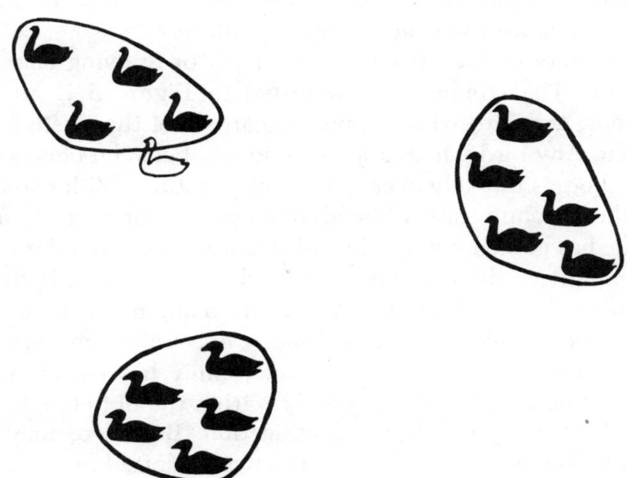

FIGURE 3

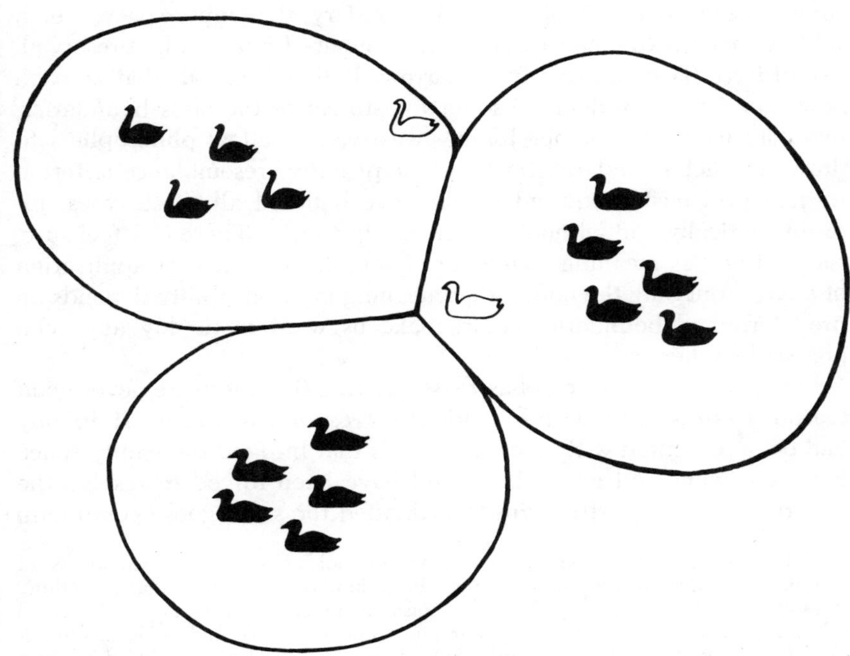

FIGURE 4

those already. In effect we would just have returned to the data-processing mechanism we had meant to replace.

Clearly, neither of the extreme techniques for drawing class boundaries will do. The compromise indicated in Figure 5 is an obvious improvement. Any bird which appears near one of the existing clusters belongs to it. Any bird which appears midway between clusters has no name, but there is unlikely ever to be such a datum. With class boundaries like these, Johnny should be able to operate successfully for some time. Yet he has gained nothing by substituting class boundaries for his original similarity criterion, and there has been some loss. If the strategic suitability of these boundaries is to be maintained, their location may need to be changed each time Johnny encounters another swan.

Figure 6 shows what I have in mind. Johnny has encountered one more swan. It lies, as it should, entirely within the old class boundary. There has been no problem of identification. But there may be one next time unless new boundaries, here shown as dotted lines, are drawn to take account of the altered shape of the swan cluster. Without the outward adjustment of the swan boundary, the very next bird encountered, though unproblematically a swan by the resemblance criterion, may fall on or even outside the old boundary. Without the simultaneous retraction of the duck boundary, the empty space, which Johnny's more experienced seniors have assured him can be preserved, would have become excessively narrow. If that is so—if, that is, each new experience can demand some adjustment of the class boundaries, one may well ask whether Johnny was wise to allow philosophers to draw any such boundaries for him. The primitive resemblance criterion he had previously acquired would have handled all these cases unproblematically and without continual adjustment. There is, I feel sure, such a thing as meaning change or change in the range of application of a term. But only the notion that meaning or applicability depends on predetermined boundaries could make us want to deploy any such phraseology here.[21]

I am not, let me now emphasize, suggesting that there are never good reasons to draw boundaries or adopt correspondence rules. If Johnny had been presented with a series of birds that bridged the empty space between swans and geese, he would have been forced to resolve the resulting quandary with a line that divided the swan-goose continuum

[21] By the same token one should here withhold phrases like 'vagueness of meaning' or 'open texture of concepts.' Both imply an imperfection, something lacking that may later be supplied. That sense of imperfection is, however, created solely by a standard that demands our possessing necessary and sufficient conditions for the applicability of a word or phrase in a world of all possible data. In a world in which some data never appear, such a criterion is superfluous.

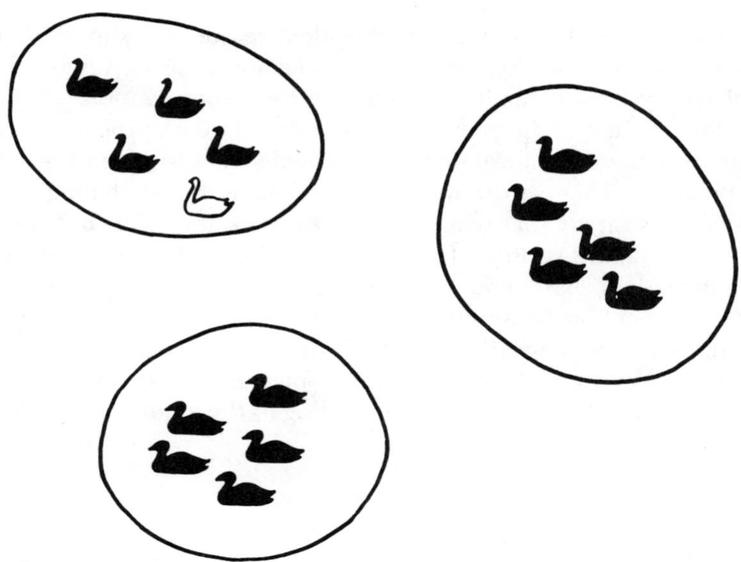

Figure 5

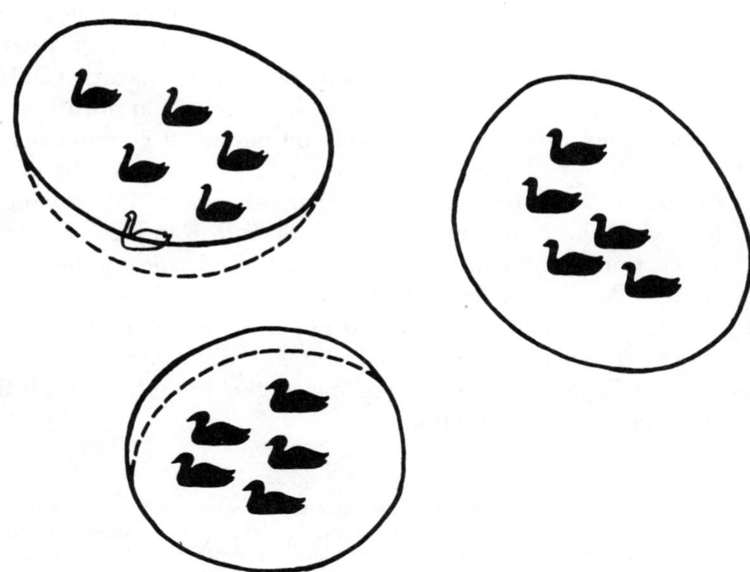

Figure 6

by definition. Or, if there were independent reasons for supposing that color is a stable criterion for the identification of waterfowl, Johnny might wisely have committed himself to the generalization, all swans are white.[22] That strategy might save valuable data-processing time. In any case, the generalization would provide an entry point for logical manipulation. There are appropriate occasions for switching to the well-known strategy that relies upon boundaries and rules. But it is not the only available strategy for either stimuli- or data-processing. An alternative does exist, one based upon what I have been calling a learned perception of similarity. Observation, whether of language learning, scientific education, or scientific practice, suggests that it is, in fact, widely used. By ignoring it in epistemological discussion, we may do much violence to our understanding of the nature of knowledge.

VII

Return, finally, to the term 'paradigm.' It entered *The Structure of Scientific Revolutions* because I, the book's historian-author, could not, when examining the membership of a scientific community, retrieve enough shared rules to account for the group's unproblematic conduct of research. Shared examples of successful practice could, I next concluded, provide what the group lacked in rules. Those examples were its paradigms, and as such essential to its continued research. Unfortunately, having gotten that far, I allowed the term's applications to expand, embracing all shared group commitments, all components of what I now wish to call the disciplinary matrix. Inevitably, the result was confusion, and it obscured the original reasons for introducing a special term. But those reasons still stand. Shared examples can serve cognitive functions commonly attributed to shared rules. When they do, knowledge develops differently from the way it does when governed by rules. This paper has, above all, been an effort to isolate, clarify, and drive home those essential points. If they can be seen, we shall be able to dispense with the term 'paradigm,' though not with the concept that led to its introduction.

[22] Note that Johnny's commitment to 'all swans are white' may be a commitment either to a law about swans or to a (partial) definition of swans. He may, that is, receive the generalization either as analytic or synthetic. As suggested in note 14, above, the difference can prove consequential, particularly if Johnny next encounters a black waterfowl that, in other respects, closely resembles a swan. Laws drawn directly from observation are corrigible piecemeal as definitions generally are not.

Exemplars, Theories and Disciplinary Matrixes[1]

FREDERICK SUPPE

Thomas Kuhn's paper "Second Thoughts on Paradigms" is a rich and suggestive paper in which he attempts, among other things, to reply to various criticisms of the account of paradigms he presented in *The Structure of Scientific Revolutions*[2]—in particular those raised by Dudley Shapere[3]—by presenting a systematic reworking of the notion. He does so by conceding that he previously used 'paradigm' ambiguously in reference to two quite distinct concepts, which he now refers to as *disciplinary matrixes* and *exemplars,* and then proceeds to systematically develop these notions in such a way as to clarify, defend, and further develop the main themes and arguments of *The Structure of Scientific Revolutions.* In the process of doing so he presents an alternative analysis of the way symbolic generalizations are attached to nature or given an empirical interpretation—an account which, he argues, provides a more accurate account of scientific knowledge than does the standard positivistic account in terms of correspondence rules.

Given its multiple aims, in critically assessing Kuhn's paper it would be legitimate to concentrate on answering any of the following questions: How successful is the paper as an answer to his critics? How much of *The Structure of Scientific Revolutions* survives under Kuhn's revised analysis of paradigms? To what extent do his arguments succeed in establishing the various new positive claims made in the paper? However valuable the answer to these questions might be, it seems to me more important to concentrate my critical efforts on the main new conceptual tools Kuhn introduces: exemplars, disciplinary matrixes, and the group-licensed primitive resemblance or similarity

[1] This is a considerably revised, expanded, and improved version of the commentary I gave at the symposium. I wish to thank Professor Kuhn for his kind indulgence of these revisions.

[2] Kuhn [1962].

[3] Shapere [1964] and [1966].

relationship. For, despite the fact that these notions are more carefully specified than the paradigm was, they too run the risk of being "too nearly all things to all people." Like the paradigm they have an intuitive appeal which prompts uncritical acceptance and invites the sort of self-defeating plastic application which Kuhn deplores. Therefore it seems particularly desirable that I critically examine these notions, point out places where I find his specification imprecise, unclear, or otherwise unsatisfactory, and make explicit what seem to me undesirable features or consequences of his revised position; by doing so I hope to provide him with a foil for further clarification of his position.

I begin with *the exemplar,* which Kuhn characterizes as "concrete problem solutions, accepted by the [disciplinary] group as, in a quite usual sense, paradigmatic" (p. 463).[4] That is, they are the accepted applications of symbolic generalizations to various concrete problems one finds in the examples and solutions to the exercises in standard textbooks and laboratory manuals. They conveniently can be analyzed as consisting of the following components: (1) A relatively informal and often elliptical description of a typical experimental setup, and a problem posed about that setup; (2) the appropriate formulas for symbolic generalizations for the type of problem; (3) a statement of the observed or measured experimental results; (4) a canonical redescription (often in the form of a diagram) of the experimental situation and results given in terms of the parameters of the symbolic generalization; (5) some sort of description how the experiment is to be translated from the original description to the canonical redescription; and (6) various manipulations which are then employed to calculate or deduce the requested results.[5] This characterization enables us to note several important features of exemplars: First, the

[4] All page references and section references are to "Second Thoughts on Paradigms," unless otherwise indicated.

[5] In the typical textbook exemplars, these various components are not clearly distinguished; in particular the fifth component tends to be quite elliptically put, or even only implicit. But they can be readily isolated and extracted. The situation here in many respects is analogous to that of translating English sentences into first-order predicate calculus expressions: there the trick is to first replace the original English sentence by an equivalent canonical-form English sentence which mirrors the syntax of predicate calculus; once this is done the remainder of the translation is automatic. Similarly, in the sciences, the trick is for the student to see how to translate the original informal description of the experiment into an equivalent canonical-form characterization whose syntax and vocabulary mirrors the syntax of the symbolic generalizations. The most problematic part of applying symbolic generalizations to nature is this step of translation to the canonical redescription.

canonical redescription of the experimental setup (4) not only describes the situation in the language of the theory's symbolic generalizations, but it does so in such a way that one or another special-case solution of the laws (for example, the basic equations of motion) of the theory is directly applicable. That particular special-case law is used in the solution of the problem (6). Thus exemplars not only illustrate how to attach symbolic generalizations to nature, but also indicate which forms of the laws or symbolic generalizations are applicable under various circumstances. Second, in illustrating the solution to the problem (6), the exemplar illustrates the ways in which the various symbolic generalizations are combined and mathematically manipulated to obtain a solution; they thus may introduce new techniques of solution, tricks of the trade, and so on, and also illustrate the sorts of approximations, and such, that the science tolerates. Thus the exempler illustrates more than how symbolic generalizations are applied to nature. And from the study of exemplars the student may learn how to (mathematically) manipulate the symbolic generalizations to obtain solutions as well as to attach symbolic generalizations to nature. Finally, in the process of translation from the informal descriptions of the phenomena (1 and 3) to their canonical redescriptions (4), various other symbolic generalizations (for example, formulas for determining friction coefficients) may be employed.[6]

The central thesis of Kuhn's paper is that it is from the study of these exemplars that one learns to apply symbolic generalizations to nature: from the study of exemplars and attempts to solve problems the student develops a *similarity* or *resemblance relation,* which is used to model the application of symbolic generalizations to new experimental situations; and it is through the acquisition of this similarity relationship, and not via correspondence rules, that the empirical generalizations come to have empirical content. While Kuhn does give some indication how the study of exemplars does lead to the development of the learned resemblance relationship, he is very nonspecific how the acquisition of the resemblance relationship affects the empirical content of symbolic generalizations. In order to assess his central thesis we will have to examine in some detail the connection between the resemblance relationship and the empirical content of symbolic generalizations. We begin by looking at the acquisition of the similarity relationship via the study of exemplars.

[6] These qualify as what Putnam calls auxiliary statements; see the summary-abstract of his paper in Session V above.

The main indication Kuhn gives us how the study of exemplars leads to the acquisition of the resemblance relation is via his Johnny example. There Johnny is taken to a zoological garden and, by a process of ostensive definition, is taught to correctly apply the names 'duck,' 'goose,' and 'swan' to various birds. Kuhn tells us that in doing so he comes to see different birds as similar, and thereby develops a resemblance relation which clusters things and associates labels with them. Thus, when Johnny next sees a bird which resembles the birds in the cluster associated with 'duck,' the response 'duck' will be elicited. Kuhn advances this as a simple illustration how the study of exemplars enables one to acquire the ability to apply symbolic generalizations to nature; we may thus assume that the two cases are analogous. The Johnny case concerns the attachment of single words to nature; so, by analogy, through the study of exemplars the student acquires a resemblance relation which clusters together various data and associates them with various words. For example, the various data might cluster and be associated with the term 'mass'. It follows that from the study of exemplars one develops a resemblance relation which enables the application of specific terms in symbolic generalizations to nature, and so the application of symbolic generalizations is through the piecemeal association of individual terms in the generalizations with features of the phenomenon to which the generalization is attached. This, then, is the picture that emerges if we view the exemplar case as strictly analogous to the Johnny case. But the resulting account seems to me defective in several respects. First, it requires that the terms in symbolic generalizations apply individually and in isolation to nature. In this respect, the analysis is subject to the same sort of objections raised against the Received View's one-time requirement that correspondence rules specify the application of individual theoretical terms to nature: the unit of application of symbolic generalizations is the generalization, not its constituent terms.[7] Second, Kuhn tells us in Section III that the symbolic generalizations applied often are special-case ones, and it is through the study of exemplars that one acquires the ability to determine the appropriate form of the generalization. Presumably the resemblance relation is supposed to play a crucial role in doing this. But if the resemblance relation only associates features of phenomena with terms occurring in generalizations, it is hard to see

[7] For discussion of the problem for correspondence rules, see Section II–A of my introduction to this volume.

how that will enable one to "see" or determine the appropriate *form* of the generalization to use, for knowing which words to use does not tell you how they should be combined to obtain the appropriate description. I conclude that if the exemplar case is strictly analogous to the Johnny case, then Kuhn's analysis is unsatisfactory.

Perhaps the problem is that I have insisted on too strict an analogy with respect to the Johnny case. If one considers Kuhn's historical case concerning the modeling of diverse phenomena on the pendulum problem (pp. 470–471), another way of construing Kuhn's thesis is suggested. In that case, what are grouped together are superficially diverse *phenomena*. Perhaps it is the case that the study of exemplars leads one to an ability to cluster as similar a wide variety of phenomena which previously seemed to have little in common. The resemblance relation then would cluster phenomena or systems, not features; and it would associate with each cluster an appropriate form of symbolic generalization. Such a picture will serve Kuhn's purposes, and in light of the pendulum case, seems to me close to what he has in mind. But if this is what Kuhn has in mind as resulting from the study of exemplars, then it is hard to see how the Johnny case is particularly relevant. For the Johnny case, and possibly Kuhn's computer simulation of it, are cases of learning language through a process of ostensive definition. And ostensive definition is a plausible means only for learning how to apply words to things; it does not give a plausible account how one learns to employ whole sentences—which are what interpreted symbolic generalizations in essence are. As such, it seems that the process involved in Kuhn's Johnny case, and possibly his computer simulation of it, cannot be the way whereby the study of exemplars leads to an ability to apply symbolic generalizations to nature.[8]

The problems we are encountering here are not simply a result of Kuhn's Johnny case being an overly simple first approximation. Rather there is a fundamental disanalogy between the exemplar case and the

[8] One might think there is the following out here: The resemblance relation comes to associate, for example, a wide variety of phenomena together and associates the description 'pendulum problem' with them; then, instead of 'pendulum problem', one associates the symbolic generalization '$F = -mg \sin\theta$' with it; thus one learns how to apply the generalization to nature. This will not do, however, for it only enables one to give the phenomena the name '$F = -mg \sin\theta$', and naming the phenomena does not enable one to correlate the various parameters in the generalization with aspects of the phenomena—which is what is required to apply the generalization *as a description* of the phenomena, or to give it empirical content.

Johnny case which Kuhn does not sufficiently appreciate.[9] The disanalogy is that exemplars are very unlike ostensive definitions. Most exemplars studied are printed in books, and have the features indicated above: the exemplar presents an informal description of an experimental setup and, *inter alia,* indicates how this description is to be translated or rendered into the language of theoretical generalizations. What the exemplars exemplify here is a connection between statements or descriptions in two different languages; they do not illustrate any *direct* application of symbolic generalizations to nature. Indeed, the connections between the informal description of the phenomenon or experimental setup and the symbolic generalizations exhibited by exemplars are somewhat analogous to the sorts of connections displayed by particular instances of correspondence rules—the primary difference being that the instances of correspondence rules also display the general form of the connection whereas the exemplars do not. In effect the exemplar says: such and such a description of a phenomenon in the informal language is to be rendered, for example, as '$F = -mg \sin\theta$' in the language of the symbolic generalizations. From the study of such sample translations, coupled with the working of exercises, (also printed and described in the informal language), the student is expected to acquire a fluency in translating from informal descriptions into the canonical descriptions of the symbolic generalizations. An analogy will help clarify the situation here. Suppose one is required to learn a second language in the following way: One first is taught the abstract grammar of the second language, but is told nothing semantical about the language. At no time is one given any definitions for particular words in the second language.[10] Instead, one is given various passages of English together with idiomatic or free translations of them into the second language. One, then, on the basis of just this, is required to begin translating other passages idiomatically into the second language;

[9] Kuhn's only indication that he is at all aware of it is in note 11 to his paper, which was added in revision. There he observes that there is a certain dissimilarity between his account and correspondence rules, in that his account attaches symbolic generalizations directly to nature, whereas correspondence rules connect words [he should have said sentences] with observation statements. What he has not yet appreciated is that exemplars are like correspondence rules in this respect, and not like ostensive definition.

[10] A more realistic assumption is that one is only given the meanings of a few words; the case is essentially the same if this more realistic assumption is made. The situation would be roughly that of learning Sanskrit where one knows the meanings of the various root morphemes, but is given no glosses for any polymorphic words. Indeed, the case under development is patterned after the typical procedure for teaching Sanskrit to Europeans and Americans—or at least the process whereby I was taught it.

these exercises are corrected, but at no time is one told any more than what the correct translation should have been. As a result of continuing this process one comes to be able to fluently translate from the one language to the other; eventually this leads to the ability to speak and think in the second language, rather than merely translate into it.[11] Learning how to apply symbolic generalizations through the study of exemplars and the working of exercises is strictly analogous. From one's prior study of mathematics one learns the grammar of the symbolic generalizations; the exemplars provide one with paradigmatic free or idiomatic translations from informal descriptions (in the first language) into descriptions in the language of the symbolic generalizations; except possibly for cognate associations, one is never given a dictionary defining the descriptive terms of the symbolic generalizations in terms of the informal language; and one's working of exercises amounts to trying one's hand at making idiomatic translations. Only after one has acquired the ability to make such translations fluently does one acquire the ability to think in the language of symbolic generalizations and apply them directly to nature.[12] Once it is realized that this is how the study of exemplars leads to the ability to apply generalizations to nature, it becomes obvious how unlike that process an ostensive definition is—how unlike the Johnny case the study of exemplars is.

If this discussion captures the essence of Kuhn's position, then I think it provides a partial explanation of his claims in *The Structure of Scientific Revolutions* that the paradigm (*qua* disciplinary matrix) partially determines or imposes constraints on what questions may legitimately be asked, what techniques may be employed in seeking solutions, and so on. For the particular language one uses restricts—particularly if it is a language of interpreted symbolic generalizations—the sorts of questions one can ask and the way descriptions can be applied to nature.

Having clarified what the resemblance relation groups together and also how the study of exemplars leads to an ability to apply symbolic generalizations to nature, we can return to our earlier question how the latter process relates to the resemblance relation.

[11] Note how similar the procedure is to that employed by a field linguist in "cracking" a language; it is something like, but not as difficult as, learning a language under radical translation circumstances.

[12] It needs to be emphasized that I am only describing how the study of exemplars teaches one to apply the generalizations to nature, which is to say, teaches one how to "set up" the problems in terms of the symbolic generalizations. This is only one of several things obtained from the study of exemplars; but it is the aspect Kuhn's analysis is concerned with here.

There is a basic sense in which things that are correctly given the same description in some language resemble each other in some respect; that this is so is virtually a tautology. But Kuhn means it as more than just this. His position seems to be that our coming to apply the same or similar descriptions to things or phenomena involves the acquisition of a *resemblance relation* which groups them together in clusters.[13] Indeed, the thrust of his Johnny case is that once one has obtained such a relation, it is the relation which determines what linguistic descriptions apply to what things or phenomena. With respect to this body of claims I wish only to make one critical observation. While the above account of the study of exemplars, coupled with the tautology indicated at the beginning of this paragraph, does lead to the conclusion that, as one comes to learn how to use the language of symbolic generalizations, one comes to see various phenomena as resembling each other; it also seems to follow that one thereby does acquire an ability to see resemblances. But nothing above, and nothing in Kuhn's paper, establishes that this involves or requires the *acquisition* or *internalization* of a resemblance *relation.* It seems to me that what requires that it be an internalized or possessed relation is a tacit assumption in Kuhn's paper that the resemblance relation will be a part of the disciplinary matrix, coupled with the requirement basic to his analysis of scientific change in *The Structure of Scientific Revolutions* that the disciplinary matrix be the common or shared *possession* of the community. It seems to me that this feature of his analysis leads him to reify the ability to see resemblances as a resemblance relation. This tendency to reify abilities into shared components seems to me one of the more undesirable features of Kuhn's approach.[14]

Kuhn tells us that his account of the acquisition of the resemblance relation is intended to replace the correspondence rule account of the Received View. He certainly is claiming that his account is intended to replace the correspondence rule account how symbolic generalizations apply to nature. But correspondence rules played another

[13] In fact, Kuhn's claims on the matter are not particularly consistent. Sometimes (for example, p. 471) he talks about an acquired *ability* to see resemblances between apparently disparate problems; this, of course, does not require that one possess any *relation* in virtue of which things are clustered. But as the paper progresses, this acquired ability gets transformed into the acquisition of a relation (for example, on pp. 472, 474, and 475, one finds stages of this transformation). This poses a problem in interpreting Kuhn. However, Kuhn indicates that he thinks this relation is the joint possession of the scientific community, and one gets the idea it is supposed to be a component of the disciplinary matrix; if so, then he seems committed to the stronger claim that one acquires a relation from the study of exemplars.

[14] See the concluding paragraphs of this paper.

function—namely, giving partial definitions to the terms occurring in symbolic generalizations—and it is not clear from what Kuhn says whether his account is also supposed to take over this function of correspondence rules. So far nothing in Kuhn's account how the study of exemplars and the solution of exercises leads to the attachment of meanings (or uses) to one's symbolic generalizations suggests that the study of exemplars defines these terms. Nonetheless, I want to argue that his general position (that is, the position in *The Structure of Scientific Revolutions* as modified by his paper in this volume) does commit him to the claim that the acquisition of the resemblance relation through the study of exemplars does, in an important sense, "define" the terms occurring in symbolic generalizations. Kuhn tells us that an individuating mark of a scientific community is its relatively full communication, where such fullness of communication does not occur between different communities. What accounts for the presence or absence of this relatively full communication, according to Kuhn, is that the members of a scientific community share a disciplinary matrix, whereas members of different communities do not have a common disciplinary matrix. From this I think we can conclude that the possessors of different disciplinary matrixes attach different meanings to whatever words they have in common; a consideration of Kuhn's other writings reinforces this suggestion.[15] Can this claim about meaning difference be accounted for solely on the basis of how one uses terms occurring in one's symbolic generalizations, in how these terms, or the generalizations they occur in, are attached to nature? I think not. Consider two hypothetical scientific communities, one of which accepts and employs relativity theory and the other of which employs classical mechanics. Further, let us assume that both communities are only concerned with phenomena which classical mechanics can predict equally well, and let us suppose that their exemplars are exactly the same, except the classical mechanics community employs the classical mechanics analogues to the symbolic generalizations used by the relativity theory community. Let us also suppose they employ the same theoretical terms (*qua* uninterpreted symbols) in their symbolic generalizations. Finally, let us suppose that they train their students in strictly analogous fashions. Under these circumstances it is clear that so long as members of the two communities confine their discussions to descriptions of phenomena in the vocabulary of their symbolic generalizations, they would have relatively full communication; only

[15] See, for example, the discussion on pp. 96ff. and in Section V of Kuhn [1962], and also Kuhn's "translation" account of the resolution of paradigm disputes in Kuhn [1970a], Section 6, which seem to presuppose this claim.

when they started to manipulate these descriptions using their respective theories would they come to disagreements. For example, they would both agree in the diagrammatic representation of a particular pendulum; but they would disagree on what laws or symbolic generalizations to employ in performing subsequent calculations. This indicates that insofar as the meanings of the terms are a function of ways in which they use them to describe phenomena, they attach the same meanings to the terms; differently put, their use of descriptive terms in the theory are such that they share the same resemblance relation for clustering phenomena. However, they do possess different disciplinary matrixes since they possess different symbolic generalizations, and one's stock of symbolic generalizations are, for Kuhn, an individuating feature of disciplinary matrixes. Since they possess different disciplinary matrixes, by the above they must attach different meanings to the terms in the symbolic generalizations; clearly the differences in meaning must be traced to something other than the resemblance relation. The only plausible source of these meaning differences is the different symbolic generalizations they accept.[16] As the primary differences in their respective symbolic generalizations are in the relations holding between their constituent terms, it follows that the various interconnections specified in the accepted symbolic generalizations contribute to the meaning of, or exert a "defining" influence on, the terms occurring in them. Indeed, the situation is very much like that maintained by one version of the Received View which claims that the conjunction of the laws of a theory with the correspondence rules "implicitly defines" the theoretical terms in the laws. Only here, it is the symbolic generalizations together with the *use* (as mediated by the resemblance relation) of the symbolic generalizations in applying them to nature which "implicitly defines" the terms occurring in the symbolic generalizations. In effect, the connections in the symbolic generalizations establish a crisscrossed network of interlocking terms or concepts, and the resemblance relation enables one to apply that whole network of concepts to nature. Since these symbolic generalizations occur in the exemplars, and the resemblance relation develops as one learns to use these generalizations in application to nature, it follows that there is an important sense in which the study of exemplars does supply the theoretical terms with a partial definition —in the sense they become "implicitly defined" as a result of learning

[16] In fact there are other possibilities, such as differences in the models they accept; for the sake of argument, we can assume that their models, and so on, do not differ significantly.

to apply symbolic generalizations to nature. The only way I can see to avoid this claim is to give up the assumption that possessors of different disciplinary matrixes invariably attach different meanings to whatever words they possess in common; doing so would in turn require that Kuhn give up or severely attenuate the various incommensurability claims made in *The Structure of Scientific Revolutions.*

Let us grant that the study of the exemplars does yield the resemblance relationship and "implicitly defines" the terms or concepts occurring in the symbolic generalizations in the manner just sketched, and now raise the question whether these alone provide the complete conceptual content of those terms or concepts? As a first step, let us limit ourselves to the sort of exemplars whose symbolic generalizations are rather low-level and not special forms or cases of some more general symbolic generalizations—say laws such as Snell's law or Boyle's law at the time when they were first advanced. Take Boyle's law—are there any contributors to the definitions of its constituent terms that do not show up in the exemplars? I would submit that there are at least the following sorts: First the words expressing the terms occurring in symbolic generalizations usually have prescientific meanings or else meanings deriving from earlier theories they occurred in, many of which carry over into the terms as they occur in the symbolic generalizations of the theory—for example, they still connote (at least partially) the prescientific idea of pressure being a force brought to bear. That is, there is something to Toulmin's thesis that theoretical terms were originally nonscientific terms which undergo a language-shift.[17] Indeed, I would go so far as to suggest that if Kuhn's account how the study of exemplars leads to an ability to correctly apply symbolic generalizations to nature is workable it is partially because the terms in the symbolic generalizations retain something of the conceptual content of the corresponding pretheoretic uses of the terms and/or the uses of these terms in the infomal precanonical description of the experiment to which the symbolic generalization is applied. Second, there are various usually unstated presuppositions required for the application of the symbolic manipulations to be legitimate.[18] For example, the symbolic manipulations employed with Snell's law presuppose the rectilinear principle of light propagation. Thus, we see that even in the very low-level laws, the conceptual apparatus depends upon more than just that conceptual content which comes from the,

[17] See Toulmin [1953], p. 13.

[18] Although they are unstated in the exemplars, they usually are given more or less explicit statements elsewhere when the law is being advanced.

study of the exemplars and thereby is supplied by the learned resemblance relation.[19]

Now let us consider a more complicated situation—one where the symbolic generalizations which show up in exemplars are special-case solutions or formulations of some more basic equations or symbolic generalizations. In such cases, the meanings of terms occurring in the generalizations depend upon all of the connections, associations, and so on already described, plus those connections required to deduce the special cases from the more general ones.[20] Typically these derivations do not proceed in the manner suggested by axiomatics, but rather require a number of physical assumptions and approximations (for example, in deriving classical from relativistic mechanics one has to assume that $(v/c)^2 << 1$).[21] This observation, taken in conjunction with Kuhn's earlier claims about the incommensurability of laws and theories under paradigm-switch, indicates that these assumptions contribute to the definition or meaning of the terms occurring in symbolic generalizations.[22] Because such physical assumptions are required for the derivation of the special-form generalizations from the more general ones, these physical assumptions establish connections that help "define" the theoretical terms that occur in the derivative low-level generalizations, whereas they did not show up in the definition of these concepts when the generalization earlier was a self-contained law not dependent upon a more encompassing theory. In such cases, the physical approximation now contributes to the definition of the concept; this approximation probably will be reflected in a changed resemblance relation, and so there is a real sense in which we now are using the terms to express different concepts than we did before. This adds to our understanding of Kuhn's incommensurability claim; however it does not necessarily establish as warranted the extreme forms of its associated with Kuhn, and especially with Feyerabend.[23]

[19] Indeed, it appears doubtful that the required sort of resemblance relation could be obtained without presupposing this other conceptual apparatus.

[20] Note that there is the definite possibility that the more general formulas may show up in no exemplars, and so that terms in symbolic generalizations may depend upon such additional generalizations for their meanings. This will be the case, for example, for the Schrödinger wave equation in quantum theory.

[21] This is the Babylonian (as opposed to Euclidean) nature of mathematics in science which Professor Feynman discusses in Feynman [1965], Ch. 2.

[22] If they do not, then Kuhn's arguments against the reducibility of classical mechanics to relativistic mechanics fail; see Kuhn [1962], pp. 100ff.

[23] But we shall see below that there is an extreme form of it which does follow —a form analogous to that discussed in Bohm's paper in Session IV above. It should be emphasized that the plausibility of the incommensurability claim, as

Turning to the *disciplinary matrix* now, Kuhn's basic characterization is that it "is the common possession of a professional discipline" and that he recognizes it as containing three kinds of elements which he refers to as symbolic generalizations, models, and exemplars (p. 463). This is insufficiently precise and invites the sort of undesirable plastic employment that the paradigm experienced. However, on the basis of the above discussion, I think that a somewhat more precise account can be given. The disciplinary matrix contains all those shared elements which make for relative fullness of professional communication and unanimity of professional judgement. These include values for judging the adequacy of scientific work,[24] models, ontological commitments, symbolic generalizations, a language, with meanings specific to that community, for interpreting symbolic generalizations, and so on. From our previous discussion we have seen the terms (alternatively the concepts they embody) occurring in symbolic generalizations constitute an interlocking network which provides the terms (or concepts) with a partial "implicit definition"; their meanings are further embellished by the resemblance relation which governs the correct application to nature of assertions in the language of symbolic generalizations. That the terms (or the concepts they embody) do constitute such an interlocking network suggests that disciplinary matrixes *inter alia* are (or supply, or include) a *conceptual framework*.[25] The fact that in *The Structure of Scientific Revolutions* Kuhn repeatedly says that paradigms (*qua* disciplinary matrixes) supply the scientist with a perspective for viewing the world, and so forth, strongly suggests that Kuhn views disciplinary matrixes *inter alia* as *Weltanschauungen*;[26] and since Kant it has been common to construe *Weltanschauungen* as conceptual frameworks. All of this strongly suggests that disciplinary matrixes centrally contain conceptual frameworks—or at least something closely analogous to them.

It was observed above that possessors of different disciplinary ma-

---

just sketched, is parasitic to the assumption that differences in disciplinary matrixes require differences in the meanings attached to the terms occurring in symbolic generalizations.

[24] It is only in Kuhn [1970a], and the "Postscript" to Kuhn [1970b], that the role of values in disciplinary matrixes becomes emphasized.

[25] I take this somewhat metaphorical characterization to indicate the sort of network which C. I. Lewis had in mind in Lewis [1929], and suggested by Quine [1953], pp. 20–46, and by Putnam [1962a].

[26] Kuhn [1962] reads as if paradigms qua disciplinary matrixes were nothing more than conceptual frameworks or *Weltanschauungen*. In his later writings, for example, Kuhn [1970a] and [1970b], Kuhn explicitly acknowledges values, and so on, as additional components of disciplinary matrixes; of course values were *tacitly* there all along.

trixes attach different meanings to the terms occurring in their constituent symbolic generalizations. We have also seen how, on Kuhn's analysis, these meanings relate to the resemblance relation and how that relation is acquired through the study of exemplars. That account strongly suggests that if different exemplars are studied then different resemblance relations will be developed. Assuming this is so, I think we have a way of substantiating Kuhn's claim that it is the difference in shared disciplinary matrixes which distinguishes the various scientific disciplinary groups (pp. 463 *passim*). Kuhn has in mind as disciplinary groups recognizable scientific communities usually comprised of no more than 100 members. Now, if one looks at the community of, say, physicists, one sees that it must include a large number of disciplinary groups. In the main all these physicists will share a common stock of symbolic generalizations, models, and pretheoretic concepts. Accordingly, on the above account, the differences in disciplinary matrixes which distinguish the various disciplinary groups will have to be largely a result of different resemblance relationships resulting from the study of different sets of exemplars. But is this possible? For do not physicists study essentially the same things in their formal course work? What this points out is that whatever exemplars there are which account for the gross differences between disciplinary groups will be exemplars which are obtained only after one finishes course work and engages in research; thus differences in resemblance relations will come only with specialization. And these exemplars will be the more esoteric state-of-the-art experiments in the recent journals, and more important, the private unpublished reports and communications which are circulated among the small groups of scientists who communicate and collaborate with each other about their current research. Only if these are counted as exemplars does one get the sort of division into conceptually distinguished disciplinary groups Kuhn postulates.[27] This points out that while the different disciplinary groups may have different disciplinary matrixes, the differences in the constituent components will be rather subtle ones and not easily identified. Presumably, major differences will show up only during crisis periods or across scientific revolutions.

In this paper Kuhn does not explicitly state what he understands a theory to be. However, in various parts of his paper (for example, pp. 464–465) there lurks implicitly the suggestion that theories are interpreted symbolic generalizations: A theory is a collection of symbolic

[27] Notice, incidentally, that if this were not so, the linkages among citations that Kuhn takes as the marks of different disciplinary groups (p. 462) would not distinguish the groups in the manner he requires.

generalizations with specific meanings attached to its constituent terms. Presumably, then, any differences in the meanings attached to a collection of symbolic generalizations will result in different theories. Moreover, at various places in *The Structure of Scientific Revolutions*[28] Kuhn's discussion seems to presuppose this is what theories are. Assuming that this is what Kuhn understands by a theory, the discussion of the preceding paragraph implies that the various different disciplinary groups within a branch of science (for example, within physics) will employ different theories which, while agreeing in the main, diverge at the fringes. However comfortable or uncomfortable this makes one, it is a corollary to this that there is even a greater proliferation of theories. The reason is as follows. Granting that one can obtain a resemblance relationship in the manner Kuhn postulates, it does not follow that all members of a given disciplinary group will obtain the same one; all that can be guaranteed is that the differences within a given disciplinary group will be sufficiently small as to preclude serious disagreements in actual applications of symbolic generalizations. But each individual member of the disciplinary group can be expected to obtain a slightly different resemblance relation, hence employ a different disciplinary matrix, and accordingly will employ a different theory. Moreover, as one assimilates an ever increasing stock of exemplars, there will be minor adjustments or refinements in the resemblance relationship, and so one's theory will change with time. Thus we find ourselves in a situation very much like the one described by David Bohm,[29] where each scientist at each time is employing a different theory. Several implications of this consequence need to be noted. Since difference in meaning means differences in disciplinary matrixes, it follows that members of a disciplinary group do not possess the same disciplinary matrix; and so they do not possess the same theory either. What they do possess are different disciplinary matrixes and theories whose differences are sufficiently minor that they do not manifest themselves in normal applications. This indicates that Kuhn is mistaken in supposing that the shared possession of a disciplinary matrix or theory is what accounts for the relative fullness of communication and unanimity of professional judgment within a disciplinary group; rather, if one maintains Kuhn's views on meaning, it will have to be the fact that the members' disciplinary matrixes are sufficiently similar, which accounts for this open communication and agreement in judgment. Of course, spelling this out will encounter the formidable problem of specifying what sorts of similarity are required and how

[28] See, for example, Kuhn [1962], pp. 96ff.
[29] See his paper in Session IV above.

similar is similar enough. One can, of course, avoid this difficulty by changing one's meaning analysis in such a way that all members of a given disciplinary group do attach the same meanings to the same symbolic generalizations. Specifying that account of meaning will not be easy; moreover, it is not clear that one can do so and still maintain Kuhn's resemblance relation. An out to this would be to give up the idea that there is a resemblance relation, maintaining that through the study of exemplars one comes to see resemblances in phenomena and associate these resemblances with certain symbolic generalizations; and in such cases, those who see the same phenomena as resembling each other and as calling for the application of the same symbolic generalizations will be able to communicate freely no matter how different the meanings are they attach to nature. So construed, I think Kuhn's basic and sound insight that one learns to use symbolic formulas through the study of exemplars remains, and something like the process discussed above is an adequate analysis. Of course, adopting this approach carries with it a price—namely, one no longer can plausibly maintain that the characteristic relative fullness of communication is to be explained in terms of a shared something possessed by all members of the disciplinary group.

This last observation brings me to one last general point. I would suggest that the individual variation, which we saw as occurring in theories under Kuhn's view and leads to different theories for different people, also will occur for a number of other components of disciplinary matrixes, such as models and values. In conjunction with the above, this leads to the following observation: If one insists that members of a disciplinary group share a common something, a common disciplinary matrix, all disciplinary groups will consist of a single individual. Kuhn's claim that members of a disciplinary group share a common disciplinary matrix thus seems ultimately to be indefensible. This raises the question, why does Kuhn have to insist on some entity such as a disciplinary matrix as a common possession? The answer is, I think, that he really does not need to. It seems to me that to account for normal science all he has to assume is that scientists in a particular scientific community are in sufficient agreement on what theory to employ, what counts as good and bad science, what the relevant questions are, how to apply theories to nature, what sorts of work to take as exemplary, and so forth, and communicate freely enough that only certain characteristic problems are seriously considered. To account for revolutions, one only needs to say that such unanimity breaks down in certain characteristic ways, and that these breakdowns typically get resolved in certain ways. All of this can be said without supposing any common possessions such as disciplinary matrixes; and what is more, it seems to me that if *The Structure of Scientific Revolutions* is divorced accordingly from the assumption of a disciplinary matrix which is the common possession of a disciplinary group, then much of the substance of that work still stands. Indeed, when so divorced I think Kuhn's view becomes a quite plausible and revealing useful analysis of the scientific enterprise. More immediately, I think that when Kuhn's analysis in "Second Thoughts on Paradigms" is similarly divorced from the assumption of shared resemblance relations, disciplinary matrixes, and the like, one does find an extremely illuminating and insightful analysis of how it is that the scientist comes to be able to apply symbolic generalizations to nature in a creative and open-ended manner.

To summarize, as one has come to expect from Kuhn, "Second Thoughts on Paradigms" is a pregnant paper loaded with original and valuable insights on the nature of the scientific enterprise. But as one also has come to expect, Kuhn has clouded these insights by his insistance on reifying his insights into shared entities—paradigms in *The Structure of Scientific Revolutions* and now disciplinary matrixes and shared resemblance relations—which are supposed to account for and explain the features of the scientific enterprise he discusses. His insights are too important, and potentially too valuable, to be clouded or obscured by such exercises in reification—and I wish he would stop populating science with new entities so that we more easily can have access to his insights.

Discussion

Professor Kuhn:[1]

Without excessively straining the normal proprieties of time and space, I cannot hope to reply point by point to Dr. Suppe's commentary. Rather than make the attempt, I here restrict myself to issues the neglect of which would risk special damage. Since misunderstandings, which cannot be unique to Dr. Suppe, are the most likely source of such damage, I am particularly grateful for the opportunity to clarify essentials which his considerable expansion of his remarks to the symposium supplies.[2]

I take up first the issue with which Dr. Suppe closes, the accusation that I am "populating science with new entities" (p. 499). If entities were the only referents for words, he would clearly be right, but I think neither of us takes so Parmenidean a position. As to entities, excepting resemblance relationships, I deal only with the standard list but am saying different things about it. For "disciplinary matrix," in particular, I would be glad to be able to substitute the standard term "theory." Before an audience composed less exclusively of philosophers I might have done so. My point would then have been that the elements which constitute the theory shared by the practitioners of a given specialty cannot be entirely represented by verbal and symbolic strings. Dr.

1 *Editor's note*: The following remarks by Professor Kuhn were written in response to my revised commentary on his contribution to this session, and replace his original comments on the version of my commentary read at the symposium. The footnotes to his reply are all written by him, and so (deviating from the previous style for discussions) are in the first person.

2 Though the first to be written, my contribution to the symposium is the last to be published of three recent essays considering problems raised by my book. The other two are: an extra chapter, "Postscript—1969," in the second edition of *The Structure of Scientific Revolutions* (Chicago: University of Chicago Press, 1970), pp. 174–210, and "Reflections on My Critics" in I. Lakatos and A. Musgrave, eds., *Criticism and the Growth of Knowledge* (Cambridge: Cambridge University Press, 1970), pp. 231–278. At some of the points where these later essays overlap my paper in this volume, readers may find evidence that I learn from experience.

Suppe's misconstruction of what I would take a theory to be shows, however, how hard it is to make a point of that sort at this time. Though he himself has grave doubts about what he calls "the received view," he can retrieve theory from my text only by selecting out precisely those abstract elements from which a theory has traditionally been constructed. What I have been trying to say, however, is that such traditional constructions are at once too rich and too poor to represent what scientists have in mind when they speak of their adherence to a particular theory. On the one hand, the traditional constructions contain a larger number of specific generalizations than are shared by those who adhere to the theory in question; on the other, they omit elements which are critically important in providing the scientist's theory with content.

Among those elements the sort I have particularly emphasized in my paper consists of concrete problem solutions. Surely philosophers have been aware of their existence, in which case my grouping them together under the rubric "exemplars" cannot have added a new entity to the universe of discourse about science. What I have hoped it might do, however, is persuade philosophers to take the role of such received solutions more seriously. My claim has been that exemplary problem solutions are one of the essential vehicles for the cognitive content of a theory. A theory consists, among other things, of verbal and symbolic generalizations *together with* examples of their function in use. The same generalizations combined with different exemplars would develop in different directions and would thus constitute a somewhat different cognitive system. On occasions, as the discussion of the *vis viva* theorem in my paper should indicate, exemplars can provide detailed knowledge of nature in the virtual absence of anything the philosophical tradition would recognize as a theory. Extending that discussion to the eighteenth-century study of vibrating strings would show how the choice of different concrete models, as the exemplars appropriate to a given problem, can produce two theories where there had been but one before.[3]

Dr. Suppe fears that any position of this sort will, for two sets of reasons, require the recognition of the existence at any given time of an impossibly large number of different theories. All physicists, he sug-

[3] For a cogent elaboration of the thesis that "the paradigm [in the sense of exemplar] is something which can function when the theory is not there," see Margaret Masterman, "The Nature of a Paradigm," in Lakatos and Musgrave, *Criticism and the Growth of Knowledge*, pp. 59–89. For the vibrating string controversy, see J. R. Ravetz, "Vibrating Strings and Arbitrary Functions," in *The Logic of Personal Knowledge: Essays Presented to Michael Polanyi on His Seventieth Birthday* (New York: Free Press, 1961), pp. 71–88.

gests by way of example (pp. 496ff), "will share a common stock of symbolic generalizations, models, and pre-theoretic concepts." Since they also "study essentially the same things in their formal course work," the differences between different disciplinary groups must derive exclusively from exemplars which can themselves differ only if they are drawn from "the more esoteric state-of-the-art experiments in the recent journals" together with "privately unpublished reports and communications." The resulting differences between disciplinary groups must therefore, he claims, "be rather subtle ones and not easily identified. Presumably major differences will show up only during crisis periods or revolutions." I take his point to be that no differences so esoteric should be equated with differences of theory and that they therefore need not much concern philosophers of science.

That analysis is, however, faithful neither to the facts of physics education nor to my paper. In most physics departments different patterns of formal course work begin, at the very latest, with the choice of fields for general examinations. (For especially bright students they begin in college.) What results from them is not only differences in exemplars but also in models and in the canonical form of some symbolic generalizations. These differences are further magnified in the course of thesis research and the recently standard postdoctoral years. Their consequence is so subtle that a standard complaint in the profession is the inability of any physicist to read more than a small subset, determined by his speciality, of the papers published in a general physics journal, like the assembled sections of the *Physical Review*. One need not follow my lead and invoke differences of theory or of disciplinary matrix to explain the existence within physics of disciplinary groups which can scarcely read each other's work. Alternatives are presumably available. But one may not, I think, follow Dr. Suppe in acting as though no alternative were needed and as though the cognitive apparatus required for even routine research could be constituted from elements which all these groups share.

More serious difficulties are presented by the second sort of theory proliferation which Dr. Suppe fears, but their gravity is not a function of the differences between my views and more usual notions. He points out that, if standard problem solutions (to say nothing of the other components of a disciplinary matrix) are a part of a theory, then no two scientists will emerge from training with quite the same theory: "all disciplinary groups will consist of a single individual" (p. 498). That difficulty is, however, equally (or as little) acute for any view of science which has recourse, for example, to the notion of pretheoretic terms or of a basic vocabulary. No two speakers acquire either their native or their professional language in exactly the same ways, and there is no reason to suppose that they would use any word or sentence in identical ways under all conceivable circumstances. It is not easy to understand why breakdowns or even apparent inhibitions of communication so seldom result from these circumstances, but that problem is not a consequence of learning from exemplars but only of the fact that language must be learned.

Dr. Suppe supposes that the difficulties of the sort just considered will vanish if we merely "assume that scientists in a particular community are in sufficient agreement about what theory to employ, what counts as good and bad science," and other matters of the sort (p. 498). But what is *sufficient* agreement? And what must one have agreed about, sufficiently or not, in order to have agreed "what theory to employ"? It is precisely questions of this sort, products of the attempt to describe normal science, that have driven me to the locutions which Dr. Suppe finds so strange, and the questions remain when the locutions are banished. Equally ineffective is Dr. Suppe's attempt to return me to better known ground by partially assimilating a disciplinary matrix to a "conceptual framework" (p. 495). The latter notion, when I first encountered it, was a source of great liberation from the confines of Dr. Suppe's "received view." But surely it was then characterized by and still retains all the plasticity and vagueness of which he complains in criticizing my position. If the term "conceptual framework" has had, as I suppose, a significant and fruitful function in philosophy of science, it provides no resting point.

Turn next to the earlier portion of Dr. Suppe's commentary where he questions the appropriateness of what he calls "the Johnny case." One of the issues he raises is, I think, of first-rate importance, but some brush must be cleared before it can be considered. Of course the Johnny case is, as Dr. Suppe emphasizes, vastly simpler than any of those which involve learning from exemplars to apply laws of nature, but I see no basis for the claim that it is barred in principle from developing in the direction required.

To understand exemplars, Dr. Suppe asserts, we must learn to deal with the employment of whole sentences. The Johnny case, he continues, being pure ostensive definition, is powerless to go beyond the application of words to things (p. 487). In two respects, however, the phrase "ostensive definition" misses central aspects of the process I have described. First, more than definition is involved: Johnny learns not only how to use certain words but also something about what the world contains and about how the newly named entities behave. Though nouns are the only linguistic entities involved, the information acquired in learning to use them is in part lawlike, a surprising characteristic for so elementary a process. Second, the procedures employed during learning transcend the usual limits of ostension: Johnny must be shown not only ducks, but also swans and geese which might be mistaken for them; he may, in addition, be allowed to attempt identifications for himself and corrected when he goes astray. If he can be imagined simultaneously to be learning syntax elsewhere, I see no reason of principle why the same extended process of "ostension" should not play a significant role in the transition from the word "duck" to the phrase "swimming duck" to the sentence "there is a duck swimming." Only one further step would then be needed before Johnny, now grown older, should be able to apply to nature a symbolic law-sketch like '$f = ma$'. He must, that is, be able not only to pick out the forces, masses, and accelerations (ducks, geese, and swans) in a particular laboratory situation, but also to recognize which mass is to be paired with which acceleration under the influence of which force. No model so elementary as mine can represent all that is involved, but why, given the long-standing inadequacy of other accounts of the process, should the attempt to make it do so be barred in principle? Fresh approaches to problems of this sort are badly needed.

Dr. Suppe's charge of "fundamental disanalogy" (p. 487) between the Johnny case and the application of exemplars does not, however, rest entirely upon the distinction between learning words and learning sentences. Exemplars, he points out, are often presented in written form. The problem of applying them is then a problem of translation from the informal verbal description of a laboratory situation to the canonical language of symbolic generalizations. Since Johnny's learning experience in the park involves nothing like translation, it cannot, he supposes, instruct us about the role of exemplars. This move to translation is important, far more so than the space I can allot to it here would suggest. Let me try, however, to indicate, first, how much more is at stake than I believe Dr. Suppe sees and, then, how I should begin to resist, not the move to translation, but his way of formulating it.

My main and most persistent criticism of the recent tradition in philosophy of science has been its total restriction of attention to syntactic at the expense of semantic problems. One posits a sense datum language, a physical thing language, or a basic vocabulary, the attachments of which to nature are unproblematic. With firm semantic ground thus apparently assured, one takes up for special scrutiny only those problems which involve the relations of words to words or sentences to sentences—for example, the manner in which "meanings" rise through the deductive structure of a theory from the unproblematic basic vocabulary of experimental reports to the otherwise undefined theoretical terms. Against such formulations I have elsewhere argued that no adequate basic vocabulary is shared in its entirety by a given theory and its postrevolutionary successor. In my contribution to the symposium I have maintained also that high level theoretical statements like the Schrödinger equation or Newton's second law do not attach to nature only through their consequences but also directly, during their passage from law-sketch to appropriate special case, a phenomenon which should make the meaning of theoretical terms more problematic. For these and other reasons, I have contended, problems of attaching word-strings to nature must be considered central to philosophy of science. That is what, more than anything else, my talk of exemplars and the Johnny case has been about. Dr. Suppe's formulation of the move to translation removes at one stroke all these elements from my position. We are restricted once more to the classical range of problems: attaching words to words. I am bound to resist.

In doing so, however, I may not simply deny the relevance of translation. Exemplars are presented in written form; when they are, "translation" is an appropriate label for the process by which they are reformulated in symbolic form. Only, there is something about learning to do these translations that Dr. Suppe misses. The student must be supplied with more than just informal descriptions and symbolic translations (compare his p. 488). For some time he also requires pictures, diagrams, and, above all, demonstration and laboratory exercises. He must, that is, learn the world to which both the informal verbal and the symbolic strings apply. His position is that of Quine's radical translator who requires not simply utterances but also the stimuli which prompt them before he can begin to learn to translate. My Johnny case was intended to apply only to those cases in which the laboratory situation is presented rather than described and for which the term "translation" is correspondingly misleading. There are others, as Dr. Suppe emphasizes, which do involve translation essentially, but they do not at all eliminate the role of exposure to the laboratory world from the process of learning from exemplars.

Those remarks will, I hope, make one brief correction of Dr. Suppe's redescription of exemplars seem less like a quibble. In listing the components into which exemplars may be analyzed, he includes as item (5), "some sort of description how the experiment is to be translated from the original description to canonical redescription" (p. 484). Elsewhere he writes that exemplars "indicate which forms of the laws or symbolic generalizations are applicable under various circumstances" (p. 485) and that an exemplar "indicates how [a particular] description is to be translated or rendered into the language of theoretical generalizations" (p. 488). But, even restricting attention to those cases in which the term "translation" is appropriate, my point would be very nearly the reverse of his. Though exposure to exemplars teaches students to translate, there need be nothing about any exemplar which "describes" or "indicates" how to translate. Exemplars may be, and sometimes are, simply presented whole, like Johnny's ducks.

I come finally to Dr. Suppe's extended remarks concerning meanings and definitions, about which I shall here have very little to say, except that I cannot see where, in this area, he thinks we disagree. Much of his argument rests on his conclusion that my views require "the possessors of different disciplinary matrices [to] attach different meanings to whatever words they have in common" (p. 491). But I can see no reason for any such conclusion: "some difference in some meanings of some words they have in common" is the most I have ever intended to claim.[4] Elsewhere Dr. Suppe's argument appears to depend upon my resisting his thesis that both pretheoretic meanings and symbolic generalizations play a role, together with exemplars, in supplying meanings for theoretic terms. But, though I would add models to his list of meaning-determiners, I would otherwise agree with much of the position he develops against me. In particular, I would agree that "there is an important sense in which the study of exemplars does supply the theoretic terms with a partial definition—in the sense that they become 'implicitly defined' as a result of learning to apply symbolic generalizations to nature" (p. 492). At least I would agree if I still felt at all confident that I knew what a "meaning" or a "partial definition" was.

With one other aspect of Dr. Suppe's commentary my agreement is even less equivocal. My presentation to the symposium was drawn from work-in-progress, and it is therefore at least as crude, preliminary, and simplistic as he claims. For good reasons I doubt that it is so plastic, so capable of being all things to all people, as the one to be found in my book. But I do not for a moment suppose it complete, and I have not stopped work.

Professor Shapere:

Prof. Kuhn talks about there being similarity relationships, and I want to ask first about this and then broaden the question. I want to start by asking whether the similarity relationships are there to be found?

[4] About other aspects of the problem of incommensurability, I have, however, changed my views. For these see, "Postscript—1969," pp. 198–204, and "Reflections on My Critics," pp. 266–277.

If that is what you mean, that sounds quite a bit like the old notion of pure observation which you seem to be very much against throughout your work. In any case, whether they are there to be found or whether they are somehow invented, presumably these communities that you talk about picked out some of them as being significant or important. But there another question comes up, and that is, are they important relationships because the community picked them out, or does the community pick them out because there is some good reason to pick them out? Or, in terms of your notion of exemplars, are the exemplars exemplars because the community licenses them or does the community license them because there are good reasons for them being considered as exemplars? I think this is important because if you take the first alternative—namely, that the exemplars (or, correspondingly, the similarity relationships) are exemplars because the community licenses them—then although you may have escaped a private-individual theory of science nevertheless you have got a private-group view on your hands, and you thus get into the same kind of relativism that you had in your book. On the other hand, if you take the other alternative—namely, that the community licenses them because there are good reasons for considering them to be exemplars—then although your reference to community may be sociologically interesting, it nevertheless is not illuminating as far as understanding the rationale behind the use or role of exemplars in science. For then no reference to the community is necessary because although the community teaches them and uses them, nevertheless the reasons for using them are things that are independent of the community. Now all of that, of course, gives rise to the wider question: how much of the relativism of the *Structure of Scientific Revolutions*[5] are you willing to keep here? In answering these questions that I just asked you, it seems that you will be showing how much of that you want to keep and how much you want to give up, because it is these alternatives that seem to me to be left unclear in your paper; and which you embrace will determine whether you want to keep that relativism, or avoid it and return to the analysis of the rationale behind scientific progress.

Professor Kuhn:

It has been clear from the beginning that I could not hope to restrict the discussion to those aspects of my book that I now feel somewhat better prepared to talk to than I was when I wrote it. As a result, I do not think there is any way of preserving a quick-question quick-

[5] Kuhn [1962]; the relativism being referred to is sketched in Shapere [1964].

answer mode, and I shall therefore have to speak to the larger questions, like Dudley's, as they come, rather than trying to store them in memory for a brief concluding summary.

As to the relativism question, let me attack it first frontally, not from the point of view of the similarity relationship. I want to say about it that, although there are all sorts of problems in the area to which Dudley points, the people who read my book and then come out and say relativism *tout court* are misreading it. I think Dudley did so in his review, and I am sorry that I have never been able to persuade him of it. Let me, however, try once more, because, if it does not work with Dudley, it may at least give some other people more of a sense of what I am after. At the end of the book I talk about an evolutionary model or an evolutionary metaphor for scientific development, and I wish people took the metaphor more seriously than they do. If you would think of science's developing in the usual evolutionary treelike pattern, then I think it not only possble, but indeed quite easy, to do the following: design a set of criteria which would permit a neutral observer to say which of two theories for the same aspect of nature was the later (the more evolved) and which was the earlier. In biological evolution such criteria include specialization and articulation; similar criteria will work for science as well. In this sense scientific development is a unidirectional and irreversible process, and that is not a relativistic view.

Nevertheless, there is a sense in which my view seems relativistic, and it is the same one that bothered people about Darwinism. When I was a high-school student, the problems showed up as standard debating topics: Is the savage happier than the civilized man? Or, is a man better than an ape? These are questions that arise when one starts viewing development as toward a particular goal laid down at the beginning of time. For science, that goal has been a theory that tells what is really there; in evolution it was provided by God's plan for men. But one has learned to get along without taking man to be the realization of a preordained goal and to see him instead as a highly evolved organism. I think one will do the same for science. I do not suggest that I have just eliminated all problems. But under these circumstances to say relativism *tout court* is to miss the point, particularly the point at which work needs to be done.

Now let me briefly apply this answer to Dudley's particular question about the similarity relationship: is it there to be found or is it there because we put it there? I said in my paper that if you model the relationship on a computer or otherwise, it will not work with merely random stimuli. In a universe of random stimuli, no processing will create data clusters that endure, for the next stimulus is as likely to fall in empty space as in a cluster. In that sense, learning a similarity relationship is learning something about nature that is there to be found. It informs you of *a* way to group stimuli in natural families, and only some groupings will do.

But in another sense the group does put them there (*or finds them already there*), and what I want most to resist about the question is the implication that it must have a yes or no answer. We have no recourse to stimuli as given, but are always—by the time we can see or talk or do science—already initiated to a data world that the community has divided in a certain way. I presume that the group might have done the division job in other ways; there are various ways to group stimuli into natural-data clusters. But it has done so in one particular way and initiates are stuck with it. It is a good way, or the group would not have survived, but there is no way to get outside it—back to stimuli—and to specify the respects in which it is good or to compare it with all the ways in which the world might have been divided. That does not mean that world-divisions of this sort are never changed, nor that choice and good reasons for it do not enter. But the choice is always between the historically given way and a single alternative that has been invented because the older way no longer functions well at particular points. I can specify good reasons for making the choice; it is not at all the case that any choice at all would do. But they are reasons that apply only at particular turning points in the evolutionary process, not to a fresh choice among all possible ways of doing the job.

Professor Bromberger:

I have a strange and surprising urge to defend the correspondence-rule philosophers. Your talk about ducks and geese is interesting, but it does not at all *show* the "reconstruction" by means of correspondence rules cannot work. In fact, it seems to me that if you are right about the facts, then it *must* be possible to come up with the right correspondence rules. Let me put it differently. It seems to me that there are three issues that you ought to distinguish. Let us think of the child and think of him as the big child who is a scientist. The first issue is, does this child, after having been taken through the park, *use* correspondence rules (or as I would prefer to call them in this case, "projection rules")?

The second issue is whether we can *formulate* these rules. The third issue is whether learning an explicit formulation of the rules could replace learning by exemplars—that is, would the classification, or the equivalence classes generated by an organism that has internalized a *formulation* of the rule, be the same as that generated by an organism that has been processed in the way you have described? Now with regard to the first issue, that is, whether or not the child uses correspondence rules, everything that you say shows that he does. A Martian child taken through the same park would probably come out with different classes; on the other hand, some other human child taken through a different park where he sees different ducks and different things probably would end up classifying in the same way. The only way to account for this is to assume not that the exemplar is common, but rather that the *effect* of the exemplar on that sort of organism is the formation and internalization of some sort of a rule which is then applied in other cases. It is just like your computer. Now the next question was, "Can we formulate this rule?" That is, the facts indicate the existence of an internal representation of the rule in the child; but can we as scientists, philosophers, logicians, linguists, or whatever formulate the rule? I think there is absolutely no a priori reason to believe that we cannot, that is, there is no reason to believe that we cannot find a reasonably constrained program that will constitute an explicit representation of the same rules. The issue is an empirical issue and is to be resolved through research.

Now, the third issue. If we can formulate the rule then again it does not seem to me that there is any reason to believe—or, for that matter, to disbelieve—that the learning of the rule (that is, of an explicit formulation) will not have the same effect as learning by exemplars. At this point we simply do not know what contingencies are involved in applying a rule. The application of a rule is a very complicated business, as is its acquisition, but there is absolutely no a priori reason to believe that the effect of direct learning must be different from that of unconscious induction from cases and tutoring. Yet you talk as if it were quite obvious that rule learning could not do the job.

Professor Kuhn:

Sylvain, I think you are confusing two points that badly need to be separated. I am not, as some readers of *The Structure of Scientific Revolutions* have thought, a mystic or a man who finds that notions like intuition, *Verstehen,* or empathy are useful to philosophy of science in their present form. Part of my answer to your question is, therefore, that I do believe there is a potentially specifiable neural mechanism by which we process stimuli into sets of similar and dissimilar data. We know little about it, but I see no reason of principle why we should not learn, which is why I bother writing computer programs. But then you ask, are there *rules*, and the answer has to be, yes and no. Yes, in the sense that our neural processing apparatus obeys rules, some of them acquired through education. But what these "rules" operate on is stimuli to which we have no conscious access, so they are not rules in the sense that we could choose to disobey them, experiment with alternates, and so on. (Are we obeying a rule when we breathe?) What we operate on with rules, in the more usual sense, are the data that are given to us after the processing "rules" have done their work.

Let me give part of that answer a bit differently to clarify what I am opposing. When a philosopher of science, at least in the current English-speaking tradition, looks for the sorts of rules which the child will have learned by the end of the afternoon in the park, he looks for something like a set of necessary and sufficient conditions for the applicability of a term. We do have some rules of that sort, but not enough. In this context it is the wrong sort of rule (or the wrong thing) to look for. Therefore, when I say similarity rather than rules, I am not saying similarity rather than some determinable processing procedure; I am saying similarity-processing procedure rather than criteria-processing.

Professor Suppes:

Professor Hempel remarked[6] that he was now putting psychology and logic closer together, and I am very sympathetic with that move, but the tendencies in your paper are too much in this direction. I think that you make some very important suggestions, but I would like to ask you how you would distinguish the history of science, the psychology of science, and the philosophy of science. As I read your paper it seems to me that you want to suggest that the philosophy of science is really to become the psychology of science. The suggestions that the philosopher must be careful not to change the science or that he will change it in applying, for example, formal methods or very explicit methods of analysis seem to me to confuse the task of studying the psychology of science and the philosophy of science. And I would also like you to comment on the same distinction in the history of mathematics,

[6] See his contribution to Session I above.

the psychology of mathematics, and the philosophy of mathematics, because it is evident that the very notable progress which has been made in the last hundred years in the philosophy of mathematics is not very much connected with the kind of psychological issues you have raised. It is a tenable hypothesis that the same kind of progress can be made in the philosophy of science. That does not mean that what you say about psychology is not important, but I want to insist on this distinction.

My final remark is very much related to what Dudley Shapere was saying. What I find difficult is the distinguishing characteristic of science. After all, one of the great philosophical problems has been, and continues to be, not only the concept of truth, but also the more general concept of scientific method. What is it, after all, that is so unique and special about science? Why do we not simply talk about a community of astrologists? What you say, for example, about being able to date the community in terms of development, and so on, I am sure would also apply to the history of astrology or to a variety of religious groups. It is the responsibility of philosophy proper not to study how astrologists operate psychologically but to understand what it is that distinguishes astrology from science.

Professor Kuhn:

Let me say that I am delighted by Pat Suppes's question and had even anticipated it, since this obviously is an issue between us. At exactly the point in my paper where I speak about the difference between being a scientist and an improver of theories, on the one hand, and being a philosopher and an anlyst of theories, on the other, there is a footnote reference to Pat as somebody who does not see the importance of maintaining the distinction. Let me then try to make my point in the following way. Although my professional identity is as an historian of science, what is on my mind when I get involved with the sort of thing I am doing here today is ultimately epistemology. I really want to know what sort of thing knowledge is, what it is all about, and why it is that it works the way it does. Now in order to do that, it seems to me the right move (I am glad somebody else said philosophy is an empirical enterprise) is to look around and try to see what is going on and what it is that people who have knowledge have got. If I then think that what I discover when I look gives me certain sorts of understanding of what goes on—makes it plausible that knowledge should be the sort of thing it is and should develop the way it does—then I can legitimately say that from the examination of scientific communities I am beginning to become a better epistemologist. But, if that sort of strategy is even conceivably legitimate, it is a mistake to ask that the person using it draw lines and say when it is psychology, when it is history, and when it is philosophy of science. Clearly it can be any of these things without the others. But that does not imply that the psychologist's data or the psychologist's generalizations, just because they are the psychologist's, cannot be illuminating to somebody who has epistemological concerns. And similarly, for the historian. I think you are making that move, and I do not think you should.

There are, of course, other things one can do besides epistemology. You do one of them and provide models of how it ought to be done. You try, that is, to improve theories—scientists do that and there is no reason why a philosopher should not do it also—and I do not want to draw lines which would exclude you. For your problem, furthermore, I think you are quite right: the more formalism you have in a scientific theory the more powerful the theory is likely to be. But the formalized theory is not the same theory, and you have not, in improving it, simply found out what was implicit in what people were doing before. The epistemologist has therefore got to be a little bit wary of accepting it as merely an explicit version of the theory one had in the first place. If theories can function without much formalism, he has to understand how and why, not provide a more formalized version.

Professor Putnam:

I said yesterday[7] that I thought philosophy of science is an empirical science; I should have added that in my view it is not compatible with saying that it involves sharp ideological clash. I think that actually your paper gives too much to positivism. I am glad to see that I was on the right track in my paper in thinking that the primary notion of a paradigm was something like an exemplar, for example, and I think that the force in seeing science as being structured by historic and paradigmatic examples and by the creative use of the imagination and the imitation of examples as long as they remain models is very much weakened by the fact that you chose to contrast the notion of an example or an exemplar with the notion of a correspondence rule. It is unfortunate because I do not think they have much to do with each other. Traditionally correspondence rules were definitions of theoretical terms in observation vocabulary, or at least in antecedent vocabulary—like defining a straight line as the path of a light ray, or the path of a stretched thread, or something of that kind; or of voltage as

[7] See the discussion in Session V above.

what the volt meter reads, and so forth. Now I claim, and I think most of the other participants agree with this, that such rules do not exist in science at all. Professor Hempel was really expressing that view in his opening lecture: that what really exists or what plays the role which these nonexistent rules of correspondence were mistakenly thought to play are in the first place theoretical analyses of empirically given things. We have a theoretical analysis of light; we just do not say, "I define a straight line as a path of a light ray"; we say "Light from a source in many conditions propagates in such a way that the normal to the wave front is a straight line," or something of that kind. Or we say that a theoretical analysis of what a stretched thread is tells us that within certain limits it is straight. Second, there are also assumptions which may contain theoretical terms about boundary conditions: a stretched thread is not in fact straight if it is a metal stretched thread in a certain kind of magnetic field, and so forth. This fact that it is a combination of assumptions about the nature of the thing, the volt meter, for example, or the nature of the conditions in which the thing is being used, tells you why a certain relationship exists. In other words, in this view it is not a definition that the volt-meter reading is approximately equal to the voltage; it is a complicated inference within a theory which includes a description of the volt meter and assumptions about fields of force acting or not acting on the volt meter, and so on. Of course, this means that a theory itself is not very consonant with some things Pat Suppes was saying—namely, that the theory itself (the total scientific theory including the theory of errors) tells you that the volt-meter reading is not exactly the same as the voltage, that it may be off by so and so much, and so forth. However, all of this is, of course, very consonant with the materialist view I hold to the effect that scientific theories are statements about the world. In my paper[8] I used the term "auxiliary statements" to refer to these statements that really play the role of correspondence rules. And what they do is specify boundary conditions and present an analysis—partially in terms of the theoretical language—of the nature of such things as light, stretched threads, volt meters, and so on. So using that terminology, I might also say that it is through the auxiliary statements that are joined on to it (or through the side theories in Robert Causey's very nice term) that I believe that a theory gets connected to the world; and I think that this is very similar to the view that Hempel was advocating. I am not sure whether he would want to consider these part of a theory or not, but the point is that Hempel was also attacking the mistake

[8] See the summary-abstract of Putnam's paper in Session V above.

of considering auxiliary statements or bridge laws to be in any way definitions. And I think that if this is right, that if this is the nature of the mistake that the people were making who were talking about correspondence rules, then you do not have the option of introducing correspondence rules in the way that you have the option of introducing an explicit definition of swan, goose, or duck. On the other hand, it is very compatible with the idea that examples do play roles; and I am not by any means wholly unsympathetic with that idea. I would like to suggest to Professor Kuhn that examples play two sorts of roles which he was not carefully distinguishing. First, if you think about what you learn when you do those problems at the end of the chapter (an experience we have all had), I think you will see that you learn two things. You learn to solve purely mathematical problems correctly—even if by "pendulum" you do not mean an actual pendulum but an ideal pendulum. It still takes a little experience to learn how to solve that sort of problem, and examples do play a role there which I think was not even mentioned or separated out; but I think that it is very important that one learns to solve mathematical problems by creatively imitating examples. Also, one learns by example what kinds of auxiliary statements to choose in trying to analyze specific kinds of empirical situations. Even if that know-how could be replaced by a set of rules, those rules would not be correspondence rules; in fact they would be the famous logic of discovery.

Professor Kuhn:

There is not a great deal I can say to this question. I think it very likely that Hilary Putnam is right (if he is not entirely right, I am not going to be able to point out now the exact place at which I want to depart from him).[9] It has been clear for some time that I constantly get into trouble because I point to a slightly out-of-date position in the philosophy of science when I want to make a point that I think of as my own. That was surely the case in the *Structure of Scientific Revolutions.* I would hope that this morning's talk has given reason to think that I have spent some time reading philosophy of science since I wrote the book, and I take the main force of Hilary's remark as, you had better go back and read some more. I shall!

I am nevertheless somewhat uneasy about the ease with which he thinks he is getting rid of my problem by saying that correspondence rules are not the way we now handle such matters. We are not going to

[9] See the footnote on his misuse of the term 'correspondence rules' on page 467 of his paper above.

talk about fitting terms to nature without ultimately having things to say about the problem of meaning, and about that problem nobody knows quite what to say at the moment. I do not myself, but I think what I am getting at with similarity relations may be one of the tools that will be helpful. Somehow, what I hear Hilary telling me, perhaps quite wrongly, is that although we do not talk about correspondence rules, we have another way, also purely linguistic, of handling the problem. If that is right, then I suspect it is just a new way to hide old problems. At the moment, I cannot see that substituting auxiliary statements for correspondence rules is going to have any bearing on the problem I have been trying to raise. You must then find an adequate body of auxiliary statements, not just partially empty boxes in Schemas I, II, and III. I think you will not find them, or enough of them, because you will still be trying to find linguistic forms to make explicit what is, in fact, tacitly embodied in the language-nature fit. But it will take more thought and reading to make me confident of this.

Professor Achinstein:

I would like briefly to reinforce Hilary's point about giving too much to positivism. The positivist—at least the extreme sort of positivist—wants to have these theoretical sentences be purely uninterpreted and then have the correspondence rules do the job of relating them to nature. You, too, have talked about a completely uninterpreted formalism and you replace the positivist's correspondence rules by your exemplars. But, now, I do not understand how these exemplars are going to work if, as a matter of fact, you do have a completely uninterpreted formalism. For example, on page 465, you mention the formula '$f = ma$', which you speak of as a purely uninterpreted equation. If I take what you mean literally—if it is purely uninterpreted—I have no reason for thinking '$mg \operatorname{Sin}\theta = -m \frac{d^2s}{dt^2}$' is going to be one form or exemplar of this law '$f = ma$'. So I do not know how your exemplars are going to work if I take you literally; they will only work if, as a matter of fact, your formalism is interpreted to begin with.

Professor Kuhn:

I think Peter Achinstein has caught a weakness in the way I raised the point, but that the difficulty is not real. I talk about uninterpreted symbolic expressions in the paper for two reasons. One of them is that I suddenly asked myself a few years ago, how on earth I could criticize formalisms as I do without facing the fact that scientists constantly do take laws and deduce consequences and do take mathematical expressions and squeeze everything one can get out of them with the rules of mathematics? It seems odd that the *Structure of Scientific Revolutions* should occasionally mention something like laws but not make much of anything of their role in science. So I want now to examine the formal elements of a science, though still without equating them with the theory. Perhaps that is why I seem to concede a little too much to positivism.

There is also another good reason for giving uninterpreted symbolic expressions a place in the disciplinary matrix, and it is methodological. Imagine yourself as Quine's imaginary linguist learning a language, but now you are examining a scientific, rather than a language, community. It is vastly easier to discover that scientists say to each other 'force equals mass time acceleration' than to discover what the devil they mean or are talking about when they say it. Though the expressions are interpreted by the men who use them, discovering the signs and discovering their interpretation are partially separate operations, particularly since the same deductions follow with or without interpretation. As to the move from '$f = ma$' to '$mg \text{ Sin}\theta = - m \frac{d^2s}{dt^2}$' I must simply have been unclear. In this context, '$f = ma$' is no longer an uninterpreted expression. The process of matching exemplars to expressions is initially a way of learning to interpret the expressions. When you can do it for yourself, you have learned the interpretation.

SESSION VII

Scientific Theories and Their Domains

DUDLEY SHAPERE

I. Framework of the Present Analysis

If we examine some relatively sophisticated area of science at a particular stage of its development, we find that a certain body of information is, at that stage, taken to be an object for investigation. On a general level, one need only think of the subject matters called "electricity," "magnetism," "light," or "chemistry"; but both within and outside such standard fields, there are more specific examples, such as what are taken to be subfields of the preceding subjects. Further, those general subjects themselves are, in many cases, considered to be related in certain ways. I will refer to such bodies of related items as *domains*, though we will find that, in the sense in which this concept will prove helpful in understanding science, and in particular in understanding the concept of a scientific "theory," more is involved than the mere relatedness of certain items.

The preceding examples are familiar ones, and there might appear to be no problem about considering them to be "fields," or, as I have called them, domains. However, this is far from being the case. In order to bring out some of the complexities involved, let us briefly review certain aspects of the history of those examples.

It is by no means obvious that all the phenomena which we today unhesitatingly group together as forming a unified subject matter or domain under the heading of "electricity" really do form such a unity. Earlier investigators had indeed associated the known phenomena: William Gilbert discovered that some twenty substances besides the previously known amber would, when appropriately rubbed, attract light bodies. His investigations led him to conclude that electric phenomena are due to something of a material nature which is liberated by the rubbing of "electricks." [1] Succeeding workers agreed, holding

[1] E. T. Whittaker, *A History of the Theories of Aether and Electricity* (New York: Thomas Nelson, 1951), Vol. I, p. 35.

that electricity consists of one (or two) fluids. However, the nineteenth century, with a larger body of apparently related information available, saw reasons to question the unity of the subject: was the "electricity" associated with physiological phenomena of the same sort (and to be explained in the same way) as that associated with inanimate objects, or was it peculiar to, and perhaps even the distinguishing characteristic of, living things? Was the "electricity" produced on the *surfaces* of certain objects by rubbing them identical with the "electricity" produced in the *interiors* of certain bodies by a voltaic cell? Even by the time of Faraday, according to Whittaker,

> the connection of the different branches of electric science with each other was still not altogether clear. Although Wollaston's experiments of 1801 had in effect proved the identity in kind of the currents derived from frictional and voltaic sources, the question was still regarded as open thirty years afterwards, no satisfactory explanation being forthcoming of the fact that frictional electricity appeared to be a surface-phenomenon, whereas voltaic electricity was conducted within the interior substance of bodies. To this question Faraday now applied himself; and in 1833 he succeeded in showing that every known effect of electricity—physiological, magnetic, luminous, calorific, chemical and mechanical—may be obtained indifferently either with the electricity which is obtained by friction or with that obtained from a voltaic battery. Henceforth the identity of the two was beyond dispute.[2]

In *De Magnete*,[3] Gilbert had called attention to a number of differences betwen electricity and magnetism, which Whittaker summarizes succinctly as follows:

> Between the magnetic and electric forces Gilbert remarked many distinctions. The lodestone requires no stimulus of friction such as is needed to stir glass and sulphur into activity. The lodestone attracts only magnetisable substances, whereas electrified bodies attract everything. The magnetic attraction between two bodies is not affected by interposing a sheet of paper or a linen cloth, or by immersing the bodies in water; whereas the electric attraction is readily destroyed by screens. Lastly, the magnetic force tends to arrange bodies in definite orientations; while the electric force merely tends to heap them together in shapeless clusters.[4]

Thus there were strong grounds for believing that electricity and magnetism constituted distinct subjects for investigation, for which dif-

[2] *Ibid.*, p. 175.

[3] W. Gilbert, *De Magnete* (New York: Dover, 1958), Bk. II, Ch. II, esp. pp. 95–97.

[4] Whittaker, *A History of the Theories of Aether and Electricity*, p. 35.

ferent explanations were to be given. Nevertheless, in spite of these clear differences, reasons accumulated over the succeeding two or three centuries for *suspecting* that these differences might prove to be superficial, and that there was some deep relationship to be found between electrical and magnetic phenomena. These considerations were very varied in kind; among them were ones like the following:

> The suspicion [in the eighteenth century] was based in part on some curious effects produced by lightning, of a kind which may be illustrated by a paper published in the *Philosophical Transactions* in 1735. A tradesman of Wakefield, we are told, "having put up a great number of knives and forks in a large box, and having placed the box in the corner of a large room, there happen'd in July, 1731, a sudden storm of thunder, lightning, etc., by which the corner of the room was damaged, the Box split, and a good many knives and forks melted, the sheaths being untouched. The owner emptying the box upon a Counter where some Nails lay, the Persons who took up the knives, that lay upon the Nails, observed that the knives took up the Nails." [5]

Subsequent investigations by Franklin, Oersted, Ampère, and Faraday (among others) of the relationships between electricity and magnetism culminated in the synthetic theories of the latter half of the nineteenth century, among which Maxwell's theory was triumphant. It is clear that in some sense Maxwell's theory provided an "explanation" of (a theory explaining) the phenomena of electricity and magnetism; nevertheless, as we shall see (and also for reasons whose character we shall see), that "theory" became part of a larger body of information which called for a further, deeper explanation.

The phenomena of electricity, particularly in the nineteenth century, also came more and more to be connected with chemical phenomena; and, through this association of electricity with chemistry, the suspicion—growing gradually into an expectation or even a demand—arose that a unified theory of electricity and matter should, in some form, be sought. Indeed, as time progressed, this form itself began to be clearer: the unity should be sought in the structure of the atom. Thus the areas which seemed to offer the possibility of precise clues to that structure—particularly the spectra of the chemical elements and the periodic table—became crucial areas of investigation. Lines of potentially fruitful research in the quest for the expected unifying theory began to be generated.

The relations between electricity and light underwent a similar development. Faraday's demonstration of the effect of a magnetic field on

[5] *Ibid.*, pp. 80–81.

the plane of polarization of a light ray provided one sort of consideration leading to the belief that there was a deeper relationship to be sought between magnetism and hence, because of the developments summarized above, electricity and light.

Even in such a cursory survey, dealing with such familiar areas of scientific investigation as electricity, magnetism, chemistry, and light, it becomes clear that the grounds for considering the elements of each such domain as constituting a *unified* subject-matter, and as exhibiting relations with other domains which lead to the formation of larger domains, are highly complex. The general situation, in these cases at least, may be summarized as follows. Although in more primitive stages of science (or, perhaps better, of what will become a science), obvious sensory similarities or general presuppositions usually determine whether certain items of experience will be considered as forming a body or domain, this is less and less true as science progresses (or, one might say, as it becomes more unambiguously scientific). As part of the growing sophistication of science, such associations of items are subjected to criticism, and often are revised on the basis of considerations that are far from obvious and naïve. Differences which seemed to distinguish items from one another are concluded to be superficial; similarities which were previously unrecognized or, if recognized, considered superficial, become fundamental. Conversely, similarities which formerly served as bases for association of items come to be considered superficial, and the items formerly associated are no longer, and form independent groupings or come to be associated with other groups. The items themselves often, in the process, come to be redescribed, often, for scientific purposes, in very unfamiliar ways. Even where the earlier or more obvious associations are ultimately retained, they are retained only after criticism, and on grounds that go beyond the mere perceptual similarities or primitive uncritical presuppositions which formed the more obvious bases of their original association.

An important part of gaining an understanding of science, and of the nature of scientific theories in particular, must be to examine the character of such grounds for the establishment of domains. But this question immediately leads to another: for in order that the area constituted by the related items be an area *for investigation*, there must be something problematic about it, something inadequate in our understanding of it. A domain, in the sense in which that term will be used here, is not *merely* a body of related information; it is a body of related information about which there is a problem, well defined usually and raised on the basis of specific considerations ("good reasons"). In addition, that problem must be considered important (also on reasonable grounds, not on the basis of some "subjective value judgment"); it must be worth making the effort to resolve. Further, as we shall see, it must —in general, though in certain rather well-circumscribed sorts of cases not necessarily—be capable of being "handled" at the current stage of science.

In earlier stages of the development of a field, curiosity, general puzzlement, or general uncritical presuppositions undoubtedly play a predominant role in generating such problems—in determining whether an area is problematic and worth investigating. With the advance of science, however, and indeed constituting in part the very notion of scientific progress, the considerations leading to certain questions being raised about a domain, and to considering them important, become more specific, precise, and subject to constraints: the generation of problems and priorities becomes more a matter of reasoning. Investigation of the character of this reasoning constitutes another aspect of the attempt to gain an understanding of science. More specifically, and more directly relevant to our present concerns, such analysis will help us to understand the nature and function of scientific theories. For as we shall see, different sorts of questions, reflecting different sorts of inadequacies, can arise, even regarding the same domain; and we shall find that only certain of these sorts of questions are answered in terms of what are commonly and appropriately referred to as "theories."

A further aspect of scientific reasoning which arises at this point concerns the ways in which, at least often when problems arise at sophisticated stages of science, it is possible to formulate promising lines of research to pursue in attempting to answer those problems, and, sometimes, to assign at least rough rankings of degree of promise to such lines of research, thereby establishing research priorities. Further, expectations—sometimes amounting to demands—arise regarding the character of any satisfactory solution to those problems, even in advance of having any such solution (and therefore certain proposed solutions are judged as more or less "attractive"). And in many cases these expectations or demands do succeed in anticipating the actual solution ultimately arrived at; but whether they do or do not, reasons are given supporting the expectations, and the character of those reasons must be analyzed. (In addition, of course, the patterns of reasoning in cases in which the actual solution is *not* in agreement with those expectations or demands must also be analyzed.) Again, in primitive stages of a science, such conclusions are no doubt based primarily on general and uncritical presuppositions.[6] But it is characteristic of sophisticated science that it tends more and more to depend on reasoned arguments for the generation of lines of research, the judgment of them as more or less "promising," and the generation of expectations regarding the character of possible answers to problems. An understanding of such reasoning is essential if we are to understand the nature of science, and in particular of scientific theories.

We may summarize the preceding discussion in terms of five major questions.

1. *What considerations (or, better, types of considerations, if such types can be found) lead scientists to regard a certain body of information as a body of information—that is, as constituting a unified subject matter or domain to be examined or dealt with?*

2. *How is description of the items of the domain achieved and modified at sophisticated stages of scientific development?*

3. *What sorts of inadequacies, leading to the need for further work, are found in such bodies of information, and what are the grounds for considering these to be inadequacies or problems requiring further research?* (Included here are questions not only regarding the generation of scientific problems about domains, but also of scientific priorities—the questions of importance of the problems and of the "readiness" of science to deal with them.)

4. *What considerations lead to the generation of specific lines of research, and what are the reasons (or types of reasons) for considering some lines of research to be more promising than others in the attempt to resolve problems about the domain?*

5. *What are the reasons for expecting (sometimes to the extent of demanding) that answers of certain sorts, having certain characteristics, be sought for those problems?*

Clearly, a further question, not explicitly emerging from our earlier discussion, also needs to be raised:

6. *What are the reasons (or types of reasons) for accepting a certain solution of a scientific problem regarding a domain as adequate?*

Of these six questions, only the last has been seriously and carefully examined by philosophers of science (in connection, largely, with discussions of "inductive logic"). In the present paper, however, I will

[6] The roots and character of some of the most general of such presuppositions have been analyzed in my essay, "The Development of Scientific Categories," forthcoming.

focus on aspects of certain of the other five which are relevant to the understanding of the nature and function of scientific theories.

It must not be supposed, however, that complete answers to one of these questions will be wholly independent of answers to the others, so that they can be dealt with in isolation from one another in a piecemeal attack; we will, indeed, discover interdependencies. Nor should it be supposed that there are not other questions which must be dealt with in the attempt to understand the nature of science—though I would argue that the above are very central ones. But in any case, a complete understanding of scientific reasoning would include a treatment of all these questions.[7] And a complete and systematic investigation of all of them would serve as a test (and at the same time, as seems to be the case in so many scientific investigations, a clarification) of three general assumptions about science, each successive one of which constitutes a stronger claim than, and presupposes the truth of, its predecessors. Traditionally, these three assumptions have been widely accepted (though not without occasional and recurrent opposition) as true of science; today, however, they are being subjected to powerful attack, in one form or another, from a number of quarters. The assumptions may be stated as follows:

I. *Scientific development and innovation are often appropriately describable as rational.* (Obviously, there is a question here of the appropriate precise sense or senses of 'rational'; however, as was indicated above, the proposed investigation itself would provide, in part at least, a specification of such a sense or senses, and thus be simultaneously a test and a clarification of the assumption. Such a procedure seems to be common in scientific inquiry, and itself requires analysis which it has never received, the classical philosophical attitude having been that "meanings" must be specified completely and precisely before any test can be undertaken—a procedure which, even if it is clear itself, is rarely if ever realized in any inquiry whatever.) I will call this the *postulate* (or *hypothesis*) *of scientific rationality.*

II. *The rationality involved in specific cases is often generalizable as principles applicable in many other cases.* (It might be supposed that the truth of II—and also perhaps of III—is a necessary condition for calling a subject or method "rational." However, at least one writer has in effect denied II while apparently maintaining I: "The coherence

[7] It is necessary to emphasize this point; for many, perhaps most, philosophers of science, even when they have raised such questions as 1 to 5, have denied that they were relevant to the attempt to understand science; for, according to those philosophers, such questions (with the possible exception of certain aspects of 2) have to do only with the "psychology," "sociology," or "history" of science, rather than with its "logic," which alone is relevant to the *understanding* of science.

displayed by the research tradition . . . may not imply even the existence of an underlying body of rules and assumptions."[8] That is, science, in its "normal" stages, operates according to an underlying rationale, even though any attempt to express that rationale in terms of explicit *rules* is, the author claims, usually [and perhaps always and necessarily] doomed to failure. Because of this possibility, it seems advisable to keep these postulates separated.) I will call this the *postulate* (or *hypothesis*) *of the generalizability of scientific reasoning.*

III. *These principles can in some sense be systematized.* This may be called the *postulate* (or *hypothesis*) *of the systematizability of scientific reasoning principles.*

The present essay can deal only with some aspects of the six questions listed above, and, in fact, will deal only with those aspects which are relevant to the concept of a scientific *theory.* It cannot pretend to deal with all aspects of that concept (or with all uses of the term 'theory'). Even within these limitations, it cannot claim completeness: it is no more than a preliminary and, in many cases, only a suggestive rather than thoroughly detailed examination of the issues.

II. Aspects of the Concept of a Domain

We have seen that, in science, items of information come to be associated together as bodies of information having the following characteristics:

(1) The association is based on some relationship between the items.
(2) There is something problematic about the body so related.
(3) That problem is an important one.
(4) Science is "ready" to deal with the problem.

Earlier, I called bodies of information satisfying these conditions *domains.* We will find that, in science, such bodies of information have other characteristics besides these four. On the other hand, we will find that, although it is generally considered desirable for (4) to be satisfied (to an appropriate degree) in order that an area can count as fully "scientific" (that is, that it can count as a "domain" in the present sense), nevertheless areas which satisfy conditions having to do with (1), (2), and (3) are often counted as "scientific" (domains) in a somewhat borderline sense even if they fail to satisfy (4). Similar qualifications will be found necessary in regard to (3).

[8] T. S. Kuhn, *The Structure of Scientific Revolutions* (Chicago: University of Chicago Press, 1970), p. 46.

Needless to say, these four characteristics of domains require further clarification. The remainder of this section will be devoted to discussion of aspects of (1), (3), and (4)—the concepts of "domain," "importance," and "readiness"—which are directly relevant to analysis of the concept of "theory" in science. The character of problems regarding domains (2), and in particular of problems whose answers are theories, will be discussed in Part III, together with related issues concerning the generation of expectations about those answers and of lines of research which indicate promise of producing such answers.

The present essay will not provide a systematic examination of reasons for associating items into domains, or for associating domains into still larger domains. Our purpose here being the analysis of the concept of "theory," we will take for granted the *existence* of such bodies of information, and concern ourselves primarily with the generation of their problematic character, with a view to understanding how problems arise which require "theories" as their answers. A few comments about the generation of domains are necessary here. First, the mere existence of *some* relationship between items or types of items is not itself sufficient to make that body of items an object for scientific investigation. After all, not much ingenuity is required to find some relationship between any set of items. But in the case of those associations in science for which I will reserve the name "domains" the associations are (for reasons which will not be examined here) well grounded, though "well groundedness is certainly a matter of degree."

Not only are the relationships well grounded; they are also distinguished, among the total set of relationships discoverable or constructible between any body of items, by being what we may call (in keeping, I think, with the frequent usage of scientists) "significant." That is, relative to the state of science at a given time, the relationships of importance in science—those which are the bases of domain-generation—serve as good reasons for suspecting the existence of further relationships, and also of more comprehensive or deeper relationships.[9]

[9] For example, the discovery of a concomitant variation of properties may in itself be only a weak indicator of a deeper relationship between two types of items or between two domains, *unless* there is reason to suppose that those properties are "significant." Thus Faraday rotation (rotation of the plane of polarization of a ray of light as a function of magnetic field strength), alluded to earlier, was an indication of a deeper relationship between magnetism and electricity precisely because polarization was a manifestation of what, in view of the Young-Fresnel theory of light, was a centrally important feature of light—namely, its transverse wave character. On the other hand, the differences between electricity and magnetism noted by Gilbert did not have to be taken too seriously because there was little or no ground, at the time or for long after, for distinguishing significant from

(The sense of "deeper" here will be examined in Part III below.) And the more relationships are found between the items of the domains, or between two domains between which some relations have been found, the stronger the suspicion will be that there is a more comprehensive or deeper relation to be found. The significance of the relations, like their well groundedness, is a matter of degree: just as the relationships which form the basis of association of the domain may be only suspected, so also their suggestion of a deeper or more comprehensive relationship may be. Or the indication may, in either case, be stronger than a mere suspicion.

This makes it clear that the suspicion of further or deeper unity involved in considering a body of information to be a domain is itself a hypothesis that may turn out to have been mistaken. In other words, that a body of information constitutes a domain is itself a hypothesis, and may ultimately be rejected: either what were originally supposed to be adequate grounds (relative to the state of science at the time) for considering the information to constitute such a unified domain should not have been as compelling as they were taken to be, or else new information, uncovered later, so altered the situation that, relative to that new state of science, the grounds for suspecting disunity (for disregarding the earlier grounds) come to outweigh those for suspecting unity. In either case, it would be found that the hope for a unifying account must be abandoned, and the previous domain, so to speak, split. Such cases are common in the history of science: although we find a general trend toward unification, the history of science does not consist of a steady, unwavering march toward greater and greater unity.[10]

---

nonsignificant features of electricity and magnetism. When due account is taken of this aspect of "significance" of relationships, Mill's methods are indicative that further research is in order, though they may not, in general, specify precisely what research to undertake. It is perhaps worth pointing out here that, as can be seen from the examples given in this note, "significance" is a function of what will later be called "background knowledge": information which, though not a part of the domain under consideration, is accepted (on presumptively good grounds) and utilized in interpreting and dealing with that domain and its problems.

[10] The reasons for suspecting a deeper unity among the elements of a body of information, and thus creating a domain for investigation, have nothing to do (or need have nothing to do) with a faith on the part of the scientist concerned in some "Principle of the Unity (or Uniformity or Simplicity) of Nature." The reasons adduced in particular scientific contexts are specific, not general, scientific, not metaphysical or aesthetic. A belief in such a general principle would in any case never be sufficient to provide or even suggest specific directions as to where to look in the search for unification—what lines of research are promising, and

A further aspect of the concept of a domain may be obtained by looking at domains from a somewhat different point of view. So far we have seen the domain as a body of information concerning which a problem has arisen. However, this description may be inverted: *the domain is the total body of information for which, ideally, an answer to that problem is expected to account.* In particular, if the problem is one requiring a "theory" as answer, the domain constitutes the total body of information which must, ideally, be accounted for by a theory which resolves that problem. (The notion of "accounting for," and the force of the qualification implied by the word "ideally," will be discussed later.)

The preceding point makes it clear that the concept of a domain is intended to replace the old "observational-theoretical" distinction as a fundamental conceptual tool for illuminating the nature of science. "That which is to be accounted for" includes, especially at sophisticated stages of scientific development (and thus at those stages where characteristically *scientific* reasoning is most apparent and predominant), elements from both the traditional "observational" and "theoretical" categories. As conceived by philosophers of science, the distinction between "observation" and "theory" has proved to be unclear, partly because what they considered "observational" is found, in actual scientific usage, to be "theory laden," but also—a point not usually emphasized by critics of that tradition—because what they considered to be "theories" are often treated in science the way "facts" or "observations" ("the given") are. But furthermore, not only did the distinction, as conceived by philosophers of science, prove unclear, but also, even to the extent to which it was clear, it provided little or no insight into scientific reasoning, but even, in its philosophical form, obscured the character of that reasoning.[11] (None of this is to say that there are not important uses of the terms "observation" and "theory" in reference to science, but only that the analyses given by philosophers of science

---

the general outlines of what a successful solution of a problem might be expected reasonably to look like. And yet, as this paper argues, sometimes such directions *are* indicated, with more or less clarity and precision, in actual scientific cases. As we shall see, the "readiness" of a scientific problem to be investigated is, in part, a function of the specificity with which such directions are indicated; thus something so general as a "faith in unity," while as a matter of sociological fact it might happen to be shared by a majority of scientists at some time, would not constitute a reason for investigating any particular problem, or for abandoning the solid ground of "ready" problems for a flight of unifying speculation.

[11] D. Shapere, "Notes toward a Post-Positivistic Interpretation of Science," in P. Achinstein and S. Barker, *The Legacy of Logical Positivism* (Baltimore: Johns Hopkins University Press, 1969), pp. 115–160; see especially Part I, pp. 115–131.

have in general failed to capture those uses.) I have argued elsewhere[12] that the distinction may have marked, rather confusedly, another problem of philosophical interest, the "epistemological" problem of the "ultimate foundations of knowledge." The solution (not yet forthcoming) of that problem would be at best only marginally relevant to the understanding of science, and would, indeed, itself be facilitated by solutions to the problems stated in Part I above.

The present analysis will recognize fully the *mutual* interdependence of "observation" and "theory," rather than considering observational and theoretical terms or propositions to be of radically distinct types. For us, what was, at a certain stage of science, a "theory" answering a problem about a domain can, at a later stage, itself become a domain (or, more usually, a part of a domain) to be investigated and accounted for. Thus Maxwell's theory, having achieved a successful unification of electricity, magnetism, and light, itself became, for reasons which will be examined later, a part of a larger domain. To put the point in another way which is natural to scientists but not to philosophers, what was a "theory" becomes a "fact"—but a "fact" concerning which there is a problem.[13] Conversely, "observations" in science are "theory laden" in certain clear ways, though, as I have argued elsewhere,[14] the objectivity of science is not thereby endangered.

Sometimes, indeed, the items of a domain are purely "theoretically determined" (which is not to say that they are, in such cases, "theories," at least in an unambiguous sense), in that no instances of them have actually been found. (They are "hypothetical entities" or "theoretical entities," but not in any of the usual senses of the positivistic tradition.[15]) Such was the case with neutrinos in the 1930s, neutron

[12] D. Shapere, "The Concept of Observation in Science and Philosophy," forthcoming.

[13] That "facts do not raise their own questions" has become a cliche. On the present analysis, there are good objective reasons why a certain problem regarding a domain is raised—and though it may not (always) be raised *by* the "facts" (or domain) which the question is *about*, it is nonetheless misleading to suggest that the alternative is that "it is *we* who pose questions *to* nature," suggesting that there is no objective ground for the questions. On the contrary, the alternative is that the questions are usually raised by (or in the light of) *other* "facts" (information which is taken for granted, presumably on good grounds) relative to the situation or "facts" under consideration.

[14] D. Shapere, "The Concept of Observation in Science and Philosophy," treats the character of "observations" in science. My concern here is with "theories."

[15] They are, for example, "hypothetical"—unconfirmed—to a degree to which the theory need not be (consider tachyons and the special theory of relativity). But they are also hypothesized as being *entities*, as positivistic "theoretical entities" were often not, as they were often looked on as not *really* referring to existent things (or even as claiming to refer to such things).

stars until the end of the 1960s (when they were found), tachyons (putative particles traveling faster than light), "superstars" (putative "stars" with masses in the range of 10^5–10^8 suns), and intermediate bosons.[16]

It is because theories and theory-determined entities, for example, can be or are parts of domains that I have preferred to speak of "items" or "elements" of domains rather than in more traditional terms like "facts," which have associations that make them unsuitable for covering the sorts of things that go together to form objects of scientific investigation. My talk of items of "information" (rather than, say, of "knowledge") is also partly motivated by the occurrence of theory-determined entities whose existence is merely proposed as a possibility; further reasons for that choice of terminology, as well as some dangers inherent in it, will appear later.

The account given thus far emphasizes that the items of a domain are generally problematic not in isolation but rather through being *related* to other such items in a body about which the problem exists: scientific research is in such cases generated by items in association with one another, rather than by "facts" in isolation from one another.

[16] There are some instructive differences between the examples mentioned. Tachyons constitute a subject for investigation only because they are *not ruled out* by the theory of special relativity. (Thus, although their investigation presupposes that theory, it is not strictly speaking an investigation *of* that theory, except insofar as it may involve a study of that theory to see if it can be extended so as either to require or rule out the existence of tachyons.) In the case of neutron stars, the existence of the entities was *required* by the theories concerned—general relativistic gravitation theory, together with broader theories of stellar evolution—if there exist (as there do) stars exceeding a certain mass, and if that excess mass is not lost prior to the star's arrival at a certain late stage of its evolution. Again, "superstars," like tachyons, are not ruled out as possible (though earlier, it had been thought that stars of masses greater than about 100 suns were ruled out on the basis of stability considerations). Unlike the case with tachyons, however, there were *other*, independent reasons for asking whether there might be superstars and, when Hoyle and others showed that there could be, for investigating their properties: namely, the need to find some way of accounting for the apparent large energies expended by radio galaxies and quasars (that is, the need to resolve a problem arising in an independent domain). Finally, the intermediate boson, still undetected in 1971, though it belongs in this general class, was proposed not on the basis either of following from or not being ruled out by a theory, but rather on the basis of analogy with another theory for another (but in many respects similar—the analogy was not an arbitrary one) domain: the intermediate boson was to play the role for weak interactions that is played by the photon for electromagnetic interactions and by the pi-meson for strong interactions. It should be added that "investigation" of such theoretically determined entities includes not only the attempt to find them, but also to investigate their properties from a purely theoretical point of view. This is particularly obvious in the case of superstars, where the motivation is to see if they could, if they existed, be the source of the energy required to account for quasars.

Philosophers of science, working within a tradition according to which all "facts" are "atomic," have been blinded to this primary source of scientific problems.

Nevertheless, though such cases are extremely common, they are not the only sources of research-generating problems in science. However, a great many other types of such problems can be treated against the background of an understanding of these. For example, there are cases which are naturally described as cases involving "*a* (single) puzzling fact or observation," in which one isolated "fact," or a single class of such facts, unrelated to any others in a domain-like class, are problematic. A paradigm case is that of the peculiar radio source discovered in the constellation Vulpecula in 1968, which was found to emit radio signals with an extremely regular and short repetition period (later, when more such objects were discovered, they were christened "pulsars"). Such cases, when they concern single, isolated facts or observations, are clearly not problematic by virtue of being members of a class of related objects. However, their problematic character arises in the same way that, we will find, many problems about domains become specific and research becomes directed: by virtue of what we will call "background information," in the light of which such isolated facts as those presently being considered appear puzzling.[17] Still other types of research-generating problems, having to do with inadequacies of theories (rather than of domains), will also be found to be interpretable *via* the concepts of "domain" and "background information."

There are certain sorts of problems, and associated research, which arise regarding domains themselves, in the sense that the solutions to those problems are not "theoretical." These have to do with, for example, determination of the extent of the domain (extending it by incorporating further items, or establishing relationships with other domains, or narrowing it in corresponding ways), or refinement of the precision of definition or measurement of the properties and relationships (particularly the domain-generating relationship) of its items. Generally, however, such investigations are not undertaken for their own sakes: to do so is to engage in purely "hack" work. They are considered appropriate to undertake only when other circumstances create the inadequacy (as when new technological developments make possible a significantly greater precision in measurement of the items or extension of the domain), or when a *theoretical* problem regarding the domain has come to be regarded as important. Recognition of the im-

[17] As we have already seen, background information also contributes to the *raising* of problems regarding domains, by determining their "significance."

portance of the domain almost invariably leads to intensive efforts to make the domain more precise, and to determine its extent more accurately. Such activity often eventuates not only in greater precision with regard to the known elements, but also in the discovery of new ones, and even, on occasion, in a shifting of the characterization of the domain itself. Such shifting may, in turn, lead to a restatement (instead of a mere refinement) of the problem which initially gave importance to the investigation of the domain. Again, however, such investigations are not undertaken (or, more accurately, are not considered important research) unless there is reason to suppose that a theoretical problem regarding the domain is important, and, further, that science is "ready" for the investigation (at least in certain respects, to be discussed in the following section, not related to the clarity and precision of the domain itself). To clarify these points, let us turn to the notions of "importance" and "readiness."

The fact that there is reason to suspect a deeper relationship between the elements of a body of information is not in itself sufficient ground for undertaking a systematic investigation of it; the domain, and the theoretical problem regarding it, must be judged as to "readiness" and "importance." Such judgments are based on a number of factors. For one thing, the grounds for suspicion of the existence of a domain-generating relationship may be more or less strong; and one factor determining whether an investigation of the domain is, at some stage of scientific development, feasible or worthwhile is the strength of these suspicions, and therefore the clarity, precision, and significance of the formulation of the domain and the theoretical problem regarding it. "Readiness" for investigation is determined partly by the precision and clarity of the domain, or at least by the precision and clarity achievable with current instrumentation, as well as by the precision with which the problem regarding the domain is stated. As was indicated at the end of the preceding section, there are also factors having to do with "readiness" which are not related to the clarity and precision of the formulation of the domain and its theoretical problem. For example, the existence of promising lines of research enters into judgment of "readiness": the domain is more ready for investigation if ways can be seen which promise solution of the problem. Mathematical techniques for dealing with the problem should also be available. As to "importance," this is largely a matter of the relation of the domain and its (theoretical) problem(s) to other domains which there is reason to believe are related to the one under consideration in such a way that there is a higher domain of which this and the others are parts. If there is reason to suppose that there is such a "higher" domain, so that a unitary theoretical explanation of the whole body appears called for, and if, for example, the domain under consideration is the "readiest" for investigation in the preceding senses, or if there is reason to think that the domain under consideration offers the clearest clues to such a theoretical explanation, then it is considered "important."

At the beginning of Part II above, it was mentioned that in some cases domains which are "important" enough need not be "ready" in order that their investigation be considered reasonable and appropriate at a certain stage, and conversely. Briefly, if the problem is deemed sufficiently important, and has achieved a certain level of precise formulation, then investigation of the area in question is often considered at least marginally appropriate despite the "unreadiness" of current science in other respects to deal with the problem. Such conditions may, indeed, as was noted previously, serve as incentives to try to *make* the state of science ready to deal with the problem: research will be generated to increase the precision of data about the domain, to develop technology for doing so, and so on. (However, in some circumstances, especially when such technological developments do not seem feasible, investigation even of domains which are recognized as important will often be looked down on as excessively "speculative," sometimes to the point of being "unscientific.") On the other hand, if the domain-generating relationship and the problem are sufficiently precise, and if current science is in other respects ready to deal with the problem, then, even though the problem is not, relative to the state of science at the time, a very important one, or not clearly important, its investigation may be considered appropriate—though such investigations may be looked on as uninteresting or even as "hack" work. Such research can, of course, *eventuate* in important results.

III. Theoretical Problems, Lines of Research, and Scientific Theories

We have examined, to the extent that is relevant to present concerns, the concept of a domain. In doing so, we have made a distinction between those problems which are concerned with the clarification of the domain itself, and other problems calling for a "deeper" account of the domain. The former type of problems will henceforth be referred to as *domain problems*; the latter I will call *theoretical problems*, inasmuch as answers to them are called "theories." Later, a third general class of scientific problems will be distinguished, which are problems regarding theories themselves; these I will call *theoretical inadequacies*. In the present part, I will consider theoretical problems and the characteristics of answers to them.

It will not, however, be possible to give a complete classification and analysis of types of such problems, and therefore of theories; I am not sure that such complete classification can or should be given. I will focus on types of theories that are, in some natural sense, paradigmatically *explanatory*, and, yet more specifically, on two types of such theories, which I will call (a) *compositional* and (b) *evolutionary*. The types of problems calling for such answers will be similarly designated. To anticipate briefly, a compositional problem is one which calls for an answer in terms of constituent parts of the individuals making up the domain and the laws governing the behavior of those parts. The parts sought need not be "elementary," though in the cases to be considered here, they are.[18] Evolutionary problems, on the other hand, call for answers in terms of the development of the individuals making up the domain; paradigm examples are the Darwinian theory of biological evolution, theories of stellar evolution, and theories of the evolution of the chemical elements. There are types of theories which do not fit into these two categories, at least not easily: the "theory" constructed on the basis of the fundamental postulates of thermodynamics is an example, as is the special theory of relativity. But the two types to be considered are centrally important, and I believe that an understanding of them is a prerequisite to an understanding of other types represented by these and other examples. At any rate, they will illustrate certain general features of "theoretical problems" and the "theories" which are answers to those problems. I will begin with three case studies, from which such general features, as well as specific features, of these two types of theories will emerge.

1. The Periodic Table of Chemical Elements

A type of domain whose analysis will prove particularly fruitful are *ordered* domains: that is, domains in which types of items are classified, and those classes themselves arranged in some pattern, for example, a series, according to some rule or ordering principle. The series may (as in the case of the periodic table of chemical elements) or may not (as in the case of spectral classifications of stars, for example, the Morgan-Keenan-Kellman system) be periodic (repeating). Orderings

[18] Such theories are related to, and indeed are a subclass of, the "existence theories" discussed in "Notes toward a Post-Positivistic Interpretation of Science" —theories, briefly, which make existence claims. Field theories are examples of existence theories which are not readily subsumable under the present heading of "compositional theories."

of domains are themselves suggestive of several different sorts of lines of further research. As we would expect from our earlier discussion, some such problems (and associated lines of research) have to do with clarification and extension of the domain: for example, refinements of measurements of the property or properties on the basis of which the ordering is made, with a view to refining the ordering; or the search for other properties which vary concomitantly with those properties.[19] Answers to such problems are not what one would naturally call "theories." (However, one might "hypothesize" that a certain property varies concomitantly with the ordering property, even though the former may not be directly measurable with current techniques, and even though there is no very clear theoretical basis for the hypothesis, though the hypothesis seems needed on other grounds. In such case, we might find the word "theory" being used.) Nor does the fact that the ordering sometimes allows predictions to be made (for example, predictions of new elements and their properties on the basis of the periodic table) turn such ordered domains into "theories." [20] (In particular, the periodic

19 In the case of ordered domains, one can speak of domain problems having to do with the *incompleteness* of the domain, because of unoccupied places in the ordering; for example, Mendeleev and other pioneers of the periodic table gave reasons for considering there to be "gaps" in their orderings—for considering certain elements to exist which had not yet been discovered. Discovery of such elements, however—though filling in those gaps—while it did increase current knowledge, did not, in any usual sense of the word, increase "understanding" or provide "explanation" of the system of elements.

20 It is true that, especially in the decade before 1870, several alternative orderings of the chemical elements had been suggested. (See F. P. Venable, *The Development of the Periodic Law* (Easton, Pa.: Chemical Publishing, 1896); J. W. van Spronsen, *The Periodic System of Chemical Elements: A History of the First Hundred Years* (New York: Elsevier, 1969); for a collection of primary sources, see D. M. Knight, ed., *Classical Scientific Papers: Chemistry, Second Series* (New York: American Elsevier, 1970). Could those proposed "orderings" be called "theories"? The question is an empirical one of usage, and what we find is that terms like "classification," "system," "table," or "law" are used; but the term "theory" is used also, but only very occasionally. This is true not only of present usage, but also, as far as I have been able to determine, in regard to the proposals made during the decade 1860 to 1870. The rarity with which the term "theory" is applied to such cases is, I think, significant. However, even to the extent to which one might be tempted to use it in reference to the ordering of the domain of chemical elements, none of the analysis given here would be vitiated. For our purposes, all that is relevant is that *once the character of the ordering had been determined, that ordering itself became part of the domain.* That is, even if the ordering is considered to have been "theoretical" at a certain stage, nevertheless once it had been settled on through the work of Mendeleev and Meyer, it became an integral aspect of the body of information which was to be accounted for—that is, it became part of the domain. (And in any case, an "ordering" would be a very different *kind* of theory from a compositional one.)

As to the use of the term "law" in reference to the periodic table, it is important to remember the historical background of that term in this connection. In

---

his paper of 1871, Mendeleev stated the "periodic law" as follows: "The properties of simple bodies, the constitution of their compounds, as well as the properties of the last, are periodic functions of the atomic weights of the elements." (D. Mendeleev, "The Periodic Law of the Chemical Elements," *The Chemical News*, Vols. XL (1879) and XLI (1880) (translation of the 1871 article); reprinted in Knight, *Classical Scientific Papers*, pp. 273–309; quotation is on p. 267. Interestingly, Freund refers to this article as "The Periodical Regularities of the Chemical Elements": I. Freund, *The Study of Chemical Composition: An Account of Its Method and Historical Development* (New York: Dover, 1968, reprint of the 1904 edition), p. 500. But "the true function, expressing how the properties depend on the atomic weights, is unknown to us." (Mendeleev, in Knight, *Classical Scientific Papers*, p. 288.) That is, Mendeleev, like nearly all other workers in the late nineteenth century, conceived this functional relationship to be a mathematical one *whose precise form remained to be discovered*; and although he was not averse to calling his periodic table a "law," it is clear that he (like others) considered the true expression of this law to be a mathematical one, and that his statement of it was only a vague one which however was clear enough to allow rough results to be achieved. Again in his Faraday lecture of 1889, Mendeleev expressed the same view: "The Periodic Law has shown that our chemical individuals display a harmonic periodicity of properties, dependent on their masses. Now, natural science has long been accustomed to deal with periodicities observed in nature, to seize them with the vise of mathematical analysis, to submit them to the rasp of experiment." (Mendeleev, "The Periodic Law of the Chemical Elements," Faraday Lecture, June 4, 1889; reprinted in Knight, *Classical Scientific Papers*, pp. 322–344; quotation on page 328.) But after discussing the inadequacies of attempted formulations of this function, and listing what he took to be requirements of an adequate expression of it, he found it necessary to conclude that "although greatly enlarging our vision, even now the periodic law needs further improvements in order that it may become a trustworthy instrument in further discoveries" (*ibid.*, p. 337). This was the universal view: that the true "law" was yet to be found (earlier, Mendeleev had explicitly declared that "I designate by the name of *Periodic Law* the mutual relations between the properties of the elements and their atomic weights, relations which are applicable to all the elements, and which are of the nature of a periodic function"; see Freund, *The Study of Chemical Composition*, p. 469). As late as 1900, this was still the view: "We have not been able to predict *accurately* any one of the properties of one of these [noble] gases from a knowledge of those of the others; an approximate guess is all that can be made. The conundrum of the periodic table has yet to be solved." (Ramsay and Travers, *Argon and Its Companions*, 1900; quoted in Freund, *The Study of Chemical Composition*, p. 500.) The relevance of this disheartened conclusion to the present point is made clear by Ida Freund's comment: "The special feature of the conundrum thus referred to by Professor Ramsey is how to find the formula for the function which would correlate the numerics of the atomic weight with the properties susceptible of quantitative measurement. Another aspect of it is that of the expression of the atomic weights themselves by means of a general algebraic formula. This problem is an attractive one, and several attempts have been made to solve it, in spite of the fact that the only indications of the direction in which success may be expected are of negative nature" (Freund, *The Study of Chemical Composition*, p. 500).

Thus, although the periodic table was widely referred to as a law, the general opinion of the time was that it could be called a "law" only in a rather loose sense, the true law being the precise mathematical expression of the "function" relating the atomic weights and the other properties of the elements and, presumably, their compounds. Views claiming that the table should be called a law table is not "explanatory," even though predictions can be made on its basis alone.[21])

On the other hand, there are other kinds of problems and lines of research suggested by ordered domains which are concerned with attempts to construct "theories." The mere existence of an ordering relation, and still more, of a periodicity in that ordering, raises the question of accounting for that order; and the more extensive, detailed, and precise the ordering, the more strongly the existence of such an account is indicated.[22] But further, the existence of such an ordering tends to make some properties appear more significant than others (for example, atomic weight), and those properties are then looked upon as furnishing "clues" to the discovery of the presumed deeper account. These and other features of ordered and periodic domains are illustrated by the case of the periodic table.

By the early 1870s, it had become finally clear that if the chemical elements were arranged in a table ordered according to atomic weights, and if due allowance were made for undiscovered elements, then certain periodicities in the properties of the elements (as well as certain "horizontal relationships") would be revealed.[23] Many investigators

---

because it permits prediction must take into account this feature of the historical situation. (van Spronsen, *The Periodic System of Chemical Elements*, makes a deliberate decision to refer to it as the periodic "system" rather than "law," and so forth.)

[21] In some respects, similar remarks hold for the multitude of conclusions about stars (for example, regarding distances, masses, intrinsic luminosity, ages, chemical composition, internal structure—few of which are "directly observable" in anything like a positivistic sense, if in any natural sense at all) which can be drawn on the basis of the Hertzsprung-Russell diagram, the astrophysical analogue of the periodic table. In this case, however, more of a "theoretical" character has become embedded in the use of the H-R diagram than in the corresponding use of the periodic table for prediction of missing elements. Indeed, a close comparison of these two cases would demonstrate clearly the absurdity of claims that scientific predictions and other conclusions always, and in some sense that is both normal and univocal, involve or presuppose the use of "theories." Such an investigation would also reveal much of importance about the interactions and interpenetrations of "theory" and "classification." The latter is, in many cases, far from being unintellectual drudge work.

[22] This is *one* motivation of the attempt, mentioned in the preceding paragraph, to refine the measurement of the ordering properties: to test the strength of the indication that there is a deeper account to be found.

[23] Relations between isolated groups of elements had been noted much earlier and held to be indications of some common composition at least of the elements so related. As early as the second decade of the century, Döbereiner had constructed "triads" of related elements: for example, he found the (then supposed) atomic weight of strontium (50) to be the mean of those of calcium (27.5) and barium (72.5), and this was taken as grounds for questioning the independent

refused to believe that any further problem was raised by these relationships; to them, the "elements" were truly fundamental, not composed of anything more elementary. This was the case particularly among working chemists, to whom the "atom" of the physicists had never been at all useful, and indeed appeared to be mere speculation.[24] However, the relationships between the elements, reflecting both order and periodicity, indicated to many that there was some more fundamental composition of the elements.[25] So extensive, detailed, and precise were those relationships that even the existence of exceptions, in

---

existence of strontium. Later, groups of more than three elements were found to be related, and again compositional theories of various sorts were suggested for those elements. Such views, of course, were based only on what are now called "vertical" rather than on "horizontal" relationships, which were disclosed fully only by the periodic table. In general, nineteenth-century science found many reasons besides the relations embodied in the periodic table for supposing the chemical elements, or at least some of them, to have common constituents; certainly there is no ground for the allegation that the view of the transmutability of the elements had died with the alchemists and was not revived until the work of Rutherford and Soddy; it is one of the liveliest strands in nineteenth-century science. A good survey is W. V. Farrar, "Nineteenth-Century Speculations on the Complexity of the Chemical Elements," *British Journal for the History of Science*, Vol. II (1965), pp. 297–323, though he neglects to include explicit discussion of the important isomeric theories of the elements.

[24] For the opposition of chemists to physical atoms, see D. M. Knight, *Atoms and Elements: A Study of Theories of Matter in England in the Nineteenth Century* (London: Hutchinson, 1967); W. H. Brock, *The Atomic Debates* (Leicester: Leicester University Press, 1967); and W. McGucken, *Nineteenth-Century Spectroscopy: Development of the Understanding of Spectra 1802–1897* (Baltimore: Johns Hopkins University Press, 1969). In this connection, perhaps Lavoisier's conception of elements as "the substances into which we are capable, by any means, to reduce bodies by decomposition" (A. L. Lavoisier, *Elements of Chemistry* [New York: Dover, 1965], p.xxiv) joined with Dalton's views and a too-rigid empiricism to discourage many chemists from "unscientific," "metaphysical" speculations about the composition of the elements. Mendeleev himself, though on other occasions he was not at all averse to such speculations, remarked in his Faraday lecture that "the periodic law, based as it is on the solid and wholesome ground of experimental research, has been evolved independently of any conception as to the nature of the elements; it does not in the least originate in the idea of an unique matter; and it has no historical connection with that relic of the torments of classical thought, and therefore it affords no more indication of the unity of matter or of the compound character of our elements, than the law of Avogadro, or the law of specific heats, or even the conclusions of spectrum analysis" (Knight, *Classical Scientific Papers: Chemistry, Second Series*, p. 332). The statement following the word "therefore," of course, is a complete *non sequitur*.

[25] The situation was, however, complicated (a) by the fact that what were and were not elements was not always clear, and (b) by the fact that atomic weights were not well known and were difficult to measure, especially without making certain assumptions. With these and other difficulties to overcome, much "theory" was used in the attempt to construct orderings of the elements before Mendeleev and Meyer. See the references in footnote 20.

which the order or the periodicity, one or the other, had to be violated if the other were satisfied, could not shake the conviction of an underlying composition which would, ultimately, remove even those anomalies. (It is perhaps significant that, for a long period, only one such anomaly was known which appeared anywhere near troublesome.[26]) Hence the conviction grew that the periodic table was to be given some deeper explanation; and in particular, since the fundamental ordering factor, the atomic weight, increased by discrete "jumps" (which were, in most cases, rather close to integral values) rather than by continuous gradations, that deeper explanation was expected to be in terms of discrete components. Thus that composition was to be understood in terms of constituent *massive* particles (whose step-by-step increase in numbers was reflected in the increases of atomic weights which furnished the ordering principle of the table), and the structure of which involved repetitions at various intervals (reflected in the periodicity of *other* properties of the domain which were "significant," that is, which were related in the periodicity of the table).

This expectation increased in strength until it reached the status of a *demand*, reinforced by the following considerations: (a) more and more other areas revealed themselves as domains in which an atomistic explanation was expected (for example, the case of chemical spectros-

[26] The one case which approached being a clear one, because of the large difference in atomic weight involved, was that of tellurium and iodine—though, as we shall see momentarily, even this case was not as clear as van Spronsen makes out. Although the ordering of cobalt and nickel was also anomalous, "The atomic weights of the latter pair of elements differed so slightly that at first the extent of the problem was not appreciated, the more so because their properties differed so little" (van Spronsen, *The Periodic System of Chemical Elements*, p. 236). The third anomaly, with regard to the order of argon and potassium, was not known until 1894, and even then there were difficulties about determining the atomic weight of argon. It was with the discovery of this anomaly, according to van Spronsen, that "the problem became extremely disturbing" (*ibid.*). Even the case of tellurium and iodine was not admitted as clear by many authorities, including Mendeleev himself, who in 1889 declared triumphantly that "the periodic law enabled us also to detect errors in the determination of the atomic weight of several elements . . . Berzelius had determined the atomic weight of *tellurium* to be 128, while the periodic law claimed for it an atomic weight below that of iodine, which had been fixed by Stas at 126.5, and which was certainly not higher than 127. Brauner then undertook the investigation, and he has shown that the true atomic weight of tellurium is lower than that of iodine, being near to 125" (Faraday Lecture, in Knight, *Classical Scientific Papers: Chemistry, Second Series*, p. 339; for an amusing if vitriolic response to Brauner's work, see Freund, *The Study of Chemical Composition*, p. 505). As to the fourth anomaly, that of the pair protoactinium-thorium, it never presented a problem, as protoactinium was discovered in 1918, five years after Moseley, Rydberg, and Van den Broek demonstrated that atomic number, rather than atomic weight, provided the fundamental ordering principle.

copy, to be discussed below); (b) atomistic explanations became more and more successful (statistical mechanics) or at least more and more promising (Kelvin's vortex atom was applied in a great many areas) in other domains; and (c) reasons accumulated, as shown in Part I, for suspecting the domain under consideration (the chemical elements related through the periodic table) to be itself related, as part of a larger domain, to others, including ones in which atomistic explanations were either expected, demanded, or actually provided. All three of these sorts of considerations were, of course, open to question: (a′) the expectations of atomistic explanations in other areas could be criticized as not being sufficiently well founded, and in any case as only expectations; (b′) the atomistic explanations advanced in other areas were perhaps not as completely successful (statistical mechanics still had its difficulties, and the vortex atom was in no case applied in precise mathematical detail[27]) or necessary (perhaps "phenomenological thermodynamics" was all that was needed in the domain of heat) as was claimed; and (c′) although some relationships between the domain under consideration and others did exist, there were also differences which might obviate the suspicion that those domains should be looked upon as parts of a higher domain requiring a unitary and, in particular, compositional explanation. But the considerations leading to the expectation of a compositional theory to account for the periodic table were strong enough to constitute reasons in favor of a search for such a theory; that expectation, and the research which it guided, were not shaken substantially by such considerations as (a′) to (c′), any more than they were disturbed by the tellurium-iodine anomaly. Nor were they shaken by the failure of successive atomistic theories to account successfully for the features of the periodic table, and still less by the opposition of the energeticists and the positivistically minded philosophers, to whom *any* atomistic explanation was unscientific. Considerations (a) to (c), when added to the indications of the periodic table itself (the domain constituted by the periodic table, that is), were strong enough to constitute reasons in favor of a search for such a theory. That the reasons were not logically conclusive did not make them any the less reasons, and good ones, relative to the state of science at the time, nor did it make action in accordance with them any the less rational.

This discussion is clearly generalizable as a principle of reasonable scientific research:

[27] For the vortex atom, see McGucken, *Nineteenth-Century Spectroscopy*, esp. pp. 165–175.

To the extent that a domain D satisfies the following conditions or some subset thereof, it is reasonable to expect (or demand) that a compositional theory be sought for D:

(Ci) *D is ordered;*

(Cii) *the order is periodic;*

(Ciii) *the order is discrete* (that is, based on a property which "jumps" in value from one item to the succeeding one), *the items having values which are* (within the limits of experimental error) *integral multiples of a fundamental value;*

(Civ) *the order and periodicity are extensive, detailed, and precise;* [28]

(Cv) *compositional explanatory theories are expected for other domains;*

(Cvi) *compositional theories have been successful or promising in other domains;*

(Cvii) *there is reason to suppose that the domain under consideration is related to such other domains so as to form part of a larger domain.*[29]

Although this principle can and will be generalized still further in a number of respects, I will refer to it (or to the more generalized version of it) as the *principle of compositional reasoning.*

In the light of this principle, one might even speak of the "degree of rationality" involved in pursuing a search for a compositional theory: the pursuit of a certain line of research in the expectation of finding a compositional theory for a given domain is more rational, the more of

[28] Thus, because it fails to satisfy this condition to a very high degree, Bode's "law," which gives a simple mathematical ordering relationship approximating the distances of the planets out to Uranus reasonably well, cannot be *clearly* included as part of a domain concerning the planets. Ordering only seven items, it is not very extensive; nor is it very detailed, not holding for Neptune or Pluto at all, and not relating to any other planetary characteristics besides distance; nor is it very precise, since it holds only approximately for the planets to which it does apply. In other words, the failure of a theory of (say) the origin of the solar system to account for Bode's "law" cannot be considered a very great weakness of that theory. For such a theory is only weakly (that is, only to the rather low degree that Bode's "law" is extensive, detailed, and precise) required to account for that "law." It is not clear, in other words, that Bode's ordering really sets a *problem* regarding the planets. To put the point more generally, membership in a domain is also a "matter of degree," and is thus subject to debate. That is, whether a theory is reasonably to be expected to account for a certain item is itself a matter which can be questioned. This kind of move in defense of a theory has often been made in the history of science.

[29] (Cv) to (Cvii) clearly have to do with determinations of the "importance" of the problem.

points (Ci) to (Cvii) are satisfied, and the more each of them is satisfied. And the demand that any acceptable theory accounting for the periodic table be a compositional theory is also the more rational, the more of (Ci) to (Cvii) are satisfied, and the more each of them is satisfied. (Such demands are therefore not "dogmatic" in the sense of being irrational, even though the explanation ultimately accepted might not be in accord with those demands. Of course, the extent to which the demands are justified should always be appreciated.) This notion of "degree of rationality" will be found also applicable to other kinds of scientific research and expectations, theoretical or otherwise.[30]

The *problem* regarding the domain, in the case of the periodic table, then becomes not merely to give an account of the domain, but more specifically, to give a compositional theory for it. Lines of research which it is reasonable to pursue are indicated by the character of the theory expected on the basis of the characteristics of the domain, and are made still more specific by other considerations to be discussed later ("background information").

2. Spectroscopy

Some of the complexity of reasoning in science, however, begins to reveal itself when we investigate another area of late nineteenth-century science which was widely expected to eventuate in a compositional theory. Almost from its inception, spectroscopy was aimed not only at the identification of chemical elements through their characteristic spectra, but also at the development of an explanatory theory having to do with atoms or molecules. As early as 1836, the British spectroscopist Talbot had written: "The definite rays emitted by certain substances, as, for example, the yellow rays of the salts of soda, possess a fixed and inviolable character, which is analogous in some measures to the fixed proportion in which all bodies combine according to the atomic theory. It may be expected, therefore, that optical researches, carefully conducted, may throw some additional light upon chemistry." [31] And half a century later, Rydberg, one of the leading figures

[30] The whole tenor of the present analysis has been in the direction of making the line between "science" and "nonscience" a matter of degree rather than a sharp distinction in terms of some "line of demarcation."

[31] McGucken, *Nineteenth-Century Spectroscopy*, p. 8. Jammer is thus in error in stating that "Mitscherlich [1864] was the first to point out that spectroscopy should be regarded not only as a method of chemical analysis . . . but also as a clue to the secrets of the inner structure of the atom and the molecule" M. Jammer, *The Conceptual Development of Quantum Mechanics* (New York: McGraw-Hill, 1966), p. 63. Mitscherlich had declared that "[The difference in the spectra of the elements and compounds] appeared to me of great importance, because by

in the field, maintained that spectral data "relate to the motions of the least parts of matter, the atoms themselves, in a way that we can expect . . . to find the most simple functions to express the relations between the form of moving bodies, their dimensions, and the active forces."[32] Hence studies of those data could be expected to lead to "a more exact knowledge of the nature of the constitution of atoms."[33]

Thus, throughout the history of the subject, an intimate connection was presumed to obtain between the characteristic lines of the spectra of chemical elements and the characteristics (usually associated in this case, especially in the nineteenth century, with vibrations)[34] of ultimate constituents of chemical substances. So widespread was this belief that one authority on the history of spectroscopy declares that "I have found no spectroscopist who did not admit an atomic theory. As we have seen, 'understanding spectra' became almost synonymous with 'understanding atoms and molecules,' and to spectroscopists atoms and molecules were as real as spectra themselves. Thus the end of the century's anti-atomistic movement, which had its origin in the application of thermodynamics to chemical phenomena, could only have met with resistance

---

the observation of the spectra a new method is found of recognizing the internal structure of the hitherto unknown elements, and of chemical compounds." A. Mitscherlich, "On the Spectra of Compounds and of Simple Substances," *Philosophical Magazine*, 4, 28 (1864), p. 169; quoted in C. L. Maier, "The Role of Spectroscopy in the Acceptance of an Internally Structured Atom, 1860–1920," Ph.D. dissertation, University of Wisconsin (1964), p. 38. Maier's comment on this passage is: "To suggest that Mitscherlich is here implying an internal structure of the elemental atoms would be a distortion in terms of the context of the times. He refers to the internal structure of elements and compounds, not of atoms and molecules. It is far more probable that Mitscherlich had reference to the utility of this new spectral distinction in deciding whether elements and compounds were actually structured into entities such as the atom and molecule than that the atoms themselves were internally structured" (pp. 38–39). Maier could not, of course, have had Jammer's later remark in mind here, but his point certainly holds against the latter. However, perhaps Jammer was thinking only of Daltonian "atoms," in which case his remark would be perfectly in order. In this connection, Maier's own reference to "elemental atoms" is confusing: as he himself notes, it is perfectly correct to interpret Mitscherlich's statement as referring to a possible internal structure of the elements (Daltonian atoms).

[32] McGucken, *Nineteenth-Century Spectroscopy*, p. 155.

[33] *Ibid.*, p. 155. It is certainly necessary to reject Dingle's assertion that "Rydberg's work, fundamentally important though it is, was purely empirical" (H. Dingle, "A Hundred Years of Spectroscopy," *British Journal for the History of Science*, Vol. I (1963), p. 209). Maier argues effectively against Dingle's interpretation (Maier, "The Role of Spectroscopy," pp. 102ff.).

[34] See Maier's discussion of what he calls "the acoustical analogy" and its guidance of the search for mathematical formulas relating the spectral lines (Maier, "The Role of Spectroscopy," Ch. III). McGucken's discussion is also highly illuminating in this connection and complements that of Maier very well (McGucken, *Nineteenth-Century Spectroscopy*).

from spectroscopists. It had apparently no influence on spectroscopy."[35]

And yet it was not until 1885 that Balmer discovered the first clear and unambiguous ordering relationship between any spectral lines. Thus, *contrary to the case of the periodic table, the conviction that a compositional theory would be found for the spectral domain was not based on ordering relationships, but preceded their discovery.* On what, then, was the expectation based that spectra would be accounted for in terms of a compositional theory? Undoubtedly it had its roots partly in considerations (Cv) to (Cvii) above (having to do with expectation or achievement of success by compositional theories in related domains), together with analogues of (Ciii) and (Civ). Although there was no *ordering* of lines in the sense of there being a known formula relating them (or even a qualitative expression of reasonable generality and precision, of their arrangements) and measurements of their positions were not related to one another by integral multiples of some fundamental value, nevertheless the lines of elements are in general discrete (though not always sharp), and furthermore maintain their relative positions, as well as a number of other characteristics (for example, under similar conditions, intensity and degree of sharpness), with great preciseness. Thus Rydberg could adduce as a reason for investigating spectra not only that they related to atomic motions, but also that spectral data were "without comparison the richest and most uniform of all relating to all of the known elements."[36]

But a further consideration, which did not emerge from our study of the case of the periodic table, enters into this case: namely, the existence, in another domain, of a way of approaching problems which, by analogy, could offer promise here. Almost from the outset, it was felt by many that the key to success in this domain lay in constructing a theory of atomistic (or molecular) vibrations on the analogy of sound: the various spectral lines of an element would prove understandable as harmonics of a fundamental vibration and could be revealed by an appropriate Fourier analysis. (Indeed, rather than believing that the discovery of an ordering formula would provide a clue to construction of an atomic or molecular theory, many spectroscopists before Balmer believed that the key to discovery of that ordering formula lay in a consideration of the harmonics of fundamental atomic vibrations.) This case differs from ones in which a theory is *related*, or for which there is good reason to suspect is related, as part

[35] *Ibid.*, p. 204.

[36] *Ibid.*, p. 155. In our terms, Rydberg here adduces the high degree of "readiness" in addition to "importance" as an argument for investigating spectra.

of a larger domain to the one under consideration.[37] In the present case, the domain from which the analogue approach is taken need not be so related, that is, what relations there are between it and the domain under consideration are either very general, very tenuous, or not very "significant." Furthermore, what is borrowed is not necessarily the theory of the original domain, but rather an analogue thereof: at best, it is possible to speak only of *adapting* that theory, not of *applying* it without alteration (as one would attempt to do if expecting to unify two related domains). (Of course, such adaptation often involves *interpreting* the current domain so as to make adaptation or application of the imported approach possible; in the present case, the lines had to be looked at—and there was good ground for such interpretation—as records of wavelengths of vibrations, and the explanatory entities, therefore, as vibrators.) Indeed, the adaptation may not, in its original application, even have been compositional. Nor, in fact, need it have been a "theory"; it may have been merely a mathematical technique or a way of approaching a problem. Needless to say, such analogical adaptations are available in the case of ordered domains also.

Thus the present case allows us to give a more general formulation of conditions (Ciii) and (Civ) for compositional theories, and to add a further condition (Cviii). In the present case, of course, with the qualification to be mentioned below, conditions (Ci) and (Cii), having to do specifically with ordered and periodic domains, are inapplicable[38]:

[37] In this kind of case, where there is not good reason to suspect that the two domains are related as parts of a larger domain, it is appropriate to speak of the importation of ideas from one domain into another as based on "analogy." Where there are such good reasons, it is more appropriate to speak of such importation as being based on "evidence" (or, more generally, on "reasons"). No doubt there are always *some* grounds, at least very weak ones, for suspecting that two domains may be related as parts of a larger domain; and to this extent, the difference between introducing new ideas on the basis of "analogy" and on the basis of "evidence" is a matter of degree—as is the distinction between principles (Cvii) and (Cviii), which will be discussed below. But this fact does not sanction the obliteration of the distinction by those who maintain that all hypotheses in science are introduced on the basis of "analogy."

[38] It should be recalled that (Ci) and (Cii) did not *have* to be fulfilled in order that a compositional theory could be reasonably expected; their fulfillment, above and beyond the fulfillment of some of the other conditions, only provided increased grounds for expecting such a theory. Condition (Ciii), concerned with discreteness and integral multiplicity, while even it is not a *necessary* condition for expecting a compositional theory, does perhaps by itself provide stronger grounds for such expectation, other things being equal, than condition (Ci) alone would. It should be noted that condition (Ci) is undoubtedly susceptible to considerable generalization.

(Ciii′) *the items of the domain have discrete values which are preserved (at least under similar conditions) from situation to situation (or, their relations to one another are preserved from situation to situation), even though no general formula (or qualitative principle) expressing the relations of those values is known.* (The existence of the preserved relations is, of course, a rational incentive to suspect the existence of such a general formula and to search for it. In this sense, (Ciii′) may be seen as implying an analogue of (Ci), namely: (Ci′) *there is reason* (in this case, in the preservation of relations of lines) *for supposing an ordering formula to exist.* If such a formula is found, as in the case of Balmer's discovery, the domain becomes, to the extent that the formula deals with a proportion of the totality of items (lines) of the domain, ordered. If the formula does not yield values of the items which are integral multiples of a fundamental value, then the rationale for expecting a compositional theory will be more complex, depending in general on (Cviii), below.

(Civ′) *a number of features of an extensive range of items of the domain are open, with techniques available, to detailed and precise description or measurement.*

(Cviii) *a theory (or, more generally, a technique or method) which has been successful or promising in another domain (even though, unlike the case of (Cvii), that domain is not related or suspected of being related as part of a larger domain to the domain D under consideration) shows promise of being adaptable, with an appropriate interpretation of the items of D, to D.*

In spite of the fact that this and other forms of reasoning take place in science, there are often alternative lines of reasoning available which lead to different conclusions; and the issue of which line has the strongest arguments in its favor is not always clear-cut. Thus, whether a certain body of information constitutes a domain or not; whether a certain item is or is not a part of a domain (that is, whether or not a theory for that domain is responsible for accounting for that item); the extent to which a certain problem is important; the extent to which the state of science is "ready" to investigate a certain problem; the degree of promise of a certain proposed line of research; whether a certain specific sort of answer to a problem is reasonably to be expected; whether a certain proposed answer to a problem is adequate—all these can be, and in any given situation in the history of science are apt to be, debated. This is not to say that such issues are *never* unambiguously clear, and still less to say that they do not, in general, become more so as science progresses: for substantive scientific knowledge, as it accumulates, imposes more and more stringent conditions on the character and interrelations of domains, the kinds of questions that can reasonably be asked regarding them, the reasons for considering those problems important and ready for investigation, the moves that it is reasonable to make in trying to answer the problems, the kinds of answers to those problems that can be expected to be found, and the conditions an answer must satisfy if it is to be acceptable. Nevertheless, in all these respects, what is maintained by scientists is of a hypothetical nature, and there is generally room for disagreement, without it being perfectly clear which side has the strongest reasons in its favor.

Thus, for example, although most, if not all, prominent spectroscopists of the nineteenth century believed with Talbot, Mitscherlich, and Rydberg that spectral lines are produced by atoms, there were some who did not believe that a study of those lines would lead, at least easily, to knowledge of the constitution of atoms. There were two distinct lines of argument by which this conclusion was arrived at. On the one hand, Kayser and Runge, two of the leading figures in the history of spectroscopy, held that, although spectral lines are ultimately produced by atoms, their study could provide us only with knowledge of *molecules*, not of atoms. Their reasons for this attitude were complex, having to do partly with experimental results and partly with conceptions of how those results could have been produced.[39] On the other hand, yet another major figure, Arthur Schuster, was pessimistic about the possibility, or at least the ease, of gaining insight through spectra even into the nature and structure of molecules, much less of atoms—not because spectra do not have their origin in the vibrations of atoms or molecules, but because spectra are too complex.

> . . . we must not too soon expect the discovery of any grand and very general law [from investigation of spectra], for the constitution of what we call a molecule is no doubt a very complicated one, and the difficulty of the problem is so great that were it not for the primary importance of the result which we may finally hope to obtain, all but the most sanguine might well be discouraged to engage in an enquiry which, even after many years of work, may turn out to have been fruitless. We know a great deal more about the forces which produce

[39] McGucken, *Nineteenth-Century Spectroscopy*, p. 156; the reasons behind this attitude are surveyed by that author on pp. 73–83.

> the vibrations of sound than about those which produce the vibrations of light. To find out the different tunes sent out by a vibrating system is a problem which may or may not be solvable in certain special cases, but it would baffle the most skilful mathematician to solve the inverse problem and to find out the shape of a bell by means of the sounds which it is capable of sending out. And this is the problem which ultimately spectroscopy hopes to solve in the case of light.[40]

These examples only illustrate some of the kinds of disagreements to which science, for all its accumulated knowledge and constraints, is subject.[41] Nevertheless, the existence of such disagreements, and the frequent unclarity as to which view is correct, do not mean that no rationale exists in science and its development: the viewpoints *often*, if not always, have reasoned arguments in their favor, even if those arguments are not always telling or accepted. And the situation may, and often does, become more clear-cut with further research. The possibility of rationally based disagreements, in fact, plays an important role in science: the possibility helps to ensure that reasonable alternatives will be explored.

[40] *Ibid.*, pp. 125–126. Maier conveys a picture of mass desertions of the field of spectroscopy: "As the complexity of spectra became apparent, more and more workers turned away from it as a method of practical analysis. . . . The field of chemical analysis was left to a few stalwarts . . ." (Maier, "The Role of Spectroscopy," p. 40). Though this is perhaps something of an exaggeration, considering the widespread employment of spectral analysis by astronomers, it was undoubtedly a very common attitude. Even Kayser, in 1910, had come to the point of declaring that "there is little prospect that in the future qualitative analysis will apply spectroscopic methods to a large extent . . . I come to the conclusion that quantitative spectroscopic analysis has shown itself as impractical" (quoted in *ibid.*, p. 41). It is interesting to note that this attitude was repeated by Niels Bohr, who finally gave a successful explanation of spectra in atomistic terms: "The spectra was a very difficult problem. . . . One thought that this is marvelous, but it is not possible to make progress there. Just as if you have the wing of a butterfly, then certainly it is very regular with the colors and so on, but nobody thought that one could get the basis of biology from the coloring of the wing of a butterfly" (quoted by J. Heilbron and T. Kuhn, "The Genesis of the Bohr Atom," in R. McCormmach, ed., *Historical Studies in the Physical Sciences* [Philadelphia: University of Pennsylvania Press, 1969], Vol. I, p. 257).

[41] A splendid example of several different kinds of disagreement of the sorts discussed here is found in the debates regarding interpretation of the photoelectric effect in the years immediately preceding Einstein's "Concerning a Heuristic Point of View about the Creation and Transformation of Light" (*Annalen der Physik*, 17 (1905), pp. 132–148; translated in H. Boorse and L. Motz, eds., *The World of the Atom* [New York: Basic Books, 1966], Vol. I, pp. 545–557) and in the succeeding years up to Compton's interpretation of his x-ray scattering experiments in 1924. Historical aspects of the case are well presented in M. Klein, "Einstein's First Paper on Quanta," *The Natural Philosopher*, No. 2 (New York: Blaisdell, 1963), pp. 57–86, and R. Stuewer, "Non-Einsteinian Interpretations of the Photoelectric Effect," in R. Stuewer, ed., *Historical and Philosophical Perspectives of Science* (Minneapolis: University of Minnesota Press, 1970), pp. 246–263.

3. Stellar Spectral Classification and Stellar Evolution

We saw that, in the case of the periodic table, the expectation of a compositional theory arose almost immediately; few workers, however, were interested in questions of the evolution of the elements.[42] On the other hand, it was not long after the first spectral classifications of stars were published that those classifications were associated with expectations (and presentations) of an evolutionary theory explaining the classification. In fact, some of the pioneers of stellar classification were among those who presented such theories. So strong and persistent was this tendency that by the end of the century, the historian of astronomy Agnes Clerke could write that "Modes of classifying the stars have come to be equivalent to theories of their evolution." [43] It will prove illuminating to examine the roots of this difference between the case of the periodic table and that of astronomical spectral classifications.

By 1863, the work of Huggins and others had established, on the basis of spectral analysis, that the stars are composed of the same elements as are found on earth. Classification of stars on the basis of spectral features began at about the same time with the work of Secchi, Vogel, and others. The resulting classifications correlated well with the colors of the stars.

At this point, there was no clear order or sequence among the different classes.[44] However, some astronomers (notably Vogel), on the

[42] For descriptions of such theories, see Venable, *The Development of the Periodic Law*, and van Spronsen, *The Periodic System of Chemical Elements*. It is highly significant that a large proportion of these evolutionary theories of the chemical elements were proposed by men whose primary work, or a considerable part of whose work, lay in fields outside chemistry. An explanation of this phenomenon will be offered shortly.

[43] A. Clerke, *Problems of Astrophysics* (London: Black, 1903), pp. 179–180. One is reminded here of McGucken's statement, quoted earlier, that in the nineteenth century, " 'understanding spectra' became almost synonymous with 'understanding atoms and molecules' " (McGucken, *Nineteenth Century Spectroscopy*, p. 204). There were, as usual, dissenters from the prevailing view: the British astronomer Maunder wrote in 1892 that "spectrum type does not primarily or usually denote epoch of stellar life, but rather a fundamental difference of chemical constitution" (O. Struve and V. Zebergs, *Astronomy of the Twentieth Century* [New York: Macmillan, 1962], p. 187). Once again we are reminded of the attitudes of some chemists toward compositional theories of the elements.

[44] Even the *Henry Draper Catalogue of Stellar Spectra*, which became the basis of modern classifications, in its first volume of 1890, divided the stars into sixteen classes denoted by the letters A through Q (with J omitted), the alphabetical order not corresponding to any ordering among the classes. It was only early in the twentieth century that some of these groups were omitted, or combined and relettered, and the order changed, ultimately becoming the present O-B-A-F-G-K-M-R-N-S ("Oh, be a fine girl, kiss me right now, sweet"), an arrangement which does provide a sequential ordering.

analogy of changes in cooling materials in terrestrial cases, proposed that the different colors (and therefore the correlated spectral classes) were indications of an *evolutionary sequence.* The hottest (and, on this view, the youngest) stars would be blue or white, while red stars were in their old age.[45]

Further, some writers, noting the presence of strong hydrogen lines in the spectra of the white (and therefore, on the theory under consideration, young) stars, conjoined to that theory an hypothesis about the composition of the elements: generally, either that of Prout, according to which all elements are composed of hydrogen (and whose atomic weights would therefore be expected to be integral multiples of that of hydrogen), or else some other view of the fundamental composition of the elements (for example, a modification of Prout's hypothesis, to the effect that the ultimate constituents had an atomic weight of one-half that of hydrogen, thus removing what was to the Prout hypothesis an embarrassing anomaly, namely that of chlorine, with a well-documented atomic weight of 35.5).[46] And on the basis of that combination of a theory of the composition of the elements and a theory of stellar evolution, they proceeded to develop an evolutionary theory of the chemical elements (Prout's own view having been, at least in its usually understood form, purely compositional): as stars age, higher elements are built up out of hydrogen, so that older stars are composed of a larger proportion of heavier elements.[47] This view, though it was not without its immediately obvious difficulties, found some support in the fact that, as a general trend, there are an increasing number of higher element lines as we proceed through the spectral classes, ordered according to color, from white to red.[48] Thus, in summary, the older stars were held to be red and composed of heavier elements—on the

[45] Other theories, for example, that of Lockyer, held that some red stars are young and heating up—according to Lockyer through meteoritic impacts—to the white stage, while others had cooled from the hotter stage. It is worth noting that an alternative view of the colors of stars had been proposed earlier: Doppler had suggested that blue stars are moving toward us, while red stars are moving away. Such an interpretation, however, would imply corresponding shifts of spectral lines, which are not observed.

[46] Such views of element composition were combined with a variety of theories of stellar evolution other than the one under consideration.

[47] There were also theories according to which greater age saw a greater *breakdown* of heavier elements, *ending* with the ultimate constituents.

[48] The existence of this trend does not itself seem to have been taken as a basis for class orderings in the early stages of astronomical spectroscopy: criteria of ordering would have had to be complex and quite beyond the knowledge of the times. It was, however, clear enough, once the classes had been ordered according to color, to provide additional support for that proposed ordering.

assumption, of course, that the *total* composition of a star was accurately reflected in the spectral observations of its surface. (It was not until 1921 that Saha demonstrated that the differences of spectra did not reflect even a difference of *atmospheric* composition, but merely one of temperature. The differences in chemical composition of most stars, though highly significant for interpretation of their energy production, internal structure, and evolution, are small. The assumption made by the early astrophysicists, however, was certainly the reasonable one to make at the time.[49])

The situation seems to have been this: while the spectral classes did admit of at least a rough ordering [50] in terms of increasing numbers and intensities of heavy element lines (coupled with decreasing intensities

[49] The history of vicissitudes in the presumed relation between spectral classification and evolution of stars is a fascinating one, worth examining for the insight it would provide regarding the rationale of scientific change. By 1928, one of the major theoreticians of astrophysics, James Jeans, could write that, although "The early spectroscopists believed that the spectrum of a star provided a sure indication of the star's age," Saha's ionization and excitation theory had shown that "The linear sequence into which the spectra of stars fall is merely one of varying surface temperature. Clearly this circumstance robs stellar spectra of all direct evolutionary significance" (J. H. Jeans, *Astronomy and Cosmogony* [New York: Dover, 1961], p. 166). "The problem of stellar evolution is now seen to be quite distinct from that of explaining the distribution of stars in the [Hertzsprung-] Russell diagram, and, furthermore, the problem can expect no assistance from the observed distribution of stars in this diagram" (*ibid.*, p. 172). Only a few more years were to pass before the pendulum began to swing back in the direction of a connection between spectral classification and stellar evolution—though that connection came to be seen as far subtler and more complex than anything envisioned by the early pioneers like Vogel and Lockyer. Those later views of a connection between spectral classification and stellar evolution, however, involve a deep penetration of "theory" into the domain (as summarized in the classification and the H-R diagram). (For example, Chalonge's system, by relying heavily on the "Balmer jump" in hydrogen spectra as a basis for spectral classification, ties itself closely to the theory of the hydrogen atom; by this means, it becomes highly useful and precise, even though it is limited in applicability to early-type stars [approximately G0 and earlier] which show hydrogen lines and the Balmer jump with sufficient clarity in their spectra.) Analysis of the modern conceptual situation in this area, though it would be very instructive as to the interrelations of "theory" and "observation," and as to the ways in which a new "theory" accounts for such a domain (consisting of an intimate mixture of older classification and later theory), and therefore as to the nature of theories, is too involved to be discussed here.

[50] As was mentioned above, the attempt to lay out such an ordering would not have been free of difficulties. For example, many spectral lines had not been identified, so that the correlation of "lateness" of spectral type with "heaviness" of composition, rather tenuous at best, could not always be assured. Again, what are now called O- and B-type stars have weaker hydrogen lines than A-type (white) ones, even though they are bluer and hence, on the theory under consideration (as well as according to modern astronomy), hotter.

of hydrogen lines), such orderings were not in general made by pre-twentieth-century pioneers [51] *except* in conjunction with a theory (or analogy) imported into the domain, namely, the color changes that take place with cooling.[52] Nevertheless, a sequential ordering of spectral classes on the basis of decreasing hydrogen and increasing heavier element lines could have been achieved, at least in rough fashion, even without importation of the "background information" (as I will call it) concerning colors of cooling bodies. And if it had been so achieved, its existence would of itself have served as good ground for suspecting that an evolutionary process might be involved, simply on the basis of the fact that the ordering was based on (depending on which end one cared to look from) increase or decrease of certain factors.

However, importation of the background information concerning color changes of cooling bodies made three further contributions to the interpretation of the sequential ordering as an indicator of a possible evolutionary process. First, it increased the strength of the suggestion that an evolutionary sequence might be involved by showing that the sequential ordering of the domain on the basis of lines could be correlated with a *temporal* order having to do with the cooling process. Second, it suggested a *direction* of the evolution—a direction which could not have been extracted from the ordering on the basis of lines alone, unless one made arbitrary assumptions (for example, that the evolution is from "simple" to "complex"). For, the final death of a star being a cold, burned-out state, the red stars should be the oldest. (Unfortunately, the suggestion was not clear with regard to the beginning of the sequence: were the white stars like Sirius the youngest, blazing forth suddenly at their birth, and gradually burning themselves down to a red old age? Or as Lockyer maintained, were certain red stars young, gradually heating up by some process, if not Lockyer's meteoritic one, to white maturity, after which they declined to a second red stage just preceding death? [53]) And third, by itself constituting the

[51] Recall the case of the *Draper Catalogue*, discussed in footnote 44.

[52] This importation was also supported by the obvious explanation of starlight in terms of the stars being hot and radiating. The resultant loss of energy by radiation would also be clearly suggestive of an evolutionary process. Again, an importation into the stellar domain is at work—in this case, supported by the newly verified view that the stars have the same composition as the earth, so that the same processes and laws can be expected to be at work in both (that is, reasons have been found for supposing the terrestrial and stellar domains to be, in this respect, parts of a larger domain).

[53] Lockyer's reasoning was apparently vindicated later by Miss Maury's discovery that, despite the fact that red stars had the same lines in their spectra, in some such stars the lines were more strongly defined than in others. Hertzsprung, in 1905, established by statistical arguments the validity of Miss Maury's conjecture that this indicated that there were two radically different types of red

outline, at least, of a theory, an answer to the evolutionary problem regarding the domain, it suggested directions which research could take: directions in which the theory needed to be laid out in detail.[54]

In spite of the residual ambiguity, in this case regarding the beginning of the temporal process of stellar evolution, we can see clearly at work here two more principles of reasonable scientific research, this time applying to the (or a) way in which a problem arises, with regard to a domain, for which an *evolutionary* answer (explanatory theory) can reasonably be expected and sought:

> (Ei) *If a domain is ordered, and if that ordering is one which can be viewed as the increase or decrease of the factor(s) on the basis of which the ordering is made, then it is reasonable to suspect that the ordering may be the result of an evolutionary process, and it is reasonable to undertake research to find such an answer (which we have called an evolutionary theory).*
>
> (Eii) *The reasonableness of such expectation is increased if there is a way (for example, by application or adaptation of some background information such as a theory from another domain, whether unrelated or [preferably] related) of viewing that sequential ordering as a temporal one, and still more if a way is provided of viewing that ordering as having a temporal direction.*

Clearly, there are also analogues for evolutionary theories of conditions (Civ) to (Cviii) which were stated earlier for the case of compositional theories. I will call (Ei) and (Eii) together the *principle of evolutionary reasoning.* It should be added that (Ei) *alone* constitutes only a

---

stars. H. N. Russell, a few years later, used this fact in his construction of a new version of Lockyer's general view of stellar evolution. See Struve and Zebergs, *Astronomy of the Twentieth Century,* pp. 195–200.

[54] This third point leads to a suggestion which I am not prepared to develop fully in the present paper. Thus far, I have been speaking of theories as answers to questions. While there is a point to this, it should be remembered that those questions themselves, in the cases considered, involve a general idea of what their answer will be like. In this sense—and it is a sense which seems *prima facie* to fit a great many cases in the history of science—a theory is *gradually developed* by a process of increasingly precise and detailed statement of the initial vague idea; there is then no single point in time at which one can say unambiguously that the theory has been *arrived at.* It would then be misleading to speak, in all cases, as if there were a single event of proposing an answer to the theoretical problem. If this suggestion is borne out, as I strongly suspect it will be, one source of philosophers' difficulties with the notion of "theory" will have been exposed: for when does an idea become precise enough to be called a "theory"? The difference would seem to be more a matter of shading than of sharpness. Theory development would then be more appropriately describable, in some cases at least, as *a process of convergence from generality to (relative) precision* than as a precisely datable event like answering a question.

weak reason for undertaking research in quest of an evolutionary theory; for, without (Eii), little or no specific direction is provided for research.

Condition (Ei) was not applied in science before the second half of the nineteenth century;[55] its acceptance as a new general reasoning principle was due in no small measure to the success of Darwin's evolutionary account of biological species. The principle was, however, only gradually accepted, and this perhaps explains (together with the very real difficulties involved in the attempt) the failure, as it seems to us, of pioneers in stellar spectroscopy to try to order the classes unless they did so with an evolutionary idea already in mind. In any case, this example shows that new reasoning principles, as well as new substantive information, can be introduced into science as part of its maturation. Today the principle seems a natural one to use—so much so, in fact, that we often have difficulty in understanding why it was not applied by earlier thinkers.

Why was it, then, that condition (Ei) was applied by a considerable number of workers in the domain of astronomical spectral classification, but only rarely in that of the periodic table, where one also had a sequential ordering, and even theories, like Prout's, of the composition of the elements? (Recall that Prout's view that elements are built of hydrogen was seen by most of its adherents only as a compositional theory, not an evolutionary one.) Perhaps chemists were so used to thinking of "elements" as "always having been there" that, despite the view of some of them that the elements were *composed* of something still more elementary, they found it difficult to think of them as having been built up in a historical sense. Astronomers, on the other hand, were more used to thinking in terms of origins and development,[56] and many of them evinced a lively interest in the new biological ideas. But there is also a less speculative and sociological answer to the question: for *astronomical evolutionary theories played the same role vis-à-vis the periodic table that the "background information" regarding cooling of hot bodies played vis-à-vis spectral classification.* (The role, namely, summarized in condition (Eii), above.) That is, having interpreted

55 The few exceptions—most notably, the Kant-Laplace "nebular hypothesis" of the origin of the solar system—are not, however, paradigm examples of evolutionary theories. They have to do with the *origin* of a system and its development only to a certain stage, after which, as far as the theory is concerned, it ceases to develop further. Such theories, while they do have much in common with paradigmatically evolutionary theories, should perhaps be distinguished from them as a separate category of "genetic theories."

56 At least in the sense of "genetic theories," if not strictly speaking of evolutionary ones; see preceding footnote. Also, the view of stars as radiating bodies called for an evolutionary theory, as was pointed out in footnote 52.

spectral sequences as temporal, theories of stellar evolution could now be applied to interpret the increasing sequence of atomic weights in turn as a temporal, and as a temporally directed, one. Without this application of (Eii), the sequence of chemical elements, even seen as composed of increasing numbers of like parts, could *at best* suggest, in accordance with (Ei), that there might be something evolutionary involved. But that alone would have provided only weak incentive and, even more important, guidance in the search for such a theory. Thus the comparative absence, among chemists, of theories of the evolution of the elements is quite understandable in terms of the need of some way of satisfying (Eii) before the search for an evolutionary theory of the elements could seem attractive.[57] And if chemists also had an occupational block against seeing the use of the "Darwinian" principle (Ei), the comparative absence among them of interest in an evolutionary theory of the elements would be still more understandable.

I would not want to claim that (Ei) and (Eii) cover all the kinds of reasoning involved whenever an evolutionary theory is suspected and sought. In particular, the case of biological evolutionary theories is undoubtedly too complex to be dealt with adequately in terms of them. But the present case does illustrate one sort of reasoning pattern involved in the expectation of and search for such theories, and a very fundamental and important one at that. (The same qualifications should be understood in regard to the reasoning principles extracted from the other two cases dealt with above, dealing with compositional theories.)

We have seen, then, that certain bodies of information, related in certain ways, raise problems of various sorts, to some of which the answers that can reasonably be expected are what are called "theories." Conversely, a "theory" is what counts as a possible answer to any one of those types of questions.

It might be objected that, although the analyses given here may be relevant to a great many questions *about* theories, they tell us nothing about the "nature" of theories, which after all is the subject of the present conference. And one might suggest an analogy: if we want to know what babies are, it is irrelevant to inquire about how they

[57] In the light of this need, it is no wonder that theories of the evolution of the chemical elements tended to be proposed by men who worked in areas other than chemistry—and, in particular, in areas in which evolutionary theories were being developed. It is almost as if a theory of chemical evolution *needed* to come from another (appropriate) area (see footnote 42). Note, too, that the application of theories from those domains to the chemical one was based on good reasons, in particular, on the similarity of composition of earth and stars, as established by spectral analysis.

arise, how they behave, what sorts of problems arise concerning them, and how to deal with those problems. (The latter three questions—with reference to theories, of course, not to babies—will be discussed in the remainder of this paper.) Similarly, it might be argued that, if we want to "understand what a scientific theory is," it is irrelevant to inquire about the rationale underlying how theories (or the need or expectation of them) arise, or how they function in science, or what sorts of problems arise concerning them, or how those problems may be dealt with. The problem about the "nature" of theories—so this objection might continue—concerns the *definition* of the term 'theory' (or alternatively, perhaps, the criteria for identifying them in the first place), and so is *presupposed* by any attempt to deal with the questions raised in the present paper.

Now, I do not wish to deny that there is a problem about formulating a definition of 'theory,' or a general set of criteria for identifying theories (if indeed either of these is what philosophers who concern themselves with the problem of the "nature" of scientific theories are after). But there are a number of important points to make about that concern. In the first place, as the present paper has tried to demonstrate, there are important, different *kinds* of theories in science, so that a selection of their common features may have to be so general as to become unenlightening. (And in any case, how are we to get at such common features if we do not first recognize and try to come to grips with the different kinds of theories actually found in science?) Furthermore, it is notorious that philosophers of science have provided no generally acceptable definition of 'theory' (or set of criteria for identifying theories), and that the usages to which philosophers, especially recently, have put the term 'theory' are often so vague and ambiguous as to be scandalous.[58] Far from *presupposing* a solution to the problem of the definition of 'theory' (or of criteria of identification of theories), a more detailed study of the roots, roles, and problems of theories might in fact *help* resolve that problem. For certainly it is easier to identify paradigm cases of theories in science than—if the experience of phi-

[58] See, for example, D. Shapere, "The Structure of Scientific Revolutions," *Philosophical Review*, 73 (1964), pp. 383–394; "Meaning and Scientific Change," in R. Colodny, ed., *Mind and Cosmos* (Pittsburgh: University of Pittsburgh Press, 1966), pp. 41–85; D. Shapere, "The Paradigm Concept," *Science*, Vol. 172 (1971), pp. 706–709. On the other hand, the older "positivistic" approach to the analysis of 'theory' (in terms of an interpreted axiomatic system) was not only very unilluminating or inadequate, but also was positively misleading, and thus positively interfered with the attempt to understand scientific theories (see my "Notes toward a Post-Positivistic Interpretation of Science," Pt. I.)

losophers is any evidence—it is to formulate a general definition of 'theory' or a set of general criteria for identification of theories.

But far more important, the investigation of the problem of 'theory' definition (or of criteria for identifying theories) can provide almost nothing in the way of understanding scientific theories. Here the analogy with babies may be turned against our hypothetical objectors: for what understanding of babies would we get if we arrived at a general definition of 'baby' or a set of general criteria for identifying babies? (Who has a problem about identifying babies anyway?) On the other hand, understanding of babies *is* gained through studying their origins and development, their behavior, the problems that can arise concerning them, and the ways in which those problems can be met.[59] The case is similar with scientific theories: the problem of the "nature" of scientific theories—the problem of "understanding what a theory is"—is interpreted in a far more illuminating and fruitful way in terms of an investigation of the questions indicated here than in terms of the problem of "definition" or "criteria of identification." It is no wonder that the work of philosophers of science has seemed so barren and irrelevant to actual science. For they have, too often, concerned themselves with relatively barren and irrelevant problems.

IV. Theoretical Inadequacies and Their Treatment

Earlier, two general classes of scientific problems were distinguished: domain problems, having to do with, for example, clarification and extension of the domain, and theoretical problems, calling for a "deeper account," a "theory," of the domain. But once a theory has been presented in answer to a theoretical problem, a further type of problem can arise, namely, problems concerning the adequacy of the theory itself. I will refer to this class of problems as *theoretical inadequacies.* These will be surveyed in the present part through an examination of Bohr's theory of the hydrogen atom (his quantum theory).[60] That theory showed the way toward resolving the problems discussed earlier in the present paper, concerning the composition of the chemical elements, the characteristic features of the periodic table, and the characteristics of the spectra of the chemical elements. However, the theory

[59] This is perhaps a linguistic remark about the term 'understanding,' rather than an empirical one about babies.

[60] N. Bohr, "On the Constitution of Atoms and Molecules," *Philosophical Magazine,* Vol. 26 (1913), pp. 1–25, 476–502, 857–875.

was seen very clearly to be inadequate in certain respects; and it is those early inadequacies, rather than the later ones, which led to the need for developing a new theory, with which we shall be concerned here. Our examination will focus on the following aspects of the case: what were considered to be inadequacies in the theory in its early phase, and the reasons for considering it to be inadequate in those respects; what were considered to be reasonable directions to move in trying to overcome those inadequacies; the reasons why those lines of research suggested themselves in the first place, and why they appeared plausible; and what were considered to be adequate solutions of those problems or removal of those inadequacies. Needless to say, only a few selected aspects of these questions, even in reference to this case, can be considered in this paper; other aspects of them, in reference to different cases, have been studied in Part II of my "Notes toward a Post-Positivistic Interpretation of Science," which should be considered to supplement, and in some respects to detail further, the present discussion.

In the course of examining inadequacies and their treatment in the Bohr case, we will also be led to touch on the question of the "function" of theories: the question, that is, of whether scientific theories are to be interpreted "realistically" (as claiming that atoms or electrons, for example, really exist), or as "instruments" for calculation or correlation of data (a view sometimes expressed by saying that theories, or at least the "theoretical terms" occurring in them, are "idealizations," "simplifications," "models," "abstractions," "logical constructs," and so on). However, this question, even though it is highly relevant to the understanding of the nature of scientific theories, will not be examined directly here, inasmuch as I have dealt with it in considerable detail elsewhere.[61]

1. Inadequacies of the Bohr Theory

A. INCOMPLETENESS

Although Bohr's theory won immediate acceptance largely through its deduction of the Balmer formula and the Rydberg constant, and its "physical interpretation" (explanation) of the hitherto unexplained ("empirical") denominators in the Balmer formula, it also gave or

[61] D. Shapere, "Notes toward a Post-Positivistic Interpretation of Science," Pt. II. The analysis given there is developed further in "Natural Science and the Future of Metaphysics," to appear in a forthcoming volume of *Boston Studies in the Philosophy of Science*.

promised to give (by being extended to other elements besides hydrogen) explanations of a large number of other features of the more general body of information already strongly suspected to be deeply related, for example, the periodic table, and, in particular, chemical valency.[62]

Nevertheless, it was realized quite early that, even for the spectral domain, the Bohr theory offered no way to account for the intensities and polarizations of the spectral lines.[63] And thus, with respect to *this* domain (which by this time was recognized as being a subdomain of a larger body of information for which a unified account was expected), the theory can be said to have been *incomplete*, in the following sense: (1) there was no reason at this stage to suppose that the theory was not fundamentally correct; and (2) there was no reason to suppose that the theory as stated could not be *supplemented* so as to account for the intensities and polarizations.

This example, when coupled with the analysis given earlier in the present paper, suggests a general notion of the completeness or incompleteness of a theory. A domain, it will be remembered, is the total body of information for which a theory is expected to account. *A theory can, then, be judged complete or incomplete relative to that body of information.* Of course, as has been pointed out, the limits of the domain are not always well defined, and it is not always generally agreed whether a certain item is part of the domain or not. Hence debate about the completeness or incompleteness of a theory is always possible. But this is not to say that the issue is never clear.

Although the theory may be complete or incomplete with regard to

62 Bohr himself did not originally approach the development of his theory with the intention of accounting for the features of spectra. In fact, "In a letter to Rutherford dated 31 January 1913, he had, in fact, explicitly excluded the 'calculation of frequencies corresponding to the lines of the visible spectrum' from the subject matter he took as his own. His program for model building [?], like that of Thomson which it closely followed, relied mainly on chemical, scarcely on optical, evidence" (Heilbron and Kuhn, in McCormmach, *Historical Studies in the Physical Sciences*, p. 257). It was not until very late in the preparation of his theory that Bohr realized the possibility of giving an account of spectral lines in terms of his theory. Nevertheless, it was the success of his theory in regard to spectra that won immediate acceptance for his theory. Heilbron and Kuhn also argue convincingly that Bohr did not approach his theory via an attempt to patch up Rutherford's theory of the atom either, entering the investigation of that theory also only relatively late in his pre-1913 work. His theoretical interests had centered on the electron theory of metals, the topic of his doctoral dissertation, and it was concern with these problems that culminated in the 1913 triology—leading him into the question of the stability of the Rutherford atom along the way.

63 Use of the correspondence principle as a basis for calculating the polarizations of the lines is not considered here as a "part of the theory." The principle was not, in any case, very successful with regard to the intensities.

some given domain, it may not even be clearly applicable to some larger domain in which its original domain has come to be included. Nevertheless, despite the fact that a domain actually undergoing investigation at a given time is usually a subdomain (on more or less strong grounds) of some broader body of related information, judgments of completeness or incompleteness of a theory are ordinarily made with respect to the specific (sub)domain for which it was designed. Nevertheless, in certain contexts, it may be judged as to completeness with respect to the total inclusive domain or some portion thereof larger than the original domain of the theory. And it is judged more highly the more features of the total domain (above and beyond those of its original subdomain) it accounts for or shows promise of accounting for (as Bohr's theory showed initial promise of being extendible to other elements than hydrogen). The stronger the grounds for supposing the original domain of the theory to be related to another domain as part of a yet larger domain, of course, the more strongly the theory is expected to account for the items of that other domain, and the more it will be likely to be judged as to completeness with respect to the more inclusive domain.

That a theory is incomplete in this sense is of course an "inadequacy"; nevertheless, it is no ground for *rejecting* the theory as false; a theory can be *incomplete*, with respect to a given domain or subdomain, without being fundamentally *incorrect*; judgments of incompleteness are not tantamount to rejection, "falsification." On the other hand, a theory can be known to be fundamentally incorrect, and yet still be useful, especially if there is no better alternative theory available; for often the limits of applicability of the theory—the location, so to speak, of the incorrectness—is known.[64] It is thus misleading and ambiguous to say that a theory is not "rejected" until a better theory is available, for the theory can continue to be *used* (and thus not "rejected" in this sense) and yet known to be incorrect (and thus "rejected" in this sense).

B. SIMPLIFICATION

We will consider two major respects in which the Bohr theory as originally presented can be said to have been a "simplification."

64 "Fundamental incorrectness" is, of course, another type of "inadequacy," the one most emphasized by philosophers of science, even to the exclusion of considering other types of inadequacies. This type of inadequacy, important though it is, will not be discussed further in the present paper; it has been dealt with, although, I would now say, not thoroughly, in "Notes toward a Post-Positivistic Interpretation of Science." In particular, an example is given there in which "the limits of applicability of the theory—the location, so to speak, of the incorrectness—is known."

(1) *Bohr ignored the motion of the atomic nucleus.* On what ground could this have been alleged to be a "simplification"? The supposition was based on two considerations, deriving from two previous bodies of knowledge:

(a) Classical electricity, according to which opposite charges attract each other (and the electron is negatively charged, while the nucleus around which, in Bohr's theory, it orbits, is positively charged);

(b) Classical mechanics, according to which, if a smaller body is moving, under an attractive force, in an orbit around a larger one, the latter also will move in response to attraction by the smaller, and both bodies will describe orbits about a common center of force.

In general, such "background information"—information which is neither part of the immediately relevant domain of the theory, nor part of the theory—serves (along with a number of other functions) as a basis for the distinction between a "simplified" and a "realistic" treatment of a subject or domain. This role of background information which is itself subject to revision makes it clear that the claim that a certain idea is a "simplification" is, in science, a hypothesis, which may turn out to have been mistaken (for example, Planck's attitude toward his quantum hypothesis).[65]

(2) *Bohr ignored relativistic effects of the high velocities required*

[65] In general, the background information is accepted as true, or at least as the best hypothesis available. In the present case, however, confusion might result from the fact that the background information leading to the distinction between a "simplified" and a "realistic" treatment of atomic motions had classically been associated with two theories that were now contradicted by the Bohr theory—the very theory to which they are here being applied in making this distinction. How is this possible? Several different sorts of considerations play a role. Often the items of information relevant to making the distinction in particular cases can be separated from the general context of the theory which is being contradicted; and even where this separation cannot be clearly accomplished, the area in which the theory is known to be incorrect may not be the area relevant to making the distinction in the case at hand.

Simplifications have much in common with what were called "idealizations" in "Notes toward a Post-Positivistic Interpretation of Science." In that article, typical cases of idealizations were analyzed in terms of three features of their use: (1) there exist certain problems to be solved; (2) mathematical techniques exist for dealing with those problems if the entities dealt with (or their properties) are considered in a certain way, even if it is known, on the basis of the theory, that those entities could not really be that way (in some cases, the allegations that the entities could not really be that way are based not on the theory at hand, but on other grounds); and (3) in many cases, it is provable that the difference between a realistic and an idealized treatment will be insignificant (for example, below the limits of accuracy required by the problem at hand; or below the limits of experimental accuracy) relative to the problem at hand.

There are, however, some differences between what were in that paper analyzed under the name "idealizations" and what are being considered here as "simplifications," though the differences are not necessarily sharp ones, and there *of his orbital electrons.* In this case, the allegation of "simplification" is again based on "background information," this time the special theory of relativity.

C. STRUCTURE

The structure of the nucleus, and any influence that structure might have on the processes dealt with explicitly by Bohr, were largely ignored. (There is no name for this type of "inadequacy"; I will propose one shortly.)

In one sense, this inadequacy might be thought of as an "incompleteness" of the theory; however, there are reasons for distinguishing it from the kind of "incompleteness" dealt with in A, above. In A, we know precisely what is wrong: incompleteness is there judged relative to a fairly well-defined domain; and we know, in A, that what has been omitted from account makes a difference. In short, we know what must be taken into account in order to obtain a better (more complete) theory. But in the present case, we do not know *how* or even *whether* any internal structure the nucleus might have will have any effect on the domain at hand, even though it is necessary, in the theory, to make reference to the nucleus and to attribute some general properties to it (for example, possession of a net positive charge balancing the charges of the orbital electrons). I propose that this type of inadequacy be called *black-box incompleteness.*[66]

2. Treatment of Inadequacies in the Bohr Theory

The present paper will deal with only one of the types of inadequacies discussed above, namely, simplifications. Problems of incompleteness

---

are borderline cases. For example, the conclusion that certain concepts are "idealizations" is, in the most typical cases, drawn from the theory at hand (as in the case of the point-charge electron considered in "Notes toward . . ."), whereas what we have here, in a perfectly natural way, called "simplifications" are employed in the original *construction* of theories (rather than in the *application* of an already constructed theory to a specific problem), and so are considered to be "simplifications" on the basis of *previous* theories or *other* knowledge, rather than, as in the case of "idealizations," on the basis of the theory itself. Again, in the case of the most typical "idealizations," we usually do not have available the mathematical techniques required for a (direct) realistic treatment (though approximation techniques may be resorted to), whereas in the case of "simplifications," as will be seen shortly, we often do.

[66] Of course, there were indications of an internal structure of the nucleus available at the time; but since those indications were independent of Bohr's theory, they are irrelevant to the present point.

(and also of fundamental correctness) have been examined in "Notes toward a Post-Positivistic Interpretation of Science."

In the case of simplifications, two situations of special interest, for our purposes, arose soon after the presentation of Bohr's theory. These two situations are related to the two respects discussed above in which Bohr's theory was considered to be a simplification.

(1) *The spectrum of Zeta Puppis and the motion of the nucleus.* This was a problem with which Bohr's theory was confronted almost immediately; its nature and resolution are summarized well by Rosenfeld and Rüdinger:

> Bohr had come to the conclusion that certain spectral lines (originally discovered in the spectrum of the star Zeta Puppis), which up to then had been believed to belong to hydrogen, must really be ascribed to helium. . . . The outstanding English spectroscopist A. Fowler, who had himself discovered some of the spectral lines in question, was, however, not yet convinced: he pointed to a small but real discrepancy between the experimental results and the values found by a simple application of Bohr's formula. Now, since Bohr's assertion was based on a correspondence argument, such a disagreement, however small, would in fact mean the breakdown of the whole basis for his theory. In the subsequent discussion in "Nature" Bohr showed, however, that Fowler's objection could be answered by taking into account the motion of the nucleus around the center of gravity of the atom. By this more exact calculation Bohr was not only able to demonstrate the finest agreement between the calculated and the observed spectral lines, but he could also predict that a series of other spectral lines from helium, so far unobserved, which according to the simple theory would coincide with some of the Balmer lines, should in fact appear very slightly displaced in relation to these. The lines were discovered the following year by Evans at the places predicted.[67]

Thus the situation was as follows: a problem arose for the theory (Fowler's objection that certain lines did not appear at the positions calculated on the basis of Bohr's theory); and a reasonable line of research in attempting to answer the problem was to look at areas in which simplifications had been made. One might even speak here of a general *principle of nonrejection of theories*: when a discrepancy is found between the predictions of a theory and the results of observation or experiment, do not reject the theory as fundamentally incorrect before examining areas of the theory in which simplifications have been made which might be responsible for the discrepancy.

[67] L. Rosenfeld and E. Rüdinger, "The Decisive Years, 1911–1918," in S. Rozental, *Niels Bohr* (New York: Wiley, 1967), pp. 59–60. For further details, see Whittaker, *A History of the Theories of Aether and Electricity*, Vol. II, pp. 113–115; Jammer, *The Conceptual Development of Quantum Mechanics*, pp. 82–85.

(2) *Sommerfeld and the fine structure of spectral lines.* In the preceding case, a problem arose which was answered by giving a more realistic treatment instead of, as earlier, a simplified one. The reverse order of events, however, might have taken place: the more realistic treatment might have been given without the problem ever having come up, and the altered prediction of the positions of the lines made. This was, in fact, the order of events in the present case: Sommerfeld, realizing the simplification involved in ignoring the relativistic effects of the high velocities of the orbital electrons, took into account those effects, giving a more realistic treatment of the situation, and in the process arriving at the prediction of a fine structure of spectral lines. Again we see how "background information," in making the distinction between simplifications and realistic treatments, also determines what counts as a reasonable line of research in the face of a problem confronting the theory (Zeta Puppis case), or even in the absence of one (Sommerfeld case). Of course, this is only one sort of case in which certain moves in science having to do with theoretical inadequacy acquire reasonableness; but it should be sufficient to show that (and even how), in dealing with such problems just as with domain problems and theoretical problems, certain moves in science sometimes, at least, are reasonable, plausible, even if they should ultimately turn out not to provide an answer to the problem at hand.

The present paper has examined a number of cases from the history of science, with a view to exposing some of the reasoning patterns existing there with regard to the generation of scientific areas, problems, and attempts to deal with those problems—all with the hope of shedding some light on the nature and function of scientific theories.[68] The patterns discerned are justly labeled "reasoning-patterns": in particular, their formulation requires no reference to psychological or sociological factors, and their operation in concrete cases is, or at least can be, independent of such factors.

Nevertheless, one of the main points of this paper has been that, although scientific development is often reasonable, there is no question here of anything that could appropriately be called a *"logic of discovery,"* for there is no *guarantee* that a certain line, or even *any* reasonable line, of research *will* eventuate in a solution of the problem.

68 It should be noted that the cases selected are all related to one another, and that their discussion leads naturally into that of a number of crucial developments in twentieth-century science. Their analysis can thus provide a background against which those more modern developments can be profitably examined.

Rather than speaking of a logic of discovery, it is less misleading, and more faithful to the spirit of science, to describe the analyses given here as having been concerned with the rationale of scientific development.

Editorial Interpolation: Shapere on the Instrumentalistic *vs.* Realistic Conceptions of Theories

Editor's note: The final version of Professor Shapere's paper deviates in certain respects from the early working draft he read at the symposium. In particular, a substantial portion of that draft was devoted to issues relating to the instrumentalistic versus realistic conceptions of theories; that discussion largely duplicated treatments of the issue Professor Shapere has published elsewhere, and to avoid excessive duplication of these other works he has only briefly discussed the issue on pp. 558–559 in this version. Since a substantial portion of the discussion following his paper dealt with his treatment of the instrumentalism versus realism issue, much of that discussion is not strictly applicable to the printed version of his paper. In as much as those portions of the discussion do relate to, and help clarify, his other writings on the instrumentalism-realism issue, it seemed desirable to publish them even though they are not directly applicable to the version of his paper printed here. In order to do so without loss of continuity in the proceedings, it has been necessary to interpolate a brief summary of his treatment of the issue. The summary which follows has been written by the editor and is based largely on Shapere [1969], Part II, augmented by portions of the working draft of his paper read at the symposium. For the full details of Professor Shapere's treatment of the issue, the reader should consult the works cited in note 61 and the discussion in note 65 of his paper above.

In the foregoing paper, the notion of a domain was discussed in an effort to clarify some aspects of the notion of a scientific theory and the roles which theories play in science. The notion of the domain is intended to replace the old "theoretical-observational" distinction as a conceptual tool for illuminating the nature of science. Domains include elements from both the traditional "theoretical" and "observational" categories. The replacement of the "theoretical-observational" distinction by the notion of a domain obviously requires reassessment or replacement of other distinctions or analyses erected on the "theoretical-observational" distinction. In particular, the instrumentalist-realist dispute over the status of theoretical terms is based on that distinction, and so must be reassessed in the light of domains.

In what follows an attempt is made to draw a distinction between realistic and nonrealistic uses of concepts in science; it is hoped that the notion of a domain and the distinction between realistic and nonrealistic uses of concepts will provide partial illumination, from opposite sides, of the concept of a scientific theory and the functions of theories in science.

The study of domains enabled us to discern various characteristic lines of reasoning in science. Further insight into modes of scientific reasoning can be obtained by examining the ways in which theories are employed. In particular, such an examination reveals that, in some instances of physical reasoning, a distinction is made between the way or ways in which entities can or cannot exist and the way or ways in which, in dealing with certain problems, it is possible and convenient to treat those entities as having characteristics which we know on purely physical grounds they could not really have. It is convenient to refer to the concepts so distinguished respectively as "existence concepts" and "idealization concepts." Not all concepts employed in physics fall under either category.

Although the notion of a rigid body from classical mechanics often is employed in reasoning with the special theory of relativity, according to the special theory of relativity it is impossible that such rigid bodies could exist. A consideration of the reasonings involved in this use of the notion of a rigid body[1] indicates that, as employed in relativistic physics, the classical concept of a rigid body must be considered an "idealization," for bodies simply cannot be classical rigid bodies under the circumstances. Moreover, that impossibility is not the result of any general philosophical thesis that all scientific concepts are idealizations; rather the reasons for the impossibility are purely scientific ones laid down by the special theory of relativity. However, even though rigid bodies are impossible, it sometimes proves useful in discussing the special theory of relativity to talk in terms of rigid bodies; and for certain kinds of problems it is not only useful but possible to do so.

Similar conclusions are forthcoming from a consideration of the Lorentz theory of the electron under which it is impossible for electrons to be geometric points, for in the solution of certain problems under certain circumstances it is convenient and possible to treat the electron *as if* it were a point particle.[2] Here, again, the treatment of electrons as geometric points is an "idealization" where the conclusion is drawn on purely scientific grounds that electrons cannot really

[1] For that consideration, see Shapere [1969], pp. 132–137.

[2] See *ibid.*, pp. 138–146, for discussion of this case.

be dimensionless points and so must be "idealizations." Furthermore, the rationale for considering electrons *as if they were* dimensionless points is scientific in character—for example, since the fields that occur when we construe point charges as localized in a point often are indistinguishable over much of the region concerned from those of simple geometrical configurations. And when it is possible to employ such "idealizations" considerable convenience results. Similar conclusions are forthcoming from a consideration of the practice in classical mechanics of localizing gravitational mass in dimensionless points.[3] To summarize what these cases reveal about "idealizations": "There often are good *scientific* reasons for distinguishing between the way in which a certain entity is asserted to be (or not to be) and the way in which it is *treated* (although, again for scientific reasons, it could not really be that kind of thing) for the sake of convenience in dealing with certain scientific problems."[4]

This conclusion enables us to understand better the logic of existence claims in physics. First, we have assertions that certain entities do or do not, might or might not, exist. These assertions make existence claims about entities that (1) are presumed to exist, although they might not exist (for example, electrons), (2) are purported entities which do not exist but once were asserted to exist (for example, ether, phlogiston), or (3) are asserted to exist by some good theorists but whose existence or nonexistence has not yet been established (for example, quarks). The terms used in these claims cut across the traditional "theoretical-observational" distinction. These terms, or rather uses of terms, may be called "existence terms"; existence terms are used to refer to entities, properties, processes, or behaviors of entities. Second, we find assertions involving expressions like "point particle" and "classical rigid body" used from the viewpoints of the theories considered in the above examples which do not designate entities purported to exist, but are related as "idealizations" to entities claimed to exist, in the ways indicated above. Thus their reference to existing things is only indirect. It is physically impossible (in the context of the theory in question) that such "idealizations" should exist. This second type of use of terms may be called "idealization terms." Thus we have distinguished two different *usages* of scientific terms and have seen that they have different *logics of usage.*

The distinction of these two types of scientific term usage does not exhaust the kinds of uses that are to be contrasted with "existence

[3] See *ibid.*, pp. 147–148.
[4] *Ibid.*, p. 149.

terms." There are a number of cases in physics called "idealizations" which are not quite like the cases examined above and might be more appropriately called "abstractions" (for example, considering a system of entities as isolated from the rest of the universe), or "approximations" (for example, calculation only within certain limits of accuracy), or "simplifications" (for example, considering electron orbits to be circular rather than elliptical). And the relations between "entities" and their "idealizations" may be other than they are in the cases considered above, in that the reasons for treating them as idealizations may be other than incompatibility with the theory's principles. It is even possible that entire theories (sets of concepts and propositions) can be "idealizations" in the sense that although it is known, for scientific reasons, that things are not really as the theory alleges, it is often convenient and possible to treat things *as if* they were. For example, although ray optics now is known to be false, it still is used as an idealization in dealing with phenomena; and it is for scientific reasons that it is known to be an "idealization." [5]

Some general conclusions about existence claims can be drawn. To say "*A* exists" is to imply at least the following: (1) *A* can interact with other things that exist ("idealizations" cannot do this); (2) *A* may have properties which are not manifesting themselves and which have not yet been discovered; (3) some properties currently ascribed to *A* may be incorrectly attributed; (4) *A* is something about which we can have different and competing theories. This last feature deserves elaboration. From the theoretical work of Ampère, Lorentz, Faraday, Milliken, and others, there was an accumulation of reasons for holding that electricity comes in discrete units. Indeed, these reasons resulted in there being a scientific domain with characteristic problems about electrons. The notion of the electron thus acquired what amounts to a theory-transcendent status; the electron was an entity about which *theories* of the electron were constructed.

The above discussion of different uses of terms in science enables us to see what is wrong with the traditional realistic and instrumentalistic construals of scientific theories, for these approaches took the position that theoretical terms occurring in a theory all either were or were not existence terms. But the above discussion indicates that both "theoretical" and "observational" terms can be used as existence terms, and that "theoretical terms" may be used with a

[5] See *ibid.*, pp. 152–154, for a discussion of the ray optics case. The preceding discussion of the logic of usage of terms in theories is based on *ibid.*, pp. 149–152.

variety of functions—as existence terms, as idealization terms, as simplifications, and so on. Thus,

> it is no wonder that both "realistic" and "instrumentalist" interpretations of science faltered with regard to their analyses of some theoretical term or other. For at least those areas of science where such terms as "existence" are appropriate, the problem may now be seen in a different way: to delineate the relationships of those terms (rather, uses) which do not have to do directly with entities as they actually exist, to those terms (or uses) which do; and to analyze the reasons for accepting existence claims.[6]

And it will be seen that the reasons determining the way or ways we can and do treat terms in certain problem situations are ones which come from *within* science; they are not metaphysical or otherwise extrascientific reasons.

The conclusions drawn above constitute, in part, a defense of a "realistic" interpretation of at least some scientific concepts.

[6] *Ibid.*, pp. 158–159; the discussion in this and the preceding paragraph is based on *ibid.*, pp. 154–158, augmented by passages from Shapere's draft manuscript at the symposium.

Heuristics and Justification in Scientific Research: Comments on Shapere[1]

THOMAS NICKLES

Dudley Shapere, in his discussion of domains, has raised in a usefully novel way some fundamental issues concerning scientific research and our characterization of it. Three of his main points are, first, that this approach reveals how significantly different are theories of one kind from those of another kind and that the standard account which maps all theories to the same structure is therefore of limited interest (p. 556). Second, "The concept of a domain . . . replace[s] the old 'observational-theoretical' distinction as a fundamental conceptual tool for illuminating the nature of science" (p. 528). Third, identifying the heuristic and justificatory roles of the "principles of reasoning" which emerge in scientific attempts to handle domains of phenomena will help us to understand the rationale of scientific decisionmaking and the establishment of research priorities, including those cases in which conflicting theories or research programs are available (esp. Part I and Part II, Sec. 3).

Following some remarks on the first two points in my first section, I shall devote most of my attention to the third, topical issue, and conclude by relating one facet of the problem of domains to the issue of intertheoretic reduction. Since I find nothing with which I strongly disagree in Shapere's presentation, my role as a commentator will be to throw into relief several points he makes, or which his discussion suggests, in a way that I believe will further illuminate and unify important issues. My differences from Shapere will turn out to be chiefly questions of emphasis.

[1] I wish to thank the editor of this volume for helpful suggestions.

Editor's note: The commentary on Professor Shapere's paper at the symposium was given by Professor Robert Stalnaker. Revisions in Professor Shapere's paper largely obviated Professor Stalnaker's commentary, and he was unable to prepare a new one. Professor Nickles very kindly agreed to fill the breach by writing this commentary. Accordingly the discussion which followed does not contain a reply to Professor Nickles's commentary.

1. The Standard Account of Theories

The standard, logical, empiricist analysis of theories as partially interpreted logical calculi is based on the observational/theoretical term distinction; so, obviously, the first two of Shapere's theses mentioned above are intimately related. Why was an account which mapped *all* scientific theories to the same simple structure nevertheless interesting? Chiefly because this structural account, based on the observational/theoretical term distinction, was supposed to exhibit the *epistemological* structure of theoretical knowledge. It was supposed to provide the *foundation* of our empirical scientific knowledge in two basic respects, conceptual and doctrinal: the partially interpreted logical structure was a rational reconstruction of the manner in which the *meaning(fulness)* of theoretical concepts depends on observational language and, second, of the manner in which theoretical statements are *justified* by their relation to the observable data. The standard analysis of theories therefore divides (quite sharply in its early versions) into a foundational account of concept formation (justification of concepts) and a foundational account of "doctrine" on theory formation (justification of statements and theories).

According to the standard account, the observational (data) statements are the sole source both of the meaningfulness of scientific language and of the justification of scientific statements.[2] By not permitting intertheoretic relations (including analogies and models, reduction, and "background knowledge" generally) to play a genuine cognitive role either in concept formation or in hypothesis confirmation, the logical positivists thereby reconstructed each theory as existing in splendid isolation on its own conceptual and empirical foundation. Let us term this austere account the *conceptual vacuum account* of theories, since the conceptual system of a theory is developed internally and no external conceptual relations to scientific tradition are deemed necessary. Theories are rationally reconstructed in a "conceptual vacuum," their only link being through a neutral observation language.

Were it correct, there is no question that this profound logico-empiricist analysis would greatly clarify the nature of theoretical research—and abstract thinking in everyday life as well. However, many philosophers today agree that the epistemological program underlying this analysis has collapsed under heavy critical attack, much

[2] I have discussed these matters in detail in Chapter I of my dissertation, Nickles [1969]. See also Quinton [1966].

of which has been directed on the observational/theoretical term distinction. But take away the epistemological program, and the uniform structural treatment of all theories is no longer of great interest. A genuine understanding of scientific research and its products therefore awaits the successful exploration of other lines of approach.

Shapere says the concept of domain can replace the observational/theoretical distinction as a conceptual tool and that studying domains will yield a more balanced view of scientific research. This claim seems legitimate in the following two respects. First, a theory must in some sense account for the domain with which it has been associated, and such a domain generally includes far more than the observational data of the positivist. At various places in his discussion, Shapere includes in the domain, besides observable phenomena, the phenomena as *ordered* in various ways (p. 534), theories (pp. 528ff.), even physical objects (p. 529)—a pretty motley collection. Shapere is not wholly successful in characterizing domains (the idea remains a bit nebulous), a point to which I shall return in Section 3. Nevertheless, his approach has merit in loosening up the idea that theories are created with reference to and justified by observational data only. The "evidence" for a theory includes not only data, but also data ordered or organized (in ways which need not be expressible in observational language [3]) and even laws and other theories (which of course cannot be expressed in observational language). To this list I would add conservation and invariance requirements and other conditions imposed on a given theory by another theory or by extratheoretic "framework principles." This point shows how far traditional, formalistic, confirmation theories fall short of capturing the intricacies of scientific justification.

Shapere's discussion brings out a second way in which attention to domains instead of to the observational language and the observational/theoretical dichotemy opens up a whole new dimension of scientific justification. I refer to the emergence of "principles of reasoning" which Shapere traces in his case studies. Such principles and the multitude of more theory-specific rules, demands, and values which arise in any established scientific discipline are important in several ways. One is that such principles themselves have a justificatory or evaluative function, so that recognizing their existence further corrects the view that scientific justification moves in one direction only, from observable data upward to theory. Shapere also says these principles

[3] See Patrick Suppes's contribution to the present volume, the editor's introduction Secs. V–B–2–c, V–C, and the references given there.

are sometimes based on analogies to other theories in other domains. The heuristic importance of models and analogies is universally recognized, and Miss Hesse [1963] has made a strong case for their importance in concept formation. I would urge, along with Hesse and Shapere, that they may also serve in a justificatory capacity. In short, attention to models and analogies as one type of intertheoretic relation ignored by the conceptual vacuum approach can help to correct the latter in several ways. Finally, it is worth emphasizing as a separate point the *heuristic* importance of items like Shapere's principles of reasoning. I shall have much to say about the connection of heuristics and justification in the next section, where I discuss the important implications the emergence of principles of reasoning and valuation have for our general conception of scientific method.

The preceding two paragraphs indicate how domains in Shapere's sense and items like his principles of reasoning (which emerge in the historical development of a domain) might become elements in a new account of scientific justification and reasoning, one which will replace the attempt to provide an epistemological foundation for scientific claims. Since domains in a theoretical science are never completely theory-neutral, Shapere's approach also would eliminate the dangerous assumption of a completely neutral observation language. Although I have here discussed only the former, it is not difficult to see why the collapse of the foundational account of doctrine (justification of statements and theories) was accompanied by the collapse of the foundational account of concept formation (justification of concepts). Both, after all, were based on the observational/theoretical term distinction. And since 1950 Hempel has stressed that "Theory formation and concept formation go hand in hand, neither can be carried on successfully in isolation from the other." [4]

2. The Rationality of Scientific Decisions

Shapere's discussion of principles of reasoning as having a central role in many scientific decisions between competing theories or lines of research raises extremely important issues concerning the rationality of

[4] Hempel [1965b], p. 113. Actually Carnap's, Bridgman's, and Reichenbach's views on concept formation were under critical attack prior to the attack on the observational/theoretical term distinction and the foundational theory of doctrine, as Hempel's article shows (see my note 9). Hempel [1965b] attempted to reduce some problems of concept formation to problems of theory formation, that is, to combine the previously distinct groups of problems.

scientific decisionmaking and scientific method. Shapere is directly concerned only with the rationality issue, however, and I am uncertain how he would relate that to the now-to-be-discussed issue of scientific method with which it is more or less intertwined.

The standard, logical empiricist account of scientific method (particularly confirmation theory and concept formation) is largely based on three distinctions, the first of which we have just discussed:

(1) The observational/theoretical term distinction (and the conceptual vacuum analysis of theories to which it leads).
(2) The sharp distinction of context of discovery from context of justification.
(3) The fact/value distinction, to put it crudely; more accurately, the theory/methodology distinction, which is made to support two doctrines:
 (α) theory systems are value-neutral,
 (β) methodology is theory-neutral, that is, independent of theoretical developments.

A prominent conclusion, or perhaps assumption, of the standard account is the doctrine of the methodological unity of science, the view that all sciences worthy of the name employ the same methods, logically speaking, of concept formation and theory testing and that theories (and explanations and predictions) have the same structure in all scientific disciplines. Intimately related to the above distinctions, the doctrine of unity of method nevertheless deserves special emphasis. I shall make five comments, A to E.

A. Having already observed how (1) coupled with the conceptual vacuum analysis of theories has shaped the standard approach to scientific confirmation and concept formation, let us turn directly to (2). While (2) may be a legitimate distinction of research contexts (see note 6), it is typically introduced to support the view that scientific methodology is concerned wholly with the justification of scientific ideas; how they are discovered is a matter for psychology, sociology, and history. Of course (2) is a reaction against Baconian inductivists and others who have espoused fail-safe, "mechanical" methods of discovery and is a recognition of the importance of creative originality in science. Still, the fact that our methods of justification are far from mechanical or fail-safe has not led philosophers to deliver justification over to psychology and sociology. And it sounds a bit strange to hear logical empiricists and Popperians alike emphasizing that there is no way to discover theories but that scientific method nevertheless starts with theories as *given,* when one of their chief objections to any methodology starting from the observable facts as given is precisely that such "methodologies" provide no methodological directive. Surely a method which directs us to "theorize" is no better a methodological directive than one whose first command is "observe."

Much of Dudley Shapere's discussion is concerned with discovery. Neither he nor I am urging a return to the method of Bacon and of Boyle, but I know that Shapere would agree that putting discovery altogether outside methodology and the sphere of reason is to move to the opposite extreme. He may also share my belief that his historical case discussions (principles of reasoning and the like) support the view that discovery and justification in science are but opposite sides of the same coin. Or, to employ Hempel's metaphor, they go hand in hand. If this view is correct (and further support will be offered below), it is a serious error to divorce context of discovery from context of justification if this means altogether excluding the former from methodology. Constraints governing validation or corroboration are also constraints governing discovery. And to a great extent, vice versa.[5] Rarely if ever are theories or research programs mere bolts out of the blue, free of all rational constraint.[6] The stories about Poincaré's intuitions and Kekulé's discovery of the benzene ring in a dream are "exceptions which prove the rule." It would be a mistake to say even in these cases that the constraints are all on the side of justification. (Ideas derived from dreams are not *usually* deemed worthy of serious scientific development and test.) To put discovery under some degree of rational control is surely not to belittle it. Niels

[5] These remarks will perhaps explain and partly justify my contention (near the end of Sec. 1) that since models and analogies play an obvious heuristic role in scientific thinking, we must expect they will play a justificatory role in ranking scientific priorities, and so on. I am not of course saying that heuristic thinking is self-justifying or that heuristic considerations alone adequately justify substantive scientific assertions. But they may serve as a constraint even here. When nature violates our heuristic expectations, a puzzling problem is created just as when she appears to contradict our theories.

[6] That philosophers have neglected discovery in their emphasis on justification was a favorite theme of the late N. R. Hanson. I was pleased to discover that Peter Achinstein outlines views similar to mine in his contribution to this volume. However, to the extent that we regard the very *same* constraints as functioning in both heuristics and justification, to satisfy heuristic constraints in the discovery process is simultaneously to justify the result (insofar as it can be justified with reference to those constraints). This idea, which will probably be criticized as Baconian, serves to blur the context of discovery/context of justification distinction itself and not merely to question its use. (As for its use, I think the view of theoretical discoveries as bolts out of the blue has encouraged the view, implicit in many discussions of theory structure, that the uninterpreted calculus is *given,* the starting point of philosophical analysis.)

Bohr repeatedly referred to new theoretical advances as "rational generalizations" of older theoretical ideas—*rational* generalizations.

Karl Popper and a few others have recognized the importance of scientific tradition and background knowledge even while adhering to the discovery/justification dichotemy. Popper, for example, advances a kind of methodological "correspondence principle": any new theory must yield its highly corroborated predecessor as a first approximation (see section 3 for further discussion).[7] My complaint remains that Popper's emphasis is still on corroboration or "context of justification" to the neglect of discovery. Bohr certainly had more than justification in mind with his correspondence principle.

B. Supported by the doctrine of the unity of method, the familiar logical empiricist and Popperian reconstructions of scientific method are characterized by the same uniformity as typifies the analysis of theory structure. By stopping with some useful but very general logical points about verification and falsification, and so on, the methodologist is practically assured that his conclusions will find some application in almost every corner of science. Actually, as Shapere indicates, these principles alone do not afford an adequate account of actual research. They do not often play the dominant role in the rational determination of research priorities, even in developed sciences like physics. And it was a surprising and profoundly disturbing discovery that where these methodological rules *did* supposedly apply, scientists too often ignored them (see the dispute over falsification of theories). With the old set of methodological rules or standards in hand, it is hard to avoid the conclusion that scientists are irrational in some of the most important matters, especially during revolutionary periods. This was Kuhn's message in *The Structure of Scientific Revolutions* [1962].

In reaction to the charge that fundamental scientific decisions and commitments are irrational, we can do one of four things: (a) accept the depressing charge at face value; (b) reject the charge as historically unfounded or reject the relevance of historical evidence and retain the present methodology unaltered; (c) decide that it is more likely that our methodology is at fault than science and attempt to produce a more adequate account of scientific research (It perhaps borders on incoherence to suggest that science is *so* radically irrational?); (d) dig still deeper: the shortcomings of our methodological accounts may be symptoms of a deeper *maladie* which we may label a mistaken (and often tacit) conception of rationality and justification. On this last view, it might not be sufficient to recognize other means

[7] For Popper's methodological correspondence principle, see his work [1959] and Agassi [1961]. See also Lakatos's discussion of heuristics in his [1970].

of justification than observational data so long as we retained our old conception of rationality and justification.[8]

As I understand him, Shapere is concerned with (c) rather than (d), although (c) and (d) may be deeply interrelated. An appreciation for the subtle, nonobservational constraints on theoretical research, for Quine's centralities and priorities, and for the detailed physical (biological, chemical . . .) theoretic, that is, discipline-specific considerations, which figure so prominently in actual scientific decision-making, may be a large step toward a direct discussion of rationality; or, it may be our last hope of avoiding a direct confrontation over this great issue.

C. Shapere's discussion of the emergence of "principles of reasoning" raises or suggests another fundamental issue concerning both the logical empiricist and Popperian accounts of scientific methodology and bearing on the rationality problem, namely, the issue, raised by (3), whether method and theory are independent, as the doctrine of unity of method demands. Both logical empiricists and Popperians have divorced the methodological form of science from its empirical theoretic content, and have assumed that critical standards of evaluation and reasoning belong to method. The result is (α) a sharp separation of the valuational and empirical theoretic components of the total scientific enterprise (the value-neutrality of theory systems) and (β) the belief that there is a correct account of method which, once found, will survive future theoretical developments to endure forever (the theory-neutrality of method).

Somewhat as Reichenbach attempted to separate the conventional or concept formational component in theories from the purely empirical component in his account of coordinative definitions[9]—a kind of Kantian attempt to isolate man's contribution from nature's—so the doctrine of the value-neutrality of theories distills off all valuational aspects of scientific research and condenses them in the methodology—the rules of the game of science. Popper [1959] in fact regards these

[8] My impression is that both Kuhn and Popper are concerned with alternative (d). On Popper, see Agassi [1961] and Bartley [1964]. F. L. Will launches a thoroughgoing attack on the traditional theory of justification and makes positive suggestions toward a new approach in Will [1973].

[9] Reichenbach [1957] contended that all empirical statements must be relativized to a set of coordinative definitions, for example, standards of measurement. Such conventions establish a precise observational meaning for terms like 'meter,' 'temperature,' 'simultaneous.' Relative to a specified concept system of this sort, the remaining component of theories is purely factual—nature's contribution. Thus, this account in effect isolates man's conceptual contribution from nature's factual, empirical one. A somewhat similar two-component account of theories may be found in P. W. Bridgman's operationism. See Bridgman [1927].

methodological rules as conventions—a kind of "social contract" theory of methodology and valuation. Although there are important differences between Popper's and the positivists' views on method, both are expressions of the sharp separability of theory and value.

Kuhn [1970b], by contrast, emphasizes that theory systems or "paradigms" include a normative or valuation component. Theoretical systems to a certain extent incorporate valuational standards of correct scientific practice.[10] Although Kuhn says little about methodology in this connection, we can take this claim of his as an attack on component (α), the doctrine of the value neutrality of theory systems. Just as Quine [1951], Hempel [1950], and Putnam [1962] have demolished the attempt to separate the conventional or a priori from the empirical elements of science (the analytic/synthetic distinction and the attempt to sharply separate concept formation from theory formation), so Kuhn can be viewed as attacking the attempt to separate theory and value.

I will not even attempt to decide this issue here, though it is an important one to raise. The connection of this dispute to the rationality problem is easily seen. If Kuhn is in fact correct that theory systems carry with them sets of values (and this idea needs careful study to determine just what sort of values these are and how they function), then the question of rational decisionmaking is seriously complicated by the fact that we no longer have two theory systems competing on neutral, methodological ground; rather, competing systems of values and standards become part of the problem.

D. We turn now to (β), the doctrine that methodology is theory neutral, that even radically new directions in theoretical research cannot be allowed to affect methodological standards of evaluation. In an interesting passage, Shapere tells us that one component of the "Principle of Evolutionary Reasoning"

> was not applied in science before the second half of the nineteenth century; its acceptance as a new general reasoning principle was due in no small measure to the success of Darwin's evolutionary account of biological species. The principle was, however, only gradually accepted, and this perhaps explains in part . . . the failure, as it seems to us, of pioneers in stellar spectroscopy to try to order the classes unless they did so with an evolutionary idea already in mind. In any case, this example shows that new reasoning principles, as well as new substantive

[10] See especially Kuhn's "Postscript" to Kuhn [1970b]. We might compare the theory/value dichotemy with the observational/theoretical distinction. Thus it might be suggestive to extend some well-worn metaphors to say theories are "value-laden" and scientific values (that is, methodological rules and constraints) are "theory-laden."

> information, can be introduced into science as part of its maturation. Today the principle seems a natural one to use—so much so, in fact, that we often have difficulty in understanding why it was not applied by earlier thinkers [p. 554].

This statement by no means commits Shapere to a Kuhnian position on the matter of theory and value just discussed, but it does strongly suggest a second line of attack against the absolute separation of theory and methodology. For Shapere here points out the close connection between method and scientific development. If there is such a connection, presumably method will be most strongly affected by major theoretical developments, an influence which should be reflected even in a philosophical reconstruction of scientific methodology.[11]

I think that many writers assume the theory neutrality of method in sense (β)—the "static" view of method according to which there is a final correct account of method which will not and should not be altered by future theoretical developments. This could probably be termed the standard view. Of course, most philosophers would here introduce a sharp distinction between scientific methods (techniques) and Scientific Method—the *logic* of science, methodology as studied by philosophers. While scientific techniques change, these philosophers would say, the logic of science does not change. As Scheffler [1967] puts it, in his elaboration of what he terms the "standard view," "Underlying historical changes of theory, there is . . . a constancy of logic and method, which unifies each scientific age with that which preceded it and with that which is yet to follow. Such constancy comprises not merely the canons of formal deduction, but also those criteria by which hypotheses are confronted with the test of experience and subjected to comparative evaluation [pp. 9–10]."

Now I do not deny that there is some truth to this view. Constancy there has been, and the philosopher need not devote long paragraphs to the techniques of washing test tubes. But once we go beyond the allegedly simple logical relationships to which many philosopher-methodologists have confined themselves, the distinction between methods and Method is, in many instances, difficult or impossible to

[11] The terms 'method' and 'methodology' are of course ambiguous between scientific procedures as practiced, the logical or conceptual steps involved in these (it is hard to avoid begging important questions in drawing this distinction), the conceptual steps as explicitly expounded by scientists and philosophers, and the latter as philosophically explicated or reconstructed. In this last case methodology is no longer merely descriptive but is partly legislative. I have generally tried to use 'method' for the first two and 'methodology' (= analysis of method) for the last two meanings; the adjectival form 'methodological' covers both. I do not believe the ambiguity is harmful to my discussion.

draw. How do we know that future theories will not *continue* to yield new methodological insights—or even past theories examined more carefully? How do we know there will not be advances in the *philosophical* discussion of epistemology and methodology? We do not know.

Shapere's discussion is rather noncommital but suggestive on this as well as the value-neutrality issue. Perhaps it is too soon to ask what will be the far-reaching conclusions of the kind of investigation he advocates.

The basic thought behind the attack on the theory-neutrality of method is, of course, not new. In the nineteenth century it was explicit in the work of Whewell and was perhaps best expressed by Peirce, who wrote, "Each chief step in science has been a lesson in logic." [12]

If we do give up the view that method is theory-neutral in all conceptually significant respects, this is tantamount to giving up the common assumption that any specific methodological account, even as "philosophically purified," will apply universally to all theories at a given time or to a single theoretical tradition over long periods of time. It is to give up the doctrine of unity of method (in any deep sense extending beyond general epistemology). It is to give up the idea that science has ever advanced far enough to give us an absolutely privileged position regarding method, one which would enable us to say that our account is final, aside from a few details.

Historians of science have learned not to evaluate historical figures as good or bad according as their results agreed with ours (that is, with the "correct" results). Is there a similar lesson for philosophers of science to learn about methodology, or do the real differences between historical and philosophical accounts of method and rationality here intervene? Is our evaluation of previous methodologies —Descartes, Newton, Berkeley, Whewell, Duhem, Bridgman, and so on—as good or bad relative to our own "correct" account also subject to the vicissitudes of time? [13] We might even ask a familiar sort of question in a new form: is the growth of insight and sophistication of

[12] C. S. Peirce [1877], Sec. 1, the first of a series of six papers entitled "Illustrations of the Logic of Science." On the contemporary scene, Stephen Toulmin has been a leading exponent of this viewpoint. The following declaration is interesting and suggestive, whatever one may think of Toulmin's controversial conception of logic: "Great logical innovations are part and parcel of great scientific, moral, political or legal innovations. In the natural sciences, for instance, men such as Kepler, Newton, Lavoisier, Darwin and Freud have transformed not only our beliefs, but also our ways of arguing and our standards of relevance and proof: they have accordingly enriched the logic as well as the content of natural science ([1964], p. 257)."

[13] And therefore "whiggish"? See Butterfield [1951].

our *philosophical* accounts of methodology cumulative? Such questions are perhaps too large to call for immediate commitment one way or another. However, it is worth pointing out that if there is any substance to the criticism of standard methodology for its deliberate neglect of scientific *discovery,* or for its absolute separation of theory and method, then we can truthfully say that the current standard methodology leaves out something that was important to Whewell and to Peirce.

E. Exactly how Shapere's "principles of reasoning" and the other heuristic and justificatory constraints are to alter philosophical accounts of method is not clear. Although much of confirmation theory and (for example) the rule that falsified theories are to be rejected have come under attack, presumably *some* of the old logical principles will remain a part of methodology. The result that universal law statements cannot be verified surely holds for any lawful science. And some of Popper's conventional rules of the game, such as the inadmissibility of ad hoc hypotheses (whatever they are) will probably also survive. So it is not as if we were throwing out general methodology altogether. Perhaps we are only supplementing it substantially in discipline-specific ways. It is also worth noting that, like Popper's methodological conventions, Shapere's constraints do not have the status of inviolable logical results such as the unverifiability of law statements. In this sense, these constraints do not constitute a logic of justification, a logic of discovery, or a logic of anything, and are not claimed to. Such constraints neither guarantee success nor rule out the admissibility of a bold new theory which violates some of them (but such a theory had better indicate why the violated constraints were inappropriate). Although they are not logical constraints on theorizing, we may term them "conceptual" or "rational" constraints. Shapere is right to give them more than a psychological role.

3. Domains and Intertheoretical Reduction

In this concluding section I shall attempt to partially answer the first two of the central questions concerning domains which Shapere lists in the first part of his paper. (All six questions are closely related, as he points out.) These questions are:

1. What considerations (or, better, types of considerations . . .) lead scientists to regard a certain body of information as a *body* of information—as constituting a unified subject-matter or domain to be examined or dealt with?

2. How is the description of the items of the domain achieved and modified at sophisticated stages of scientific development?

Much of Shapere's discussion concerns relatively unsophisticated stages of scientific development. Lack of theoretical sophistication is especially evident in the early history of electricity and magnetism, with which Shapere opens his paper, but even the spectral lines in the Bohr discussion were only being brought under a quantitative, explanatory theory for the first time. My partial and necessarily sketchy answer to the two questions for theoretically *advanced* stages of research is that theories and intertheoretic reduction play the central role. In advanced research, a domain is largely determined and unified by a theory, and as one theory succeeds another the domain is modified and usually enlarged. Intertheoretic reduction can help us to understand theory succession and the modification of domains. Shapere himself finds it convenient to describe such domains as "the total body of information which must—ideally—be accounted for by a theory" (p. 528). But where Shapere was most interested in the incompleteness of theories—that is, why phenomena not yet unified by the theory are nevertheless included in the theory's domain—I shall be most concerned with that part of the domain the theory does handle more or less successfully.

Better, let us recognize an ambiguity in talk about domains in theoretically advanced research. First, there are domains in Shapere's sense—what any adequate theory *should* relate and account for. Then there are domains in a different sense—what a particular, available theory *does* account for successfully (by then-current standards). Consider "the domain" of Maxwell's electromagnetic theory. In one, not very theoretical, sense of 'domain,' electric, magnetic, and optical phenomena were being formed into a *common* domain prior to Maxwell's theory (for example, Shapere mentions Faraday's experiments on magnetically induced polarization). But in another sense, Maxwell's theory united two or more previously *distinct* domains—domains as determined by previous theories. Frequently unification of domains is achieved *by* unifying, that is, by reducing, distinct preexisting theories. (One of the preexisting theories may itself become the reducing theory.) My distinction of two kinds of domains is meant to capture the distinction we discover in the Maxwell example.

Domains in the second, theory-determined sense are domains of particular theories and therefore *relatively* easy to pin down: they are those items unified or accounted for (in various ways) by the theories in question (but not merely a class of "observational sentences"). By contrast, domains in Shapere's sense, although very important, are elusive and hard to describe with precision. I earlier noted what a motley collection of items such domains contain, as Shapere describes them. Perhaps it would have helped had he told us whether such domains are most usefully construed as collections of phenomena (for example, physical objects and their behavior), as linguistic descriptions of these, or as sets of questions of various forms raised by our acquaintance with the phenomena.

The fact is, though, that domains (in Shapere's sense) under any construal are profoundly affected by the advent of a theory. A theory imposes a high degree of organizational structure on a domain and thereby sometimes transforms it almost beyond recognition (see, however, note 14). This fact makes domains in Shapere's sense all the more elusive; in passing from relatively nontheoretical to highly theoretical contexts, they practically lose their identity. Once we *are* in highly theoretical contexts, therefore, I think a domain in Shapere's sense is best construed as the domain determined by the successes of the particular theory (that is, the domain in our second sense) *plus* those phenomena, described in the language of that theory, for which the theory is so far unable to account. (This suggestion does not, I think, contradict anything Shapere says.) We can then still distinguish the domain as what the theory *does* successfully account for from the domain as what the theory *should* account for, and we are therefore left with a means for saying that a theory is incomplete. (As Shapere points out, a theory may be incomplete either by yielding false answers or by failing to provide answers at all over a portion of its domain.)

So much for Shapere's first question. It is of course true that domains even in the theory-determined sense are altered by the advent of a new theory, but normally in a fairly controlled way. Elaborating this point will constitute my answer to Shapere's second question.

I want to suggest that in theoretical contexts the old theory imposes interesting constraints on the structural form of the new theory. Although it is difficult to be precise in abstraction from any particular theoretical context, we may say that the internal structure of a theory imposes constraints on the form of any succeeding theory for this domain and thus tends to limit the degree to which the domain will be transformed. (However, these constraints are not of an absolute, logical nature.) To demonstrate the interplay between domains and theories, we can turn this point around and say, as Shapere prefers to do, that not only do theories structurally determine domains but domains in turn impose structural constraints on future theories. Thus even philosophers skeptical of the justificatory force of highly theoretical constraints, so far removed from the "hard" empirical data, may be willing to acknowledge that a theory may impose structural constraints on future theoretical research in a less direct manner—*via* the domain. For once we recognize that the domain of phenomena is not merely a collection of observational data but is organized and structured by the theory, we see that even the bland requirement that future theories must give an equally good account of the present theory's domain will quite probably impose constraints on the internal structure of the new theory. Shapere provides interesting support for this last point. In this manner, structure may be subtly transmitted from theory to theory via the domain.

Describing domains in terms of theories rather than the other way around therefore need not defeat Shapere's purpose of getting at theories through an analysis of domains. There is no reason why the analysis cannot move in both directions at once, illuminating both theories and domains as it does so.[14] And the same can be said for theoretical reduction: the topics of domains, theory structure, and reduction are intertwined in such a way that discussion of each can illuminate the others.[15] It is to reduction that I now briefly turn for

[14] Many items in the domain are unified simply by being redescribed in a common, limited theoretical vocabulary in a way that does not depend on a developed theory. Indeed, this is often the case when no developed theory yet exists but only a theoretical program based on a few technical predicates and a leading principle believed to be fundamental, for example, Newton's initial realization that a falling stone and a "falling" moon were describable as phenomena of the same type. Furthermore, the entrenchment of predicates (and the *promise* of research programs based on them) can be explained partly in terms of the number and diversity of phenomena that these predicates (or "variables") can redescribe. Finally, ability to extend our redescriptions to new phenomena and problems is a special case of the kind of scientific knowledge required to extend theories to "new domains" (theoretical redescription is the key to such extension) and to model new and difficult problems on older, familiar ones. For a valuable discussion of this kind of knowledge, see Kuhn's [1970b], "Postscript."

[15] Not only can reduction help us clarify the domains issues, but a clear concept of domain could also help us state improved conditions on reduction and to distinguish different types of reduction. A useful condition on the reduction of predecessor theories to successors would be that the reduced and reducing theories must apply to the same domain, or that the domain of the reducing virtually includes the domain of the reduced theory. This informal requirement is in certain respects an improvement on some logical reconstructionist attempts to employ the concept of a "domain" of individuals in the formal semantic sense. (Semantic domains do sometimes tell us roughly what a theory is "about," but it is pretty clear that they cannot serve to explicate 'domain' in Shapere's sense.) The informal requirement on reduction might remove the objection that Patrick Suppes's analysis fails to distinguish genuine reduction from mere modeling and a similar objection, based on the Wiedmann-Franz law, which Sklar [1967], p. 109, raises against Nagel's analysis. For useful discussion and references, see Schaffner [1967].

further development of the above ideas. My discussion will relate intertheoretic reduction to the domains problem, will show that reduction is one key to understanding the importance of tradition and background knowledge in science, and finally, will tie these matters in with the metamethodological issues discussed earlier.

First let me draw a rough distinction between domain-preserving and domain-combining reductions. Many scientific theories are involved in reductions of both kinds. The special theory of relativity (STR) together with its reduction of classical mechanics (CM) was chiefly domain-preserving in that its main function was not to unify two vast, preexisting domains of phenomena but to replace a defective predecessor theory. We can term STR the *successor* theory to CM as *predecessor*. (It is interesting to note, however, that the problems which sparked the development of STR did not lie wholly within CM but in an apparent incompatibility of CM with electromagnetic theory. Einstein's 1905 paper began with some puzzling features of the electrodynamics of moving bodies. In other words, anomalies may arise between as well as within theories covering essentially different domains, a fact for which the conceptual vacuum approach to theories cannot account. Such anomalies reveal the existence of intertheoretic constraints and of framework principles, which are being violated.)

Domain-combining reductions, in which two preexisting theories and their domains are brought together under one theory, generally involve ontological reduction and consolidation of theoretical postulates in a way that domain-preserving reductions of predecessor theories by their successors do not. It is one thing to "identify" the Lorentz electron with its successor concept or entity, the Bohr electron, and quite another thing to identify light with electromagnetic radiation.[16] Philosophers of science have been more interested in ontological reduction and in consolidation of postulates than in trying to understand the significance of domain-preserving reduction in theoretical research. Actually, they have assimilated the two kinds of reduction in an account which works better for domain-combining than for

[16] To be sure, the electromagnetic theory of light did not *perfectly* agree at all points with the older physical optics, and there is a significant difference between the Lorentz and Bohr electrons. Nevertheless, either to regard the latter as a full-fledged ontological reduction *or* to overemphasize the "change of meaning" in the word 'electron' between the two theories would obscure important distinctions and seriously undermine any account of scientific *tradition*. As I have argued in Nickles [1973a], the familiar "meaning change objection" to intertheoretic reduction leads to a position strongly resembling the conceptual vacuum account and thereby undermines any attempt to analyze the role of tradition or background knowledge in science.

domain-preserving reduction. The chief importance of a domain-preserving reduction of a successor theory to its predecessor resides in its justificatory and heuristic functions in theoretical research. I shall end with a word about each of these functions.

As its name implies, the latter sort of reduction "preserves domains" and thereby plays a significant justificatory role in research. If theory T_1 reduces T_2 (for example, by showing that some of T_1's equations go over into those of T_2 as an appropriate limit is taken), virtually the entire confirmatory support of T_2 is therefore transferred to its successor T_1, that is, T_1 is shown by the reduction to account at least as well for T_2's domain as does T_2 itself. (In general the two theories will be logically incompatible, so this kind of reduction $\neq$ explanation.) And the domain here includes not just experimental data but the data as structured in various ways, experimental laws, theoretical constraints, framework conditions, and so on. In other words, this mode of confirmation by reduction almost *automatically* takes into account the very things that traditional, formalistic confirmation theories seem (so far) quite incapable of handling.[17] For much the same reason, reduction is therefore a relatively tidy and economical way for the *scientist* to confirm a new theory or to readily evaluate the plausibility and fruitfulness of a new theoretical proposal.[18] (To be sure, thorough testing of a successor theory involves far more than reduction of its predecessor.) Such advantages are undreamt of on the conceptual vacuum approach, which, ignoring tradition and background knowledge, attempts to provide each major theory with its own independent conceptual and empirical foundation. Each new theoretical program, on this latter account, starts completely from scratch.

We can therefore suggest what amounts to a new "principle of reasoning" or a new constraint or demand on theorizing, that successor

[17] My account here is somewhat idealized. When a major conceptual change occurs, not all of the old questions can significantly be raised with the new scheme. That a reduction is "domain-preserving" does not mean that the old domain survives unaltered. For example, the new theory may be a statistical theory while the old one was not, and the new *theory* may lead us to reconstrue old "deterministic" *data* as really statistical-probabilistic. See also Shapere's discussion of chlorine, and so on, and the periodic table. The confirmatory function of reduction has been pointed out by Lawrence Sklar.

[18] Walter Heitler [1949], p. 195, argues that quantum theory is *complete* since it contains a complete theory (classical mechanics) as a special case. If quantum theory *does* reduce to classical mechanics, then Heitler is right *in one sense*, because a reduction of this type guarantees the completeness of a successor theory relative to the domain determined by its predecessor; the reduction is domain-preserving. However, both theories may be incomplete relative to their domains in Shapere's wider sense. And the issue in quantum mechanics involves still another sense of completeness.

theories reduce to their predecessors in this way.[19] It is to Popper's credit that he has recognized the importance of a constraint of this sort in his methodological "correspondence principle" mentioned earlier: each successor theory must yield its highly corroborated predecessor as a first approximation.

Actually, the requirement that a new theory be domain-preserving by means of theoretical reduction can be strengthened to say that a new theory must be domain-*increasing*: it must constitute an attempt to remove the incompleteness which plagues the old theory. That is, it must account not only for the domain (in our second sense) determined by the old theory's successes but also for the domain in Shapere's wider sense, relative to which the old theory is incomplete. Otherwise, the new theory would have no more empirical content than the old and would preserve the incompleteness of the old (assuming the old questions could still be raised within the new theory).

We know that Bohr's correspondence principle was used as a *heuristic* principle helping to guide physicists to "rational generalizations" of incomplete or otherwise defective quantum theories already at hand. Elsewhere, I have attempted to show that the correspondence principle was more than an attempt to patch up Bohr's early quantum theory and represented more than the obvious justificatory demand that any new theory must account for the successful observational *predictions* of the old theory.[20] In fact it was a more or less successful attempt to impose deeper "structural" requirements on the internal makeup of a future theory and thus to serve as a valuable guide in constructing such theories.

Once again I would insist that justification in science goes hand-in-hand with discovery or heuristics. There is no mechanical procedure for either, but to the extent that detailed theoretical constraints can be established, these constraints can aid discovery as well as justification. It is wrong to think of rational constraints as *essentially* justifica-

[19] For more detailed discussion of this and other points made in this section, see Nickles [1973b]. I there introduce a new concept of reduction—"reduction$_2$"—which is not only philosophically suggestive but also which (I think) better fits the usage of physicists. Reduction$_2$ is based on the idea of reducing one thing to another by performing an operation on the former, for example, a successor theory reduces$_2$ to its predecessor (not *vice versa*) if applying an appropriate operation (for example, a mathematical limit) to some equations of the successor yields the formalism of the predecessor. Reduction$_2$ therefore involves a reversal of terminology, since other accounts of reduction invariably say the *less* fundamental science or theory reduces to (is reduced by) the *more* fundamental one.

[20] Ch. III of Nickles [1969]. A paper on Bohr's correspondence principle and its philosophical significance is currently in preparation.

tory. In this commentary, I have suggested that such constraints may be found in the patterns of intertheoretic reduction and in other intertheoretic relations such as invariance requirements and, of course, in the analogies and models discussed by Shapere.[21]

My remarks, especially in this last section, have been exploratory and rather sketchy. How much illumination the sort of study outlined by Shapere and myself will bring remains to be seen, but, to appropriate the words of Kuhn, this kind of philosophical study of history might well work a "transformation" in our image of science and its methods. Whether further study of reduction or the correspondence principle will yield interesting results which can be, to some extent, generalized to other cases, we cannot yet say.[22] Nor is it clear just how deeply the *Korrespondenzdenken* really influenced the development of the "new" quantum theory of Heisenberg. But until there are good reasons to the contrary, I think we should take seriously Heisenberg's [1964] remark, in agreement with earlier statements of Bohr (for example, Bohr [1949]), that his "first draft of the quantum mechanics . . . for me represented in a certain sense the quintessence of our discussion in Copenhagen—a mathematical formulation of Bohr's correspondence principle [pp. 99f.]."

[21] If this is correct, it is easy to see the importance of regarding reduction as an intimate relationship of theories and their internal structures. This central feature of reduction is neglected in the well-known positivistic account of Kemeny and Oppenheim [1956], in which, roughly, T_1 reduces T_2 if T_1 accounts for T_2's domain—observational data only. Nagel's [1961] classic analysis of reduction is a big improvement on this score.

[22] It is interesting to note that H. A. Kramers views the reduction of Planck's radiation law to the Rayleigh-Jeans laws as supporting Bohr's stronger correspondence claims about polarization and intensity of spectral lines. See p. 328 of Kramers's important doctoral dissertation, Kramers [1919].

Discussion

Professor Cohen:

I have a question and a comment. The question deals with whether or not Dudley Shapere is proposing to recapture the thinking of a past age or to apply anachronistically but heuristically the canons of our own times.

Whenever historians or historically minded philosophers discuss reality or existence, the first concept that comes to my mind is phlogiston. And so I am led to ask Dudley Shapere the obvious question: Are you thinking about the reality that might have been associated historically with this concept some 200 or more years ago? Are you trying to guess something about the state of people's minds two centuries ago? Or, are you making a logical analysis as of our own day?

Now to the comment. I wish that some more attention had been paid to exploring and developing detailed aspects of the so-called "logic of discovery." Even though this actual expression was not a prominent feature of the presentation, it comes at once to mind in relation to Dudley Shapere's main theme. He presented the notion that a close examination of a certain classification of stars seemed to demand a particular theory; and the relation between electricity, magnetism, and light was invoked, eventually leading to the demand for the extension of these related theories to matter. I would like to suggest that sometimes this "demand" may be more apparent than real; that, in an analysis made when looking backward from our own day, we may envisage such "demands" which cannot be documented from the records of past times.

Let me take as my primary example the inverse-square law in its application to the forces of gravitational attraction and of electrical attraction and repulsion. If we conceive of anything that spreads out uniformly from a center through space—whether a set of material particles, the radiation of light or heat, the effect of a force, an influence, a field—simple geometry tells us that this type of phenomenon follows the law of the inverse square. For example, if the intensity of a given phenomenon be measured by the number of particles striking a unit area of any one of a nest of concentric spheres, then the intensity (if the radiation be uniform) must be related to the way in which the surface itself stretches out. On purely logical grounds, and without experiments, we may conclude that the diminution of the intensity of illumination accords with a law of the inverse square of the distance from the source. On such purely logical grounds, then, we might be led to assume that any scientist who knew the inverse-square law of illumination and was interested in a sort of gravitation would necessarily be led to conceive that this gravitation must also follow the inverse-square law.

Historically, however, this sequence of thought just is not what happened. Kepler actually discovered the inverse-square law for light, or illumination, but he believed he had found a very different law for his variety of "gravitation." He held that his "gravitation" did not diminish as the inverse square of the distance, but rather as the simple inverse ratio of the distance. In this instance we conclude that for Kepler there were other factors involved than the simplest logic of mere analogy.

A somewhat similar episode presents itself to us in the eighteenth century. Following the success of the Newtonian paradigm, would it not seem obvious that scientists should have demanded an inverse-square law for magnetism and for electricity, just as for gravitation? Would we not expect that this demand would have been so pressing that scientists would not merely endeavor to establish such a law, but that they would welcome it with enthusiasm and alacrity just as soon as it was announced? I remember that when I first learned that the inverse-square law for electrical force had been discovered before the time of Coulomb (to whose name we generally attach the law), I was terribly puzzled, because quite obviously this result had not been generally accepted. For a long time I thought that the lack of acceptance was not so much a conscious rejection as a consequence of ignorance, due to the fact that the "discovery" was embedded in Priestley's history of electricity, and was not made the subject of a paper in the *Philosophical Transactions* to announce the 'discovery,' if we may use that word. Now Priestley, as I always told my students, discovered Coulomb's law on the basis of a "Faraday experiment" in the form in which the latter had been discovered by Benjamin Franklin. (So much for eponymy in science!) Franklin had found that a charge given to an insulated conductor is found to be wholly on the outer surface, that there is no charge discernible on the inside. Priestley assumed, from the symmetry of the situation, that the same result would hold for a hollow, charged, insulated sphere. He then applied a theorem proved by Newton in the *Principia*, that the absence of a force field inside of a hollow sphere results only if the force varies as the inverse square. Hence, Priestley concluded, the law of electrical force must be an inverse-square law.

In my research on the history of electricity, summarized in my monograph on *Franklin and Newton,* I found that Priestley's discovery could hardly be said to have been buried in an obscure history book. Rather, his *History and Present State of . . . Electricity*[1] was a kind of "Bible" of all "electricians"; anybody interested in acquiring a knowledge of what had been done in electricity, as well as the current state of theory, read that book. It came out in five editions in English, and was translated into French and German. The book was widely and thoroughly read, but there is no evidence of an acceptance of the inverse-square law of electrical action. This lack of response may have been due to the fact that the Franklinian phenomenon had been demonstrated experimentally only for hollow cylinders and not for hollow spheres; possibly the Priestley application of a Newtonian theorem was too mathematical and apparently abstract. (Cavendish did perform the experiment of the charged hollow sphere and found it worked exactly as in the case of the cylinder, but his results did not become public until well into the nineteenth century.) I think this historical episode may thus be a "cautionary tale" for those who look back at the science of the past to conclude from today's vantage point that a given conclusion may have been—in some sense—"demanded."

Perhaps an even more striking example comes from post-Coulomb science. It was known in the early nineteenth century that electricity follows an inverse-square law, that magnetism follows an inverse-square law, and that gravitation follows an inverse-square law. Thus the same form of law can be written for all three types of phenomena: F is equal to G or y or k times the product of masses, charges, or magnetic pole-strengths, divided by the inverse square of the distance. Today we might be apt to conclude from our analysis that there must therefore have been a strong feeling among scientists that this formal similarity of the three laws should lead to some kind of unified theory (possibly a "unified field theory"). We know that Faraday made significant experiments and studies on the interrelations between various types of physical phenomena. Yet the record shows very little general scientific concern for a unified or a simple all-embracing theory

[1] Priestley [1767].

until the latter part of the century. Perhaps the reason was that gravitation presents only attraction and not repulsion, and insofar differs from electricity and magnetism. Furthermore, despite the purely formal (or mathematical) similarity of the three laws, there is a profound physical difference among these. Consider the very nature of the constants—G is a universal constant, while the dialectic constant and the magnetic constant characterize the very specific variety of matter (or absence of matter) between the charged or magnetic bodies.

It follows that great care is required whenever we conclude that a given situation must have "demanded" a particular conclusion. In the case of the three inverse-square laws, our conclusion may depend on whether we concentrate on similarities or differences. Or, whether, looking back, we decide that the similarities may have been more important than the differences. Possibly a reason for the lack of active conviction that there should be a unitary force (not yet a field theory) might be found by studying carefully the development of electrical thought between Priestley and Coulomb, and especially between Coulomb and Gauss. Perhaps there we would find significant factors which would *not* have demanded a unified theory quite to the extent we might otherwise initially have expected.

Professor Shapere:

First let me just say something about phlogiston: Yes, it involved an existence claim; it is one of those concepts which was found not to refer to anything but there were good reasons for making the claim, even though in the light of later science they no longer seem like such good reasons. Some concepts of this sort retain a use in science even after their existence claims have been rejected. Phlogiston happens to not be of that sort, and so in that respect it belongs with a number of other concepts which originally, I would take it, involved existence claims: 'ether', 'caloric', 'phlogiston', and so forth, are examples.

Now, the point about whether there is more apparent unity than real unity: I agree with you that in many cases this is so; in fact, I like all of your comments and I think they were comments, not questions, from here on in. There also is one thing that I think needs to be said, which is that there is not a constant drive toward unity or an unambiguous drive toward unity in any of these cases, but rather there are always differences. As I suggested, there were differences known in many of these cases and you have to go very deeply into the reasons when there were reasons why people investigated this sort of relationship rather than that sort of relationship. As a matter of fact, as far as I know, the question of the relations between electricity, magnetism, gravitation, and so on, has appealed to some people; and you find discussions of the possibility of there being some deeper unity behind scientific theories in discussion of the tridimensionality of space and the connection between the tridimensionality of space and these laws—the existence of these laws and their particular mathematical form being used by some thinkers as arguments in favor of the tridimensionality of space and furthermore for the view that physical theories should be giving an ultimate explanation in terms of the characteristics of space. The Kepler case is interesting, but of course Kepler was thinking of the spreading of gravitational effects on a plane and not spherically. This explains why he did not think of the parallel between light intensity and gravitation; so I hope that is in agreement with your remarks.

Professor Putnam:

I have two comments on which I would like Dudley to comment. The first concerns something that occurred to me during your discussion today that has occurred to me before; but I never realized before that it contradicts the verbal formalization I have been using. The point is that the better theory need not explain what the earlier theory explained. The case I have in mind is that Newtonian gravitation was not overthrown by general relativity, but rather was overthrown by special relativity. Special relativity is a better theory even though it is not a theory of gravitation. So now I would not say that the theory is finally overthrown by a better theory; I would rather say that in general the good ideas—those ideas which have had really major successes in practice—are not shown to be false by experiment alone. I still think that formulation is correct for a wide class of cases (although the job of delimiting those cases certainly remains and is, I think, an important problem for philosophy of science). But, in general, I now want to say, it requires ideas as well as experiments to overthrow an idea, although the overthrowing idea need not always be a replacing idea. Special relativity overthrew Newtonian gravitation without replacing Newtonian gravitation; and I think your examples today were examples of cases in which theories say that other theories must be wrong although the theory that says the other theory must be wrong does not necessarily tell you how to replace the other theory.

Now the other comment I have is not so much on your paper as on something which suddenly occurred to me on reflecting on the whole discussion of these four days. I think it is very interesting and very important. In this discussion on March 29, 1969, we have a group of fairly skilled philosophers of science talking for seven sessions with virtually no discussion of what probably would have been the characteristic problem ten years ago and certainly would have been twenty years ago, which is precisely the central problem behind the Received View—namely, "How do new terms (in the Hempelian sense) acquire meaning?" I think that is a very important development, and I think it is a healthy development in part. The fact that you no longer talk about certain problems can be a healthy development in science because it may mean that you are onto something new; on the other hand, it can be unhealthy if it means that we simply sweep the old problem under the rug. I would like to suggest that the machinery for dealing with that problem is contained in some of the ideas that have been circulating at this conference and in the papers that a number of us have written, including some of the things you have said today. I would like to talk for a couple of minutes about what I think the machinery is, a kind of completion of the historical remarks I just made.

I think the answer is this: I have already suggested that the main problem is "When do you have a new term?," and I agree that theories usually do not introduce new terms; they talk about electrons and electricity and gravitation, and so on, just like the theories before them did. Occasionally you do get a new term or a term which was not previously a scientific term—although like 'electricity' it may have been used in ordinary language. When you do get a new term, I think the key problem is not to say "what it means"; I think as a philosopher of language (in part), I would say you really would not be very interested if I told you what I think most scientific terms mean. You would say that if that is what their meaning is, who should care about their meaning? For example, in the case of 'electricity' I think very little is literally contained in the meaning of the word. I think most people know the meaning of the word, but that does not mean they know anything very much about electricity. I think the interesting question is, "How do you say what the word refers to? How do you say what answers to the concept?." The statements or indications the scientist gives of what his term refers to may or may not be a meaning explanation. I think it is quite unimportant in extensional contexts (and that means in virtually all empirical science) whether the indications he gives of what he is using the term to refer to or to denote is or is not also a meaning explanation; but what kind of indications do you give of what a term refers to?

Here I want to suggest a principle which I have called, not in print, but in a number of lectures, *the principle of charity.* Like all principles of charity it is to be used with judgment and with prudence: you know, if it costs too much do not be so charitable. In its first approximation the principle has two parts. First of all let me take the case of saying what the terms of an older or preceding theory referred to. If you want to know, for example, what Bohr was referring to when he used the term 'electron', and we are answering this question from the standpoint of present theory, the principle says: First look around the world from the spectacles of your present theory and see if there are entities which pretty well answer to the properties and the causal mechanisms that Bohr assigned to electrons; second, if there are such entities—even if they are not perfect—do him the charity of saying that those are the entities he was referring to, rather than saying that he was referring to nothing at all. Sometimes we are not that charitable, as in the case of phlogiston. There we could be charitable and say there is phlogiston—it is just the absence of oxygen—but we feel that it would cost too much to say this. In the case of the electron, we do not feel it would cost too much, and I think the reasons we feel it does not cost too much have to do with ideas like preserving substance (with electrons being substances), the fact that they have a rest mass, and so forth; and that Bohr already knew that, and that he knew that the hydrogen atom had exactly one of them, and so forth. There is so much that he was right about that we do not feel it costs as much to be charitable; so I would say that it is in the light of this kind of principle—the idea that older theories may not have been exactly right but that they were right enough so that we feel some of the mechanism that they postulated was right—that we are able to say a term can refer even though it may have analytically contained a property that is not possessed by the thing it refers to; just as if I refer to Professor Hempel as "that bachelor," it is clear from the context that I am referring to Professor Hempel. We do not say that I did not refer to anyone; we say I referred to Professor Hempel, because it is clear from the context what the reference was.

You might say, "How is this going to help you with the new term? With the new term, it's not a matter of standing later in time with what you pretend to be better apparatus, and then you say what terms refer to." With respect to introducing a new term, here I think the answer is that usually (although not always) the new terms refer to things which at least belong to classes that we already have. You know, you say I am postulating a new kind of force here. Although the term I introduce may be a new term, the term 'kind of force' is by no means a new term; and here I think that we must say this if we look from the point of view of your paper. So I think this bears directly on what you said on the term 'electron'. You see, there is a whole series of theories which are using the same term, say 'electron'; it becomes quite standard practice that each one applies the principle of charity to the preceding terms so that each term says, "Yes, I too am talking about what he was calling electrons," and you get a tradition of saying, "Let's say all these theories are talking about the same things." You then get the kind of situation you characterized by saying something to the effect that 'electron' was something like an extratheoretic term. And I am suggesting that the procedure that you described whereby theoretic terms become extratheoretic terms arises from this practice of applying the principle of charity to preceding terms. Since theoretical terms in the new theory usually do refer to kinds of entities for which we already have a name, and since we are interested in getting an idea of what the guy is referring to, one can see why this is methodologically important: It is why using what I have called broad-spectrum concepts[2] to indicate the sort of thing the term stands for is methodologically important. In fact, even if the answer is negative—even if the answer is that you are introducing this term this time to stand for a thing for which there not only is no extensional name in the previous literature, but which does not even fall into a class which has a name in previous literature—I want to say that it would be important to say that. When you introduce the notion of spin for the first time, you can at least say that it is not referring to any of the things you think it might be referring to. I want to suggest that along these lines, which are roughly speaking along extensional or denotational lines, one might be able to get an answer to the meaning problems we would have been discussing if this conference had been held ten or fifteen years ago. And I think these extensional lines do not pose as many problems as the old problems of meaning —many of which are still around.

Professor Causey:

I would like to add a footnote to Professor Cohen's remarks. I think that he was pointing out a very serious and a very natural question which we would want to ask of Professor Shapere. What does

[2] Cf. Putnam [1962].

Shapere's discussion (of the idealizations, simplifications, and so on, that scientists use) have to do with the instrumentalist-realist dispute? Professor Shapere has apparently given us a rather Austinian view of how scientists consider various modes of existence of entities. I think this is very interesting, and I think that there are lots of questions we would want to ask him about particular cases. For instance: Is it really a case of idealization? Is it simplification? Is it approximation? Is it something else?

However, right now I am concerned with the following question: Has Professor Shapere really given us good reasons for accepting a kind of realistic view of theories? I think Professor Cohen's question about phlogiston was not meant just to be answered "Yes," but rather was a question intended to generate some skepticism about some of the entities that theories presumably refer to. Now I personally think that we should interpret our theories realistically, and I think that in most cases—except perhaps in some very interesting idealizations, as you have pointed out—scientists do interpret their theories realistically. But I wonder if we really can give a philosophical argument in favor of this. Is it not simpler just to say, "Well, this is the best thing to do?"

Professor van Fraassen:

I think Professor Shapere would really like to dismiss the ontological issue of instrumentalism and realism as inappropriate to the philosophy of science; and I would agree at least to the extent that I think philosophy of science should be ontologically neutral as far as we can possibly make it. But I am afraid that Professor Shapere's approach in terms of domains leads at once to ontological issues and, as a matter of fact, necessarily to realism. And neither of these two consequences is a virtue in my opinion. Let me try to explain why I think his approach makes it impossible for him to be anything but a realist To use a simple example, let us agree that Bohr's theory of the atom is incorrect. Now an instrumentalist can say that Bohr's theory of the atom is incorrect or false. What he cannot say is, "Bohr's theory is about atoms, but he says wrong things about them," because, of course, according to the instrumentalist there are no atoms. It is true that he can speak the language of the prevalent theory when he is speaking with the vulgar, so he can say that a person is referring to an atom. But this would have to be true for him in just a purely formal sense: the subject term of the statement correctly describes this entity within the framework of the theory. Professor Putnam has just counseled us to be charitable here, but it is the kind of charity that only a realist like Professor Putnam could afford. Consider now the notion of a domain; at one point Professor Shapere emphasized that the domain is a pretheoretical notion. Now I assume he was using Professor Hempel's term, and meant that the domain is described in the pretheoretical language but the pretheoretical language is the language of an old theory and the new theory entails that the old theory is wrong. And so the instrumentalist could not say that there is a domain identified by this pretheoretical description because it is exactly the kind of description that for him cannot constitute reference at all. So for the instrumentalist there could be no such thing as reference to a domain described in pretheoretical terms. In order to follow Shapere's approach at all one would have to be a realist.

Professor Shapere:

Well, I will reply to just a couple of these points and say that I agree with most of the things that Professor Putnam said. As to Professor Causey's one point—have I really given reasons for a realistic view of theories?—there seems to be some contradiction between Professor Causey's interpretation and Professor van Fraassen's, since Professor van Fraassen thinks that I must be a realist and Professor Causey thinks I have not given any good reasons for being one. But, anyway, he reraises the question of phlogiston, and he says this makes us doubt on the question of realism. Of course, the kind of realism that I am defending here is the realism of existence claims. One can claim that phlogiston exists and phlogiston still may not exist; so that kind of realism is all that is at issue here. I would like to thank Professor van Fraassen very much for showing that I am very consistent. I do not quite understand what the difficulty is here: He does not like the fact that talking about domains as I did requires you to be a realist. It seems to me that if there is any use for the concept of a domain in the sense that I have outlined it, it is to discuss existence claims, and if it is true that that requires one to be a realist, so much the better.

The Structure of Scientific Theories

STEPHEN TOULMIN

Every tradition originates to meet a need, and falls into disuse when it has become demonstrably counterproductive. So, when the agenda for this symposium says, "*Traditionally* philosophers of science have construed scientific theories as axiomatic calculi in which theoretical terms and statements are given a partial observational interpretation by means of correspondence rules," [1] we must assume that the axiomatic model will be no exception to that general rule. As a concluding postscript, therefore, I shall be asking two questions:

(1) When and how did this tradition originate in the first place?
(2) Are recent discontents with the axiomatic model genuine signs that it has begun to be more of a hindrance than a help to the philosophy of science?

Let me begin by recalling the historical context in which philosophy of science took the axiomatic road, and then consider the current demands for a change of direction against that background.

To European eyes, the word "traditionally" was an odd choice. Certainly the tradition in question is an extremely new one. Though the roots of the axiomatic model go back into the late nineteenth century, it has had a central place in philosophy of science for less than fifty years, and—even so—philosophers have by no means been unanimous about its significance. The crucial moment was the confluence in Vienna after World War I of Mach's logico-historical criticism and empiricist epistemology with Russell's symbolic logic and Einstein's relativistic physics. And the first thing to notice here is the fact that, from the very outset, the philosophical partners to the resulting alliance had differing motives and were aiming at different goals.

For instance, the book to which all supporters of the axiomatic model look back as a prototype—rightly, since it remains one of the model's

[1] P. vii above; emphasis added.

most thoroughgoing and illuminating applications—is *The Principles of Mechanics* by Heinrich Hertz. Hertz, like his master Helmholtz and his successors Wittgenstein and Cassirer, was philosophically more a Kantian than he was a Humean empiricist. In expounding the theory of mechanics as an axiomatic calculus, to which a physical interpretation was given subsequently, Hertz's purpose was heuristic. For this method of exposition provided a perspicuous way of distinguishing those aspects of theoretical mechanics which had a direct empirical reference from those other aspects—notably, its general form, or mode of articulation—which were a feature rather of our "model" (*Bild*) or "representation" (*Darstellung*); and in this way, Hertz claimed, it was possible to undercut the confused speculations about the nature of *force* which had obstructed the progress of nineteenth-century physics.

On the other hand, Hertz was not concerned with taking an epistemological stand on the model, any more than Wittgenstein did later in his *Tractatus*: still less did he suggest that our confidence in the theoretical terms or statements of mechanics is to be justified by treating them as derivative, logically and epistemologically, from "sensory observations" or *Protokolsätze*. The epistemological interpretation was added by the Vienna Circle philosophers, and by Bertrand Russell in England. As the immediate successors of Ernst Mach they welcomed the added strength that the axiomatic model for science apparently gave to Mach's own neo-Humean "scientific epistemology." As they saw it, this model could be used not only to separate out the formal articulation of physical theories from their empirical applications, but with its help, we could also go on to provide our tentative, hypothetical belief in the general entities and propositions of scientific theory with an epistemological foundation, by relating them back to the indubitable, categorical, and particular evidence of the senses.

To this day, several leading topics in the "traditional" philosophy of science look back to this Machian program for epistemology; for example, the "theoretical"/"observational" distinction on which Dudley Shapere concentrated much of his fire at this symposium. For the logical empiricists, who have been most fully committed to this "traditional" program in philosophy of science, the data of observation have always been "hard," particular, and epistemologically fundamental: theoretical knowledge, by contrast, has been in their eyes derivative, general, and "soft." For a Kantian like Hertz, however, the distinction between "theory" and "observation" cuts along quite different lines. For him, empirical questions about observed motions could be stated in a form relevant to mechanics, only in the theoretical terms defined within a prior *Bild* or *Darstellung*. So, on this view, we do not "construct" the general terms and statements of theory out of particular sense data or observation statements: rather, the empirical data of physics are themselves already general and related.

In its fully developed form, the traditional (or Viennese) philosophy of science incorporated into itself two further elements: the symbolism of mathematical logic and the methodological program of the unified science movement. At its most grandiose, the ambition was to establish epistemological foundations, not merely for individual theories considered singly, nor merely for an "ideal type" of theory, but—in principle, at any rate—for positive scientific knowledge *in its entirety*. What Klein had done by mapping pure geometry onto arithmetic, what Peano and Russell had done by founding pure mathematics in formal logic, what Hamilton and Hertz had done by converting physical dynamics into "rational mechanics," the advocates of unified science planned to do for the whole of natural science. By adding further primitive terms, postulates, and correspondence rules, they hoped to incorporate all genuine branches of science into a single axiomatic edifice; and, since the central (or logico-mathematical) portions of this edifice were best presented in the formalism of symbolic logic (particularly the lower functional calculus), that same notation could presumably be adapted to serve the purposes of the whole. On this program, the value of the axiomatic model was not just heuristic or epistemological: it now became the obligatory form for expounding a coherent and unified scientific theory, or *Weltbild*.

If we bear in mind the variety of aims with which the axiomatic model was originally introduced, we shall understand better the different preoccupations of the philosophers who have worked within the resulting tradition; and we shall also understand better the many varied doubts and hesitations that have been current in recent years. For neo-Humeans who, like Mach, regard "sensory observations" as clear, certain, and comparatively well understood, the crucial problem has been to see how these particular "hard data" can be used to underpin the general terms and statements of scientific theory: this topic has preoccupied all those philosophers of science who have—from one point of view or another—debated the theory of verification, falsification, corroboration, and/or confirmation. For neo-Kantians, who have no such confidence in "immediate sensations," the question has been, rather, how mathematical theories or models can serve as "representations" of phenomena at all. Correspondingly, challenges to the Viennese program have been based, sometimes on formal, sometimes on epistemological grounds, and sometimes on more general philosophical considerations. Certain philosophers (like Hilary Putnam) have argued that the operative question in actual scientific practice is not whether theoretical concepts or principles are "true," "false," or "partly confirmed," but whether—when combined with all necessary "auxiliary statements"—they "do an explanatory job." Others (including myself) have attempted to ridicule the traditional interpretation for treating "All swans are white" as a "typical theoretical statement" in science; in return, they have insisted on the conceptual incongruity between theoretical concepts or principles and their alleged foundations in "direct sensory observations."

Among supporters of the axiomatic model, again, the status of the "correspondence rules," by which theoretical terms and statements are reputedly given a "partial observational interpretation," has itself been in doubt. Philosophers with strongly epistemological aims have seen these rules as playing the part of "ostensive definitions," and so as "analytic"; others have construed them, rather, as putting forward tentative empirical correlations between theory and observation, and so as "synthetic"; while still others (like W. V. Quine, echoing Pierre Duhem and Charles Sanders Peirce) have seen their status as variable, and have refused to describe them as either "synthetic" or "analytic."

If supporters of the traditional program have agreed on any one *positive* point, it is what we may call the Central Axiom of the Viennese tradition. They all assume that, at any stage in its historical development, the established intellectual content of a science or scientific theory can be exhaustively represented as a "logical system"—that is, that the theoretical concepts and conclusions of the science are related to one another, and to the observational evidence on which they are based, in a formal network of logical relations—and that the consistency, richness, and logical structure of this network determine the validity, and/or degree of establishment, of the theoretical concepts and conclusions in question. Logic and philosophy of science are thus concerned with the ex post facto "justification" of scientific concepts and hypotheses, as determined by their logical relations, both to one another, and to the empirical evidence on which they are based. Conversely, all supporters of the Viennese tradition agree on one *negative* point; namely, that the intellectual discoveries as a result of which the theoretical terms and statements of a science change—by which new hypotheses are arrived at and new concepts introduced—as between one moment in the development of a science and another, are a matter for psychologists or sociologists rather than philosophers. Unless and until the new concepts and hypotheses can take their place in a revised "logical system," whose "structure" can be scrutinized and compared with that of its predecessor, no question of "justification" arises, and the philosopher has nothing to get a grip on. As the resulting slogan puts it: "There is no Logic of Discovery."

Seen against this historical background, the problems currently under discussion—of which this symposium provides a good sample—can be divided into two broad classes, each with a number of subdivisions. To begin with, suppose that we concede more or less of the traditional approach; then we may ask:

(1) Can the axiomatic model be used equally well *in all cases* to analyze, and judge, the intellectual content of any particular temporal cross-section of a natural science?

If, however, we challenge that approach, and reject the traditional dichotomy between the "logic of justification" and the "psychology of discovery," we may ask, further:

(2) Can the axiomatic model be used *at all* to analyze, and judge, the ways in which the intellectual content of a natural science develops, from one temporal cross-section to the next?

Robert Causey states the contrast between these two questions admirably in his comment on David Bohm. The picture of a science as a "logical structure" gives us (he says) only a static "snapshot" of its content: the newer questions that younger philosophers of science are now pressing begin to arise when we ask for a "moving picture," showing how the intellectual content of the sciences develops historically.

Let us consider each of these two broad classes of problems in turn. Under heading (1) there are four distinct groups of subproblems. To begin with, those who are still ready to construe the logical structure of scientific theories on the traditional axiomatic model can nevertheless ask:

(1a) Is there any *standard and compulsory symbolism,* or form, for analyzing the axiomatic structure of all scientific theories whatever?

One stage more generally, those who accept the snapshot view of science as a "logical structure," but hesitate to restrict themselves within the axiomatic framework, can ask:

(1b) Is the axiomatic form the only legitimate "logical structure" for science, or may there be *other logical forms* into which the content of a scientific theory may legitimately be analyzed?

Either way—whether the "logical structures" of all scientific theories are construed on the axiomatic model, or not—one must consider their empirical application as well as their formal articulation, and this will give rise to the third question:

(1c) What is the nature of the "correspondence" by which the formal elements in a scientific theory acquire an *empirical relevance or interpretation*?

Finally, there are those who would more radically challenge the whole picture of scientific theories as "logical structures," and who would ask instead:

(1d) Can the intellectual content of a natural science, at any one temporal cross-section in its development, be expressed as a *systematic network of logical relations* at all?

To begin by taking up question (1a): On an historical note, none of the participants in this symposium—and few contemporary philosophers of science anywhere—are still interested in defending, in full, the original program for a Unified Science. To that extent, the tide of logical positivism has already receded from its high watermark. The claims made for the axiomatic model today are, at most, epistemological or heuristic. In the present symposium Patrick Suppes alone has put the axiomatic model to work, using the formal symbolism of mathematical logic; yet even he has done so, not in a conventional manner, but in order to raise some novel questions. Supposing that the axiomatic model is used as an instrument of analysis, he asks, may we not end up by employing a variety of axiomatic forms in different cases, when considering different sciences or epochs? In one respect, at least, his call for a *taxonomy* of axiomatic systems thus represents a significant departure from the earlier program, which looked forward to the establishment of a single, common, axiomatic form or structure for analyzing the intellectual content of any genuine science, at any time.

The next question (1b) represents only one step beyond Suppes's suggestion. For if various different forms of axiomatic structure are available and it is a matter of history which of those forms is exemplified by a particular science at a particular time, then is it not also a matter of history (one may inquire) whether certain sciences at certain stages do not equally and legitimately exemplify other, *non-axiomatic* forms of logical structure? In the introduction to his *Principles of Mechanics*, Hertz himself emphasized that his axiomatic exposition of dynamics represented only one of several alternative *Bilder*, all of which were logically coherent and empirically applicable to the same phenomena. Alternative systems of logical articulation may quite legitimately be used—though not all with equally perspicuousness—to represent phenomena, whether in Hertz's own chosen field of mechanics or in other natural sciences. In view of this admission by "the father of axiomatics," one may surely go on to ask whether the points that he made in his account of axiomatic systems (as scientific *Bilder* for the *Darstellung* of phenomena) cannot be broadened and generalized, so as to apply to theories having other logical forms also. This is, in fact, a subject to which that great admirer of Hertz, Ludwig Wittgenstein, repeatedly used to return in his later years; and many of his ideas on this subject are taken up and developed in W. H. Watson's book, *On Understanding Physics*.

There are, for instance, natural sciences whose internal articulation is more naturally displayed in taxonomic, rather than in axiomatic, form. (Aristotle himself having been a marine biologist, it is no accident that his logical *syllogistic* was immediately applicable to the biological systematics of his time.) Likewise, there are natural sciences—for example, geometrical optics—whose standard explanatory procedures employ graphical, rather than mathematical, techniques; there are sciences constructed around the use of computer programs, and so forth. With a little care, one can make the same heuristic distinction in each case that Hertz was so insistent on: namely, the distinction between the internal structure, or formal articulation, in which the theoretical concepts and statements of the science are linked (corresponding to Part I of Hertz's *Principles*) and the external relevance, or empirical application, of the resulting articulated theory (corresponding to Hertz's Part II).

Granted, then, that this point does not depend on the use of the axiomatic model, what reason then remains to claim priority for the axiomatic analysis—still more to make it *obligatory*? So long as philosophers were aiming to construct a single, integrated Unified Science, such claims were all very well; but, once that ambition is abandoned, other arguments must be found for insisting on "axiomatics-or-nothing." No abstract, formal, system (we might reply) can ever specify—still less *guarantee*—its own empirical relevance, or range of application. So we must surely investigate separately, in each particular case, just what form of articulation—axiomatic, taxonomic, graphical, or whatever—is appropriate to a scientific theory covering this or that subject matter, at this or that stage of historical development. And, even if the appropriate form does in fact turn out to be axiomatic, it will still surely remain an open question in each case, just which item from Patrick Suppes's "taxonomy of axiomatic forms" applies to that particular example. This being so, it is particularly impressive to find Carl Hempel, at this symposium, warning philosophers not to overrate "the importance of formalization, including axiomatization, as essential to proper scientific procedure." Seeing that Hempel has played such a major part in the development of logical empiricism, it is interesting to find him, so to say, outflanking Patrick Suppes on the left. Hempel's readiness to rethink old positions in this way not only does him credit personally, but also is an indication of the problems that still remain even within the Viennese tradition.

Whatever the answers to these first two questions, the third problem arises: namely (1c) to explain what sort of "correspondence" exists between the theoretical terms and statements of science and their empirical applications. Over this point, the philosophers of science participating in the present symposium are in manifest disarray. At one extreme are those, like Carl Hempel, who would be content to make somewhat minor adjustments to the traditional account of empirical interpretation, while on the other hand there are those, like Hilary Putnam, for whom the notion of "correspondence rules" only serves to conceal profound confusions about the explanatory application of scientific theories—as well as those who, like Dudley Shapere, would argue that "correspondence rules" appear necessary only because the distinction between "theoretical" and "observational" statements has been misconceived, and wish to see this particular question completely restated.

Over this third question, the most intriguing and surprising paper in this symposium is the one by Thomas Kuhn. Here he spells out in a new way his views about the nature and role of "paradigms" in science; and in doing so he shows himself to be far nearer than he had previously appeared to the traditional logical empiricist position. One notable feature of Kuhn's earlier account of "paradigms" was its complete neutrality over all the logical and epistemological disputes that have bedeviled recent philosophy of science. This was, in fact, one of the *virtues*, for it left one free to suppose that different scientific theories, constructed around different "paradigms," might have quite different kinds of logical structure and derive epistemic support from quite different sources. In his present paper, however, Kuhn takes a very definite stand on these logical and epistemological issues. For this purpose, he draws a fresh distinction between two separate aspects of paradigms, which he calls "disciplinary matrices" and "exemplars" respectively; and he defines these in terms that Mach or Russell need scarcely find objectionable. As Frederick Suppe rightly remarks in his commentary, the term "disciplinary matrix" can be construed to mean "conceptual framework" or "logical system," while Kuhn's "exemplars" have the same role as the traditional "ostensive definitions." It is therefore no accident that, of all the symposiasts, only Kuhn still argues explicitly for *sense data* ("green there," "triangle here," and so on) to serve as the minimal elements of experience, to which all our knowledge must ultimately be led back—as in Mach's *Analyse der Empfindungen.* Meanwhile, his account of the manner in which Johnny learns "symbolic labels" from "exemplars" is in close agreement with Russell's arguments in *Human Knowledge*, according to which one "universal" alone is absolutely indispensable: namely, that of "resemblance."

The clearest opposition over this third question is that between Hempel and Putnam. Hempel concedes that the distinction between "internal principles" (which connect theoretical terms together within a science) and "bridge principles" (which connect theoretical terms to prescientific terms, or to extrascientific experience) is nowhere near as cut and dried as it was assumed to be in the heyday of logical empiricism. Hempel, like Carnap, is now prepared to treat philosophical questions about the historical development of scientific theories out of prescientific ideas more seriously than he used to do. His concessions, however, do not go far enough to satisfy Putnam, whose account of "auxiliary statements" and "explanatory schemata" represents not so much a mature refinement of the traditional analysis as early steps toward a quite novel analysis of "explanatory success" in science.

As in his paper attacking Karl Popper's theory of corroboration, so here Putnam's claim that, if there exists no "logic of discovery" there exists no "logic of testing" either (that is, no formal "algorithm" for confirmation, verification, corroboration, falsification, call it what you will) is a radical challenge to the philosophical program of the Vienna Circle and all its associates. For Putnam determinedly ignores most of the logical barriers erected in Vienna between (for example) theory and practice, or between concepts and their application, and he deliberately thrusts the task of judging scientific ideas back into the arena of everyday life and practice, from which Mach originally tried to extract it. The theoretical ideas of a science are not something separate, and apart from, ideas in general, for example, from the ideas that guide practice in technology, politics, and other areas of extrascientific life. To that extent, there is nothing specially "tentative" or "hypothetical" about them—nothing that divorces them (say) from the terms in which the results of our observations are reported. For Putnam, the only distinction that then remains between a scientific theory and its "experiential foundation" is the distinction between that theory formulated and considered in the abstract—in purely intellectual terms—and the same theory when used to structure our forms of life and allowed to prove its explanatory success in the world of practice.

So much for the questions that arise, within the scope of the Central Axiom of the Viennese tradition: once we move on to questions (1d) and (2), however, we have to question that axiom. The new issues that have to be considered, as a result, can be illustrated from Dudley Shapere's contribution to the symposium. The examples he cited make it clear *both* (in reply to question (1d)) that the internal relations linking the terms and statements of a science, at any time, are not necessarily "logical" or "axiomatic" at all, *and also* (in reply to (2)) that a natural science consequently needs to be considered, not as a "logical system" merely, but, more generally, as a "rational enterprise," having as its current outcome a sort of concepts and propositions where interrelations are less strict and rigorous than those of any mathematical system, axiomatic or otherwise.

In practice (as Shapere shows) actual natural sciences tolerate a substantial degree of logical "gappiness," incoherence, and even inconsistency. In some fields, for example, quantum electrodynamics, the current explanatory procedures may even require us to contradict ourselves: assuming, for the purposes of certain calculations, that *p*—for example, "the electron has zero radius"—while for other calculations, we must assume that *not-p*—for example, "the electron has non-zero radius." Yet physicists are perfectly well able to live with these contradictions and learn to recognize in what situations each kind of calculation is appropriate. If we wish to understand how actual sciences operate, therefore, we must abandon the assumption that the intellectual contents of natural sciences actively in debate have "logical" or "systematic" structures: we must instead consider how such sciences can succeed in fulfilling their actual explanatory missions, despite the fact that, at any chosen moment in time, their intellectual contents are marked by logical gaps, incoherences, and contradictions.

Why have supporters of the Viennese tradition overlooked these logical gaps and inconsistencies—or at any rate, regarded them as inessential to science? The reasons are apparently connected with two ambiguities, or unclarities, in the Central Axiom of the tradition, the axiom which question (1d) calls in doubt. For it is frequently left unclear, first, whether it is only a *particular theoretical calculus or algorithm* within a natural science that is to be construed as a "logical system," or rather the intellectual content of *the entire science*. And it is often left obscure, also, whether the notion of "logical structure" is intended as a *descriptive pattern* for expounding and analyzing actual natural sciences, or whether it is proposed rather as a *prescriptive ideal* for judging and criticizing them.

The origin of those ambiguities is intelligible, when we recall the starting point of the axiomatic approach: that is, Hertz's analysis of theoretical mechanics. For, from its birth in Newton's *Principia* right up to Hertz's time, the theory of mechanics was presented as a formal axiom system, and was conceived of as providing (at least in principle) the intellectual basis for an all-embracing, mechanistic account of the physical world. As such, it acquired something of the same comprehensive character as a branch of pure mathematics. Kant, for instance, placed Newtonian dynamics on a par with Euclidian geometry; and, by the present time, "rational mechanics" has become a strictly mathematical subject, capable of standing on its own, like pure geometry, without reference to any active, empirical scientific problems.

Thus in mechanics—and in mechanics alone—the intellectual content of an entire physical science could apparently be expounded as a single mathematical calculus. Here was a complete natural science free of logical gaps and incoherences. So in this case, for once, it was unnecessary to distinguish the science as a whole from the particular algorithms and families of concepts that it comprised. As a picture of an *ideal* natural science, free of irrelevant intellectual blemishes, the Hertzian account of mechanics had an evident charm. The temptation to hold theoretical mechanics up as a mirror to other branches of science, and to demand that other sciences be construed on the same model and achieve the same logical coherence, seemed irresistible.

Yet the very formal perfection of theoretical mechanics ought surely to have ruled it out as the "type example" of a natural science, and prevented us from extrapolating conclusions about the "logical structure" of mechanics, so as to apply to natural sciences generally. Rather, we need to recognize how *exceptional* a science mechanics really is. Whereas the concepts and postulates of mechanical theory are all interdefined, and can be introduced all of a piece—so forming, quite naturally, a simple coherent "logical system"—most natural sciences comprise a number of distinct, and more or less loosely connected concepts, or families of concepts, which were introduced at different times in the past, with different problems and explanatory tasks in view. Rather than forming a tight logical system, the concepts of the typical natural science are an aggregate, or congeries: at any chosen moment of time, they do not all have the same empirical range of application, only some of them are logically interdependent, and certain of them may even be mutually inconsistent.

The significance of this point is apparent when we face the implications of question (2): that is, when we look to see in what terms we are to describe the manner in which the intellectual content of a natural science develops from one historical cross-section to another.

For it is (as Shapere emphasizes) precisely the gaps, incoherences, and contradictions in the ideas of a typical natural science that give rise to the *conceptual problems* of the science, and so compel the scientists concerned to introduce *conceptual changes* into its intellectual content. In a subject like rational mechanics, the only remaining problems are formal ones, and there is room for mathematical refinements alone: in more typical sciences, there is room for conceptual changes also, and this is what keeps them "scientific." Far from a typical science forming a complete logical system, it is its logical gaps and inconsistencies that keep the subject alive as an active, developing field for scientific inquiry; and its very *a*typical, *un*systematic, *non*axiomatic character is what generates the real head of steam behind its problems.

With this in mind, we may think it better to speak (with Shapere) not of "theoretical calculi and their structures," but rather of "scientific enterprises and their problems." In order to understand the true nature and function of scientific concepts, we need to analyze not just their *logical relations* with the other concepts of the same theoretical calculus, but also the *rational procedures* by which conceptual problems are dealt with in a developing science. The crucial defect of the traditional approach on this view lies in its equation of the "rational" with the "logical." By declining to admit into philosophical discussion any intellectual relation that is not amenable to formal analysis, the Viennese empiricists eliminated from philosophy the whole subject of "conceptual change"—the whole question of how conceptual problems of a nonformal kind arise and are dealt with rationally within scientific enterprises. Having focused on the nature of "logical systems," the Viennese tradition in the philosophy of science thus ended by giving a misleading picture of the intellectual content of a natural science—even on the "snapshot" level.

This objection cannot be swept aside with the bare assertion that "there is no logic of discovery." That overworked epigram is no longer capable of making any but a rhetorical point. For the question at issue here is not whether any formal (or quasi-formal) relations exist between concepts and theories current during successive cross-sections of a science, or any algorithms for comparing their respective merits: it is, rather, what kinds of rational procedure are involved in the introduction, establishment, and improvement of scientific concepts, in cases where there is *no pretense* that formal, mathematical, or "logical" relations exist between concepts current during successive cross-sections, and where there may be no exact correspondence, either, between the empirical fields of application of earlier and later concepts. Once we recognize the nature of this problem for what it is, we shall be equally disinclined either to deny with the logical empiricists the existence of any "logic of discovery," or to attempt (with N. R. Hanson) to resurrect C. S. Peirce's "logic of abduction"—or, for that matter, to strike rhetorical gestures (with Paul Feyerabend) on behalf of *Wissenschaftstheoretische Anarchismus*, on the grounds that, once our basic theoretical concepts are questioned, any man is at liberty to think as he pleases. (On this point it is interesting to note how David Bohm, in the present symposium, even out-Feyerabends Feyerabend.) The question that has now to be faced—though, as Robert Causey rightly pointed out, not very much has yet been said about it—is in what the "rationality" of scientific procedure consists, when the conceptual problems and changes under consideration are essentially *non*mathematical and *in*formal.

If we are so short of answers to this question, some of us would argue, that is the price we are paying, in today's philosophy of science, for fifty years of domination by the Viennese logical empiricists and their associates. The time has now come to move beyond the static, "snapshot" pictures of scientific theory to which philosophers of science have confined themselves for so long, and to build up a "moving picture" of scientific problems and procedures, in terms of which the intellectual dynamics of conceptual change in the sciences will become intelligible and the nature of its "rationality" apparent.

As matters stand, we can do no more here than indicate the major problems to be covered in such a new account—problems that Putnam, Nickles, and Shapere have helped to define, but about which much more will have to be said. To begin with, the task is no longer the chimerical one, of devising formal algorithms for the testing of new scientific concepts and theories: it is, rather, to characterize, both in intellectual and in practical terms, the *explanatory missions* of the different sciences for the sake of which new scientific concepts and theories are introduced. Once we have done this, we can then inquire what kinds of "rational consideration" serve to establish some new concept, or hypothesis, *either* as a "possibility" that needs to be taken seriously, *or* as a "valid explanation" of the phenomena under discussion. The "rational considerations" which make a new concept a *possibility* will not necessarily lend themselves to analysis in the existing schemata of symbolic logic; yet the discussion of novel "possibilities" (like the discussion of methodological maxims and intellectual strategies) will now be quite as much the legitimate concern of philosophy as the discussion of established (or "justified") concepts, theories, and explanations. Within a dynamic account of natural science, accordingly, much that the logical empiricists dismissed as "psychology of discovery," and much that Tom Kuhn has claimed for "sociology of science," will have to be reclaimed as a proper field for philosophical inquiry.

To sum up: if many philosophers have difficulty today with the "traditional," or logical empiricist, approach to philosophy of science, this is for reasons of several fundamentally different kinds—some of them highly specific and technical; others much more general and philosophical. To begin with the minimal difficulties: there are those contemporary philosophers who accept that the logical structure of scientific theories is (or should be) axiomatic, but question the original Unified Science ideal of a single, unitary, and compulsory axiomatic form. Then, there are those who concede that scientific theories have an essentially logical structure, but question whether that structure is necessarily axiomatic. Again, there are those who allow that scientific theories have an intellectual structure, but question whether this structure is usefully construed on "logical" or "mathematical" models, and are much more concerned about the practical application of the resulting theories. Finally—and most radically—there are those who believe that it is no longer useful to discuss the concepts and hypotheses of the natural sciences in terms of "structure" or "system" at all, let alone in the static terms associated with terms like "logical structure" and "axiomatic system."

Correspondingly, how much of the traditional analysis any contemporary philosopher of science will retain depends on just how radically he is prepared to question the traditional approach. At one extreme, he may be content to stand by the axiomatic model, continuing to use the sybolism of mathematical logic to discuss all the different axiomatic forms that have found an application in one natural science or another. (This now seems to represent the minimum acceptable change in the classical, logical empiricist doctrine.) At the other extreme, he will argue that the very idea of presenting the intellectual content of a science as a "logical structure" involves an artificial abstraction: one that has a limited application to a few, untypically coherent sciences, like theoretical mechanics, and then only to single temporal cross-sections of an historically developing intellectual activity. And he will prefer, as a defense against this abstraction, to see questions about "the logical structure of scientific systems" replaced at the center of philosophy of science, by questions about "the rational development of scientific enterprises."

If philosophers of science do decide to move on from the traditional, static, or "snapshot" view of *theoretical calculi* to a more "kinematic" view of *scientific enterprise*, they will find themselves facing a whole new range of questions. They will have, for instance, to ask

> how, in any scientific enterprise, the failure of current concepts to fulfill all the *explanatory ambitions* of the science gives rise to *conceptual problems*;
>
> how the theoretical approach to current conceptual problems is governed by alternative *intellectual strategies*;
>
> how novel ideas are put into circulation, and rationally criticized, as *theoretical possibilities*;
>
> how alternative inquiries are then judged, as *empirically relevant* or *irrelevant* to the claims of these possibilities;
>
> how certain ways ahead from the current problem-situation are thus selected out as providing *acceptable explanations*;
>
> how, in due course, the revised concepts win a firm place in the current body of scientific thought, and become *established changes*;

and so, in short, how the concepts, and families of concepts, current in any one temporal cross-section of the science concerned *develop rationally* into those of successive later cross-sections. And all of these questions must be answered (as I. B. Cohen insisted at the symposium) not in abstract, formal terms, but in a way that pays proper historical attention to the explanatory ambitions directing the development of the various "scientific enterprises."

Once philosophy of science reaches that stage, however, it will no longer be concerned with the "traditional" view of scientific theories or "axiomatic calculus." Instead, a whole new tradition will have been born.

AFTERWORD—1977

Frederick Suppe

Introduction[1]

For over thirty years logical positivism (or logical empiricism as it later came to be called) exerted near total dominance over the philosophy of science. The Received View, together with its incorporated borrowings from earlier empiricisms, provided the basic framework for posing problems about the nature of scientific knowledge and also imposed constraints on what would count as appropriate solutions to these problems: Singular knowledge of directly observable phenomena was nonproblematic, whereas the remaining knowledge science purported to provide was problematic at best. According to the Received View, knowledge of phenomena that are not directly observable was possible only if theoretical-language assertions were verifiable or at least testable. The instrumentalist/realist controversies over the interpretation of theoretical-language assertions in effect were debates over whether verifiability or testability were sufficient conditions for obtaining knowledge about nondirectly observable phenomena. The connected problems of confirmation and induction focused on how one could exploit limited singular knowledge about directly observable phenomena so as to obtain general knowledge about directly observables and (if theories are construed realistically) about nondirectly observable phenomena as well. Induction was viewed as the only plausible means for confirming generalizations, and with few exceptions induction was construed probabilistically; thus the possibility of obtaining general scientific knowledge depended on the ability to develop probabilistic inductive logics which would be justified in a manner that begged no epistemic questions. Problems concerning intertheoretic reduction were construed as the question how, within the confines of the Received View, a later theory could incorporate earlier theories as special cases (see pp. 53–56 above). For years many positivists, especially those of an instrumentalist persuasion, had denied that theories

[1] I am grateful to my colleague Dudley Shapere for helpful advice and criticism of the draft version of this piece. Several portions of this essay incorporate research done under the support of NSF Grant GS-39677. Support for the writing of this essay was provided by a grant from the University of Maryland General Research Board. A number of the developments and theories presented in this essay were given brief and preliminary discussion in Suppe [1975].

could be explanatory; and Hempel's development of his covering-law models of explanation constituted an attempt to show that theories could be explanatory on the Received View.

Only in the 1960s did logical positivism's program for the philosophy of science come under serious intensive challenge. Although most aspects of positivistic philosophy of science were subjected to critical attack, by far the most fundamental and damaging were those aimed at the Received View. By the end of the decade these had been so successful that most philosophers of science had repudiated the Received View. The consequences of this rejection were far reaching and catastrophic, for in rejecting the Received View one also called into question the positivistic conception of what the main philosophical problems were about scientific knowledge and what constitutes acceptable solutions to those problems. Reinforced by sustained attacks on positivistic treatments of reduction, explanation, induction, and confirmation, the result was widespread confusion and disagreement among philosophers as to what the main problems in philosophy of science were, how they should be approached, and what would constitute acceptable solutions to them. The 1969 Illinois Symposium on the Structure of Scientific Theories (pp. 244–599 above) occurred in the midst of this disarray, and thus provides a particularly vivid account of a discipline in search of a new direction. The foregoing proceedings of that symposium provide a graphic portrait of the diversity of views prevalent then as to where philosophy of science ought to head; and they also reveal the extent to which such viewpoints were subjected to rational assessment and evaluation by debating the few pivotal theses and questions summarized on pages 234–235 above.

Much has happened to philosophy of science in the eight years since the symposium: (1) Positivistic philosophy of science has gone into near total eclipse; (2) the more extreme *Weltanschauungen* views of Feyerabend, Hanson, and Kuhn no longer are serious contenders for becoming a replacement analysis; and (3) philosophy of science is coalescing around a new movement or approach which espouses a hard-nosed metaphysical and epistemological realism that focuses much of its attention on "rationality in the growth of scientific knowledge" and proceeds by the examination of historical and contemporary examples of actual scientific practice. (4) To an extent that is only coming to be appreciated, these latter developments have profound implications for a number of basic issues in epistemology. This Afterword will detail these four main recent developments in subsequent sections, providing in the process a coherent perspective on, and guide to, present-day philosophy of science. Hopefully my long editorial introduction, the proceedings of the symposium, and this Afterword collectively will provide a helpful account not only of where philosophy of science is today, but also how it came to be there.

I. Swan Song for Positivism

Virtually all of the positivistic treatment of science has come under sustained attack since the 1950s. In addition to the successful attacks on the Received View already detailed (pp. 62–118), positivistic treatments of intertheoretic reduction, explanation, and (more recently) induction and confirmation have been challenged. Gradually the cumulative effect of these challenges has been that these other positivistic analyses are, or are coming to be, widely viewed as inadequate. Thus the last vestiges of positivistic philosophy of science are disappearing from the philosophical landscape—as is well testified to by Carl G. Hempel's recent public lectures where, continuing in the vein of his symposium paper in Session I above, he increasingly has been calling into question more and more of the positivistic program and the products of his earlier efforts on its behalf.

To the extent that attacks on these other aspects of the positivistic program have exerted an influence in shaping current philosophical work on theories and the activity of scientific theorizing, it is desirable that we give brief consideration to them.

A. Explanation and Intertheoretic Reduction

In 1948 Carl Hempel and Paul Oppenheim published their "Studies in the Logic of Explanation"[2] in which they argued that realistically construed theories and laws could provide causal explanations; their account came to be known as the *deductive-nomological (D-N) model of explanation*. In subsequent papers Hempel extended this account to cover statistical explanations as well via his *inductive-statistical (I-S) model of explanation*.[3] Collectively the D-N and I-S models constitute the *covering-law*

[2] Hempel and Oppenheim [1948], reprinted in Hempel [1965].

[3] His first attempt at I-S explanation, which was seriously defective, was in Hempel [1962]. A much improved version, which we shall confine our attention to, is found in Hempel [1965a].

model of explanation—so called because one explains an event by subsuming it under an appropriate law or laws that "covers" the occurrence of an event E. According to Hempel, an explanation of some event (whose description is known as the *explanandum*) consists of a suitable *argument* wherein the explanandum "correctly follows" from the premises (known as the *explanans*) of the argument. For D-N models this means the argument must be logically valid; and for I-S explanations this means the explanans must make the explanandum highly probable. Thus, covering law explanations take one of the following two forms where the L_i are appropriate laws and the C_i are factual conditions.[4]

$$\begin{array}{lccl} \text{(D-N)}\ L_1, \ldots, L_n & & \text{(I-S)}\ L_1, \ldots, L_n & \\ & \text{Explanans} & & \\ \underline{\quad C_1, \ldots, C_m \quad} & & \underline{\underline{\quad C_1, \ldots, C_m \quad}} & \text{[with high probability]} \\ \qquad E & \text{Explanandum} & \qquad E & \end{array}$$

The explanans must contain essentially at least one lawlike generalization—a universal one in the case of D-N explanations and a statistical one in the case of I-S ones; Hempel does not characterize what it is to be a universal or a statistical lawlike generalization.[5] Statements in the explanans must either be true or else highly confirmed.[6] For I-S explanations, in order to avoid certain paradoxes and ambiguities, a *requirement of maximal specificity* is imposed on the explanans which says, roughly, that "in formulating or appraising an I-S explanation, we should take into account all that information provided by . . . [the set of sentences accepted at the time] which is of potential *explanatory* relevance to the explanandum event; i.e., all pertinent statistical laws, and such particular facts as might be connected, by the statistical laws, with the explanandum event."[7]

On the D-N model, the explanandum E may be either a (description of an) event or a law or theory. In the former case, an explanation is an argument which, if it were advanced prior to the explanandum event E, would have enabled one to predict the occurrence of E; thus there is a

[4] In [1965a], Hempel allows a third form, *deductive statistical* explanations; I am construing them as a special version of D-N explanations wherein the explanandum is a probabilistic statement.

[5] An attempt, which proved defective, was made for universal ("causal") laws in Hempel and Oppenheim [1948]; no subsequent attempts were made by Hempel. For a discussion of some of the problems involved in characterizing universal lawlike generalizations, see pp. 36–45 above. In many respects, the problems are even greater for statistical lawlike generalizations, and virtually no progress has been made in characterizing this notion.

[6] Hempel and Oppenheim [1948] required that they be true; this condition was relaxed in Hempel [1965a].

[7] Hempel [1965a], pp. 400–401; italics his. Motivation for this condition is provided in discussion beginning on p. 394 of the same work.

symmetry between D-N explanation and prediction.[8] This symmetry thesis was the focus of early criticism of the D-N model, with numerous attempts being made to generate counterexamples to it. Toulmin pointed out that evolutionary theory could explain but thus far had yielded no significant predictions.[9] Scriven and others generated a number of cases where a body of information either enabled one to predict E but did not explain E, or else clearly would be accepted as explaining E but would not enable one to predict the occurrence of E.[10] Hempel later replied to these criticisms by (1) construing 'prediction' to include retrodiction so as to accommodate the evolution case; (2) dismissing a number of the putative counterexamples as inappropriate to the D-N model since the predictions were implicitly statistical or probabilistic; and (3) invoking a doctrine wherein it was maintained that intuitively satisfying "explanations" which did not afford predictions of E were only "explanation sketches" which, if fully spelled out, *would* enable predictions. Hempel did concede, however, that there may be predictions which do not afford explanations.[11] Little else was resolved in these disputes since they tended to involve Hempel and his critics arguing at cross-purposes—the critics being concerned with the pragmatics of actual explanations whereas Hempel was trying to provide an analysis of what a "logically ideal" explanation should be.

More damaging objections to the symmetry thesis were raised by Bromberger, who adduced a number of cases which clearly show the D-N model inadequate. It will suffice to present only one. Using geometric optics, we can form a law of coexistence which correlates the height of a flagpole, the angle of the sun to the horizon, and the length of the shadow cast by the flagpole. Using this law and initial conditions about the height of the flagpole and the sun's angle, we can explain the length of the shadow in accordance with the D-N model. However, if we take our initial conditions as being the length of the shadow and the sun's angle, using the law the D-N model allows us to (causally!) explain the height of the flagpole. But only the former case is a genuine explanation, the latter being spurious; since the D-N model sanctions both as genuine, the D-N model is defective. Bromberger concludes that the D-N model provides necessary but not sufficient conditions for causal explanations.[12] In a quite

[8] Hempel and Oppenheim [1948] maintained this symmetry also held when E was a law or theory. In his [1962], Scriven argues that the symmetry thesis makes no sense in this case. In [1965a] Hempel accepts the criticism and drops the claim.

[9] See Toulmin [1961], Ch. 2.

[10] See Scriven [1962] and [1958]. A comprehensive discussion of much of the debate over the symmetry thesis is found in Part I of Scheffler [1963].

[11] See Hempel [1965a], pp. 359–376, 423–424.

[12] See Bromberger [1966].

complicated analysis he then attempts to augment Hempel's D-N model so as to obtain sufficient conditions. Following a suggestion of Hempel's that explanations provide answers to explanation-seeking why questions,[13] Bromberger attempts to determine what additional conditions are required by employing erotetic logic to provide an analysis of what it is to be an answer to an explanation-requesting why question. Roughly his analysis is that laws (which he calls "general rules") are only descriptions of what will happen in idealized conditions, but they can be extended so as to specify those circumstances in which phenomena are not idealized and deviate from the idealized behavior described by the laws; such expansions of general rules he calls "abnormic laws."[14] Explanations are possible only when such deviations occur—where one answers the why question by citing those factors which, via the abnormic law, were responsible for deviations from the idealized behavior described by the general rule. While there is much merit to this view, Bromberger's development of it is fundamentally defective since it entails that all *ceteris paribus* conditions for a law or theory are finitely specifiable—which generally is not the case.[15] Thus Bromberger's attempt to salvage the D-N model fails, and counterexamples such as the flagpole case remain.

Key to both the D-N and the I-S models is the requirement that explanations must be *arguments* which yield, deductively or with high probability, the explanandum *E*. Salmon and Jeffrey have argued that it is possible to give perfectly good statistical explanations of highly improbable events—as when I use half-life laws to explain the emission of an electron from a radioactive substance, where the probability of an electron emission at the time is very low. Since Hempel's I-S model can explain only explanandum events *E* which are highly probable given the explanans, it is inadequate. To modify his I-S account to allow the explanation of low-

[13] Hempel [1965a], pp. 334–335.

[14] Toulmin [1961] defends a similar view (reading 'ideal of natural order' for 'law')—as does the *semantic conception of theories* (see pp. 221–230 above). However, these two approaches differ from Bromberger in that they do not suppose that the extensions to other circumstances are *finitely* specifiable, hence do not presume the existence of his abnormic laws.

[15] See Bromberger [1966] for his analysis of answers to why questions. When conjoined with his b- and p-predicament analysis of explanations given in an earlier paper and summarized on pp. 230–231 above, an account of answers to explanation-requesting why questions is obtained. The line of criticism just given has been indicated in my [1975], but has not been developed in detail in print; however, it follows straightforwardly from his definition of a (general) abnormic law. Other criticisms of Bromberger's program are found in Achinstein [1971], pp. 68–70.

Despite defects in Bromberger's approach, I am convinced that a number of his key insights (and similar ones by Toulmin—see note 14) are right-headed. Also the attempt to link problems of explanation with answers to various sorts of questions is, as shall be seen later (Section III-3-C), a promising move. A more recent attempt to analyze explanation via erotetic logic is found in Chap. V of Tondl [1973]; see also note 544 on p. 215 above.

probability E, one will have to give up the requirement that statistical explanations are "correct" arguments.[16] Construing causal explanations as limiting cases of statistical explanations, Salmon further concludes, on the basis of conditions of symmetry, that explanations are not arguments at all.[17] Rather, Salmon, Jeffrey, and Greeno suggest that "an explanation is an *assembly of facts statistically relevant* to the explanandum, *regardless of the degree of probability* that results";[18] causal explanations are just limiting cases where a probability of 1 is conferred on the explanandum event by the assembly of facts. Of course, not just *any* assembly of facts will qualify as a statistical explanation, and so the viability of this positive suggestion will depend on whether it can be developed into an adequate analysis; the central problem concerns adequately specifying the key notion of statistical relevance.[19] For our purposes, the important point is that Hempel's I-S model is defective, hence by implication so is his D-N model, since explanations are not arguments. It should be noted that Bromberger's attempt to construe causal explanations as answers to why questions tacitly concedes the same point. Thus the positivistic treatment of explanation seems to be fundamentally defective, and current work on explanation is attempting to explore and develop new approaches to understanding scientific explanation of events.[20]

When the explanandum in a D-N explanation is a law or theory, the explanandum law or theory is explained by the laws or theory in the explanans. It was seen on pages 54–55 above that this is equivalent to *reducing* the explanandum law or theory to the explanans laws or theory in accordance with Nagel's second form of theory-reduction. This positivistic treatment of *intertheoretic reduction* has been subject to considerable criticism. First, there are Feyerabend's criticisms discussed on pages 172–174 above. Although these criticisms are defective since they rest on Feyerabend's extreme and untenable doctrines on meaning and

[16] See Salmon [1966], pp. 7–10 and Jeffrey [1966].

[17] Salmon [1966], pp. 30, 37.

[18] *Ibid.*, p. 11. See also Jeffrey [1966] and Greeno [1966].

[19] Salmon has attempted to provide such a detailed development on pp. 29–88 of his [1966]. A number of features of his analysis have been challenged recently; see Lehman [1972], pp. 500–506; John Meixner's recent Ph.D. dissertation completed at Johns Hopkins University; and pp. 143–144 of my [1975]. Not too convincing replies to Lehman are found in Salmon [1973], pp. 397–402, and Koertge [1975]. Most of these objections involve challenges to the adequacy of Salmon's characterization of statistical relevance.

[20] In addition to the criticisms already indicated, further controversy over Hempel's "covering-law" model of explanations has surrounded Hempel's claims that, to the extent that they are genuinely explanatory, historical explanations will fit either his D-N or I-S "covering-law" models; an extended controversy over this issue, which involves subsidiary debates over the possibility of "singular historical laws" and so on, is found in works such as Hempel [1942], pp. 35–48 (reprinted on pp. 231–243 in Hempel [1965]; Dray [1957], [1964], and [1966]; Gardiner [1959]. As interesting as this controversy is, it is peripheral to our central themes here and so will not be detailed.

incommensurability, a legitimate objection lurks buried in his discussion—namely, that the reduced theory often is false whereas the reducing theory is true, which precludes the required sort of sound deduction of the former from the latter augmented by further definitions and hypotheses. Second, Schaffner, Sklar, and Nickles have argued that one finds in science a variety of different reduction phenomena, only some of which are captured by the positivistic analysis (namely, Nagel's elaboration and improvement of Kemeny and Oppenheim's basic analysis—see pp. 54–55 above). Sorts of reductions they display which are not captured include partial reductions, reductions which involve the ontological identification of parameters from different theories, and so on.[21] Third, a number of recent studies based on Shapere's notion of scientific domains (introduced in his symposium paper in Session VII above) and related notions indicate that reduction in science typically involves the combining of domains or relating different scientific fields in ways that are quite unlike the positivisitic treatment of reduction. Thus it is beginning to emerge that intertheoretic reduction, in at least many cases, is not between theories at all, but rather between scientific fields or domains. These developments will be discussed in Section III-B-3 below.[22] Whether there are any genuine cases of intertheoretic reduction in science which fit the positivistic account is increasingly suspect;[23] regardless, it now is clear that their account fails to capture or adequately represent the sorts of reductions science typically is concerned with. And contemporary philosophical work on reduction increasingly repudiates or ignores the positivistic treatment.

B. Induction and Confirmation

For logical positivism a central epistemic problem was showing how the observational procedures employed enabled science to provide general or theoretical knowledge: How is it possible that observing a finite number of instances of a generalization (law or theory) can enable one to know that the generalization holds in all the unexamined cases (of which there normally is a potential infinity)? The standard empiricist answer is "by induction"—which leads to the epistemological problem of showing that

[21] See Schaffner [1967], pp. 137–147; Sklar [1967], pp. 109–124; and Nickles [1973b], pp. 181–201. A number of articles have appeared recently which try to present analyses of various of these recently identified different types of reduction (for example, microreductions).

[22] See Nickles's symposium paper in Session VII above; Nancy Maull [Roth] [1974]; and Darden and Maull [Roth] [forthcoming]. Somewhat related to these developments is Schaffner [1970].

[23] My historian-of-science colleague Stephen Brush has tried, without success, to find

inductive inferences *do* provide knowledge. For empiricists such as Hume, this required showing that induction was capable of *proving* the truth of a generalization G on the basis of the examined instances of G. Hume argued that such "inductive proof" was possible only if the premises of the argument included some sort of known *induction hypothesis* (such as "the future will be like the past") to the effect that the examined instances of G are typical of all situations or events falling within the scope of G. Such an induction hypothesis itself was a contingent generalization, which in turn had to be justified. But, it could be justified only inductively, which required recourse to still another induction hypothesis, which in turn required inductive justification—and so on into an infinite regress. Thus Hume concluded there is no possible justification for induction and so general empirical knowledge is impossible.[24]

With the move to *physicalism* (see pp. 14–15 above and also pp. 45–47), logical positivism gave up the classical empiricist demand that knowledge must be justified (*proved*) with certainty: Observation-language assertions could be checked via intersubjective agreement among normal observers and so were extremely likely to be true. Thus direct-observation reports had a high probability of being true; more generally, the positivists counted as knowledge any true beliefs for which one had evidence that rendered the truth of the belief highly probable. Thus it no longer was necessary for induction to *prove* the truth of a generalization G; all that was required to obtain general knowledge G was that the available evidence about G's instances render it highly probable that G is true. Inductive inference thus becomes inferences from evidence about various *confirming instances* $g_1, \ldots, g_n$ of G to the conclusion that G *most probably* was true. But such inferences are valid only if one assumes a *probabilistic induction hypothesis* to the effect that the probability of G given $g_1, \ldots, g_n$ is high—that is, that $P(G, g_1 \& \ldots \& g_n) = r \approx 1$. Since a variety of different probabilistic induction hypotheses is possible, if probabilistic induction is to yield general knowledge, we must employ probabilistic induction hypotheses which we *know* to be true. Thus we face a probabilistic analogue to the traditional empiricist problem of justifying induction.

The problem of justifying probabilistic induction becomes intertwined with a related problem of interpreting the meaning of the conditional probability operator, $P(C, E) = r$. The standard Kolomogorov axiomatiza-

---

any source wherein the claimed paradigm instances of the positivistic account are shown actually to meet the conditions of either Nagel's or Kemeny and Oppenheim's analyses; see his paper forthcoming in Suppe and Asquith [1977] for further discussion of this point.

[24] See Hume [1902], Section IV. A large body of literature has emerged since Hume wrote the *Enquiry*, trying to get around his arguments. Some of the more influential recent attempts are discussed in Skyrms [1966], Chap. II. See also Section III-D below for related discussion.

tion of this operator is consistent with a number of different interpretations or models:[25] The *frequency-theory interpretation* construes $P(C, E) = r$ as being the ratio of C-type events among E-type events. More precisely, if $C(n)$ is the number of C-type events in n examinations or "trials" of E-type events, then

$$P(C, E) = r \text{ if and only if } \underset{n \to \infty}{\text{Limit}} \frac{C(n)}{n} = r.$$ [26]

The *logical theory of probability* construes $P(C, E) = r$ as asserting a logical or analytic relation between two statements, C and E, and a real number r.[27] The *subjective interpretation* construes $P(C, E) = r$ as being a measure of a person's willingness to bet in the face of uncertainty as determined by a rational set of beliefs and values.[28]

Probabilistic induction allows one to conclude that C on the basis of E only if $P(C, E) \approx 1$. Thus in determining whether we can legitimately infer C inductively from E we must determine the correct value r for $P(C, E)$. Doing so is particularly difficult on the frequency theory. For the available evidence we have about the occurrence of C-type events under circumstances E will concern a *finite* number of tests. That is, having made n trials we only will know that $C(n)/n = r'$. But $P(C, E)$ is defined in terms of an infinite sequence of E-type events or trials; and it can be shown that $C(n)/n = r'$ is compatible with $\underset{n \to \infty}{\text{Limit}}\ C(n)/n$ being any value r between 0 and 1. Thus to conclude anything about $P(C, E)$ from knowledge of $C(n)/n$ (for any n) requires recourse to some further induction hypothesis that enables us to extrapolate $P(C, E)$ from $C(n)/n$. Minimally

[25] For Kolomogorov's axiomatization, see [1950].

It is standard to distinguish *empirical probabilities* and *inductive probabilities*—the former being used to make factual assertions about the world and the latter to assess the extent to which a body of evidence supports or gives warrant to an hypothesis; typically philosophical theories of probability take one of these types as basic, analyze it, and then attempt to show how it can be used to characterize or analyze the other. For present purposes we need not be particularly concerned with these distinctions.

[26] See Reichenbach [1949] and Salmon [1966]. Closely related to frequency theories are propensity theories. Like the frequency theory, propensity theories see infinite sequences as playing an important role in defining empirical probabilities; but they view these sequences as possible histories of some underlying system, identifying empirical probabilities with "propensities" of the underlying systems—that is, as *dispositional attributes* of the system which produces its various possible histories. For present purposes, we need not distinguish propensity from frequency theories of probability. For a survey of various attempts to develop propensity theories, see Kyburg [1974], pp. 358–375.

[27] See Keynes [1921]; Carnap [1950], [1952], and [1963c]. As the following work indicates, in his later years Carnap moved increasingly toward a "subjective approach" to probability: Carnap and Jeffrey [1971].

[28] See de Finnetti [1972]; Good [1950]; Savage [1954]; Kyburg and Smokler [1964]; and Burks [1977]. Carnap's later work also should be consulted. Proponents of subjective interpretations have not been particularly concerned with providing the sorts of total or "global" justification or induction that Hume and later empiricists insisted on.

this induction hypothesis will have to assert that $C(n)/n = r'$ makes it highly probable that $P(C, E) = r$ (for some value r); but this induction hypothesis itself requires justification—which leads to an infinite regress analogous to Hume's. Various attempts have been made to get around this problem—such as Reichenbach's "self-corrective" procedure wherein one estimates $P(C, E)$ on the basis of $C(n)/n$ for some value of n, then samples more E, uses the additional information to correct one's estimate of $P(C, E)$, and so on. But it can be shown that this method fails, as it succumbs to more complicated regress arguments.[29]

On the logical theory, $P(C, E) = r$ can be determined a priori since the assertion is analytic. On Carnap's system probabilities are determined in terms of state descriptions and structure descriptions, where these descriptions are specified relative to some selected set of objects $a_1, \ldots, a_m$ and properties $P_1, \ldots, P_n$. A *state description* specifies for each of the objects $a_1, \ldots, a_m$ whether or not it possesses each of the properties $P_1, \ldots, P_n$. Since each of the objects a_i either possesses or lacks each of the P_j $(1 \leq j \leq n)$, we can construe the combined presence and absence of the P_j characteristic of a_i as a *complex property*; since there are n different P_j, there will be 2^n complex properties, $Q_1, \ldots, Q_{2^n}$, that could be characteristic of each of the a_i. A *structure description* specifies for each complex property Q_k $(1 \leq k \leq 2^n)$ how many of the $a_1, \ldots, a_m$ possess Q_k. It is possible for more than one state description to be characterized by the same structure description; all state descriptions characterized by the same structure description are said to be *isomorphic*. For example, let S_1 and S_2 be two different state descriptions such that interchanging all occurrences of a_1 and a_2 in S_1 yields S_2; then precisely the same number of objects $a_1, \ldots, a_m$ possess each of the Q_k in S_1 as do in S_2, and so S_1 and S_2 are isomorphic state descriptions. In terms of these notions *unconditional probabilities* are defined:

(*) Let S be a state description, let v be the number of structure descriptions, and let w be the number of state descriptions isomorphic to S. Then $P(S) = 1/(w \times v)$. For any statement C,

$P(C)$ = the sum of the probabilities of state descriptions in which C holds.

The conditional probability, $P(C, E)$, is defined in terms of unconditional probabilities:

$$P(C, E) = P(C \,\&\, E)/P(E).$$

When E describes a finite body of evidence and C is a statement, $P(C, E)$ is identified with the *degree of confirmation* of C provided by evidence E. Unfortunately, however, on this system, whenever C is a universal generalization having a potentially unlimited number of instances and E is

[29] See Burks [1977], Ch. 3, Sec. 4.

evidence about particular instances of C, $P(C, E) = 0$. Thus, on Carnap's system the probability of a generalization being true given available evidence about its instances always will be zero. Hence probabilistic induction is incapable of yielding general knowledge; neither empirical laws nor scientific theories are knowable. Still, all was not lost. For suppose our law is of the form $(x)\ (Fx \supset Hx)$; although $P((x)(Fx \supset Hx), E) = 0$ for any E, given suitable E Carnap's system does allow $P((Fa \supset Ha), E) = 1$ where a describes a particular situation. That is, although one cannot know that a law or theory is true, on Carnap's system one *can* have inductive knowledge that the *next* case examined will be in accordance with that law or generalization. And Carnap mounted a strong defense of these features of his system pointing out that no scientist in his right mind would be willing to bet that a law or theory held for all systems anywhere in the universe (that is, was true), but scientists regularly are willing to bet that the next case will be in accordance with that law or theory: "it now seems to me that the role of universal sentences in the inductive procedures of science has generally been overestimated. . . . The predictive inference is the most important inductive inference."[30] Even if Carnap is right on this, it still remains the fact that on his approach to inductive logic there are no justifiable a posteriori induction hypotheses which enable one to have general knowledge, so the probabilistic analogue to the traditional problem of justifying induction remains.

Unsatisfied with this outcome, Hintikka and his Finnish colleagues have attempted to modify Carnap's basic approach to inductive logic so as to obtain probability measures which assign nonzero probabilities to generalizations. Whereas Carnap's state descriptions are descriptive of individuals and their attributes, their approach (roughly) is to construe state descriptions as being about *kinds* of individuals. Whenever the potentially infinite instances of a law or theory involve only a finite number of kinds of individuals, an appropriate analogue to (*) generally will make $P(C, E) \neq 0$.[31] This approach has the effect, however, that $P(C, E) = r$ no longer can be construed as analytic, for the determination of $P(C, E) = r$ depends now on various contingent metaphysical truths about how the world parcels into kinds. Thus the problem of justifying probabilistic induction is reopened—now becoming the question how we justify these

[30] Carnap [1945], pp. 72–97 (reprinted on pp. 35–61 in Foster and Martin [1966], p. 52 in this reprinting). The Foster and Martin volume is a useful reprinting of a number of classic positivistic treatments of induction and related issues. A useful discussion of this aspect of Carnap's inductive logic, as well as various changes his inductive logic underwent over the years, is found in Lakatos [1968a].

[31] See Hintikka [1965], [1968], [1975], and [1976]; Hilpinen [1968]; Niiniluoto and Tuomela [1973]. A symposium on systems of inductive logic which can confer non-zero probabilities on generalizations (with I. Niiniluoto, S. Uchii, W. Harper, and P. Teller) is forthcoming in Asquith and Suppe [1977].

metaphysical assumptions which underlie probabilistic inductive inferences to generalizations. Using a subjective theory of inductive probability, Arthur Burks has been able to develop an inductive logic in which generalizations can receive nonzero probabilities. Just as Hintikka's approach involves metaphysical assumptions that in effect make only a finite number of cases relevant to the assessment of $P(C, E)$, so too does Burks's approach; in his case the metaphysical assumptions are that a near-determinism is characteristic of the world and that a Keynesean-like "principle of limited variation" holds. A number of other probabilistic inductive confirmation theories have been developed which confer nonzero probabilities on generalizations. Abner Shimony assumes that at any time there is some finite set of *seriously proposed hypotheses* which do not exhaust all logical possibilities, and to these he assigns finite probabilities regarding all the nonseriously proposed ones as having zero probability. From this he develops an explication of inductive probabilistic inference.[32] A related approach is developed by Harold Jeffreys.[33] And Mary Hesse argues that "though strictly universal generalizations may have an essential role in science, they do not have to be *confirmable*."[34] Rather, she maintains that most theories, particularly those which reasonably can be taken as true or known, have strictly finite domains of applicability; underlying this claim is a view which "reinterprets theories as expressions of analogies between their instances, in virtue of which analogical inferences can be made to other finite sets of instances," and such "inference (and also use of universal terms) can be analyzed without loss into inference from particulars to particulars, or at most to generalizations in finite, though large, domains."[35] Since inductively confirmable theories have only finite numbers of instances, there is no problem conferring nonzero probabilities upon them on the basis of finite evidence.[36] What is common to all these approaches to inductive logic is that in one way or another they make only a finite number of instances relevant to the

[32] Shimony [1970].

[33] Jeffreys [1957].

[34] Hesse [1974], p. 180; italics hers.

[35] *Ibid.*, p. 194.

[36] Although Hesse's *Structure of Scientific Inference* focuses on the role of inference in confirming theories, given her earlier views on the role of analogy in scientific discovery (for example, in her [1966]; see also pp. 97–102 above), one would expect that she would view her analogical account of inductive inference as also giving a model for the sorts of inferences involved in scientific discovery; thus far she has not attempted any such extension in a systematic way.

Closely related to Hesse's work on scientific reasoning, and on models, is the work of R. Harré in his [1960], [1964], [1970], and [1972]. Although his work does concern a number of contemporary issues (for example, growth of scientific knowledge) and is highly regarded in some quarters, it has not been particularly influential in shaping what I take to be the most important recent developments and trends in philosophy of science, and so, because of space limitations, his work will not be discussed.

testing of universal generalizations, and such means ultimately rest on various assumptions about the sorts of regularities characteristic of the world. Thus it would appear that one can obtain nonzero probability measures for generalizations only if one makes certain fairly strong metaphysical assumptions to the effect that certain patterns of regularity are characteristic of the world. Burks argues that such assumptions are pragmatic presuppositions of induction which can be established on neither a priori or empirical grounds.[37]

In his *Gambling with Truth*,[38] Isaac Levi distinguishes *global induction* and *local induction*. In local induction "justification is demanded only when the need for such justification arises in the context of specific inquiries."[39] Moreover,

> Supplying this justification requires an appeal to evidence, which will include observation reports and theoretical assumptions, as well as much of the apparatus of logic and mathematics. In short, evidence will consist of the investigator's findings and beliefs that are relevant to the problem at hand and are not likely to be questioned by any participant in the inquiry or by anyone who is qualified to evaluate its results. Evidence is not ruled out as illegitimate solely because of the possibility that in some future inquiry it may be shown to be false. . . . Global justification is more demanding. Following Descartes, the globalist wishes to show that *all* his beliefs (at least those he holds at a given time) are justified.[40]

Initially logical positivism was concerned with global induction: Reichenbach's "self-corrective" method and Carnap's analytic inductive method were attempts to prove the truth of probabilistic induction hypotheses which would enable us to obtain general knowledge; both failed to do this. More recent work in inductive logic has given up the attempt to develop a more global inductive logic. The approaches of the Hintikka school, Burks, and others mentioned above strictly speaking are dealing with local induction, showing how, given certain deeply held metaphysical presuppositions or beliefs, one can justify generalizations inductively; they do not attempt to establish that these contingent metaphysical generalizations are themselves most probably true. Rather they are defended as *presuppositions* of induction. Other recent work on inductive logic is concerned with even more local induction—focusing on the inductive justification or confirmation of laws and theories relative to large bodies of information—roughly what Shapere calls scientific domains and

[37] Burks [1977], Chap. 10; his presupposition theory of induction is developed in Chapters 4, 5, and 8–10.

[38] Levi [1967].

[39] *Ibid.*, p. 3.

[40] *Ibid.*, p. 4; italics added. See also Adler [1976]. Adler's perspective is similar to that adopted in the discussion which follows.

related background information[41]—or on inductive decision procedures for deciding what hypotheses to accept or reject on the basis of such accepted information. Examples of such work on local induction include Levi's *Gambling with Truth*, portions of Mary Hesse's analogical theory of inductive inference discussed above, and work on "testing models of scientific inference."[42] Characteristic of these approaches to local induction is a focus on the development of probabilistic or statistical theories for determining when to rationally accept or reject generalized hypotheses such as laws or theories.

In short, although positivistic work on induction and confirmation continues to exert an influence on work in inductive logic, the focus of such work today is quite different from that of the positivists. Whereas they viewed the problem of induction and confirmation as developing a global theory of induction, present-day focus is on developing theories of (more or less) local induction—which is quite a different problem than logical positivism was concerned with. Today even the importance of global induction is coming to be seriously challenged. In addition to the long-standing Popperian challenge, based on Popper's denial that generalizations can receive nonzero probabilities and so the acceptance and rejection of laws and theories must be done on nonprobabilistic grounds,[43] recent work on observation and epistemology is questioning whether inductive confirmation plays any role in obtaining general scientific knowledge (see Section III-D below). Work on the growth of scientific knowledge indicates that the acceptance or rejection of general hypotheses *as true* plays a relatively minor role in the rational evaluation of hypotheses—science being concerned for the most part with evaluating, for example, whether an hypothesis is *sufficiently promising* to warrant further investigation, development, and so on (see Sections III-B-4, and especially III-D below). In short, philosophy of science increasingly is coming to question the importance of inductive confirmation to the ongoing epistemic enterprise of science, thus relegating even issues of local induction to a relatively minor role in scientific reasoning and further repudiating the central importance ascribed to induction and confirmation by the positivistic program.[44]

[41] See his symposium paper in Session VII above as well as the discussion in Section III-B-3 below.

[42] For example, Giere [1977].

[43] Popper's views on this are sorted out, given detailed exposition, and critically discussed in Lakatos [1968a], Pt. III. Popper develops these views at various places in his [1959] and [1965]. Feyerabend and Kuhn are fellow travelers on this point.

[44] In discussing induction and confirmation, I have ignored Hempel's attempt to develop a *qualitative* notion of confirmation in his [1945a], pp. 1–26, 97–121 (reprinted in his [1965]). Although this attempt generated a lot of critical discussion and tends to be discussed heavily in philosophy of science courses, it seems to me a relatively unimportant episode in positivis-

To conclude, virtually all of the positivistic program for philosophy of science has been repudiated by contemporary philosophy of science. The Received View has been rejected, as have its treatments of explanation and reduction. Its developments in inductive logic and confirmation theory continue to be influential, but the focus of such work has shifted from a positivistic-like concern with global induction to the development of probabilistic treatments of local induction. Also, the importance of induction and confirmation is coming to be sharply downgraded in contemporary philosophical thinking about the scientific enterprise and the knowledge it provides. Positivism today truly belongs to the history of the philosophy of science, and its influence is that of a movement historically important in shaping the landscape of a much-changed contemporary philosophy of science.

---

tic treatments of confirmation, and so I have chosen to ignore it here. A good critical discussion of it is found in Chapter 4 of Lambert and Brittan, Jr. [1970]; a revised 2nd ed. is being issued by Dickenson Publishing Co.

In his [1955], Nelson Goodman focuses on the systematic interconnections between laws and theories, counterfactuals, induction and confirmation—the focus of his discussion being to introduce a "new riddle of induction" which he claims can be resolved so as to justify induction and lay a basis for noncircular characterizations of laws and counterfactuals. Although his treatment is of considerable interest, and has generated a substantial body of critical literature in response, his "solution" to the "new riddle of induction" is not widely accepted. Moreover, his work is not particularly central to contemporary work on local induction and so it will not be discussed in detail here.

It will be recalled from pp. 36–45 above that Goodman earlier had argued that the problem of induction was intimately intertwined with related problems of analyzing the notions of scientific laws and counterfactual conditionals, the implication being that an independent analysis or solution of any one problem would lay a foundation for resolving the others. We indicated there that various attempts had been made to use modal logic to analyze counterfactual conditionals. We should mention briefly two more recent developments along this line: Lewis [1973] presents a particularly sophisticated modal logic of counterfactual and other subjunctive conditionals, which improves on the treatment in R. Stalnaker [1968]. And in his [1977], Arthur Burks not only develops a modal logic of subjunctive conditionals, but also incorporates it into his inductive logic in such a way that universal generalizations involving the causal modalities can receive non-zero probabilities on the basis of finite evidence. Lewis's and Burks's modal logics employ two quite different approaches in their development.

II. The Waning of the *Weltanschauungen* Views

As previously indicated (see pp. 125–126 above), an important factor leading to the demise of the Received View and the positivistic program in the philosophy of science was the challenge provided by the newly emerging *Weltanschauungen* analyses of Feyerabend, Hanson, Kuhn, and others.[45] For a while it was held that a viable replacement for positivistic philosophy of science would be some sort of *Weltanschauungen* analysis. Gradually, however, key tenets of these various *Weltanschauungen* analyses came under increasingly heavy attack by a number of authors including Achinstein, Shapere, and Scheffler. (See pp. 191–221, as well as pp. 135–188 *passim*, above). By the time of the symposium, these attacks had been sufficiently effective that many philosophers of science were questioning the very tenability of these *Weltanschauungen* approaches. Such doubts occupy a prominent place in a number of the papers, and especially the discussions, at the symposium. Since the symposium these doubts have increased to the point that the *Weltanschauungen* analyses are not widely viewed as serious contenders for a viable philosophy of science. Contemporary philosophy of science, although strongly influenced by these *Weltanschauungen* views, has gone beyond them and is heading in new directions. The *Weltanschauungen* views, in a word,

[45] Toulmin's work also was influential. At the time I wrote the introduction to this volume, his most recent work (for example [1961] and [1959], pp. 1–29, 203–227) clearly espoused a moderate *Weltanschauungen* analysis which avoided a number of the objections raised against the more extreme versions advocated by Hanson and especially Bohm, Kuhn, and Feyerabend. But his *Weltanschauungen* tendencies are defective in other ways; see Shapere [1960], pp. 376–385. His more recent work (discussed in Section III-B-2 below) appears to be an attempt to retreat from, and disassociate himself from, the *Weltanschauungen* perspective. In discussing this later work, it is more natural to group him with Lakatos and Shapere as I do below. Thus in this section I intend to exclude him from consideration, confining my attention to the more *extreme Weltanschauungen* analyses of Feyerabend, Hanson, and Kuhn. Bohm's work is not discussed since I am unaware of any recent elaborations or further development of his philosophical views that warrant consideration here.

today are *passé*, although some of their authors continue to develop them and they continue to be much discussed in the philosophical literature. This section examines what has happened to the *Weltanschauungen* views during this period of their declining influence and importance. A particular focus will be on those aspects of the story which have influenced contemporary approaches to the growth of scientific knowledge and the emergence of scientific realism as what is becoming the dominant philosophical approach to understanding science.

A. Hanson

Norwood Russell Hanson died in 1967 at the age of forty-three and so was denied the opportunity to clarify and further develop his views. A number of works have been published posthumously, including two textbooks,[46] a collection of essays,[47] a collection of fragments,[48] and several essays in other volumes.[49] Much of these works is concerned with replowing familiar Hansonian ground—an amplified version of his arguments against sense data theories of perception,[50] his views on theories, interpretation, and the theory-ladenness of observation,[51] and on retroduction and the logic of discovery,[52] and so forth. Although sometimes helpful in clarifying or illustrating his position, these writings do not significantly advance his views beyond the earlier versions summarized and discussed above (pp. 151–166). One area where substantial "new material" is found is that of scientific explanation. Expanding his earlier ideas about the connection between conceptual organization and causality (see pp. 159–161 above), Hanson attempts to improve on the Hempelian account of explanation. In a projected history of planetary theory, he intended to argue on historical grounds that only briefly in the seventeenth century does one find symmetry between prediction and explanation such as is required by Hempel's D-N model. More typical are the Greek cosmologists whose theories provided explanations without predictions and Ptolemy's theory which afforded predictions without explanations.[53] Moreover, it is possible to

[46] Hanson [1971] and [1969].
[47] Hanson [1971a].
[48] Hanson [1973].
[49] These include Hanson [1967], [1969a], and [1970]. It should be noted that the last essay is a different work than the essay of the same title found both in Hanson [1971a] and in Colodny [1970].
[50] Hanson [1969], pp. 69–198.
[51] For example, Hanson [1967] and [1969a].
[52] For example, Hanson [1971a], pp. 288–300.
[53] Hanson [1973]; see also pp. 103–126 in Hanson [1971a].

satisfy the conditions for Hempelian D-N explanations without thereby obtaining any *understanding* of the phenomena that supposedly has been explained. Essential to scientific explanation is "rationally comprehending the 'go' of things,"[54] and so Hempel's model is deficient.

> What can be wrong with our seeking examples of scientific theory which are capable both of explaining *á la* Hempel and of providing understanding and illumination of the nature of the phenomena in question? Even if distinguishable, the two are genuinely worthwhile objectives for scientific enquiry; they are wholly compatible. And, it may be noted, the second is unattainable without the first. So although Hempel's account of scientific explanation may not be sufficient, it seems to be necessary. Ontological insight, unstructured by quantitatively precise argument and analysis, is mere speculation at best, and navel-contemplatory twaddle at worst.[55]

Thus Hanson's view appears to be that a scientific explanation is a D-N covering-law explanation which conceptually organizes the phenomena in such a way as to make sense of, or render comprehensible, the nature of the phenomena. Unfortunately, Hanson does not provide anything in the way of a precise characterization of what it is to make sense of, or render comprehensible, the nature of a phenomenon, and so his account is at best suggestive. Furthermore, it is hard to square the passage just quoted with his view that, for example, Greek cosmological theories were explanatory without being predictive. To accept Hempel's D-N covering-law model as specifying necessary conditions for explanation entails that explaining *E* implies the predictability of *E*. One possible resolution, suggested but not confirmed by various passages,[56] is that Hanson intended the quoted passage to apply to just causal explanations, and that he would allow the existence, if not the legitimacy of, other noncausal modes of "explanation" as well—including Greek cosmological theories, anatomical drawings of the heart, and so on.

Thus, although the Hansonian corpus has been much expanded by posthumous publication, relatively little in the way of new doctrines or views has emerged. Furthermore, other than the publication of Willard Humphrey's *Anomalies and Scientific Theories*,[57] little attempt has been made by others to approach the philosophy of science from within the general perspective provided by Hanson's position. We will see, however, that Hanson has exerted some influence on attempts to deal with problems on the growth of scientific knowledge from a different perspective (see note 213 below).

[54] Hanson [1971], p. 45.

[55] *Ibid.* Judging from discussion preceding this passage, I conjecture that Hanson is discussing Hempel's D-N model, and does not intend this to apply to Hempel's I-S model.

[56] See, for example, *ibid.*, p. 50.

[57] Humphreys [1968].

B. Feyerabend and Kuhn

Kuhn views science as consisting of episodes of normal science punctuated by occasional scientific revolutions. During normal science, a scientific community sharing the same disciplinary matrix or theory focuses its attention on further articulating the theory and solving various puzzles raised by it. Occasionally the puzzles concerning the theory prove to be intractable theoretical anomalies which cause the scientific community to doubt the theory and consider alternatives to it, thus starting a scientific revolution. The revolutionary proliferation of alternative theories continues until one of them emerges as victor, and a new scientific community coalesces around, and gives allegiance to, that theory—at which time normal science reemerges. Kuhn maintains not only that this pattern regularly is exemplified in the history of science, but also that ideally science *ought* to proceed in this manner. Feyerabend deplores the dogmatism inherent in Kuhn's normal science—doubting whether normal science actually occurs in science, but maintaining that even if it does, it should not. Rather he maintains that science *ought* to proceed via the proliferation of a variety of theories which are incompatible with each other. Despite the fact that Kuhn and Feyerabend differ radically on how science does and ought to proceed, underlying their positions are remarkably similar epistemologies—although recent changes in Kuhn's position (see below) have resulted in some divergence.

Although other aspects of their views on science have been subjected to criticism, the bulk of attack has been aimed at the epistemological positions that underly their views, the charges being that their positions lead to an extreme subjective idealism which is incompatible with the objectivity of science; that their doctrines on meaning, incommensurability, and the theory-ladenness of observation make impossible any rational basis for comparing the empirical adequacy of competing theories; and that it debases knowledge into the joint prejudices of the members of a scientific discipline who accept the same theory.[58] Other than publishing a few rejoinders in which he concedes little,[59] Feyerabend generally has ignored and refused to take seriously these criticisms, preferring instead to develop increasingly extreme versions of his general views. This attitude, coupled with the widely held perception that a number of the objections raised are serious and even devastating, has seriously eroded the credibil-

[58] Kuhn's and Feyerabend's positions (as of the time of the symposium), as well as some of the objections raised against them, are summarized on pp. 135–151 and 170–180 above; other criticisms are discussed and developed on pp. 191–221.

[59] See Feyerabend [1965], pp. 266–274, and [1965b].

ity of Feyerabend's work. In contrast, Kuhn has taken seriously some of the objections raised against his view and has attempted to modify his position to escape them. The net effect of these modifications has been that he has given up much of what was most distinctive, original, and exciting about his position—retreating to a position that increasingly resembles the very positivism he earlier was concerned to overthrow. Thus, in both the case of Feyerabend and of Kuhn, their reactions to the critical attacks leveled against their earlier work have played a significant part in the declining influence of their work during the 1970s. This section discusses their responses to criticism and the changes their views have undergone since the symposium, in the process attempting to provide an overall assessment of their work and its limited influence on contemporary philosophy of science.

There is little point in speculating about why Feyerabend has chosen the counterproductive practice of largely ignoring major criticisms of his views—a practice which is especially perplexing since, as we now will argue, a case can be made that some (but not all) of these criticisms rest on misinterpretations of his basic epistemological views—views which he developed in one of his early papers, "An Attempt at a Realistic Interpretation of Experience,"[60] and has continued to assume tacitly and without significant change in his subsequent writings. In summary, the view he develops there is as follows: Although he rejects the positivistic observational/theoretical distinction, sense can be made of an observation language. The observation language for a class *C* of observers will be, roughly, those sentences which members of *C* are *caused* to accept or reject in response to sensory phenomena, where there is a consensus among the members of *C* whether to accept or reject the sentence.[61] Such assent or dissent is to *uninterpreted sentences*, not statements, and so such assent or dissent leaves open the question of the interpretation of sentences in the observation language and is compatible with different members of *C* assigning different interpretations to the same sentences.[62] Moreover, experience can play no decisive role in determining which interpretations are correct, if by correctness of interpretation one means that the interpreted sentences "fit" or "correspond with" the way the world is.[63] Since experience cannot determine the correctness of interpretations of observation-language sentences, it cannot supply those interpretations either. Rather, "the interpretation of an observation-

[60] Feyerabend [1958], pp. 143–170. The account which follows is defended in far greater detail in my [forthcoming c].

[61] Feyerabend [1958], pp. 144–145.

[62] *Ibid.*, pp. 145–146.

[63] *Ibid.*, Secs. 4, 5.

language is determined by the theories which we use to explain what we observe, and it changes as soon as those theories change."[64] Since only interpreted sentences (statements) can be true or false in any correspondence sense, and members of C can accept and reject the same body of observation sentences while assigning different interpretations to them, on Feyerabend's view there is no connection between truth and the acceptance of observation sentences—one is caused to accept observation sentences which, as the observer interprets them, may be true or false. And since it is impossible to ascertain experientially the truth or falsity of observation sentences, a correspondence notion of truth—"fitting the world"—can bear no epistemic burden.

Feyerabend's extreme doctrines on meaning are such that no terms common to different global theories will have the same meanings, and all statements of a theory are analytic.[65] Thus all of the observation-language implications of the theory, as interpreted by the theory, will be analytically true. But there is no automatic correlation between the class of observation sentences rendered analytically true by the theory and the class of observation sentences which one is caused to assent to. This allows the possibility that an observer may be caused to reject an observation-sentence which, as interpreted by the theory he subscribes to, is analytically true; or he may be caused to accept an observation sentence which, as interpreted, is analytically false. Thus there can be a clash between theory and observation—though Feyerabend's insistence on referring to such clashes as "falsification of a theory" is highly misleading.

In much the same manner, proponents of different theories can "compare the relative merits" of their respective theories: If S_1 holds T_1 and S_2 holds T_2, where T_1 entails observation sentence O and T_2 entails not-O, and if both S_1 and S_2 are caused to accept observation sentence O, then they can agree that T_1 has passed an observational test that T_2 fails. Since S_1 and S_2 can agree on the acceptance of the observation sentence O despite the fact that, interpreting it via T_1 and T_2 respectively, they mean different things by O, it is possible for them to "debate" and "compare" the observational adequacy of T_1 and T_2 despite the incommensurability of these two theories.

If it is granted that the foregoing is an accurate representation of Feyerabend's basic epistemological views, it follows that some of the criticisms summarized on pages 179–180 and 200–202 above misfire. First, in attempting to show defective Feyerabend's doctrines on meaning and incommensurability, several authors have charged that they make the

[64] *Ibid.*, p. 163; italicized in the original.

[65] See Feyerabend [1965a], pp. 180, 214, and 227, note 19. His meaning doctrines are discussed on pp. 171–174, 176, 199, and 200 above.

testing of theories circular. On *some* versions of this criticism (for example, Achinstein's which is presented as the fifth objection on pp. 201–202 above), it is assumed tacitly that the observation sentences are interpreted—that is, are statements. Such arguments misinterpret Feyerabend's position and do not preclude the sort of conflict between theory and observation that has just been considered. However, such conflicts must take the form of rejecting analytically true assertions on the basis of experience under circumstances where one *knows* the rejected assertion is a logical consequence of the theory; anyone who did this while accepting Feyerabend's meaning doctrines and their consequences would have to engage in the *highly irrational behavior* of rejecting *on the basis of experience* a proposition which he *knew* to be analytically true or else accepting *on the basis of experience* a proposition which he *knew* to be analytically false. Second, on pages 178–179 it was noted that Feyerabend's doctrines on the proliferation and testing of theories require the comparative testing of incommensurable theories, and that he proposed three procedures for such comparative evaluation; objections were raised to all three. The objection to the third procedure (p. 179) tacitly presupposed that observation reports would have to be statements (interpreted sentences), the charge being that on this procedure testing the competing theories' predictions would require there to be an observation report that assigned the same meanings to its constituent terms as do the competing theories—which is precluded since via his meaning doctrines two global theories must assign different meanings to each term they have in common. This objection clearly misfires on Feyerabend's position since advocates of the two theories can possess the same stock of observation-language (uninterpreted) sentences and be caused to accept or reject the same observation sentences by common experiences, despite the fact they interpret them differently. The fact that Feyerabend himself has maintained that the sort of comparability his view necessitates does not require that the predictions of the two theories be compared against an observation *statement* that is neutral with respect to the two theories[66] supports the interpretation of Feyerabend being advanced here. Third, the charge that "subjective" views such as Feyerabend's lead to an extravagant subjective idealism clearly is unwarranted; such charges would be warranted *if* Feyerabend were committed to a correspondence notion of truth, which he is not. Rather Feyerabend maintains a gratuitous metaphysical realism which plays no role whatsoever in his epistemology

[66] See the works cited in note 59 above. The considerations raised here also apply to the latter part of the similar third objection to Feyerabend's meaning doctrines argued on p. 201 above. Although they do not affect the second objection there, it does serve to point out the very idiosyncratic notions of 'falsification,' 'contradiction,' 'disagreement between theories,' and so forth, Feyerabend employs.

other than presumably being involved in the causal processes terminating in the acceptance or rejection of observation sentences.[67]

Although the interpretation of Feyerabend's views presented above enables him to escape certain lines of criticism which erroneously construe observation sentences as *statements*, it is possible to raise much the same objections when observation reports are uninterpreted sentences. For the account of comparability attributed to him above presupposes that persons who subscribe to different, incommensurable, theories possess the same stock of sentences—or, as Feyerabend puts it, have "an inbuilt syntactic machinery that *imitates* (but does not describe) certain features of our experience."[68] This amounts to granting him that no interpretation is involved in the syntactic decomposition of language into sentences, phonemes, and so on. In effect, this is to grant Feyerabend that, although there is no neutral "interpreted" observation language, there is a *common* syntactical language that can be presupposed in the comparison of theories. Although this supposition is weaker than the positivist's "neutral observation language," it is not that much weaker. And this not only is to concede to the positivist most of what Feyerabend wants to take back, but also is incompatible with his general doctrines on incommensurability.[69]

In addition, there are a number of other weighty objections that can be raised against Feyerabend's position: *First*, it has been seen that his view makes the rejection of a global theory on the basis of observation a fundamentally irrational process. *Second*, part of that irrationality stems from the fact that his doctrines on the theory-ladenness of meaning entail that theories are analytically true. This *prima facie* is an unacceptable consequence, and in the absence of any good reasons why we should accept his meaning doctrines, it is not incumbent upon us to accept either the consequence that theories are analytically true or the resulting irrational process for rejecting theories on the basis of observation. *Third*, his realism is an empty one wherein the correspondence of a theory with reality plays no role in its acceptability or truth; finding out how the world is ceases to become a legitimate aim or concern of science on his view. *Fourth*, his position commits him to a view of "knowledge" where the truth of ϕ has no bearing on whether one knows that ϕ; knowledge yields

[67] For charges that the "subjective" views lead to such an idealism, see Scheffler [1967], p. 19. Feyerabend espouses his metaphysical realism in [1958]. The interpretation of Feyerabend just given is developed and defended at length in Section 2 of my "Kuhn's and Feyerabend's Relativisms" [forthcoming c].

[68] Feyerabend [1970b], pp. 214–215.

[69] For an extended discussion of these points, see pp. 59–62 of Shapere [1966]. On those pages Shapere presents devastating criticisms of Feyerabend's views which construe observation reports as uninterpreted sentences, showing the incompatibility of the supposition of the common syntactic language with Feyerabend's incommensurability doctrines.

to mere belief, and Feyerabend capitulates totally to the skeptic.[70] *Fifth*, it becomes very unclear what Feyerabend's motives are for insisting that the proliferation of mutually inconsistent theories is preferable to the employment of a single set of theories insisted on by radical empiricism (see p. 171 above). Popper's insistence on theory proliferation had as its aim discovering truths about the world (see p. 169); but Feyerabend has expelled truth from science and epistemology, and so this cannot be his motive. Perhaps his point is only that science is "more fun" if done his way.[71] Collectively, these objections are weighty indeed, displaying how bizarre, implausible, and unattractive is Feyerabend's view of science.[72]

Although Feyerabend has changed certain of his views in recent writings,[73] these modifications do little to make his position more acceptable. In earlier versions of his position, Feyerabend assumed that any conflict between a theory's predictions and an accepted observation statement falsified the theory.[74] Given this assumption it was plausible to suppose (with Popper) that proliferation and falsification would converge on the truth. But, as has been seen, this assumption is incompatible with Feyerabend's basic epistemology: On his view, a conflict between theoretical prediction and accepted observation sentence is compatible with either the theory or the accepted observation sentence (as interpreted by the theory) being false. It follows that the failure of a theoretical prediction to cohere with observation does not necessarily falsify the theory on Feyerabend's view. Further, it follows that the practice of proliferating theories, testing them, and rejecting those which fail to cohere with observation need not converge on an accepted body of true theories.

Feyerabend eventually came to realize this, and in "Against Method: Outline of an Anarchistic Theory of Knowledge," he attempts to rework his position to rectify these shortcomings. Basically his approach is to dip into the history of science to find cases where people successfully maintained theories in the face of "disconfirming observational tests," using

[70] For more on this point, see my "Kuhn's and Feyerabend's Relativisms," where I argue that Feyerabend is the ultimate eighteenth century empiricist—carrying Hume's skeptical program to its logical limits by denying even the possibility of knowledge of sensory experience.

[71] See Feyerabend [1970a], especially p. 229. Below we will discuss briefly a change in his position which apparently supplies another's motive.

[72] For additional criticisms of Feyerabend views, consult the works by Achinstein, Scheffler, and Shapere, cited in the introduction to this volume, as well as Hesse [1963], pp. 98–108; Kordig [1970], pp. 399–404; Giedymin (1971), pp. 28–48; Suppe, "Kuhn's and Feyerabend's Relativisms" [forthcoming c]; and Townsend [1971]. There are, of course, other critical discussions.

[73] For example, Feyerabend [1965a], [1970], and [1969].

[74] See pp. 29–30 of his [1962].

these to argue that science is better off if one has the options of resolving conflicts between theory and observation by rejecting the theory or by rejecting the observation.[75] Thus, "there is not a single [methodological] rule, however plausible, and however firmly grounded in epistemology, that is not violated at some time or other."[76] "[T]here is only one [methodological] principle that can be defended under all circumstances, and in all stages of human development. It is the principle: *anything goes*."[77] This methodological rule leads him to augment his proliferation doctrines with a *principle of counterinduction*.

> Let us apply this . . . to the rule that "experience," or "the facts," or "experimental results" . . . measure the success of a theory, so that agreement between the theory and "the data" is regarded as favoring the theory (or as leaving the situation unchanged), while disagreement endangers or perhaps even eliminates. This rule is an essential part of all theories of induction, including even some theories of corroboration. Taking the opposite view, I suggest introducing, elaborating, and propagating hypotheses which are inconsistent either with well-established *theories* or with well-established *facts*. Or, as I shall express myself: *I suggest proceeding counterinductively in addition to proceeding inductively*.[78]

Moreover, if resort to *ad hoc* hypotheses is necessary to persist in maintaining a theory which conflicts with observation, Feyerabend maintains such resort is wholly legitimate.[79]

These changes clearly eliminate an inconsistency in his earlier views. But what is the epistemological point of such counterinductive proliferation of theories and facts? Feyerabend sees it as exemplifying Hegel's dialectical method, and accepting that method he concludes that counterinductive proliferation of theories ultimately must lead to knowledge and truth.

> Knowledge is part of nature and is subjected to its general laws. The laws of dialectic apply. . . . According to these general laws, every object participates in every other object and tries to change into its negation. . . . To understand the process of negation we must attend to those other elements which are fluid, about to turn into their opposites, and *which may, therefore, bring about knowledge and truth, "the identity of thing and concept."* . . . the identity itself cannot be achieved mechanically, i.e., by arresting some aspect of reality and fiddling about with the remaining aspects, or theories, until agreement is achieved. . . . We must rather proceed dialectically, i.e. by an *interaction* of concept and fact (observation, experiment, basic state-

[75] The historical cases are presented in Feyerabend [1970] and [1965a]. Severe criticisms of his historical analyses are given on pp. 34–41 of McMullin [1970].

[76] Feyerabend [1970], p. 22.

[77] *Ibid.*, p. 26; italics his.

[78] *Ibid.*, p. 26; italics his.

[79] *Ibid.*, pp. 63–69.

> ment, etc.) that affects *both* elements. The lesson for methodology is, however, this: Do not work with stable concepts. Do not eliminate counterinduction. Do not be seduced into thinking that you have at last found the correct description of "the facts" when all that has happened is that some new categories have been adapted to some older forms of thought, which are so familiar that we take their outlines to be the outlines of the world itself.[80]

What are we to make of these changes in Feyerabend's position? *First*, other than possibly involving a rejection of his gratuitous metaphysical realism in favor of a subjective idealism, these changes not only are compatible with, but also appear to presuppose, his previous epistemological views outlined above.[81] Thus all of our previous objections to Feyerabend's view of science stand.[82] *Second*, Hegel never made a convincing case that his dialectical process would lead man into knowledge of, or becoming one with, the Absolute; and Hegel's dialectic involved much more structure for resolving "contradictions" than Feyerabend's method of proliferation and counterinduction provides. Thus, Feyerabend's assumption that his anarchistic theory of knowledge will lead to, or converge on, truth and knowledge is doubly unconvincing. In short, other than perhaps to the most fanatical Hegelian, Feyerabend's philosophy of science has little to recommend itself and is losing whatever importance and influence it once had within philosophy of science.

Unlike Feyerabend, Thomas Kuhn publicly has taken criticisms of his views seriously and has attempted to address himself to them in a number of recent articles beginning with his symposium contribution in Session VI above.[83] Often Kuhn's responses take the form that his critics have misinterpreted him or else that, when in the critic's opinion particularly significant and telling objections are raised, he is incapable of seeing where his critics think there are disagreements between them other than in nuances; and he has been selective in which criticisms he chooses to address.[84] However, he has taken a number of the many criticisms of his position seriously and has made conscientious attempts to either clarify or

[80] *Ibid.*, p. 36; some italics added.

[81] It seems to be relatively clear that Feyerabend is committing himself to a Hegelian notion of truth wherein concept and object become one in the Absolute; but introducing this notion of truth, at least in Feyerabend's mind, apparently does not involve the introduction of the usual correspondence notions of truth (see *ibid.*, p. 116, n. 105).

[82] I suspect he would dismiss them with a wave of the hand on the grounds that they presuppose an untenable view of scientific knowledge, whereas his Hegelian view has it right. Similarly I am inclinded to dismiss Feyerabend's views as clearly being irrelevant to the sort of knowledge science claims to provide and has provided.

[83] The other papers are Thomas Kuhn, "Postscript" to the second edition of his [1970b]; also his [1970] and [1970a].

[84] For examples of these patterns of response, see his [1970a], and pp. 500–506 above.

else modify his position in response to them. In his symposium paper, we already have seen how he has acknowledged that his use of the notion of a "paradigm" was extremely plastic and confused two quite distinct notions, and attempted to rectify this difficulty by replacing the notion of a paradigm by a new notion of an exemplar together with the more structured notion of a disciplinary matrix. As a comparison of my account of his pre-symposium views on pages 135–151 above and his *Structure of Scientific Revolutions* hopefully illustrates, this does provide a basis for clearer exegesis of his position and precludes a number of misinterpretations of his views that were occasioned by problems with his notion of a paradigm. Nevertheless, much of his position still is quite unclear, and his new notions of disciplinary matrixes and exemplars do not resolve many of the problems surrounding his old notion of a paradigm.[85]

Another significant effort at clarification has been his attempt to work out a more detailed account of his views on theory-laden observation and the theory-ladenness of meaning. Since this is done in his symposium paper above, and since I have commented on this attempt at length in my commentary paper in Session VI above, my discussion here of these developments will be kept brief. As indicated earlier in this book, a major concern of Kuhn's has been to deny both the observational/theoretical distinction and the correspondence-rule account of the interpretation of theoretical terms provided by the Received View. Rather on his view one interprets and applies the symbolic generalizations of a theory to nature by modeling such attachments on a shared stock of exemplars. His paper in the present volume (see Session VI above) attempts to explain how this occurs via his analogy with how a boy Johnny comes to learn how to use the terms 'duck,' 'swan,' and 'geese' via acquiring a "learned resemblance relation" through the study of exemplars (ducks, geese, and swans identified by his father). The learned resemblance relation acquired through this process determines the meanings of the ("theoretical") terms 'duck,' 'swan,' and 'goose.' Kuhn maintains that essentially the same process is involved in learning how to apply symbolic generalizations to nature and in learning to understand the theory. In both cases one eventually learns how to apply the appropriate descriptions, theories, and so on, in response to sensory phenomena.

Kuhn's analysis here is remarkably similar to Feyerabend's treatment of observation.[86] On Kuhn's view, as one comes to belong to a scientific (or

[85] For a particularly effective, and devastating, critique of Kuhn's attempt to eliminate the problems surrounding paradigms with his new replacement notions, see Shapere [1971]; see also my contribution to symposium Session VI above.

[86] Much of what follows is based on my "Kuhn's and Feyerabend's Relativisms" [forthcoming c] which should be consulted for fuller defense of points.

other linguistic) community, one's sensory stimuli cause one to give assent to, or dissent from, sentences or symbolic generalizations; and like Feyerabend's sentences, Kuhn's symbolic generalizations are uninterpreted (see p. 464 above). Both Kuhn and Feyerabend maintain that the interpretation of these sentences is provided by the theory one possesses; for Kuhn the theory is the disciplinary matrix (see pp. 500–501 above), and so *inter alia* includes the symbolic generalizations, and also the learned resemblance relations acquired from the study of exemplars that play a major part in interpreting these symbolic generalizations. However, Feyerabend and Kuhn apparently disagree on how the theory interprets the sentences or symbolic generalizations—Feyerabend denying such interpretations are provided by experience and Kuhn maintaining that the resemblance relation is acquired via the experience of studying exemplars. Although Kuhn clearly is committed to the view that observation yields knowledge and that in coming to learn to apply symbolic generalizations to nature one thereby acquires knowledge,[87] like Feyerabend he denies that any correspondence notion of truth plays a role in such knowledge. "There is, I think, no theory-independent way to reconstruct phrases like 'really there'; the notion of a match between the ontology of a theory and its 'real' counterpart in nature seems to me to be elusive in principle."[88] Rather, for Kuhn scientific knowledge is the collective opinion of a scientific community. "I regard scientific knowledge as intrinsically a product of a congeries of specialists' communities."[89] "Members of a given scientific community will generally agree which consequences of a shared theory sustain the test of experiment and are therefore true."[90]

At a number of places in *Structure of Scientific Revolutions*, Kuhn seems to be maintaining meaning and incommensurability doctrines as extreme as Feyerabend's (see pp. 146–148 above and p. 200, note 508, above). Such doctrines coupled with their remarkably similar treatments of observational knowledge, via considerations raised in discussing Feyerabend above, would seem to preclude the rational assessment of the relative merits of competing theories during revolutionary science, thus subjecting Kuhn to the charge that scientific progress on his view is fundamentally irrational. And, indeed, a number of critics have leveled this charge at him.[91] A central concern of Kuhn's recent work has been to

[87] See Kuhn's "Postscript" [1970b], pp. 175, 196; and his [1970a], pp. 253, 265, 270, 272, and 275.

[88] Kuhn, "Postscript" [1970b], p. 206; his most sustained defense of this view is found in his [1970a], pp. 264–266.

[89] *Ibid.*, p. 253.

[90] *Ibid.*, p. 264.

[91] See, for example, Scheffler [1967], and Shapere [1964], pp. 383–394, [1971], and [1966].

disassociate himself from such "irrationality" charges by showing how the rational comparison of competing theories is possible on his view. Key to these attempts has been the adoption of a doctrine on the theory-ladenness of meanings somewhat weaker than Feyerabend's wherein disciplinary matrixes or theories determine meanings in such a way that at least *some* of the terms two of them have in common are given different interpretations, but not *all* of them *need* be.[92] This makes provision for the possibility of there being some shared interpretation of terms used to describe observations, hence, for a common body of facts expressible in these terms. These shared meanings also provide a common vocabulary for exploring and investigating the different meanings competing theories attach to other terms, thus allowing the possibility that proponents of the two competing theories may come to find there are further facts they can agree on.[93] Of course, this does not preclude the possibility that two competing theories may fail to share such common terms, thus preventing rational assessment of their competing merits in this way (though he does suggest that this difficulty can be circumvented by adopting linguists' monolingual field techniques for "cracking" a language). Further, because proponents of different theories share different values (for example, as to what facts ought to be accommodated by a viable theory), agreement on which facts competing theories can accommodate may not settle questions as to which is the more adequate theory. In such cases "rational persuasion" may be needed to convince your opponents that your theory is preferable.[94]

While these recent moves of Kuhn do allow for the rational comparison of competing theories in at least some circumstances, thereby avoiding the necessity for taking recourse to highly irrational procedures akin to Feyerabend's, these moves do commit Kuhn to working out extremely difficult problems concerning the individuation of meanings and theories which have been discussed at length on pages 200–203;[95] and as the discussion on pages 203–208 indicates, a satisfactory solution to them will lead to a position that requires repudiating many of the most characteristic, distinctive, and interesting of Kuhn's views. Finally, it is clear that

[92] See his "Postscript" [1970b], p. 198.

[93] See *ibid.*, pp. 201–204, and [1970a], pp. 238, 261–262, 268–269, and 297.

[94] "Postscript" [1970b], pp. 199–200; the "translation" possibility is discussed on pp. 266–271 of his [1970a].

[95] The prospects for working out such problems is not that promising, judging from the recent literature on meaning change and the comparability of theories. See, for example, Fine [1967], pp. 231–240; Hesse [1969], pp. 46–52; Leplin [1969], pp. 69–75; Giedymin [1971a], pp. 30–48; Martin [1971], pp. 17–26, and [1972], pp. 252–256; Scheffler [1967]; Putnam [1973], pp. 199–221, [1973a], and [forthcoming]; Fine [1975]; and Shapere [1966] and [1975a].

Kuhn's account of the assessment of competing theories is at best fragmentary and seriously incomplete. For there now is overwhelming evidence that there are rational considerations regularly used in nonnormal science to evaluate which hypotheses or theories are most promising, worthy of further investigation, and so on, without thereby accepting them as correct or established. Such rational procedures often involve a scientific community having an agreed-upon body of information, what Shapere calls a scientific domain, outside of normal science.[96] Kuhn's analysis implies the absence of such scientific domains outside normal science and denies the need for such assessment within normal science, hence cannot accommodate such forms of rational hypothesis and theory evaluation. Thus, although Kuhn's recent modifications in his views do allow room for *some* rationality in scientific progress, in no way can they accommodate the full diversity of rational evaluation procedures employed regularly in the growth of scientific knowledge. In short, although Kuhn rejects the positivistic view that the context of discovery is not a legitimate concern for philosophy of science, his position allows no room for many, if not most, of the rational procedures involved in the context of actual scientific discovery, thereby conceding the positivistic view for all but normal science. The full force of these criticisms should become apparent after the discussion in Section III-B below.

Despite his sustained efforts to reply to critics and clarify, modify, or improve his position when he feels his critics have a legitimate objection, since the symposium Kuhn's views have undergone a sharply declining influence on contemporary philosophy of science. Why? Several reasons seem to be involved. *First*, as Kuhn has modified and attenuated his views, it has seemed to many that he was retreating toward a neo-positivistic view. For example, as I tried to show in my contribution to Session VI of the symposium, his treatment of the interpretation of terms in theories is very much like the positivistic account of the interpretation of theoretical terms extended to apply to observation terms as well, with the correspondence rules being replaced by a kind of "operant conditioning" procedure for acquiring a learned resemblance relation.[97] *Second*, there is the growing perception, defended briefly above, that Kuhn's account unnecessarily but essentially shortchanges the role of rationality

[96] For the evidence, see, for example, Shapere's symposium contribution in Session VII above, as well as other works of his and Darden's discussed in Section III-B-3 below. See also the papers by Buchdahl, Stuewer, Stein, and Schaffner in Stuewer [1970a].

[97] In my "Kuhn's and Feyerabend's Relativisms," *op. cit.*, I argue that Kuhn's (and Feyerabend's) concessions to positivistic and earlier empiricist views on epistemology are mighty indeed—which says something about how much of positivism Kuhn has conceded or retreated to.

in the growth of scientific knowledge. *Third*, there is a growing skepticism over Kuhn's claims that the history of science exemplifies his views on how science oscillates between normal and revolutionary science, despite brief attempts of his to counter such doubts.[98]

> The cyclic pattern which he [Kuhn] describes for science is much too simplistic. In fact, rarely can any of the stages be found exemplified very clearly in the course of science. The periods which he had previously described as pre-paradigm contained paradigms not that different from those of normal science. Nor does normal science alternate with revolutionary science; both are taking place all the time. Sometimes a revolution occurs without any preceding state of crisis. In short, the most one can say for Kuhn's three stages of scientific development [pre-paradigm, normal, and revolutionary] is that they are abstract, ideal types which certain episodes in science occasionally approximate, just the sort of abstract rational reconstructions which Kuhn found so objectionable in the work of philosophers such as Hempel.[99]

Fourth, there is the growing realization that Kuhn's position commits him to a metaphysical and epistemological view of science which is fundamentally defective since it makes discovering how the world really is irrelevant to scientific knowledge, reducing scientific knowledge to the collective beliefs of members of scientific disciplines. Collectively these factors have led increasing numbers of philosophers of science to reject Kuhn's approach as irredeemably flawed, although not as hopeless as Feyerabend's.

Philosophy of science today is ceasing to view the *Weltanschauungen* analyses as offering promising avenues for the development of an adequate understanding of science, the activity of scientific theorizing, or the nature of the knowledge resulting from such activities. It is seeking such understanding in new directions. Yet the directions in which contemporary philosophy of science is heading are profoundly influenced by the repudiated *Weltanschauungen* analyses: Like the *Weltanschauungen* analyses, they view the history of science, as well as contemporary scientific practice, as providing important evidence to be used in developing and evaluating their philosophical analyses. But the focuses of contemporary philosophy of science are quite different—evaluating the patterns of reasoning used to suggest hypotheses as being promising or worthy of further development, or to decide which are crucial problem areas for investigation, and so on; and attempting to provide detailed analyses of theories and models that reflect the conceptual devices actually employed

[98] See, for example, the critical discussions by Popper, J. W. N. Watkins, L. Pearce Williams, and Stephen Toulmin in Lakatos and Musgrave [1970], and Kuhn's reply on pp. 241–249 and especially pp. 249–259 of the same volume.

[99] Quote on p. 397 of Hull [1975].

in science as well as ones that could be employed, with an emphasis on their practical employment in the ongoing rational activity of scientific theorizing. Thus a premium is placed on the role of rationality in the growth of scientific knowledge—that premium being placed in large part in response to its absence in positivistic philosophy of science and its near absence in the work of Kuhn and Feyerabend. Further, contemporary work in philosophy of science increasingly subscribes to the position that it is a central aim of science to come to knowledge of how the world *really* is, that correspondence between theories and reality is a central aim of science as an epistemic enterprise and crucial to whatever objectivity scientific knowledge enjoys—in sharp repudiation of the "sociological" views of knowledge found in the more extreme *Weltanschauungen* analyses while acknowledging the defects of positivistic and earlier empiricist treatments. This has led to an emphatic belief that an adequate philosophy of science must embrace a "hard-nosed" metaphysical and epistemological realism wherein how the world *is* plays a decisive role in the epistemic efforts and achievements of science. Doing so requires calling into question a number of deeply held traditional beliefs about knowledge and is leading to sustained efforts by philosophers of science to rethink many of the most basic issues concerning the nature of a posteriori knowledge and its metaphysical underpinnings. The remainder of this Afterword will focus on detailing these contemporary developments in philosophy of science.

III. Historical Realism

Contemporary philosophy of science rapidly is becoming philosophy *of science*— a discipline concerned with science as actually practiced yet at the same time doing philosophy. Science, as practiced, involves an ongoing process of observation, experiment, recourse to prior theory, reliance on various metaphysical principles, and so on, exploited via reason and argument to suggest hypotheses, evaluate their promise for further development, debate their adequacy, develop them further, accept or reject them as true or false, and so on—the point of the enterprise being to obtain systematic knowledge that provides understanding of the world we live in. Whether or not its use of it is very good, far more of science is concerned with reasoning, argument, and marshaling evidence than with manipulating nature in the laboratory. In short, a central and characteristic activity of science is *the use of reason* in the suggestion and development of hypotheses and theories and in evaluating the knowledge claims made by those who advance such hypotheses and theories. Contemporary philosophy of science increasingly is coming to realize that there are "patterns of reasoning in the construction or discovery (as well as the ultimate acceptance or rejection) of scientific hypotheses and theories, and that a great deal of illumination of the scientific enterprise can be attained by examining them,"[100] and that the philosophical examination of them is central to a viable philosophy of science:

> The problem of the nature of the world in which we live, and the problem of how we are able to find out about that world, or at least are able to make rationally warranted claims about it, have always been at the heart of philosophy. . . . That science and its methods constitute a paradigm case of knowledge and the knowledge-acquiring process should be beyond dispute. It follows that *an investigation of the character of the knowledge-claims of science and of the methods by which those knowledge-claims are justified, is of fundamental importance to philosophy.*[101]

Such an investigation requires paying close attention to actual scientific practice, both historical and contemporary, all in the aim of developing a

[100] Shapere [1974], p. 141.
[101] *Ibid.*, p. ix; italics added.

systematic philosophical understanding of the justification of knowledge claims. Such is the focus of recent work by Imre Lakatos, Stephen Toulmin, and Dudley Shapere, which will be examined in Section B below.

Although the philosophical examination of rationality in the growth of scientific knowledge is coming to occupy an increasingly central place in contemporary philosophy of science, it is not doing so at the expense of work on questions such as the nature of scientific theories, explanation, reduction, and so on. But it is strongly affecting how such questions are approached and what would count as adequate solutions to such problems.

> What is needed is a closer examination of actual scientific development and practice—of the jobs performed by terms and statements in their actual employment in science, and of the respect in which those jobs change and remain the same as science develops. This means a return to an examination of the "content" of science, of the ways in which uses of terms like "space," "time," "explanation," "cause," "law," which are employed in or talking about scientific theories are similar or different in different contexts, and how those uses are like, or depart from, the uses of corresponding terms in more ordinary (nonscientific) contexts. . . .
>
> [This] . . . should not be taken as recommending that the problems, methods, and results of the logical empiricist approach be abandoned as useless. . . . But there is much promise that, at the very least, such new, broader approaches will reveal features of science that tended to be passed over by the logical treatment.[102]

Since theories often serve as vehicles for the knowledge claims science rationally develops and evaluates, an adequate philosophical analysis of theories must reflect their nature *as actually employed* in the reasoning activities of science. Moreover, theories often function as conceptual devices in science (see Section III-C below); that is, they can be employed to achieve a variety of different ends in science (for example, as factual descriptions, idealizations, heuristic accounts, and so on), which ends are reflected in the various ways science reasons about them, and an adequate analysis of theories must be able to account for, and explain, these various employments. The evaluation of theories often involves assessing their ability to solve theoretical problems about domains by *explaining* the underlying unity of scientific domains (see pp. 533–534 above), so an adequate account of theoretical explanation must reflect this usage of theories. Similarly, reasoning about hypotheses and theories in science often involves considerations about the relations between theories and the unification of different scientific domains,[103] so an adequate analysis of

[102] Shapere, "Introduction" to his [1965], p. 29.

[103] See Thomas Nickles's symposium contribution in Session VII above, as well as Dudley Shapere, "On the Introduction of New Hypotheses in Science," forthcoming, and the works cited in note 212 below.

intertheoretic "reduction" must reflect actual scientific reductive practices and accommodate the sorts of considerations involved in reasoning about such possible "reductions." Recent work on several of these problems from such an approach (including the semantic conception of theories introduced on pp. 221–230 above) will be discussed later in Section C.

Underlying most contemporary work on the growth of scientific knowledge, as well as work on the nature of theories, explanation, intertheoretic reduction, and so on, is the basic assumption that science can and does yield knowledge descriptive of how the world really is, and that observational interaction between man and that world plays an important role in obtaining such knowledge. Thus a strong commitment to both a metaphysical realism and an epistemological realism is characteristic of the new philosophy of science today, and such commitment virtually precludes "sociological" views of knowledge such as are embraced by Kuhn and Feyerabend. Throughout the history of modern philosophy, a major theme in epistemology and metaphysics has been to show how the then contemporary science could yield the sort of knowledge it claimed to.[104] Current philosophical examinations of the epistemic practices science engages in are yielding results which have profound implications for metaphysics and epistemology. For it increasingly is becoming clear that the epistemic practices science engages in can yield knowledge only under an epistemology which differs sharply from those which have tended to predominate recently. These metaphysical and epistemological implications of contemporary philosophy of science will be discussed in Section D.

Out of these recent developments on the growth of scientific knowledge, the nature and use of theories and conceptual devices in actual scientific practice, and the metaphysical and epistemological foundations of science is emerging a new movement in philosophy of science. I have chosen to call this perspective "historical realism" because of the central role history of science plays in its investigation and because of its strongly realistic metaphysical and epistemological biases. The examination of historical realism begins by looking at its relationship to history of science.

A. History and Philosophy of Science

At the time of the symposium there was wide diversity of opinion over whether there was any essential connection between the history of sci-

[104] See Part I of my [forthcoming c] for discussion in support of this point.

ence and philosophy of science, and if so, what that connection was. The extent of disagreement over this issue is revealed in Cohen's and Achinstein's papers, and especially the discussion which followed, in Session III above.[105] As the preceding discussion indicates, the new movement coalescing in philosophy of science today presupposes a resolution to this question, and it is desirable to clarify what that answer is.

A common distinction in history of science is between *external history* and *internal history*. Although the distinction is somewhat vague, internal history tends "to regard the history of science as the history of rational thought about nature, evolving according to its own inner logic, and requiring for its understanding only the attempt on the part of the historian to 'think the scientist's thoughts after him.'"[106] On the other hand, external history "is the view of science as an irreducibly social and cultural phenomenon, subject alike to rational and irrational influences, to magic as well as mathematics, religious sectarianism as well as logic, politics and economics as well as philosophy, and which is itself one of the major causative influences upon the general historical scene and inseparable from it."[107] And, of course, a given historical work can be some combination of internal and external history. Given its emphasis on the (historical) examination of reasoning in science, it may seem that contemporary philosophical work on the growth of scientific knowledge is just internal history of science done by philosophers of science. Such a view is seriously mistaken, however.[108] *First*, not all philosophers working on the growth of scientific knowledge confine themselves to just the considerations of internalist history. For example, a central theme of Stephen Toulmin's *Human Understanding*[109] is that an adequate account of the evolution of scientific concepts must be based on both internalist and externalist historical concerns. *Second*, and more important, although, when done well, philosophical work on the growth of scientific knowledge involves doing good internal history of science, the internalist historian of science and the historically oriented philosopher of science differ significantly in the nature of their concern with reasoning in scientific progress. It is important that we try to delineate what that difference is.

Ernin McMullin has written suggestively on the difference between

[105] See also Stuewer [1970a], which is concerned with the relationships between history of science and philosophy of science.

[106] Hesse [1970], p. 135.

[107] *Ibid.*

[108] But it is a very common view. For example, nearly all reviewers, whether their reviews are critical or laudatory, have made this mistake in looking at and assessing Shapere's *Galileo: A Philosophical Study* [1974]. The one significant exception is David Hull's review [1975]. The following discussion draws freely from Hull's review as well as Maull [Roth] [1976].

[109] Toulmin [1972].

the concerns with, and uses of, history by the historian of science and the historically oriented philosopher. History of science

> is *not* of itself a mode of understanding science, in the ordinary sense of discovering and explaining regularities in the practice of science. Its goal is to establish the singular, not the universal (as does epistemology or psychology). Insofar as it provides "understanding," it is an understanding of the past singular in its complexity and contingency, a different sense, therefore, of 'understanding.' To achieve it, the historian may make use of a variety of sciences . . . as well as philosophy. But that does not mean that his own effort falls in the same methodological category as theirs. There is ultimately a quite fundamental division here. The historian is concerned with what happened just because it *did* happen. He may call upon universals of all sorts in his effort to establish what happened or why it happened. But his goal is not the assertion of a universal, a pattern, or the interlinking of such patterns. This is the task of the philosopher.[110]

Is it really the case, as McMullin suggests, that what distinguishes the historian from the historically oriented philosopher is that the former "tries to recreate the singular in all its individuality; he emphasizes context and distrusts generalizations,"[111] whereas the latter generalizes philosophical theses from the history and uses the history to supply evidential warrant for his philosophical claims? A glance at such historical works as Butterfield's *The Origins of Modern Science: 1300–1800*,[112] Cohen's discussion of "transformations" of concepts (pp. 318, 322–327 above), and Gerald Holton's *Thematic Origins of Scientific Thought: Kepler to Einstein*,[113] to say nothing of Koyré's earlier work, suggests strongly that historians of science *often* are concerned with the development of generalizations about the historical events they discuss. Accordingly, McMullin's characterization fails to capture the difference we seek.[114]

Since both the historian and the historically oriented philosopher generalize from the historical cases they examine, perhaps the difference lies in the sorts of generalizations they draw. In establishing his generalizations, the historian is concerned to discover patterns of regularity in the growth of science—patterns which regularly occur unless there are spe-

[110] McMullin [1967], pp. 54–55.

[111] *Ibid.*, p. 58.

[112] Butterfield [1958].

[113] Holton [1973].

[114] In fairness to McMullin, it should be noted that he is characterizing idealized historians and philosophers, and is quite aware that these idealizations characterize widely separated points on "the intellectual spectrum in their approaches to science" ([1967], p. 58) and that in actual practice a work, for example, by a "historian," can combine both history and philosophy. My point is that this happens very often, and so McMullin's idealized characterization fails to get at the significant difference between internalist historians and historically oriented philosophers of science.

cial complicating factors which interfere with or alter the progress of science; and when such deviations do occur, the historian will look for those complicating factors in an attempt to understand why the expected patterns were not realized in that episode. By contrast, the historically oriented philosopher of science is concerned with generalization primarily as a prelude to critical analysis and evaluation. First he examines the patterns of reasoning involved in the advancement, evaluation, and justification of scientific hypotheses. Then, having identified the reasoning patterns used in a particular historical episode, he asks whether the reasoning in question was good or not. Do the reasons advanced really make the hypothesis plausible? Does the evidence adduced strongly favor the truth of the hypothesis as claimed? If the philosophical examination yields affirmative answers to these questions, the philosopher can abstract the reasoning pattern and generalize that "when, or to the extent that, the following factors are present such and such a sort of theory is likely to be true," or that "it is reasonable to accept the theory as being established," and so on.[115] And if the philosophical evaluation is that the reasoning patterns are deficient, the philosopher becomes concerned with what alternative reasoning patterns *could* or *should* have occurred given the available information in the scientific domain of the time and available background knowledge.[116] In dealing with these issues, the philosopher is free to invent alternative reasoning patterns that were feasible at the time which can be evaluated as to their adequacy; and if such invented patterns of reasoning are both feasible and successful, the philosopher may generalize from them just as he does from actually exemplified patterns which pass the test of philosophical scrutiny. In such historically oriented philosophy, two focuses can be discerned: (1) the discovery how science in fact does reason about its subject matter and evaluate its hypotheses, and (2) through the evaluation of such reasoning patterns, displaying how actual scientific practice does or could lead to knowledge about the world.

[115] See, for example, pp. 534–557, especially pp. 541, 546, and 553, in Shapere's contribution to symposium Session VII, for illustrations of this approach. Shapere is of the opinion that there are more basic reasons than those presented in this section for approaching the philosophy of science through the history of science; these are discussed in Section B-3 below.

[116] See Shapere, "Remarks on the Relations between History and Philosophy of Science, and on the Notion of Rationality in Science," unpublished but circulated manuscript, n.d. There Shapere makes the observation that the sense of 'could' in question is not that of logical possibility, but rather concerns what the "natural" or expectable thing would be given the instrumentation, mathematical techniques, and physical ideas available at the time, *or* that at the given stage of science the ideas and techniques could have been developed with relative ease, *or* whether certain ideas or techniques were feasible only after certain later developments had occurred. And such assessments of what could have happened lay the basis for assessing what should have happened had the scientists in question been more accurate, or careful, or aware—that is, had they been doing their job well.

Collectively these two focuses ultimately should lead to a philosophical understanding of science as an epistemic enterprise. Thus, although both the internalist historian and the historically oriented philosopher are concerned with reason in the growth of scientific knowledge, and their concerns may overlap (as when the historian asks why somebody did not draw conclusions which it seems he could or should have), ultimately their focuses are quite different—the historian in explaining historical episodes and possibly generating historical generalizations useful in explaining such episodes, and the historically oriented philosopher in showing how the reasoning patterns science does or could employ justify science in claiming to provide knowledge about the world, and in analyzing what the nature of that knowledge is.

It is important to realize that, on the approach just outlined, the philosopher is not resorting to historical material merely to *illustrate* his philosophical views. Rather, the history of science functions as *evidence* for his philosophical views. For he is claiming that much of what science characteristically does *is* rational and capable of yielding knowledge, although he also recognizes that not all of science is rational and thus that not everything science does yields knowledge. He is also concerned with whether, or how, the techniques, concepts, information, and so on, available to science (at a given time) could or should have enabled science to obtain knowledge had better reasoning occurred. His aim is to establish a philosophical theory of rationality, reflective of good science as actually practiced, wherein such actual science is capable of yielding knowledge; and in order to substantiate any claims to have established such a theory of rationality (or a portion thereof), the historical evidence must play an essential role. This is not to say, however, that the philosophical conclusions about rationality are simple inductive generalizations such as an historian might make. The resulting philosophical findings are not *mere summaries* of reasoning patterns science exemplifies, but rather concern which reasoning patterns compatible with actual scientific practice *could* yield knowledge and are feasible in the sense that science reasonably *should* be expected to use them under specifiable circumstances.

Although the historical evidence provides essential evidential warrant for the historically oriented philosopher's findings, it does not provide the entire warrant. Part of what the philosopher does is *evaluative* in nature—claiming that various patterns of reasoning from evidence to hypotheses *do* make it plausible to suppose a certain type of theory will be true, or *do* justify certain knowledge claims, and so on. And such evaluation does not generally consist in showing that the reasoning patterns are logically valid—that the conclusions drawn are entailed by the available evidence—for it is clear that few of the reasoning patterns employed in science meet this standard. Deductive logic is one pattern of rationality in reasoning, but it is not the only one; and good reasoning in science typically yields conclusions that go beyond the logical entailments of deductive logic.[117] Viewing the patterns of reasoning propounded by philosophers as "different systems of rules of the scientific game," Imre Lakatos is prompted to conclude from this observation that "these *scientific games* are without any genuine epistemological relevance *unless* we superimpose on them some sort of metaphysical (or, if you wish, 'inductive') principle which will say that the game, as specified by the methodology, gives us the best chance of approaching the Truth. Such a principle then turns the pure conventions of the game into fallible conjectures; but without such a principle the scientific game is just like any other game."[118] To the extent that Lakatos is suggesting that part of the warrant for the historically oriented philosopher's conclusions about viable patterns of reasoning in science rests on more basic epistemological considerations not validated by the historical evidence, his point is correct.[119] Ultimately these epistemological considerations underlie the philosopher's evaluation of whether identified patterns of reasoning do or do not support the conclusions drawn from them, and will have to be evaluated using the usual repertoire of techniques from philosophy. Thus the evidential warrant for the historically oriented philosopher's findings about rationality in the growth of scientific knowledge is part historical and part philosophical.[120]

As mentioned above, the new movement coalescing in philosophy of science today is concerned with the analysis of theories, explanation, reduction, and so on, as well as the reasoning patterns employed in the growth of scientific knowledge. But in attempting to analyze such epis-

[117] See McMullin [1970], pp. 50–52, 55–56; Shapere, "Remarks on the Relations between History and Philosophy of Science," note 73; Lakatos [1971], pp. 101, 108–109; and Toulmin [1972], Sec. A *passim*.

[118] Lakatos [1971], pp. 108–109.

[119] It is less than clear whether this is his point or not, since it occurs in a context where he is trying to show both the superiority of his research program methodology over others and that all history is reconstructed history (see note 120).

[120] Some writers (for example, Lakatos [1971], pp. 105–108) doubt whether history can provide such a warrant on grounds that all internal history must presuppose (explicitly or implicitly) a rationality theory, and so either is circular or question-begging. Good discussions of this sort of historiographical claim, which cannot be given detailed consideration here, are found in McMullin [1970], and Hesse [1970]. Suffice it to say that Lakatos does not make a convincing case since it depends essentially on the erroneous supposition that recognizing the pattern of reasoning used by an historical figure requires accepting that pattern as rational. This supposition may be plausible for Lakatos's own idiosyncratic notion of internal history (Lakatos [1971], p. 123, n.1), but it is not for what is usually understood as internal history.

Another set of reasons for viewing examination of historical case studies in doing philosophy of science will be raised when we consider Shapere's views in Section B-3 below.

temic devices, it demands that viable analyses characterize such devices as actually employed in science, and so actual scientific practice, both historical and contemporary, plays an essential evidential role in the evaluation of such analyses. Ultimately, this reflects a deep conviction that philosophy of science must show how science, as actually practiced, is capable of yielding knowledge about the world. And an adequate philosophical analysis of epistemic devices such as theories must display how they bear the epistemic burdens actual science imposes on them. Thus the evidential warrant for such philosophical analyses of epistemic devices consists partially of evidence about actual scientific practice as to the devices employed and the uses to which they are put, together with philosophical considerations which are used to establish that such devices can bear the required epistemic burdens. For example, examination of the various uses of the term 'theory' in science indicates that it means various things in various contexts—including scientific fields (such as in 'electromagnetic theory') or an evolving body of theory (such as 'the old quantum theory') or conjecture or hypothesis (as in Freud's theory that homosexuality is an arrested state of psychosexual development), and so forth. But one very central use of 'theory' involves an epistemic device which is used to characterize the state-change behavior of isolated systems within a general class of phenomena. Through an examination of actual scientific attempts to formulate, manipulate, and employ the latter sort of epistemic devices, one can discover that they invariably involve postulating a class of states of systems, specify laws indicating how if isolated such systems change over time, admit of alternative linguistic descriptions or formulations, and are used to characterize how natural classes of phenomena would behave if isolated, and so on. Having discovered such invariant features of the epistemic devices referred to by this sense of 'theory,' the philosopher can then attempt to provide a precise analysis of this kind of theory. The semantic conception of theories presented earlier (pp. 221–230 above) is offered as such an analysis, and its adequacy depends in part on the extent to which it provides a precise characterization of this kind of theory and the uses to which such theories are put in science. Such adequacy does not depend on whether its characterization is one the scientist would give or recognize—any more than the philosopher's reconstruction of reasoning patterns found in science need be accounts the scientist would offer. Rather what counts is that the analysis be an accurate reconstruction of the devices actually employed, and that it can explain how theories bear the epistemic burdens they are called upon to bear in actual usage. Showing that the latter is the case requires recourse to epistemological and other considerations. Thus, as with philosophical analyses of rationality in the growth of scientific knowledge, the evidential warrant for philosophical analyses of the epistemic devices employed by science includes both information about past and present scientific practice and other epistemological or philosophical considerations.

B. Rationality and the Growth of Scientific Knowledge

Having clarified several facets of the concerns and approaches of the newly emerging philosophy of science (see also Section III-B-3 below), we turn now to a consideration of the findings being yielded—concentrating first on work by Lakatos, Toulmin, and Shapere on the growth of scientific knowledge and, then, in Section C, looking at attempts to analyze various conceptual devices employed, for example, in the use of theories by science in its epistemic endeavors. Finally, in Section D we will look at the implications of this work for metaphysics and epistemology.

1. Lakatos[121]

In the history of the philosophy of science, philosophers often have been concerned to establish *methodologies*, or canons of rationality, for *doing* science—which, if followed, would enable science to obtain knowledge. This was a central goal of Descartes' method of doubt, which method he attempted to exploit in developing his theory of mechanics; and it was a central motive in the development of inductivist methodologies by Bacon and his later empiricist successors. In the twentieth century, we find the same motives in the development of inductive-verification and later inductive-confirmation methodologies by logical positivists.[122] Common to all these methodologies is their concern to establish canons of rationality which, if followed, will enable science to obtain knowledge; and much of the focus of the associated epistemological and metaphysical investigations concerned establishing that the recommended methodologies did make possible scientific knowledge

[121] This section is a revision of a paper, "Falsification, Research Programmes, and the Growth of Scientific Knowledge," I presented before the Washington, D.C., Philosophy Club in a symposium with Peter Achinstein, Carl Kordig, and William Wallace. I am grateful to my colleague Michael Gardner for helpful comments on that earlier version.

[122] For a brief historical survey of empiricist inductive methodologies from Bacon to logical positivism, see Part I of my "Kuhn's and Feyerabend's Relativisms" [forthcoming c].

or showing what the limits of such knowledge were. Invariably these methodologies were set forth as *normative* recommendations on how science *ought* to be practiced. Sometimes it further was claimed that these methodologies were *descriptive*—as in Whewell's inductive philosophy—claiming to reflect actual scientific practice insofar as science was done well. Although such descriptive claims often involved a fair amount of historical distortion, such methodologies have exerted substantial influence on science at various times, and so one finds in the history of science deliberate attempts to do science in accordance with them. Thus to varying degrees of approximation, these methodologies do provide examples of reasoning patterns actually exemplified at times in the history of science. Yet, from the history of science we know that much of the reasoning involved in science, including the achievement of some of science's more spectacular successes, is not in accordance with the prescriptions of these "inductivist" or "falsificationist" methodologies. In particular, there is mounting historical evidence that much of scientific reasoning is not "inductive" in anything like the empiricist or positivistic sense.

Motivated sometimes by historical considerations and sometimes by epistemological doctrines, a number of philosophers of science recently have sought to develop improved, noninductive, methodologies for doing science; such attempts by Popper and Feyerabend already have been considered (see pp. 160–180 and Section II-B above). Imre Lakatos's work on the growth of scientific knowledge is a further example of such an approach; as one critic puts it, "Lakatos himself has simply taken over Popper's own argument at the point where it breaks off."[123] Whereas Popper's methodology involves conjecture of bold theories which one seeks to overthrow by falsifying empirical tests, Lakatos takes exception on two grounds. *First*, the locus of scientific progress is not the isolated theory, but rather that science does and ought to focus on the development of some key insights into an ever improving sequence of related theories which he calls a *research program. Second*, it often is rational to persist in the development of these key insights in the face of experimental evidence which appears to falsify them. "The main difference from Popper's . . . is that in my conception criticism does not—and must not—kill as fast as Popper imagined. Purely negative, destructive criticism, like 'refutation' or demonstration of an inconsistency does not eliminate a [research] programme. Criticism of a programme is a long and often frustrating process and one must treat budding programmes leniently. One may, of course, show up the degeneration of a research programme, but it is only *constructive criticism* which, with the help of

[123] Toulmin [1972], p. 482.

rival research programmes, can achieve real success."[124] In developing his methodology of research programs, Lakatos's motives are *normative*—establishing a methodology to use in the criticism of scientific practice.[125]

Lakatos's research program methodology is concerned with how a mature science develops a particular theoretical perspective on the world by the carrying out of what he calls a research program. Research programs are reminiscent of Kuhnian "normal science," though the guiding principles of a research program, Lakatos's positive and negative heuristics, are very *unlike* Kuhn's paradigms or disciplinary matrixes; for "one must never allow a research programme to become a *Weltanschauung*, or a sort of scientific rigour."[126] What Kuhn "calls 'normal science' is nothing other than a research programme that has achieved monopoly. . . . The history of science has been and should be a history of completing research programmes (or, if you wish, 'paradigms'), but it has not been and must not become a succession of periods of normal science: the sooner competition starts, the better for progress. 'Theoretical pluralism' is better than 'theoretical monism.'"[127] Indeed, one of Lakatos's motives is to "rework" Kuhn's views so as to obtain an account wherein the growth of scientific knowledge is rational. "Indeed, my concept of a 'research programme' may be construed as an objective, 'third world' reconstruction of Kuhn's sociopsychological concept of paradigm."[128] Unlike paradigms, according to Lakatos it is possible for the relative merits of research programs to be compared and assessed.

Lakatos begins his reworking of Kuhnian paradigms into research programs with the observation that the basic concept of the logic of discovery is not the theory, but rather *series of theories*. "It is a succession of theories and not one given theory which is appraised as scientific or pseudo-scientific."[129] When the theories in such a succession or series are connected with a *continuity* reminiscent of Kuhn's normal science, the series become *research programs*.[130] "The main problems of the logic of discovery cannot be satisfactorily discussed except in the framework of a

[124] Lakatos [1970], p. 179; some italics in the original deleted. Much of this work is concerned with criticisms of Popper's methodological doctrines, as well as those of others. Also, he devotes considerable space to criticizing Kuhn's views. For the most part these criticisms will be ignored here.

[125] See, for example, *ibid.*, p. 184. In addition to the works cited below, Lakatos develops his research program views in the following works: [1963–64], pp. 1–25, 120–139, 221–243, 296–342; "Changes in the Problem of Inductive Logic"; and [1968], pp. 149–186.

[126] Lakatos [1970], p. 155.

[127] *Ibid.*; italics deleted.

[128] *Ibid.*, p. 179, n. 1; the "third world" is Popper's term for the world of propositions, truth, standards—the world of objective knowledge.

[129] *Ibid.*, p. 132; italics deleted.

[130] *Ibid.*

methodology of research programs"[131] since the history of science is the history of research programs.[132] Research programs are defined in terms of *problem shifts*: Let T_1, T_2, T_3, . . . be a series of theories where each subsequent theory results from adding auxiliary clauses to, or from the semantical reinterpretation of, the previous theory in order to accommodate some anomaly, where each theory in the series has as much empirical content as the unrefuted content of its predecessor. A problem shift is *theoretically progressive* if each theory has some excess empirical content over its predecessor—that is, it predicts some novel, hitherto unexpected, fact. A problem shift is *empirically progressive* if some of this excess empirical content is corroborated—that is, each new theory leads us to the actual discovery of some new *fact*. The problem shift is said to be *progressive* if it is both theoretically and empirically progressive; otherwise it is *degenerating*.[133]

Problem shifts can be developed by trial and error, and according to Lakatos this *is* what happens in immature science; but in "mature" science the series of theories is generated in accordance with a research program having "heuristic power."[134] Such *research programs* consist of methodological rules for the development of a problem shift; these rules comprise a *negative heuristic* that tells us what paths of research to avoid and a *positive heuristic* telling us what paths to pursue.[135] The negative heuristic amounts to the key idea or insight of the problem shift, the theories in that problem shift being different models or attempts to spell out that idea in accurate detail. For example, in the research program of Cartesian mechanics, the mechanistic clockwork view of the universe served as the negative heuristic, discouraging work on theories such as Newton's which involved action at a distance.[136] The negative heuristic of a research program thus isolates a "hard core" and forbids us to modify or reject this core; rather "we must use our own ingenuity to articulate or even invent auxiliary hypotheses which form a *protective belt* around this core."[137] Only the elements of this protective belt are to be modified in the face of anomalies. Precisely what this irrefutable hard core consists in is determined by methodological decision. Nowhere does Lakatos tell us what considerations are involved in making such a decision. His account of rationality in the growth of scientific knowledge assumes the negative

[131] *Ibid.*
[132] *Ibid.*, n. 1.
[133] *Ibid.*, p. 118.
[134] *Ibid.*, p. 175.
[135] *Ibid.*, p. 132.
[136] *Ibid.* There Lakatos indicates that the same principle also served as a positive heuristic, encouraging people to discover auxiliary hypotheses to circumvent apparent counterevidence such as was provided by Kepler's ellipses.
[137] *Ibid.*, p. 133.

(and positive) heuristic as *given*, and thus has nothing to say about rationality in the choice of research programs to follow.

The positive heuristic "consists of a partially articulated set of suggestions or hints on how to change, develop the 'refutable variants' of the research program, how to modify, sophisticate, the 'refutable protective belt.'"[138] It "sets out a programme which lists a chain of ever more complicated models simulating reality: the scientist's attention is riveted on building his models following instructions which are laid in the positive part of his programme; he ignores the *actual* counterexamples, the available data."[139] The positive heuristic of a research program can be formulated as a *metaphysical principle*; this principle determines what problems scientists rationally choose to work on.[140]

A successful research program is one that generates a series of theories (a problem shift) which *consistently* is theoretically progressive and *intermittently* is empirically progressive.[141] Mature science consists of research programs, whereas immature science consists of a "mere patched up pattern of trial and error";[142] but sometimes, in ways Lakatos does not specify, research programs emerge from a long, preliminary process of such trial and error.[143] The mature and rational way of doing science is to undertake a research program, developing a theoretically progressive problem shift by trying to falsify theories (theories being roughly the negative heuristic and auxiliary hypotheses formulated as a model) and then modifying them by the addition of new hypotheses or the semantic reinterpretation of the theory—all this being done under the guidance of the positive heuristic. Once embarked upon, a research program should be stopped or rejected only if it is seen to be degenerating; and even then it rationally can be continued if it continuously is theoretically progressive and intermittently is empirically progressive. Whether a research program is degenerating or not is something that can be assessed only with historical hindsight, so it often is reasonable for scientists to continue working on a degenerating research program.[144] It is irrational to continue a research program once it clearly is degenerating. Moreover, since Lakatos denies the possibility of inductively confirming a theory,[145] and is of the opinion that all hard cores of research programs are likely to be

[138] *Ibid.*, p. 135.
[139] *Ibid.*
[140] *Ibid.*, pp. 136–137.
[141] *Ibid.*, p. 135. Notice that the definition here allows successful research programs to be degenerating in virtue of only intermittently being empirically progressive.
[142] *Ibid.*, p. 175.
[143] *Ibid.*, p. 133, n. 4.
[144] *Ibid.*, pp. 155–173.
[145] *Ibid.*; pp. 99–103 and 175 of his "Replies to Critics" (pp. 174–182 in Buck and Cohen [1971]).

false, no amount of testing of a research program's problem shift can establish the validity of its theories. Thus, it is irrational to suppose that your theory is true, and so science ought to encourage the proliferation of competing research programs.

In the development of a research program, sometimes one program will be grafted onto an older research program with which it blatantly is inconsistent;[146] for example, Copernican astronomy was grafted onto Aristotelian physics. In such cases, one can attempt to reduce the old research program to the new one by explaining the postulates of the new one in terms of the old program, or one can accept the inconsistency as some basic property of nature, or one can take the intermediate tack of exploiting the heuristic power of the inconsistent grafted program without resigning one to accept the inconsistency; according to Lakatos, only the latter approach is reasonable.[147] It also is possible for competing research programs to coexist without one being grafted to the other; such coexistence is reasonable so long as the research programs can be rationally reconstructed as progressive problem shifts. Indeed, coexistence of research programs is (and ought to be) the rule, not the exception, in the history of science.[148]

Other than illustrating the above ideas with historical examples, the foregoing pretty much exhausts what Lakatos has to say about rationality in the growth of scientific knowledge. Although Lakatos does not purport to offer a comprehensive theory of rationality in the growth of scientific knowledge,[149] such rationality avowedly is one of his major concerns. It thus is rather surprising how little he has to say about rationality: Research programs should be proliferated; so long as a research program remains progressive, it should be pursued in accordance with the positive heuristic, and the negative heuristic should not be tampered with; and it is rational to exploit heuristically the inconsistent grafting of two research programs so long as you do not believe in the inconsistency. Notice how much is left uncovered. Some possible positive heuristics are better than others—some are more rational and some positively irrational to follow. Thus, contra Lakatos, sometimes it will be irrational to follow a theoretically progressive and empirically intermittently progressive problem shift just because the positive heuristic is not a reasonable one.[150] Closely re-

[146] Lakatos [1970], p. 142.

[147] *Ibid.*, pp. 144–145.

[148] *Ibid.*, pp. 155–157.

[149] Lakatos, "Replies to Critics," p. 179 in Buck and Cohen [1971].

[150] Lest one erroneously think that the progressiveness of the program precludes this, it should be noted that inappropriate positive heuristics can make for a theoretically progressive problem shift which indeed predicts new facts. For example, this can happen if one has

lated is the fact that, in modifying theories in a problem shift to resolve anomalies, certain modifications are reasonable to make whereas others are not; the factors involved are not unlike those which favor the introduction of certain sorts of theories, and not others, which Shapere discusses in Session VII of the symposium; and such reasonableness has no obvious connections with whether a problem shift is progressive or not. Furthermore, it would be quite irrational to work on a research program whose problem shift begins with a theory one has good reasons to believe is inappropriate, or to continue developing a progressive problem shift if evidence became available which strongly suggested a different sort of theory, one incompatible with your problem shift, is likely to be correct. Yet in both these cases, Lakatos's account allows such practices to be rational. These difficulties can be traced to the fact that, in dealing with rationality in the development of research programs, Lakatos totally ignores the extent to which what is theoretically reasonable is conditioned by the subject matter of the science or by the constitution of what Shapere calls the scientific domain (see pp. 518–565 above). Such considerations are, of course, precisely the sort which are involved in the development of a research program, in deciding which research program to adopt—something Lakatos said he was not going to discuss.[151] But the price of not discussing it is saying very little about rationality in the pursuit of research programs. And what he does say exaggerates the importance of being theoretically or empirically progressive in deciding whether it is fruitful to pursue a research program.

Considerations about how the domain influences what is scientifically rational also enable us to show Lakatos is mistaken in claiming that immature science consists of a "mere patched up pattern of trial and error" whereas mature science consists of research programs. At any stage in its development, a science focuses on some body of phenomena which is thought to be related in some significant ways. The science has available various putative facts about such phenomena where such data typically suggest there is some significant connection between the phenomena. In a word, the facts concern a "natural" grouping of phenomena. For example, in pre-Aristotelean Greek astronomy there were associated various "facts" about the movements of the sun, the planets, the moon, and the stars. Initially all such phenomena were probably grouped on the basis that they were celestial; by Eudoxus' time, the association had been intensified by the addition of general facts such as those concerning the

---

a problem shift in which initial theories are approximately true but following the heuristic produces subsequent theories which become increasingly more erratic in predicting phenomena.

[151] *Ibid.*, p. 133, n. 4.

planets and the sun making various synodic paths along the ecliptic. Clearly, such facts indicated, rationally, an intimate connection between such facts about the movements of different celestial bodies without indicating the precise nature of that connection. Thus the very association of such facts raised difficult questions: What underlying mechanism was responsible for such correlated regular behavior of these different celestial bodies, and why did the planets undergo retrograde motion? That is, the very questions Greek astronomy focused on were suggested, forcefully, by the associated body of astronomical facts. More important, the available data indicated that, except for retrograde motion, the motion of celestial bodies was uniform and circular. This strongly suggested that an adequate explanation of the associated astronomical data would be in terms of uniform circular motions. And, indeed, all known Greek attempts to explain celestial phenomena did proceed in terms of uniform circular motions. They varied, however, as to whether the earth was flat, whether the stars were located on a rotating sphere, cylinder, or hemisphere. Prior to Eudoxus, Greek astronomy clearly fails to be a problem shift in Lakatos's sense; and although a case can be made that Eudoxus', Aristotle's, and Callipus' astronomical theories apparently *do* qualify as a problem shift, they clearly do not constitute a research program; for what was the hard core? Certainly not the idea that celestial motions were a function of uniform circular motions concentric around the earth (which was the heart of their three theories), for Aristotle himself, in commenting on the phenomenon of planets changing their apparent size, comments that this may have to go.[152] Accordingly, a negative heuristic seems to be nonexistent. It follows, then, that pre-epicyclic Greek astronomy qualifies as immature under Lakatos's account, hence is "a mere patched up pattern of trial and error."

But it clearly is not. For, as has been seen, the association of data about related celestial phenomena not only rationally posed certain problems, but also strongly suggested a particular approach to solving these problems. Although various mechanisms were postulated, and found wanting, as to why the celestial phenomena behaved as they did, with some reservations such as Aristotle's, they all involved the key idea of uniform circular motion of celestial bodies, and gradually led to the postulation of more refined mechanisms which could account for more and more of the phenomena with increasing accuracy. The move from Thales to Callipus was anything but "a mere patchwork of trial and error."

What is significant here is not merely that the body of associated data or putative facts about celestial phenomena posed certain problems and also

[152] See Toulmin and Goodfield [1961], Chap. 1–3, for a good discussion of Greek astronomy.

strongly suggested the sort of theory which could account for them, but rather that such associated bodies of data *generally* are present in science, pose certain significant problems, and rationally suggest certain sorts of theories as being appropriate for explaining the underlying unity of such data. For such problematic associated data constitute what Dudley Shapere has termed a *scientific domain* in his contribution to Session VII of the symposium above—a number of *items of information* or putative facts (perhaps including accepted laws and theories) which come to be associated together as a *body of information* having the following characteristics: the association is based on some well-grounded, significant, relationships between the items of information which are suggestive of deeper unities among the items; there is something problematic about the body so related; the problems are important; and, usually, the science is "ready" to deal with them. And Shapere and his associates have been able to demonstrate that for a wide variety of cases (including one, the Bohr program, Lakatos explicitly views as being "mature"), scientific domains *do* pose problems in this way, and, possibly aided by a certain amount of background information or knowledge, rationally suggest or favor certain types of theories as likely candidates for explaining the underlying unities of the domain information.[153] Moreover, their case studies indicate this occurs long before anything like a Lakatosian research program emerges.[154] Minimally, these findings indicate that from its most primitive to its most advanced stages, there is a rational basis for theorizing. Thus, contra Lakatos, there is a rationality to theorizing even in the primitive "immature" stages of science.

Even if Lakatos's research program account were augmented so as to incorporate rationality considerations of the sort mentioned, his account still would be deficient on three counts: *First*, Lakatos's characterization of a problem shift requires that the theories T_1, T_2, T_3, . . . be such that T_{i+1} is obtained from T_i either by adding new auxiliary hypotheses or by semantically reinterpreting terms in T_i; what is not allowed is the deletion or replacement of any of the portion of T_i that is not hard core. This "continuity" requirement thus precludes a number of reasonable means for modifying theories in the progress of carrying out a fruitful research program.[155] *Second*, in his account of mature science, Lakatos attaches too

[153] In addition to cases concerning the periodic table, spectroscopy, and the Bohr quantum theory in Shapere's "Scientific Theories and Their Domains" (pp. 518–565 above), other cases are given in his [1974b]; in Darden [1975]; and in Maull [Roth] [1974]. Much of this work will be discussed in Section 3 below. Further works will be cited there.

[154] See especially Darden [1975].

[155] See Chap. 4 of Suppe [1967] for discussion of this point. There I develop a model of rational theory development that anticipates Lakatos's research programs (and also Toulmin's evolutionary approach discussed in Section 2 below), but is more sophisticated with

much importance to theory development viȧ testing and modifying theories in response. On the one hand, theoretical development often is little influenced by experimental results—shifts in theory being due to "thought experiments," reassessment of items in the domain, and so on; such has been characteristic of much of the development of general relativity theory. On the other hand, the implication of the characterization of mature science provided by Lakatos's research programs methodology is that scientific progress consists *just* in the development of improved theories in accordance with a plurality of methodologies. But such a view clearly is mistaken. For, as Shapere shows in his symposium paper above (see Session VII), scientific domains raise a variety of different sorts of problems, including what he calls domain problems, which do not require theories for their solution. But such domain problems (which are concerned with clarifying the domain itself) *do* play an important role in theorizing. For example, Shapere convincingly shows that work on solving domain problems played an important role in the development of a theory able to explain the organization of the periodic table (see pp. 534–540 above). By focusing *exclusively* on the modification of theories within a problem shift, Lakatos's research program analysis leaves out an often important way of developing theories. *Third*, in the development of theories adequate for dealing with a class of phenomena, the lack of suitable concepts, or the employment of unsuitable concepts, often is a major obstacle. And Toulmin has shown, convincingly, that much of rationality in science concerns the development of appropriate concepts, and that one's concepts play an important role in determining what theoretical moves are appropriate in trying to explain a body of phenomena.[156] Other than allowing semantic reinterpretation of terms in the generation of problem shifts, Lakatos totally ignores this aspect of theory development and its bearing on rationality in the growth of scientific knowledge.

It may seem that my criticisms of Lakatos amount to attacking him unfairly for not dealing with issues he said he was not going to consider. This is to miss the main point of my comments. What I am claiming is that, although being theoretically and empirically progressive is sometimes a relevant factor in deciding rationally how to go about scientific theorizing, many other factors also are involved in such rational assessment and often take precedent over considerations of empirical and theoretical progressiveness. Thus, either for doing science or for the his-

---

respect to allowable modifications in theory. It is deficient, however, in that it does not take into account fully the sort of rationality considerations discussed above, and also in that the second and, to an extent, the third objections below apply to it.

[156] See Toulmin [1972] and Section 2 below where this is discussed.

torical assessment of past science, Lakatos's account misplaces the locus of rationality.[157] Hence it is a seriously defective account.

One of Lakatos's prime motives in developing his research programs methodology is to use it for the evaluation of episodes in the history of science. Maintaining the questionable thesis that all history of science *must* reconstruct history from the perspective of *some* scientific methodology,[158] Lakatos contrasts his research programs methodology with several others, including inductivist, conventionalistic, and falsificationist ones—the focus of the contrast being to determine which methodology is most appropriate for doing history of science. He argues that the other methodologies are inadequate since they are at odds with, hence falsified by, "the basic appraisals of the scientific elite"[159] as revealed in history. But, he maintains, his research programs methodology is *corroborated* in virtue of passing the same historical test, and thus is superior.[160] This is a most perplexing series of doctrines, as McMullin has pointed out:[161]

> For if the history used in the test is reconstructed history, then the use of it to test a methodology is either question-begging or circular depending whether or not a different or the same methodology is used to effect the reconstruction. And if it is actual, unreconstructed, history then Lakatos' research-programs methodology fails to pass the test just a surely as do the other methodologies he considers; for Lakatos himself acknowledges that a number of the historical episodes he examines do not proceed in accordance with his research-programs methodology, although they could and should have.[162]

Thus Lakatos's arguments in support of his research programs methodology are no more convincing than the methodology is itself.

What, then, are we to conclude about Lakatos's treatment of rationality

[157] It should be noted that Lakatos acknowledges that *only* with historical hindsight and reconstruction can one assess whether a research program is progressive. If he is correct, this virtually precludes *de facto* progressiveness from figuring centrally in a scientist's own reasoning, and suggests that the factors that are or ought to be involved in scientific reasoning about theories are other than Lakatos has identified.

Other criticisms of Lakatos's position are found in Toulmin [1972], Vol. I, pp. 479–484; in McMullin [1970]; in the articles by Kuhn, Feigl, Hall, and Koertge which follow Lakatos's "History of Science" in Buck and Cohen [1971]; and in Maxwell [1974], pp. 123–153 and 247–295. There Maxwell is concerned to develop an "aim-oriented theory of scientific discovery."

[158] Lakatos [1971], pp. 105–108. This appears to imply that unreconstructed history is impossible—which seems to be incompatible with Lakatos's own practice of indicating how his own reconstructed histories deviate from the actual (unreconstructed?) history by presenting the *actual* history in footnotes. Making coherent sense of his views here is difficult, if not impossible.

[159] *Ibid.*, p. 111; see also pp. 108–116.

[160] *Ibid.*, pp. 116–122.

[161] McMullin [1970], pp. 31–34.

[162] See Section 3c of Lakatos [1970].

in the growth of scientific knowledge? Certainly it is not a very illuminating account of the role of reason in the development of scientific theories, and it certainly would be a mistake to insist that science *must* be done in accordance with it. Yet, as his own historical examinations show, it does provide at least a *partial* account of ways in which theoretical advance in science *could* have occurred under at least *some* circumstances. In short, we can conclude that Lakatos has exposed *partially* one reasoning pattern in the growth of scientific knowledge which, in some circumstances, *is* characteristic of good reasoning in science; but even in the cases he examines, much of the reasoning involved is not reflected in his account.[163] Moreover, it is at best *a* pattern of good reasoning, and very often science does, and ought to, employ other, incompatible, patterns in proceeding rationally. Other than this limited achievement, Lakatos's work does little to illuminate the role of rationality in the growth of scientific knowledge.

2. Toulmin

Earlier Stephen Toulmin's views on science were examined (pp. 127–135). Briefly these views were that the function of science is to build up systems of explanatory techniques; a variety of *representational devices*, including models, diagrams, and theories is employed to describe and reason about phenomena. Theories consist of ideals of natural order (which provide ways of looking at or representing phenomena), laws, and hypotheses which are stratified nondeductively via meaning relationships. In science, theories, techniques for representing phenomena, and terminologies are introduced in one fell swoop; and when the terminology involves words or concepts already in prior use, their incorporation into theory involves some change in meaning or a *language shift*. Theories and other representational devices are neither true nor false, but statements about their scope or range of application are; thus the fruitfulness of theories is judged relative to the presuppositions and interests of scientists, and not their truth.[164] Science is not a static enterprise; rather its concepts, interests, presuppositions, theories, and other representational devices are dynamically evolving.

[163] To see this, contrast Lakatos's discussion of the Bohr research program (*ibid*., pp. 140–154) with Shapere's on pp. 558–564 above.

[164] But assertions to the effect that such and such law, model, or whatever represents this or that phenomenon to within measurement error and so forth, *are* true or false. Thus Toulmin's "instrumentalism" is much more benign than that of, say, instrumentalist positivists who denied that theoretical assertions are descriptive of anything; and it escapes many of the standard objections against instrumentalism (see pp. 27–36 above).

In his "Postscript" (pp. 600–614 above), Toulmin commented on the state of philosophy of science at the time of the symposium and where he thought it should be headed. Since the symposium, he has published Volume I of his *Human Understanding*[165] in which he attempts to extend his earlier views on science, together with ideas on reasoning presented in his earlier book, *The Uses of Argument*,[166] along those lines. Actually, the scope of *Human Understanding* is much broader than accomplishing just this, being an attempt to provide "a systematic reanalysis of the problem of human understanding, and of the role of 'concepts' in the growth and expression of knowledge."[167] His approach is the ambitious attempt to "consider, first, our current ideas about the historical evolution of human knowledge and understanding—i.e. the *growth* of concepts— . . . secondly, those about the development of such understanding within the lifespan of human individuals—i.e. the *grasp* of concepts—[and, thirdly,] what we can then learn about the *worth* of concepts—i.e. the foundations on which their intellectual authority rests, and the standards against which it is to be appraised."[168] The first issue is the focus of Volume I of *Human Understanding*, the second and third being the respective focuses of the announced, but not yet published and overdue, Volumes II and III; thus our discussion here must confine its attention to developments in just the first volume concerning the growth or evolution of concepts and their collective use by disciplines.

Toulmin rejects those views which construe "scientific concepts as terms in formal calculi or as names for empirical classes, in favor of a procedural analysis, linking them to the alternative 'techniques of representation' in explanatory practice,"[169] where to represent (*darstellung*) a phenomenon is "to 'demonstrate' or 'display' it, in the sense of setting it forth, or exhibiting it, so as to show in an entirely public manner what it comprises, or how it operates: as when an hydraulic system of tubes and pumps is used to provide a simplified representation, or explanatory model, of a complex electrical circuit."[170] It is important to note that the linkage of concepts with "techniques of representation" is not that of identifying concepts with words, theories, models, axiomatic calculi, or other representational devices; rather such devices are *means for expressing* or symbolizing concepts with varying degrees of adequacy. But since the public use of concepts requires resort to such representational devices, "theories, techniques of representation, and terminologies are in-

[165] Toulmin [1972].
[166] Toulmin [1964].
[167] Toulmin [1972], pp. 9–10.
[168] *Ibid.*, pp. 11–12.
[169] *Ibid.*, p. 192.
[170] *Ibid.*, p. 195.

troduced together, at one swoop";[171] so, for Toulmin, providing an analysis of the growth of scientific concepts indirectly provides an analysis of the growth of theories, techniques of representation, terminologies, and, presumably, of the growth of scientific knowledge.

Given his special sense of 'concept,' it is clear that conceptual diversity is characteristic of the history of science; and it is implausible to suppose that there is any fixed, absolute, and unchanging set of concepts adequate for doing science. Thus conceptual *relativity* is characteristic of science; but prior attempts to accommodate such relativity have succumbed to conceptual *relativisms*, such as Collingwood's, Kuhn's, and Feyerabend's, wherein there is no basis for the rational evaluation of theories, concepts, and so on, and science ceases to be objective. A central goal of Toulmin's is to provide a *model of conceptual change* which reflects conceptual relativity without becoming trapped in a conceptual *relativism*. From a sustained analysis of both "absolutist" positions which deny conceptual relativity and of such relativisms, he concludes that they both rest on the erroneous assumption that rationality is an attribute of a conceptual or logical system; and he argues that the correct view is that "rationality is an attribute . . . of the human activities or enterprises of which particular sets of concepts are the temporary cross-sections: specifically, of the procedures by which the concepts, judgments, and formal systems currently accepted in these enterprises are criticized and changed."[172] When the enterprise is science, it is a *collective* activity involving groups of scientists; thus rationality in science is an attribute of the *collective* use, evaluation, criticism, and alteration of concepts. And rationality in the growth of scientific concepts is to be understood in terms of the *process* whereby scientific disciplines evaluate and change their concepts—which process Toulmin sees as being evolutionary in nature. Toulmin's central task, then, is to develop an evolutionary model of conceptual change within scientific disciplines and evaluate its adequacy—both with respect to its fidelity to actual scientific practice and its ability to account for conceptual relativity without becoming a conceptual relativism.

Toulmin's approach to developing his model is quite straightforward: Maintaining, correctly, "that Darwin's populational theory of 'variation and natural selection' is one illustration of a more general form of historical explanation; and that this same pattern is applicable also, on appropriate conditions, to historical entities and populations of other kinds,"[173] he

[171] Toulmin [1953], p. 146.

[172] Toulmin [1972], p. 134; the analysis leading up to this conclusion is on pp. 41–130.

[173] *Ibid.*, p. 135. Taken abstractly, the "explanatory pattern" is that of a "parallel-processing" *adaptive system*. For a precise statement of the characteristics of adaptive systems, as well as rigorous proof of the fact that biological natural selection is but one of a wide variety of [robust] adaptive systems, see Holland [1975]. There Holland demonstrates

attempts to show that the pattern applies to the process of conceptual change within scientific disciplines. In the genetic natural selection case, we have populations of *genotypes—types* of chromosomes (organized strings of genes). Often genotypes are *variants* on each other. For example, in *Drosophila* body color is controlled by a particular gene location on a pair of chromosomes. A variety of different genes, known as *alleles*, can occupy this location—including a dominant one (B) for grey body color and a recessive one (b) for black body color; body color is determined, roughly, by the paired alleles occupying this location on the paired chromosomes—BB, Bb, and bB producing grey bodies and bb producing black bodies. Within a population, genotypes which are appropriately related constitute *species*. Since more than one chromosome, and more than one genotype, may share genes in common, genes typically will occur a number of times within the population of genotypes. Thus the population of genotypes also may be viewed as a *gene pool*—which has various genes in various proportions. Through a process of reproduction and, to a lesser degree, mutation, makeup of the gene pool changes over time—the relative proportions of the genes being changed. The means for most such changes in the makeup of the gene pool are the death and birth-via-reproduction of organisms bearing those genes. If an organism dies without reproducing, its genes disappear from the gene pool without being replicated. But if the organism survives long enough to reproduce, then multiple copies of its genes are replicated and added to the pool. Depending on the collective reproductive behavior of a particular genotype, the proportion of its genes increases or decreases. The mechanisms whereby such proportions change include the reproductive mechanisms of crossover and inversion of paired chromosomes, as well as mutation. Roughly speaking, the *fitness* of a genotype is its reproduction rate relative to other genotypes;[174] the "fitter" genotypes are those which tend to have enough members surviving to reproduce in substantial quantities relative to other genotypes in the population.[175] "Fitness" applies to

---

that the general pattern not only encompasses genetic natural selection phenomena, but also a variety of phenomena falling within economics (such as the "von Neumann technology"), game theory, pattern recognition, control and function optimalization, and physiological psychology. A briefer version of Holland's results is found in his [1976].

[174] The account just given oversimplifies the biology, in effect being a special case where a genotype is identified with the contents of a single gene position rather than entire chromosomal makeups. Since Toulmin's model has no analog to epistatic or "linked effects" of coadapted alleles, this special case is the appropriate expository foil. Another oversimplification is corrected in note 175.

[175] What counts in natural selection is the passing on of genes and their relative proportion in the gene pool, not that all surviving members reproduce. To the extent that social organizations which divide the reproductive and food gathering, rearing and support activities between members of a genotype or species have the effect of enhancing reproduction rates of genes both reproducing and nonreproducing members carry, the activities of the

species only indirectly—the fitter species being those which consist, to an appreciable degree, of relatively fit genotypes.

The key ingredients, then, in natural selection are a population of entities forming a "pool" and grouping into "species"; mechanisms for altering the proportion of various types of entities in that "pool" over time; and some objective notion of relative "fitness" for these types of entities or the "species" they form. In Toulmin's evolutionary model of conceptual change, the population forming a "pool" will be a collection of concepts, methods, and "fundamental aims";[176] his species will be "more or less separate and well-defined 'disciplines,' each characterized by its own body of concepts, methods, and fundamental aims."[177] Over time the conceptual content of a discipline can change quite drastically, and more slowly so can its aims and methods. "Yet each discipline, though *mutable*, normally displays a recognizable continuity, particularly in the selective factors that govern changes in its content."[178] Such continuity and change consist in the generation of intellectual novelties (variant concepts, methods, and fundamental aims), only a few of which win acceptance, thereby surviving and winning an ongoing place in the conceptual pool associated with a discipline.[179] The mechanisms whereby such conceptual variants (mutant concepts?) succeed in winning widespread acceptance in the discipline ("survive to reproduce in volume") or fail to are of two sorts: *reasons* and *causes*. The reasons constitute rational processes for the evaluation of intellectual novelties or conceptual variants; and the causes

---

nonreproducing organisms can enhance the fitness of their own genotypes or species; such is the case with bees. The newly emerging, and controversial, field of *sociobiology* is concerned with the investigation of such "social" factors which confer evolutionary advantage or increase fitness. See Wilson [1975]; a useful and fair evaluation of the sociobiology controversy surrounding Wilson's book is Wade [1976]. With respect to humans, one of the more interesting suggestions to emerge from sociobiology is that having a certain proportion of the human population be homosexual confers evolutionary advantage (for hints see Wilson [1975], p. 555). An appraisal of the sociobiology controversy from the perspective of philosophy of science is found in the symposium on sociobiology (with Richard D. Alexander, Richard Lewontin, Stuart Kauffmann, and Michael Ruse) in Suppe and Asquith [1977]. A philosophical attempt to apply sociobiology to the scientific enterprise is found in Hull [forthcoming].

[176] Often Toulmin writes as if the pools were just of concepts; but if his disciplines are to be species analogues, the pools will have to include methods and fundamental aims as well. Exegesis is hampered by the fact that his drawing of the analogy between natural selection and conceptual evolution is not that precise; for example, his setting forth of natural selection theory does not approach the precision of the account given above.

[177] Toulmin [1972], p. 139.

[178] *Ibid.*, italics added.

[179] *Ibid.*, pp. 139–140. Toulmin never gives an adequate account of what the continuity consists in; on pp. 340–347 he suggests an account on the analogy of the "interfertility" definition of species, raises problems with the account that are serious, then drops the issue without showing how to avoid the difficulties. The problems are analogous to those in defining 'species' in biology. See Hull [1964], pp. 37–70; and Section 1 of Suppe [1974].

are those various social and other factors, such as the "intellectual politics" of disciplines which sometimes override reason, and in any case are an important force in shaping the accepted intellectual content of a discipline.[180] Reasons correspond to the sorts of factors studied by internal history and causes concern the sort of factors studied by external history (see Section III-A above); thus the actual course of intellectual development or evolution of a scientific discipline depends on both sorts of factors, reasons and causes; and an adequate model or picture of a particular discipline's course of development must combine both internal and external history.[181] At least in Volume I of *Human Understanding*, Toulmin does not seem to be particularly concerned with fitness notions (this presumably concerning the "worth" of concepts, and so being the concern of Volume III which has not appeared), so it is difficult to tell what his analogue to the fitness of genotypes or species would be.

Toulmin devotes several hundred pages to developing and motivating the foregoing analogies, thereby providing his evolutionary model with texture and detail. Like Darwin, and unlike contemporary natural selection theory, Toulmin's focus is on the species—his disciplines—not the changing gene pool or collected genotypes. His first task is to characterize what it is to be a scientific discipline. Taking a clue from Shapere's discussion of scientific domains (pp. 518–565 above), he notes that "the same type of object will fall within the domains of several different sciences, depending on what questions are raised about it"[182] and what it is that makes a problem "problematic" will be from the point of view of a specific discipline. Thus "the nature of an 'intellectual discipline' always involves both its concepts and also the men who conceived them, both its subject matter or 'domain' and also the over-arching intellectual ambitions uniting the men who work within it."[183] So a discipline is a continuing histori-

[180] Toulmin [1972], pp. 222–224.

[181] *Ibid.*, pp. 300–307. "Intellectual ecology" is Toulmin's term for this combined approach to explaining scientific change via his evolutionary model which, in taking into account both reasons and causes, combines internal and external history; see *ibid.*, pp. 307–318. His view of intellectual ecology is broad indeed—encompassing not only internal and external history, but also sociology of science, the psychology of scientific research, and philosophy of science. Moreover, he sees intellectual ecology as extending beyond science to other "compact disciplines" such as judicial law, and so on. The scope which he claims for his intellectual ecology approach, and the profound implications he sees it as having, are displayed quite graphically on *ibid.*, pp. 504–508. These aspects of his work cannot be considered in detail here.

[182] *Ibid.*, p. 149.

[183] *Ibid.*, p. 154. As will be seen in Section 3 below, Shapere rejects the move to such a "social" approach to dealing with the growth of scientific knowledge; specifically, he denies that the psychology, or "intellectual ambitions," of people working in a discipline is essential to determining what is problematic about the domain. This is the most insignificant difference of opinion between Toulmin's and Shapere's positions.

cal entity whose continuity is part intellectual and part professional—a discipline being characterized intellectually by a *geneology of problems* and professionally by a *geneology of institutional authority.*[184]

This "geneology of problems" is to be characterized in terms of an evolutionary account "how the intellectual ideals characteristic of a scientific discipline act as the link between its explanatory techniques, its concepts, its theoretical problems, and empirical applications."[185] Although "the content of a science is . . . transmitted from one generation of scientists to the next by a process of *enculturation*,"[186] thus providing a *transmit*—the set of concepts representative of a historically developing discipline—which "links the ideas of successive generations into a single conceptual geneology."[187] Although providing for a degree of conceptual and cultural stability, the result usually is not a conceptually stagnant discipline. For characteristic of a scientific discipline at any time is some set of *intellectual ideals* or *explanatory ideals* as to what a *complete* explanation would be of those features of the natural world comprising the scientific domain of the discipline; but inevitably the "current ideas [of the discipline] fall short, in some remediable respects, of our intellectual ideals."[188] Thus the scientific problems facing a discipline at a given time are posed by the differences between the intellectual explanatory ideals of the discipline and its current capacity to account for the phenomena in the scientific domain.[189] Some of these problems require the discovery of new facts, others may require the introduction of conceptual novelties, and so on. Thus, in dealing with its scientific problems, members of a discipline often are involved in the generation of *conceptual novelties* which are advanced in competition with prior concepts; Toulmin gives nothing in the way of indicating the role of reason in the generation of these conceptual novelties. The pool of concepts characteristic of a discipline consists of a variety of "conceptual variants" generated in the attempt to resolve the discipline's scientific problems. Of these conceptual variants, only a few are *selected* for perpetuation, for becoming a part of the discipline's repertoire and transmit. Such selection depends on intellectual and professional factors. The intellectual selection factors concern the rational

[184] Toulmin discusses the former in *ibid.*, Chaps. 2 and 3, and the latter in Chap. 4.
[185] *Ibid.*, p. 155.
[186] *Ibid.*, p. 159.
[187] *Ibid.*, p. 158.
[188] *Ibid.*, pp. 150–151. On p. 152, Toulmin seems to identify intellectual or explanatory ideals with the "ideals of natural order" of his *Foresight and Understanding*; but, at least as we interpreted and characterized ideals of natural order on pp. 128–129 above, they do not seem to be the same thing as intellectual or explanatory ideals. Determining what the connections are between these various ideals is complicated by the fact that his various statements about them on pp. 152, 153, and 174 of [1972] are inconsistent.
[189] Toulmin [1972], p. 152.

evaluation of conceptual variants—the selection in favor of or against concepts on the basis of reasons—for example, by showing that one particular conceptual innovation is most successful in resolving the conceptual problems of the science. Such evaluations are comparative—concerning its relative ability to resolve problems compared to other available conceptual variants. These evaluations take into account a variety of factors including predictiveness, coherence, scope, precision, intelligibility, and so on. But sometimes the evaluation involves a reappraisal of the fundamental aims of the discipline, a reassessment of the explanatory ideals of a discipline. For one way to solve a problem is to eliminate it; and as the problems facing a discipline are determined by the difference between the ideals and explanatory achievements of the discipline, changing the explanatory ideals sometimes can eliminate the problem. In such cases, the focus of intellectual debate is not so much on choosing between competing conceptual variants as between competing explanatory ideals or intellectual strategies. And in such cases, to the extent the evaluation is rational, the reasoning consists of "broader arguments involving the comparison of alternative intellectual strategies, in the light of historical experience and precedents."[190] And, of course, which competing explanatory ideals are selected will affect which conceptual variants win out in the comparative evaluation of relative abilities to solve scientific problems.

Thus, through such procedures of reasoned comparison of conceptual variants and explanatory ideals, selection occurs among the innovations and novelties produced by members of a discipline. And, says Toulmin, this endows science with the requisite objectivity—not the objectivity of the empiricists and positivists which involved the matching of hypothesis against facts. Rather, objectivity rests in the fact that our conceptual and strategic judgments are exposed to criticism in the light of experience in ways that "involve prospective estimates of the consequences to be expected from alternative intellectual policies, and so amount to 'rational bets' . . . with the possibility of making the natural world itself a more intelligible object of human understanding. So, in the nature of the case, these strategic issues have an epistemic aspect."[191]

Although reasoned intellectual choice typically is, and should be, a strong factor influencing the development of a discipline, other factors are involved. For scientific disciplines have associated with them formal and informal organizations—power structures—which exert considerable influence on which conceptual variants, proposed revisions in explanatory ideals, and the like do get selected. Such professional organization confers

[190] *Ibid.*, p. 237. The foregoing is based on pp. 222–242.

[191] *Ibid.*, p. 246; the objectivity of intellectual selection discussion occurs on pp. 242–260.

intellectual authority on certain people, and the reception given by those in position of intellectual authority to proposed intellectual novelties often plays an important role in the reception of such novelties. On the one hand, acceptance of an innovative idea by those in authority may promote the selection of the idea for perpetuation, and rejection by those in authority may be sufficient to remove an idea from serious contention. On the other hand, the putting forth of new ideas by "young Turks" may lead to the toppling of established authority and a change in the professional power structure. Thus an important part of conceptual change involves the evolution of the professional organization of scientific disciplines and the mechanisms for the transfer of intellectual authority. Although these issues, which Toulmin deals with through an "ecological analysis," are important to a full understanding of the scientific enterprise, we will ignore them here. Our concern is with rationality in the growth of scientific knowledge; and to the extent that transfer of authority is based on being the author of those intellectual novelties, which, on the basis of reasoned evaluation, are most successful or promising, we have already considered what Toulmin has to say on the matter. And to the extent that transfer of authority concerns other factors, it is not directly concerned with rational aspects of scientific change.[192]

The foregoing narrative does not convey the richness of Toulmin's insights about science and the often perceptive observations he makes on aspects of the scientific enterprise and on particular episodes in the history of science. In this respect, *Human Understanding* is a very impressive piece of work that is well worth reading. But such insights are embroidery that embellish, but do not add substantially to the detailed articulation of, his evolutionary model of conceptual change and the role of rationality therein. All this illustrative detail notwithstanding, the foregoing captures the essential ingredients of his position and reflects the vagueness of his highly metaphorical articulation of it. Thus his account is exciting, insightful, fascinating, and vague.

Vagueness aside, a number of criticisms can be raised against his evolutionary model. *First*, one of his motives in developing it was to provide a comprehensive account of conceptual change which can provide a basis for historical explanation.[193] How adequately does it achieve this

[192] This is not to say these are irrational aspects, however. Similarly, we will ignore here Toulmin's consideration of the extent to which his evolutionary model applies to "less compact" fields which do not qualify as disciplines in his sense, as well as his application of the model to the resolution of various "innate structure" contentions concerning the language capabilities of humans. The professional aspects of scientific disciplines are discussed in Chapter 5, and these other two issues in Chapters 6 and 7 respectively of his *Human Understanding* [1972].

[193] See *ibid.*, pp. 135–142, 300–307, 336, 362 *et passim*.

goal? Perhaps the best way to answer this is to evaluate the model in accordance with Toulmin's own account of explanation—as presented in his *Foresight and Understanding* and summarized on pages 127–128 above. On that account phenomena occurring in accordance with an ideal of natural order are self-explanatory, and deviating phenomena are to be explained in terms of laws, and so on, which account for deviations from the expectations provided by that ideal. If Toulmin's evolutionary model is to provide a basis for explaining the evolutionary course of a discipline, then presumably it is to be an ideal of natural order. As an ideal of natural order, it specifies that for "compact" disciplines (for example, developed sciences) having a certain sort of organizational structure, (1) the evolutionary development of the discipline should occur via a process of speculative propounding of conceptual variants and intellectual novelties in response to scientific problems, or else proposing a change in the problems, and (2) such novelties, and so forth, will be selected for or against on the basis of reasons unless institutional or other factors cause different factors to be selected. For such compact disciplines, it would seem that *any* pattern of conceptual change is in accordance with the model, and thus is self-explanatory. If so, the model provides *no* explanation of *particular* patterns of conceptual development for compact disciplines; and for other disciplines, explanations for courses of conceptual change, disunity in the field, and so forth, will be in terms of those factors in virtue of which the subject fails to be a compact discipline.[194] Such a construal may be unfair, however. Toulmin's explanatory ideal may be that science, ideally, is an organized compact discipline which proceeds in its acceptance and rejection of intellectual novelties by means of *reasoned* evaluation. Thus, when a subject undergoes conceptual change via rational evaluation by the members of a compact discipline, then the conceptual development of the science requires no explanation; but when it proceeds otherwise, then conceptual development will deviate from this ideal in ways to be explained either on the basis of poor reasoning (lapses in rationality) or else on the basis of not being a compact discipline (for example, in virtue of features characteristic of what Toulmin calls "diffuse" and "would-be" disciplines). So interpreted, Toulmin's model is capable of providing historical explanations of the development of scientific and other subjects; thus the latter interpretation is the more charitable one, and I will adopt it. So interpreted, Toulmin's model has some potential as an explanatory tool; but its adequacy becomes marred by the fact that Toulmin has precious little to say about what constitutes "good reasoning" in the evaluation of intellectual novelties other than to say it involves "rational bets" as to which of the available competing intellectual novelties is the

[194] This seems to be the thrust of *ibid.*, Chap. 6.

best way to proceed. But in the absence of some sort of account as to what constitutes a rational bet, we are left in the dark. This being, apparently, the focus of the promised third volume of *Human Understanding*, it is impossible to assess now how adequate his evolutionary model is for explaining or understanding the historical developments of various intellectual subjects, disciplines, and so on.[195]

Second, we noted in our account of genetic natural selection theory that an important part of the theory is developing objective measures of fitness for populations of genes, genotypes, or species; indeed, the explanatory force of evolutionary theory lies in its ability to rate comparative fitness in various environments. Toulmin says relatively little about fitness. For conceptual populations—pools of conceptual variants—presumably fitness will be acceptance or rejection for propagation of intellectual novelties or conceptual variants; for scientific disciplines, it is very unclear what fitness would consist in. Toulmin gives us no real hint, and the only plausible candidate would seem to be following procedures in the development of one's concepts which tend to converge on truth, knowledge, or "fruitful" ways of representing phenomena that adequately do represent phenomena.[196] *Third*, to continue the latter point, Toulmin does view his account as being, *inter alia*, an epistemic enterprise, as having an epistemic dimension. But it is unclear precisely what the epistemic connection is that Toulmin sees. Although Toulmin denies that

[195] Toulmin might reject my demand here for criteria of good reasoning as being too absolutist—noting that the evolution of "improved" criteria of "good reasoning" is characteristic of the history of science, and so there will be a relativity of criteria of good reasoning. But if he makes this move, it is hard to see how he simultaneously can use his model as an ideal of natural order (along the lines of our second interpretation) and also avoid the *relativism* of "good reasoning" being whatever a discipline or subject takes to be good reasoning. But see note 198, Subsection 3, and Section D below for further discussion.

[196] There are potential difficulties with both these "fitness" notions. As to the first, the population model of natural selection theory requires there to be pluralities of genes; the analog here would be that conceptual populations would have to include multiple copies of conceptual variants, and propagation as part of the transmit would have to consist in the continuation of these copies over time in substantial numbers. The only plausible candidates for these multiple copies would seem to be "conceptual variants accepted by people," the number of copies in the population being the number of people accepting them. For an example of an evolutionary account of scientific change from this perspective, see Chapter 4 of my [1967]. I have serious doubts about such a model, for reasons connected with my third criticism below: Briefly, an adequate account of rationality in the growth of scientific knowledge is going to have to show how rational evaluation procedures have an epistemic payoff, how they favor achieving knowledge; and such an account will have to proceed in terms of *rational acceptability*.But the population model under consideration is in terms of *acceptance*, not acceptability. Still, to make contact with the second "fitness" notion, there is the possibility that an acceptance model might provide a useful framework for a comparative evaluation of which of the acceptance practices of two competing disciplines are most likely to converge on the truth without presupposing an ideal or ultimate account of rational acceptability. (Such was the attempt of my dissertation [1967].) Whether such an approach can prove successful presently is less than clear to me.

theories, laws, and so on, are true or false—only statements about their scope are—his view of knowledge is a realistic one wherein what correctly represents the world is essential to knowledge.

> Complete scientific knowledge . . . involves knowledge both of the explanatory procedures of a science and of their application to Nature. . . . Nor can any abstract general theory ever, in and by itself, 'explain' or 'represent' natural phenomena. . . .
>
> The empirical knowledge that a scientific theory gives us is always the knowledge that some general procedure of explanation, description, or representation (specified in abstract, theoretical terms) can be successfully applied (in a specific manner, with a particular degree of precision, discrimination, or exactitude) to some particular class of cases (as specified in concrete, empirical terms).[197]

It would appear, then, that the epistemic part of science involves getting reasonably accurate explanatory representations (*Darstellungen*) of particular phenomena, and that the epistemic dimension of his evolutionary model concerns the ability of science to evolve such representative techniques. But not every historically evolving discipline need evolve such techniques. Our second interpretation of the "explanatory force" of Toulmin's model (above) suggests that Toulmin is committed to the thesis that to the extent that a subject proceeds rationally, the *odds* are that it will converge on representational techniques which both yield knowledge about and are explanatory of particular phenomena; and that "compact" disciplines do so more efficiently than do noncompact ("diffuse" or "would-be") ones. If so, then this is a thesis that requires arguing for, and such arguments are not likely to be forthcoming in the absence of some account of what rational evaluation of conceptual novelties consists in, of what constitutes good reasoning in science—something Toulmin has said precious little about.[198]

Fourth, there is good reason to claim that, without serious modifications (along lines that reinforce the above comments), Toulmin's model is incapable of accounting for the epistemic success of science. For on the notions of fitness suggested by his model, those disciplines which are most fit are those which converge efficiently on the production of concepts which adequately represent nature and thus are relatively efficient in producing knowledge. On Toulmin's account such fitness will be a rating of the "variation and selection" procedures used in developing the

[197] Toulmin [1972], pp. 172–173. He credits the early Wittgenstein for the origin of these doctrines. See also *ibid.*, p. 243 and Sects. 2.4 and 3.3 *passim*. Its similarity to Carnap's views on inductive confirmation (Section I-B above) of generalizations as opposed to singular predictive inferences is worth noting.

[198] This is not to say that fully explicit criteria of "good reasoning" are required. They are not, as shall be seen when we consider Shapere's work in the next section. Discussion in Section D will pursue this point still further.

discipline's transmit. Toulmin's account views the introduction of conceptual novelties as being analogous to mutation—they are spontaneously generated possible solutions to scientific problems facing the discipline; but there is overwhelming evidence now, resulting from work on fitness and the efficiency of geneticlike adaptive systems, that recombination of the population (for example, gene pool, transmit, and so on) of variants by just mutationlike operators fails to produce an efficient (robust) adaptive system.[199] In terms of Toulmin's model, this means that if spontaneous, mutationlike, generation of conceptual variants is the process for providing conceptual novelties in science, scientific disciplines will be relatively inefficient in producing knowledge—that is, will be relatively inefficient epistemic enterprises. To be epistemically reliable and successful, the production of conceptual variants will have to be conditioned by the present state of the discipline in ways that are analogous to "cross-over," "inversion," and so on, operators which operate on linked alleles ("strongly correlated items of the domain"). Thus the role of reason in the production of conceptual variants is of crucial epistemic importance to any evolutionary attempt to deal with the growth of scientific knowledge; and the fact Toulmin ignores this aspect of the problem is a serious deficiency in the analysis—just as it was in Lakatos's research programs analysis.

What emerges from these connected points is that for all its many merits, Toulmin's *Human Understanding*, Volume I, and the evolutionary model he develops there, says precious little about *rationality* in the growth of scientific *knowledge*, although it is possible to conjecture (as we did) ways in which he could exploit the developments there in deriving an account of rationality in the growth of scientific knowledge. Presumably it is Toulmin's intent to draw such epistemic connections in the projected third volume of that work. But as things presently stand, he has shed little systematic illumination on either the rational evaluation of scientific concepts or on how such rational evaluation enables science routinely to provide knowledge about the world. And it is virtually impossible to ascertain whether he is succeeding in his attempt to obtain an account of conceptual relativity that does not succumb to relativism.

3. Shapere[200]

At a number of places in this volume, we have discussed or encountered Dudley Shapere's penetrating critical discussions of Kuhn,

[199] For the rigorous evidence, see Holland [1975]; virtually the entire book is involved in proving this important finding.

[200] While this section focuses on Dudley Shapere's work some attention will be given to related work by two of his former students, Lindley Darden and Nancy Maull [Roth]. I am

Feyerabend, and logical positivism; throughout his critical writings,[201] there are several persistent underlying themes or assumptions:

> *Postulate of Scientific Rationality*: Scientific development and innovation are often appropriately describable as rational.
> *Postulate of the Generalizability of Scientific Reasoning*: The rationality involved in specific cases is often generalizable as principles applicable in many other cases.
> *Postulate of the Systematizability of Scientific Reasoning Principles*: These principles can in some sense be systematized.[202]

One of his basic objections against both the extreme *Weltanschauungen* views of, for example, Kuhn and Feyerabend and the views of logical positivism is that they deny, fully or in part, these postulates and thereby present highly distorted and inaccurate pictures of the scientific enterprise; and, as a result, the parasitic accounts they give of scientific knowledge have little to do with the knowledge actually produced by science. It is his view not only that these postulates must underlie an adequate philosophy of science, but also that the systematic examination of the "reasoning patterns" actually employed in science is a primary source of information about the nature of scientific knowledge and the theories, models, and conceptual devices science employs. Thus the key to developing an adequate philosophical understanding of science as an epistemic enterprise is the detailed examination of actual scientific practice, from which one generalizes and evaluates the reasoning patterns encountered.[203] Of course, Shapere acknowledges that in the process of generalizing these reasoning patterns and in analyzing the conceptual devices they employ, other techniques and methods, including some of those employed by the more formally inclined positivists, may be appropriate;[204] but the adequacy of such analyses or constructions must be judged both on their philosophical merits *and* by their fidelity to actual scientific practice. And, if philosophy of science is pursued in this way, the reasoning patterns discerned, and the portrait of scientific knowledge which follows, will be such that "their formulation requires no reference to psychological or sociological factors, and their operation in concrete cases is, or at least can be, independent of such factors."[205] Accordingly, it

---

grateful to Professors Shapere, Darden, and Maull for access to various unpublished or forthcoming manuscripts of theirs.

[201] They include Shapere's [1960], pp. 376–385; "Introduction" to his [1965]; [1966]; [1969]; [1971]; [1967]; and [1963].

[202] See pp. 524–525 above.

[203] Shapere maintains this not just for philosophy of science, but for philosophy in general.

[204] See, for example, the "Introduction" to his [1965], p. 29.

[205] "Scientific Theories and Their Domains" (pp. 518–565, above), p. 564.

is both unnecessary and inappropriate to present the sorts of "socio-psychological" views of scientific knowledge that, for example, Kuhn does and Toulmin flirts with.

But Shapere's motives for approaching philosophy of science historically do not stem merely from a desire to steer a middle ground between the excesses of logical positivism and the *Weltanschauungen* analyses. A more basic motivation is that he sees such an historical approach, focusing on the examination of reasoning patterns in actual science, as being absolutely essential to solving what he takes to be the *fundamental problem* in philosophy of science—making sense of and determining how science has arrived in a justified way at its present, extremely *weird*, beliefs about how the world is. For example, the pictures of the world provided by quantum theory and general relativity theory border on the bizarre. No naive consideration of logical possibilities would have included such pictures among the logically possible. Thales and Aristotle could not have arrived at quantum theory; no naive examination of experience could have suggested such a view of the world. If logical possibilities and experience cannot explain how anybody could rationally have arrived at the quantum picture of the world, what could? Shapere's answer is that we have to look at how our ideas about the universe have developed and changed—at the kinds of beliefs held earlier about the world and why they rationally *had* to be changed. And, here, a *further* question needs to be raised—namely, whether concepts, propositions, reasoning patterns, and methods that prove to be stable in the history of science and govern the ways changes of ideas take place are stable because they are independent of the *content* of science at any stage—as was supposed by Plato in his doctrines on forms, Kant with his categories, and logical positivism with its logical and metascientific views. Or is it the case that, more in keeping with Aristotle, the logical and methodological criteria whereby science develops are influenced or determined by the *content* of the science at the time. That is, to what extent does the content of knowledge claims have a "feedback" influence on what the concepts for science should be. It is Shapere's position not only that the content of science *does* impose constraints on what is a legitimate scientific concept, problem, or hypothesis, but also that these constraints become tighter and tighter as science develops and the scientific alternatives allowed become more surprising. It is these constraints imposed by "feedback" from the content of science that suggest and render plausible extremely "weird" views about the world such as are provided by contemporary physics. Such an approach to philosophy of science—one that involves a larger attack on that tradition in the philosophy of science (having its origins in Plato and extending down through Kant to the positivists, Feyerabend, and Kuhn) which denies that "facts raise their own questions" and suggest solutions to them—makes historical and philosophical examination of reasoning patterns in science absolutely essential. Without such examination, there is little chance of either answering Shapere's fundamental problem in philosophy of science or determining the extent to which the content of science influences the specific directions of that science's subsequent development.[206]

Shapere's assertion of his three postulates (or assumptions as he sometimes calls them), and the attendant view on what philosophy of science ought to be, is anything but dogmatic; in a sustained series of historical case studies, he has vindicated those postulates by repeatedly discerning "reasoning patterns" involved in scientific innovation and development, shown how they can be generalized into principles of good scientific reasoning, and displayed a number of instances where the content of science does impose constraints on and influence the direction of subsequent development of the science. And through case studies, he also has shown how the examination of reasoning patterns used in employing theories, models, and conceptual devices such as idealizations adds to our understanding of the "nature" of those devices.[207] The cases in question cover the whole spectrum of what Kuhn calls "pre-paradigm," "normal," and "revolutionary" science. Thus, contra Kuhn and fellow travelers, the postulates of rationality, generalizability, and systematizability are vindicated by the history of science,[208] as is his view that the content of science influences its further development. Shapere *is* correct when he insists that such compatibility is a necessary condition for being an adequate philosophical account of scientific knowledge. Establishing these three postulates does not, in itself, fully establish the superiority of Shapere's further views on how philosophy of science ought to proceed in obtaining a philosophical understanding of science; those views can be vindicated only by the development of such a philosophy of science—something which Shapere has begun to do, and is continuing to do. We now turn to an examination of the view of science that is emerging from his work.[209]

[206] The foregoing paragraph is based on conversation with Shapere; these themes are echoed on pp. 525–533, especially note 10 on pp. 527–528 and note 13 on p. 529, of Shapere's symposium contribution above.

[207] A number of instances are found in Shapere's "Scientific Theories and Their Domains," pp. 518–565 above. See also his [1969] (part of which is summarized on pp. 565–570 above); [1974]; [1974b]; [1974c]; [1975]; Shapere and Edelman [1974]; as well as several unpublished works cited below. See also Section C below.

[208] Acceptance of them, and the particular case studies Shapere has done, underlies a number of our criticisms of Lakatos and Toulmin, as well as of the *Weltanschauungen* analyses, above.

[209] Although much of what follows is at least hinted at in his symposium contribution

Central to Shapere's account of scientific knowledge and its growth is his notion of a *scientific domain* which he introduced in his symposium contribution, "Scientific Theories and Their Domains" (pp. 518–565 above). Scientific domains are characterized as a number of *items of information* (putative facts, including, perhaps, accepted laws and theories) which come to be associated together as a *body* of *information* having the following characteristics: the association is based on some well-grounded, significant, relationship between the items of information which are suggestive of deeper unities among the items; there is something problematic about the body so related; the problems are important; and, usually, science is "ready" to deal with them.[210] That is, at any given stage in an area of science, the science is concerned with a body of information (domain) which *generates* problems; and scientific progress focuses on attempting to solve those problems. In saying that the domain generates problems, Shapere is claiming that the very association of items in the domain, together sometimes with appropriately related *background information*, rationally poses or raises problems.[211] A variety of such problems can be discerned: *Domain problems* are concerned with clarification of the domain itself; *theoretical problems* are those calling for a "deeper" account of the domain and answers to them are theories; *theoretical inadequacies* are problems regarding theories themselves (see p. 533 above). Not only does the associative organization of a domain pose

---

(above), as well as in the other works cited in notes 201 and 207 above, I have relied on the following unpublished manuscripts (which have been presented various places or circulated) by Shapere which develop them more fully; "Interpretations of Science in America"; "The Concept of Observation in Science and Philosophy"; "What Can the Theory of Knowledge Learn from the History of Knowledge?"; "On the Introduction of New Hypotheses in Science, and on the Notion of Rationality in Science"; "Explanation and the Structure of Reality"; "On the Role of Conceptual Devices in Science"; and "On the Relationship between Science and the Humanities." The first four of these are in the process of being reworked as Parts I–IV respectively of a monograph-length work entitled "The Concept of Observation in Science and Philosophy" for publication in a future volume of the Pittsburgh series in philosophy of science.

Since these works are expected to undergo revision before publication, and some of them exist in several versions, page references for quoted passages will not be given. All quotations from these works are with the kind permission of Professor Shapere.

[210] See pp. 525–533 above. Although domains are, from one perspective, constituted by the items of information dealt with by the "scientific community" of practitioners in the area, the notion of a domain ultimately is not a sociological one. For what constitutes a domain is not collectivity of opinion among a group of scientists; rather it is the conceptual interconnections of the items and the existence of reasons for their association that groups the items into a domain. That is, the association of items of information into a domain must be grounded in reason. Thus domains are not sociological entities, although they are historical subjects associated with groups of scientists who work with them.

[211] As was indicated above, it is here that Shapere most severely parts company with most of recent philosophy of science—including not only the positivists, Popper, Kuhn, and Feyerabend, but also Toulmin and, apparently, Lakatos.

various problems, but often it tends to "favor" certain types of solutions to these problems in the sense that the domain, possibly augmented by appropriate "background information," rationally suggests certain sorts of solutions. That is, there are good reasoning patterns which allow one to conclude, on the basis of such information, that a particular kind of theory is needed, or that a particular approach to eliminating theoretical inadequacies is appropriate. (Examples of such reasoning patterns are given on pages 541, 545–546, 553, and 558–564 of Shapere's symposium contribution above.)

Although Shapere initially tended to identify domains with scientific fields such as genetics, subsequent investigation has revealed that *scientific fields* are not domains, but rather are a broader concept. In an important historical study of the emergence of genetics as a field,[212] Lindley Darden has argued that fields are areas of science containing scientific domains, about which there are central problems, augmented by certain explanatory factors and goals, accepted experimental techniques and methods, and concepts and laws which are interrelated. And she has shown, through her emergence-of-genetics case study, that an area of science that fails to qualify as a field can develop into a field. Moreover, fields can exist prior to the emergence of a theory solving their central problems; and the elements in the field (domain items, explanatory factors, and so on) play an important role in the discovery of such a theory—in ways that can be generalized into reasoning patterns. In the cases examined thus far, arguments from analogy play an important role.[213] Fields, then, are not domains, although they contain them;

[212] Darden [1974]. The importance of this work rests not only in its philosophical contributions, but also in its well-defended challenge to previous views on the history of genetics. Refined versions of her dissertation work, which extend it further, are found in her [1976]. Nancy Maull [Roth] further develops the notion of a field and the theoretical relations between fields in [1974]. Combined presentations of their results are found in Darden and Maull [Roth] [1975] and [forthcoming].

[213] In her [1974] and [1976], Darden discerns "the following general schema for a pattern of reasoning in hypothesis-construction:

problem posed by fact	generalize →	general form of the problem	analogize to →	general forms of similar problems with solutions ↓
plausible solution to this problem	← particularize	general form of solution to problem	← construct	general forms of other known solutions

The pattern of reasoning is used for each of the facts in turn. The use of the same explanatory factor in each case results in a hypothesis made up of a set of postulates all of which involve the same explanatory factors" ([1976], p. 142). Further, the following conditions are necessary for the plausibility of a hypothesis constructed using this reasoning pattern: (a) the postulate provides a possible solution to the problem posed by the fact; (b) it is a form of solution found in the world or else likely to be found given our general empirical rather fields constitute a variety of sophisticated science and have characteristic reasoning patterns that are not found in primitive or other stages of science.[214]

Since the development of a scientific area starts from, and is conditioned rationally by, a scientific domain, and since domains are not static but evolve, detailed investigation of domains and their functions is crucial to a philosophical understanding of the scientific enterprise. On page 523 above, Shapere poses six focal problems concerning domains, the answers to which are intended to serve as building blocks for his philosophy of science.

1. What considerations (or, better, types of considerations, if such types can be found) lead scientists to regard a certain body of information as a *body* of information—that is, as constituting a unified subject matter or domain to be examined or dealt with?
2. How is description of the items of the domain achieved and modified at sophisticated stages of scientific development?
3. What sorts of inadequacies, leading to the need for further work, are found in such bodies of information, and what are the grounds for considering these to be inadequacies or problems requiring further research?
4. What considerations lead to the generation of specific lines of research, and what are the reasons (or types of reasons) for considering some lines of research to be more promising than others in the attempt to resolve problems about the domain?
5. What are the reasons for expecting (sometimes to the extent of demanding) that answers of certain sorts, having certain characteristics, be sought for those problems?
6. What are the reasons (or types of reasons) for accepting a certain solution to a scientific problem regarding a domain as adequate?

These questions obviously are not independent, and so cannot be dealt

knowledge; (c) it is a solution embodying the explanatory factors characteristic of the scientific fields (*ibid.*).

In her dissertation, Darden acknowledges the influence on her work of Hanson's work on the role of analogy in scientific discovery. However, as one easily can discern from a comparison of Hanson's views (pp. 162–165 above), and the reasoning pattern just sketched, her view is quite different from Hanson's and is much more sophisticated. And, like Shapere, she does not claim to be developing a *logic* of discovery, if by that one means either an algorithm or a *fixed* canon of reasoning. Rather her interest is in what patterns of reasoning *do* occur in actual science, and she fully expects that in addition to the reasoning pattern given above, historical research will uncover other good patterns of reasoning in scientific discovery; and she is willing to allow that these may be an open-ended variety of such patterns and that new ones may continue to emerge as science progresses.

[214] The notion of a field bears certain relations to "broader" parts of science such as Lakatos's *research programs* and Kuhn's *paradigms*, most closely resembling Toulmin's *disciplines*; yet there are differences. For example, central problems and techniques do not figure in Toulmin's notion of a discipline, and the notion of a field is not tied to Toulmin's "evolutionary epistemology." For a discussion of the differences between fields and these other broader parts of science, see the opening section of Darden and Maull [Roth] [forthcoming].

with in isolation from each other. Thus far, in working toward the solution of these questions, Shapere has focused, and continues to focus, on five interconnected issues: (a) the ways in which "observational facts" come to be grouped together into domains, and how the associations come to be modified and the items of the domain redescribed; (b) the rationale for introducing new hypotheses in science which radically contradict established theory; (c) the role of "background information" in science; (d) the way in which scientific objectivity and rationality are maintained in the face of "interpretation" of "observation" by "theory"; and (e) the role of "conceptual devices" such as "idealizations," "simplifications," "models," and so on, in science—particularly in the description of domain items and in the formulation of solutions to problems about domains. We now will examine Shapere's views on the first four of these—trying to keep in mind that our examination is based on "works in progress." His views on the fifth, "conceptual devices," issue will be considered in Section C below.

Observation and Theory: In introducing his notion of a scientific domain, Shapere tells us that "the concept of a domain is intended to replace the old 'observational-theoretical' distinction as a fundamental conceptual tool for illuminating the nature of science" (p. 528 above). In doing so he is rejecting positivistic views on a theory-neutral observation language; but he also is attempting to do so in a way that avoids "the relativism consequent on the views of Kuhn and Feyerabend."[215] From an examination of logical positivism's views on observation and theory (see pp. 45–50 above), he concludes they rest on an argument, the key moves of which can be summarized in the following progression:

(i) Observation must be independent of, neutral with respect to, the theory to be assessed.
(ii) "Interpretation" always is in terms of "theory."
(iii) Observation must be neutral with respect to *all* theory.
(iv) The observation-language must be the *same* for all theories.

In parallel fashion, he finds that the Feyerabend-Kuhn view makes the following chain of inferences:

(i′) Observation, if it is to be relevant, must be interpreted.
(ii′) That in terms of which interpretation is made is always theory.
(iii′) The theory that interprets is the theory to be tested.
(iv′) The theory to be tested is "the whole of science" (or a branch thereof).
(v′) This whole forms a unity ("paradigm" or "high-level background theory").
(vi′) This unified whole not only serves as a basis of interpretation, but also determines ("defines") what counts as an observation, problem, method, solution, and so forth.

[215] Shapere, "Interpretations of Science in America."

Both (i) and (i′) are plausible, and appear to constitute adequacy criteria for any philosophy of science; and the former motivates logical positivism's views on theory and observation whereas the latter motivates Feyerabend's and Kuhn's. But from (i) and (i′) these two schools of thought progress to (iv) and (vi′), despite the fact that there are serious logical gaps in the progression; and on no plausible interpretation of them do either (iii) through (iv) follow from (i) and (ii) or (iii′) through (vi′) follow from (i′) and (ii′). Rejecting (iii) through (iv) and (iii′) through (vi′) as unacceptable, Shapere argues that the fact neither set of conclusions follows from (i) or (i′) allows one to accept *both* (i) and (i′); and he attempts to develop an analysis of observation and theory based on both (i) and (i′).[216]

His approach is to begin with an examination of the scientific use of 'observation' and 'direct observation' in astrophysics; and he finds that astrophysicists regularly write, for example, of *detecting* neutrino fluxes as yielding *direct observations* of the center of stars. Moreover, the astrophysical use of 'observation' or 'direct observation' (as well as 'detection' and 'probe') is not used in opposition to 'theoretical,' but rather in opposition to 'experimental'—experiment involving interfering with processes which will allow us to test our hypotheses at will and in the most convenient manner, whereas observation generally does not involve such interference or manipulation. Analyzing the astrophysical use of 'direct observation,' he concludes that:

> the expression 'x is directly observed', as used in contexts like those . . . about direct observation of a stellar core, may be explicated as follows:
> 1. Information is received by an appropriate receptor.
> 2. The information is transmitted directly (*i.e.*, without interruption or interference) to the receptor from the entity x said to be observed. (We shall see later that this second condition can be relaxed some.)
>
> That the usage of 'observation' as restricted to reception by the human senses is a special case of this general notion should be obvious.[217]

An "appropriate receptor" is understood as being an instrument able to detect the presence of an interaction (be it an electromagnetic, "strong," "weak," or gravitational interaction), and therefore the presence of the entities interacting, according to the precise rules of current particle physics. Notice that this makes the specification of what counts as directly observable depend on the current state of physical knowledge, and can change as that knowledge changes. In particular, what counts as an "ap-

[216] The foregoing is based on the latter portion of *ibid*. In this work he ignores (ii) and (ii′) which are common to both views; however, he would deny both (ii) and (ii′) (personal communication).

[217] Shapere, "The Concept of Observation in Science and Philosophy."

propriate sensor," "interruption," and "interference" depends on current scientific theory.

Suppose we make a photographic observation of several stars through a telescope. The configuration of dots on the developed photographic plate (the positivist's uninterpreted observation) does not constitute that which is observed. Only when the dots are shown to be *images* of something, conveying *information* via understood *general* processes (for example, that in general there is a precise relationship between brightness of a star and the radius of the corresponding star image), and that this information is *reliable* under the particular instrumental and environmental conditions of the photographing event, do we obtain *data* or *evidence* that constitutes observation. That is, the end product of observation is data or evidence; and such evidence or interpretation is obtained from the photographic plate by recourse to *background information*—including detailed knowledge about the photographic process (for example, relative emulsion shrinkage factors in processing for various degrees of exposure that affect the size of the star images and the distances between them), the general character of telescopes, the physical processes whereby the information is initiated by the entity and transmitted to and received by the receptor (and this may be crucial when, for example, the image is spectroscopic), and the biases and idiosyncrasies of the particular instrument (receptor).

The background (and, possibly, domain) information used in the interpretation of observations is, of course, fallible and liable to possible revision, evaluation, and assessment; so, too, then are the observations obtained. What one observes is not determined solely by the available background information. Observations are undertaken in the expectation that they will be *relevant* to the solution of one or more problems associated with a domain. Such relevancy requires that the interpretation of observation be done in terms of the descriptive vocabulary used to give expression to items of information already in the domain, specify what is problematic about the domain, and formulate theories as solutions to those problems. Appropriate descriptive forms for observations thus play important roles in determining what background information is appropriate for interpreting raw data of an observation and influencing what sorts of theories are advanced. The importance of these points emerges when it is realized different domains or fields may have overlapping phenomena which are described quite differently, resulting in quite different theoretical accounts of the phenomena. For example, in early stages both genetics and cytology were concerned with heredity and theorized about hereditary material (now called genes); but the cytological characterizations were in terms of spatial locations on microscopic structures, whereas genetic accounts were in terms of postulated genes having characteristic breeding patterns but no spatial locations. In developing theories and interpreting observations, the two fields relied on different background information.[218]

In the characterization of direct observation quoted above, it was said that the transmission of information to a receptor should be without interruption or interference; this requires qualification. Interference or interruption is allowable in direct observation so long as known background and domain information enable us to take into account, and *precisely* correct for, any such interruptions or interference. By contrast, *nondirect observations* are those cases where, in order to interpret what is detected by a receptor as relevant information, the available information is only *approximate*—for example, depending on approximations, idealizations, simplifications, and so forth—or involves models, hypotheses, or theories that are not yet adequately established. This is the working direct observation/nondirect observation contrast actually employed in science. Since "theory" is involved in both, "it is not a contrast adequately characterized by a contrast between two different sorts of concepts, one 'observational,' the other 'theoretical.'"[219] This point is further underscored when one realizes that theories characteristically underlie the design of observational apparatus, belong to domains, provide explanations for the unities underlying domains, establish connections between phenomena occurring in related domains, and so on.[220] And theories can be established or problematic, approximate or exact, simplifying or not, and so on. Theory can be involved in both direct and nondirect observation, depending on whether it is established, approximate, and so on. We will see, below, that Shapere maintains this "theory-ladenness" of observation (a dangerously loaded term in philosophical contexts) does not compromise the objectivity of scientific knowledge.

The characterization of direct observation is such that direct observation is a source of knowledge given that the background and other information used in the interpretation is knowledge. This is not always the case for nondirect observation. Suppose, for example, that we have two competing, not yet established, theories or models that could be used to yield different, incompatible, interpretations of what a receptor detects—hence could be used to obtain incompatible nondirect observations. Usually

[218] Later, cytological and genetic accounts were unified. For discussion of differential description of phenomena by overlapping fields, see Maull [Roth] [1974], Ch. I.

[219] Shapere, "The Concept of Observation in Science and Philosophy."

[220] Shapere has tended to focus on theories involving only one domain, although not to the exclusion of those which connect several domains; the latter sort, interfield theories, are identified and discussed in the works by Darden and Maull cited in note 212 above.

these variant interpretations will rely in part on an overlapping body of noncontroversial background theory. Thus, we can *unload* the problematic portions of the interpretation in such a way as to provide an interpretation, hence description, which is common to the competing models or theories, and is epistemically nonproblematic; for "if the two interpretations are to be considered competitors, theory-unloading . . . must be possible so that at some level a common vocabulary (of those two theories, not necessarily a philosopher's dream of a universal common 'observational vocabulary') will remain."[221] And the interpretations of observation resulting from such "theory unloading" not only can be used to test the competing theories and indicate what further direct observations are needed for such testing, but also can provide us with observational knowledge if the unloaded interpretation depends only on background and other knowledge. Several connected points are involved here. *First*, different "levels of description" or interpretations of what a receptor detects are possible, and they characteristically involve different vocabularies; some levels of description or interpretation may be epistemically nonproblematic and others problematic given the present domain and background knowledge. *Second*, the nonproblematic observations available may be insufficient to establish or suggest theories that are adequate for resolving theoretical problems about domains; in such cases, importation of knowledge from other disciplines as background knowledge may enable the reinterpretation or redescription of existing items in the domain in such a way as to provide data sufficient to establish theories that solve domain problems.[222] *Third*, items in the domain may be at different levels of description, and what is problematic about the domain may be generated in part by gaps between the levels of description sanctioned by what is known and the levels of description one has reason to suspect should apply; often the reasons for suspecting a certain level of description should apply indicate the sort of theory needed to establish interpretations of observation at that level. *Fourth*, establishing theory sufficient to show the correctness of observational interpretations at a particular level of description may suffice to explain the underlying unity of the domain and (fully or partially) resolve the crucial problems about domains.

It might be thought that the foregoing picture precludes scientific progress other than by the importation of knowledge from other disci-

221 Shapere, "The Concept of Observation in Science and Philosophy."

222 This often involves interfield theories of the sort discussed by Darden and Maull in the works cited in note 212. These works supply a wealth of case studies documenting this phenomenon. Although often called, or claimed to be, cases of reduction, on Maull's views such uses of interfield theories typically do not involve reducing one field to another. Further discussion of this point is given in Section C below.

plines; and since these disciplines also face the same problems in establishing the adequacy of their observational interpretations, one might be tempted to conclude that ultimately no scientific knowledge involving "theoretical interpretations" is possible—that is, that scientific knowledge is limited to descriptions of the reception of signals by a human sense (the "uninterpreted observations" of the positivists). Shapere would deny it, for science *does* yield knowledge about more than just sensory experience, and in doing so it employs characteristic reasoning patterns. There *are* characteristic reasoning patterns whereby science *does* justify or establish the theories which afford observational knowledge that depends on those theories for its interpretation and description. And this is why the examination of case studies, and the discernment of reasoning patterns employed therein, is crucial. The case studies he has done in his symposium contribution above indicate that there are patterns of reasoning which make it reasonable to expect that a particular *kind* of theory is required. And the items of information in the domain, at their established levels of description, often severely restrict the plausible candidates to such a degree that even single theory-unloaded observations can decide piecemeal between different candidate features of the correct theory—the theory being "*gradually developed* by a process of increasingly precise and detailed statement of the initial vague idea."[223] Or it may be the case that theory-unloaded observations may suffice to establish an approximate solution—that is, to establish that such and such a simplified theory, idealization, or model is approximately correct. That fact then may be used to interpret observations which can be used to decide other features of the correct theory. In turn, these features may be used to interpret data that can decide between plausible improvements on that simplified approximate theory. In many respects, Kepler's theory of the planetary orbits was obtained in just this manner.[224]

One should not suppose that observation affords the only means for establishing theories—be they the theories used to interpret observations or the theories used to explain the underlying unities of domains and resolve other problems raised by domains. As noted above, observation is to be contrasted with experiment. And through the causing of controlled interferences or interactions of phenomena, we can set up experimental situations that inform us which of competing plausible descriptions or interpretations is appropriate and/or whether certain hypotheses (possibly involving new levels of description) are appropriate. For experimentation to yield knowledge, the experimental designs must be in accordance with established background or other knowledge. And the alternative forms of

[223] Shapere, "Scientific Theories and Their Domains," p. 533 above, n. 54.
[224] See Toulmin and Goodfield [1961], pp. 203–204, for illustrations.

description or hypotheses which experiment can be used to decide between will not be just any logically possible alternatives, but rather those one has good reasons to suppose might be true. Although purely observational science is possible, it is more typical for a science to combine observation and experiment. In all but the most primitive stages of science, "theory" is involved in the interpretation of observational and experimental outcomes.[225]

Whether observation or experimentation is used, what emerges from the above considerations is that we find characteristic reasoning patterns employed in successful science whereby, working from items in domains which rest on nonproblematic direct observations or experiments, one is able to establish the appropriateness or approximate correctness of theories and observational interpretations which involve new levels of description. Through this process, science advances from primitive stages where "obvious sensory similarities or general presuppositions" usually determine the interpretation of items in the domain and their association to more sophisticated stages wherein the items of the domain are interpreted on the basis of "theory." As science establishes the appropriateness of such "deeper" levels of description and interpretation, the frontiers of direct observation and experimental knowledge are expanded and the domain items are reassociated in new ways conditioned by the altered interpretation and description of the items in the domain, and by the incorporation of the new nonproblematic interpreting theory into the domain. As the domain items become reinterpreted and the interconnections of the items become reconstituted, the problems associated with a domain change. Sometimes this process is done relative to a fixed body of background information; sometimes it involves the importation of new information from other areas. Sometimes it involves noticing similarities between the differently described contents of different domains and the establishment of various "domain-combining" (interfield) or "domain-preserving" (intrafield) theories.[226] Since similarities are partially a

[225] It should be noted that, thus far, Shapere has written very little on experiment as opposed to observation. However, it seems clear that he would analyze experimentation analogously to observation, the main differences in the account involving "interfering" manipulation of phenomena and the interactions between phenomena and receptors.

[226] For these, see Nickles's symposium contribution above, especially pp. 586–588. In [1974], Chap. III, Nancy Maull [Roth] basically accepts Nickles's views on reduction except she denies that "domain-preserving" reductions are deductive; she maintains that so-called "reductive" phenomena typically do not involve reducing one field to another. In their forthcoming "Interfield Theories," Darden and Maull [Roth] argue against a view, which they attribute to Shapere, that "domain-combining" reductions result in the creation of one new domain or field out of several others. It is not clear to me how significant their disagreement is. What *is* important here is that, whatever the detailed analysis of such "reductive" phenomena, it is one pattern whereby domains evolve and science progresses in the attainment of new knowledge and the resolution of problems posed by domains or fields. Shapere discusses the evolution of domains in his [forthcoming c].

function of how the domain items are described, different descriptions or redescriptions of phenomena may affect which similarities are noticed.

Although characteristic reasoning patterns govern the development of domains and the solution of problems associated with them, it should not be supposed that there is some fixed canon of rationality characteristic of good science for all time. An examination of the history of any well-developed science will reveal not only that different reasoning patterns have been employed at various stages in the science, but also that which patterns are appropriate rationally depends on the nature (contents and organization) of the science at the time. As science progresses, it has to develop new, more sophisticated patterns of reasoning if it is to continue expanding knowledge of its phenomena.[227] And there is no reason not to suppose that, as sophisticated branches of science continue to develop, they will evolve new, hitherto unexemplified patterns of reasoning in justifying and accepting their knowledge claims, and thus in the development of their domains. It should be clear, then, that on Shapere's view the epistemological point of case studies from which one generalizes patterns of sound reasoning is not the production of some exhaustive list of good reasoning patterns such that only they should be used in doing good science. What emerges from a variety of such case studies is that no fixed list is to be expected. That itself is a significant finding about scientific knowledge. Indeed, in Section D we will see that its implications for epistemology are profound. We note that although Shapere's approach does eschew the need for establishing "ultimate" criteria of "good reasoning" in science, it does presuppose that an able philosopher knowledgeable of the relevant science and its history is able to "recognize" good reasoning and thus evaluate the worth of the reasoning patterns exemplified in various scientific episodes.

The Introduction of Radical New Hypotheses: The picture of the growth of scientific knowledge presented thus far concerns "relatively continuous" lines of scientific development wherein past understanding is added to and extended in ways that generate new problems and lead to new findings. But not all scientific progress, not all development or evolution of domains, occurs in such a manner. At crucial junctures in science we find new hypotheses being introduced which radically contradict established theory that is part of the domain. And on occasion such new hypotheses are treated seriously, explored, and even accepted. When this happens, rather dramatic reorganizations of domains occur and as a result

[227] A particularly illuminating example of this is the changing notion of simplicity, and the increasingly subtle simplicity arguments, that have occurred over the history of the theory of general relativity and geometrodynamics. Unfortunately the history of these changes has not been written.

the problems generated by the domain to which the science addresses itself undergo a radical change. The introduction of radical new hypotheses is itself a rational matter, and characteristic reasoning patterns can be discovered for justifying their introduction, treating them seriously, and exploring and developing them. In his "On the Introduction of New Hypotheses in Science," Shapere explores one such case, namely Einstein's introduction of the quantum hypothesis. In 1900 Max Planck had introduced the assumption that a material oscillator of frequency v could emit or absorb energy only in multiples of hv (h being Planck's constant); he introduced this as a simplifying assumption required to apply combinatorial techniques in an attempt to derive the "black-body" radiation law. Although he wavered on this in private, publically he did not attribute any physical significance to the assumption. In 1905 Einstein published his photoelectric effect paper[228] in which he seriously called into question the general validity of the electromagnetic theory of light and attached *physical* significance to the idea of discrete quanta (as Planck had not) in cases of instantaneous absorption of radiant energy—an idea which was completely at variance with the prevailing undulatory electromagnetic theory of light. In urging his quantum light hypothesis, Einstein offers a number of arguments in its defense. From an examination of Einstein's reasoning in his 1905 photoelectric paper, Shapere discerns the following "good" reasoning pattern in Einstein's argumentation:

> In the case of the introduction of radical new hypotheses, generally . . . serious consideration of the latter nevertheless is not irrational if (or to the extent that) it can be shown:
>
> (1) that there is a certain fact;
> (2) that that fact is a member of a set of facts [a domain] for which a unitary explanation (theory) is expected (on independent reasonable grounds)—i.e. that this fact is a member of the domain of facts for the explanation of which a certain theory or type of theory is responsible;
> (3) that the classical theory for this domain of facts fails to explain this particular fact (or that it does so only by the additional assumption of arbitrary and/or artificial hypotheses); and
> (4) that the new hypothesis does explain this particular fact easily.[229]

In the case of Einstein's paper, the fact in question was the photoelectric effect. In virtue of reasoning patterns such as the above, Shapere's philosophy of science can make sense of, and explain, the introduction of radical new hypotheses in science—something which no other philosophy of science (including Kuhn's, Feyerabend's, and those which focus on either confirmation or falsification) is able to do.

[228] Einstein [1905]. For historical discussions, see Stuewer [1970] and Klein [1963] and [1967].

[229] Shapere, "On the Introduction of New Hypotheses in Science."

Several comments are in order on the above rationality principle for the introduction of radical new hypotheses. *First*, the case from which it is obtained is unique in some respects—differing in various ways from, for example, the case of introduction of the transverse-wave theory of light, or introduction of the concept of a "field," or introduction of the idea of intrinsic and variable characteristics of space; and it may be that there are other reasonable grounds than those applying to the quantum case which *also* make it reasonable to seriously consider a radical new hypothesis. *Second*, this pattern of reasoning indicates how it is that an existing domain and the problems it generates rationally favor one hypothesis over others, and thus condition the path scientific development in an area will take. *Third*, one might dispute this reasoning pattern on the grounds that bizarre new hypotheses would be sanctioned as rational by it.[230] Shapere's reply to this general line of criticism is that such bizarre hypotheses fail to be *scientific hypotheses*, and that his conditions (1) through (4) are sufficient conditions *only* relative to the assumption that the hypothesis is a scientific hypothesis. Although he has not yet supplied an analysis of what it is to be a scientific hypothesis,[231] the distinction he is drawing attention to is one that underscores a point that permeates his work on rationality in science: Contrary to what many philosophers of science have suggested, although science often is concerned with choosing between various possible options on the basis of evidence, the notion of *possibility* is not that of logical possibility. Most logically possible hypotheses are eliminated from consideration, or are ignored completely, by science. Only very few of the logically possible hypotheses, explanations, or theories ever are a matter for serious scientific consideration; rational science only seriously considers hypotheses which warrant consideration. And which hypotheses warrant consideration is a rational matter conditioned by the domain, its organization, and the problems it generates. Roughly speaking, the notion of "scientific hypothesis" involved in Shapere's reply is that of a hypothesis which rationally warrants consideration given the current state of the domain. Certain minimal conditions are required for a possible hypothesis which accounts for the facts to be a *candidate* for consideration, for it to be a scientific hypothesis. Shapere is

[230] This form of criticism was raised by Peter Achinstein in the commentary on Shapere's "On the Introduction of New Hypotheses in Science" at a meeting of the Washington, D.C., Philosophy Club in spring, 1976. The reply given below is, roughly, the one Shapere gave in response to Achinstein.

[231] And the argument of his above paper *does not* require that he supply such an analysis. For the purposes of his argument there (which is concerned to establish, contra Kuhn, that there *can* be good reasons for the introduction of radical new hypotheses), a critic would have to show that Einstein's quantum hypothesis was not in any plausible sense a scientific hypothesis. Shapere sees the analysis of a scientific hypothesis as involving the notions of being arrived at as a result of an actual deduction, precise, accurate, and so on (personal communication).

concerned with the further issue of what makes a candidate hypothesis warrant *serious* consideration—his reasoning pattern given above being one answer when the hypothesis is a radical new hypothesis. Similarly, in the "continuous" pattern of development considered above, the use of observational or experimental evidence to decide between competing theories, hypotheses, or interpretations of receptors' detections was a choice between theories, hypothesis, and so on, which rationally warranted serious consideration—not just between any old hypothesis or theory that was logically possible.[232] Thus, whether "normal" or "revolutionary" (to use Kuhn's misleading locutions), the current state of the domain (augmented where appropriate by background information) plays a strong role in determining the directions in which a science rationally can proceed; and the introduction of new hypotheses, whether radical ("revolutionary") or not ("normal"), can, should be, and usually is a matter of rational debate and evaluation.

Background Information: In discussing the interpretative aspects of observation, it was seen that background information plays a crucial role. There are severe constraints on what background information reasonably can be resorted to in working within a domain; and, as will be seen below, these constraints are crucial to the objectivity of scientific knowledge. Although Shapere's work on background information is only in its formative stages, the following very preliminary and general list of constraints on the scientific employment of background information presently is serving as a basis for his work on this topic:

i. Background information is to be employed only where and when necessary; and that necessity is determined by the character of the domain and the techniques for dealing with it and its problems. In particular,
ii. The domain to which it is applied must be describable or redescribable with precision and completeness in terms of the background information utilized (or, conversely, the background information must be expressible or re-expressible in terms suitable in detail to the domain).
iii. The background information must have been successful in application to a well-defined domain.
iv. The background information itself must be from some field that coheres with successful concepts and theories of other domains.[233]

[232] See, for example, the discussion on pp. 526–527 of "Scientific Theories and Their Domains" above, especially notes 9 and 10. In passing, it is worth noting that ignoring such a notion of hypotheses that rationally warrant consideration, and arguing for equal consideration of any possible theory or hypothesis, is part of what is wrong with extreme proliferation doctrines such as Feyerabend's. And, in subtler form, the same defect occurs in Lakatos's and Toulmin's positions—in ways that connect with some of our criticisms given above.

[233] Shapere, "Observation, Theory, and Objectivity in Science," unpublished manuscript. In condition iv it is not clear whether he means 'field' in Darden's sense (see above) or in the informal sense of scientific "area."

Although these constraints are only provisional "working hypotheses" and require much further analysis—a fact of which Shapere is acutely aware—his motivations for thinking that some variation on or refinement of these constraints is needed emerge from his views on the objectivity of scientific knowledge, and the connections between objectivity and rationality on his view. Indeed, condition (i) is just Shapere's refinement of the classical notion that scientific objectivity consists of "looking at the facts without letting anything else influence you."

Objectivity and Rationality in Science: A persistent theme in Shapere's criticisms of extreme *Weltanschauungen* analyses is that they destroy the objectivity of scientific knowledge, making knowledge be subjective and irrational, reducing knowledge to sociocultural group prejudice. While rejecting such views of scientific knowledge as unacceptable, he also rejects the positivistic account of objectivity that rests on its untenable observational/theoretical distinction (see pp. 45–50, and 66–86 above); and he sees his work on rationality in the growth of scientific knowledge as providing a new approach to scientific objectivity:

> My work . . . has attempted to show how [rational] considerations leading to scientific development can, in some cases and in some senses, emerge from the subject-matter (domain) in science, and so provides a basis for reformulating the traditional notion of "objectivity" (and therefore of "rationality," though the exact relationships between these concepts remain to be analyzed) in terms of two conditions.
>
> I. An activity or proposition in science is objective if the considerations on which it is based come solely from the subject-matter (or domain) with which it is concerned.
>
> . . . Objectivity, as far as this condition goes, is intimately associated with the degree of delineation of a domain, the development of techniques for raising and dealing with problems, proposing and accepting or rejecting answers to them, etc. (A corollary to this condition is that the "psychology" of the researcher, or the "sociological context" of a scientific development, insofar as they are not part of the subject-matter of that scientific development, are irrelevant to the question of its objectivity, even when they provide circumstances (a "climate") in which that development is promoted or fostered.)
>
> However, the first condition alone is not a sufficient condition for (scientific) objectivity, because the mere existence of a subject-matter and associated techniques, no matter how well delineated, does not necessarily make its pursuit "objective" or "rational". (Nor . . . is it sufficient for the purposes of scientific reasoning.) An additional condition is the following:
>
> II. The subject-matter or domain is consistent or coherent with the main body of domains, techniques, and accepted theories of other well-delineated domains, etc.[234]

[234] Shapere, *ibid.*

Shapere is aware not only that both of these conditions require further elaboration, but also that jointly they do not constitute a sufficient condition of scientific objectivity and rationality.

> This is partly because a specification of the objectivity of a particular move or proposition in science must include satisfaction not only of these general conditions, but also of more specific considerations arising in connection with the type of move it is—that is, with whether it has to do with the formation and modification of domains (including their redescription), the raising of problems concerning them, the proposal and ranking of alternative lines of research, the expectations of solutions of certain sorts, or the acceptance of a specific solution as adequate. . . . And, correspondingly, a complete account of the concept of 'objectivity' (and of 'rationality') in science will include, at least, a specification of the reasoning-patterns involved (at any given stage of science) in each of the six questions posed above. (And we see that, inasmuch as those reasoning-patterns in each case may, as I have argued . . . be satisfied only to some degree, scientific objectivity and rationality are, to *that* extent, 'demarcated' from their opposites only as a matter of degree.)[235]

Although Shapere never puts it this way in his writings, I think the following perspective can help illuminate his views on objectivity of scientific knowledge. For several centuries now it has been standard to analyze knowledge as "justified true belief":

S knows that *P* if and only if
(a) '*P*' is true;
(b) *S* believes that *P*;
(c) *S* has adequate evidence for believing that *P*.

The items in a domain are "putative facts"—what is asserted by various statements or propositions expressing knowledge claims that have been accepted. That is, the items in the domain are propositions which people believe on the basis of what has been judged to be adequate evidence. In science, reasoned debate is the normal means of evaluating proposed knowledge claims; and a claim is accepted and admitted to the domain only if the evidence adduced in its support is sufficient for the claim to pass muster under the prevailing rationality standards of the science. As is usually the case, the evidence which can be adduced in support of a knowledge claim never is sufficient to *guarantee* the truth of the claim. But, under various canons of rationality, a body of evidence may provide *sufficient warrant* for the claim that it becomes *reasonable* to accept the claim, attribute to it the status of knowledge, and allow it to enter the domain. Such entry into the domain does not place the claim beyond subsequent reevaluation or reassessment, for the evidence on which it is

[235] *Ibid.*

admitted to the domain always *underdetermines* the truth of the claim, and so it is possible (but not, if the canons of rationality are good ones, probable) that, despite the supporting evidence, the claim is in fact false—hence does not really constitute knowledge. Thus, room must be left for reassessment of knowledge claims on the basis of subsequently obtained evidence. From this perspective, then, science is objective if it allows entry into the domain only of those knowledge claims which the evidence rationally supports. And, as has been seen in our discussion of observation and theory, the ways in which the domain rationally favors particular lines of research, makes plausible only certain sorts of theories, and so on, play an important part in the evidential evaluation of knowledge claims. Thus Shapere's condition I is a central ingredient in scientific objectivity, for on his view, rationality and objectivity go hand in hand. And we see why, at any given time, the particular canons of methodology being employed in the evaluation of knowledge claims play an important role in the objectivity of the knowledge purportedly being provided by that science. Yet, because the assessment of knowledge claims by a science is fallible, a further test of objectivity is the coherence between what is discovered in one area of science and in related areas of science—hence Shapere's condition II.

However central rationality clearly is to the objectivity of scientific knowledge, rationality alone is not sufficient to escape a "subjective" view of knowledge and thereby to obtain a viable notion of objectivity, for part of scientific objectivity consists in the fact that science is concerned with establishing *facts* about the *real* physical world. The point of the rational evaluation of knowledge claims by science is to determine whether the claims do or do not express facts *about* the world—to determine whether what the claims assert is descriptive of how the world *actually* is. Thus part of the objectivity of science on Shapere's view consists in the items in domains being putative *facts*—that is, on adopting some realistic view of truth wherein the truth of scientific claims depends on whether what the claims assert corresponds with the way the world is. It is important to note that such a correspondence is precisely what Kuhn and Feyerabend deny is of any relevance to the scientific enterprise.[236] Thus Shapere's notion of scientific objectivity ultimately involves the embracement of a metaphysical realism with respect to truth together with the claim that, as a matter of fact, there are patterns of good reasoning which do enable one to rationally assess whether or not a particular knowledge claim is *likely* to be true, where patterns of such assessment significantly involve the or-

[236] See the discussion of them in Part II-B above, as well as more extended discussion of this point in my "Kuhn's and Feyerabend's Relativisms," [forthcoming c].

ganization of the domain and "emerge from the facts" constituting the domain.[237]

One possible objection to Shapere's views on objectivity deserves brief consideration. Shapere characterizes background information roughly as information which is not part of the domain under immediate consideration, or of a theory proposed to account for it. *Prima facie* the employment of background information would appear to conflict with condition I on objectivity in science. And such conflict would, indeed, occur if severe restrictions were not imposed on what background knowledge may be resorted to, "so that we are again threatened by an obliteration of the distinction between the objective and the subjective, the rational and the irrational or non-rational."[238] Shapere's provisional list of constraints on the employment of background information (given above) suggests the sort of restrictions that must be imposed if the use of such information is to be consistent with condition I on scientific objectivity; in particular, condition (ii) guarantees the compatibility of such employment with condition I.

Two characteristics stand out when one reads Shapere's work on the growth of scientific knowledge: Although the scope of his views and interests is wide-ranging and ambitious, he proceeds in an extremely cautious and careful way resisting the temptations to generalize prematurely or to force all science into patterns exemplified by particular case studies. To be sure, he insists that science does and should proceed rationally and that philosophy of science ought to proceed by examining the patterns of reasoning involved; and he does focus his efforts on answering his six questions given above in the attempt to solve what he sees as the fundamental problem in philosophy of science discussed above (as he has done in the work summarized and discussed here which bears importantly on all six of them). But in doing so he resists the temptation to suppose that all science at all times employs the same reasoning patterns or follows the same methodology. Indeed, the denial that this is so lies at the very heart of his philosophy of science. It is becoming an increasingly dominant theme of his that as sophisticated science proceeds, it develops improved patterns of reasoning not previously employed in ways that are conditioned by the content of the science, and that much of scientific progress consists in such development of increasingly subtle improved

[237] Shapere's views on facts and objectivity are further developed in his "The Influence of Knowledge on the Description of Facts," forthcoming in Suppe and Asquith [1977]. In Section D below we will indicate how such a view of objectivity in science has profound implications for various contemporary issues in epistemology.

[238] Shapere, "Observation, Theory, and Objectivity in Science."

patterns of reasoning for evaluating knowledge claims. Or, as he likes to put it, "We learn how to learn as we learn."[239]

Since much of what is reported here is from work in progress and subject to revision and refinement, and since I think Shapere's general approach and views are essentially right-headed, I will not attempt to go into any systematic critical evaluation of his specific views; indeed, doing so would require detailed historical examinations which available space precludes. Instead, in presenting his views I have tried to indicate those areas where further development and refinement of them is in order. The single area where the most further work is needed is on the explicit development of the views on facts, knowledge, and knowledge claims underlying his entire approach to objectivity and rationality in science; and I have tried to ferret out the basic views on these issues which are only tacit in his discussions to date. In Section D, below, a more detailed general discussion of these and related epistemological and metaphysical issues will be given. Another area where further work is needed is in the mechanics of domain formation and modification—of which the developments on "observation and theory" discussed above constitute only a crude beginning. Shapere himself is aware of how much more work is needed in these areas, and continues to work steadily and carefully on adding more to the picture, thus increasing our philosophical understanding of the scientific enterprise.

4. Conclusions on the Growth of Scientific Knowledge

During the last five or six decades there have been important shifts in philosophical thinking about scientific discovery and the growth of scientific knowledge. The positivists distinguished the context of discovery and the context of justification, dismissing the former as the subject matter of history or psychology. The only aspects of the growth of scientific knowledge relevant to philosophy were the inductive justification or confirmation of knowledge claims and the incorporation of older theories into more comprehensive theories via intertheoretic reduction. The resulting view of scientific knowledge was a static one which, ignoring the dynamics of scientific progress and being tied to an untenable observational/theoretical distinction and associated epistemology, led to a highly distorted portrait of science and the knowledge it provided, which had little to do with the epistemic activities science actually was engaged in. Rejecting such a view, a group of "young Turks"—including Hanson,

[239] Shapere, "On the Introduction of New Hypotheses in Science."

Feyerabend, and Kuhn—started examining scientific practice and the history of science and developed *Weltanschauungen* views that, unfortunately, made scientific knowledge a social phenomenon in which science became a subjective and, to varying degrees, an irrational enterprise.

More recently philosophers such as Lakatos, Toulmin, and Shapere have attempted to steer a middle course between these two extremes wherein science is a rational enterprise concerned with obtaining objective knowledge of the real world. In the first such attempt examined, that of Lakatos, it was seen that his analysis of research programs at best identified one of a number of possible reasoning patterns for attempting to obtain scientific knowledge; and that as a reasoning pattern it was seriously defective in that it focused on a few possibly relevant factors in assessing a line of research to the exclusion of other factors which often are more significant to such assessment. Indeed, reasoning and rationality proved to be of relatively little importance in his account of research programs. Reasoning was given more of a place in Toulmin's evolutionary model of scientific development; but, although *provision* was made to afford reason a place, Toulmin has little to say about the role of reason. And we raised considerations that suggested strongly that if he is to allow sufficient place for reason in his account, significant alterations in his position will be required; in particular, it seems his evolutionary view of knowledge, wherein whatever conceptual variants survive the selection process qualify as knowledge, will have to be revised to preclude irrational selections from qualifying as knowledge. Only when we get to Shapere's work do we find an account where reason is accorded a sufficiently detailed and central place in a philosophical account of the growth of scientific knowledge. Although very much in the state of developing work in progress, and much more work is needed, out of Shapere's work is emerging the outlines of a promising and coherent philosophical portrait of the growth of scientific knowledge; and it is an approach which goes beyond the mere attempt to steer a "middle course" between the extremes of positivism and the *Weltanschauungen* analyses, constituting a larger attack on the tradition in philosophy of science from whence those two extremes arise. Whether the particular details of his account prove correct, approximately correct, or end up by being replaced, his work does constitute a promising approach and perspective for work in philosophy of science; and it is my perception that, increasingly, philosophical work on the growth of scientific knowledge is coalescing in the general direction and approach exemplified by Shapere's work.

C. Conceptual Devices

Although observation and theory figure centrally in Lakatos's, Toulmin's, and Shapere's accounts of the growth of scientific knowledge, it is significant that there is virtually no talk of "verification," "inductive confirmation," or "refutation" of theories or hypotheses. This is no accident, and a number of factors explain their absence. *First*, if an account of the growth of scientific knowledge is to reflect actual scientific practice, then its focus must be some larger unit of science than the particular theory—Lakatos's problem shifts and research programs, Toulmin's disciplines, Shapere's domains, and Darden's fields all being offered as candidate analyses of these larger units. And when one looks at how observation and experiment are employed in evaluating sophisticated theories within these larger units, one finds that the focus typically is not what philosophers of science have characterized as inductively confirming a theory as true or refuting it as false. When a sophisticated theory is undergoing active development, it is commonplace for scientists working on it to suppose that the present version of the theory is defective in various respects, which is to say that it is literally false, at best being only an approximation to the truth or a promising candidate; and if one is convinced this is so, it would be pointless to attempt to either refute or inductively confirm the theory. What *is* to the point is to use observation and experiment to discover shortcomings in the theory, to determine how to improve the theory, and to discover how to eliminate known artificialities, distortions, oversimplifications, and errors in the descriptions, explanations, and predictions of reality that the theory affords.[240] It is to these ends that science ordinarily uses data to "test" its current theories—and not the inductive confirmation or refutation of them which has so occupied the attention of philosophy of science in the past. Thus we find Lakatos trying to specify when a problem shift and research program are worth continuing to develop in the face of known deficiencies; we find Toulmin discussing how conceptual variants are selected for propagation as active candidates for development, and the role of explanatory ideals in guiding the development of theories and other representational devices; and we find Shapere discussing reasoning patterns for deciding what sort of theory is worth developing, how to decide what sorts of improvements

[240] For example, my physicist colleague Charles Misner recently has argued that we do not know which parts of a theory adequately describe or represent phenomena over what ranges until that theory has been superceded over much of its original claimed scope by improved theories, the improved theories telling us where the earlier theory was correct in its representation of reality. Implicit in this view is the denial that either the inductive confirmation or the refutation of a theory warranting serious development is terribly important to the working scientist.

(removal of theoretical inadequacies) are in order, and so on. Except in primitive sciences which eschew, or are little concerned with, the development of comprehensive explanatory theories, one finds little concern with refutation or inductive confirmation of theories in actual scientific practice. Rather the focus is on the use of reason, observation, and experiment to develop a promising theory.[241] *Second*, in the process of developing a comprehensive theory, at various stages one's theory may not purport to be a "true" theory; rather the theory is introduced as an "idealization," an "abstraction," a "simplification," a "model," or even as a "fiction"; or one has a theory in a particular stage of development where one does not know which of these statuses the theory has, and one's concern with reason, observation, and experiment is to determine what the cognitive status of the theory is. That is, the operant question in the

[241] Although Kepler's determination of the elliptical orbits for the planets often is viewed as being a paradigm exemplification of such refutation and inductive confirmation exercises, this is an exaggeration. Prior to having access to Tycho's massive bodies of data, he had concluded that certain approximate relationships ("the distant planets move slower than the inner ones") were characteristic of planetary motion and that these had to be explained in terms of some solar force whose action fell off as the distance increased. Most of the theoretical apparatus here (including the "approximate relationship") was taken from Copernicus, and data did not figure that centrally in his work. Only after Tycho pointed out to him that a number of his views in the *Mysterium Cosmographicum* were at odds with the data, did Kepler join Tycho and start working closely from the data. After gaining access to Tycho's data, he concluded, partially from the data but more from "Pythagorean" prejudices, that a single geometric figure explainable by the action of his simple solar force had to be the orbit. Before getting to the question of the shape of the orbit, he introduced his second law (his inverse speed proportion, equal areas in equal times law) which was a refinement of Copernicus' earlier conjecture about the relation between speed and distance. Then he turned to the question of the orbit, first trying circular orbits, then other orbits such as an egg-shaped orbit, and finally, as a mathematical construction, an elliptical orbit—which happened to fit the data adequately. But, for Kepler, this was not the end of the matter, for he felt that his account of the orbits should be part of a more general theory which also explained the number and the relative distances of the planets—which he then spent ten years working on unsuccessfully. Although Kepler did use data to test various hypothesized orbits for the planets, his use does not fit the usual patterns of refutation and inductive confirmation advanced by philosophers of science. For the elliptical orbits were part of a more comprehensive planetary theory; and much of that theory was incorrect—for example, his account of the solar force was seriously defective and had to be corrected by Newton. Indeed, his account of the planetary orbits was only approximately correct, as it was not able to account for various orbital perturbations. Since his theory and description of the orbits was, strictly speaking, false, his use of data in establishing it is at odds with the philosopher's model of inductive confirmation. Sometimes he used the data to test hypothetical orbits he was convinced were false—for example, when he first tested elliptical orbits while being convinced an "egg-shaped" orbit was correct; and the point of such a test could not have been to either confirm or refute the hypothesis of an elliptical orbit. Thus, although Kepler used data to test various hypotheses, that use does not exemplify the inductive confirmation or refutation models advanced by philosophers of science. Further, such models totally ignore the ways Kepler used the available data to determine which orbits were promising enough to warrant careful evaluation on the basis of data or how he used the outcomes of tests of hypotheses to suggest improved hypotheses.

development of theory often concerns whether a theory provides a *realistic* account of phenomena or whether it is some sort of *conceptual device* falling short of providing a realistic account; or it may be how such a conceptual device can be modified to provide a more realistic treatment.[242] *Third*, on pages 566–570 above we examined Shapere's treatment of the instrumentalistic and realistic construal of theoretical terms in theories; and we saw that he maintained, on the basis of convincing historical case studies, that one and the same theory can contain some theoretical terms which are "existence concepts" that are construed realistically and some terms which are "idealization concepts" that treat entities as having characteristics we know they cannot possess. Still others may be "abstraction concepts," "approximations," or "simplifications." And depending which theoretical terms or concepts are the locus of evaluation, different employments of observational or experimental data will be appropriate. Insofar as the concern is with such conceptual devices which, in contrast to existence concepts, do not admit of a realistic interpretation, both refutation and inductive confirmation are beside the point.

The item of present concern is that in its development and use of theories, laws, and hypotheses, science can advance and employ them with a variety of different statuses—as purportedly true descriptions of classes of phenomena, as idealizations, simplifications, or approximations of phenomena. Which status a concept, theory, law, or hypothesis—or a portion thereof—is accorded is determined on the basis of current scientific knowledge and may vary with the content of what is taken as knowledge; that is, whether the theory, and so on, is taken as providing a realistic treatment or as being a conceptual device is established by characteristic reasoning patterns based on factual claims currently accorded the status of knowledge.

Although such conceptual devices as idealizations, abstractions, simplifications, and so forth, can be employed in advancing a theory, law, or hypothesis—for example, it is *advanced as* an idealization or simplification, and so on—these devices also can be employed in the *application of* a theory to a particular situation. For example, although the Lorentz theory of the electron implies that electrons cannot be geometrical points, nevertheless for certain applications of Lorentz's theory it is convenient and possible to treat the electron *as if* it were a point-particle and make calculations on that basis. Here we are employing the conceptual device of a simplification or idealization in our application of the Lorentz theory to a particular problem. Sometimes the resort to such a conceptual device

[242] The sense of 'conceptual device' being used here is that of Shapere, "On the Role of Conceptual Devices in Science."

in the application of a theory is justified by the fact that the resulting calculations yield results which are "close enough"—for example, accurate within measurement error; in other cases, simplifying the situation in ways that fundamentally falsify it may lead to results that are *exactly* the same as if the calculations had taken into account the full complexity of the situation. For example, in the development of the kinetic theory of gases, one can develop much of the theory without taking the existence of molecular collisions into account, which is an unrealistic simplification of the situation; yet when the number of molecules striking a square centimeter of the surface per second is calculated, taking into account such collisions, the result is exactly the same as one obtains when molecular collisions are ignored. And in still other cases, one resorts to conceptual devices to make approximate calculations in order to determine rough orders of magnitude, or to estimate solutions, and so forth.[243]

When conceptual devices are employed in the application of theory to a particular phenomena, the description or account of the phenomena which results strictly speaking falsifies the situation and so fails to provide a realistic account. Similarly, when a theory (or portion thereof) is advanced as a conceptual device, it provides an unrealistic account of the phenomena which is a "falsification" of the situation. But not all applications or propoundings of theory are unrealistic; a theory may be advanced as providing a realistic portrayal of a particular phenomena or of a class of phenomena. Or it may be an open question whether a particular theory is realistic, and if so, "how realistic" an account the theory provides. That theories do admit of such a diverse variety of statuses in being advanced or applied is revealed by the ways in which science reasons about and evaluates its theories on the basis of the domain, background information, and the results of observation and experiment.[244] And a necessary condition for the adequacy of any philosophical analysis of the nature or structure of theories, or laws, is that the analysis be able to accommodate such diversity of statuses. More generally, an adequate account of theories must be able to accommodate the various use of theories encountered in actual scientific practice. The semantic conception of theories (see pp. 221–230 above) is the only serious contender to emerge as a replacement for the Received View analysis of theories; since much, but not all, of its development occurred prior to the present emphasis on the growth of

[243] This paragraph, as well as portions of earlier ones, is based on and summarizes a number of points made in Shapere's [1969] (summarized on pp. 566–570 above), and his "On the Role of Conceptual Devices in Science." A central theme of Shapere's in these works is that whether something is a conceptual device or not is determined by the content of the science, especially the background information, at the time.

[244] For the evidence, see the works cited in note 243 and also on pp. 557–565 of Shapere's contribution to Session VII of the symposium.

scientific knowledge, it is worth reassessing it in the light of more recent findings about the actual employment of theories in science.[245]

It will be recalled that the semantic conception construes theories as extralinguistic entities that admit of alternative and even inequivalent linguistic formulations. Structurally a theory consists of a domain of states of phenomenal or physical systems together with one or more laws. The states consist of *n*-tuples of attributes which could be possessed simultaneously by particulars in causally possible phenomenal systems; these attributes are the values of the defining parameters for the theory. The laws for the theory are relations over states which determine time-directed sequences constituting possible behaviors or histories of phenomenal systems within the theory's scope. The theory is empirically true just in case the class of histories determined by the laws of the theory is identical with the class of causally possible histories of isolated systems. Subsequent development of the semantic conception has established that although theories with multiple laws are possible, they are equivalent to theories containing just single laws; and it has been shown that laws of succession, interaction, and coexistence are special cases of more general classes of laws which *inter alia* include the laws characteristic of "adaptive" phenomena, and functional and teleological systems.[246]

In all published discussions of the semantic conception, the focus has been on theories which are propounded as being true. In such cases, in advancing a theory one is claiming that the behaviors of causally possible *isolated* phenomenal systems within its scope will be precisely those which correspond to time-directed state sequences sanctioned by the laws of the theory. Extended discussion has been given how theories so propounded can be used to make predictions about nonisolated systems by recourse to auxiliary hypotheses and theories, and how the empirical truth of such theories can be tested and confirmed. In doing so it provides a quasi-realistic interpretation of theories wherein the defining parameters of a theory's states are interpreted as being characteristic of particulars participating in the phenomenal systems comprising the theory's scope, and any other "theoretical" apparatus is descriptive of regularities in the state-change behaviors of isolated phenomena. Accordingly, when propounded as true, the semantic conception of theories provides idealized

[245] Although published accounts of the semantic conception have little to say about the relations between theories and the growth of scientific knowledge, the subject was considered at length in Chapters 3 and 4 of my [1967]. The discussion there concedes far too much to both inductivist accounts of the growth of scientific knowledge as well as to Kuhn. The discussion which follows supercedes the discussion there and marks a number of changes in view.

[246] For these recent developments, see Suppe [1976a]. Earlier works on the semantic conception are cited in the notes to pp. 221–230 above.

characterizations of how actual systems *would* behave *were* they isolated. Thus, one form of conceptual device, that of "idealized" isolated systems, is built into the analysis and is consistent with providing a "realistic" account of phenomena. Careful examination of the use of scientific theories indicates that theories sometimes *are* propounded as true, and when so propounded they do provide the sort of idealized characterization given by the semantic-conception's quasi-realistic interpretation of theories. And when such theories are applied to nonisolated phenomena within their scopes, auxiliary hypotheses are employed in the manner claimed. Thus to the extent that science does advance theories as being true, the semantic conception appears to provide an accurate account of their nature or structure.[247]

But the foregoing discussions of conceptual devices and the growth of scientific knowledge indicate that theories, especially during their periods of active development, generally are not advanced as being true; rather they are advanced as being an approximation to the truth, or as a simplification, or as a promising first step toward what eventually will prove to be a correct theory, and so forth. Can the semantic conception accommodate these other statuses accorded to theories during their periods of active development? It is my considered opinion that it can. Although the detailed historical investigations needed to fully substantiate such a claim are yet to be made, the basis for defending such a claim is fairly clear. Whether advanced quasi-realistically as true or whether advanced as some less realistic conceptual device, in presenting a theory about the state-behavior of a class of systems one is presenting some sort of structure specifying a class of possible state-change behaviors of systems and claiming that this class stands in *some* relationship to causally possible behaviors of a class of phenomenal systems. When the theory is advanced quasi-realistically, one is claiming that the theory-induced class of behaviors is identical with that of the class of isolated causally possible systems. Recent results, yet unpublished, indicate that this claim can be true only if each such isolated system actually occurs in the history of the

[247] For detailed discussion of the application of theories to phenomena, see my [1974a]. The account there attaches far too much importance to both testing and inductive confirmation of theories; in particular, I would want to take back much of Section 8 of that work as being fairly irrelevant to the actual practices whereby sophisticated science evaluates its theories. Further, for deep-seated epistemological reasons (hinted at in the next section and developed at length in a forthcoming book, *Facts, Theories, and Scientific Observation*), I now think probabilistic inductive confirmation is irrelevant to scientific knowledge, and only of limited value in the evaluation of scientific knowledge claims.

The idealized quasi-realistic treatments of phenomena provided by true theories, described above, raise a host of problems for the employment of theories in technology which philosophy of technology is only just coming to appreciate. See Edwin Layton's contribution to the symposium on philosophy of technology in Suppe and Asquith [1977].

real world.[248] But it is possible to propound a theory claiming that other relationships hold between the theory-induced behaviors and the behaviors of the causally possible systems. For example, when the conditions on isolated systems required for empirical truth are not met, one could advance the theory *as if* they could be met—as a kind of simplification known to be false. Or, one could acknowledge that the two classes of behaviors are not identical but claim that, within the limits of measurement error characteristic of a particular technique, they are indistinguishable—that is, advance the theory as being an approximation. And so on. The point here is that whether a theory serves as a nonrealistic conceptual device or not, and if so what kind, appears to concern what sort of relationship holds between the characterization of possible state-change behaviors provided by the theory and the actual behaviors of phenomena within its scope. An open-ended variety of such relationships is allowed by the semantic conception. Moreover, once historical case studies identify various conceptual devices that theories can function as, it would seem that the precise structural account of theories provided by the semantic conception could be exploited beneficially in the detailed analysis of those conceptual devices. Indeed, it seems to me that an adequate understanding of the variety of ways theories are employed in science can best be achieved by a judicious mixture of historical examination of patterns of reasoning about theories and the more traditional and formal analysis characteristic of the semantic conception.

Although varying in specific detail, in the work of Lakatos, Toulmin, Shapere, and Darden we find the idea that, on at least one pattern of development, science begins with a fairly vague idea of the general form of a theory, and then proceeds to add details to that picture or pattern, gradually developing an increasingly more detailed and fully articulated theory. Be it Lakatos's negative heuristic, Toulmin's explanatory ideal, Shapere's "process of increasingly precise and detailed development of the initial vague idea" (p. 553, above, note 54), or Darden's explanatory factors and techniques—there is some reason to suppose that in the early stages of the development of a theory, things are sufficiently vague that nothing corresponding to the precise structures of the semantic conception exists. Whether this is an inadequacy of the semantic conception is unclear. At such stages, is the initial vague idea a theory—in the sense of 'theory' the semantic conception is concerned to analyze? [249] Although

[248] These findings, which are based on fairly involved metaphysical results concerning the physical interpretation of the causal modalities, will be reported in Chapter VII of my [forthcoming b].

[249] Recall from p. 658 above that there are a number of senses of 'theory' encountered in science, and the semantic conception is concerned to analyze only one of them, albeit the most significant one for scientific knowledge.

detailed examination of case studies is needed to answer this question, I suspect the answer is negative. But even if the answer is negative, important questions remain as to what relations hold between the initial vague idea and the resulting theory, and is this a worthwhile area for further investigation. For example, is it plausible to construe the initial vague idea, and subsequent articulations of it, as providing increasingly precise specifications of some theory under development; or should we construe them as indicating the kind of theory it is reasonable to expect where we do not have such a theory yet, or ??? Here again, there is scope for historical case studies being undertaken in the future development and evaluation of the semantic conception.[250] Although inconclusive, the foregoing discussion does indicate that the semantic conception not only has considerable potential for compatibility with findings emerging about the role of theories in the growth of scientific knowledge, but also how such findings indicate promising directions for further development of both the semantic conception and our understanding of the use of conceptual devices in science.

Work on the growth of scientific knowledge, and reasoning patterns involved therein, also has revealed several kinds of theories which previously have escaped notice or tended to be ignored by philosophers analyzing theories.[251] In his symposium paper above, Shapere identifies two of these—*compositional theories* and *evolutionary theories*—which he characterizes respectively as providing "an answer [to a theoretical problem] in terms of constitutent parts of the individuals making up the domain and the laws governing the behavior of those parts" and as providing "answers in terms of the development of the individuals making up the domain" (p. 534 above). Although he does not provide detailed "structural" analyses of such theories, it is relatively clear from the characterizations quoted that the laws of such theories concern patterns of state-change and so fall within the scope of the semantic conception analysis.[252] A

[250] A closely related issue emerges if we take seriously Toulmin's metaphor about populations of conceptual variants. During the development of a theory, various people working in a discipline often can agree on what are the "established" or "accepted" portions of the theory, although they may be experimenting with various variations on or emendations of the theory. In such a case, are there a number of variant theories being employed? And what sense, if any, can be made of the idea that these are *versions* of the *same* theory. Some relatively deep issues about how theories are, in fact, individuated in science are involved here. And since considerations on the individuation of theories were invoked in arguing for the semantic conception (see pp. 221–222), they bear on its adequacy.

[251] In addition to the kind of theories discussed below, other newly identified types of laws characteristic of theories are identified and characterized in my [1976a].

[252] In case this is not obvious, the following comments may help: First, the attributes serving as parameter values for states can be properties or relations on the semantic conception; hence "part-whole" relations of the sort required by compositional theories can be built

third type of theory, *interfield theories*, has been identified by Darden and Maull in their related work on the emergence of fields in biology and so-called "reductive" phenomena. Such theories serve to make explicit the connections between related, noncompeting, fields which take different, complementary, approaches to dealing with aspects of the same or overlapping phenomena. The identification of interfield theories has resulted from a number of careful historical case studies which indicate that the developments they analyze as interfield theories "are often mistakenly thought to be the derivational reduction of one field to the 'more general,' 'more fundamental,' and 'more powerful' theories of another field."[253] Interfield theories function to make explicit and explain relations between fields by, for example, providing a specification of the physical location of an entity or process postulated in another field ("genes are in chromosomes"), specifying the physical nature of an entity or process postulated in another field ("biochemistry gives the physical-nature of the represser of the operon theory"), specifying the structure of entities or processes the function of which is investigated in another field ("physical chemistry provides the structure of molecules whose function is described biochemically"), or linking causally the entities postulated in one field which are causes of effects studied in another field ("the theory of allosteric regulation provides a causal explanation of the interaction between the physico-chemical structure of certain enzymes and a characteristic biochemical pattern of their activity").[254] To the extent that interfield theories connect the entities or processes of two fields in such a way as to provide behavioral characterizations of the specified correlations or connections, it is clear that they describe state-change behaviors of the sort with which the semantic conception is concerned.[225] Thus further vindication of the semantic conception is provided by its ability to accommodate subsequently discovered varieties of theory employed by science.

---

into the characterization of states; thus the laws can include part-whole relations in their characterizations of behaviors. In evolutionary theories, "generational time" sometimes is more appropriate than chronological time; nothing in the semantic conception precludes recourse to discrete time metrics, even ones which do not qualify as extensive measurement scales. These possibilities are discussed in Chapter II of my [1967].

[253] Darden and Maull [Roth] [1975], p. v–108. The case studies are presented in their works cited in note 212 above.

[254] Darden and Maull [Roth] [1975], p. 7. For fuller discussion, see Maull [Roth] [1974], Chap. III.

[255] It is less than clear whether providing such behavioral characterizations is an essential feature of interfield theories on their account, though I suspect that there is little point to interfield theories if they do not. If they do not, then interfield theories appear to be just theories in the sense of 'hypothesis' or 'established hypothesis.'

There is reason to suspect that in later, more sophisticated areas of science, interfield theories might sometimes perform the sort of functions analogies play in earlier stages of science in the reasoning pattern given in note 213. If so, an important connection between interfield theories and conceptual devices would be established.

In his symposium paper, Shapere argues that theories provide answers to theoretical problems about domains. In discussing Bromberger's work on explanation from an erotetic logic (logic of questions and answers) perspective (Section I-A above), we indicated that this seemed a promising and right-headed approach, even though his particular treatment of explanations was defective. Shapere's work on domains provides deep reasons for supposing that the erotetic approach to theoretical explanation is sound. To date little published work has been done on investigating how, on the semantic conception, theories can provide explanations or answer theoretical problems calling for an explanation of the underlying unities of domains. Shapere's work makes it clear, however, that the adequacy of the semantic conception depends in part on whether its characterization pinpoints what it is about theories that enable them to explain the underlying unities of domains. Thus exploring how, on the semantic conception and from an erotetic approach, theories can provide such explanations is of crucial importance. Unpublished but extensive preliminary investigations strongly suggest that the semantic conception will be able to provide an erotetic account of theoretical explanation which avoids the known defects of Hempel's, Bromberger's, Salmon's, and other approaches to causal and statistical explanation.

In many respects this section has raised more questions than it has provided, or even suggested, answers to.[256] This is not inappropriate since its primary aim has been to show how work on the growth of scientific knowledge bears on more traditional issues such as analyzing the structure of theories. To this end I have tried to reexamine the semantic conception in the light of such work. And what the discussion reveals is the extent to which work on the growth of scientific knowledge alters and refocuses not only the sorts of issues relevant to evaluating the adequacy of structural analyses of, for example, theories, but also plays a significant role in the development and refinement of such analyses. Although it presses the point less strongly, I hope that the present discussion indicates the extent to which historically based work on the growth of scientific knowledge and structural analyses of, for example, theories can complement each other; indeed, I would suggest that *both* are required if we are

[256] There are other problems deserving investigation as well. To indicate just one more: On a suitably powerful theory of automata (logical machines), the theory structures of the semantic conception qualify as automata. Using the same class of automata, fairly comprehensive theories of simulation modeling have been developed. See Zeigler [1976a] and his [1976]. An alternative but related approach, which is somewhat critical of Zeigler's, is found in Burks [1975], pp. 295–308. Collectively these results provide a theoretical basis for investigating the similarities and differences between theories and one important class of models. For the automata background and a brief survey of its connections to issues of theories and modeling in philosophy of science, see my [1976], pp. 303–305.

to approach anything like an adequate and comprehensive philosophical understanding of science and the knowledge it provides.

D. Toward a Metaphysical and Epistemological Realism

On several occasions we have suggested that recent work on the growth of scientific knowledge has profound implications for epistemology, and that those implications are tied intimately to historical realism's commitments to a metaphysical and epistemological realism. Underlying those commitments are the beliefs that science is one of our paradigm examples of a successful epistemic enterprise, hence that how science goes about achieving knowledge is indicative of the nature of knowledge. Despite occasional flirtations with instrumentalism, science generally is concerned to obtain knowledge or truths about the real, physical, psychological, or social world; even when it employs conceptual devices in the search for such truth, they are judged to be conceptual devices in virtue of falling short of a standard of correctly representing how the world really is and the characteristic regularities of that real world. In short, science overwhelmingly is committed to a metaphysical and epistemological realism; and accepting science as a paradigm knowledge-yielding enterprise commits one to a realistic philosophical analysis of scientific knowledge and truth.[257] If one grants these points, then one is committed to a realistic analysis of knowledge and truth that is compatible with actual scientific practice. And actual scientific practice, as revealed by recent work on objectivity and the growth of scientific knowledge, apparently *is* at odds with *most* recent philosophical analyses of knowledge. To see this, hence to discern the implications of work on the growth of scientific knowledge for a realistic philosophical account of knowledge, we first must sketch the current state of epistemology and the history of how it got to where it is.

Over much of the history of philosophy a central aim of epistemology has been to vindicate the epistemic claims of then contemporary science; such were principle motives of Locke for writing his *Essay*, Kant for writing his *Critique of Pure Reason* and *Metaphysical Foundations of Natural Science*, and the positivists for developing the Received View. A

[257] Indeed, in its instrumentalistic phases science is committed to a metaphysical and epistemological realism—such instrumentalisms being nothing other than a realism coupled with the assertion that realistically construed knowledge is limited to knowledge of, for example, positivism's directly observable. See my [1973] for defense of this view on instrumentalism.

secondary motive of epistemology historically has been to identify the epistemological excesses of science and indicate how a reformed science could yield knowledge; such was the motive of Bacon's *Novum Organon*, Descartes' *Discourse on Method* and *Principles of Philosophy*, Berkeley's *New Theory of Vision*, Whewell's *Philosophy of the Inductive Sciences*, Mach's *Analysis of Sensations*, and the positivists' concern with cognitive significance. Often, as in the case of the positivists, these two motives were combined. In short, to an overwhelming degree the history of epistemology (and metaphysics) is the history of the philosophy of science—although histories of philosophy tend to give scant attention to this fact.[258]

During the modern period, a standard epistemological view emerged. At the heart of this view was the contention that knowledge is justified true belief—that is, that

(1) *S* knows that *P* if and only if
  (a) '*P*' is true;
  (b) *S* believes that *P*;
  (c) *S* has adequate evidence for believing that *P*.

Although rarely articulated until recently, it was standard, at least tacitly, to interpret 1-c as embodying the so-called *K-K thesis*,

(2) '*S* knows that *P*' entails that '*S* knows that he knows that *P*.'[259]

This thesis, which in effect says that one cannot know that *P* unless one knows that one's claim to know that *P* is correct, plays a central role in modern and contemporary discussions of epistemology—underlying Cartesian-like skeptical challenges to knowledge: Suppose *S* claims to know that *P*; from (1) and (2) together, this implies that *S* knows that '*P*' is

[258] Although he tends to underemphasize it, Frederick Copleston does tend to cover the scientific influences and connections in his *A History of Philosophy* [1946–65]; (a paperback edition has been released by Image). Although flawed in various respects and quite elementary, John Losee's *A Historical Introduction to the Philosophy of Science* [1972] does have the merit of correctly viewing the history of metaphysics and epistemology as being in large part the history of philosophy of science. W. T. Jones, *History of Modern Philosophy* [1952], also has the merit of stressing the connections between developments in science and the history of philosophy, although he ultimately underplays the connection. In *Knowledge and Society* [1974], Arnold Levison shows how a number of methodological issues in the philosophy of social science (for example, the holistic vs. reductionistic controversies) arise out of the history of modern philosophy. Despite a few works such as these which are aware of the intimate genetic connections between the history of science and the history of epistemology and metaphysics, contemporary philosophical accounts of the history of philosophy seriously distort matters as a result of paying inadequate attention to such connections; the history of philosophy sorely is in need of being completely rewritten.

[259] The K-K thesis was brought to contemporary attention by J. Hintikka in his *Knowledge and Belief* [1962]; the designation 'K-K thesis' is based on a mnemonic device employed in that book to refer to various axioms, postulates, and principles of his modal logic of knowledge and belief claims.

true, that *S* knows that he believes that *P*, and *S* knows that he has adequate evidence for believing that *P*. The skeptic then challenges either the first or third of these implications by showing the evidence *S can adduce* is compatible with the falsity of '*P*.' Obtaining a concession on this latter point, he concludes *S* did not know that *P* after all. It is important to note that the skeptic's line of attack essentially requires the K-K thesis (2) as well as (1); for it is consistent to deny (2) while maintaining a version of (1),[260] and if this is done, the skeptic's conclusion that *S* does not know fails to follow. With a few exceptions (for example, Dretske and Goldman), virtually all recent discussions of epistemology tacitly or explicitly concede the K-K thesis.

During the seventeenth through early twentieth centuries, it was common to interpret the justification clause (c) of (1) along the lines of the "building-block" model: A body of *base knowledge* was postulated which was *incorrigible*; such base knowledge either consisted of something like Descartes' clear and distinct ideas or else what have come to be known as sense data (see pp. 152–154 above). Any other knowledge which was possible had to be obtained, via operations of the understanding or mind, from base knowledge in such a way that it was adequately justified; typically this meant that the supporting base knowledge had to render the derivative knowledge indubitable or incorrigible. Causal and phenomenalistic theories of perception attempted to show how this enabled one to have knowledge of physical objects (given a suitable metaphysical account of what it was to be a physical object). Theories of induction were introduced to show how general knowledge, such as scientific laws and theories claimed to provide, was possible. Hume's skeptical attacks (aided at places by Berkeley) succeeded in showing that, if base knowledge was limited to incorrigible knowledge of sensation and a priori knowledge, neither knowledge of physical objects nor inductively obtained general knowledge was possible since the available base knowledge never was sufficient to endow them with the certainty or indubitability demanded of knowledge under the prevailing interpretation of (lc). It is important to note that acceptance of the K-K thesis was crucial to these Humean skeptical attacks, and without recourse to it, his lines of attack fail. The heart of Hume's attack consists in showing that one cannot know the induction hypothesis needed to infer the derivative knowledge that *P* from what one already knows, hence that one does not know that one's evidence is adequate; but this yields his skeptical conclusions only if resort is made to the K-K thesis.

[260] Whether it is consistent depends on how clauses (la-c) are construed or interpreted. For a discussion of the relationship of the K-K thesis to various common versions of (1), see Hilpinen [1970]. Criticisms of parts of his discussion are found toward the end of my [1973a].

Despite Kant's attempts to get around such difficulties via his transcendental subjective-idealist philosophy, Hegel's dialectical attempts, and the transparently unsuccessful nineteenth-century empiricist attempts of Mill and others to vindicate induction, Hume's pervasive skepticism constituted the last empiricist word on the matter until logical positivism made the move to physicalism. Although not widely acknowledged or recognized, this move amounted to denuding the building-block model of knowledge of the requirement that the evidence satisfying (1c) makes belief that *P* be certain in the sense of being incorrigible or indubitable.[261] Rather, for base knowledge of sensation and a priori knowledge, potential intersubjective agreement provided sufficient evidence or justification for knowledge despite the possibilities of collective delusion; and observational evidence which, under a suitable probabilistic inductive logic, conferred a high probability on generalizations was sufficient for obtaining general knowledge. We saw in Section I-B, however, that attempts to establish such a "global" inductive logic also failed; what we neglected to say then was that the successful attacks on, for example, Reichenbach's "self-corrective method" depend essentially on acceptance of the K-K thesis—just as did Hume's attacks on non-probabilistic induction. Thus the head of skepticism once again is raised. Responses to such skeptical challenges to induction include Popper's falsification doctrines, Kuhn's view of normal *vs.* revolutionary science, and Feyerabend's and Lakatos's proliferation doctrines. All of these tacitly involve acceptance of the K-K thesis; moreover, both Kuhn's and Feyerabend's denial that any correspondence notion of truth is relevant to scientific knowledge (see Section II-B above) stems from their contention that one generally cannot know that such a correspondence holds; hence, via tacit invocation of the K-K thesis, that scientific knowledge is impossible if such a correspondence truth condition is imposed. But, their argument continues, scientific knowledge is possible, and so (1c) cannot be construed as involving any such correspondence in its satisfaction. Thus the K-K thesis crucially underlies Feyerabend's and Kuhn's extreme views on scientific knowledge.[262]

The physicalistic positivistic move of weakening the "adequate evidence" requirement of (1c) to something like "evidence making *P* highly probable or likely" was seconded by a number of authors influenced by the later Wittgenstein's private language arguments against the incorrigi-

[261] It did, however, retain the remainder of the "building-block" model—which has continued to be prominent in contemporary epistemology, albeit divorced from the notion that base knowledge is incorrigible.

[262] The foregoing discussion of the history of modern epistemology, the role of the K-K thesis therein, and the sources of Kuhn's and Feyerabend's extreme epistemological doctrines are spelled out much more fully and defended at length in my [forthcoming c].

bility of sense data.[263] For example, A. J. Ayer, Roderick Chisholm, and Norman Malcolm advanced versions of (1) wherein the evidence satisfying (1c) need not be sufficient to guarantee the truth of '*P*,' yet satisfied some other warrant or testability criterion the satisfaction of which was compatible with the falsity of '*P*.'[264] Unfortunately all attempts to develop such versions of analysis (1) of knowledge have succumbed to some variation on the so-called Gettier paradoxes. In a much discussed article,[265] Edmund Gettier argues that any version of (1) which, in addition, maintains

(3) It is possible for *S* to have adequate evidence for believing that *P* when '*P*' is false;
(4) For any proposition *P*, if S has adequate evidence for believing that *P*, '*P*' entails '*Q*,' and *S* accepts *Q* as a result of this deduction, then *S* has adequate evidence for believing that *Q*;

is liable to counterexamples wherein cases which clearly fail to qualify as knowledge are sanctioned by (1) as such. For example, suppose S has strong (adequate) evidence for believing that Jones owns a Ford (*P*) since Jones always in the past has been known by *S* to drive a Ford and Jones just offered him a ride in a Ford. *S* also has a friend, Brown, about whose whereabouts he is uncertain, and by sheer chance constructs the proposition (*Q*)

Either Jones owns a Ford or Brown is in Barcelona.

S accepts the entailment of *Q* from *P*, and believes *Q*. Since Brown just happens to be in Barcelona, *S* satisfies (1), (3), and (4) with respect to *Q*, and so knows that Jones owns a Ford or Brown is in Barcelona. But since, as a matter of fact, unbeknownst to S Jones sold his Ford yesterday and is driving a rented Ford, Gettier says our intuitions are that S does not know that *Q* because the truth of *Q* depends on Brown being in Barcelona (since Jones does not own a Ford) for which S has *no* evidence whatsoever. Hence, Gettier concludes that satisfying (1a-c), as interpreted by (3) and (4), is not a sufficient condition for knowing that.[266] In response to Gettier's article, dozens of papers have been written attempting to modify (1) so as to avoid Gettier's or related counterexamples. Almost without exception[267] these attempts have left (3) unchallenged and have attempted

[263] See Wittgenstein [1953], especially the discussion between paragraphs 243–420.

[264] See Ayer [1956], Chaps. 1 and 2; Chisholm [1957]; and Malcolm [1963]. Although some authors (for example, Malcolm) deny that they have so weakened the notion of certainty, an overwhelming case that they do is made by Roderick Firth in his [1967].

[265] Gettier [1963].

[266] In stating (3) and (4) and in presenting the example, some alterations in Gettier's presentation have been made for expository purposes; they do not alter the substance of his argument, however.

[267] The chief exceptions are Thalberg [1969]; Goldman [1967]; various articles by F. Dretske, including his [1971]; and my [forthcoming a].

to modify clause (1c), for example, by adding a further condition on the justification of knowledge claims or the notion of adequate evidence, in such a way as to restrict the applicability of (4) in a manner that blocks counterexamples. Unfortunately all these attempts have in turn succumbed to new counterexamples which are variations on Gettier's.[268] The result has been a depressing philosophical quagmire.

The failure of numerous such attempts to avoid the Gettier paradoxes by modifying (1c) so as to weaken (4) raises the obvious question, why not give up (3)? For denying (3) alone is sufficient to block all the known Gettier-like counterexamples. Why has this move been so little attempted? One reason immediately comes to mind: To do so would be to require that adequate evidence for believing that *P guarantee* the truth of *P*, for example, make the truth of *P* be indubitable or incorrigible. This would reintroduce a wholesale skepticism with respect to both observational knowledge of physical reality and also general inductive knowledge. Further, the "private language" arguments and other related attacks on the incorrigibility of our knowledge of sensations[269] give reason to doubt that *any* a posteriori knowledge can meet such a stringent standard. Thus rejecting (3) seems an unpromising move. But such a conclusion, although understandable, is mistaken. For, as Goldman and Dretske have seen,[270] the former sorts of skepticism result only if one accepts the K-K thesis; and the incorrigibility of sensations is a problem only if one supposes that knowledge of the physical world *must* be obtained *inferentially* from incorrigible *knowledge* of the contents of sensation.[271] Reject both of these and one can reject (3) and thus block the Gettier and related paradoxes without succumbing to a pervasive skepticism. Thus far the few attempts along these lines[272] have construed adequate justification satisfying (1c) as involving "causal" regularities obtaining between the circumstances described by '*P*' and belief that *P* such that one would not believe that *P* unless '*P*' were true; thus the fact of believing that *P* when such conditions are met is sufficient to guarantee the truth of '*P*,' which entails denial of

[268] The following very incomplete list includes some of the more influential attempts, as well as criticisms of them: Clark [1965]; Sosa [1965], [1970], and [1969]; Turk-Saunders and Champawat [1964]; Lehrer [1965]; Lehrer and Paxton [1969]; Chisholm [1973]; Harman [1968], [1970], and [1970a]; and Skyrms [1967]. A useful summary of the controversy is found in Chapter 4 of Ackerman [1972]. Of course, additional works on the controversy have been written and continue to be published in substantial volume.

[269] For the classic version of the "private language" argument, see Wittgenstein [1953]. The most important attack to my mind is Sellars [1956].

[270] See Goldman [1967] and Dretske [1971] and [1969], pp. 137–139.

[271] Involved in the latter move is a rejection both of the observational/theoretical distinction of the positivists and of the so-called "myth of the given"; for the latter see Sellars [1956].

[272] See the works by Goldman, Dretske, and myself cited in notes 267 and 270 above.

(3).[273] However, if skepticism is to be avoided, the exploitation of such "causal" regularities in obtaining a posteriori knowledge must not require prior knowledge of those regularities, for were this required it would be impossible to obtain our "first" pieces of knowledge about the physical world, hence resulting in a pervasive skepticism. Denial of the K-K thesis thus is essential to the viability of this approach, such denial enabling one to evidentially exploit the "causal" regularities involved in, for example, perception in obtaining knowledge without knowing what those regularities are.

The denial of the K-K thesis and (3) in this latter approach carries with it a separation of the role evidence plays in *justifying knowledge* and the role of evidence in the *defense of claims to know* that *P*. For example, in the perceptual or observational case the evidence we *can adduce* in defense of *claims* to know that *P* always falls short of what is required to *guarantee* the truth of *P*—a fact we have seen the skeptic is well aware of and attempts to exploit in conjunction with the K-K thesis. Thus if (3) is denied, the evidence we can adduce in defense of a claim to know that *P* generally will fall short of what is required to justify the belief that *P* under (1) if (3) is denied. In the latter case on, for example, Dretske's approach, the adequate evidence required by (1) will consist in being in an experiential state which "triggers" the belief that *P* under circumstances where one could not be in that state unless '*P*' were true (the 'couldn't' here being one of physical or causal impossibility); but to know that *P* one need not know that such regularities hold between the circumstances described by '*P*,' being in that experiential state, and believing that *P*. The separation in the roles evidence plays in satisfying (1c) on this approach and in defending or justifying claims to know that *P* is made possible by denial of the K-K thesis and has been defended on independent grounds by others.[274] Such an approach allows knowledge, both singular and general, about the physical world and avoids the Gettier paradoxes. In all versions to date it allows one to know that *P* under circumstances where one is very ill-equipped to defend one's claim to know that *P*, which fact has been the focus of criticisms of this approach.[275]

[273] Such attempts have themselves been subject to objections and counterexamples; Dretske [1971] and Skyrms [1967] criticize Goldman's formulation. Easily countered objections to Dretske's formulations are advanced in Pappas and Swain [1973]; far more troubling objections to Dretske, and indeed to the whole approach, are found in Martin [1975]. A "hard-line" response to Martin and reworking of Dretske's analysis are found in my [forthcoming a].

[274] See Woozley [1952–53] and A. White [1957].

[275] Such is the thrust of Martin [1975]. A defense of this characteristic of the analysis is given in my [forthcoming a].

Our survey of the recent history of epistemology has revealed two approaches: One, the dominant approach, maintains the K-K thesis; it thereby requires the evidence adequate for knowing that *P* to be identical with the evidence adequate for the defense of a *claim* to know that *P*, and thus far has succumbed to variations on the Gettier paradoxes. The other, the minority approach, denies the K-K thesis, thereby allowing the evidence required to know that *P* to be sufficient to guarantee the truth of '*P*' while allowing the evidence one can *adduce* in defense of a *claim* to know that *P* is insufficient to guarantee the truth of '*P*,' and avoids the Gettier paradoxes. It is worthwhile to ask which of these two approaches is *most promising*, which is most likely to lead to an adequate philosophical analysis of knowledge including scientific knowledge; and it is important to stress that this is quite a different question than asking whether extant incarnations of either approach are adequate as they stand. In the present context, we narrow the question to whether recent findings emerging from work on the growth of scientific knowledge favor or are incompatible with either approach.[276]

For a number of reasons it is my contention that recent work on the growth of scientific knowledge strongly favors denial of the K-K thesis and developing an analysis of knowledge sharing a number of features in common with the minority approach just sketched: *First*, if one accepts the K-K thesis, then on any version of (1) it follows that to know that *P* one must know that 'P' is true; if a correspondence notion of truth is imposed, this requires knowing that the sort of correspondence imposed does obtain. We have seen at the beginning of this section that an adequate epistemology of science must involve a correspondence notion of truth. In general, however, the evidence we can adduce in defense of knowledge claims is insufficient to establish that such a correspondence obtains; indeed, requiring that one be able to establish that such a correspondence holds between '*P*' and the world in order to know that *P* leads to a vicious infinite regress that precludes knowledge about the world.[277] Thus, the

[276] The conclusions argued for in what follows do not depend essentially on this narrowed focus; indeed, a widened focus only reinforces them. See my [forthcoming b] for the wider defense.

[277] For defense of these claims, see my [1973a]. Virtually the same considerations, coupled with tacit acceptance of the K-K thesis, lead Feyerabend and Kuhn to deny the relevance of any correspondence notion of truth to scientific knowledge (see Section II-B above) and leads them directly to their unacceptable views on the nature of scientific knowledge; for defense of this, see my [forthcoming c].

Denying the K-K thesis does not automatically resolve all problems about the incorporation of a correspondence notion of truth into a realistic epistemology; indeed, the problems involved in specifying the nature of the correspondence are formidable but manageable. For background discussion, see White [1970]; for detailed discussions of the specific problems and attempts to resolve them, see Sellars [1963a] and my [1973a] and Chap. VII of my [forthcoming b].

realistic pretensions of science in its epistemic efforts call for a denial of the K-K thesis.

Second, we have seen that a characteristic feature of science is that it develops canons of rationality for evaluating knowledge claims and deciding what to admit into the domain as knowledge. Moreover, we have seen (from one perspective in Shapere's work, and from another perspective in Toulmin's work) that these canons of rationality change, evolve, and become more sophisticated as science develops; for example, straightforward inductive confirmation is characteristic of relatively primitive stages of science whereas, for example, general theory of relativity evaluates evidence much more efficiently (so efficiently, indeed, that only six or seven direct tests of the basic tenets of the theory have been attempted). In a number of cases in diverse branches of science, theories or general hypotheses are "confirmed" or accepted on the basis of *single* observations or experiments. These changing standards of rationality pose a problem for any epistemology of science that insists on the K-K thesis and on identification of the evidence adequate for the *evaluation* of *knowledge claims* with the evidence required for *knowledge*. If these are insisted on, and we accord science the status of a paradigm epistemic enterprise, there are two primary options: (a) We can adopt an extreme epistemic relativism wherein changes in canons of rationality amount to changes in what counts as knowledge, making knowledge be whatever a science accepts and allows to enter into the domain. This option is unacceptable since it destroys the objectivity of scientific knowledge in precisely the ways Kuhn's and Feyerabend's accounts do. (b) We can impose some fixed standard of knowledge against which the canons of rationality, and the evaluation of knowledge claims thereupon, are judged adequate or deficient. Perhaps the most noteworthy feature to emerge about the evaluation of scientific knowledge claims is that as science gets sophisticated it bases its evaluations on smaller and more selective data bases. If our fixed standard of knowledge is tied to, reflects, and sanctions the inefficient knowledge-evaluation standards of primitive science—for example, an "inductive" standard—then it is likely that the later, more sophisticated, evaluation techniques evolved by science will fail to qualify (since, for example, the number of instances or pieces of data is insufficient). And if this fixed standard is tied to those encountered in more sophisticated science, surely the evaluation procedures of more primitive science will fail to qualify as adequate, thus denying sophisticated science its primitive origins which provided the epistemic base for developing its later, more sophisticated, procedures. Moreover, pegging the standards to the presently most sophisticated evaluation standards is sure to disqualify yet-to-be-developed improved, more efficient, means for assessing knowledge claims. The general point can be put differently: What data are sufficient for sanctioning a knowledge claim as legitimate depends on the patterns of reasoning employed to evaluate the claim in light of the data. Thus what qualifies a knowledge claim as acceptable will depend on both available data and patterns of reasoning. And work on the growth of scientific knowledge informs us there is an open-ended variety of the latter. Thus the attempt to establish a fixed pattern for the justification of knowledge claims by data seems hopeless. In short, if we want to insist on the K-K thesis and avoid a Kuhn-Feyerabend-like epistemological relativism, it appears we will have to opt for an impossible fixed standard for the evaluation of knowledge claims which cannot hope to reflect the growing diversity of standards for evaluating knowledge claims which science has developed and can be expected to develop as it becomes increasingly sophisticated. This seems to call for (although it does not prove the necessity of) a philosophical analysis of knowledge which eschews the K-K thesis.

Third, science's evaluatory procedures for assessing knowledge claims, hence for admission of items into domains, although generally reliable, are fallible. Sometimes false claims are admitted. And an adequate account of knowledge must be able to make sense of how this is. The most promising explanation of this phenomenon is to say that science uses evidence to determine the *likelihood* that various putative knowledge claims are true—that is, to assess whether what is *claimed* as knowledge is in fact known. As Lakatos puts it, "scientific games are without any genuine epistemological relevance unless we superimpose on them some sort of metaphysical (or if you wish 'inductive') principle which will say that the game, as specified by the methodology, gives us the best chance of approaching the Truth."[278] That is, the patterns of reasoning, or methodologies, used by a science are *fallible* means for evaluating the truth of putative knowledge claims; but if they are good ones, they *tend* to accept only true knowledge claims. Yet the very idea of having fallibly good or adequate reasons for assessing the truth of knowledge claims presupposes some *independent* standard of what knowledge is. And this seems to require a separation of the role of evidence in the rational evaluation and defense of knowledge claims from the role evidence plays in obtaining knowledge—especially if we are to allow the canons of rationality for assessing knowledge claims to evolve without compromising the objectivity of knowledge. Such a separation is most likely to be obtained if the K-K thesis is denied, and so the second, minority, approach to analyzing knowledge seems more promising in the light of what is known about the growth of scientific knowledge.

[278] Lakatos [1971], pp. 108–109.

Finally, I want to briefly allude to one other consideration. From our studies in the growth of scientific knowledge, we know that scientific observations get increasingly sophisticated as a science advances; in particular, as science becomes more sophisticated, its observation reports, which ultimately involve perceptual evidence, cease to describe what the observer directly sees, and become descriptive of micro or other nondirectly seeable entities, processes, or events. That is, the interpretative aspects of observations become increasingly more subtle, theoretical, and removed from what we directly perceive.[279] If the K-K thesis is insisted on, such observational knowledge of what we cannot directly perceive will be possible only if we have known theories detailing the correlations between the behaviors of such entities and our perceptual experiences; but such theories can be established only on the basis of evidence about such nondirectly perceivable entities—which evidential knowledge seems to be precluded since we do not already have the theory required to obtain such knowledge.[280] Thus it would seem that accommodating the findings about observation in actual scientific practice into an account of scientific knowledge requires rejecting the K-K thesis.

Having made a case for the "minority position" which involves a denial of the K-K thesis and appears to accord more closely with the actual means whereby science evaluates putative knowledge claims in the attempt to undergo objective growth in scientific knowledge, it is worth considering what the implications of such an approach are for recent efforts in philosophy of science to develop inductive logics and whether the epistemic premium placed on such attempts is warranted. Through its separation of the roles evidence plays in obtaining knowledge and in the defense of knowledge claims, the "minority approach" is able to insist that the evidence required for knowledge that *Q guarantee* the truth of '*Q*' while allowing the *available* evidence that can be marshaled in defense or evaluation of a knowledge *claim* to fall short of this standard. Such a position precludes the possibility that probabilistic induction can play *any* role in obtaining knowledge, for the evidence supporting *Q* that is exploitable by probabilistic induction always will fall short of what is

[279] These themes are developed and defended by Shapere (see Section III-B-3 above) as well as by Dretske in his [1969], especially Chapter VI; Sellars in his [1956] and [1965]; Aune in his [1967]; and myself in [1974a], Secs. 4 and 5, and in a more sustained fashion in my [forthcoming b].

[280] The problem here is a variation on the standard one besetting causal theories of perception which maintain the K-K thesis; for example, Bertrand Russell's [1929] succumbs to such difficulties. Although not identified as such and somewhat obscure, the basic move of avoiding these difficulties in a manner that involves denying the K-K thesis seems to have been advanced first in Grice [1961].

required to *guarantee* the truth of 'Q'. However, such evidence (E) may make it reasonable to *accept* Q as being established as known—for example, because $P(Q, E) \approx 1$ and E meets various "maximal relevant evidence" requirements.[281] Although induction thus can play *a* role in the evaluation of knowledge claims and the determination of which ones to admit into the domain, the lessons we have learned from studying the growth of scientific knowledge suggest that such probabilistic inductive evaluations are relatively inefficient and characteristic of relatively unsophisticated stages of science. As science evolves, it becomes more sophisticated and efficient in its evaluation of knowledge claims, thereby rendering the inductive logics developed by philosophy of science increasingly less relevant to understanding the means whereby sophisticated science evaluates and passes on putative knowledge claims. The implications, then, of recent work on the growth of scientific knowledge are that probabilistic inductive logic is irrelevant to scientific knowledge, and that it is of limited value in understanding how science evaluates putative knowledge claims.

In the preceding discussion, my attempt has not been to resolve the current controversies in epistemology over how knowledge ought best to be analyzed, to prove the limited value of inductive logic, or to prove the necessity of denying the K-K thesis; such attempts would be inappropriate here, and in any case would require far more space than is available to me. Moreover, I am in the process of writing a separate detailed account and defense of my views on scientific knowledge.[282] Rather, my aims here have been more limited—to place current work in philosophy of science into the larger epistemological context and to show how recent work on the philosophy of science, especially on rationality in the growth of scientific knowledge, bears importantly on contemporary issues in epistemology. Although I have tried to make a case that such work favors and reinforces a particular approach to analyzing knowledge—an approach

[281] The nature of such requirements is controversial, as is evidenced by the controversy between Hempel (in his [1965a]) and Salmon (in his [1970]) over the appropriate evidential bases in statistical explanation. In his "On the Role of Conceptual Devices in Science," Shapere convincingly argues, from considerations such as were raised in Sections III-B-3 and III-C above concerning actual scientific practice, that the relevant data base E for an "inductive logic" of "confirmation" should meet the following condition, which is quite at odds with those previously advocated: "In the application of inductive logic to a given knowledge situation, the total evidence *available* and *required* for the problem at hand must be taken as a basis for determining the degree of confirmation (or of warranted confidence in a prediction)" where what is required depends on the nature of the conceptual devices employed, hence ultimately on the content of the existing science.

[282] This is my *Facts, Theories, and Scientific Observation* which, hopefully, is nearing completion and will be released within a year or two.

which is in opposition to the dominant approach recently evidenced in epistemology—I will be content if I have convinced the reader that philosophy of science and epistemology are handmaidens. Good philosophy of science must come squarely into contact with the basic issues in epistemology and metaphysics; and the attempt to do epistemology or metaphysics without regard to science is dangerous at best. Although this is a lesson our philosophical forebears such as Locke and Kant knew well, it is one that lately has been ignored all too much. Recent developments in philosophy of science not only give grounds for hope that philosophy once again is learning that lesson, but also provide guidance for acting on that lesson in the attempt to develop a viable epistemology of knowledge.

IV. Conclusion: Philosophy of Science Today

In this volume we have been concerned to detail where philosophy of science is today, show how it got there, and indicate where it is heading. In doing so, we have focused on one important and pivotal conference in philosophy of science, the 1969 Illinois Symposium on the Structure of Scientific Theories, held at a time in which philosophy of science was in an acute state of disarray. We allowed a select body of important philosophers and other involved scholars to address themselves to that confused state of the field, focusing on one central problem—the nature of scientific theory—and to do their best to discover a new focus, a new direction. And we invited them to evaluate, discuss, and consider each other's positive suggestions under public scrutiny. The published proceedings of the symposium in this volume constitute the record of that forward-looking encounter. The *mere* recording in print of these informed and conscientious reactions to the then disordered house of philosophy of science would have been of only limited value; there is little point to a profession airing its laundry in public unless it is done in an instructive manner. To that instructive end, the symposium proceedings have been sandwiched between two long essays of mine—the critical introduction on pages 3–241 and this Afterword. In the former work, I attempted to present a critical history of how philosophy of science went from what Toulmin calls a "compact discipline" into the disordered "would be" discipline evidenced at the symposium. In doing so, I attempted to provide an account of how positivistic philosophy of science originated as a philosophical-scientific response to dramatic advances, and attendant foundational problems, in physical science, but then lost sight of the science as it developed doctrines about science which had increasingly less relevance to what the most successful branches of science were engaged in doing. Then I detailed the growing critical response to positivistic philosophy of science which, correctly, castigated it for being irrelevant philosophy of science. I looked at the alternative philosophies of science which were being advanced as superior in virtue to their claimed fidelity to actual science, as well as the healthy and growing skeptical doubts whether these *Weltanschauungen* analyses, for all their history of science trappings, had any more to do with actual science than did positivistic philosophy of science. A few other trends or significant developments in evidence at the time were sketched. This provided the background not only for comprehending the disarray of the symposium but also for understanding the views and positions being espoused by the symposium participants.

The Afterword was written eight years after the symposium when philosophy of science had emerged substantially from the chaos evidenced in 1969, was finding a new direction, and appeared to be making impressive strides (to the point that it could be claimed a new "movement" was coalescing). My attempt here was, again as critical history, to show how philosophy of science has been, and is succeeding at, working itself out of the confused state so much in evidence at the symposium, and how it is finding new direction and is advancing our understanding of the scientific enterprise. In telling this recent story, I have tried to indicate what I see as the most promising recent developments in philosophy of science and what, in my considered judgment, are the most promising directions for further work in philosophy of science and the most fruitful lines of research to be followed. In doing so, hopefully I have provided a helpful perspective for viewing and understanding the field of philosophy of science—its recent past, the present state, and its burgeoning promise. I have taken definite, but considered, critical and evaluative stands on recent literature in the field; and I have tried to marshal evidence that, in my reflective opinion, substantiates those judgments. Although the account given clearly reflects a substantial and informed body of professional opinion on recent developments, my intent has been, to adapt a phrase from Rousseau, that it represent "the general will" among philosophers of science today and thus provides a reliable guide to future philosophical advances in understanding the scientific enterprise.

Bibliography

The following is a comprehensive but selected bibliography of main works on the structure of theories and related topics. It includes virtually every work cited in this volume. Additional references on related problems in philosophy of science can be found in the quite extensive (but now somewhat dated) annotated bibliography in Wartofsky [1968].

Works are listed alphabetically by author, and where more than one work by an author is included, they have been arranged in chronological order.

Achinstein, P.

1963. "Theoretical Terms and Partial Interpretation," *British Journal for Philosophy of Science*, 14, 89–105.

1964. "On the Meaning of Scientific Terms," *Journal of Philosophy*, 61, 475–510.

1965. "The Problem of Theoretical Terms," *American Philosophical Quarterly*, 2, 193–203.

1968. *Concepts of Science*. Baltimore, Md.: Johns Hopkins Press.

1969. "Approaches to the Philosophy of Science," pp. 259–291 in Achinstein and Barker [1969].

1971. *Law and Explanation*. Oxford: Oxford University Press.

Achinstein, P., and S. Barker

1969. *The Legacy of Logical Positivism*. Baltimore, Md.: Johns Hopkins Press.

Ackerman, R. J.

1972. *Belief and Knowledge*. Garden City, N.Y.: Anchor.

Adler, J. E.

1976. "Evaluating Global and Local Theories of Induction," pp. 212–223 in Suppe and Asquith [1976].

Agassi, J.

1961. "The Rȯle of Corroboration in Popper's Methodology," *Australasian Journal of Philosophy*, 39, 82ff.

Aldrich, V.

1970. "Review of Fred I. Dretske, *Seeing and Knowing*," *Journal of Philosophy*, 67, 994–1006.

Alexander, H. Gavin

1958. "General Statements as Rules of Inference," pp. 309–329 in Feigl, Scriven, and Maxwell [1958].

Alston, W.
1964. *Philosophy of Language*. Englewood Cliffs, N.J.: Prentice Hall.
Alston, W., and G. Nakhnikian, eds.
1963. *Readings in Twentieth Century Philosophy*. Glencoe, Ill.: Free Press.
Andrade e Silva, J., and G. Lochak
1969. *Quanta*. New York: World University Library.
Aune, B.
1967. *Knowledge, Mind, and Nature*. New York: Random House.
Austin, J.
1961. *Philosophical Papers*. Oxford: Oxford University Press.
1962. *How to Do Things with Words*. Cambridge, Mass.: Harvard University Press.
Ayala, F., and T. Dobzhansky, eds.
1974. *Studies in the Philosophy of Biology*. London: Macmillan.
Ayer, A. J.
1946. *Language, Truth, and Logic*. London: Gollanez, 1936; 2nd ed.
1956. *The Problem of Knowledge*. Baltimore, Md.: Penguin.
———, ed.
1959. *Logical Positivism*. New York: Free Press.
Bacon, Francis
1620. *Novum Organon*. Part 2, *Instauratio magna*. London: J. Billium.
Barcan, Ruth C.
1946a. "A Functional Calculus of First-Order Based on Strict Implication," *Journal of Symbolic Logic*, 11, 1–16.
1946b. "The Deduction Theorem in a Functional Calculus of First-Order Based on Strict Implication," *Journal of Symbolic Logic*, 11, 115–118.
1947. "The Identity of Individuals in a Strict Functional Calculus of Second Order," *Journal of Symbolic Logic*, 12, 12–15.
Bar-Hillel, Y., ed.
1975. *Proceedings of the 1964 Congress for Logic, Methodology, and the Philosophy of Science*. Amsterdam: North Holland.
Bartley, W. W., III
1964. "Rationality Versus the Theory of Rationality," in Bunge [1964].
Baumrin, B., ed.
1963. *Philosophy of Science. The Delaware Seminar*. Vol. I, 1961–62. New York: John Wiley.
1963a. *Philosophy of Science. The Delaware Seminar*. Vol. II. New York: Interscience.
Beadle, G., and M. Beadle
1967. *The Language of Life*. Garden City, N.Y.: Doubleday.
Beer, A., and K. Strand, eds.
1975. *Copernicanism Yesterday and Today*. New York: Pergamon.
Bergmann, G.
1951. "Comments on Professor Hempel's 'The Concept of Cognitive Significance'," *Proceedings of the American Academy of Arts and Sciences*, 80, 78–86. Reprinted in Bergmann [1954].
1951a. "The Logic of Psychological Concepts," *Philosophy of Science*, 18, 93–110.
1954. *The Metaphysics of Logical Positivism*. New York: Longmans, Green.
1957. *Philosophy of Science*. Madison: University of Wisconsin Press.

Bergmann, G., and Kenneth Spence
1941. "Operationism and Theory in Psychology," *Psychological Review*, 48, 1–14. Reprinted in Marx [1951].

Bernoulli, Daniel
1738. *Hydrodynamica, sive de viribus et motibus fluidorum, commentarii opus academicum*. Strasbourg: J. R. Dulseckeri.

Beth, E.
1948. *Natuurphilosophie*. Gorinchem: Noorduyn.
1949. "Towards an Up-to-Date Philosophy of the Natural Sciences," *Methodos*, 1, 178–185.
1961. "Semantics of Physical Theories," pp. 48–51 in Freudenthal [1961].
1963. "Carnap's Views on the Advantages of Constructed Systems over Natural Languages in the Philosophy of Science," pp. 469–502 in Schilpp [1963].

Birkhoff, G.
1940. *Lattice Theory*. New York: American Mathematical Society.
1960. *Hydrodynamics*. Rev. ed. Princeton, N.J.: Princeton University Press.

Birkhoff, G., and J. von Neumann
1936. "The Logic of Quantum Mechanics," *Annals of Mathematics*, 37, 823–843. Reprinted on pp. 105–125 of von Neumann [1962], Vol. IV.

Black, Max
1962. "Models and Archetypes," pp. 219–243 in Black [1962a].
1962a. *Models and Metaphor*. Ithaca, N.Y.: Cornell University Press, 1962.

Blake, R., C. J. Ducasse, and E. Madden
1960. *Theories of Scientific Method*. Seattle: University of Washington Press, 1960.

Bohm, David
1951. *Quantum Theory*. Englewood Cliffs, N.J.: Prentice Hall.
1952. "Quantum Theory in Terms of Hidden Variables," *Physical Review*, 35, 166ff.
1957. *Causality and Chance in Modern Physics*. London: Routledge and Kegan Paul.
1957a. "A Proposed Explanation of Quantum Theory in Terms of Hidden Variables at a Sub-Quantum Mechanical Level," pp. 33–40 in Körner [1957].
1965. *The Special Theory of Relativity*. New York: Benjamin.
1971. "Quantum Theory as an Indication of a New Order in Physics. Part A. The Development of New Orders as Shown through the History of Physics," *Foundations of Physics*, 1, 359–381.
1971a. "On the Role of Hidden Variables in the Fundamental Structure of Physics," in T. Bastin, ed. *Quantum Theory and Beyond*. Cambridge: Cambridge University Press.

Bohr, N.
1913. "On the Constitution of Atoms and Molecules," *Philosophical Magazine*, 26, 1–25, 476–502, 857–875.
1931. "Maxwell and Modern Theoretical Physics," *Nature*, 128, 691.
1934. *Atomic Theory and the Description of Nature*. Cambridge: Cambridge University Press.
1935. "Can Quantum Mechanical Description of Physical Realty Be Considered Complete?," *Physics Review*, 48, 696–702.

1949. "Discussions with Einstein," pp. 199–242 in Schilpp [1949].
1958. *Atomic Physics and Human Knowledge*. New York: John Wiley.
1963. *Essays 1958–1962 on Atomic Physics and Human Knowledge*. New York: Random House.

Boorse, H., and L. Motz, eds.
1966. *The World of the Atom*. New York: Basic Books.

Braithwaite, R. B.
1953. *Scientific Explanation*. New York: Harper Torchbooks.
1954. "The Nature of Theoretical Concepts and the Role of Models in an Advanced Science," *Revue International de Philosophie*, 8, 34–40.

Bridgman, P. W.
1927. *The Logic of Modern Physics*. New York: Macmillan.
1936. *The Nature of Physical Theory*. Princeton, N.J.: Princeton University Press.
1938. "Operational Analysis," *Philosophy of Science*, 5, 114–131.
1951. "The Nature of Some of Our Physical Concepts," *British Journal for the Philosophy of Science*, 1, 257–272; 2, 25–44, 142–160. Reprinted as a separate monograph, New York: Philosophical Library, 1952.

Broad, C. D.
1965. "The Theory of Sensa," pp. 85–129 in Swartz [1965].

Brock, W. H.
1967. *The Atomic Debates*. Leicester, England: Leicester University Press.

Brodbeck, May
1959. "Models, Meaning, and Theories," pp. 373–403 in Gross [1959].
1962. "Explanations, Predictions, and 'Imperfect' Knowledge," pp. 231–272 in Feigl and Maxwell [1962].
1968. *Readings in the Philosophy of the Social Sciences*. New York: Macmillan.

Brody, B.
1970. *Readings in the Philosophy of Science*. Englewood Cliffs, N.J.: Prentice Hall.

Brody, B., and N. Capaldi, eds.
1968. *Science, Methods, and Goals*. New York: Benjamin.

Bromberger, S.
1960. "The Concept of Explanation," Ph.D. thesis, Harvard University.
1963. "A Theory about the Theory of Theory and about the Theory of Theories," pp. 79–106 in Baumrin [1963a].
1965. "An Approach to Explanation," pp. 72–105 in Butler [1965].
1966. "Why Questions," pp. 86–111 in Colodny [1966].

Brown, T. M.
1969. "The Electrical Current in Early Nineteenth-Century Electricity," pp. 61–103, in McCormmach [1969].

Bub, J.
1968. "The Daneri-Loinger-Prosperi Quantum Theory of Measurement," *Il Nuovo Cimento*, 57B, 503ff.
1969. "What Is a Hidden Variable Theory of Quantum Phenomena?," *International Journal of Theoretical Physics*, No. 2, 101–123.

Büchner, Ludwig Friedrich
1855. *Kraft und Stoff*. Frankfort a.M.: Meidinger Sohn.

Buck, R., and R. Cohen, eds.
1971. *PSA 1970: In Memory of Rudolf Carnap. Boston Studies in the Philosophy of Science*, Vol. VIII. Dordrecht, Holland: Reidel.

Bunge, M.
1959. *Causality—the Place of the Causal Principle in Modern Science*. Cambridge, Mass.: Harvard University Press.
1964. *The Critical Approach to Science and Philosophy*. New York: Free Press.

Burks, A. W.
1949. "Icon, Index, and Symbol," *Philosophical and Phenomenological Research*, 9, 673–689.
1951. "The Logic of Casual Propositions," *Mind*, 60, 363–382.
1955. "Dispositional Statements," *Philosophy of Science*, 22, 175–193.
1975. "Models of Deterministic Systems," *Mathematical Systems Theory*, 8, 295–308.
1977. *Cause, Chance, and Reason*. Chicago, Ill.: University of Chicago Press.

———, ed.
1970. *Essays in Cellular Automata*. Urbana: University of Illinois Press.

Burtt, E. A.
1949. *The Metaphysical Foundations of Modern Science*. London: Routledge and Kegan Paul.

Bush, R. R., and W. K. Estes, eds.
1959. *Studies in Mathematical Learning Theory*. Stanford, Calif.: Stanford University Press.

Bush, R. R., and F. Mosteller
1955. *Stochastic Models for Learning*. New York: John Wiley.

Butler, R. J.
1965. *Studies in Analytical Philosophy*. 2nd Ser. Oxford: Blackwell.

Butterfield, H.
1951. *The Whig Interpretation of History*. New York: Scribners.
1958. *The Origins of Modern Science: 1300–1800*. New York: Macmillan.

Campbell, Norman R.
1920. *Physics: The Elements*. Cambridge: Cambridge University Press. Republished under the title *Foundations of Science*. New York: Dover, 1957. Reprinted in part in Feigl and Brodbeck [1953].
1921. *What Is Science?* London: Methuen, reprinted New York: Dover.
1928. *An Account of the Principles of Measurement and Calculation*. New York: Longmans, Green.

Cantor, Georg
1932. *Gesammelte Abhandlungen*. Berlin: Springer.

Căpek, M.
1961. *The Philosophical Impact of Contemporary Physics*. Princeton, N.J.: Van Nostrand.
1971. *Boston Studies in the Philosophy of Science*, Vol. VII. Dordrecht, Holland: Reidel.

Carnap, Rudolf
1923. "Über die Aufgabe der Physik und die Andwendung des Gründsatze der Einfachstheit," *Kant-Studien*, 28, 90–107.
1928. *Der Logische Aufbau der Welt*. Berlin: Welkreis-Verlag.

1932. "Die physikalische Sprache als Üniversalsprache der Wissenschaft," *Erkenntnis*, 2. A revised English translation can be found in Alston and Nakhnikian [1963].
1932a. "Überwindung der Metaphysik durch Logische Analyse der Sprache," *Erkenntnis*, 2; English trans., pp. 60–81 in Ayer [1959].
1934. *Logische Syntax der Sprache*. Vienna: Springer, 1934; trans. as *Logical Syntax of Language*. London: Kegan Paul, 1937.
1936–37. "Testability and Meaning," *Philosophy of Science*, 3, 420–468; 4, 1–40, reprinted as a monograph by Whitlock's Inc., New Haven, Conn., 1950. Excerpts reprinted in Feigl and Brodbeck [1953].
1939. *Foundations of Logic and Mathematics*. Chicago, Ill.: University of Chicago Press.
1942. *Introduction to Semantics*. Cambridge, Mass.: Harvard University Press.
1945. "On Inductive Logic," *Philosophy of Science*, 12, 72–97.
1947. *Meaning and Necessity*. Chicago, Ill.: University of Chicago Press; enlarged ed., 1956.
1950. *Logical Foundations of Probability*. Chicago, Ill.: University of Chicago Press; 2nd rev. ed., 1962.
1950a. "Empiricism, Semantics, and Ontology," *Revue internationale de Philosophie*, 11, 208–228; reprinted in Linsky [1952] and the enlarged 1956 edition of Carnap [1947].
1952. *Continuum of Inductive Methods*. Chicago, Ill.: University of Chicago Press.
1952a. "Meaning Postulates," *Philosophical Studies*, 3, 65–73.
1955. "Meaning and Synonymy in Natural Languages," *Philosophical Studies*, 6, 33–47.
1956. "The Methodological Character of Theoretical Concepts," pp. 33–76 in Feigl and Scriven [1956].
1959. "Beoabuchtungssprache und theoretische Sprache," pp. 32–44 in *Logic: Studia Paul Bernays Dedicata*, Bibliotheque Scientifique, 34, Neuchâtel: Éditiones du Griffon.
1963. "Carl G. Hempel on Scientific Theories," pp. 958–966 in Schilpp [1963].
1963a. "Physical Language as the Universal Language of Science" in Alston and Nakhniknan [1963].
1963b. "Intellectual Autobiography," pp. 3–84 in Schilpp [1963].
1963c. "Replies and Systematic Expositions," pp. 859–1013 in Schilpp [1963].
1966. *Philosophical Foundations of Physics*. New York: Basic Books.

Carnap, R., and R. Jeffrey, eds.
1971. *Studies in Inductive Logic and Probability*. Vol. I. Berkeley: University of California Press.

Cassirer, Ernst
1910. *Substanzbegriff und Functionsbegriff*. Berlin: B. Cassirer. Translated in *Substance and Function and Einstein's Theory of Relativity*. Chicago, Ill.: Open Court, 1923.

Chisholm, R.
1946. "The Contrary to Fact Conditional," *Mind*, 55, 289–307; reprinted in Feigl and Sellars [1949].

1957. *Perceiving*. Ithaca, N.Y.: Cornell University Press.
1973. "On the Nature of Evidence," pp. 224–250 in Chisholm and Swartz, eds. [1974].

Chisholm, R., and W. Sellars
1958. "Intentionality and the Mental," pp. 597–639 in Feigl, Scriven, and Maxwell [1958].

Chisholm, R., and R. Swartz, eds.
1974. *Empirical Knowledge*. Englewood Cliffs, N.J.: Prentice Hall.

Chomsky, N.
1957. *Syntactic Structures*. The Hague: Mouton.
1959. "Review of Skinner's *Verbal Behavior*," *Language*, 35, 26–58.
1968. *Language and Mind*. New York: Harcourt, Brace, and World.

Church, A.
1949. Review of Ayer [1946]. *The Journal of Symbolic Logic*, 14, 52–53.
1956. *Introduction to Mathematical Logic*. Vol. I. Princeton, N.J.: Princeton University Press.

Clagett, Marshall
1959. *The Science of Mechanics in the Middle Ages*. Madison: University of Wisconsin Press.

Clark, M.
1965. "Knowledge and Grounds: A Comment on Mr. Gettier's Paper," *Analysis*, 24, 46–48.

Clavelin, M.
1968. *La philosophie naturelle de Galilée, essai sur les origines et la formation de la mécanique classique*. Paris: Librarie Armand Colin.

Clerke, A.
1902. *History of Astronomy during the Nineteenth Century*. London: Black.
1903. *Problems of Astrophysics*. London: Black.

Clifford, W. K.
1885. *Common Sense of the Exact Sciences*. New York: Appleton.

Cohen, Hermann
1871. *Kant's Theorie der reinen Erfahrung*. Berlin: B. Cassirer, 1902–12.
1902–12. *System der Philosophie*. 3 vols. Berlin: B. Cassirer.

Cohen, I. B.
1950. "A Sense of History in Science," *American Journal of Physics*, 18, 343–359.
1962. "The First English Version of Newton's 'Hypotheses non fingo,'" *Isis*, 53, 379–388.
1963. "Pemberton's Translation of Newton's *Principia*, with Notes on Motte's Translation," *Isis*, 54, 319–351.
1964. "'Quantum in se est': Newton's Concept of Inertia in Relation to Descartes and Lucretius," *Notes and Records of the Royal Society of London*, 19, 131–155.
1966. "Hypotheses in Newton's Philosophy," *Physis*, 8, 163–184.
1967. "Dynamics: The Key to the 'New Science' of the Seventeenth Century," *Acta historiae rerum naturalium necnon technicarum* (Czechoslovak Studies in the History of Science), Prague, Special Issue 3, 79–114.
1967a. "Newton's Second Law and the Concept of Force in the *Principia*," *The Texas Quarterly*, 10, 127–157.

1967b. "Newton's Use of 'Force' or Cajori *vs.* Newton: A Note on Translations of the *Principia*," *Isis*, 58, 226–230.

1969. "Newton's *System of the World*: Some Textual and Bibliographical Notes," *Physis*, 11, 152–166.

1971. Introduction to Newton's *Principia*. Cambridge, Mass.: Harvard University Press; Cambridge: Cambridge University Press.

Forthcoming. *Transformations of Scientific Ideas: Newtonian Themes in the Development of Science*. Cambridge: Cambridge University Press.

Cohen, M. R.

1931. *Reason and Nature*. New York: Harcourt, Brace.

Cohen, M. R., and E. Nagel

1934. *Introduction to Logic and Scientific Method*. New York: Harcourt, Brace.

Cohen, R. S., and M. W. Wartofsky, eds.

1965. *Boston Studies in the Philosophy of Science*, Vol. II. New York: Humanities Press.

1967. *Boston Studies in the Philosophy of Science*, Vol. III. Dordrecht, Holland: Reidel.

1969. *Boston Studies in the Philosophy of Science*, Vol. IV. Dordrecht, Holland: Reidel.

1969a. *Boston Studies in the Philosophy of Science*, Vol. V. Dordrecht, Holland: Reidel.

1970. *Boston Studies in the Philosophy of Science*, Vol. VI. Dordrecht, Holland: Reidel.

Colodny, R., ed.

1962. *Frontiers of Science and Philosophy*. Pittsburgh, Pa.: University of Pittsburgh Press.

1965. *Beyond the Edge of Certainty*. Englewood Cliffs, N.J.: Prentice Hall.

1966. *Mind and Cosmos: Explorations in the Philosophy of Science*. Pittsburgh, Pa.: University of Pittsburgh Press.

1970. *The Nature and Function of Scientific Theories*. Pittsburgh, Pa.: University of Pittsburgh Press.

1972. *Paradigms and Paradoxes*. Pittsburgh, Pa.: University of Pittsburgh Press.

Cooper, Lane

1935. *Aristotle, Galileo, and the Tower of Pisa*. Ithaca, N.Y.: Cornell University Press.

Copi, I. M.

1958. "Artificial Languages," pp. 96–120 in Henle [1958].

Copleston, F.

1946–65. *A History of Philosophy*. 8 vols. Westminster, Md.: Newman.

Craig, William

1953. "On Axiomatizability within a System," *Journal of Symbolic Logic*, 18, 30–32.

1956. "Replacement of Auxiliary Expression," *Philosophical Review*, 65, 38–55.

Cramér, Harold

1946. *Mathematical Methods of Statistics*. Princeton, N.J.: Princeton University Press.

Crane, Diana
1969. "Social Structure in a Group of Scientists: A Test of the 'Invisible College' Hypothesis," *American Sociological Review*, 34, 335–352.
Crosland, M. P.
1961. "The Origins of Gay-Lussac's Law of Combining Volumes of Gases," *Annals of Science*, 17, 1–26.
Danto, A., and S. Morgenbesser, eds.
1960. *Philosophy of Science*. New York: Meridian.
Darden, Lindley
1974. "Reasoning in Scientific Change: The Field of Genetics at Its Beginnings." Ph.D. dissertation, University of Chicago.
1976. "Reasoning in Scientific Change: Charles Darwin, Hugo de Vries, and the Discovery of Segregation," in *Studies in the History and Philosophy of Science*, 7, 127–169.
Darden, L., and Nancy Maull [Roth]
1974. "The Unity of Science: Interfield Theories," pp. v–108 in *Contributed Papers: Fifth International Congress of Logic, Methodology, and Philosophy of Science.* London, Ontario, Canada: International Union of History and Philosophy of Science.
Forthcoming. "Interfield Theories," *Philosophy of Science*.
Davidson, Donald
1967. "Truth and Meanings," *Synthese*, 17, 304–323.
Davis, M.
1965. *The Undecidable*. New York: Raven.
de Broglie, L.
1954. *The Revolution in Physics*. London: Routledge and Kegan Paul.
De Finetti, Bruno
1951. "Recent Suggestions for the Reconciliations of Theories of Probability," pp. 217–226 in Neyman [1951].
1972. *Probability, Induction, and Statistics*. New York: John Wiley.
Dennis, W., ed.
1951. *Current Trends in Psychological Theory*. Pittsburgh, Pa.: University of Pittsburgh Press.
Dijksterhuis, E. J.
1961. *The Mechanization of the World Picture*, trans. C. Dikshoorn. Oxford: Clarendon Press.
Dingle, H.
1963. "A Hundred Years of Spectroscopy," *British Journal for the History of Science*, 1.
Dobzhansky, T., and F. Ayala, eds.
1975. *Problems of Reduction in Biology*. London: Macmillan.
Donagan, Alan
1964. "Historical Explanation: The Popper-Hempel Theory Reconsidered," *History and Theory*, 4, 3–26. Reprinted on pp. 127–159 of W. Dray, ed., *Philosophical Analysis and History*. New York: Harper and Row, 1966.
Drake, Stillman
1957. trans. *Discoveries and Opinions of Galileo*. Garden City, N.Y.: Doubleday.

1970. *Galileo Studies: Personality, Tradition, and Revolution*. Ann Arbor: University of Michigan Press.

Dray, W.

1957. *Laws and Explanation in History*. Oxford: Oxford University Press.

1964. *Philosophy of History*. Englewood Cliffs, N.J.: Prentice Hall.

———, ed.

1966. *Philosophical Analysis and History*. New York: Harper and Row.

Dretske, F.

1969. *Seeing and Knowing*. Chicago, Ill.: University of Chicago Press.

1971. "Conclusive Reasons," *Australasian Journal of Philosophy*, 49, 1–22.

Dugas, René

1955. *A History of Mechanics*. Trans. J. R. Maddox. Neuchâtel: Editiones du Griffon.

Duhem, Pierre

1906. *La théorie physique, son objet et sa structure*. Paris: Chevalier et Rivière.

1954. *Aim and Structure of Physical Theory*. New York: Atheneum.

Dundon, S. J.

1969. "Newton's 'Mathematical Way' in the *De mundi systemate*," *Physis*, 11, 195–204.

Einstein, A.

1905. "Über einen die Erzeugung und Verwandlung des Lichtes betreffenden heuristischen Gesichtspunkt," *Annalen der Physik*, 17, 132–148; translated as "On a Heuristic Viewpoint Concerning the Production and Transformation of Light" on pp. 545–557 of Boorse and Motz [1966].

Einstein, A., B. Podolsky, and N. Rosen

1935. "Can Quantum-Mechanical Description of Reality Be Considered Complete?," *Physical Review*, 47, 777–780.

Einstein, D., and L. Infield

1947. *Evolution of Physics*. Cambridge: Cambridge University Press.

Estes, W. K., and P. Suppes

1959. "Foundations of Linear Models," pp. 137–139 in Bush and Estes [1959].

Farrar, W. V.

1965. "Nineteenth-Century Speculations on the Complexity of the Chemical Elements," *British Journal for the History of Science*, 2, 297–323.

Feigl, H.

1948. "Some Remarks on the Meaning of Scientific Explanation" (a slightly modified version of comments first published in *Psychological Review*, 52), pp. 510–514 in Feigl and Sellars [1949].

1950. "Existential Hypotheses," *Philosophy of Science*, 17, 35–62.

1950a. "Logical Reconstruction, Realism, and Pure Semiotic," *Philosophy of Science*, 17, 186–195.

1951. "Principles and Problems of Theory Construction in Psychology," pp. 179–213 in Dennis [1951].

1954. "Operationism and Scientific Method," *Psychological Review*, 52, 250–259, reprinted with some alterations in Feigl and Sellars [1949].

1956. "Some Major Issues and Developments in the Philosophy of Science of Logical Empiricism," pp. 3–37 in Feigl and Scriven [1956].

1970. "The 'Orthodox' View of Theories: Remarks in Defense as Well as Critique," pp. 3–16 in Radner and Winokur [1970].

Feigl, H., and May Brodbeck, eds.
1953. *Readings in the Philosophy of Science.* New York: Appleton-Century-Crofts.
Feigl, H., and G. Maxwell, eds.
1961. *Current Issues in the Philosophy of Science.* New York: Holt, Rinehart, and Winston.
1962. *Minnesota Studies in the Philosophy of Science*, Vol. III. Minneapolis: University of Minnesota Press.
Feigl, H., and M. Scriven, eds.
1956. *Minnesota Studies in the Philosophy of Science*, Vol. I. Minneapolis: University of Minnesota Press.
Feigl, H., M. Scriven, and G. Maxwell, eds.
1956. *Minnesota Studies in the Philosophy of Science*, Vol. II. Minneapolis: University of Minnesota Press.
Feigl, H., and Wilfred Sellars, eds.
1949. *Readings in Philosophical Analysis.* New York: Appleton-Century-Crofts.
Feyerabend, P.
1958. "An Attempt at a Realistic Interpretation of Experience," *Proceedings of the Aristotelian Society*, New Ser., 58, 143–170.
1960. "Professor Bohm's Philosophy of Nature," *British Journal for the Philosophy of Science*, 10, 321–338.
1962. "Explanation, Reduction, and Empiricism," pp. 28–97 in Feigl and Maxwell [1962].
1962a. "Problems of Microphysics," pp. 189–283 in Colodny [1962].
1963. "How to Be a Good Empiricist—A Plea for Tolerance in Matters Epistemological," pp. 3–40 in Baumrin [1963a].
1963a. Review of Hanson [1963]. *Philosophical Review*, 73 (1963), 264–266.
1964. "Realism and Instrumentalism—Comments on the Logic of Factual Support," pp. 280–308, in Bunge [1964].
1965. "On the Meaning of Scientific Terms," *Journal of Philosophy*, 62, 266–274.
1965a. "Problems of Empiricism," pp. 145–260 in Colodny [1965].
1965b. "Reply to Criticism," pp. 223–261 in Cohen and Wartofsky [1965].
1968–69. "On a Recent Critique of Complementarity," *Philosophy of Science*, 35, 309–331; and 36, 82–105.
1969. "Linguistic Arguments and Scientific Method," *Telos*, 3, 43–63.
1970. "Against Method: Outline of an Anarchistic Theory of Knowledge," pp. 17–130 in Radner and Winokur [1970].
1970a. "Consolations for the Specialist," pp. 197–230 in Lakatos and Musgrave [1970].
1970b. "Problems of Empiricism, Part II," in Colodny [1970].
Feyerabend, P. K., and G. Maxwell, eds.
1965. *Mind, Matter, and Method—Essays in Philosophy of Science in Honor of Herbert Feigl.* Minneapolis: University of Minnesota Press.
Feynman, R.
1965. *The Character of Physical Law.* Cambridge, Mass.: MIT Press.
Fine, A.
1967. "Consistency, Derivability and Scientific Change," *Journal of Philosophy*, 64, 231–240.

1975. "How to Compare Theories," *Nôus*, 9, 17–32.
Finkelstein, David
1968. "The Physics of Logic." Trieste: International Center for Theoretical Physics.
Firth, R.
1965. "Sense Data and the Percept Theory," pp. 204–270 in Swartz [1965].
1967. "The Anatomy of Certainty," *Philosophical Review*, 26, 3–27, reprinted on pp. 203–223 of Chisholm and Swartz, eds. [1974].
Flew, A.
1960. *Essays in Conceptual Analysis*. London: Macmillan.
Fodor, J., and J. Katz
1964. *The Structure of Language: Readings in the Philosophy of Language*. Englewood Cliffs, N.J.: Prentice Hall.
Foster, M. H., and M. L. Martin, eds.
1966. *Probability, Confirmation, and Simplicity*. New York: Odyssey.
Frank, P.
1950. "Comments on Realistic *vs.* Phenomenalistic Interpretations," *Philosophy of Science*, 17, 166–169.
1950a. "Metaphysical Interpretations of Science," *British Journal for the Philosophy of Science*, 1, 60–91.
1957. *Philosophy of Science*. Englewood Cliffs, N.J.: Prentice Hall.
1961. *The Validation of Scientific Theories*. New York: Collier Books.
Frege, G.
1879. *Begriffschrift*. Halle a/S: L. Nebert.
1894. *Die Grundlagen der Arithmetik*. Breslau: W. Koebner.
1893–1903. *Grundegesetze der Arithmetik*. Jena: H. Pohle.
Freud, S.
1961. *The Complete Psychological Works of Sigmund Freud*, 24 vols. New York: Liveright.
Freudenthal, H.
1961. *The Concept and the Role of the Model in Mathematics and Natural and Social Sciences*. Dordrecht, Holland: Reidel.
Freund, I.
1968. *The Study of Chemical Composition: An Account of Its Method and Historical Development*. New York: Dover.
Galilei, Galileo
1914. *Dialogues Concerning Two New Sciences*, trans. Henry Crew and Alfonso de Salvio. New York: Macmillan.
1953. *Dialogues Concerning the Two Chief World Systems—Ptolemaic and Copernican*, trans. Stillman Drake. Berkeley: University of California Press.
Gallie, W. B.
1957. "What Makes a Subject Scientific?," *British Journal for the Philosophy of Science*, 8, 118–139.
Gardiner, P., ed.
1959. *Theories of History*. Glencoe, Ill.: Free Press.
Gårding, L., and A. Wightman
1954. "Representations of the Anticommutation and of the Commutation Relations," *Proceedings of the National Academy of Sciences*, 40, 617–626.

Garfield, E.
1964. *The Use of Citation Data in Writing the History of Science*. Philadelphia, Pa.: Institute for Scientific Information.
Geach, P.
1962. *Reference and Generality*. Ithaca, N.Y.: Cornell University Press.
Gettier, E., Jr.
1963. "Is Justified True Belief Knowledge?," *Analysis*, 23, 121–123.
Giedymin, J.
1971. "Consolations for the Irrationalist?," *British Journal for the Philosophy of Science*, 22, 28–48.
1971a. "The Paradox of Meaning Variance," *British Journal for the Philosophy of Science*, 22, 30–48.
Giere, R.
1977. "Testing vs. Information Models of Statistical Information," pp. 19–70 in R. G. Colodny, ed., *Logic, Laws, and Life*. Pittsburgh Press.
Gilbert, W.
1958. *De Magnete*. New York: Dover.
Gleason, H.
1961. *An Introduction to Descriptive Linguistics*, rev. ed. New York: Holt, Rinehart, and Winston.
Gödel, K.
1931. Über formal unentscheidbare Satze der Principia Mathematica und verwandter Systeme," *Monatshefte für Mathematik und Physik*, 1931; translation in Davis [1965].
1934. "On Undecidable Propositions of Formal Mathematical Systems," mimeographed, 1934; reprinted in Davis [1965].
Goldman, A.
1967. "A Causal Theory of Knowledge," *Journal of Philosophy*, 64, 357–372.
Good, I. J.
1950. *Probability and the Weighing of Evidence*. London: Charles Griffin.
Goodman, N.
1947. "The Problem of Counterfactual Conditionals," *Journal of Philosophy*, 44, 113–128; reprinted in Linsky [1952] and as Chap. 1 of Goodman [1955].
1949. "On Likeness of Meaning," *Analysis*, 10, 1–7; reprinted in a revised form in Linsky [1952].
1950. "An Improvement in the Theory of Simplicity," *The Journal of Symbolic Logic*, 15, 228–229.
1951. *The Structure of Appearance*. Cambridge, Mass.: Harvard University Press.
1955. *Fact, Fiction, and Forecast*. Cambridge, Mass.: Harvard University Press.
1959. "Recent Developments in the Theory of Simplicity," *Philosophy and Phenomenological Research*, 19, 429–446.
Greeno, James G.
1966. "Explanation and Information," pp. 89–104 in Salmon [1966].
Grice, H. P.
1961. "The Causal Theory of Perception," *Proceedings of the Aristotelian Society*, Supp. Vol. 35, 121–152.
Grice, H. P., and P. F. Strawson
1956. "In Defense of a Dogma," *Philosophical Review*, 65, 141–158.

Gross, L., ed.

1959. *Symposium on Sociological Theory*. New York: Harper and Row.

Grünbaum, A.

1963. *Philosophical Problems of Space and Time*. New York: Knopf.

1963a. "The Special Theory of Relativity as a Case Study of the Importance of the Philosophy of Science for the History of Science," in Baumrin [1963].

Hagstrom, W. O.

1965. *The Scientific Community*. New York: Basic Books.

Hahn, H., R. Carnap, and O. Neurath.

1929. *Wissenschaftliche Weltauffassung: Der Wiener Kreis*. Vienna: Wolff.

Hankins, T.

1967. "The Reception of Newton's Second Law of Motion in the Eighteenth Century," *Archives Internationales d'Histoire des Sciences*, XXe, 43–65.

1970. *Jean d'Alembert, Science and the Enlightenment*. Oxford: Clarendon Press.

Hanna, J. G.

1968. "An Explication of 'Explication'," *Philosophy of Science*, 35, 28–44.

Hannequin, Arthur

1899. *Essai critique sur l'hypothèse des atomes dans la science contemporaine*. 2nd ed. Paris: Félix Alcan.

Hanson, N. R.

1958. "The Logic of Discovery," *Journal of Philosophy*, 55, 1073–1089, reprinted in Brody and Capaldi [1968].

1958a. *Patterns of Discovery*. Cambridge: Cambridge University Press, 1958.

1959. "On the Symmetry between Explanation and Prediction," *Philosophical Review*, 68, 349–358.

1960. "More on The Logic of Discovery'," *Journal of Philosophy*, 57, 182–188.

1961. "Is There a Logic of Scientific Discovery?," pp. 20–35 in Feigl and Maxwell [1961].

1963. *The Concept of the Positron: A Philosophical Analysis*. Cambridge: Cambridge University Press.

1967. "Observation and Interpretation," pp. 89–99 in Morgenbesser, ed. [1967].

1969. *Perception and Discovery: An Introduction to Scientific Inquiry*. San Francisco: Freeman, Cooper.

1969a. "Logical Positivism and the Interpretation of Scientific Theories," pp. 57–84 in Achinstein and Barker [1969].

1970. "A Picture Theory of Theory Meaning," pp. 131–141 in Radner and Winokur [1970].

1971. *Observation and Explanation: A Guide to Philosophy of Science*. New York: Harper and Row.

1971a. *What I Do Not Believe, and Other Essays*. S. Toulmin and H. Wolff, eds. Dordrecht, Holland: Reidel.

1973. *Constellations and Conjectures*. W. C. Humphreys, ed. Dordrecht, Holland: Reidel.

Harman, G.

1968. "Knowledge, Inference, and Explanation," *American Philosophical Quarterly*, 5, 164–173.

1970. "Induction: A Discussion of the Relevance of Theory of Knowledge to the Theory of Induction," pp. 83–100 in M. Swain, ed. [1970].

1970a. "Knowledge, Reasons, and Causes," *Journal of Philosophy*, 67, 841–855.

Harrah, David

1959. "Gallie and the Scientific Tradition," *British Journal for the Philosophy of Science*, 10, 234–239.

1963. *Communication: A Logical Model*. Cambridge, Mass.: MIT Press.

Harré, R.

1960. *An Introduction to the Logic of the Sciences*. New York: St. Martins.

1964. *Matter and Method*. New York: St. Martins.

1970. *The Principles of Scientific Thinking*. Chicago, Ill.: University of Chicago Press.

1972. *The Philosophies of Science*. New York: Oxford University Press.

Hawkins, D.

1964. *The Language of Nature*. San Francisco: Freeman.

Hebb, D. O.

1949. *Organization of Behavior*. New York: John Wiley.

Heelan, P.

1970. "Quantum and Classical Logics: Their Respective Roles," *Synthese*, 21, 2–33.

Heilbron, J., and T. S. Kuhn

1969. "The Genesis of the Bohr Atom," pp. 211–290 in McCormmach [1969].

Heisenberg, W.

1930. *The Physical Principles of the Quantum Theory*. New York: Dover.

1958. *Physics and Philosophy: The Revolution in Philosophy*. New York: Harper.

1967. "Quantum Theory and Its Interpretation," pp. 94–108 in Rozenthal [1967].

Heitler, W.

1949. "The Departure from Classical Thought in Modern Physics," pp. 179–198 in Schilpp [1949].

Helmer, O., and P. Oppenheim

1945. "A Syntactical Definition of Probability and of Degree of Confirmation," *Journal of Symbolic Logic*, 10, 25–60.

Helmholtz, H. L. F. von

1863. *Tonempfindungen*. Translated as *On the Sensations of Tone*. London: Longmans, Green, 1912.

1921. *Schriften zur Erkenntnistheorie*, P. Hertz and M. Schlick, eds. Berlin.

1927. *Handbuch der physiologischen Optik*, translated as *A Treatise on Physiological Optics*. New York: The Optical Society of America.

Hempel, C.

1942. "The Function of General Laws in History," *Journal of Philosophy*, 39, 35–48.

1945. "Geometry and Empirical Science," *American Mathematical Monthly*, 52, 7–17, reprinted in Feigl and Sellars [1949] and in Wiener [1953].

1945a. "Studies in the Logic of Confirmation," *Mind*, 54, 1–26, 97–121, reprinted in Hempel [1965].

1946. "A Note on the Paradoxes of Confirmation," *Mind*, 55, 79–82.

1950. "Problems and Changes in the Empiricist Criterion of Meaning," *Revue Internationale de Philosophie*, 11, 41–63, reprinted in Linsky [1952].
1950a. "A Note on Semantic Realism," *Philosophy of Science*, 17, 169–173.
1951. "The Concept of Cognitive Significance: A Reconsideration," *Proceedings of the American Academy of Arts and Sciences*, 80, 61–77.
1951a. "General Systems Theory and the Unity of Science," *Human Biology*, 23, 313–322.
1952. *Fundamentals of Concept Formation in Empirical Science*. Chicago, Ill.: University of Chicago Press.
1954. "A Logical Appraisal of Operationalism," *Scientific Monthly*, 79, 215–220; reprinted on pp. 123–133 of Hempel [1965].
1958. "Theoretician's Dilemma," pp. 37–98 in Feigl, Scriven, and Maxwell [1958], reprinted in Hempel [1965] and in Shapere [1965].
1958a. "Empirical Statements and Falsifiability," *Philosophy*, 33, 312–318.
1962. "Deductive-Nomological vs. Statistical Explanation," pp. 98–169 in Feigl and Maxwell [1962].
1963. "Implications of Carnap's Work for the Philosophy of Science," in Schilpp [1963].
1965. *Aspects of Scientific Explanation and Other Essays in the Philosophy of Science*. New York: Free Press.
1965a. "Aspects of Scientific Explanation," pp. 331–496 in Hempel [1965].
1965b. "Empiricist Criteria of Cognitive Significance: Problems and Changes," pp. 101–133 in Hempel [1965].
1966. *Philosophy of Natural Science*. Englewood Cliffs, N.J.: Prentice Hall.
1969. "On the Structure of Scientific Theories," pp. 11–38 in the *Isenberg Memorial Lecture Series, 1965–1966*. East Lansing: Michigan State University Press.
1970. "On the 'Standard Conception' of Scientific Theories," pp. 142–163 in Radner and Winokur [1970].

Hempel, C. G., and P. Oppenheim
1945. "A Definition of 'Degree of Confirmation'," *Philosophy of Science*, 12, 98–115.
1948. "Studies in the Logic of Explanation," *Philosophy of Science*, 15, 135–175; reprinted with a postscript in Hempel [1965], pp. 245–295.

Henkin, L., P. Suppes, and A. Tarski, eds.
1959. *The Axiomatic Method with Special Reference to Geometry and Physics*. Amsterdam: North Holland.

Henle, P., ed.
1958. *Language, Thought, and Culture*. Ann Arbor: University of Michigan Press.

Herbst, P.
1960. "The Nature of Facts," pp. 134–156 in Flew [1960].

Hermes, H.
1938. "Eine Axiomatisierung der allgemeinen Mechanik," *Forschungen zur Logik und Grundlegung der exakten Wissenschaften*. Neue Folge, Heft 3. Leipzig.

Hertz, Heinrich
1894. *Die Prinzipien der Mechanik*. Leipzig: J. A. Barth.
1894a. *Principles of Mechanics Presented in a New Form*. New York: Macmillan, reissued by Dover, 1956.

Hesse, M.
1952. "Operational Definition and Analogy in Physical Theories," *British Journal for the Philosophy of Science*, 2, 281–294.
1953. "Models in Physics," *British Journal for the Philosophy of Science*, 4, 198–214.
1958. "Theories, Dictionaries, and Observation," *British Journal for the Philosophy of Science*, 9, 12–28.
1962. *Forces and Fields*. New York: Philosophical Library.
1963. "A New Look at Scientific Explanation," *Review of Metaphysics*, 17, 98–108.
1965. *Forces and Fields*. Totowa, N.J.: Littlefield, Adams.
1966. *Models and Analogies in Science*. Notre Dame, Ind.: University of Notre Dame Press.
1969. "Fine's Criteria of Meaning Change," *Journal of Philosophy*, 65, 46–52.
1970. "Hermeticism and Historiography: An Apology for Internal History of Science," pp. 134–160 in Stuewer [1970].
1974. *The Structure of Scientific Inference*. Berkeley: University of California Press.

Heyerdahl, T.
1950. *The Kon Tiki Expedition*. London: Longmans, Green.

Hilpinen, R.
1968. "Rules of Acceptance and Inductive Logic," *Acta Philosophica Fennica*, Fasc. XXL.
1970. "Knowing that One Knows and the Classical Definition of Knowledge," *Synthese*, 21, 109–132.

Hintikka, J.
1962. *Knowledge and Belief*. Ithaca, N.Y.: Cornell University Press.
1965. "On a Combined System of Inductive Logic," pp. 21–30 in Hintikka [1965a].
1965a. *Studia Logico-Mathematica et Philosophica in Honorem Rolf Nevanlinna*. Helsinki: *Acta Philosophica Fennica*, Fasc. XVIII.
1968. "Induction by Enumeration and Induction by Elimination," pp. 191–216 in Lakatos, ed. [1968].
1975. "Towards a Theory of Inductive Generalization," pp. 274–288 in Bar-Hillel [1975].

Hintikka, J., and I. Niiniluoto
1976. "An Axiomatic Foundation for the Logic of Inductive Generalization," pp. 57–81 in Przełecki, Szaniawski, and Wójcicki [1976].

Holland, J. H.
1975. *Adaptation in Natural and Artificial Systems*. Ann Arbor: University of Michigan Press.
1976. "New Perspectives in Nonlinearity or What to Do When the Whole Is More Than the Sum of Its Parts," pp. 240–255 in Suppe and Asquith [1976].

Holton, Gerald
1969. "Einstein, Michelson, and the 'Crucial Experiment'," *Isis*, 60, 133–197.
1973. *Thematic Origins of Scientific Thought: Kepler to Einstein*. Cambridge, Mass.: Harvard University Press.

Hook, S., ed.
1950. *John Dewey: Philosopher of Science and of Freedom*. New York: Dial.

Hooker, C.
1972a. "The Impact of Quantum Theory on the Conceptual Bases for the Classification of Knowledge," pp. 284–318 in Wojciechowski [1974].
1972b. "The Nature of Quantum Mechanical Reality: Einstein *vs.* Bohr," pp. 67–302 in Colodny [1972].
1972c. "Physics and Metaphysics: A Prolegomena for the Riddles of Quantum Theory," in Hooker [1972d].
1972d. *Contemporary Research in the Foundations and Philosophy of Quantum Theory*. Dordrecht, Holland: Reidel.
1975. "On Global Theories." *Philosophy of Science*, 42, 152–179.

Hoyle, F.
1961. *Frontiers of Astronomy*. London: Mercury Books.

Hull, C. L.
1943. "The Problem of Intervening Variables in Molar Behavioral Theory," *Psychological Review*, 50, 273–291.

Hull, D.
1964. "The Logic of Phylogenetic Taxonomy," Ph.D. dissertation, Indiana University.
1975. "Review of Carl G. Hempel's *Philosophy of Natural Science*, Thomas S. Kuhn's *The Structure of Scientific Revolutions* (2nd ed.), and Dudley Shapere's *Galileo: A Philosophical Study*," *Systematic Zoology*, 24, 395–401.
Forthcoming. "Altruism in Science: A Sociobiological Explanation."

Hume D.
1902. *An Enquiry Concerning Human Understanding*. 2nd ed. L. A. Selby-Biggie, ed. Oxford: Oxford University Press.

Humphreys, Willard C.
1968. *Anomalies and Scientific Theories*. San Francisco: Freeman, Cooper.

Hutten, E. H.
1953–54. "Role of Models in Physics," *British Journal for the Philosophy of Science*, 4, 285–301.
1956. *The Language of Modern Physics: An Introduction to the Philosophy of Science*. London and New York: Macmillan.

Jammer, Max
1957. *Concepts of Force*. Cambridge, Mass.: Harvard University Press.
1961. *Concepts of Mass*. Cambridge, Mass.: Harvard University Press.
1966. *The Conceptual Development of Quantum Mechanics*. New York: McGraw-Hill.

Jauch, J. M.
1968. *Foundations of Quantum Mechanics*. Reading, Mass.: Addison-Wesley.

Jeans, J. H.
1961. *Astronomy and Cosmogony*. New York: Dover.

Jeffrey, R. C.
1956. "Valuation and Acceptance of Scientific Hypotheses," *Philosophy of Science*, 23, 237–246.
1966. "Statistical Explanation vs. Statistical Inference," pp. 19–28 of Salmon [1966].

Jeffreys, H.
1957. *Scientific Inference*. 2nd ed. Cambridge: Cambridge University Press.
Jones, W. T.
1952. *History of Modern Philosophy*. New York: Harcourt, Brace, and World.
Jørgensen, J.
1953. "The Development of Logical Empiricism," Vol. II, No. 9. *The International Encyclopedia of Unified Science*. Chicago, Ill.: University of Chicago Press.
Kahl, R., ed.
1963. *Studies in Explanation. A Reader in the Philosophy of Science*. Englewood Cliffs, N.J.: Prentice Hall.
Kaplan, A.
1964. *The Conduct of Inquiry*. San Francisco: Chandler.
Kemeny, John G.
1951. Review of Carnap [1950]. *The Journal of Symbolic Logic*, 16, 205–207.
1959. *A Philosopher Looks at Science*. Princeton, N.J.: Van Nostrand.
Kemeny, John G., and P. Oppenheim.
1952. "Degree of Factual Support," *Philosophy of Science*, 19, 307–324.
1956. "On Reduction," *Philosophical Studies*, 7, 6–19.
Kessler, M. M.
1965. "Comparison of the Results of Bibliographic Coupling and Analytic Subject Indexing," *American Documentation*, 16, 223–233.
Keynes, J. M.
1921. *A Treatise on Probability*. London: Macmillan.
Kim, J.
1962. "Explanation, Prediction, and Retrodiction: Some Logical and Pragmatic Considerations," Ph.D. thesis, Princeton University.
Klein, M.
1963. "Einstein's First Paper on Quanta," pp. 57–86 in *The Natural Philosopher*, No. 2. New York: Blaisdell.
1967. "Thermodynamics in Einstein's Thought," *Science*, 157, 509–516.
Kneale, W.
1949. *Probability and Induction*. Oxford: Clarendon Press.
Knight, D. M.
1967. *Atoms and Elements: A Study of Theories of Matter in England in the Nineteenth Century*. London: Hutchinson.
1970. *Classical Scientific Papers: Chemistry, Second Series*. New York: American Elsevier.
Kockelmans, Joseph J., ed.
1968. *Philosophy of Science: The Historical Background*. New York: Free Press.
Koertge, N.
1975. "An Exploration of Salmon's S-R Model of Explanation," *Philosophy of Science*, 42, 270–274.
Kolomogorov, A. N.
1950. *Foundations of the Theory of Probability*. New York: Chelsea.
Kordig, C. R.
1970. "Feyerabend and Radical Meaning Variance," *Nous*, 9, 399–404.

Körner, S.
1955. *Kant*. Baltimore, Md.: Penguin Books.
1960. *Conceptual Thinking*. New York: Dover Publications.
1966. *Experience and Theory*. New York: Humanities Press.
———, ed.
1957. *Observation and Interpretation*, Proceedings of the Ninth Symposium of the Colston Research Society. New York: Academic Press, Inc., and Dover; London: Butterworth.

Koyré, A.
1937. "Galilée et l'experience de Pise: à propos d'une légende," *Annales de l'Université de Paris*, 441–453, reprinted in Koyré [1966].
1939. *Etudes galiléennes*. Paris: Herman, reprinted, 1966.
1939a. "La Loi de la Chute des Corps," *Etudes galiléennes, histoire de la pensée* (Paris: Herman).
1943. "Traduttore-traditore, a propos de Copernic et de Galilée," *Isis*, 34, 209–210.
1943a. "Galileo and Plato," *Journal of the History of Ideas*, 4, 400–428, reprinted in Koyré [1968].
1961. *La révolution astronomique*. Paris: Herman.
1965. *Newtonian Studies*. Cambridge, Mass.: Harvard University Press; London: Chapman and Hall.
1966. *Etudes d'histoire de la pensée scientifique*. Paris: Presses Universitaires de Paris.
1968. *Metaphysics and Measurement: Essays in Scientific Revolution*. London: Chapman and Hall; Cambridge, Mass.: Harvard University Press.

Kraft, V.
1953. *The Vienna Circle*, trans. by Arthur Pap. New York: Philosophical Library.

Kramers, H. A.
1919. *Intensity of Spectral Lines*. Copenhagen: Andr, Fred, Høst and Son, reprinted on pp. 3–108 of his *Collected Scientific Papers*, Amsterdam: North Holland.

Kuhn, Thomas S.
1957. *The Copernican Revolution*. Cambridge, Mass.: Harvard University Press; reissued by Random House in 1959.
1962. *The Structure of Scientific Revolutions*. Chicago, Ill.: University of Chicago Press.
1970. "Logic of Discovery or Psychology of Research," in Lakatos and Musgrave [1970].
1970a. "Reflections on My Critics," pp. 231–278 in Lakatos and Musgrave [1970].
1970b. *The Structure of Scientific Revolutions*, enlarged ed. Chicago, Ill.: University of Chicago Press.

Kyburg, H. E., Jr.
1968. *Philosophy of Science: A Formal Approach*. New York: Macmillan.
1974. "Propensities and Probabilities," *British Journal for the Philosophy of Science*, 24, 358–375.

Kyburg, H. E., and H. Smokler, eds.
1964. *Studies in Subjective Probability*. New York: John Wiley.

Lakatos, I.

1963–64. "Proofs and Refutations," *British Journal for the Philosophy of Science*, 14, 1–25, 120–139, 221–243, 296–342.

1968. "Criticism and the Methodology of Scientific Research Programmes," *Proceedings of the Aristotelian Society*, 69, 149–186.

1968a. "Changes in the Problem of Inductive Logic," pp. 315–417 in Lakatos, ed. [1968].

1970. "Falsification and the Methodology of Scientific Research Programmes," pp. 91–196 in Lakatos and Musgrave [1970].

1971. "History of Science and Its Rational Reconstruction," pp. 91–136, in Buck and Cohen [1971].

———, ed.

1968. *The Problem of Inductive Logic*. Amsterdam: North Holland.

Lakatos, I., and A. Musgrave, eds.

1970. *Criticism and the Growth of Knowledge*. Cambridge: Cambridge University Press.

Lambert, K., and G. Brittan, Jr.

1970. *An Introduction to the Philosophy of Science*. Englewood Cliffs, N.J.: Prentice Hall.

Lange, Friedrich Albert

1866. *Die Geschichte des Materialismus und Kritik seiner Bedeutung in der Gegenwart*. Leipzig: J. Baedeker, trans. as *The History of Materialism and Criticism of Its Present Importance*. London: Routledge and Kegan Paul, 1957.

Langford, C. H.

1941. Review in *The Journal of Symbolic Logic*, 6, 67–68.

1942. "Moore's Notion of Analysis," pp. 319–342 in Schilpp [1942].

Laplace, P.

1814. *Théorie analytique des probabilities*, 2nd ed. Paris, reprinted, with changes made in later editions, as Vol. 7 of Laplace, *Oeuvres complètes* (Paris: Académie des Sciences, 1886). The introduction to this work (first inserted in the 2nd ed.) has been translated into English as Laplace [1951].

1882. *Traité de méchanique céleste*, Vol. 5 of *Oeuvres complètes* (Paris: Académie des Sciences, 1882).

1951. *A Philosophical Essay on Probabilities*, trans. from the 6th French ed. by E. W. Truscott and F. L. Emory. New York: Dover.

Lavoisier, A. L.

1965. *Elements of Chemistry*. New York: Dover.

Lehman, H.

1972. "Statistical Explanation," *Philosophy of Science*, 39, 500–506.

Lehrer, K.

1965. "Knowledge, Truth, and Evidence," *Analysis*, 25, 168–175.

Lehrer, K., and T. Paxton

1969. "Knowledge: Undefeated Justified True Belief," *Journal of Philosophy*, 66, 225–237.

Leinfellner, W., and E. Köhler, eds.

1974. *Developments in the Methodology of Social Science*. Dordrecht, Holland: Reidel.

Leonard, Henry S.
1937. Review of Carnap [1936–1937]. *Journal of Symbolic Logic*, 2, 49–50.

Leplin, J.
1969. "Meaning Change and the Comparability of Theories," *British Journal for the Philosophy of Science*, 20, 69–75.

Levi, I.
1967. *Gambling with Truth*. New York: Knopf.

Levison, A.
1974. *Knowledge and Society*. Indianapolis, Ind.: Pegasus.

Lewis, C. I.
1929. *Mind and World Order*. New York: Dover.
1946. *An Analysis of Knowledge and Valuation*. La Salle, Ill.: Open Court.

Lewis, C. I., and C. H. Langford
1932. *Symbolic Logic*. New York: Dover.

Lewis, D.
1973. *Counterfactuals*. Cambridge, Mass.: Harvard University Press.

Lewis, H. D., ed.
1956. *Contemporary British Philosophy: Personal Statements*. New York: Macmillan.

Lindzey, Gardner
1953. "Hypothetical Constructs, Conventional Constructs, and the Use of Physiological Data in Psychological Theory," *Psychiatry*, 16, 27–33.

Linsky, L., ed.
1952. *Semantics and the Philosophy of Language*. Urbana: University of Illinois Press.

Losee, J.
1972. *A Historical Introduction to the Philosophy of Science*. New York: Oxford University Press.

Lyndon, R.
1966. *Notes on Logic*. Princeton, N.J.: Van Nostrand.

MacCorquodale, K., and P. Meehl
1948. "On a Distinction between Hypothetical Constructs and Intervening Variables," *Psychological Review*, 55, 95–107, reprinted in Feigl and Brodbeck [1953] and, with omissions, in Marx [1951].

Macdonald, G.
1957. *The Epidemiology and Control of Malaria*. London: Oxford University Press.

Mach, Ernst
1868. "Über die Definition der Masse," *Carls Repertorium* (Munich), 4, 355–359.
1886. *Beiträge zur Analyse der Empfindungen*. Jena. Trans. as *The Analysis of Sensations*. New York: Dover, 1959.
1919. *The Science of Mechanics*, trans. Thomas J. McCormack. 4th ed. Chicago, Ill.: Open Court.
1962. *History and Root of the Principle of Conservation of Energy*, trans. P. E. Jordain. Chicago, Ill.: Open Court.

Madden, E. H., ed.
1960. *The Structure of Scientific Thought*. Boston, Mass.: Houghton Mifflin.

Maier, C. L.
1964. "The Role of Spectroscopy in the Acceptance of an Internally Structured Atom, 1860–1920," Ph.D. thesis, University of Wisconsin.

Malcolm, N.
1963. *Knowledge and Certainty*. Englewood Cliffs, N.J.: Prentice Hall.

Margenau, H.
1935. "Methodology of Modern Physics," *Philosophy of Science*, 2, 48–72 and 164–187.
1950. *The Nature of Physical Reality*. New York: McGraw-Hill.

Martin, M.
1971. "Referential Variance and Scientific Objectivity," *British Journal for the Philosophy of Science*, 22, 17–26.
1972. "Ontological Variance and Scientific Objectivity," *British Journal for the Philosophy of Science*, 23, 252–256.

Martin, R.
1975. "Empirically Conclusive Reasons and Scepticism," *Philosophical Studies*, 28, 215–217.

Martin, R. M.
1952. "On 'Analytic'," *Philosophical Studies*, 3, 42–47.

Marx, Melvin H., ed.
1951. *Psychological Theory*. New York: Macmillan.

Masterman, Margaret
1970. "The Nature of a Paradigm," pp. 59–90 in Lakatos and Musgrave [1970].

Mates, Benson
1951. "Analytic Sentences," *Philosophical Review*, 60, 525–534.
1965. *Elementary Logic*. New York: Oxford University Press.

Maull, Nancy. See [Roth], Nancy Maull

Maxwell, G.
1962. "The Ontological Status of Theoretical Entities," pp. 3–27 in Feigl and Maxwell [1962].
1962a. "The Necessary and the Contingent," pp. 398–404 in Feigl and Maxwell [1962].

Maxwell, James Clerk
1892. *A Treatise on Electricity and Magnetism*. 3rd ed. Oxford.

Maxwell, N.
1974. "The Rationality of Scientific Discovery," *Philosophy of Science*, 41, 123–153, 247–295.

McCormmach, R., ed.
1969. *Historical Studies in the Physical Sciences*. Vol. I. Philadelphia: University of Pennsylvania Press.

McGucken, W.
1969. *Nineteenth-Century Spectroscopy: Development of the Understanding of Spectra 1802–1897*. Baltimore, Md.: Johns Hopkins Press.

McKinsey, J. C. C., A. Sugar, and P. Suppes
1953. "Axiomatic Foundations of Classical Particle Mechanics," *Journal of Rational Mechanics and Analysis*, 2, 253–272.

McKinsey, J. C. C., and P. Suppes
1953. "Transformations of Systems of Classical Particle Mechanics," *Journal of Rational Mechanics and Analysis*, 2, 273–289.

McMullin, E.
1967. *Galileo, Man of Science*. New York: Basic Books.

1970. "The History and Philosophy of Science: A Taxonomy," pp. 12–67 in Stuewer [1970a].
Meehl, Paul
1970. "Nuisance Variables and the Ex-Post-Facto Design," pp. 373–402 in Radner and Winokur [1970].
Mehlberg, H.
1958. *The Reach of Science*. Toronto: University of Toronto Press.
Meiland, J., and M. Krausz, eds.
1977. *Relativism*. Princeton, N.J.: Princeton University Press.
Meyerson, E.
1930. *Identity and Reality*, trans. K. Loewenberg. London: Allen and Unwin, reprinted by Dover Publications, New York, 1962.
Michelson, A. A.
1881. "The Relative Motion of the Earth and the Luminiferous Ether," *American Journal of Science*, 22, 120–129.
Michelson, A. A., and E. W. Morley
1887. "On the Relative Motion of the Earth and the Luminiferous Aether," *Philosophical Magazine*, 24, 449–463.
Mill, J. S.
1936. *A System of Logic*. New York: Longmans, Green.
Mises, Richard von
1951. *Positivism. A Study in Human Understanding*. Cambridge, Mass.: Harvard University Press.
Moody, Ernest A.
1951. "Laws of Motion in Mediaeval Physics," *Scientific Monthly*, 72, 18–23.
1951a. "Galileo and Avempace," *Journal of the History of Ideas*, 12, 163–193, 375–422.
Morgenbesser, S.
1958. Review of Bergman [1957]. *Journal of Philosophy*, 55, 169–176.
———, ed.
1967. *Philosophy of Science Today*. New York: Basic Books.
Morgenbesser, S., P. Suppes, and M. White, eds.
1969. *Essays in Honor of Ernest Nagel: Philosophy, Science, and Method*. New York: St. Martin's.
Mulchkhuyse, J.
1960. *Molecules and Models: Investigations on the Axiomatization of Structure Theory in Chemistry*. Thesis. Amsterdam.
Mullins, N. C.
1966. "Social Networks among Biological Scientists," Ph.D. thesis, Harvard University.
1968. "The Microstructure of an Invisible College: The Phage Group," manuscript read at annual meeting of the American Sociological Association, Boston.
1972. "The Development of a Scientific Society," *Minerva*, 10, 51–82.
Nagel, E.
1949. The Meaning of Reduction in the Natural Sciences," in Stauffer [1949], reprinted in Wiener [1953].
1951. "Mechanistic Explanation and Organismic Biology," *Philosophy and Phenomenological Research*, 11, 327–338.
1954. Review of Toulmin [1953], *Mind*, 63, 403–412.

1956. *Logic without Metaphysics*. Glencoe, Ill.: Free Press.
1957. "A Budget of Problems in the Philosophy of Science," *The Philosophical Review*, 66, 205–226. Review of Braithwaite [1953].
1961. *The Structure of Science*. New York: Harcourt, Brace.

Nagel, E., P. Suppes, and A. Tarski, eds.
1962. *Logic, Methodology, and Philosophy of Science: Proceedings of the 1960 International Congress*. Stanford, Calif.: Stanford University Press.
1966. *Logic, Methodology, and the Philosophy of Science—Proceedings of the 1964 International Congress for Logic, Methodology, and the Philosophy of Science*. Amsterdam: North Holland.

Nash, Leonard K.
1963. *The Nature of the Natural Sciences*. Boston, Mass.: Little, Brown.

Neugebauer, O.
1969. *The Exact Sciences in Antiquity*. 2nd ed. New York: Dover Publications.

Neurath, O., R. Carnap, and C. Morris
1938–69. *International Encyclopedia of Unified Science*. 2 vols., issued in 10 parts each volume. Chicago, Ill.: University of Chicago Press.

Newton, Sir Isaac
1934. *Mathematical Principles of Natural Philosophy and His System of the World*, trans. Andrew Motte in 1729, rev. trans. by Florian Cajori. Berkeley: University of California Press. This contains a translation of Newton's *Philosophiae Naturalis Principia Mathematica*.
1968. *The Mathematical Principles of Natural Philosophy*, trans. by Andrew Motte, 1729, intro. by I. B. Cohen, 2 vols. London: Dawsons of Pall Mall.
1969. *A Treatise of the System of the World*, trans. by I. B. Cohen. London: Dawsons of Pall Mall.

Neyman, J.
1951. *Proceedings of the Second Berkeley Symposium on Mathematical Statistics and Probability*. Berkeley: University of California Press.

Nickles, T.
1969. "The Structure and Interrelationships of Physical Theories," Ph.D. thesis, Princeton University.
1973a. "Reduction and Conceptual Change," typescript.
1973b. "Two Concepts of Intertheoretic Reduction," *Journal of Philosophy*, 70, 181–201.

Nietzsche, F.
1967. *The Will to Power*. W. Kaufmann, trans. and ed. New York: Random House.

Niiniluoto, I., and R. Tuomela
1973. *Theoretical Concepts and Hypothetico-Inductive Inference*. Dordrecht, Holland: Reidel.

Northrop, F. S. C.
1947. *The Logic of the Sciences and the Humanities*. New York: Macmillan.

O'Conner, D. J.
1950. "Some Consequences of Professor A. J. Ayer's Verification Principle," *Analysis*, 10.

Pap, A.
1949. *Elements of Analytic Philosophy*. New York: Macmillan.

1953. "Reduction Sentences and Open Concepts," *Methodos*, 5, 3–28.
1955. *Analytische Erkenntnistheorie*. Wien: J. Springer.
1962. *An Introduction to the Philosophy of Science*. New York: Free Press.

Pappas, G. S., and M. Swain
1973. "Some Conclusive Reasons against Conclusive Reasons," *Australasian Journal of Philosophy*, 51, 72–76.

Passmore, John
1957. *A Hundred Years of Philosophy*. London: Duckworth.

Pearce, G., and P. Maynard, eds.
1973. *Conceptual Change*. Dordrecht, Holland: Reidel.

Pearson, Karl.
1892. *Grammar of Science*. New York: C. Scribners and Sons, reissued in 1937 by J. M. Dent, London.

Peirce, Charles
1877. "The Fixation of Belief," *Popular Science Monthly*, 12, 1–15; reprinted in Vol. V of Peirce [1931–58].
1931–58. *Collected Works*. C. Hartshorne, P. Weiss, and A. Burks, eds. 8 vols. Cambridge, Mass.: Harvard University Press.

Petersen, A.
1963. "The Philosophy of Niels Bohr," *Bulletin of the Atomic Scientists*, 19, Sept. issue, 8–14.
1968. *Quantum Physics and the Philosophical Tradition*. Cambridge, Mass.: MIT Press.

Pike, Kenneth
1966. "A Guide to Publications Related to Tagmemic Theory," pp. 365–394 in Sebeok [1966].

Pitcher, G., ed.
1964. *Truth*. Englewood Cliffs, N.J.: Prentice Hall.

Poincaré, Henri
1902. *La Science et l'hypothèse*. Paris: E. Flammarion, translated as *Science and Hypothesis*. New York: The Science Press, 1905. It was reissued by Dover in 1952.
1952. *Science and Method*. New York: Dover.

Polanyi, Michael
1958. *Personal Knowledge*. Chicago, Ill.: University of Chicago Press.

Popper, Karl
1935. *Logik der Forschung*. Wien: J. Springer.
1949. "A Note on Natural Laws and So-Called 'Contrary-to-Fact Conditionals'," *Mind*, 58, 62–66.
1950. *The Open Society and Its Enemies*. Princeton, N.J.: Princeton University Press.
1956. "Three Views Concerning Human Knowledge," in Lewis [1956], reprinted as Ch. 3 of Popper [1965].
1957. "The Aim of Science," *Ratio*, 1, 24–35.
1959. *The Logic of Scientific Discovery*. London: Hutchinson.
1965. *Conjectures and Refutations: The Growth of Scientific Knowledge*. 2nd ed. New York: Basic Books.
1970. "Normal Science and Its Dangers," pp. 51–58 in Lakatos and Musgrave [1970].

Preston, David
1971. "The German Jews in Science," Ph.D. thesis, University of Illinois.
Price, D. J.
1965. "Networks of Scientific Papers," *Science*, 149, 510–515.
Price, D. J., and D. de B. Beaver
1966. "Collaboration in an Invisible College," *American Psychologist*, 21, 1011–18.
Priestley, J.
1767. *On the History and Present State of Electricity*. London: Printed for J. Dodsley.
1965. *Priestley's Writings on Philosophy, Science, and Politics*. John A. Passmore, ed. New York: Collier.
Przełęcki, M., K. Szaniawski, and R. Wójcicki, eds.
1976. *Formal Methods of the Methodology of Science*. Wrocław: Ossolineum.
Putnam, H.
1962. "What Theories Are Not," pp. 240–251 in Nagel, Suppes, and Tarski [1962].
1962a. "The Analytic and the Synthetic," pp. 350–397 in Feigl and Maxwell [1962].
1963. "An Examination of Grünbaum's Philosophy of Geometry," pp. 205–255, in Baumrin [1963].
1965. "How Not to Talk about Meaning," pp. 205–222 in Cohen and Wartofsky [1965].
1969. "Is Logic Empirical?," pp. 216–241 in Cohen and Wartofsky [1969a].
1971. "On the 'Corroboration' of Theories," in Schilpp [1971].
1973. "Explanation and Reference," in Pearce and Maynard, eds. [1973].
1973a. "Meaning and Reference," *Journal of Philosophy*, 70, 699–711.
Forthcoming. "The Meaning of Meaning" in Vol. VII or VIII of *Minnesota Studies in the Philosophy of Science*, K. Gunderson, ed.
Quine, W. V. O.
1951. "Two Dogmas of Empiricism," *Philosophical Review*, 60, 20–43, reprinted in Quine [1953].
1953. *From a Logical Point of View*. Cambridge, Mass.: Harvard University Press. 2nd ed., 1962.
1959. *Methods of Logic*. Rev. ed. New York: Holt, Rinehart, and Winston.
1960. *Word and Object*. New York: Technology Press of MIT and John Wiley.
1963. "Carnap and Logical Truth," pp. 385–406, in Schilpp [1963].
1966. *The Ways of Paradox and Other Essays*. New York: Random House.
Quinton, A.
1966. "The Foundations of Knowledge," pp. 55–86, in Williams and Montefiore [1966].
Radner, M., and S. Winokur
1970. *Minnesota Studies in the Philosophy of Science*. Vol. IV. Minneapolis: University of Minnesota Press.
Ramsey, Frank Plumpton
1931. *The Foundations of Mathematics and Other Logical Essays*. London: Kegan Paul; New York: Harcourt Brace.

Rapoport, A.
1958. "Various Meanings of 'Theory'," *American Political Science Review*, 52, 927–988.

Ravetz, J. R.
1961. "Vibrating Strings and Arbitrary Functions," pp. 71–88 in *Personal Knowledge: Essays Presented to Michael Polanyi on His Seventieth Birthday*. New York: Free Press.

Reichenbach, Hans
1924. *Axiomatik der relativistischen Raum-Zeit-Lehre*. Braunschweig: F. Vieweg.
1925. "Uber die Physikalischen Konsequenzen der Relativistischen Axiomatik," *Zeitschrift für Physik*, 34, 32–48.
1928. *Philosophie der Raum-Zeit-Lehre*. Berlin: W. de Gruyter.
1938. *Experience and Prediction*. Chicago, Ill.: University of Chicago Press.
1944. *Philosophic Foundations of Quantum Mechanics*. Berkeley and Los Angeles: University of California Press.
1947. *Elements of Symbolic Logic*. New York: Macmillan.
1949. *The Theory of Probability*. Berkeley: University of California Press.
1951. *The Rise of Scientific Philosophy*. Berkeley and Los Angeles: University of California Press.
1954. *Nomological Statements and Admissible Operations*. Amsterdam: North Holland.
1957. *Philosophy of Space and Time*. New York: Dover. Translation of Reichenbach [1928].
1962. *Rise of Scientific Philosophy*. Berkeley: University of California Press.

Rescher, N.
1958. "On Prediction and Explanation," *British Journal for the Philosophy of Science*, 8, 281–290.
1958a. "A Theory of Evidence," *Philosophy of Science*, 25, 83–94.
1970. *Scientific Explanation*. New York: Free Press.

———, ed.
1968. *Studies in Logical Theory*. American Philosophical Quarterly Monograph Series. Oxford: Basil Blackwell.

Robinson, Abraham
1963. *Introduction to Model Theory and the Metamathematics of Algebra*. Amsterdam: North Holland.
1966. *Non-Standard Analysis*. Amsterdam: North Holland.

Rorty, R., ed.
1967. *The Linguistic Turn: Recent Essays in Philosophical Method*. Chicago, Ill.: University of Chicago Press.

Rosen, Edward
1966. "Kepler's Harmonics and His Concept of Inertia," *American Journal of Physics*, 34, 610–613.
1967. Trans. and commentator. *Kepler's Sommium*. Madison: University of Wisconsin Press.

Rosenbleuth, W., and N. Wiener
1945. "The Role of Models in Science," *Philosophy of Science*, 12, 318–321.

Rosenfeld, L., and E. Rüdinger
1967. "The Decisive Years, 1911–1918," pp. 38–73 in Rozenthal [1967].

[Roth], Nancy Maull

1974. "Progress in Modern Biology: An Alternative to Reduction." Ph.D. dissertation, University of Chicago.

1976. "Reconstructed Science as Philosophical Evidence," pp. 119–129 in Suppe and Asquith [1976].

Rozeboom, William W.

1956. "Mediation Variables in Scientific Theory," *Psychological Review*, 63, 249–264.

Rozenthal, S., ed.

1967. *Niels Bohr*. New York: John Wiley.

Rubin, H., and P. Suppes

1954. "Transformation of Systems of Relativistic Particle Mechanics," *Pacific Journal of Mathematics*, 4, 563–601.

Rudner, R.

1966. *Philosophy of Social Science*. Englewood Cliffs, N.J.: Prentice Hall.

Russell, Bertrand

1903. *Principles of Mathematics*. Cambridge: Cambridge University Press.

1929. *Our Knowledge of the External World*. London: Allen and Unwin.

1948. *Human Knowledge*. New York: Simon and Schuster.

Russell, P.

1955. *Man's Mastery of Malaria*. London: Oxford Press.

Ryle, G.

1949. *Concept of Mind*. London: Hutchinson's University Library.

Salmon, W.

1966. *The Foundations of Scientific Inference*. Pittsburgh, Pa.: University of Pittsburgh Press.

1970. *Statistical Explanation and Statistical Relevance*. Pittsburgh, Pa.: University of Pittsburgh Press.

1973. "Reply to Lehman," *Philosophy of Science*, 40, 397–402.

Savage, L. J.

1954. *The Foundations of Statistics*. New York: John Wiley.

Schaffner, K. F.

1967. "Approaches to Reduction," *Philosophy of Science*, 34, 137–147.

1969. "Correspondence Rules," *Philosophy of Science*, 36, 280–290.

1970. "Outlines of a Logic of Comparative Theory Evaluation with Special Attention to Pre- and Post-Relativistic Electrodynamics," pp. 311–354 in Stuewer [1970a].

Schaffner, K. F., and R. Cohen, eds.

1974. *PSA 1972: Proceedings of the 1972 Biennial Meetings of the Philosophy of Science Association. Boston Studies in the Philosophy of Science*. Vol. XX. Dordrecht, Holland: Reidel.

Schagrin, M. L.

1963. "Resistance to Ohm's Law," *American Journal of Physics*, 31, 536–547.

Scheffler, I.

1957. "Prospects for a Modest Empiricism," *Review of Metaphysics*, 10, 383–400, 602–625.

1957a. "Explanation, Prediction, and Abstraction," *British Journal for the Philosophy of Science*, 7, 293–309.

1963. *The Anatomy of Inquiry: Philosophical Studies in the Theory of Science*. New York: Knopf.

1967. *Science and Subjectivity*. Indianapolis, Ind.: Bobbs Merrill.

Schilpp, P., ed.

1942. *The Philosophy of G. E. Moore*. New York: Tudor.

1949. *Albert Einstein: Philosopher-Scientist*. New York: Tudor, reissued as a Harper Torchbook, 1959.

1963. *The Philosophy of Rudolf Carnap*. LaSalle, Ill.: Open Court.

1971. *The Philosophy of Karl R. Popper*. LaSalle, Ill.: Open Court.

Schlick, M.

1918. *Allgemeine Erkenntnislehre*. Berlin: J. Springer.

1931. "Die Kausalitaet in der gegenwaertigen Physik," *Die Naturwissenschaften*, 19, 145–162.

1936. "Meaning and Verification," *Philosophical Review*, 45, 339–369, reprinted in Feigl and Sellars [1949].

1938. *Gesamelte Aufsätze*. Vienna: Gerold, reissued by G. Olms, Hildesheim, 1969.

1949. *Philosophy of Nature*. New York: Philosophical Library.

Schon, D.

1959. "Comments on Mr. Hanson's 'The Logic of Discovery'," *Journal of Philosophy*, 56, 500–503.

Scriven, M.

1958. "Definitions, Explanations, and Theories," pp. 99–195 in Feigl, Scriven, and Maxwell [1958].

1959. "Truisms as the Grounds for Historical Explanation," pp. 443–475 in Gardiner [1959].

1959a. "Explanation and Prediction in Evolutionary Theory," *Science*, 130, 477–482.

1962. "Explanations, Predictions, and Laws," pp. 170–230 in Feigl and Maxwell [1962].

1963. "The Temporal Asymmetry between Explanations and Predictions," pp. 97–105 in Baumrin [1963].

Sears, F. W., and M. W. Zemansky

1955. *University Physics*. Vol. 1, 2nd ed. Reading, Mass.: Addison-Wesley.

Sebeok, T. A., ed.

1966. *Current Trends in Linguistics*. Vol. III. The Hague: Mouton.

Sellars, W.

1948. "Concepts as Involving Laws and Inconceivable without Them," *Philosophy of Science*, 15, 287–315.

1949. "Realism and the New Way of Words," pp. 424–456 in Feigl and Sellars [1949].

1953. "Inference and Meaning," *Mind*, 62, 313–338.

1953a. "Is There a Synthetic Apriori?," *Philosophy of Science*, 20, 121–138.

1956. "Empiricism and the Philosophy of Mind," pp. 253–329 in Feigl and Scriven [1956].

1958. "Counterfactuals, Dispositions, and the Causal Modalities," pp. 225–308 in Feigl, Scriven, and Maxwell [1958].

1961. "The Language of Theories," pp. 57–77 in Feigl and Maxwell [1961]; reprinted as Chap. 4 of Sellars [1963].

1963. *Science, Perception, and Reality*. London: Routledge and Kegan Paul.

1963a. "Truth and Correspondence," pp. 197–224 of Sellars [1963].

1965. "Scientific Realism or Irenic Instrumentalism," pp. 171–204 in Cohen and Wartofsky [1965].

Shankland, R. S.

1955. "New Analysis of the Interferometer Observations of Dayton C. Miller," *Review of Modern Physics*, 27, 167–178.

1963. "Conversations with Einstein," *American Journal of Physics*, 31, 47–57.

Shapere, D.

1960. "Mathematical Ideals and Metaphysical Concepts," *Philosophical Review*, 69, 376–385.

1963. "Space, Time, and Language: An Examination of Some Problems and Methods of the Philosophy of Science," pp. 139–170 in Baumrin [1963a].

1964. "The Structure of Scientific Revolutions," *Philosophical Review*, 73, 383–394.

1966. "Meaning and Scientific Change," pp. 41–85 in Colodny [1966].

1967. "Philosophy and the Analysis of Language," in R. Rorty, ed. [1967].

1969. "Notes toward a Post-Positivistic Interpretation of Science," pp. 115–160 in Achinstein and Barker [1969].

1971. "The Paradigm Concept," *Science*, 172, 706–709.

1974. *Galileo: A Philosophical Study*. Chicago, Ill.: University of Chicago Press.

1974a. "Natural Science and the Future of Metaphysics," pp. 161–171 in R. Cohen and M. Wartofsky, eds., *Methodological and Historical Essays in the Natural and Social Sciences*. Dordrecht, Holland: Reidel.

1974b. "On the Relations between Compositional and Evolutionary Theories," in F. Ayala and T. Dobzhansky, eds. [1974].

1974c. "Discovery, Rationality, and Progress in Science: A Perspective in the Philosophy of Science," pp. 407–419 in Schaffner and Cohen [1974].

1975. "Copernicanism as a Scientific Revolution," in A. Beer and K. Strand, eds. [1975].

1975a. "Fine on Reference and Theory Change," presented at 1975 Western Division meetings of the American Philosophical Association.

Forthcoming a. "The Concept of Observation in Science and Philosophy."

Forthcoming b. "The Development of Scientific Categories," in *Dictionary of the History of Ideas*. New York: Scribners.

Forthcoming c. "The Influence of Knowledge on the Description of Facts," in Suppe and Asquith [1977].

———, ed.

1965. *Philosophical Problems of Natural Science*. New York: Macmillan.

Shapere, D., and G. Edelman

1974. "A Note on the Concept of Selection," pp. 202–204 in Ayala and Dobzhansky [1974].

Shimony, Abner

1970. "Scientific Inference," pp. 79–172 in Colodny [1970].

Skinner, B. F.

1953. *Science and Human Behavior*. New York: Macmillan.

1957. *Verbal Behavior*. New York: Appleton-Century-Crofts.

Sklar, L.

1967. "Types of Inter-theoretic Reduction," *British Journal for the Philosophy of Science*, 18, 109–124.

Skyrms, B.
1966. *Choice and Chance*. Belmont, Calif.: Dickenson.
1967. "The Explication of X Knows that P'," *Journal of Philosophy*, 65, 373–389.
Smart, J. J. C.
1956. "The Reality of Theoretical Entities," *Australasian Journal of Philosophy*, 34, 1–12.
1965. "Conflicting Views about Explanation," pp. 147–170 in Cohen and Wartofsky [1965].
1968. *Between Science and Philosophy*. New York: Random House.
Sneed, J.
1971. *The Logical Structure of Mathematical Physics*. Dordrecht, Holland: Reidel.
Sosa, E.
1965. "The Analysis of 'Knowledge that P'," *Analysis*, 25, 1–8.
1969. "Propositional Knowledge," *Philosophical Studies*, 20, 33–43.
1970. "Two Concepts of Knowledge," *Journal of Philosophy*, 67, 59–66.
Spector, M.
1965. "Models and Theories," *British Journal for the Philosophy of Science*, 16, 121–142.
1966. "Theory and Observation," *British Journal for the Philosophy of Science*, 17, 1–20, 89–104.
Spence, Kenneth W.
1944. "The Nature of Theory Construction in Contemporary Psychology," *Psychological Review*, 51, 47–68, reprinted in Marx [1951].
Stalnaker, Robert C.
1968. "A Theory of Conditionals," in Rescher [1968].
Stauffer, Robert C., ed.
1949. *Science and Civilization*. Madison: University of Wisconsin Press.
Strawson, P. F.
1950. "Truth," *Proceedings of the Aristotelian Society*, Supp. Vol. 24; reprinted in pp. 32–53 of Pitcher [1964].
Struve, O., and V. Zebergs
1962. *Astronomy of the Twentieth Century*. New York: Macmillan.
Stuewer, R.
1970. "Non-Einsteinian Interpretations of the Photoelectric Effect," in Stuewer [1970a].
1970a. *Minnesota Studies in the Philosophy of Science*, Vol. V. Minneapolis: University of Minnesota Press.
Suppe, Frederick
1967. "The Meaning and Use of Models in Mathematics and the Exact Sciences," Ph.D. thesis, University of Michigan, 1967.
1971. "On Partial Interpretation," *Journal of Philosophy*, 68, 57–76.
1972a. "Misidentification, Truth, and Knowing That," *Philosophical Studies*, 23, 186–197.
1972b. "What's Wrong with the Received View on the Structure of Scientific Theories?," *Philosophy of Science*, 39, 1–19.
1973. "Theories, Their Formulations, and the Operational Imperative," *Synthese*, 25, 129–164.

1973a. "Facts and Empirical Truth," *Canadian Journal of Philosophy*, 3, 197–212.
1973b. "Seeing: The Doctrine of an Incorrigible Given," forthcoming as Chapter 3 of *Facts, Theories, and Scientific Observation*.
1974. "Some Philosophical Problems in Biological Speciation and Taxonomy," pp. 190–243 in J. Wojciechowski, ed. [1974].
1974a. "Theories and Phenomena," pp. 45–92 in Leinfellner and Köhler, eds. [1974].
1975. "Post World War II Developments in American Philosophy of Science," *Ruch Filozoficzny*, 33, 135–168.
1976. "Logic, Computers, and Humanity—A New Course," *Teaching Philosophy*, 1, 259–321.
1976a. "Theoretical Laws," pp. 247–267 in Przełęcki, Szaniawski, and Wójcicki [1976].
Forthcoming a. "Conclusive Reasons, Causality, and Knowledge."
Forthcoming b. *Facts, Theories, and Scientific Observation*.
Forthcoming c. "Kuhn's and Feyerabend's Relativisms," in Meiland and Krausz, eds. [1977].

Suppe, F., and P. Asquith, eds.
1976. *PSA 1976: Proceedings of the 1976 Biennial Meetings of the Philosophy of Science Association*. Vol. I. East Lansing, Mich.: Philosophy of Science Association.
1977. *PSA 1976: Proceedings of the 1976 Biennial Meetings of the Philosophy of Science Association*. Vol. II. East Lansing, Mich.: Philosophy of Science Association.

Suppes, P.
1957. *Introduction to Logic*. New York: Van Nostrand.
1959. "Axioms for Relativistic Kinematics with or without Parity," pp. 291–307 in Henkin, Suppes, and Tarski [1959].
1959a. "A Linear Model for a Continuum of Responses," pp. 400–414 in Bush and Estes [1959].
1961. "The Philosophical Relevance of Decision Theory," *The Journal of Philosophy*, 58, 605–614.
1961a. "A Comparison of the Meaning and Use of Models in Mathematics and the Empirical Sciences," pp. 163–177 in Freudenthal [1961].
1962. "Models of Data," pp. 252–261 in Nagel, Suppes, and Tarski [1962].
1967. "What Is a Scientific Theory?," pp. 55–67 in Morgenbesser [1967].
1967a. "Set Theoretic Structures in Science," mimeographed, Stanford University, 1967.
1968. "The Desirability of Formalization in Science," *Journal of Philosophy*, 65, 651–664.
1969. "Stimulus-Response Theory of Finite Automata," *Journal of Mathematical Psychology*, 6, 327–355.
1969a. *Studies in the Methodology and Foundations of Science*. Dordrecht, Holland: Reidel, 1969.

Suppes, P., and R. C. Atkinson
1960. *Markov Learning Models for Multiperson Interactions*. Stanford, Calif.: Stanford University Press.

Swain, M., ed.
1970. *Induction, Acceptance, and Rational Belief*. New York: Humanities.

Swartz, R.
1965. *Perceiving, Sensing, and Knowing*. Garden City, N.Y.: Anchor Books.

Tarski, Alfred
1935. "Einige methodologische Untersuchungen über die Definierbarkeit der Begriffe," *Erkenntnis*, 5, 80–100, trans. in Tarski [1956].
1936. "Der Wahrheitsbegriff in den formalisierten Sprachen," *Studia Philosophica*, 1, 261–405, trans. in Tarski [1956].
1941. *Introduction to Logic and to the Methodology of Deductive Sciences*. New York: Oxford University Press.
1944. "The Semantic Conception of Truth," *Philosophy and Phenomenological Research*, 4, 341–375, reprinted in Feigl and Sellars [1949] and in Linsky [1952].
1956. *Logic, Semantics, Metamathematics*, trans. by J. H. Woodger. Oxford: Clarendon Press.

Thackary, A.
1973. *Dalton Studies*. Cambridge, Mass.: Harvard University Press.

Thalberg, I.
1969. "In Defense of Justified True Belief," *Journal of Philosophy*, 66, 794–803.

Todhunter, I.
1949. *A History of the Mathematical Theory of Probability*. New York: Chelsea.

Tondl, L.
1973. *Scientific Procedures*. Dordrecht, Holland: Reidel.

Toulmin, S.
1953. *The Philosophy of Science: An Introduction*. London: Hutchinson.
1959. "Criticism in the History of Science: Newton on Absolute Space, Time, and Motion," *Philosophical Review*, 68, 1–29.
1961. *Foresight and Understanding*. London: Hutchinson; New York: Harper and Row Torchbook, 1963.
1964. *The Uses of Argument*. Cambridge: Cambridge University Press. First published in 1958.
1967. "Conceptual Revolutions in Science," in Cohen and Wartofsky [1967].
1967a. "The Evolutionary Development of Natural Science," *American Scientist*, 55, 456–471.
1970. "Does the Distinction between Normal and Revolutionary Science Hold Water?," pp. 25–38 in Lakatos and Musgrave [1970].
1972. *Human Understanding*, Vol. I. Princeton, N.J.: Princeton University Press; Vol. II and III to follow.

Toulmin, S., and J. Goodfield
1961. *The Fabric of the Heavens*. New York: Harper and Row.

Townsend, B.
1971. "Feyerabend's Pragmatic Theory of Observation and the Comparability of Alternative Theories," pp. 202–211 in Buck and Cohen [1971].

Truesdell, Clifford
1967. "Reactions of Late Baroque Mechanics to Success, Conjecture, Error, and Failure in Newton's *Principia*," *Texas Quarterly*, 10, 238–258.

Turk-Saunders, J., and N. Champawat
1964. "Mr. Clark's Definition of Knowledge," *Analysis*, 25, 8–9.

Vaihinger, Hans.
1911. *Philosophie des Als-Ob*. Berlin: Reuter and Reichard, trans. as *Philosophy of As-If*. New York: Harcourt, Brace, 1924.
van Beuren, H. G.
1960. *Imperfections in Crystals*. Amsterdam: North Holland.
van Fraassen, B.
1967. "Meaning Relations among Predicates," *Nôus*, 1, 161–179.
1968. "The Labyrinth of Quantum Logic," pp. 224–254 in R. S. Cohen and M. Wartofsky (eds.), *Logical and Empirical Studies in Contemporary Physics. Boston Studies in the Philosophy of Science*. Vol. XIII. Dordrecht: Reidel, 1974.
1970. "On the Extension of Beth's Semantics of Physical Theories," *Philosophy of Science*, 37, 325–339.
1972. "A Formal Approach to the Philosophy of Science," pp. 303–366, in Colodny [1972].
van Spronsen, J. W.
1969. *The Periodic System of Chemical Elements: A History of the First Hundred Years*. New York: Elsevier.
Varadarajan, V. S.
1968. *Geometry of Quantum Theory*. Princeton, N.J.: Van Nostrand.
Venable, F. P.
1896. *The Development of the Periodic Law*. Easton, Pa.: Chemical Publishing.
von Neumann, J.
1955. *Mathematical Foundations of Quantum Mechanics*. Princeton, N.J.: Princeton University Press.
1962. *Collected Works*, 6 vols. New York: Pergamon Press.
Von Wright, G. H.
1951. *An Essay in Modal Logic*. Amsterdam: North Holland.
Wade, N.
1976. "Sociobiology: Troubled Birth for a New Discipline," *Science*, 191, 1151–55.
Walker, A. G.
1943–49. "Foundations of Relativity: Parts I and II," *Proceedings of the Royal Society of Edinburgh*, 62, 319–335.
Wang, Hao
1955. "Notes on the Analytic-Synthetic Distinction," *Theoria*, 21, 158–178.
Warnock, G.
1965. "Seeing," pp. 49–67 in Swartz [1965].
Wartofsky, M. W.
1963. Ed. *Boston Studies in the Philosophy of Science*, Vol. I. Dordrecht, Holland: Reidel.
1968. *Conceptual Foundations of Scientific Thought*. New York: Macmillan.
Watson, W. H.
1938. *On Understanding Physics*. Cambridge: Cambridge University Press.
1963. *Understanding Physics Today*. New York: Cambridge University Press.
Weyl, H.
1949. *Philosophy of Mathematics and Natural Science*. Princeton, N.J.: Princeton University Press.

Wheelwright, Philip
1954. *The Burning Fountain*. Bloomington: Indiana University Press.

White, A.
1957. "On Claiming to Know," *Philosophical Review*, 66, 180–192.
1970. *Truth*. London: Macmillan. Garden City, N.Y.: Anchor.

White, Morton G.
1950. "The Analytic and the Synthetic: An Untenable Dualism," pp. 316–330 in Hook [1950], reprinted in Linsky [1952].
1956. *Toward Reunion in Philosophy*. Cambridge, Mass.: Harvard University Press.

Whitehead, A.
1929. *The Aims of Education*. New York: Macmillan.

Whitehead, A., and Bertrand Russell
1910–13. *Principia Mathematica*. 3 vols. Cambridge: Cambridge University Press.

Whiteside, D. T., and M. A. Hoskin, eds.
1967–72. *The Mathematical Papers of Isaac Newton*. 4 vols. Cambridge: Cambridge University Press.

Whittaker, E. T.
1951. *A History of the Theories of Aether and Electricity*. 2 vols. New York: Thomas Nelson.

Whorff, B. L.
1956. *Language, Thought and Reality: Selected Writings*. John B. Carroll, ed. Cambridge: MIT.

Wiener, Philip P., ed.
1953. *Readings in Philosophy of Science*. New York: Scribners.

Will, F.
1973. *Induction and Justification*. Ithaca, N.Y.: Cornell University Press.

Williams, B. A. O., and A. Montefiore, eds.
1966. *British Analytical Philosophy*. London: Routledge and Kegan Paul.

Wilson, E. O.
1975. *Sociobiology*. Cambridge, Mass.: Harvard University Press.

Wittgenstein, Ludwig
1922. *Tractatus Logico-Philosophicus*. London: Routledge and Kegan Paul. Trans. under the same title by D. F. Pears and B. MacGuinness, as Wittgenstein [1963].
1953. *Philosophical Investigations*. Oxford: Blackwell.
1963. *Tractatus Logico-Philosophicus*. Pears and McGuinness, trans. London: Routledge and Kegan Paul.

Wohlwill, E.
1883–84. "Die Entdeckung des Beharrungsgesetzes." *Zeitschrift für Völkerpsychologie*, 14, 365–410; and 15, 70–135.

Wojciechowski, J., ed.
1974. *Conceptual Basis of the Classification of Knowledge*. Munich: Verlag Dokumentation.

Woodger, J. H.
1937. *The Axiomatic Method in Biology*. Cambridge: Cambridge University Press.
1939. *The Technique of Theory Construction*. Chicago, Ill.: University of Chicago Press.

Woozley, A. D.

1952–53. "Knowing and Not Knowing," *Proceedings of the Aristotelian Society*, 53, 151–172.

Zeigler, B.

1976. "The Hierarchy of System Specifications and the Problem of Structural Inference," pp. 227–239 in Suppe and Asquith, eds. [1976].

1976a. *Theory of Modeling and Simulation*. New York: John Wiley.

Notes on Contributors

Peter Achinstein received his Ph.D. in philosophy at Harvard and currently is Professor of Philosophy and Chairman of the Philosophy Department at Johns Hopkins University. He specializes in the philosophy of science, has published a number of articles in the area, is the author of two books, *Concepts of Science* and *Law and Explanation*, and is coeditor of *The Legacy of Logical Positivism*. He held a Guggenheim Fellowship, was a delegate to the International Union for History and Philosophy of Science, and was on the social science advisory panel for the National Science Foundation.

David Bohm received his Ph.D. in physics at the University of California at Berkeley, and currently is Professor of Physics at Birkbeck College, the University of London. He is a physicist-philosopher who specializes in collective theory and the physical and philosophical fundamentals of relativity and quantum mechanics; he is perhaps the best-known critic of the Copenhagen interpretation of quantum theory, and has advanced the "hidden-variable" hypothesis as an alternative. He is the author of *Quantum Theory* and *Special Theory of Relativity*. In the philosophy of science he has published *Causality and Chance in Modern Physics* and is coeditor of *Quanta and Reality: A Symposium*.

Sylvain Bromberger received his Ph.D. in philosophy at Harvard and currently is Professor and Chairman of Philosophy at the Massachusetts Institute of Technology. He specializes in the philosophy of science, the philosophy of language and erotetic logic, and has published a number of quite important papers in these areas. He delivered the Thalheimer Lecture at Johns Hopkins University in 1969.

Jeffrey Bub received his Ph.D. in physics at Birkbeck College, the University of London, and currently is Associate Professor of Philosophy at the University of Western Ontario. He specializes in the philosophical foundations of physics with special reference to quantum theory, and in problems concerning the role of space and time in modern physics. He has written numerous articles on the foundations of quantum theory—a number of them coauthored with David Bohm.

Robert L. Causey received his Ph.D. in logic and the methodology of science at the University of California at Berkeley, and currently is Associate Professor of Philosophy at the University of Texas. He specializes in the philosophy of science and questions concerning the impact of science on society. He is the author of a technical report on measurement and has published articles and reviews in various scientific and philosophical journals.

I. Bernard Cohen received his Ph.D. in the history of science at Harvard, and currently is Professor of the History of Science there. He specializes in the history of physical thought, the history of science in America, and the interactions of science and sociology. One of the world's distinguished historians of science, he was president of the International Union of the History and Philosophy of Science, and has been editor of *Isis* and a vice-president of both the American Association for the Advancement of Science, and the American Academy of Arts and Sciences, and is a member of various other professional societies. The books he has authored and edited include an edition of Newton's *Principia* with variant readings (in collaboration with Alexandre Koyré), *Isaac Newton's Papers and Letters in Natural Philosophy*, *Benjamin Franklin's Experiments*, *Franklin and Newton*, *Some Early Tools of American Science*, *Birth of a New Physics*, and *Rømer and the First Determination of the Velocity of Light*.

Carl G. Hempel received his Ph.D. from the University of Berlin and is Emeritus Stuart Professor of Philosophy at Princeton University. One of the nation's most distinguished philosophers of science, he has made important contributions to the "covering law" analysis of scientific explanation, and is closely identified with the standard analysis of the structure of scientific theories. He published numerous important articles in the philosophy of science and is the author of the books *Fundamentals of Concept Formation in Empirical Science*, *Aspects of Scientific Explanation*, *Philosophy of Natural Science*, and *La Formazione dei Concetti e della Teorie nella Scienza Empirica*; he coauthored *Der Typusbegriff im Lichte der Neuen Logik*. He has served on the editorial board of several journals, is a past president of the Eastern Division of the American Philosophical Association, has held Guggenheim and Fulbright Fellowships, has had an appointment at the Center for Advanced Studies in the Behavioral Sciences, is a Fellow of the American Academy of Arts and Sciences and a member of the American Philosophical Society.

Thomas S. Kuhn received his Ph.D. in physics at Harvard and is M. Taylor Pyne Professor of the History of Science at Princeton, where he also has been Director of the Program in History and Philosophy of Science. He is a distinguished historian of science and author of the highly influential book *The Structure of Scientific Revolutions*. In addition he is the author of *The Copernican Revolution* and has published a large number of papers in physics and the history of science. He has been a Junior Fellow at Harvard, Lowell Lecturer, a Guggenheim Fellow, Centennial Visiting Scholar at Swarthmore, Isenberg Lecturer at Michigan State, a Fellow of the Center for Advanced Studies in the Behavioral Sciences, and a Fellow of the American Academy of Arts and Sciences. He has held offices in a number of scholarly societies, a number of consultantships, and is past president of the History of Science Society.

Thomas Nickles received his Ph.D. from Princeton University and currently is Associate Professor of Philosophy at the University of Nevada at Reno. He specializes in the philosophy and history of physical and social sciences, and has published a number of articles on intertheoretic reduction and explanation in those areas. In 1974 he was an invited symposiast at the Philosophy of Science Association biennial meetings.

Hilary Putnam received his Ph.D. in philosophy at UCLA and currently is Professor of Philosophy at Harvard. He specializes in philosophy of science and mathematical logic, and in various papers has made a number of important contributions to these fields. He has been a National Science Foundation Fellow, a Rockefeller Fellow, a Guggenheim Fellow, and a member of the Minnesota Center for the Philosophy of Science. He is president of the Philosophy of Science Association.

Dudley Shapere received his Ph.D. in philosophy at Harvard and currently is Professor of Philosophy in the History and Philosophy of Science program at the University of Maryland at College Park. He specializes in the history and philosophy of science and analytic philosophy. He is the author of a number of articles in these areas, is author of *Galileo: A Philosophical Study*, has edited an anthology, *Philosophical Problems of Natural Science*, and is preparing a volume on the relations between science and philosophy in the history of those subjects. He has been Chairman of programs in History and Philosophy of Science at the Universities of Chicago and Illinois, on the editorial boards of several journals, a member of the NSF Advisory Panel for History and Philosophy of Science and Program Director for the NSF Program in History and Philosophy of Science, Secretary of Section L of AAAS, and has been Sigma Xi lecturer for a number of years.

Frederick Suppe received his Ph.D. in philosophy at the University of Michigan and currently is Associate Professor of Philosophy and Chairperson of the program in History and Philosophy of Science at the University of Maryland at College Park. He specializes in philosophy of science, history of the philosophy of science, epistemology, and automata theory, and has published widely in those areas; he is coeditor of *PSA 1976*. Currently he is completing a book *Facts, Theories, and Scientific Observation*. He was cochairman (with Alan Donagan) of the Symposium on the Structure of Scientific Theories; has been an invited participant in a number of symposia here and abroad; was Chairperson of the Program Committee for the 1976 Biennial Meetings of the Philosophy of Science Association; was on the Advisory Board to the National Workshop on Teaching Philosophy, where he directed workshops on "philosophy and the computer" and on "philosophy and sex"; is an elected member of Sigma Xi; has received ACLS and NSF grants; and received the *Amicus Poloniae* award from Poland.

Patrick C. Suppes received his Ph.D. in philosophy from Columbia and currently is Professor of Philosophy, Statistics, and Education at Stanford, where he also is Director of the Research Institute for Mathematical Studies in the Social Sciences. He specializes in the philosophy of science and mathematical methods in the social sciences. He has published many articles in these and related areas, as well as authoring *Axiomatic Set Theory, Introduction to Logic*; coauthoring *Markov Models for Multiperson Interactions, Experiments in Second-Language Learning*, and *Decision Making: An Experimental Approach*. He has edited a number of volumes, including *Aspects of Inductive Logic* and *Logic, Methodology, and the Philosophy of Science*. He has been a Fellow at the Center for Advanced Studies in the Behavioral Sciences, National Science Foundation Fellow, has received the Butler Silver Medal at Columbia, the Johnson Memorial Award, and a research award of the Social Science Research Council. He is a Fellow of the American Academy of Arts and Sciences.

Stephen Toulmin received his Ph.D. at Oxford and currently is a Professor in the Committee on Social Thought at the University of Chicago.

He specializes in the philosophy of science, the history of scientific ideas, and epistemology. He has published a number of articles in those areas, and is the author of *Reason in Ethics, The Uses of Argument, Philosophy of Science, Foresight and Understanding, Human Understanding,* and *Knowledge and Action,* and is coauthor of *The Fabric of the Heavens, The Architecture of Matter, The Discovery of Time,* and *Wittgenstein's Vienna*; and edited *Physical Reality.* He has been a director of the Nuffield Foundation, a counselor for the Smithsonian Institution, an officer of AAAS, Sigma Xi lecturer, and is a consultant to the National Commission for the Protection of Human Subjects.

Bas C. van Fraassen received his Ph.D. at the University of Pittsburgh and currently is Professor of Philosophy at the University of Toronto. He works on the philosophy of physics, space and time, and logic. He is the author of many articles in these areas and has authored *An Introduction to the Logic of Time and Space, Formal Semantics and Logic,* and is coauthor of *Derivation and Counterexample.* He is editor of the *Journal of Philosophical Logic.*

Index

Index for the Afterword